Frommer's

EUROPE'S GREATEST DRIVING TOURS

by

Michael Spring

Macmillan • USA

ABOUT THE AUTHOR

Michael Spring is the publisher of Macmillan Travel. In former lives, he was the editorial director at Fodor's, the travel expert on the CNN Travel Show, and host of WNCN's (New York) "Mike Spring on Travel." His books include *The Great Weekend Escape Book* (Dutton), *The American Way of Working* (Bantam), and *A Student's Guide to Julius Caesar.* Though he spends most of his life these days orchestrating other people's adventures, he has never lost his lust for travel.

MACMILLAN TRAVEL
A Simon & Schuster Macmillan Company
1633 Broadway
New York, NY 10019

Find us online at **http://www.mgr.com/travel** or
on America Online at Keyword: **Frommer's.**

ISBN 0-02-861550-6
Library of Congress Catalog Card Number: 96-78292

Editor: Ron Boudreau
Production Editor: Lori Cates
Design by Scott Meola
Digital Cartography by John Decamillas and Ortelius Design

Manufactured in the United States of America

CONTENTS

LIST OF MAPS

INTRODUCTION

I wrote this guide for anyone who hates rubbing suitcases with strangers on guided tours, but who needs help deciding where to go and how to organize his or her time.

I hope you'll see me as your travel agent and close friend, who sat down with you and helped plan the vacation of your life. Because friends value honesty, I tried to leave you with the truth. There are many places you won't hear about because I wouldn't send friends there or wouldn't choose to go back myself.

I've chosen the most popular trips in each of seven European countries and shown you how to make do with a little money and how to spoil yourself with a lot. Though I suggest you take these trips by car, there are many public transportation options. Major car-rental companies are **Avis** (☎ 800/331-1212), **Hertz** (☎ 800/654-3001), and **National/European** (☎ 800/CAR-RENT). If you're looking for a bargain, try **Kemwel** (☎ 800/678-0678). If you're staying abroad more than 3 weeks, consider leasing a car from a company like **Renault** (☎ 800/221-1052).

To get you started, each chapter begins with the following sections: "Before You Go," "Arriving & Departing," "Getting Around," and "Essential Information." Travel books that I found particularly helpful in formulating my own ideas are listed under "Reading" in most "Before You Go" sections. Under "The Itinerary," I give directions for 3 to 5 days, 5 to 7 days, and 7 to 14 days—but you can combine them into longer trips. You can visit the countries individually or in the order I've presented them, starting in Ireland and moving southeast as far as Italy and then west to complete the circuit in Spain. Then in the "Exploring" section I take you on a day-by-day trip along the proposed route, suggesting things to do and places to stay and eat. The following abbreviations are used for credit cards: AE (American Express), DC (Diners Club), MC (MasterCard), and V (Visa).

Here are some of the highlights:

Austria:	Medieval towns along the Danube.
England:	Salisbury Cathedral and the Cotswold countryside.
France:	St-Tropez at dawn and the perched village of Peillon.
Germany:	The royal castles and Heidelberg.
Ireland:	Slea Head, on the wild west coast of the Dingle Peninsula.
Italy:	The Temple of Neptune in Paestum and the hill town of Ravello.
Spain:	The Alhambra and the white villages of Andalusia.

Because I'm asking you to trust me, I'd better say a word about my sensibilities. I've omitted many chain hotels because they could be anywhere in the world, and I'm partial to hotels that capture the spirit of a place, that are one of a kind, that could be nowhere other than where they are. On the other hand, I know that age is no guarantee of atmosphere or charm and that many modern hotels have twice the character of so-called historic inns listed in the guides. I dislike yellow water glasses, all-weather carpeting, soft mattresses, and furnishings that are cute, overdone, or deliberately old-fashioned. I like to fall asleep in rooms softened with age. My favorite hotel organization is **Relais & Châteaux** (☎ **800/546-4777**; on the World Wide Web at http://www.integra.fr/ relaischateaux), because the properties it represents are historic buildings that are exquisitely furnished and maintained.

While every care has been taken to ensure the accuracy of the information in this guide, the passage of time will always bring change, and consequently the publisher cannot accept responsibility for errors that may occur. All quoted prices and opening times are based on information supplied to us at press time. Hours and admission fees may change, however, and prudent travelers will avoid inconvenience by calling ahead.

Frommer's wants to hear about your travel experiences, both pleasant and unpleasant. When a hotel or restaurant fails to live up to its billing, let us know and we'll investigate the complaint and revise our entries when the facts warrant it.

Send your letters to Michael Spring at Macmillan Travel, 1633 Broadway, New York, NY 10019.

I R E L A N D

The Southern Coast
& the Wild West

Southwestern Ireland offers a wonderful range of scenery—wild mountain passes, rich green farm country, and romantic seascapes. The view changes from one moment to the next. The weather changes, too, creating a sense of expectancy, as if you had stumbled on an unfinished bit of creation. If you're addicted to blue skies, stay away; Ireland is for those romantic fools who know that only on a misty day can you see forever.

Throughout the region you can piece together Ireland's history in ancient ruins, the Blarney Stone, restored mansions, and the daily life of the inhabitants. All the major towns have crafts stores selling everything from Waterford crystal to hand-knit Aran sweaters as well as seafood restaurants serving fish as fresh as the day's catch. The west coast has a lively pub life where you can hear traditional Irish music—not made just for tourists. On the wild and unspoiled Dingle Peninsula the people still study and speak Gaelic.

You can also enjoy a summer's worth of outdoor activities: angling for shark or salmon, teeing off on championship golf courses, ambling along a riverside, or climbing some of the country's highest peaks. Killarney's romantic lakes invite rowing parties, and you can explore the Gap of Dunloe by pony cart.

BEFORE YOU GO

GOVERNMENT TOURIST OFFICES

The major source of information is the **Irish Tourist Board.** It produces numerous publications, many of them free and all of them useful.

HIGHLIGHTS ALONG THE WAY

- Seascapes and spectacular mountain passes on the Dingle Peninsula, where *Ryan's Daughter* was filmed.

- A wealth of outdoor sports—golf, tennis, boating, fishing, and hiking—along the Ring of Kerry and among the beautiful mountains and lakes of Killarney.

- The greatest collection of ancient monuments in Ireland, including the Rock of Cashel, where St. Patrick is said to have baptized Ireland's first Christian king.

- The Blarney Stone.

In the U.S.: 345 Third Ave., New York, NY 10017 (☎ 800/223-6470 or 212/418-0800).

In Canada: 160 Bloor St. East, Toronto, ONT M4W 1B9 (☎ 416/929-2777).

In the U.K.: Irish Desk, British Travel Centre, 12 Regent St., Piccadilly Circus, London SW17 4PQ (☎ 0171/839-8416).

In Ireland, local **Tourist Information Offices** will (for a nominal fee) reserve accommodations and provide extensive information on all aspects of the surrounding areas. They're normally open Monday to Friday from 9am to 6pm and Saturday from 9am to 1pm. The main office is in Dublin at 14 Upper O'Connell St. (☎ 01/2844768). There are also offices at Dublin Airport (same number as above) and in Shannon (☎ 061/471664).

WHEN TO GO

The main tourist season runs from June to mid-September. The attractions of Ireland aren't as dependent on the weather as those in most other northern European countries, and the scenery is just as attractive in off-peak fall and spring. Accommodations are more economical in winter, though some of the smaller attractions are closed from October to March. In all seasons you can expect rain.

CURRENCY

The unit of currency in Ireland is the **pound,** or **punt** (pronounced *poont*), written as **IR£** to avoid confusion with the pound sterling. The currency is divided into the same denominations as in Britain, with IR£ divided into 100 pence (written *p*). There's likely to be some variance in the rates of exchange between Ireland and the United Kingdom (which includes Northern Ireland). This usually favors the visitor. Change U.K. pounds at a bank when you get to Ireland (pound coins not accepted); change Irish pounds and pound coins before you leave.

Dollars and British currency are accepted only in large hotels and shops licensed as *bureaux de change*. In general, visitors are expected to use Irish currency. Banks give the best rate of exchange. Ireland's rate of exchange at press time was about $1.64 U.S. = IR£1 (or 1 U.S.$ = 61 Irish pence); and $2.19 Canadian = IR£1 (or $1 Canadian = 46 Irish pence). Comparisons between the currencies of Ireland and Britain are more equivalent: IR£1 = 98 British pence.

CUSTOMS

Two categories of duty-free allowance exist for travelers entering the Irish Republic: one for goods obtained outside the European Union, on a ship or an aircraft or in a duty-free store within the European Union; and the other for goods bought in the European Union, with duty and tax paid.

In the first category, you may import duty-free: 200 cigarettes or 100 cigarillos or 50 cigars or 250 grams (8.8 oz.) of smoking tobacco; 2 liters (.53 gal.) of wine, and either 1 liter of alcoholic drink over 22% volume or 2 liters of alcoholic drink under 22% volume (sparkling or fortified wine included); 50 grams (1.8 oz.) of perfume and one-quarter liter of toilet water; and other goods to a value of IR£124 per adult or IR£73 for those under 15.

In the second category you may import duty-free: 800 cigarettes or 400 grams (14 oz.) of tobacco or 400 cigarillos or 200 cigars; 1½ liters (.40 gal.) of alcoholic beverage of more than 22% volume or a total of 3 liters of alcoholic beverage of not more than 22% volume or sparkling or fortified wines, plus 4 liters of other wine; 75 grams (2.6 oz.) of perfume and three-eighths of a liter of toilet water; and other goods to a value of IR£73 per person regardless of age.

Goods that can't be freely imported include firearms, ammunition, explosives, drugs (narcotics, amphetamines), indecent or obscene books and pictures, oral smokeless tobacco products, meat and meat products, poultry and poultry products, plants and plant products (including shrubs, vegetables, fruit, bulbs, and seeds), domestic cats and dogs from outside the United Kingdom, and live animals from outside Northern Ireland.

Note that in both categories tobacco and alcohol allowances apply only to those 17 and older. If you have nothing more than the duty-free allowance when you arrive, walk straight through the green "Nothing to Declare" channel. If you have more than your duty-free allowance, however, you must go into the red channel and declare the goods you're bringing in.

Visitors may import any quantity of currency, whether foreign or Irish, and nonresidents may export any amount of foreign currency, provided it's declared on arrival.

LANGUAGE

Officially, the Irish language is the first language of the Republic, but the everyday language of the majority of Irish people is English. Except for in the northwest, most signs are written in Irish with an English translation underneath. There's one important exception to this rule, with which you should familiarize yourself: *Fir* and *mna* translate respectively into *men* and *women*. The *Gaeltacht*—areas in which Irish *is* the everyday language of most people—comprises only 6% of the land, and all its inhabitants are, in any case, bilingual.

IRELAND

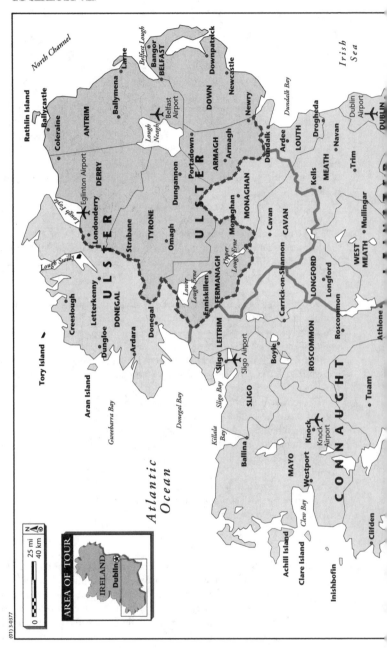

SPECIAL EVENTS & NATIONAL HOLIDAYS

Special Events

Mid-June: Liberties Festival, Dublin.

June 16: Bloomsday (honoring James Joyce), Dublin.

Late September–early October: Dublin Theater Festival.

National Holidays

January 1 (New Year's Day); March 17 (St. Patrick's Day); Easter and Easter Monday; the 1st Monday in May, June, and August; the last Monday in October; December 25 (Christmas); December 26 (Boxing Day).

READING

Don Fullington, *An American's Ireland* (Panafast, New York).

Steve MacDonogh, *A Visitor's Guide to the Dingle Peninsula* (a detailed guide sold locally).

Sean O'Suilleabhain, *Irish Walk Guides No. 1, Southwest* (available at local bookstores).

ARRIVING & DEPARTING

BY PLANE

Flying to Dublin and returning from Shannon will save you about 3½ hours of driving time (224km/140 miles) and money spent on gas. The scenery grows more beautiful as you head west toward Shannon, so, on the principle that it's better to save the best for last, see Dublin first and fly home from Shannon. Three airlines operate between Ireland and the United States: **Aer Lingus** (☎ 800/223-6537 in the U.S. or 212/557-1110 in New York State); **Delta** (☎ 800/241-4141 in the U.S. or 800/722-9230 in Georgia or 514/337-5520 in Canada); and **Aeroflot** (☎ 800/535-9877 or 202/429-4922).

Aer Lingus flies direct to Dublin and Shannon from New York and Boston; fares to Dublin are slightly higher. Delta flies to Shannon direct from Atlanta. Aeroflot flies to Shannon from Washington, D.C.

Aer Lingus (☎ 0181/899-4747 in the U.K.) and **Ryan Air** (☎ 0171/435-7101 in the U.K.) have frequent services from the United Kingdom (London and most major regional airports) to both Dublin and Shannon. **British Midlands** (☎ 0181/9905127 in the U.K. or 800/788-0555 in the U.S.) has frequent service from London Heathrow to Dublin.

BY CAR, TRAIN & BUS

All car ferry services from Britain are also served by motor coach and rail services to accommodate foot passengers. You can go direct from both Liverpool and Holyhead to Dun Laoghaire, a few miles south of Dublin. The crossing from Liverpool takes 7 hours and from Holyhead takes 3½ hours. If you're picking up the itinerary at Kilkenny or Cork, go via Fishguard or Pembroke to Rosslare, about 3½ hours. Crossings from Holyhead, Liverpool, and Fishguard are run by **Sealink British Ferries**—contact BritRail at 1500 Broadway, New York, NY 10036 (☎ 800/677-8585 or 212/575-2667 in New York). In the United Kingdom contact **Sealink Travel** (☎ 01233/647074) for the nearest office. Pembroke to Rosslare is operated by **B & I Line**—contact Lynott Tours, 350 Fifth Ave., Suite 2619, New York, NY 10118 (☎ **800/ 221-2474** or 212/760-0101 in New York). In the United Kingdom, contact the line at 150–151 New Bond St., London W1Y 0AQ (☎ **0171/491-8682**).

GETTING AROUND

BY CAR

Driving is on the left, as in Britain, and drivers and front-seat passengers must wear seat belts. Most road signs have both kilometers and miles posted. Expect to be confused. There's a general speed limit of 88 kilometers per hour (55 m.p.h.) on most roads; in towns, the speed limit is 48 kilometers per hour (30 m.p.h.). In some areas, the limit is 64 kilometers per hour (40 m.p.h.); this will always be clearly posted. At junctions, traffic from the right takes precedence.

Rented cars won't have automatic transmission unless you request it in advance. If you're under 21 or over 70, you may be excluded from certain fly/drive packages; be sure to check. All the major car-rental companies have outlets in Ireland, as do a number of Irish firms.

One of the most reasonably priced Irish car-rental companies is **Dan Dooley** (☎ **062/53103**), which has desks at both Shannon and Dublin airports. Arrangements can be made in the United States by calling **800/331-9301** (or 201/381-8948 in New Jersey).

Aer Lingus has some attractive fly/drive packages. Some include prepaid vouchers for meals and/or accommodations.

BY PUBLIC TRANSPORTATION

This is the one trip I advise you definitely to make by car. Trains and buses do exist, but they won't get you to many of the most beautiful, out-of-the-way spots. If you must go by public transport, your best bet is simply to skip the south coast and take the train directly from Dublin to Killarney. From here you can take local buses or sign up for daily excursions to all local points of interest, including the Ring of Kerry and the Dingle Peninsula. Rented bikes will get you everywhere you want to go in the Killarney area.

Should you want to go from Dublin to Cork, the train takes 2 hours and 40 minutes. A bus goes from Cork to Kinsale in 50 minutes. The train from Cork to Killarney, via Mallow, takes 1 hour and 50 minutes. The train from Dublin to Killarney via Mallow takes 3 hours and 45 minutes. From Dingle, the bus to the Tralee train station takes 80 minutes. From Tralee, the train back to Dublin takes 3 hours and 35 minutes.

If you plan to travel extensively, consider purchasing the **Irish Explorer,** a money-saving pass allowing unlimited travel within the Republic. An 8-day combined bus/rail pass sells for $150 per person, a

5-day rail-only pass going for $100. The pass can be purchased through bus and rail ticket offices in Ireland or before you go by contacting **CIE Tours International,** 100 Hanover Ave., P.O. Box 501, Cedar Knoll, NJ (☎ **800/243-8687** or 201/292-3438).

ESSENTIAL INFORMATION

IMPORTANT ADDRESSES & NUMBERS

VISITOR INFORMATION   Some of the smaller offices on the itinerary are open only in high season as indicated.

Bantry:	Tourist Information Office (☎ **027/50229**); open mid-June to mid-September.
Cashel:	Tourist Information Office, Town Hall (☎ **062/61333**); open March to September.
Cork:	Tourist House, Grand Parade (☎ **021/273251**).
Dingle:	Tourist Information Office (☎ **066/51188**); open May 21 to October 1.
Kilkenny:	Tourist Information Office, Shee's Alms House, Rose Inn Street (☎ **056/51500**).
Killarney:	Tourist Information Office, Killarney Town Hall, opposite St. Mary's Church on Main Street (☎ **064/31633**).
Kinsale:	Tourist Information Office, Pier Road (☎ **021/772234**); open mid-May to mid-October. (Outside these months you might look up Peter Barry at the Scilly Store opposite the Spaniard Inn or call him at 021/774026.)

EMBASSIES   **U.S. Embassy,** 42 Elgin Rd., Ballsbridge, Dublin (☎ **01/688777**). **Canadian Embassy,** 65 St. Stephen's Green, Dublin (☎ **01/4781988**). **U.K. Embassy,** 33 Merrion Rd., Dublin (☎ **01/269-5211**).

EMERGENCIES   **Police** (☎ **999**). **Ambulance** (☎ **999**). **Doctor:** in Kilkenny (☎ **056/21702**); in Cork City, County Cork, and County Kerry (☎ **021/545011**). **Dentist** (☎ **01/679-4311**). There are no late-night or all-night pharmacies in Ireland.

OPENING & CLOSING TIMES

BANKS   Banks are open Monday to Friday from 10am to 12:30pm and 1:30 to 3pm (until 5pm on selected days).

MUSEUMS   Museums are usually open Monday to Friday from 10am to 5pm, Saturday from 10am to 1pm, and Sunday from 2 to 5pm. Always make a point of checking, as hours can change unexpectedly.

SHOPS   Shops are open Monday to Saturday from 9am to 5:30pm, closing earlier on Wednesday, Thursday, or Saturday, depending on the locality.

GUIDED TOURS

The following agents will organize full-day and half-day trips by private chauffeur-driven car or coach in the Killarney area:

KILLARNEY   Contact **Castlelough Tours,** High Street (☎ **064/32496**); **Cronin's Tours,** College Street (☎ **064/31521**); or **Deros Bus Tours,** Main Street (☎ **064/31251**). **Destination Killarney,** Scotts Gardens (☎ **064/36238**), will make all the arrangements for your stay, lining up accommodations, entertainment, special-interest tours, and sporting activities in one tailor-made package.

CORK   Try **Discover Cork**, Belmont, Douglas Road (☎ **021/293873**), which will prearrange special-interest tours for 10 or more in the Cork area.

SHOPPING

VAT REFUNDS   Visitors from outside Europe can take advantage of the "cash-back" system on the **value-added tax (VAT)** if their purchases total more than IR£50. A cash-back voucher must be filled out by the retailer at the point of sale. You pay the total gross price, including VAT, and receive green and yellow copies of the invoice; you must retain both. These are presented to—and stamped by—customs as you leave the country. Take the stamped form to the cashier and you'll be refunded the VAT on the spot.

BEST BUYS   It's not necessary to go to Waterford to buy **Waterford glass;** the price is the same everywhere in Ireland, even at the factory store. The factory may have a wider selection, but there are no "seconds" available at reduced prices. Part of what you're paying for is the name, so consider buying other Irish glass made in Kilkenny, Cork, Galway, and Dublin, at considerably lower prices.

Almost every town has a shop or two selling handwoven **tweeds,** undyed wool sweaters (the so-called **Aran knitwear**), and **linen.** Some of the knitted goods are made by hand, others—the less expensive ones—are made by machine. Some fabrics and knitwear are made locally, so goods vary from shop to shop. Prices vary, too: Aran-style sweaters, for instance, cost up to 40% more at the airport. The rule is to buy what you like when you see it, for you probably won't see one exactly like it again.

The **Design Workshop,** The Parade (☎ 056/22118), in Kilkenny has a large selection. Irish poplin is woven only in Cork.

Ireland is famous for its hand-thrown **pottery.** Some of the best shops are in Kinsale, Dingle Town, and Dunquin (on the west coast of the Dingle Peninsula).

The best bet for Irish crafts, fabrics, and knitwear is the **Blarney Woolen Mills and Shop (☎ 021/385280),** at the entrance to Blarney Castle, 8.1 kilometers (5 miles) north of Cork.

The tradition of Celtic ornamentation has inspired the jewelry and silver work of present-day Irish craftspeople. Particularly popular are designs based on the Book of Kells.

In **Cork,** try the **Queen's Old Castle Shopping Centre** on St. Patrick's Street (☎ 021/275044). The best store for jewelry and silver is **Manton's,** Winthrop Street (☎ 021/276245). For antiques, try **Macurtain Street** across St. Patrick's Bridge or the **Paul Street–Cornmarket area.** Many shops and department stores sell locally made Glengarriff lace.

In **Kinsale,** you'll find several tasteful craft shops as you walk about town, notably **Boland's Craft Shop** on Pearse Street (☎ 021/772161). Antiques, hand-knits, and more crafts can be found in the narrow, twisty **Main Street.**

SPORTS

In **Bantry,** if you plan to spend more time, you can arrange to angle for trout and salmon by contacting **Justin McCarthy,** Main Street (☎ 027/51133); to go bike riding, contact **Kramers Bicycles Ltd.,** Glengarriss Road (☎ 027/50278). You can play golf at the **Bantry Golf Club,** Cahir (☎ 027/50579). Although it doesn't have headquarters in Bantry, you can call **Dolphin Watersports (☎ 064/42238)** for arrangements for sailing, windsurfing, and jet-ski rental.

In **Killarney,** ponies or jaunting cars are available at the Muckross Road exit from town (near the Tourist Information Office), as well as at the entrance to the Gap of Dunloe and at the entrances to Muckross Abbey and Muckross House. Horseback rides through other areas of the National Park can be arranged through **Donald O'Sullivan** at the Killarney Riding School, Ballydowney (☎ 064/31686). The salmon season is normally from January 1 to September 30, but dates vary. To fish for salmon or sea trout by rod and line, you need a state national license, costing IR£25 annually or IR£10 for 21 days. It's available from **The Central Fisheries Board,** Balnagowan House, Mobhi Boreen, Glasenvin, Dublin 9 (☎ 01/8379206). No license is required for brown trout, rainbow trout, or coarse fish. On privately owned waters a permit is also necessary, costing on average IR£5 to IR£15 a day. For detailed information contact the **Killarney Tourist Information Office** (☎ 064/31633). For golf, the **Killarney Golf and Fishing Club** (☎ 064/31034) has two championship courses, at Mahoney's Point

(4km/2½ miles) from Killarney on the road to Killorglin, and at Killeen. For boat hire and tours, contact **Henry Clifton** at Ross Castle (☎ 064/32252) or **Dermit O'Donoghue,** High Street (☎ 064/31068).

For bike rental, contact **O'Callaghan Bros.,** College Street (☎ 064/ 31175), or **O'Sullivan's,** Bishop's Lane New Street (☎ 064/31282).

In **Kinsale,** if you plan to spend some time in the area, there's golf at the **Kinsale Golf Club** (☎ 021/772197); tennis at the **Kinsale Community Tennis Club,** Kilcan (no phone); and windsurfing at the **Oysterhaven Boardsailing Centre** (☎ 021/770738). Walking tours of historic Kinsale can be arranged by calling **021/772044;** they cost IR£1.50 per person. Departures are based on demand.

DINING

Your safest bet as you travel along the coast is fresh fish, particularly salmon (either poached or grilled). Other favorites are sea- and brown trout, sole grilled on the bone, oysters, and lobster. For meat dishes, try Irish mutton, spring lamb, or steaks.

Simplicity is the keynote of native Irish cooking, with such unpretentious dishes as Irish stew, bacon and cabbage, spring chicken with fresh vegetables, roast pork with applesauce, and eggs with homemade whole-meal bread. The leading restaurants lean toward French cuisine — either classic or modern, with an emphasis on fresh local produce. The more imaginative establishments try to blend French and Irish influences: like a sauce made with Irish whiskey or Bailey's Irish Cream.

The word *whiskey* is derived from the Irish *uisce beatha,* meaning "water of life." A great way to try it is by ordering an Irish coffee, which is topped with a thick layer of fresh cream.

For quick, inexpensive lunches, you can't go wrong with pub grub and a pint of cider, stout, or lager. Tipping isn't expected at bars.

Some of the more expensive establishments add a 12% or 15% service charge; elsewhere a tip of 10% is adequate. At press time there were 0.61 Irish pounds (IR£) to the dollar.

CATEGORY	COST
Expensive	Over IR£28
Moderate	IR£16–IR£28
Inexpensive	Under IR£16

Prices are per person and include a first course, main course, and dessert, but no wine or tip.

ACCOMMODATIONS

The choice is yours between hotels — some modern high-rises, others restored mansions — and private homes offering a bed and breakfast. My vote would be to stay either in the best hotels or in private guest houses,

THE ITINERARY

ORIENTATION

Ireland is small enough that you can enjoy a wide range of scenery with a minimum amount of driving. This itinerary takes you around the south and southwest coasts, primarily through Cork and Kerry counties. You can begin at either Shannon or Dublin and end at either airport. As you head south to Cork, you can stay in friendly guest houses or historic homes. The road along the southern coast wanders through rich green farmland bordering the sea. As you head west, the scenery grows wilder. You pass through Killarney and the Ring of Kerry, with their ruins, historic sites, and opportunities for enjoying the outdoors as well as the local life. Finally, you can take an unforgettable trip around the Dingle Peninsula. From here you'll return to either Shannon or Dublin.

THE MAIN ROUTE

3–5 DAYS

One Night: *Cashel or Mallow.*
Day excursions to the Rock of Cashel and the Blarney Stone.
One or Two Nights: *the Killarney area.*
Day excursion through the Gap of Dunloe and around the Ring of Kerry.

or in a combination of the two. The exclusive hotels have the atmosphere and amenities many travelers want. The second- and third-class hotels— many of them older hotels lacking the funds for renovations—aren't in themselves objectionable, but the private homes are usually cleaner, friendlier, and more modern. The Irish Tourist Board publishes an indispensable guide to Irish bed-and-breakfast establishments, which shows pictures of each home and gives information on prices and facilities, including availability of rooms with private bath. It publishes a similar listing of hotels.

Bed-and-breakfast reservations can be made through Tourist Information Offices in major Irish towns or by writing to the **Central Reservations Service,** 14 Upper O'Connell St., Dublin 1 (☎ 01/

One Night: *Dingle.*
Day excursion around the Dingle Peninsula.

5–7 Days

Day excursion to Kilkenny, the Rock of Cashel, and the Blarney Stone.

One Night: *Cashel, Mallow, or Kinsale.*

Three Nights: *the Killarney area.*
Day excursions through the Gap of Dunloe, across the lakes of Killarney, and around the Ring of Kerry.

Two Nights: *Dingle.*
Day excursions around the Dingle Peninsula and to the Blasket Islands.

7–14 Days

Day excursion to Kilkenny and the Rock of Cashel.

One Night: *Mallow or Shanagarry.*
Day excursion to Cork and the Blarney Stone.

One Night: *Kinsale.*
Day excursion to the Beara Peninsula.

One Night: *Ballylickey.*

One Night: *Kenmare.*

Five Nights: *the Killarney area.*
Day excursions through the Gap of Dunloe, across the lakes of Killarney, around the Ring of Kerry, and to the Skellig Islands.

Three Nights: *Dingle.*
Day excursions around the Dingle Peninsula and to the Blasket Islands.

605-7777). A 10% deposit is taken; for accommodation in private homes, a small fee is required to cover at least the cost of the phone call and a 25% deposit is taken. Hotel reservations can, of course, also be made through your travel agent at home.

Published rates don't always include taxes and service charges; it pays to ask beforehand. The larger chain hotels that cater to the package-tour trade have gone the way of the world and begun charging extra for breakfast: Tourists should boycott them on principle. It's not just a matter of dollars and cents: A breakfast "on the house" has always been part of the Irish (and British) experience, giving Americans the sense that they're guests in a foreign home.

At press time there were 0.61 Irish pounds to the dollar.

CATEGORY	COST
Very Expensive	Over IR£160
Expensive	IR£120–IR£160
Moderate	IR£80–IR£120
Inexpensive	Under IR£80

Prices are for two people in a double room based on high-season (June—Sept) rates.

EXPLORING

If your time is limited, take Routes N7 and N8 directly from Dublin to Cashel—a 2½-hour drive. With more time or a keen interest in Irish history, you can make a side trip to Kilkenny (2¼ hours), following Route N7 southwest from Dublin to Dorrow and Route N77 south to Kilkenny.

KILKENNY

Kilkenny (*Cill Chainnigh,* Canice's Church) is billed as the best example of a medieval town in Ireland, but its historic roots are less than obvious to the casual visitor. Even with its narrow side streets with names like Collier's Lane, you'll have to use some imagination to envision its antiquity. What makes a side trip here worthwhile is St. Canice's Cathedral, with its ancient stone tower; the restored medieval Black Abbey; a restored 16th-century home, the Rothe House (a rare sight in a country whose past is so often glimpsed only in broken stone and rubble); and Kilkenny Castle.

Anyone who wants to understand Anglo-Irish relations has to go back at least to the infamous 1366 Statutes of Kilkenny, which were meant to strengthen English authority in Ireland and to keep the Irish and the Anglo-Norman settlers apart. No Irish cattle could graze on English land. Marrying the Irish was punishable by death. Anglo-Norman settlers—many of whom went native—had their estates forfeited for speaking Gaelic, giving their children Irish names, or dressing in Irish clothes. Wearing Irish-made underwear was enough to get a person thrown in jail. The native Irish weren't allowed within the town walls and had to live in shantytowns—in their own country! The intermingling of Irish and Anglo-Norman elements was well under way when the Statutes of Kilkenny went into effect; if this fusion had been allowed to continue, who knows, there might be no civil war in Northern Ireland today.

By the early 17th century the Irish Catholics had had enough and formed the Confederation of Kilkenny, which governed Ireland for 6 years and tried to bring about reform. Pope Innocent X sent money and guns. Cromwell responded in 1650 by overrunning the town, sacking the cathedral, and using it to stable his horses.

KILKENNY

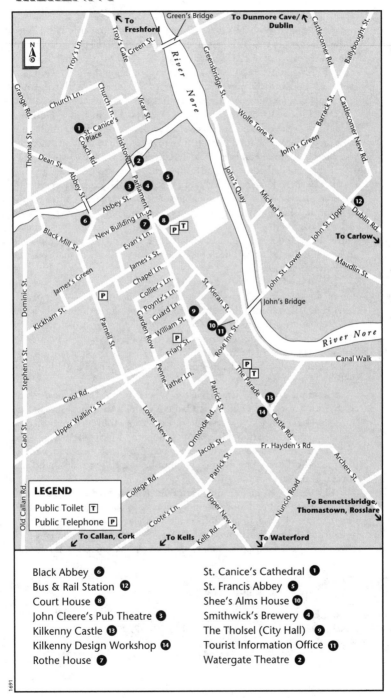

Black Abbey ❻	St. Canice's Cathedral ❶
Bus & Rail Station ⓬	St. Francis Abbey ❺
Court House ❽	Shee's Alms House ❿
John Cleere's Pub Theatre ❸	Smithwick's Brewery ❹
Kilkenny Castle ⓭	The Tholsel (City Hall) ❾
Kilkenny Design Workshop ⓮	Tourist Information Office ⓫
Rothe House ❼	Watergate Theatre ❷

Begin your tour at **St. Canice's Cathedral,** one of the finest in Ireland, despite Cromwell's defacements. The round tower is all that's left of the 6th-century monastic settlement around which the town developed. The cathedral, mostly Early English, is 13th-century (restored in 1866), with a 12th-century marble font, a library you should ask to see, and a stone seat built into the north wall, said to be St. Canice's. Within the massive walls is a Gothic structure with what one Irish writer calls "all the exultant sensuality of the Provençal love poetry that the Normans brought to Ireland." The knights in full armor stare upward at eternity, their faces more Irish than French. The tower is one of the few in Ireland you can climb. Free admission. Open daily 9am–1pm and 2–6pm.

From the cathedral, return to the road, turn right, and make your first left past the hairdresser's shop to reach the **Black Abbey,** a recently restored 13th-century friary, named after the black capes of the Dominican friars. Note how the transept is longer than the nave—a good example of how the Irish played tricks with Gothic forms, which never suited them, and a sad reminder of what the Irish could've accomplished architecturally if they had been permitted to develop styles that reflected their own Celtic sensibilities.

From the Black Abbey, turn left and follow narrow Abbey Street—one of the town's more medieval-looking streets—to Parliament Street. Turn right. Two blocks down on your right and across the street is the late 16th-century **Rothe House (☎ 056/22893),** the restored home of a Tudor merchant. Ask to see a small costume collection hidden away in an armoire. Admission IR£2 adults, IR£1 children, IR£1.50 seniors. Open Apr–Oct, Mon–Sat 10:30am–5pm, Sun 2:30–5pm; Nov–Mar, Sun 2:30–5pm.

Continue down Parliament Street. Where the road splits, bear left on St. Kieran Street. On your left is **Dame Kyteler's Inn,** the 14th-century house of Dame Alice "the witch." Perhaps because four husbands died on her, she was accused of holding witch's sabbaths, sacrificing black cocks, and mixing their innards with herbs, bugs, and the hair and nails of unbaptized children. She escaped without her maid, Petronilla, who was burned at the stake.

On your right at the junction of St. Kieran Street and Rose Inn Street is **Shee's Alms House,** founded as a hospital for the poor in 1582, now occupied by the Tourist Information Office.

From John's Bridge, left out of Shee's Alms House, you can look across the River Nore to **Kilkenny College (☎ 056/61544),** the former

TAKE A BREAK

*Turn left out of Shee's Alms House and left again at the edge of the River Nore to discover **Tynan's Bridge House,** John's Bridge (☎ 056/21291), one of the country's oldest pubs and a good bet for lunch.*

St. John's College, where Jonathan Swift, William Congreve, and Bishop George Berkeley were educated.

Return to the bridge without crossing it and continue along the path beneath **Kilkenny Castle (☎ 056/21450),** which underwent major restoration in 1991. A narrow break in the wall takes you up a flight of stairs to the castle. There's some lovely woodwork, an impressive Grand Hall, and a gallery of modern Irish art, but if you have only a passing interest in the arts, you may want to pass by. Admission IR£3 adults, IR£1.25 children and students, IR£2 seniors; 4 and under free. Open Tues–Sat 10am–7pm, Sun 2–5pm.

Two good alternatives are the extensive grounds and the **Kilkenny Design Workshop (☎ 056/22118),** located in the castle's stables. One of the best in the country, it sells locally made woven textiles, silver and metal work, hand-knits, and crystal. Open daily 9am–6pm.

Dunmore Cave (☎ 056/627726), 11.3 kilometers (7 miles) north of Kilkenny on N78 (follow signposts for Castlecomer and Athy), is modest in size yet has some beautiful formations that children in particular will enjoy. The bones found here belonged to 44 hapless individuals—25 of them children—who were probably seeking refuge from a Viking attack. Scholars theorize that the coins found here fell from the armpit of a Viking: The Irish didn't use coins then, and the Vikings in those pocketless days wound them in a screw of cloth they attached with beeswax to their armpit hair. A Viking probably dropped them in battle. "When you enter, a sudden Chilliness seizes all part of the body," wrote an earlier visitor, "and a Dimness surrounded our lights, as if the Place were filled with a thick Fog. . . . Our Faces, through this Gloom, looked as if we were a Collection of Ghosts, and the Lights in our Hands seemed as if we were making a visit to the infernal Shades." Admission IR£2 adults, 60p children and seniors. Open mid-June to Sept, daily 10am–7pm; Oct to mid-Mar, Sat–Sun 10am–5pm; mid-Mar to mid-June, Tues–Sat 10am–5pm, Sun 2–5pm.

DINING

Dame Kyteler's Inn, St. Kieran St. (☎ 056/21064). The former home of Ireland's famous "witch" used to be a byword for touristic ballyhoo with its Friday-night Witch's Banquet. Owner John Flynn has banished cabaret and fancy dress and restored some dignity to the stonework and exposed beams of the 14th-century interior. However, he can't resist serving witch's broth—a homemade vegetable soup—along with hybrid versions of French cuisine, like pan-fried chicken cooked in whiskey, cream, and mushroom sauce or poached salmon served with a sauce of fresh herbs, white wine, and cream. Weekend reservations advised. Casual. MC, V. Moderate.

Langton's, 69 John St. (☎ 056/65133). This popular city-center pub/restaurant has been nominated "Pub of the Year" three times. Its Edwardian interior, replete with mahogany paneling, polished brass, and potted plants, has been refurbished. The Edwardian theme is continued in the 90-seat restaurant, where a rear extension opens onto a walled garden. Fresh meat and fish are the menu's strength: Try the peppered sirloin steak or roast spring lamb. Weekend reservations advised. Neat but casual. AE, DC, MC, V. Moderate.

ACCOMMODATIONS

Butler House, 15–16 Patrick St., Kilkenny, Co. Kilkenny (☎ 056/65707; fax 056/65626). The elegant Georgian house, once the dower house of Kilkenny Castle, is on a main street of the town but can be approached through the craft workshops opposite the castle, which lead into the back garden. The rooms are decorated in good modern taste with oatmeal-and-white decor, large potted plants, and modern prints. Avoid rooms facing Patrick Street; they're noisier and generally smaller. 14 rms with bath. Facilities: restaurant (wine license). AE, MC, V. Moderate.

Hotel Kilkenny, College Rd., Kilkenny, Co. Kilkenny (☎ 056/62000; fax 056/21994). The Kilkenny is a little closer to the city than the Newpark (below), and its public rooms have a little more character; otherwise, there's not much difference between the two. This property also has a charming Victorian house supplemented by modern cinderblock extensions that provide executive-style comfort in identical rooms. A pretty glass conservatory dominates the facade. 80 rms with bath. Facilities: restaurant, bar, indoor pool, saunas, sun bed, Jacuzzi, gymnasium, two lighted tennis courts, nightclub with disco Wed, Fri, and Sun. AE, MC, V. Expensive.

Lacken House, Dublin Rd., Kilkenny, Co. Kilkenny (☎ 056/61085; fax 056/62435). This compact Georgian guest house, a 7-minute walk from the center of Kilkenny, is set on an acre of grounds. The basement restaurant (expensive) has a high reputation for creative French-influenced cuisine. The rooms are decked out in Laura Ashley prints. 8 rms with bath. Facilities: restaurant (dinner only; closed Sun–Mon). AE, DC, MC, V. Inexpensive.

Newpark Hotel, Castlecomer Rd., Kilkenny, Co. Kilkenny (☎ 056/22122; fax 056/61111). This hotel in the rural suburbs about 1.6 kilometers (1 mile) from town has a Victorian house at the center of its modern extensions. The busy lobby is a popular meeting place for business travelers and also copes with tour bus trade in summer. The newer the rooms are, the more modern the furnishings; go for one in the old block. 84 rms with bath. Facilities: two restaurants, bar, indoor pool, saunas, sun beds, gymnasium. AE, DC, MC, V. Expensive.

ON TO CASHEL

Whether or not you visit Kilkenny, you'll be passing through Urlingford on the Dublin-Cork Road (N8) and then heading south to Cashel. It'll add another 45 minutes to your trip to head west through Thurles and stop at the **Abbey of Holycross** en route to Cashel. You'll find it worth the time if you want to join the faithful who since the late 12th century have been making pilgrimages to this Cistercian Abbey to see a piece of the Cross.

CASHEL

For anyone who cares about the past, a visit to the **Rock of Cashel** (*Causeal,* stone fort; ☎ 062/61437) is a high point for a trip to Ireland. The rock rises like a stone castle, 59.9 meters (200 ft.) above the town, and contains Ireland's best examples of medieval architecture. It was here, it's believed, that St. Patrick baptized the Irish King Aengus, who thus became Ireland's first Christian ruler; here that St. Patrick plucked the shamrock he used to explain the doctrine of the Trinity, which gave Ireland its national emblem; here that you can glimpse the Gaelic Ireland that has survived in spite of the Normans, the Danes, the British, and the tourists. Admission IR£2.50 adults, IR£1 children, IR£1.75 seniors. Open May–Sept, daily 9am–7:30pm; Oct–Apr, daily 9:30am–4:30pm. Optional 50-min guided tour.

The most romantic route to the Rock is along the **Bishop's Walk,** a 10-minute hike from the Cashel Palace Hotel.

The rock dominates the surrounding landscape, which in the 5th century was covered with dense oak forests. Legend has it that the devil, flying back to England, took a bite from a nearby hillside and dropped it here in the Golden Vale. Ask a guide to point out the "bite" in the side of the Slieve Bloom Mountains.

As you enter this royal city, you'll see ahead of you a rough stone with an ancient cross, where Patrick is said to have baptized King Aengus. Patrick was old then and drove his staff into the earth to support himself. After the ceremony, it was discovered that the staff had passed through the king's foot and the grass was soaked with blood. Aengus never cried out because he thought that suffering was part of the Christian experience.

The stone is a replica; the actual one is on display in the museum across from the entrance. One piece is missing from the triple cross, which symbolizes the three crosses on Calvary. Carved on the back is the figure of a robed bishop. It's believed that the stone beneath the cross was once a coronation stone for pre-Christian Irish kings and, before that, a sacrificial altar. How emblematic of the blend of pagan/Celtic and Christian elements in the Irish character.

Behind the cross are **Cormac's Chapel,** the country's best-preserved Romanesque ruin, and the **cathedral.** When English writer and traveler H. V. Morton called the chapel "whimsical"—an example of "gay Norman"—he was referring to its individuality, to the refusal of its builders to submit to foreign influences. Built by well-traveled Irish monks half a century before the Normans came, it has a uniquely Irish double roof, high-pitched to keep the rain away without pushing the walls out. The eastern end isn't pointed directly east, as in other Romanesque churches, because the chapel was dedicated to Our Lady and built so that on her feast day, May 1, the sun streamed through two windows (now blocked up) and fell directly on the altar below. Similarly, the cathedral was built a few degrees off so that the sun could shine through three lancet windows and illuminate the altar on another feast day, March 17. Notice how the chancel arch (the rounded arc separating the body of the chapel from the "front") is lopsided, symbolizing the drooping of Christ's head on the cross. Each column in both the chapel and the cathedral has a different shape, as if each had been carved by a different artist faithful to his own vision. How contrary to European models, and how sad that these Celtic anomalies were eventually stuffed into an English form.

Compare the rough, simple chapel, built in the earliest days of Christianity, to the relatively grand, sophisticated Gothic cathedral, built in a later age when Christianity was more established and faith more formalized. Ironically, it's the more modest chapel that has survived.

DINING

Bishop's Buttery, in the Cashel Palace Hotel, Main St. (☎ 062/61411). This is the Cashel Palace's version of a coffee shop. Elaborate Celtic-design hangings remind you you're in a palace, but the flagstone floor suggests you've ended up in the servants' quarters. Try the substantial Irish stew: mutton, onion, carrots, and potatoes; or Colcannon, a traditional mix of leeks, floury potatoes, butter, cream, and nutmeg. No reservations. Casual. AE, DC, MC, V. Moderate.

Chez Hans, Rockside (☎ 062/61177). The heavily paneled nave of an old church gives this restaurant a unique ambiance. The menu features an Irish variation on French cuisine: turkey breast with lemon balm sauce, duck flavored with fresh thyme and honey, and delectable chicken with a sabayon of leeks and Cashel Bleu cheese followed by delicious homemade ice cream. The wine list is predominantly French. Be prepared for somewhat leisurely service. Reservations advised. Jacket/tie advised. MC, V. Closed Sun–Mon, first 3 weeks Jan. Dinner only. Expensive.

ACCOMMODATIONS

Cashel Palace Hotel, Main St., Cashel, Co. Tipperary (☎ 062/61411; fax 062/61521). A conversation piece, this 18th-century mansion was for 140 years the palace of the Archbishop of Cashel. The Palladian architect Sir Edward Pearce also designed Parliament House in Dublin, now the Bank of Ireland. One room has a 3.6-by-5.4-meter (12-by-18-ft.) bathroom, with 4.7-meter (16-ft.) ceilings. Running along the wall and across the mirror is a family of Beatrix Potter rabbits—the work of the Right Rev. Dr. Robert Wyse Jackson, Bishop of Limerick, who resided here as dean of Cashel from 1946 to 1961. The staff is friendly and accessible. The Four Seasons Restaurant is outstanding. The Cellar Bar is a favorite with locals. Ask for a room facing the back so you can enjoy the panoramic view of the Rock of Cashel rising behind the hotel. 20 rms with bath. Facilities: three restaurants, bar. AE, DC, MC, V. Very Expensive.

CAHIR

Cahir (pronounce it *care*), 17.6 kilometers (11 miles) south of Cashel, has a fully restored 15th-century **castle** (Cahir center: ☎ 052/41011), with a massive keep, high enclosing walls, and spacious courtyards. The entrance fee includes a 12-minute audiovisual show. Admission IR£2 adults, IR£1 children, IR£1.50 seniors; family ticket IR£5. Open June–Sept, daily 10am–7:30pm; Oct–May, Tues–Sat 10am–6pm, Sun 2–6pm.

ACCOMMODATIONS

Kilcoran Lodge Hotel, Cahir, Co. Tipperary (☎ 052/41288; fax 052/41994). A few miles south of Cahir, on your right, this rural retreat makes an ideal overnight stop on the Cork-Dublin road. The restaurant and lounge bar are cheerful and homey, with a spectacular view of the distant mountains. A few rooms have antiques; ask for one that's quiet and in the original hunting lodge. Those in the wings aren't as pleasant. 23 rms with bath. Salmon and trout fishing on grounds. Facilities: restaurant, bar, indoor pool, sauna, sun beds, Jacuzzi. AE, DC, MC, V. Expensive.

ON TO CORK

The fastest route from Cahir to Cork is along the Dublin-Cork Highway (N8) to Mitchelstown and Fermoy. If you appreciate beautiful scenery, however, it's worth an extra half an hour turning off N8 at Clogheen, driving over the mountains to Lismore, and heading west to Fermoy. About 48 kilometers (30 miles) northwest of Fermoy is the town of Buttevant. Cross-country horse racing is said to have begun here in 1752 when Edward Black challenged a neighbor to race to the church at St. Leger, 6.4 kilometers (4 miles) away. The steeple gave them a point to head toward—hence the term steeplechase.

At Fermoy you have two choices: (1) To skip Cork and the south coast and head directly west on Route N72 to Killarney. This makes sense if time is limited and you want to reach the west coast as soon as possible. The road takes you through Mallow, which has one of Ireland's better hotels. (2) To head south to Cork and the south coast. It's the latter route we'll be following.

CORK

Cork (*Corcaigh,* marsh) is so named because the area within the arms of the River Lee—the center and the oldest part of Cork—is filled-in marsh-land. If you're looking for a colorful old town with memorable walks, historic hotels, and first-class restaurants, Cork is *not* the place to visit, or at least not to stay. If you have a passing curiosity, plan to spend a morning or an afternoon, then overnight in Shanagarry (to the east), Mallow (to the north), or Kinsale (to the south). You may want to spend more time in Cork if you have a serious interest in its history as a center for the struggle for independence.

The Anglo-Normans invaded in 1172 and the native chieftain was forced to marry a Norman woman. The townspeople, led by merchants, won a good deal of independence over the years, but in 1492 they took up the cause of Perkin Warbeck, pretender to the throne, and the mayor and leading citizens were executed and Cork lost its charter. The city surrendered to Cromwell in 1649, and in 1690 had to surrender to William III. The Fenian movement, the secret revolutionary society that sought independence from England by force, began here in 1858. These early terrorists played an important role in the War of Independence (1919–21), earning the city the name of Rebel Cork, which it kept until independence was won in 1922. The British burned down much of the city in 1920, so many of the buildings are relatively new.

It was here that William Thackeray composed *Vanity Fair* with the help of his mother-in-law, and here that writers Frank O'Connor and Sean O'Faolain were born. It was nearby at Youghal that Edmund Spenser wrote the *Faerie Queene*, with financial help from the mayor, an Englishman named Sir Walter Raleigh. Raleigh may have been polite to women, but he recommended a ruthless policy against the Irish, helping to suppress rebellions and recommending assassination of their leaders.

You can tour the city's high points in about 2 hours. Begin near **St. Patrick's Bridge,** beneath the statue of Theobald Mathew (1790–1861), who championed at least one side of the Irish character by leading a nationwide temperance campaign. He looks young and dashing, but his right hand is raised, either to bless you or to say "no."

Follow St. Patrick's Street, the main street of town, toward the center of the island. Turn right on Academy Street to Emmet's Place and see the modern Irish landscapes on display in the **Crawford Municipal School of Art Gallery** (☎ 021/273377). Free admission. Open Mon–Fri 10am–4:30pm, Sat 10am–5pm.

From the Gallery, follow Paul Street. On your right is the **City Park Shopping Centre,** where you can compare Waterford glass to less expensive Cork crystal. Turn right on Corn Market Street, which contains the remnants of a once-thriving street market. Continue to the river. Turn left and walk to the bridge, crossing over and following Shandon Street to Church Street. Turn right to **St. Ann's Shandon Church.** Sing "The Bells of Shandon" as you climb the 36-meter (120-ft.) bell tower for a gull's-eye view of the town: "With deep affection / And recollection," wrote Fr. Francis Sylvester Mahoney, "I often think of / Those Shandon bells, / Whose sounds so wild would / In the days of childhood / Fling around my cradle / Their magic spells." Is it any wonder many locals prefer Father Francis to O'Connor or O'Faolain?

Return down Shandon Street, recross the bridge, and continue along North Main Street. At the **Hilser Jewelry Store,** 95 S. Main St. (☎ 021/270713), which is worth a visit, turn left on Washington Street and right on Grand Parade, past an enclosed vegetable-and-meat market, to the **Tourist Information Office** (☎ 021/273251).

CORK

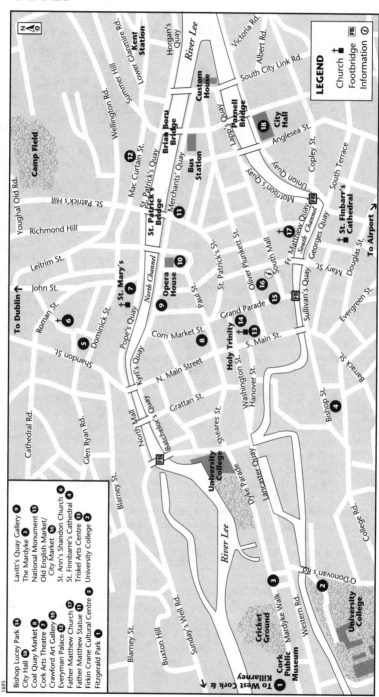

LEGEND
✝ Church
FB Footbridge
ⓘ Information

Bishop Lucey Park ⑭
City Hall ⑱
Coal Quay Market ⑧
Cork Arts Theatre ⑦
Crawford Art Gallery ⑫
Everyman Palace ⑯
Father Matthew Church ⑰
Father Matthew Statue ⑪
Firkin Crane Cultural Centre ⑫
Fitzgerald Park ①

Lavitt's Quay Gallery ⑨
The Mardyke ③
National Monument ⑮
Old English Market/
City Market ⑩
St. Ann's Shandon Church ⑥
St. Finnbarre's Cathedral ④
Triskel Arts Centre ⑬
University College ②

TAKE A BREAK

Turn right out of the Tourist Information Office and follow Grand Parade around to the right into Patrick Street. In a narrow alleyway, Market Lane, on your right, is The Vineyard (☎ 021/274793), which has been in the same family since 1903; its dark wood-paneled interior has recently been restored to the original Edwardian design. On weekdays at 6pm it hums with lively locals enjoying a "quick one" after work.

On Tobin Street, opposite the Tourist Information Office, is the **Triskel Arts Center** (☎ 021/965011)—check out its program of exhibitions, poetry readings, and lunchtime theater. If you plan to spend the evening in the area, find out what's happening at the **Opera House,** Lavitt's Quay (☎ 021/270022), which hosts both plays and recitals by visiting companies and popular artists.

DINING

Arbutus Lodge, Middle Glanmire Rd., Montenotte (☎ 021/501237). The best reason to overnight in Cork is to dine at the Arbutus. This luxurious restaurant, in a late Victorian house on lovely grounds overlooking the River Lee high above the city, has won numerous awards. Monogrammed tableware and personalized napery enhance a dining room furnished with polished antiques and modern Irish paintings. Those on a budget can sample the cuisine at lunch in the bar, but I recommend splurging on dinner. Haute cuisine interpretations of Irish home cooking are a feature. Try, for example, mussels in a garlic-laced cream sauce, flavored with Pernod and with almonds added; grilled black sole; or a savory chicken covered with a coating of wild mushrooms fresh from the forest. The rack of lamb is a classic, perfectly prepared. Ninety percent of the produce is local. The wine list at the Arbutus is among the best in the country. Reservations required. Jacket/tie advised. AE, DC, MC, V. Closed Sun. Expensive.

Clifford's, 18 Dyke Parade (☎ 021/275333). Michael Clifford, once the head chef at the Arbutus, runs this small, fashionable city-center restaurant in a converted Georgian building. A high standard is maintained in the fixed-price set menu that features dishes such as locally smoked fish, gratinée of Castletownbere prawns with scallops, and a terrine of chicken and leeks with Milleens cheese. Reservations advised. Jacket/tie required. AE, DC, MC, V. Wine license only. Closed Sun; no lunch Mon and Sat. Moderate.

ACCOMMODATIONS

Arbutus Lodge, Middle Glanmire Rd., Montenotte, Cork, Co. Cork (☎ 021/501237; fax 021/502893). Here's a place to satisfy anyone seeking a smaller hotel in town, a 7-minute drive from the city center. The rooms in this late Victorian house set in a garden overlooking the city are individually decorated, some with antiques. The restaurant is exceptional (see "Dining," above). 20 rms with bath. Facilities: restaurant, bar. AE, DC, MC, V. Expensive.

Gabriel House, 1 Summerhill St., St. Luke's, Cork, Co. Cork (☎ 021/500333; fax 021/500178). This plain but friendly guest house, which used to belong to the Christian Brothers, is convenient for rail and bus stations. Most of the rooms overlook gardens and the River Lee. Refreshments are available 24 hours. 20 rms with bath. Facilities: restaurant (wine license). AE, MC, V. Inexpensive.

Imperial Hotel, South Mall, Cork, Co. Cork (☎ 021/274040; fax 021/275375). A sedate old-fashioned institution, the Imperial is in the heart of Cork's legal-and-banking district. The spirit of an earlier age prevails in the carefully refurbished public rooms with high ceilings, marble floors, and chandeliers. Choose between a room renovated in the modern style or one with antique furniture. 100 rms with bath. Facilities: two restaurants, two bars. AE, DC, MC, V. Closed Dec 24–Jan 3. Expensive.

Jurys Hotel, Western Rd. by Washington St., Cork, Co. Cork (☎ 021/276622; fax 021/27447). This modern two-story hotel with a striking smoked-glass facade is on the banks of the River Lee, a 5-minute walk from the downtown area. Cork's Pub is a lively bar, and the Fastnet Restaurant is better than hotel average. Despite the cinder-block walls, the rooms are spacious and comfortable, and the public rooms big enough to absorb the package-tour crowds attracted by the facilities. 184 rms with bath. Facilities: two restaurants, two bars, indoor/outdoor heated pool, Jacuzzi, saunas, gymnasium, two tennis courts, squash courts. AE, DC, MC, V. Closed Dec 25–27. Expensive.

NEARBY ACCOMMODATIONS

Your choice of hotels outside Cork depends on your schedule. If you plan to tour Cork in the afternoon and take the slower but more scenic drive along the south coast, it makes sense to spend the night in Kinsale, which has several decent hotels and restaurants (see the town listings below). In a class by themselves, however, are Ballymaloe House in Shanagarry and Longueville House in Mallow.

Ballymaloe House, Shanagarry, Midleton, Co. Cork (☎ 021/652531; fax 021/652021). Since this isn't directly on our proposed route, it would make sense staying here only if you plan to spend a few days in the Cork area; you arrive at the hotel in the evening, spend the night, then continue to Cork the next morning on your way west; and/or you're willing to go out of your way to stay in a tranquil family-run country hotel rich in charm and character. The hotel, part of it dating back to the 17th century, sits on 160 hectares (400 acres) of rolling farmland. William Penn, Oliver Cromwell, and Bishop Berkeley stayed here—in the days before it had swimming, tennis, and croquet. The restaurant, lined with the paintings of Jack Yeats (William Butler's brother), is first-rate, particularly for Sunday dinner. To reach Shanagarry, pick up N25 at the traffic circle outside Cork City, where N8 from Dublin terminates. Turn off N25 at Midleton and follow signs for Cloyne and Ballycotton. Ballymaloe is

WHAT TO SEE & DO WITH CHILDREN

Ireland is geared to family travel, making it ideal to visit with children of any age. Most hotels and private homes can make arrangements for baby-sitters.

Almost every town along the route offers swimming, hiking, biking, fishing, and pony rides. Families can rent ponies or pony carts for trips through the Gap of Dunloe. They can also take boat trips on the lakes of Killarney. The grounds of **Muckross House,** on the shores of two of Killarney's most beautiful lakes, are a safe and scenic place for kids to bike. Killarney has several bike-rental shops.

Kids will love **Blarney Castle** and a walk through its **Rock Close.** They should also enjoy exploring **Muckross Abbey,** near Killarney, and climbing to the dizzying heights of the **Great Blasket Island,** off the coast of Dingle.

3.2 kilometers (2 miles) beyond Cloyne on the Ballycotton road. 32 rms with bath. Facilities: restaurant, bar, outdoor heated pool, croquet, tennis court. AE, DC, MC, V. Closed Dec 24–26. Expensive.

Longueville House, Mallow, Co. Cork (☎ 022/47156; fax 022/47459). This place, just west of Mallow on the N72 Killarney road, is 35.2 kilometers (22 miles) north of Cork, so you wouldn't want to stay here unless you plan to spend a few days in the area; you arrive at the hotel in the evening, spend the night, then in the morning continue south to Cork or west to Killarney; or you're willing to go out of your way for a night in one of Ireland's best-loved country hotels. The Georgian mansion sits on 200 hectares (500 acres) overlooking the Blackwater River, which supplies some of the country's top restaurants with its fresh fish. In spite of the owner's efforts to modernize the hotel, it has managed to keep its old-world charm, with an elegant drawing room, a basement billiards room, and lots of molded plaster, Waterford chandeliers, and beautiful inlaid mahogany doors. The Presidents' Restaurant is outstanding. Ask for a room with traditional furnishings overlooking the ruins of Dromineed Castle. 20 rms with bath. Facilities: restaurant, bar. Fishing on grounds. AE, MC, V. Closed Dec 23–Feb 28. Very Expensive.

BLARNEY CASTLE

Kissing the Blarney Stone is like standing for the Hallelujah Chorus of Handel's *Messiah*—it's something you do. But the romantic ruins of **Blarney Castle** (☎ 021/385252) are also worth a visit, and so are the Woolen Mills—the largest emporium of Irish crafts in the country—located on the castle grounds. The castle is 8.1 kilometers (5 miles), a 10-minute drive, north of Cork off the main (N22) Killarney road—follow the signs. If you're staying in Mallow, stop off at the castle en route south to Cork.

Why is there so much blarney about a simple stone? As the story goes, an emissary named George Carew was sent by Elizabeth I to get the Lord of Blarney Castle, Cormac McDermot MacCarthy, to transfer his allegiance from his clan to her; in other words, to surrender his fortress.

Again and again MacCarthy agreed, but at the last moment he always found another reason to delay. His excuses were so frequent and reasonable that Carew became a joke at Elizabeth's court. Elizabeth is reported to have told Carew in exasperation, "This is all Blarney talk; what he says he never means." And so the word *blarney* has come to stand for smooth talk—charming, basically harmless, but meant to deceive.

High up on the battlements of the ancient castle, embedded in the outside wall, is the Blarney Stone. Kissing it is said to give one the gift of eloquence, which makes a person irresistible to the opposite sex. Of all visitors to the castle—Germans, Japanese, and so on—Americans, the manager says, are most likely to kiss the stone and be on their way, neglecting the romantic 15th-century castle and the beautiful castle grounds.

Visitors, including the Irish, have been kissing the stone since the 18th century. No one knows exactly why. The most plausible explanation is that the stone had some significance to the MacCarthy clan—perhaps as the stone on which the chieftain sat—and it was later incorporated into the battlements.

What will surprise you is the considerable effort you must make to kiss the stone. After climbing 127 very steep stone steps, you have to lie on your back and lean backward over the edge of the 42.75-meter (150-ft.) wall. Visitors were once dangled by their heels over the side of the castle, but in 1912 a hapless pilgrim fell ineloquently to the ground and an iron guard rail was installed. Ninety-year-olds have kissed the stone, so there's no reason why you can't, too; and a photographer will take your picture to prove it. Admission IR£3 adults, IR£2.50 seniors, IR£2 children. Open May, Mon–Sat 9am–6:30pm; June–Aug, Mon–Sat 9am–7pm; Sept, Mon–Sat 9am–6:30pm; Oct–Apr, Mon–Sat 9am to dusk; year-round, Sun 9am–5:30pm.

The path leading to the castle veers left to the **Rock Close,** a grove of ancient yew trees—some of the oldest in the world—and weirdly shaped boulders. The paths were probably laid out by an 18th-century owner of the castle, but when you see the witch's stone and wander through her kitchen, you'll agree with those who believe this was once a center of Druid worship.

Blarney Castle House (☎ 021/385252), next door to the castle, was built in 1784 in the style of a Scottish baronial mansion with picture-book turrets and fancy stepped gables. The interior features a fine stairwell and numerous family portraits. Admission IR£3 adults, IR£2.50 seniors, IR£2 children. Open June to mid-Sept, Mon–Sat noon–6pm.

ACCOMMODATIONS

Blarney Park, Blarney, Co. Cork (☎ **021/385281;** fax 021/381506). If you must overnight in Blarney (not a thing I recommend because of the package-tour crowds), this modern low-rise is your best bet. It's pleasantly located a few minutes' walk from the hubbub of the castle green.

76 rms with bath. Facilities: restaurant, bar, indoor pool, saunas, gymnasium, tennis. AE, DC, MC, V. Expensive.

KINSALE

Kinsale (*Ceann Saile*, head of the tide), 28.8 kilometers (18 miles) southwest of Cork, is one of Europe's top deep-sea fishing and sailing centers. It also holds an important place in Irish history, for it was here, in 1601, in the Battle of Kinsale, that the Irish, aided by some 4,000 Spaniards, held the town for 10 weeks before surrendering to English forces. This was the final effort by the medieval chiefs to fight the British; after the battle, the Irish were outlawed from the town (as in Kilkenny) and not permitted to live within its walls until the late 18th century. It was from Kinsale that the *Cinque Ports* set sail in 1703 with a sailor named Alexander Selkirk. Selkirk was marooned on the lonely Pacific island of Juan Fernandez and became the model for Defoe's *Robinson Crusoe*.

Kinsale today is one of Ireland's most attractive, sophisticated harborfront towns, with a reputation for good food. It's here that the annual Gourmet Food Festival is held in early October. Even if you don't plan to spend the night, it's worth stopping for lunch and a short walk around town.

TAKE A BREAK

A 5-minute climb in the Scilly/Summercove direction will take you to the **Spaniard Inn** *(☎ 021/772436), one of Ireland's most famous dives, situated on a hairpin bend overlooking the harbor on the road to Charles Fort. Inside, a big log fire is always burning in the grate of the small front bar, which has a fishing net, wood beams, and sawdust on the floor. This is the place to meet the locals over a glass of Guinness.*

The **museum** at the Old Courthouse, Market Place (☎ 021/772044), in the 17th-century Market House has models of local ships and examples of Kinsale lace. Admission 35p. Open Mon–Sat 11am–5pm, Sun 3–5pm. The 12th-century **St. Multose Church** has a Norman tower and some stocks for unruly children.

DINING

Blue Haven, 3 Pearse St. (☎ 021/772209). This old town house has earned international acclaim for its seafood. Inexpensive bar lunches are served in the lounge bar, patio, and conservatory, which are decorated with swagged curtains, hanging plants, and nautical brass. The quieter main restaurant overlooks a floodlit garden with a cherub-adorned fountain. Try wood-smoked salmon with lemon-butter sauce or phyllo parcels of crab with caviar sauce. Medallions of hake flavored with Pernod is one of the many delectable offerings from the sea, but you can also order meat dishes like a roulade of pork flavored with champagne and served with oyster mushrooms. Reservations advised. Casual. AE, DC, MC, V. Expensive.

Man Friday, Scilly, Kinsale, opposite the Spaniard Inn (☎ 021/772260). The log-cabin atmosphere of this restaurant is reminiscent of Robinson Crusoe's tropical paradise, complete with stone walls and floor, rough-hewn beams, and potted palms. Many diners prefer the conservatory that offers a sweeping view of the harbor. The restaurant attracts a cross-section of locals and offers main courses that include vegetables. Two of the best-recommended dishes are the Polynesian pork kebabs, served with a zesty and spicy sauce, and the Irish lamb, a dish that the staff praises more than any other. Reservations advised at all times. Neat but casual. AE, MC, V. Dinner daily and Sun lunch. Moderate.

The Vintage, Main St. (☎ 021/772502). This is a charming front-parlor restaurant, hidden away in a narrow back street a minute from the center of town. It has a loyal clientele of discerning locals and occasional celebrity visitors. The original front room, which has been discreetly extended, still gives you the impression of dining in a quietly chic, antiques-filled private home. Hot oysters in a sauce of dry white wine, cream, and sorrel and guinea fowl with red cabbage and apples are among the unusual specialties on the menu. Reservations advised. Jacket/tie advised. AE, DC, MC, V. Closed Sun in winter. Dinner only. Expensive.

ACCOMMODATIONS

Acton's Hotel, Pier Rd., Kinsale, Co. Cork (☎ 021/772135; fax 021/772231). Kinsale's biggest hotel is constantly being refurbished. It has a delightful seafront location on the town pier approach, but be sure to specify a room with a view; half of the rooms overlook a noisy back street. The bar and lobby, which are subject to invasions from the conference room, bus tours, and weddings, are taken over by jazz buffs on Sunday for a popular brunch jazz session. 56 rms with bath. Facilities: restaurant, bar, gymnasium, sauna, indoor pool. AE, DC, MC, V. Expensive.

Blue Haven, 3 Pearse St., Kinsale, Co. Cork (☎ 021/772209; fax 021/774268). This carefully renovated town house is the first choice of those who value atmosphere and attention to detail above spaciousness, though some feel the decor verges on the precious. The rooms are small but individually decorated with antiques and paintings by local artists. The owner-managers have won numerous international awards. 18 rms with bath. Facilities: restaurant, bar. AE, DC, MC, V. Closed Jan 9–25. Expensive.

Old Bank House, 11 Pearse St., Kinsdale, Co. Cork (☎ 021/774075; fax 021/774296). This refurbished Georgian guest house sits in the center of town and has been acclaimed as one of the top 100 places to stay in Ireland for the past several years. The windows in the spacious rooms are double-glazed against traffic noise and the decor is sumptuous, with antique furniture and tastefully coordinated draperies and carpets.

9 rms with bath. Facilities: restaurant (wine license). AE, MC, V. Closed Dec 23–26. Moderate.

The Old Presbytery, Cork St., Kinsale, Co. Cork (☎ 021/772027). A tall, thin Victorian town house, this is among the most attractive of Kinsale's B&Bs. It's wittily furnished with a strange assortment of antiques and bold primary colors. Host Ken Buggy bakes his own bread daily and serves an above-average breakfast. 6 rms, 5 with bath. No credit cards. Inexpensive.

ON TO SKIBBEREEN & BANTRY

The narrow road from Kinsale to Skibbereen and Bantry twists and turns through rich green farm country, cultivated to the edge of the sea. The roller-coaster ride drops you down into hollows among fat sheep and peaceful cows, then up over the crests of hills where you can look out over a patchwork quilt of meadows extending in every direction, each patch a different shade of green. Beyond them you can see the colorful fishing boats and the sea. There's a domestic beauty here—a sense of fullness— you won't find elsewhere in Ireland. When you reach Balleydehob, the landscape becomes starker and leaner, and suddenly you realize you're in the west. Gone are the prosperous farms and the happy, gentle land- scapes; you're now in a world of wild seascapes and stone. You're sure to prefer one world to the other; but the joy of this trip is that you'll have an opportunity to experience both. There's a shortcut from Skibbereen Island to Bantry, but it's not worth saving a few minutes and missing some panoramic views of the coast.

Dining

West Cork Hotel, Bridge St., Skibbereen (☎ 028/21277; fax 028/22333). Tiny front-parlor restaurants come and go like wildflowers in this area. If you see one open, give it a try; otherwise, join the lawyers, doctors, priests, and merchants of Skibbereen at this reliable hotel restau- rant. Ignore the tacky modern decor and concentrate on the plainly cooked fresh Irish produce. There's always a choice of roast meat at lunch—generous portions of pork, lamb, beef, chicken, or ham—accom- panied by a seemingly endless succession of potatoes and vegetables. At dinner, hearty eaters should try the mixed grill. Reservations advised for parties of four or more. Casual but neat. AE, DC, MC, V. Inexpensive.

TIMOLEAGUE

Just 26 kilometers (16 miles) west of Kinsale is **Timoleague,** where you can stop and walk through the 600-year-old ruins of the largest Franciscan friary in Ireland. Just inland from the abbey, signposted in the town, is **Timoleague Castle Gardens** (☎ 023/46116). The castle is no more, but the pleasant Victorian manor has two large walled gardens— one for flowers, one for fruits and vegetables—and fine mature shrubbery. Outside the gates is a tiny gray stone Church of Ireland that'll surprise you with a dazzling interior: Its walls are entirely covered in mosaic and gold leaf, donated by an Indian maharajah in the 1890s. Admission IR£1.20 adults, 60p children. Open mid-May to mid-Sept, daily noon–6pm.

CASTLETOWNSHEND

If you have time to visit only one seaside village off the main road, stop in **Castletownshend.** Baltimore would be a good choice, too, but getting there involves a 25.6-kilometer (16-mile) round-trip from the coastal road, whereas Castletownshend is only a few miles away and requires no back-tracking. Leave the coastal road at Rosscarbery and follow signs to Glandore, Unionhall, and Castletownshend. The town has only one main street that slides steeply down to the sea, passing around an ancient sycamore that keeps the tour buses away.

TAKE A BREAK

*Stop for a drink at **Mary Ann's** (☎ 028/36146) —one of the noblest pubs in Ireland. Mary Ann, who never married, died in 1966, but the pub itself is some 300 years old. Play snooker (a type of billiards) or darts or enjoy your drink under the trees in the garden. Bar food is available in high season or by arrangement only in off-season. You'll surely sigh at the bland, tasteless furnishings that destroy the atmosphere of so many venerable old Irish hotels and pubs; so drink a toast to Mary Ann, who understood the beauty that comes with age. A restaurant has been added to the pub, accommodating large crowds on occasion. Restaurant food is served Tuesday to Saturday.*

ACCOMMODATIONS

If you want to build memories on your trip, consider spending a night in one of Castletownshend's two guest houses. Both can arrange for fishing, riding, golf, and tennis.

Bow Hall, Castletownshend, Co. Cork (☎ 028/36114). Bow Hall is as close as you'll come in Ireland to an American country inn—not surprising, as it's run by a family of bright, eager Midwesterners who fell in love with Ireland in the 1970s and decided to stay. The 17th-century house is bright and cheery, with American-made quilts and several summers' worth of books. Nowhere in Ireland will you be made to feel more of a welcome guest in a private home. It's no-smoking. Contact Mrs. Vickery here. 3 rms with bath. No credit cards. Moderate.

The Castle Guesthouse, Castletownshend, Co. Cork (☎ 028/36100). The water's-edge seat of the Townshend family that gave the town its name is the sort of place a pair of glassy-eyed teenagers might find themselves trapped in—in a late-night horror movie. Its torn carpets and peeling wallpaper evoke the ghostly presence of a bygone age. Anyone young at heart and/or in love should stay here—but probably only in the "Studio," with its fabulous antiques, or in a room called "Army." By the time you arrive here, four modern rooms may have been added. Contact Mrs. Rosemary Salter-Townshend here. 4 rms, 1 with bath. Lunch and dinner by arrangement. MC, V (but not for the Studio). Moderate.

BANTRY

Bantry (*Beann traighe*, the race of Beann) is delightfully situated at the head of Bantry Bay, one of the most beautiful bays along the Irish coast. If you're only passing through, try to find time to tour Bantry House, one of the great houses of Ireland—one of the very few whose furnishings do justice to their surroundings.

Bantry House (☎ 027/50047) has been the seat of the Earls of Bantry since 1765. The brick Georgian mansion was enlarged by the second Earl, who filled it with treasures from his travels around Europe—Flemish tapestries, fireplaces from Versailles, floor tiles from Pompeii. In one small dressing room is a dollhouse that's kept safe for examination by young visitors. If you can't spend the night here (see "Accommodations," below), consider staying for tea or homemade soups. Admission IR£5 adults, IR£3.50 students and seniors; under 16 free. Open daily 9am–6pm.

DINING

Larchwood House, Pearson's Bridge (☎ 027/66181). Clearly signposted midway between Bantry and Ballylickey, this is a cozy little restaurant at the back of a large modern country house overlooking a river valley. Owner/chef Sheila Vaughan is an ambitious and imaginative cook. Filet of brill with elderflower sauce and loin of veal with port and cream are the sort of main courses featured on her well-varied set menu. Reservations suggested. Casual but neat. AE, DC, MC, V. Wine license only. Closed Sun Easter–Oct and Sun–Wed Nov–Easter. Expensive.

ACCOMMODATIONS

Bantry House, Bantry, Co. Cork (☎ 027/50047; fax 027/50795). Imagine staying in a B&B among the treasures and sumptuous gardens of this magnificent mansion. A selection of comfortable and stylishly decorated rooms in both wings can now be rented overnight—the best one is the family room. 8 rms with bath. MC, V. Moderate.

Hillcrest House, Ahakista, Durrus, near Bantry, Co. Cork (☎ 027/67045). This place is about 20 kilometers (12½ miles) from Bantry, but if you've ever dreamed of staying in a whitewashed farmhouse on top of a pine-covered hill with great ocean views, then this is for you. The interior has been modernized with no loss of character, and if you like, you can lend a hand on the 20-hectare (48-acre) dairy farm. Contact Mrs. A. Hegarty here. 4 rms with bath. Closed Nov–Mar. Inexpensive.

BALLYLICKEY

From Bantry, head north 4.8 kilometers (3 miles) around the head of the bay to **Ballylickey.**

ACCOMMODATIONS

Ballylickey Manor House, Ballylickey, Co. Cork (☎ 027/50071; fax 027/50124). Ballylickey has a sophistication not easy to find on the west coast of Ireland. The ambiance is more country French than Irish—which will be a plus or minus, depending on why you're here. The four rustic pine chalets around the pool seem out of place; your best bets are the elegant rooms and suites in the recently rebuilt 300-year-old main house. Furnishings are a blend of Cork and Provence—and, difficult as it is to believe, it works. The hotel is surrounded by gardens on a hillside overlooking the bay. The grounds include a pool and private streams for fishing. The candlelit French country restaurant is in itself a good reason to stay. 11 rms with bath. Facilities: restaurant, bar, fishing on grounds, golf nearby. MC, V. Closed Nov–Mar. Moderate.

Sea View House Hotel, Ballylickey, Co. Cork (☎ 027/50462; fax 027/51555). This hotel is next door to the Manor House, though their spacious wooded grounds conceal this fact. The large three-story Victorian structure, once a home, has been turned into a pleasantly old-fashioned hotel. All rooms have a selection of attractive antique furniture, but if you want one with the promised sea view be sure to say so when you book. Here, as elsewhere along the coast, the owners can arrange for riding, boating, fishing, and golf. 17 rms with bath. Facilities: restaurant, bar. AE, DC, MC, V. Closed Nov 15–Mar 14. Moderate.

GLENGARRIFF

From Ballylickey, head west around the island-studded bay to the tourist center of **Glengarriff** (*Leann Gargh,* rugged glen), which, because of its sheltered location, is famous for its semitropical vegetation.

The top attraction is **Garinish Island,** a 10-minute boat ride from town. Barren 50 years ago, it now has a lovely Italian garden with plants and shrubs from around the world. Shaded paths lead to Roman statues, Grecian temples, a miniature Japanese garden, and an old Martello tower. It's also called Bryce Island, after the family who gave it to the nation. George Bernard Shaw was a frequent visitor when he was living in the neighborhood, writing *Saint Joan.*

If time permits, or if you're partial to seascapes, follow a 107.2-kilometer (67-mile) circular route around the Beara Peninsula from Glengariff to Castletownbere, then north to Kenmare. The scenery is similar to but less spectacular than that of the Ring of Kerry and the Dingle Peninsula, which you'll see later on, so you may prefer to head directly north from Glengarriff to Kenmare. This is a beautiful drive through wild mountain scenery, with cloud shadows racing across purple mountains and pillars of golden gorse.

KENMARE

Kenmare (*Ceann mara*, head of the sea) is a delightful tourist center at the head of the Kenmare River, 32 kilometers (20 miles) south of Killarney. If you want a single base from which to explore the entire west coast, you're better off closer to Killarney, which is central both to the Ring of Kerry and to the Dingle Peninsula. Kenmare, however, has the Park Hotel, which is the number-one hotel on your itinerary. Kenmare is also much more sophisticated and uncommercial. If you want to enjoy outdoor sports for a few days or need a place to overnight before heading around the Ring of Kerry, Kenmare is ideal. At the very least, you should stop for lunch at one of its first-class restaurants or have a deli make a picnic lunch for you. Sandwiches come on homemade brown bread—that's how sophisticated Kenmare is. If you're here on Monday, the Town Fair on Main Street has some good buys on hand-knit sweaters.

DINING

The Lime Tree, Kenmare (☎ 064/41925). Located in a charming old stone house, this is a good bet for dinner if you'd rather not splurge in the Park Hotel next door. Main courses include mussels in garlic butter, smoked chicken with curried rice salad, and rack of lamb with a sauce of red currants and almonds. Reservations advised in high season. Casual but neat. MC, V. Closed Sun and Nov–Apr 1. Dinner only. Moderate.

Park Hotel, Kenmare (☎ 064/41200). The menu at this stately old hotel restaurant, which looks like a Victorian château, is accurately self-described as "progressive Irish with a Pacific Rim flavour." Perhaps begin with a warm salad of squab pigeon with a *brunoise* of foie gras—flavored with a lavender-and-apple vinaigrette—then move succulently on to filet of Scottish salmon with a compote of leeks and red peppers or a daring dish of beef filet with a chartreuse of oxtail, the meats enhanced with a demiglaze of truffles and port. Ask for a window table overlooking lawns sweeping down to the bay. Reservations advised. Jacket/tie required. AE, DC, MC, V. Expensive.

The Star Restaurant, Gortamullen, Kenmare (☎ 064/41099). This light, bright modern restaurant is half a mile outside town and specializes in local seafood. Try pan-fried monkfish with Irish Mist and dill sauce. They also serve steaks, veal, and roast duckling. Reservations advised high season. Casual. MC, V. Closed Oct–Apr Mon–Thurs. Moderate.

ACCOMMODATIONS

Lansdowne Arms, Main St., Kenmare, Co. Kerry (☎ 064/41368; fax 064/41114). Kenmare's original coaching inn was established by the Marquis of Lansdowne when the town was first laid out in the 1790s. It has a friendly, homey atmosphere. The rooms are basic but adequate for an overnight stop, and there's live entertainment in the bar most nights. 25 rms with bath. Facilities: restaurant, bar. MC, V. Inexpensive.

Park Hotel Kenmare, Kenmare, Co. Kerry (☎ 064/41200; fax 064/41402). This former bishop's palace nearly a century old is on 11 beautifully kept acres overlooking Kenmare Bay. Here at last is a historic Irish hotel with rooms as distinguished as its public areas. Some rooms have four-posters, Liberty fabrics, and antique furniture from stately mansions of England and Holland. Others are smaller and more modern, but also decorated with flawless taste. The grounds are a natural garden of dracaena palms, gladiolus, rhododendrons, fuchsia bushes, and other flora typical of southwestern Ireland. In its first incarnation, the Park Hotel belonged to the chain of Great Southern Hotels built at the turn of the century for the English gentry who wanted their comforts away from home. 47 rms with bath. Facilities: restaurant, bar, tennis, 18-hole golf course. DC, MC, V. Very Expensive.

Rockvilla, Templenoe, Kenmare, Co. Kerry (☎ 064/41881). Mrs. Sheila Fahy's home is 6.4 kilometers (4 miles) outside Kenmare on the Sneem/Ring of Kerry Road. She offers plain Irish hospitality in a comfortable modern house set in an acre of gardens. Unlike most B&Bs, this one has a chef in residence who prepares an à la carte evening meal of local seafood or steak. 6 rms, 5 with bath. Facilities: restaurant (dinner only; wine license only), tennis. V. Inexpensive.

ON TO KILLARNEY

Kenmare is the starting point for drives around the Ring of Kerry to Killarney—a full day's trip. By taking this circular route, however, you'll miss the sensational drive north over the mountains from Kenmare to Killarney. Be sure to include this drive on an excursion from Killarney to Ladies' View.

THE RING OF KERRY

The famous **Ring of Kerry** is a road that skirts the coast of the Iveragh Peninsula, with dramatic seascapes, fine mountain scenery, and restaurants and hotels for every taste and budget. It's less wild than the Dingle Peninsula to the north, but it also has more amenities. If you have time for only one side trip from Killarney, tour the Dingle Peninsula instead; the Ring of Kerry is better suited for those who plan to stay in one of its resorts and take advantage of the outdoor activities—tennis, fishing, hiking, riding, and golf. The 176-kilometer (110-mile) drive around the Ring is a full-day trip. Start in Kenmare, as most day-trippers will be heading in the opposite direction. The most dramatic views are west of Parknasilla on the south coast and west of Glenbeigh on the north coast—particularly around Cahirciveen.

TAHILLA

The village of **Tahilla** (17.6km/11 miles west of Kenmare, 4.8km/3 miles east of Parknasilla) consists of a Catholic church, a petrol pump, a post office, a school, and lots of grazing cows and sheep.

Accommodations

Tahilla Cove Country House, Tahilla, Co. Kerry (☎ 064/45204; fax 064/45104). This modest but unusual guest house was built on a slope amid a subtropical garden in its own private cove. The comfortable chintz-covered furnishings aren't particularly original or inspired, but the location is remarkably peaceful and the sight of the long, drawn-out sunset above the restless sea is hypnotic. In fact, there's almost nothing to do here but exist; but the secluded, out-of-the-way atmosphere and the friendliness of the hosts, Dolly, Deirdre, and James Waterhouse, make this a worthwhile stop. Stay if you're passing through or if you want to take a few days off to fish or to rest. Some rooms are plainer than others; of the four in the main house, no. 6 is best. The tiny bar is popular with local fishers. The Sunday menu includes scallops, salmon, and lobster. 9 rms, all with bath. Facilities: restaurant, bar. AE, DC, MC. Closed Oct 15–Apr 15. Moderate.

PARKNASILLA

Parknasilla (24km/15 miles west of Kenmare), on the shores of the Kenmare River at the edge or the sea, is a center for sailing, fishing, tennis, pony trekking, and golf. Thanks to the Gulf Stream, the vegetation is tropical.

Accommodations

Parknasilla Great Southern Hotel, Parknasilla, Co. Kerry (☎ 064/451622; fax 064/45323). This is one of those elegant turn-of-the-century hotels built for the English upper classes so they could brave the wilderness in comfort. The architect also designed the Park Hotel in Kenmare. (The Park seems to attract more Americans; the Parknasilla, more Europeans.) Among the most famous guests have been General de Gaulle, Princess Grace, the Dutch royal family, and George Bernard Shaw, who wrote much of *Saint Joan* while staying here in Suite 216. The atmosphere has an institutional edge but also conjures up the glamour of a bygone age. The rooms are a bit plain but tasteful. Guests, most of whom prefer to stay in the old section, are greeted by a porter in frock coat and striped pants. 84 rms with bath. Facilities: restaurant, bar, indoor saltwater pool, sauna, horse trekking, sailing, windsurfing, waterskiing, angling, tennis, nine-hole golf course. AE, DC, MC, V. Closed Mar 1–10. Very Expensive.

SNEEM

The grassy central green in **Sneem** (27km/17 miles west of Kenmare) is more typically an English village than an Irish one. Nevertheless, Sneem has won several government awards for its attractiveness. The latest and the best of its charms is a "sculpture park"—a field by the river in which small stone-built pyramids with stained-glass insets were erected by Cork artist James Scanlon. Opened in 1990, it already looks like an integral

COUNTY KERRY

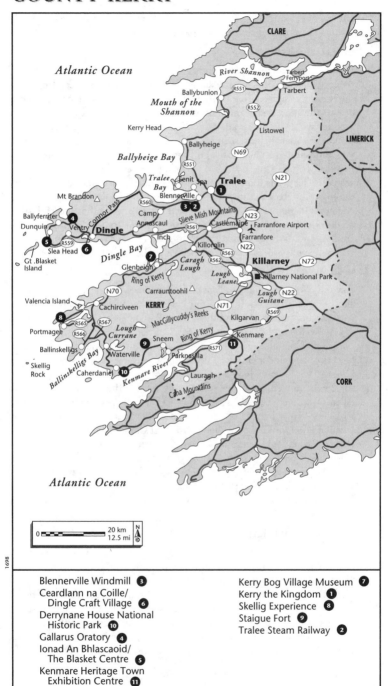

Blennerville Windmill **3**
Ceardlann na Coille/
  Dingle Craft Village **6**
Derrynane House National
  Historic Park **10**
Gallarus Oratory **4**
Ionad An Bhlascaoid/
  The Blasket Centre **5**
Kenmare Heritage Town
  Exhibition Centre **11**

Kerry Bog Village Museum **7**
Kerry the Kingdom **1**
Skellig Experience **8**
Staigue Fort **9**
Tralee Steam Railway **2**

part of the landscape. Stroll down the lane beside the sweater shops toward the Catholic church to explore it.

STAIGUE FORT

Beyond Sneem, the road winds inland for a few miles through wild scenery, meeting the coast again at Castlecove. Just past Castlecove, on the right, is a sign leading you 2.4 kilometers (1½ miles) to **Staigue Fort,** one of the most remarkable prehistoric monuments in Kerry. You may wonder what the fuss is all about, as there's nothing to see but a circular wall of dry masonry 5.4 meters (18 ft.) high. But let your imagination lift you thousands of years back in time, to when the fort contained two thatched cottages and was used to shelter farmers and their animals from wolves. The walls, constructed without mortar, are 3.8 meters (13 ft.) thick at the base. Along the interior of the walls are several well-constructed flights of stairs. Staigue Fort is one of the finest of some 35,000 surviving ring forts scattered throughout Ireland, dating from the Iron Age to early Christian times. In spite of their name, they were not used as military forts but as homesteads and cattle enclosures.

CAHERDANIEL

Beyond Westcove is the village of **Caherdaniel.** In the vicinity, near the shores of Derrynane Bay, is the curious **hermitage of St. Crohane,** carved from solid rock. Slightly under 3.2 kilometers (2 miles) southwest of Caherdaniel is **Derrynane House** (☎ **066/75113**), the former home of Daniel O'Connell (1775–1847), one of the most famous and revered fathers of Irish independence. If you know nothing of O'Connell and care little for Irish history, you'll have no reason to visit—just as an Irish person might not go out of his or her way to visit the birthplace of Ethan Allen on a tour of the United States. O'Connell was committed to non-violence. While living here he defended the poor in court, helped win emancipation for Catholics (he was the first Catholic Irishman to sit in the British Parliament), demonstrated to the Irish the power of numbers, and helped win back for them a sense of pride and self-respect. Admission IR£7 adults, 80p children and seniors. Open mid-June to Sept, daily 10am–1pm and 2–7pm, Sun 2–5pm; Oct to mid-June, Tues–Sat 10am–1pm and 2–5pm, Sun 2–5pm. Free admission to park, which is open daily.

THE SKELLIG ISLANDS

The views become more spectacular as you head north around the western rim of the peninsula. The road climbs above the sea, beneath smooth brown hills and sheep-colored rocks. Neat white cottages stand like sentinels among the green fields, running down to the edge of the sea. There's something noble about this effort to claim every inch of available soil—a human drama you're not aware of in the richer country to the east.

The islands rising offshore are the **Skelligs.** Severe erosion has been caused by visitors to the islands. There's an excellent view of the monastic remains from the boat, and you can observe the large numbers of nesting seabirds without disturbing them. **Desmond Lavelle** (☎ 066/ 76124), a skilled boat owner on Valentia Island (connected with a bridge to the mainland of County Kerry, north of Waterville), is the author of several books about the islands. He leads boat tours to the Skelligs every day, weather permitting, between Easter and late October for no more than a dozen participants. If you're young at heart and want a real adventure, this is the one trip you'll want to take; the memory will linger for a lifetime. The 14.4-kilometer (9-mile) voyage from Valentia is made only when seas are relatively calm, and even then the sea can be rough; be sure to take motion-sickness pills before sailing. The cost of IR£20 per person includes a departure at 11am; a 90-minute boat trip in the waters around The Small Skelligs, site of an estimated 27,000 pairs of nesting gannets, a local sea bird; then a 2-hour guided walking tour (not by Mr. Lavelle, but by a colleague) of Big Skellig (also known as Skellig Michael) for a view of the ruined monasteries and local ecology. The experience ends with a return to Valentia between 4 and 4:30pm.

The **Great Skellig** or **Skellig Michael** (Michael is the patron saint of high places) is the largest of the three—an enormous mass of rock rising more than 209.9 meters (700 ft.) above the sea. In former times Skellig Michael was a place of pilgrimage. The ruins on its summit are from an early Christian monastery, the earliest dating from around A.D. 750. They include two small oratories, a small early church, a larger 10th-century church, six beehive cells, and several burial enclosures and crude crosses. En route to Skellig Michael you'll pass **Little Skellig,** home of 20,000 pairs of gannets, the second-largest gannetry in the North Atlantic.

WATERVILLE

The road from Derrynane House crosses the 209.9-meter (700-ft.) Pass of Coomakesta, then winds down to **Waterville** (*An Coirean,* little waterfall). The popular angling center is on a strip of land between Ballinskelligs Bay and Lough Currane, one of the loveliest lakes in Ireland. Like Parknasilla, Waterville is a popular tourist destination with a few good restaurants and hotels. Outdoor activities are plentiful, including sailing, tennis, hiking, and riding; but the main attractions are fishing and playing golf on an 18-hole championship course. You also have the exhilarating feeling of being on the ocean.

Dining

The Huntsman, Waterville (☎ 066/74124; fax 066/74124). This restaurant features plainly cooked fresh fish: lobsters from the tank (broiled and served with roe), creamy seafood bisque, scampi Newburg, salmon with hollandaise, and delicious homemade bread. The color scheme is a soothing combination of burgundy and rose with oak parquet floors. Though the restaurant serves daily from March to November, call ahead from December to February, as it's likely to be closed if the weather is bad.

Today the Huntsman is also a B&B, offering 10 rooms with bath (moderate). Neat but casual. AE, DC, MC, V. Moderate.

Accommodations

Butler Arms, Waterville, Co. Kerry (☎ 066/74144; fax 066/74520). This is a large, established, residential-type hotel, neither sophisticated nor elegant, but friendly and old-fashioned in a distant-aunt sort of way. The best bets are rooms facing the sea. Ask for no. 215 or something comparable. Free salmon and sea trout fishing is offered on Lough Currane and on private lakes—all arranged by the hotel staff. 30 rms with bath. Facilities: restaurant, bar, tennis, deep-sea and freshwater angling, pony trekking. AE, DC, MC, V. Closed Oct 20–Apr 18. Expensive.

The Smuggler's Inn, Cliff Rd., Waterville, Co. Kerry (☎ 066/74330; fax 066/74422). On Waterville's mile-long sandy beach, the small family-run guest house has old-world charm. The rooms are basic but pretty and clean, with panoramic sea views. Chef/proprietor Harry Hunt runs a seafood restaurant. 10 rms with bath. Facilities: restaurant (moderate), bar. AE, DC, MC, V. Closed Nov 7–Mar 1. Inexpensive.

CAHIRCIVEEN

Cahirciveen (take it slowly: Ka-*her*-sigh-veen), at the foot of 373.5-meter (1,245-ft.) Mount Bentee and overlooking Valentia Harbor (where boats leave for the Skelligs), is the shopping center of the western end of the Ring of Kerry. Of all the towns on the Ring, Cahirciveen has the most charm, in part because it enjoys a life independent of the tourists passing through. Stop for a pint at the Anchor, one of the town's most famous pubs (but unknown to tourists), where writers and artists touch mugs with local farmers and fishers.

Accommodations

Mount Rivers, Mount Rivers, Carhan Rd., Cahirciveen, Co. Kerry (☎ 066/72509). This bed-and-breakfast is one of the friendliest on the Ring. Books are everywhere in this late 19th-century home at the far end of town. Contact Mrs. N. McKenna. 5 rms with bath. Closed Oct–Mar. No credit cards. Inexpensive.

GLENBEIGH

The road northeast from Cahirciveen to **Glenbeigh** is scenically the highlight of the drive around the Ring of Kerry. Across the bay is the Dingle Peninsula, which you'll be exploring in future days. Glenbeigh is the starting point for some of the best hikes in western Ireland, around the Glenbeigh Horseshoe, near Commasaharn Lake, and along the slopes of Drung Hill. Ask locally for details or consult the *Irish Walk Guides No. 1* (see "Reading," earlier in this chapter).

A few minutes west of Glenbeigh is a 3.2-kilometer (2-mile) spit of land jutting into Dingle Bay, with soft yellow sand backed by high dunes and breaking surf. Across the bay, on the Dingle Peninsula, is a similar spit, perfect (at low tide) for walking or swimming. If the weather is right, don't wait for Dingle; in Ireland you never know when you'll see the sun again.

CARAGH LAKE

A few miles northeast of Glenbeigh, on the Ring Road toward Killorglin, you'll see signs on your right pointing to **Caragh Lake.** This is a beautiful expanse of water, set among broom- and heather-covered hills with majestic mountains beyond. Much of the lakeside property is privately owned — as is much of the Killarney area — by Germans. If you're making a quick tour of western Ireland and want to see as much as possible, it makes little sense to base yourself on Caragh Lake. Stay here either as a starting or an ending point for a trip around the Ring of Kerry or as a place to stay put for a day or two that's near a lake and off the beaten track.

Accommodations

A hundred yards back from the lake are two lovely secluded hotels surrounded by woods and gardens. Though both provide access to the lake and their own boats for rowing and fishing, neither is close enough to enjoy lakeside views.

Ard na Sidhe, Caragh Lake, near Killorglin, Co. Kerry (☎ 066/69105; fax 066/69282). With a name pronounced *sheen,* meaning "hill of the fairies," this is a secluded and peaceful Victorian mansion, with imposing gray walls covered with creeper, 4.8 kilometers (3 miles) from the Ring Road. The interior is tastefully furnished with antiques and open fireplaces. The hotel is now run by the same German group that manages Hotel Europe and Dunloe Castle (see "Killarney," below). The rooms are a bit bare but have nice traditional furnishings, and the main house is preferable to the annex. 20 rms with bath. Facilities: restaurant, bar, boating, fishing. AE, DC, MC, V. Closed Oct 2–Apr 25. Expensive.

Caragh Lodge, Caragh Lake, near Killorglin, Co. Kerry (☎ 066/69115; fax 066/69316). Another secluded country house on the lake shore, 1.6 kilometers (1 mile) from the Ring Road, the Lodge is smaller, friendlier, and more relaxed than its neighbor. The lounges and the dining room are furnished with antiques and overlook the lake. It's on 3.6 hectares (9 acres) of parkland with rare and subtropical trees and shrubs. 9 rms with bath. Facilities: restaurant (wine license only), sauna, fishing, tennis. AE, DC, MC, V. Closed mid-Oct to Easter. Expensive.

KILLORGLIN

The best time to visit **Killorglin** is during the 3-day Puck Fair in August, which is attended by people from all over Ireland. On the evening of the first day, a procession assembles at the bridge and a large billy goat, horns bedecked with ribbons, is borne in triumph through the streets to a platform on a square in the center of town. Here Puck is enthroned for 2 days, presiding over a great cattle-, horse-, and sheep fair, with nonstop dancing and entertainment. The tradition is a holdover either from pagan times or from colonial days, when the stampeding of goats gave warning of the approach of English forces. Killorglin is a pleasant 22.5-kilometer (14-mile) drive from Killarney.

KILLARNEY

There are two Killarneys—one is a spectacular region of mountains and island-studded lakes, wooded shores, and romantic glens; the other, a tourist-infested town whose population more than triples in summer. The town—more a place of transit than a destination—is in the wrong place: on a flat plain more than a mile from the lakes. The only reason to come here is to satisfy a nostalgia for noise, traffic, and fast food; mingle with the under-25 crowd; shop; or dine at one of the quality restaurants. Fortunately, there are hundreds of guest houses and hotels in the countryside, so you don't need to visit the town too often.

What makes the scenery around Killarney so breathtaking is the rare combination of lushness and grandeur, of tropical vegetation and wild mountain scenery. A climate warmer than anywhere else in the British Isles encourages the growth of Mediterranean strawberry trees, cedars of Lebanon, and wild fuchsia sprouting from gray stone walls. Happiness, you'll find, has very little to do with the mind here. There are historic buildings to check off as you tour the country, but most of your time will be spent getting back in touch with yourself: biking along the shores of Muckross Lake, hiking to some windswept peak, angling for salmon, or simply watching the morning mist uncurl from a mountain lake.

A full-day pony- or pony-cart ride through the Gap of Dunloe and a boat trip through the three lakes of Killarney makes a memorable excursion. Hotels can make arrangements for you to rent private ponies or a boat. The trip was the standard Killarney adventure in the 19th century; today most visitors haven't time for a full day of anything and make do with the pony trip alone, which is the least rewarding part of the tour.

If you're crossing the Gap on your own, drive west 7.2 kilometers (4½ miles) on Route R562 to Beaufort and follow the signs another 2.4 kilometers (1½ miles) to the Gap of Dunloe. Men with pony carts—known locally as "jaunting cars"—will "assault" you along the way, but it's best to wait until you reach Kate Kearney's Cottage at the entrance, where the rates are regulated (but be sure to agree on a fee before you set off).

Have some ale or a cup of Irish coffee at Kate Kearney's Cottage and toast the lady who was famous in her day for her moonshine and her beauty. Wrote Lady Morgan:

Oh, did you ne'er hear of Kate Kearney,
She lived on the banks of Killarney;
From the glance of her eye
Shun danger and fly

For Fate's in the glance of Kate Kearney.
For that eye is so modestly beaming,
You'd ne'er think of mischief she's dreaming.
Yet, oh, I can tell
How fatal's the spell
That lurks in the eye of Kate Kearney.
Though she looks so bewitchingly simple,
Yet there's mischief in every dimple,
And who dares inhale
Her sigh's spicy gale
Must die by the breath of Kate Kearney.

Kate never married. When the law came after her, she disappeared—some say to Australia or New Zealand. The Irish loved her because she flouted the law and the law was British; and they continue to love wild, voluptuous women who flout the codes by which they're told to live.

On any given summer day, the pony carts make some 300 ninety-minute trips about halfway through the Gap and back, so don't expect to feel like Lewis and Clark. It's a scenic romantic trip, though, past a series of clear mountain lakes through a rift in the great MacGillycuddy's Reeks—surely an improvement over seeing the world framed through a car window. As the ponies leave their own trail markers along what is essentially an unimproved dirt road, you'll want to think twice about squishing forth on foot. If you're traveling off-season or want, because of health or children, to take a pony cart, a trip through the Gap is a great treat; otherwise, I suggest you take your feet or your rented ponies and explore other, equally spectacular areas of this beautiful country, including the **Horse's Glen,** described in Charles Kidney's *Visitor's Guide to Killarney.* A trip through the Gap makes sense, too, if you're leaving the crowds behind and taking a boat ride through the lakes.

The most romantic of the three lakes, **Upper Lake,** is also the least accessible. A road runs along a section of it, so, for the right price, you may be able to arrange through your hotel or a tour agency to have a boat put in the water for you or to get one at Lord Brandon's Cottage, at the western end of the lake. The cottage is a tea shop serving soup and sandwiches daily from Easter to September from 10am to dusk.

Ross Castle, a 16th-century stronghold of the O'Donoghue clan and the last castle to fall to Cromwell's army in 1652, is no longer open but operates a boat concession on the castle grounds, on the western shore of **Lower Lake.** You can row yourself around (rowboat hire is IR£2 per person per hour)—a memorable experience, particularly at dawn or dusk—or allow yourself to be taken to **Innisfallen Island.** (A covered, heated launch costs IR£5 one way.) If you have an interest in antiquity or a fondness for romantic ruins, you'll want to visit the remains of a 7th-century abbey on Innisfallen, which, like the Rock of Cashel, goes back to the earliest days of Christianity. Brian Boru, the last High King of Ireland,

and St. Brendan, who probably "discovered" America centuries before Columbus, are said to have been educated here. H. V. Morton writes that "there was once a Frenchman who said that Ireland was the jewel of the west, that Kerry was the jewel of Ireland, that Killarney was the jewel of Kerry, and that the little uninhabited isle of Innisfallen was the jewel of Killarney. I have nothing to add to this."

Another delightful half-day excursion from Killarney is south on Route N71 to **Muckross Abbey, Muckross House,** and **Torc Waterfall,** and around the southern shore of the three lakes to **Ladies' View** (32.2km/20 miles round-trip). This will take you along a section of the spectacular road between Killarney and Kenmare that you missed by driving from Kenmare around the Ring of Kerry. The abbey and house are in wooded parklands along the tranquil shores of Muckross and Lower Lakes—an idyllic spot for walks, bicycle rides, or pony-cart rides (cars aren't permitted on the grounds). There are several bicycle-rental shops in Killarney.

You'll reach Muckross Abbey first—a .4-kilometer (quarter-mile) walk from the parking lot and 4 kilometers (2½ miles) from Killarney. You can rent a pony cart here to take you on a delightful 1- or 2-hour ride to Muckross House and Torc Waterfall (IR£12 to IR£24 negotiable with the guide/driver depending on the time and route; up to four people per cart). You can also arrange to ride to Muckross House and walk back. What the drivers won't tell you is that you can return to your car after seeing the abbey and then drive directly to Muckross House without their services.

The 15th-century Franciscan **abbey,** partially restored in the past 25 years, was wrecked by Cromwell's forces in 1652, but is still amazingly complete, though roofless. An ancient yew tree rises up through the cloister and branches out over the broken abbey wails. The lakefront walk called Lovers' Lane, running halfway from the abbey to Muckross House, is one of the most beautiful in the park. Look at the islands in the lake—the abbey's treasures were buried on one of them in 1589 to avoid pillage and haven't yet been found.

Muckross House (☎ 064/31440) is a 19th-century mock-Elizabethan manor house that no one knew what to do with for 32 years. It's now a craft center where blacksmiths, weavers, basket makers, and potters demonstrate their skills. Also on display are old tools and an assortment, more representative than exceptional, of 19th-century country furnishings. Admission IR£3.50 adults, IR£1.50 children. Open daily 9am–5:30pm (to 7pm July–Aug).

Muckross House is clearly not for everyone; what you shouldn't miss, however, are the **Muckross Gardens,** with their many tender and exotic shrubs, and a stroll along Arthur Young Walk to Brickeen Bridge on a narrow strip of parkland between the two lakes. Free admission. Opening hours are the same as those at Muckross House.

Unless you go by pony cart, return to Route N71 and drive to **Torc Waterfall**—7.2 kilometers (4½ miles) from Killarney. The falls are a

10-minute walk from the parking lot. Visitors whip out their cameras as the falls roar into view; if you want more privacy, continue up a long flight of stone steps for about 10 minutes to the second clearing. From here there's a marvelous view of the lakes of Killarney. If you need more exercise, bear right where the path splits and continue walking through the 8,000-hectare (20,000-acre) national park.

Return to your car and continue west another 5 minutes or so to the **Ladies' View.** If I were Irish, I'd feel a certain outrage at the fact that what's perhaps the region's most spectacular setting is named in honor of Queen Victoria's Ladies-in-Waiting—not even the queen herself—who once upon a time expressed their pleasure at the view. Stop at the cafe if you need some refueling; but the best view is at another parking area 90 meters (100 yd.) farther west. If you haven't had enough beautiful scenery, continue across the mountains to Kenmare; otherwise, return to Killarney.

A delightful way to end the day is to drive at dusk to the ruined tower on Aghadoe Heights, only 4 kilometers (2½ miles) west of town, and watch the shadows creep over Lough Leane (Lower Lake).

KILLARNEY WALKS

The easiest walk, but one of the most delightful, is along the paved paths through the wooded parklands surrounding Muckross House.

Follow the steps past Torc Waterfall for a panoramic view of the lakes of Killarney.

The most satisfying short walk—8.8 kilometers (5½ miles) or 3 to 4 hours round-trip—is to the top of 529-meter (1,764-ft.) **Torc Mountain,** where you can enjoy breathtaking views of the entire region. Follow Route N71 past the entrance to Muckross House. Where the Kenmare road veers right, an unsurfaced road (the Old Kenmare Road) runs straight ahead into the forest. Drive uphill until you reach a locked gate beside the water supply station. Walk straight (disregarding forest roads to the left) to the bridge across the Owengarriff River above Torc Waterfall. The steep east face of Torc Mountain should be ahead of you. Continue uphill (left) along the road to the open moorland, where the river runs down from a mountain lake called the Devil's Punch Bowl. Continue until you come to a weather recording station within a wire enclosure. When a bridle path joins the road on the right, begin your ascent up to the summit. Be sure to return the same way you came; descent by the steep east side of Torc would be foolhardy.

If you're partial to mountain lakes, take the 9.7-kilometer (6-mile) walk (3 to 4½ hours round-trip) to the **Devil's Punch Bowl,** the lake that feeds Torc Waterfall. The lake is 90 meters (300 ft.) below the summit of 689.9-meter (2,300-ft.) **Mangerton Mountain.** You should be able to arrange in advance to make most of the trip by pony, but because the ascent is gradual the summit is accessible on foot to all age groups. Take Route N71 from Killarney toward Muckross House. Just past the Muckross Hotel (you might stop here for further details), take the road left to the Mangerton Viewing Park. At the upper end of the woods, swing right, past the car park, to the end of the surfaced road. Park by the concrete bridge. From here an old pony path leads up the mountain. The path swings right to an estate boundary fence, which runs left to the Punch Bowl. Just beside the outlet from the Punch Bowl is Bachelor's Well. Drink from its magic waters and you'll remain single all your life.

To enjoy what may be the wildest region in the country take a walk to the **Horse's Glen.** There are three lakes here suitable for swimming and fishing: Lough Garagarry, Lough Managh, and Lough Erhogh. The starting point, near Muckross Hotel, is only 9.7 kilometers (6 miles) from Killarney, yet the lakes are seldom visited.

DINING

Foley's Seafood and Steak Restaurant, 23 High St. (☎ 064/31217). This smart pub/restaurant is either fun and lively or crowded and smoky, depending on your preferences. In either case, it has lots of atmosphere, thanks in part to the colorful characters playing turn-of-the-century ballads. The menu features local produce in classic French dishes (sole meunière, steak au poivre), and 200 wines are offered. Reservations advised in high season. Neat but casual. AE, DC, MC, V. Moderate.

Gaby's, 17 High St. (☎ 064/32519). With crowded tables and wood-slat benches, this place gets low grades for atmosphere but high honors for the freshness of its fish. Try lobster bisque, black sole in cream sauce, seafood mosaic (an enormous shellfish platter), or fresh or smoked salmon. No reservations. Neat but casual. AE, DC, MC, V. Closed Sun Oct–May. Moderate.

Panorama Restaurant, in the Hotel Europe, Fossa (☎ 064/31900). The best of the many hotel restaurants in town overlooks the lakes, with live Irish entertainment most nights. The menu features such local specialties as oxtail soup, Irish stew, Dingle Bay lobster, and sea trout with toasted almonds. Reservations advised. Jacket/tie required. AE, DC, MC, V. Expensive.

Sheila's, 75 High St. (☎ 064/31270). In a town bedeviled by tourist traps, this friendly family-run spot offers excellent value. Now run by Sheila's daughter, it has fed the people of Killarney and its visitors for nearly 40 years. Simply furnished with pine tables and paper place mats, it features such Irish specialties as corned beef with cabbage and Irish stew (lamb with carrots, onion, and potatoes). Wine license only. MC, V. Inexpensive.

ACCOMMODATIONS

Aghadoe Heights Hotel, Aghadoe, Killarney, Co. Kerry (☎ 064/31766; fax 064/31345). This is a modern hilltop hotel 3.2 kilometers (2 miles) northwest of Killarney, whose main attraction is its exquisite view over Lower Lake. The interior is furbished in a luxurious country-house style. Antique china cabinets sit oddly beside the picture windows of its low-ceilinged public rooms, but all you'll really be looking at is the remarkable view. The rooms are plushly furnished and have floor-to-ceiling picture windows; ask for one with the lake view. 57 rms with bath. Facilities: restaurant, bar, tennis, indoor pool, sauna, gymnasium, fishing, access to two championship golf courses. AE, DC, MC, V. Very Expensive.

Arbutus Hotel, College St., Killarney, Co. Kerry (☎ 064/31037; fax 064/34033). This former shelter for monks is small and unpretentious — the best budget hotel for those who want to stay in town. It has turf fires and traditional music in its oak-paneled bar. The Buckley family has owned and managed it for more than 65 years. 34 rms with bath. Facilities: restaurant, bar. AE, DC, MC, V. Closed Jan 1–Feb 14. Moderate.

Cahernane, Muckross Rd., Killarney, Co. Kerry (☎ 064/31895; fax 064/34340). This 1877 Victorian mansion was once the home of the Earls of Pembroke. If you're looking for a small, peaceful hotel with a certain amount of character, this is the place. The public areas have rich wood paneling and a sense of the past. The guest rooms in the main building vary considerably in furnishings and size, and the best bet is no. 26. Ask for a room with a lake view. Avoid the rooms in the modern wing, which are undistinguished. 48 rms with bath. Facilities: two award-winning restaurants with a choice of 200 wines, bar, tennis court, fishing, horse-back riding, putting green. AE, DC, MC, V. Closed Nov–Mar. Very Expensive.

Carriglea, Muckross Rd., Killarney, Co. Kerry (☎ 064/31116). Here's a clean, friendly, reasonably priced guest house on a farm set back from a main road. I find the rooms in the main house generally preferable to those in the annex. More amusing than offensive is the extraordinary collection of clashing colors, as if one person were responsible for the curtains, another for the bedspreads, and so on (nos. 1 and 8 are a bit more color-coordinated). The public areas are fussy in a delightfully proper Victorian way. Contact Mr. and Mrs. M. Beazley. 9 rms with bath. Breakfast only. No credit cards. Closed Nov–Mar. Inexpensive.

Castlerosse, Killarney, Co. Kerry (☎ 800/528-1234 or 064/31144; fax 064/31031). This Best Western has a peaceful setting with lovely views, plus lower prices than many other of Killarney's modern hotels. The ambiance is "Turnpike Modern" — each room with its own parking place. The rooms are clean, charmless, functional, and ample. 110 rms with bath. Facilities: restaurant, bar, tennis, sauna. AE, DC, MC, V. Closed Nov 26–Mar 1. Expensive.

Dunloe Castle, Beaufort, Killarney, Co. Kerry (☎ 064/44111; fax 064/44583). Just south of Beaufort, on the road to the Gap of Dunloe, 7.2 kilometers (4½ miles) west of Killarney, this isn't a castle but a modern hotel under the same German management as the larger, more expensive and somewhat more elegant Hotel Europe (below). The public areas have classical statues and lovely terra-cotta floors, but the rooms are Butcher-block modern. Still, the castle is much classier than Killarney's mass-market hotels. 120 rms with bath. Facilities: two restaurants, two bars, indoor pool, sauna, gymnasium, tennis, horseback riding. AE, DC, MC, V. Closed Oct–Apr 18. Expensive.

Hotel Europe, Killorglin Rd., Fossa, Killarney, Co. Kerry (☎ 064/31900; fax 064/32118). This spacious modern hotel is under the same German management as Dunloe Castle (above). Though a bit impersonal (banquet facilities for 600), it attracts a well-heeled, educated clientele and has an old-fashioned elegance you won't find in hotels catering exclusively to the package-tour trade. Ask for an upstairs room facing the lake. 205 rms with bath. Facilities: two restaurants, two bars, indoor pool, sauna, gymnasium, tennis, horseback riding, fishing. AE, DC, MC, V. Closed Nov–Feb. Expensive.

Kathleen's Country House, Tralee Rd., Killarney, Co. Kerry (☎ 064/32810; fax 064/32340). Situated a mile outside town on Tralee Road, this is an imaginatively designed modern guest house set in its own grounds in the open countryside with pleasant views of the wooded valley. The spotless rooms, catering to nonsmokers, are spacious, light, and airy, with modern pine furniture. Kathleen herself is always on hand to ensure that everything runs smoothly. Her restaurant serves only fresh produce and organic vegetables. 15 rms with bath. Facilities: restaurant (dinner only; wine license). No credit cards. Inexpensive.

Killarney Great Southern Hotel, Killarney, Co. Kerry (☎ 064/31262; fax 064/31642). This good chain hotel hasn't entirely lost that old-world feeling it had at the turn of the century, when the British came by train and talked of Empire over their afternoon tea. The rambling creeper-clad town-center hotel dates from 1864 and is surrounded by pleasant gardens. Guests have included Caroline Kennedy and Pat Nixon. 180 rms with bath. Facilities: two restaurants, two bars, indoor pool, sauna, tennis. AE, DC, MC, V. Closed Jan 3–Mar 1. Expensive.

Tullig House, Tullig, Beaufort, Killarney, Co. Kerry (☎ 064/44183). A B&B near Dunloe Castle, Tullig House is a basic but romantic and peaceful farmhouse where kids can help feed the chickens and milk the cows. The owner, Mrs. Debbie Joy, serves hearty, honest Irish fare. 8 rms, 4 with bath. Facilities: restaurant (wine license only). No credit cards. Closed Oct–Mar. Inexpensive.

THE DINGLE PENINSULA

The **Dingle Peninsula** is the wild west of Ireland—visually, because it has the grandest scenery; historically, because it has the most impressive number of Iron Age and early Christian monuments; and spiritually, because it was never tamed by the English (as the Ring of Kerry was) and has kept alive those Gaelic traditions that have all but disappeared from the rest of the country. The circular route around the peninsula from Killarney to Tralee is 166.4 kilometers (104 miles) and should take the better part of a day.

On a day's outing you'll drive through magnificent coastal scenery and cross the most spectacular mountain pass in Ireland. You'll walk or swim along soft, sandy beaches, visit quality craft shops, and dine in first-rate restaurants and pubs. Should you want to spend more than a day here, you can base yourself in any number of charming guest houses and explore the Blasket Islands, play golf, go fishing, and hike some of the most dramatic trails in Ireland. The best places to stay are in the far west, around the towns of Dingle, Ventry, Dunquin, and Ballyferriter.

INCH STRAND

From Killorglin, head north to Castlemaine and then west along the southern coast of Dingle about 16 kilometers (10 miles) to the town of **Inch,** where John Millington Synge's *The Playboy of the Western World* was filmed. If the weather is behaving and the is tide low (check the tides the night before), park your car, take off your shoes and socks, and let the wind blow through your hair as you wander out along **Inch Strand,** a wide sandy beach stretching 3.2 kilometers (2 miles) into the bay. (When you leave your hotel in the morning, bring a towel and wear a bathing suit under your clothes.)

From Inch continue west along the road to **Anascaul.** A right turn off the coastal road takes you to the South Pole Inn, named in honor of the local sailor who went to rescue Robert Scott and found him dead in his tent, having failed in his mission to reach the South Pole in 1912. Could anything be more wonderfully incongruous, and more appropriate, than a South Pole Inn in a tiny fishing village in western Ireland?

DINGLE

The road west from Anascaul is pleasant, but the real adventure begins in **Dingle** (*Daungean,* stronghold), the district's chief town and touring center. Dingle was a Norman administrative center, a walled city in Elizabethan times, and chief port of Kerry in the old Spanish trading days. Today it's a center of Gaelic studies that attracts students from around the world—its existence doesn't depend solely on tourists. You'll want to walk around town, shopping for knitted goods, pottery, and yarn in several sophisticated craft shops, such as **The Weaver's Shop,** Green Street (☎ **066/51688**), and photographing many of the colorful old houses.

TAKE A BREAK

*As you wander through town, refuel with a lunch visit to **An Café Liteartha,** Dykegate Street (☎ **066/ 51388**), a cafe/bookstore with a marvelous collection of Irish books and records, many in Gaelic.*

From Dingle you can arrange for a boat trip from Dunquin (16km/10 miles west) to the Blasket Islands (see "Dunquin," below). There's pony trekking in Ventry, 6.4 kilometers (4 miles) to the west;

golf at Sybil Head, near Ballyferriter; beaches at Ventry and Dunquin; deep-sea fishing off the coast of Dingle; trips to ancient monuments; spectacular drives around Slea Head and over the Coner Pass; and an endless variety of hikes to mountain ridges and lakes.

The high point of my visit to Dingle was an evening at **O'Flaherty's Pub,** Bridge Street (☎ **066/51461**), drinking bitter with strangers and listening to local traditional music played with guitars, flutes, accordions, and spoons. This is a place of great character where locals and tourists join together in the fun.

Dining

The Armada, Strand St. (☎ **066/51505**). This popular seafood restaurant near the pier offers homemade chowders, fresh Dingle cod, and seafood curries. Reservations advised. Casual. AE, DC, MC, V. Closed Mon and Nov–Mar. Moderate.

Beginish, Green St. (☎ **066/51588**). The food here is Dingle's best, an imaginative menu with French overtones but the freshest of Irish products. Mrs. Pat Moore, the host/chef, presides over this collection of small dining rooms. The freshest available seafood is prepared without oversaucing or destroying natural flavors. Vegetarians are welcomed and tempted with an array of well-flavored meatless dishes. In tastefully decorated rooms, dine on filet of brill served in white-wine sauce with leek fondue or filet of Irish lamb in phyllo pastry with mushroom duxelles. The wine carte offers some 100 selections (many half bottles). Reservations advised. AE, DC, MC, V. Closed Mon. Moderate.

Doyle's, John St. (☎ **066/51174**). This is the town's second best, most sophisticated seafood restaurant. At the table across from mine was a Canadian couple who'd come here on their 20th anniversary and were back for their 30th. The menu depends on the day's catch but usually features cockle-and-mussel soup with garlic, grilled black sole, salmon cooked in parchment, and salmon poached sometimes with a sharp sorrel sauce. Reservations advised. Casual. AE, DC, MC, V. Closed Sun and mid-Nov to mid-Mar. Moderate.

Half Door, John St. (☎ **066/51600**). Next door to Doyle's, though not quite as good, this is nevertheless a leading seafood place noted for the freshness of its catch. Popular dishes include crab quiche, trout in oatmeal, mussels in garlic, seafood au gratin, and a variety of less-tempting meat dishes. Reservations advised. Casual. AE, DC, MC, V. Closed Tues and mid-Nov to mid-Mar. Moderate.

Accommodations

The Tourist Office has a complete list of hotels and guest houses.

Ballymore House, Ballymore, Ventry, Co. Kerry (☎ **066/59050**). A friendly B&B 2.4 kilometers (1½ miles) beyond Cleevaun, this is a good choice. Contact Mrs. S. Birmingham. 7 rms, 5 with bath. No credit cards. Inexpensive.

Benner's Hotel, Main St., Dingle, Co. Kerry (☎ 066/51638; fax 066/51412). This famous 260-year-old hotel is better than ever following a major face-lift in the early 1990s. Plump chintz sofas in the lobby and polished wood paneling create a charming old-world welcome. All the rooms have country pine antiques, and some contain four-posters. 24 rms with bath. Facilities: restaurant, bar. MC, V. Moderate.

Cleevaun, Lady's Cross, Dingle, Co. Kerry (☎ 066/51108; fax 066/51108). This B&B is more comfortable and modern than many of Ireland's aging hotels, with rooms that are spotless and cheery. The living room has a helpful collection of books on the Dingle area. Contact Mrs. C. Cluskey. 8 rms with bath. No credit cards. Closed Nov–Mar. Inexpensive.

Mrs. Conner, Dykegate St., Dingle, Co. Kerry (☎ 066/51598). A good bet if you're on a budget, this modern bed-and-breakfast is in the center of town. The rooms are plain, unfussy, clean, and pleasant. 15 rms with bath. AE, DC, MC, V. Inexpensive.

Dingle Skellig Hotel, Dingle, Co. Kerry (☎ 066/51144; fax 066/51501). This extraordinary and rather bizarre modern building on the edge of the sea is supposed to remind you of the area's early Christian beehive-shaped hermit cells. It received a major renovation in the early 1990s and offers the town's best sporting facilities. Its bar has traditional music. 50 rms with bath. Facilities. restaurant, bar, indoor pool, sauna, gymnasium, tennis. AE, DC, MC, V. Closed Nov 15–Apr 3. Expensive.

VENTRY

There's a magnificent horseshoe of soft sand in **Ventry;** follow the signs to the beach. Ventry Harbor was the scene of the ancient romantic tale "The Battle of Ventry Strand," which, as told in a 15th-century manuscript now in the Bodleian Library at Oxford, describes how the King of the World, Daire Doon, landed at Ventry in an attempt to invade Ireland and was defeated in a battle that lasted a year and a day. One of the loveliest walks in the region is to the lake on **Eagle Mountain,** to the west of Ventry. Inquire about the route in Ventry.

DUNBEG

Past Ventry, about 3.2 kilometers (2 miles) before Slea Head, look carefully for a small sign on the left pointing to a fort called **Dunbeg,** romantically situated on a promontory 27 meters (90 ft.) above the sea. This is the country's most notable example of an Iron Age promontory defense fort — a refuge of last resort. Note the underground tunnel, called a souterrain, leading from the center of the fort to an escape hatch in front of the entrance; when the enemy entered the fortification, the people inside could crawl out and trap the invaders within. Notice, too, the drainage system to stop the water coming down the mountain and the guard rooms with spy holes on either side of the entrance. Because of sea erosion, the fort will probably disappear by the end of the century.

SLEA HEAD

The road is cut from the slopes of Mount Eagle, and the views, if the weather is right, are as spectacular as any in Ireland. Where the land juts into the sea you'll see the rusted hulk of a Spanish freighter sunk in a storm in 1982. Beneath the black cliffs is a magnificent beach, perhaps 90 meters (100 yd.) deep at low tide. **Slea Head** points to a group of islands and rocks known as the **Blaskets.** The largest, Inishmore, or the Great Blasket, has an abandoned village you can explore on a day trip from Dunquin. Boats to the island leave from Dunquin Harbour (call 066/56455 for reservations and schedules). The island was the home of a remote and self-contained Irish-speaking community with a rich oral literature. In time, the younger islanders married into an easier life on the mainland, and in 1954 the remaining people were resettled near Dunquin. A walk along the high cliffs of the Great Blasket, above the crying gulls, is a memory to cherish for a lifetime.

The Blaskets acquired a new importance at the turn of the century, when there was a revival of interest in Irish culture; playwright J. M. Synge spent two weeks here in 1905, and it's believed that the character of Pegeen Mike in *The Playboy of the Western World* was inspired by his hostess. What's extraordinary is the literary outpouring from such a small, remote settlement: Maurice O'Sullivan's *Twenty Years A-Growing,* Thomas O'Criffan's *The Islander,* and Peig Sayers's *Peig.* Synge also wrote about the Blaskets, and so did the Englishman Robin Flower. What fun you can have reading their books (available in American libraries and many Irish tourist shops), then visiting the Blaskets and trying to identify the homes.

DUNQUIN

If it interests you, ask at the public house in **Dunquin** for directions to the *Ryan's Daughter* schoolhouse, on a nearby cliff. The film was shot nearby.

Of all the pottery stores on the Dingle Peninsula, the finest is **Louis Mulcahy** (☎ **066/56229**) in Clogher, 2.4 kilometers (1½ miles) past Dunquin. In addition to pottery, you can buy beautiful handwoven blankets, coveralls, wall hangings, and scarves. Shopping is possible here Monday to Friday from 9am to 8pm and Saturday and Sunday from 10am to 8pm.

BALLYFERRITER

From **Ballyferriter** you can look down on Smerwick Harbour, where the old fortress of **Dún an Óir** (Fort of Gold) stands on a rock promontory. It was here in 1580 that some 600 Italian, Spanish, and Irish troops, supported by the Pope, held out against English Protestant forces and were butchered by Lord Grey's troops. Grey's secretary was none other than poet Edmund Spenser, who loved Ireland (but not the Catholics) and advocated starvation and genocide to bring the Irish under the sway of the Faerie Queene (Elizabeth I). Unsuccessful in its efforts to conquer England through the back door (Ireland), Spain made a frontal attack 8 years later, with a 130-ship armada. The force was routed in the English

Channel. The ships that weren't destroyed fled around the top of Scotland and down the west coast of Ireland. Twenty-five Spanish ships were lost off the Irish coast, including two wrecked near the Blasket Islands. (Ironically, there's a modern Spanish ship aground there today.)

Accommodations

Dún an Óir Hotel, Ballyferriter, Dingle Peninsula, Co. Kerry (☎ 066/ 56133; fax 066/56153). Not to be confused with the Fort of Gold is this modern hostelry with a name that is its only Gaelic attribute. The hotel is essentially a complex of small white buildings squeezed together on a grassy field in the middle of the countryside, with virtually no trees or landscaping, supposedly reminiscent of a typical Kerry village. In its favor, however, is the fact that it's the only modern resort on the western end of the peninsula; its motelish rooms are softened by tasteful fabrics, and the setting is as peaceful as anyone could wish. 22 rms with bath. Facilities: restaurant, bar, outdoor pool, sauna, tennis, 18-hole golf course. Closed Oct 7–Apr. AE, DC, MC, V. Moderate.

GALLARUS ORATORY

Don't take the road south from Ballyferriter back to Ventry; follow signs toward the village of Ballydavid and **Gallarus Oratory.** The 7th- or 8th-century Oratory is one of the country's best-preserved early Christian churches and an unrivaled example of the use of corbeling—successive levels of stone projecting inward from both side walls until they meet at the top. Though made of unmortared stone, it's still water tight after more than 1,000 years. The two stones with holes in them on either side of the entrance were probably meant to hold the ends of wooden doorposts.

KILMALKEDAR CHURCH

Kilmalkedar Church, 3.2 kilometers (2 miles) north of Gallarus, is one of the finest examples of Romanesque (Early Irish) architecture in the country. Churches such as this replaced the more modest beehive huts in the 13th century, when a local and decentralized church developed into a formal system of dioceses and parishes. This church was founded in the 7th century, but the present structure, standing in a graveyard, dates from the 12th. Note how—as at Cormac's Chapel at Cashel, by which it was inspired—the native craftspeople integrated foreign influences with local traditions: keeping the blank arcades and round-headed windows, for instance, but using stone roofs, sloping doorway jambs, and weirdly sculptured heads.

In the immediate vicinity you can "sample" a great variety of ancient Irish monuments. Just to the right of the entrance to the churchyard, beside a tomb, is a stone with mysterious decorations. It's usually regarded as a sundial but could also be an early cross or even a pre-Christian monument. Nearby is an ogham stone with a hole in it. The writing on these stones, dating from the late Stone Age and early Christian periods, consists of up to five strokes on either side of an imaginary vertical guideline. It begins on the bottom, continuing upward and, if necessary, down the other side. The lines represent letters in the Roman alphabet, but the language itself is an early form of Irish. Most inscriptions commemorate the deceased and give details of their ancestry.

Near the church is **Caherdorgan Stone Fort,** which contains five almost complete beehive huts; **St. Brendan's House,** a two-story 15th-century building, now roofless but otherwise well preserved, where the local clergy probably lived; and the **Chancellor's House,** a two-room medieval building. The chancellor was a cathedral dignitary who occasionally resided here.

THE CONOR PASS

From Gallarus Oratory, return to the town of Dingle, then head north across the **Conor Pass,** Ireland's most spectacular high-level crossing. The parking area at the head of the pass is a good starting point for the ascent of **Ballysitteragh** (614.9m/2,050 ft.) to the west or **Slievanea** (605.9m/2,020 ft.) to the east. Neither walk should take more than an hour round-trip. You don't need a marked path on these treeless slopes; just head for the summit. The climb is gradual, so anyone with perseverance can make it to the top.

From the top of Conor Pass you can look down and see **Brandon Bay.** It was from here that St. Brendan the Navigator (484–577) is believed to have set sail at age 59 in a boat of skins and wood for "the Land of Promise." He got as far as Iceland, landing once on the back of a whale, which he thought was an island. On his second trip he may have reached either Newfoundland or Labrador, and "discovered" America more than 900 years before Columbus. In 1977 three men sailed 4,830 kilometers (3,000 miles) to Newfoundland in a replica of Brendan's boat, proving that it could be done.

St. Brendan was a Kerryman from Tralee who founded an important monastery at Clonfert, in County Galway, and later became the patron saint of the Dingle Peninsula. **Ballybrack,** 9.6 kilometers (6 miles) north of Dingle, is the starting point for a grueling 3½-hour (one-way) hike to Brendan's hermitage (**St. Brendan's Oratory**) on the top of the peninsula's most famous landmark, **Brandon Mountain.** Don't go if the summit is shrouded in mist—it usually is. The route follows an ancient pilgrim route, the Saint's Road, to the high point of an enormous 6.4-kilometer (4-mile) ridge. Brandon was a sacred mountain in pagan times, when there was an annual pilgrimage to the summit to celebrate the festival of the Celtic god Lugh. After Christianity was introduced, the event was transformed into a pilgrimage in honor of Brendan.

CAMP

Head down the Conor Pass to Kilcummin and right (east) to Tralee. If you want one final hike, visit a great prehistoric stone fort, one of the country's highest, on a 614.9-meter (2,050-ft.) spur of the 813.6-meter (2,712-ft.) **Cahercontree Mountain.** The fort can be reached from **Camp,** following signs to the Promontory Fort. Ask locally for details.

ADARE

From Tralee take Route N21 east to Limerick, then head either north to Shannon Airport or east to Dublin. If you need to spend the night near Shannon, consider staying in **Adare,** 16 kilometers (10 miles) southwest of **Limerick. Adare Manor** (☎ 061/396566; fax 061/396124), a vast Victorian country house on an 840-acre estate at the edge of the village, was opened as a luxury hotel under American ownership in 1988. Its July classical music festival, with symphony orchestras under a marquee and chamber music in the house, is establishing itself as a major event on the Irish music and social calendar. Voted the tidiest town in Ireland, it has some lovely thatched cottages on the banks of the Maigue River, three medieval abbeys, a 13th-century castle, and a popular inn with good food.

Accommodations

Dunraven Arms Hotel, Adare, Co. Limerick (☎ 061/396633; fax 061/396633). Old-world character envelops this country-house–style inn in the center of the village. For a special treat, try the Princess Grace and Prince Rainier Suite, named in honor of their visit. You'll find good classic French cuisine in the Maigue Restaurant, including eel in white-wine sauce and stuffed pork steak. 66 rms with bath. Facilities: restaurant, bar, horseback riding. AE, DC, MC, V. Expensive.

E N G␣2␣A N D

Bath, the Cotswolds &
Stratford-upon-Avon

W ithin just 2 hours of London you can discover an extraordinary variety of scenery and architectural styles. Salisbury is the site of the country's most perfect cathedral, and not far away are the mysterious pillars of Stonehenge. Wells, like Salisbury, is a famous cathedral town. Bath is the most sophisticated city in England after London, with theater, shops, and Georgian and Roman architecture. The National Trust town of Lacock, where the newest houses were built in the 18th century, is nearby. To the north are the stone villages and rich, rolling fields of the Cotswolds. Stratford-upon-Avon is the birthplace of the Bard as well as home to the Royal Shakespeare Theatre. Blenheim Palace, where American-born Jenny Jerome Churchill gave birth to Winston, and the colleges and chapels of Oxford University are other highlights.

The region is rich in churches that were built and expanded over hundreds of years—each reconstruction reflecting the styles and values of a new age. Norman architecture (1066–ca. 1150) was named for the Normans, who brought their variant of the Romanesque style when they conquered Britain in 1066 and grafted it onto the English Saxon Romanesque style begun by Edward the Confessor (1003?–1066). Early English (ca. 1150–ca. 1250) is, in effect, Early Gothic. Decorated (ca. 1250–ca. 1350) is mature Gothic. Perpendicular (ca. 1350–ca. 1520) is Late Gothic, an original and distinctively British style. In contrast to the Decorated style, the Perpendicular is marked by a stress on straight verticals and horizontals, window tracery with complex designs emphasizing the vertical, and fan vaulting (ceiling ribs fanning outward).

BEFORE YOU GO

GOVERNMENT TOURIST OFFICES

The major source of information is the **British Tourist Authority** (BTA).

In the U.S.: 40 W. 57th St., New York, NY 10019 (☎ 212/581-4700); John Hancock Center, Suite 3320, 875 N. Michigan Ave., Chicago, IL 60611 (☎ 312/787-0490); World Trade Center, 350 S. Figueroa St., Suite 450, Los Angeles, CA 90017 (☎ 213/628-3525); 2305 Cedar Springs Rd., Suite 210, Dallas, TX 75201 (☎ 214/720-4040).

In Canada: 94 Cumberland St., Suite 600, Toronto, Ontario M5R 3N3 (☎ 416/925-6326).

In the U.K.: Thames Tower, Black's Road, London W69EL (☎ 0181/846-9000).

HIGHLIGHTS ALONG THE WAY

- Three of England's greatest cathedrals—at Salisbury, Winchester, and Wells.

- The Roman city of Bath—a fashionable spa in the 18th century and today a sophisticated tourist center with elegant shops, music festivals, and first-class hotels and restaurants.

- The mysterious standing stones of Stonehenge.

- Stratford-upon-Avon—the Bard's birthplace and home to the Royal Shakespeare Theatre.

- The picturesque stone villages of the Cotswolds.

- Dining and lodging in restored manor homes and Elizabethan inns.

WHEN TO GO

The main tourist season in Britain runs from mid-April to mid-October. Spring is the time to see the countryside at its freshest and greenest. During July and August, when most of the British take their vacations, accommodations in the most popular resorts and areas are in high demand and at their most expensive.

In the main, the climate is mild, though the weather is changeable and unpredictable at any time of year. Summer temperatures can reach the 80s and the atmosphere can be humid, whereas in winter there can be heavy frost, snow, and thick fog. A good guide to what each day will be like is carried in the early-morning radio forecast.

CURRENCY

The unit of currency in Britain is the **pound sterling £,** divided into 100 **pence** (p). The bills are 50, 20, 10, and 5 pounds (Scotland has £1 bills). Coins are £1, 50, 20, 10, 5, 2, and 1p. At press time the exchange rate was about U.S. $1.60 and Canadian $2.15 to the pound sterling.

SPECIAL EVENTS & NATIONAL HOLIDAYS

Special Events

March–December: Royal Shakespeare Theatre season at Stratford-upon-Avon.
April: English Bach Festival, Oxford.
May–June: Bath International Festival, music and the arts, at Bath and Avon.
May: Royal Windsor Horse Show.
July: International Festival of Music at Cheltenham.
End of July: Southern Cathedrals Festival, concerts and church music, at Salisbury and Winchester.

National Holidays

January 1 (New Year's Day); Good Friday; Easter Monday; 1st Monday in May (May Day); 4th Monday in May (Spring Bank Holiday); last Monday in August (Summer Bank Holiday); December 25 (Christmas); December 26 (Boxing Day).

CUSTOMS

For visitors to England, goods fall into two categories—purchases made in a non–European Union country or bought tax free within the European Union, and purchases on which tax was paid in the European Union. In the former category, limits on imports by individuals (17 and older) include 200 cigarettes, 50 cigars, or 250 grams (8.8 oz.) of loose tobacco; 2 liters (.53 gal.) of still table wine, 1 liter of liquor (over 22% alcohol content), or 2 liters of liquor (under 22%); and 2 fluid ounces of perfume. In the latter category—items on which tax was paid in the European Union—limits are *much* higher: An individual may import 800 cigarettes, 200 cigars, *and* 1 kilogram (2.2 lb.) of loose tobacco; 90 liters (23.8 gal.) of wine, 10 liters (2.6 gal.) of alcohol (over 22%), *and* 110 liters (29 gal.) of beer; plus unlimited amounts of perfume.

READING

Philip A. Crowl, *The Intelligent Traveller's Guide to Historic Britain* (Congdon & Weed).

ARRIVING & DEPARTING

BY PLANE

London-bound international flights arrive at Heathrow, Gatwick, or Stanstead airport. Heathrow is the most convenient, with a direct subway (tube) to central London, followed by Gatwick.

Airlines serving London and other major cities in Britain include **American Airlines** (☎ 800/433-7300), **British Airways** (☎ 800/247-9297), **Delta** (☎ 800/241-4141), **Northwest Airlines** (☎ 800/447-4747), **TWA** (☎ 800/892-4141), and **United** (☎ 800/538-2929).

British Airways flies to London from more American cities than any other airline: Boston; New York; Philadelphia; Baltimore; Washington, D.C.; Miami; Orlando; Tampa; Detroit; Chicago; Los Angeles; San Francisco; Seattle; and Anchorage. It's also the only airline that flies the Concorde there—from New York to London in 3 hours.

ENGLAND

NORTH SEA

AREA OF TOUR

ENGLAND

London

Glasgow
Edinburgh

SCOTLAND

Northumberland Nat'l Park

Newcastle upon Tyne

Belfast
Carlisle

NORTHUMBRIA

NORTHERN IRELAND

Solway Firth

THE LAKE DISTRICT

Isle of Man

Lake District Nat'l Park

North York Moors Nat'l Park

IRISH SEA

Yorkshire Dales Nat'l Park

YORKSHIRE

Blackpool

York

Liverpool Bay

Leeds

Liverpool

Manchester

St. George's Channel

Peak District Nat'l Park

Chester

THE NORTHWEST

Lincoln

EAST MIDLANDS

LINCOLNSHIRE

The Wash

Nottingham

Leicester

Norwich

EAST ANGLIA

Birmingham

Ely

WARWICKSHIRE

Cambridge

Aldeburgh

Stratford-upon-Avon

THE COTSWOLDS

Bedford

WALES

Woodstock

Buckingham

Dedham

Swansea

AVON

Oxford

LONDON

Cardiff

OXFORDSHIRE

Bristol

Bath

Windsor

THAMES VALLEY

Canterbury

WILTSHIRE

SURREY

KENT

Dover

Bristol Channel

SOMERSET

HAMPSHIRE

WEST SUSSEX

EAST SUSSEX

Exmoor Nat'l Park

Salisbury

Calais

DEVON

Southampton

Brighton

Hastings

DORSET

Portsmouth

Strait of Dover

Dartmoor Nat'l Park

Lyme Bay

Isle of Wight

CORNWALL

Plymouth

Land's End

Lizard Point

English Channel

Cherbourg

Le Havre

Channel Islands

FRANCE

BY TRAIN

If you're traveling to Britain from the Continent, your Eurailpass will *not* be valid when you get there. In 1994 Queen Elizabeth and President François Mitterrand officially opened the Channel Tunnel (Chunnel) and the *Eurostar Express* passenger train began twice-daily service between London and both Paris and Brussels—a 3-hour trip. The $15-billion tunnel, one of the great engineering feats of all time, is the first link between Britain and the Continent since the Ice Age. **Rail Europe** (☎ 800/94-CHUNNEL) sells direct-service tickets on the *Eurostar* between Paris or Brussels and London. A round-trip fare between Paris and London costs $344 in first class and $242 in second. You can cut the second-class cost to $148 by making a (nonrefundable) 14-day advance purchase. In London make reservations for *Eurostar* by calling **01345/300003,** in Paris by calling **01-44-51-06-02,** and in the United States by calling **800/EUROSTAR.** *Eurostar* trains arrive and depart from Waterloo Station in London, Gare du Nord in Paris, and Central Station in Brussels.

BY FERRY OR HOVERCRAFT

Ships and ferryboats have long traversed the English Channel, and today's major carriers are P&O Channel Lines, Hoverspeed, and Sealink.

P&O Channel Lines (☎ 01304/242233) operates car and passenger ferries between Portsmouth and Cherbourg, France (three departures a day; 5 hours each way, 7 hours at night); between Portsmouth and Le Havre, France (three a day; 5½ hours each way); and between Dover and Calais, France (25 sailings a day; 75 minutes each way).

P&O's major competitor is **Stena Sealink** (☎ 01233/615455), which carries both passengers and vehicles. This company is represented in North America by **BritRail** (☎ 800/677-8585, or 212/575-2667 in New York). Stena Sealink offers conventional ferryboat service between Cherbourg and Southampton (one or two trips a day; 6–8 hours) and between Dieppe and Newhaven (four departures daily; 4 hours each way). Stena Sealink's conventional car-ferries between Calais and Dover are popular; they depart 20 times a day in both directions and take 90 minutes. Typical fares between France and England are $38.40 for a one-way adult ticket, $35.20 for seniors, and $22.40 for children.

By far the most popular route across the Channel is between Calais and Dover. One company, **Hoverspeed,** operates at least 12 hovercraft crossings daily (the trip takes 35 minutes). They also run a SeaCat (a catamaran propelled by jet engines) that takes slightly longer to make the crossing between Boulogne and Folkestone. The SeaCats depart about four times a day on the 55-minute voyage.

Traveling by Hovercraft or SeaCat cuts the time of your surface journey from the Continent to Britain. A SeaCat crossing from Folkestone to Boulogne is longer in miles but is covered faster than conventional ferryboats make the Calais-Dover crossing. For reservations and information call Hoverspeed at **01304/240-241.** Typical one-way fares are $40 per person.

By Car

If you plan to take a rented car across or under the Channel, check with the rental company about license and insurance requirements before you leave.

There are many "drive-on, drive-off" car-ferry services across the Channel. The most popular ports in France for Channel crossings are Boulogne and Calais, where you can board Sealink ferries taking you to the English ports of Dover and Folkestone.

There are special Channel Tunnel trains for passenger cars, charter buses, taxis, and motorcycles. Before boarding the train that the French call *Le Shuttle,* you stop at a toll booth and then pass through customs for both countries at one time. During the 35-minute ride (19 minutes of which are actually in the Chunnel), you stay in a bright air-conditioned carriage and can remain inside your car or step outside to stretch your legs. When the trip is over, you simply drive off toward your destination. Total travel time between the French and English highway system is about 1 hour. This car service operates 24 hours a day; it runs every 15 minutes during peak periods and at least once an hour at night.

GETTING AROUND

By Car

Driving on the left sounds frightening if you've never done it before; but when your life is on the line it's amazing how quickly it becomes second nature. The most important rule to remember is that the driver *inside* a traffic circle has the right of way. There's a 112-kilometer-per-hour (70-m.p.h.) speed limit on highways (*motorways* to the British), but most drivers ignore it. Speeds of 128 kilometers per hour (80 m.p.h.), even 144 kilometers per hour (90 m.p.h.), aren't at all unusual.

British Airways has a fly/drive package that saves you about 20% on car rentals. **BritRail Travel** (☎ **212/599-5400**) has a BritRail/Drive pass that lets you take the train and pick up a car at or near your destination. You can then leave the car at another station with no drop-off costs. (The BritRail/Drive pass won't make much sense if your trip is limited to my itinerary; distances are short and you'll probably want to travel the entire route either by car or by public transport.)

You may want to visit London first and rent a car only when it's time to leave on this trip. If you're flying to and from London, arrange both to pick up and to return your car at Heathrow Airport *after* your stay in London.

Don't be satisfied with a general road map of England. The Ordnance Survey 1:50,000 maps indicate all back roads and footpaths and allow you to discover the beauty of the countryside while avoiding heavy traffic. These maps are sold in map stores in large American cities and in gift shops throughout England.

The fastest access to the region from London is by way of the M40 motorway, which starts at Marylebone Road and runs past Oxford and Stratford to Birmingham.

By Public Transportation

You should follow my itinerary by car if you can; otherwise you'll miss many of the small out-of-the-way places. Still, it's possible to reach most of the major sites by train and bus.

There's good train service between London and Winchester (from Waterloo Station), but *not* between Winchester and Salisbury. To get from Winchester to Salisbury, you need either to backtrack to Basingstoke or to ride to Southampton. Unless Winchester Cathedral is high on your list, consider skipping Winchester and taking the train directly to Salisbury. From here buses go regularly in season to Stonehenge and direct trains run to Bath. From Bath there's regular bus service to Wells and frequent bus tours to Longleat House.

From Bath, take a train to Stratford-upon-Avon via Bristol and Birmingham. From Stratford-upon-Avon, ride to Moreton-in-Marsh, which is as close as you can get by train to the center of the Cotswolds. From Moreton-in-Marsh rent a car or a bicycle to tour the countryside. Trains go from Moreton-in-Marsh to Oxford and back to Paddington Station in London.

Give a list of towns you want to visit to the **BritRail** office, and they'll work out and issue either a single-journey ticket or a BritRail Pass, depending on which is cheaper.

You *must* purchase the BritRail Pass before you leave home. They're available from most travel agents or from one of these **BritRail Travel International offices:** 630 Third Ave., New York, NY 10017 (☎ 212/599-5400); Cedar Maple Plaza, 2305 Cedar Springs, Suite 210, Dallas, TX 75201 (☎ 214/748-0860); 800 S. Hope St., Suite 603, Los Angeles, CA 90017 (☎ 213/624-8787); 94 Cumberland St., Toronto, Ont. M5R 1A3 (☎ 416/929-3333); 409 Granville St., Vancouver, B.C., V6C 1T2 (☎ 604/683-6896).

The BritRail Pass allows unlimited rail travel through the entire British rail system for periods of 8, 14, 22, or 30 days and is available for both first- and economy-class travel. Even if you don't make full use of the pass, it saves time waiting in ticket lines. Children 5 to 15 receive a 50% reduction. There are also BritRail Youth Passes for young people 16 to 25 and Senior Citizen Passes for travelers over 60.

The least expensive way to travel is by coach (as opposed to local buses). The Britexpress Card gives you one-third off on all National Express services over a 6-month period. You can buy it from travel agencies in the United States or from **National Express** at Victoria Coach

Station, Buckingham Palace Road, London SW1 (☎ 0990/808080). Unfortunately, there's no single pass good for both trains and buses.

BritRail also sells Open to View Tickets, good for 1 month, to hundreds of castles, historic homes, and sites.

BY BICYCLE

Flat or rolling countryside, short distances between towns, plenty of traffic-free back roads—all add up to a perfect landscape for biking. Bring bikes from home or rent them in London or in towns along the route, and when you've had enough exercise put them on the train with you at little or no cost. The British Tourist Authority (see "Government Tourist Offices," above) has brochures, or you may want to join the **Cyclists' Touring Club,** 69 Meadrow, Godalming, Surrey GU7 3HS (☎ 01483/ 417217), the national body in Britain that promotes the interests of cycle tourists. Hours are Monday to Friday from 9am to 5pm.

ESSENTIAL INFORMATION

IMPORTANT ADDRESSES & NUMBERS

VISITOR INFORMATION For information on Stratford and the Cotswolds, contact the **Heart of England Tourist Board,** Larkhill Road, Worcester, Hereford and Worcester WR1 2EZ (☎ 01905/763436). Open Monday to Thursday from 9am to 5:30pm and Friday from 9am to 5pm.

For information on south-central England, contact the **Southern Tourist Board,** 40 Chamberlayne Rd., Eastleigh, Hampshire S05 9JH (☎ 01703/620006). Open Monday to Thursday from 8:30am to 5pm and Friday from 8:30am to 4:30pm.

For information on Bath and Avon, contact the **West Country Tourist Board,** 60 St. Davis Hill, Exeter, Devon EX4 4SY (☎ 01392/ 76351). Open Monday to Friday from 9:30am to 5pm.

Local tourist information centers are normally open Monday to Saturday from 9:30am to 5:30pm, but times vary according to season:

Bath:	Abbey Church Yard, Bath, Avon BA1 1LY (☎ 01225/ 462831).
Chipping Campden:	Woolstaplers Hall Museum, High Street, Chipping Campden, Gloucestershire GL55 6HB (☎ 01386/ 840101).
Cirencester:	Corn Hall, Market Place, Cirencester, Gloucestershire GL7 2NW (☎ 01285/654180).
Salisbury:	Fish Row, Salisbury, Wiltshire SP1 1EJ (☎ 01722/ 334956).
Stow-on-the-Wold:	Hollis House, The Square, Stow-on-the-Wold, Gloucestershire GL54 1AF (☎ 01451/831082).

Stratford-upon-Avon:	Bridgefoot, Stratford-upon-Avon, Warwickshire CV37 6GW (☎ **01789/293127**).
Winchester:	The Guildhall, The Broadway, Winchester, Hampshire SO23 9LJ (☎ **01962/840500**).

EMBASSIES & CONSULATES   **U.S. Embassy,** 24 Grosvenor Sq., London W1A 1AE (☎ **0171/499-9000**). **Canadian High Commission,** Mac-Donald House, Grosvenor Square W1X 0AB (☎ **0171/258-6600**).

EMERGENCIES   For **police, fire brigade,** or **ambulance,** dial 999.

OPENING & CLOSING TIMES

BANKS   Banks are open Monday to Friday from 9:30am to 3:30pm. Some have extended hours on Thursday evenings and a few are open on Saturday mornings.

MUSEUMS   Museum hours vary considerably from one part of the country to another. In large cities, most are open Monday to Saturday from 10am to 5pm; many are also open Sunday afternoons. The majority close 1 day a week. Holiday closings vary, so be sure to check individual listings.

SHOPS   Usual business hours are Monday to Saturday from 9am to 5:30pm. Outside the main centers, most shops observe an early closing day once a week, often Wednesday or Thursday. They close at 1pm and don't reopen until the following morning. In small villages, many also close for lunch. Apart from some newsstands and small food stores, almost all shops are closed on Sunday.

GUIDED TOURS

The **Heart of England Tourist Board** (☎ **019051/763436**) and the **West Country Tourist Board** (☎ **01392/76351**) have details of numerous guided tours within their regions, and the staff can book you with registered guides for outings ranging from short walks to luxury tours that include accommodations in stately homes.

BATH   Free 1¾-hour walking tours are conducted throughout the year by the all-voluntary **Mayor's Honorary Society** (☎ **01225/477786**). The free tours depart from outside the Roman Baths Monday to Friday at 10:30am and 2pm, Sunday at 2:30pm, and Tuesday, Friday, and Saturday at 7pm. A highly informative but somewhat more commercialized walking tour is conducted by the **Bath Parade Guides** (☎ **01225/447770**), costing £3 per person; it departs Saturday at 2:30pm from outside the Roman Baths. Reservations aren't needed for either tour.

   Jane Austen Tours (☎ **01225/436030**) take you in the footsteps of the author and her characters. Conducted only once a week, tours begin at Abbey Lace Shop, York Street. The cost is £3 per person, and departures are every Saturday. You'll be told the time to meet for the tour when you make a reservation.

To tour Bath by bus, you can choose among several companies—some with open-top buses leaving from the Tourist Information Centre, which can be called for changing schedules and prices. Among the best candidates are **Patrick Driscoll/Beau Nash Guides,** Elmsleigh, Bathampton, BA2 6SW (☎ **01225/46210**). These tours are more personalized than most. Another good outfitter is **Sulis Guides,** 2 Lansdown Terrace, Weston, Bath BA1 4BR (☎ **01225/429681**).

SALISBURY   Guided walking tours begin outside the **Tourist Information Centre,** Fish Row, daily at 11am from April to October. An evening walk is scheduled at 6pm daily from May to September. The cost is £2 for adults or £1 for children, and the duration is about 1½ hours. Everything from the "ghost" of the Duke of Buckingham to the legend of a bawdy housekeeper will be revealed during this grand walk.

STRATFORD-UPON-AVON   Try **Guide Friday,** The Civic Hall, 14 Rother St., Stratford-upon-Avon, Warwickshire CV37 6LU (☎ **01789/294466**), for open-top buses that pick you up and drop you off along a predetermined historic route in season only—daily from 9:30am to 6:30pm. The cost is £7 for adults, £5 for students, and £2 for children 5 to 12 (4 and under free).

WINCHESTER   From May to October guided walking tours are conducted Monday to Saturday at 10:30am and 2:30pm and Sunday at 1:30pm, costing £2 per person. Departures are from the **tourist office** (☎ **01962/840500**).

SHOPPING

If you're making large purchases, ask for forms to exempt you from payment of a 17½% **value-added tax (VAT).** Not all stores have this service.

Almost anything you could buy in London you can find in Bath—and at similar prices. Stop at any of the **National Trust shops** for potpourri, wool ties, pottery, Beatrix Potter books, and dozens of other tasteful gifts. The best and most expensive antiques are in Bath and Stow-on-the-Wold.

SPORTS

BICYCLING   For bike rentals in Bath, contact **Avon Valley Cyclery,** Dorchester Street, in the rear of the Bath Spa Station (☎ **01225/461880**), open daily from 9am to 6pm. The Avon Valley Cycle Path is a peaceful 6-kilometer (4-mile) stretch of abandoned railroad line between Bath and Bitton.

BOATING   You can rent punts and canoes on the Avon, just northeast of Bath, from the **Bath Boating Station,** Forester Road (☎ **01225/ 466407**). Call this same number for canal-boat cruises.

FISHING   The River Test, running through Stockbridge, is incomparably the best trout-fishing river in England. There are also good streams for trout fishing near Bibury and Fairford. All are privately owned. Your best bet is to stay in a hotel catering to anglers: **Bibury Court Hotel,** Bibury GL7 5NT (☎ **01285/740337**); **Swan Hotel,** Bibury GL7 5NW (☎ **01285/740695**); or **Wroxton House Hotel,** Wroxton St. Mary, Wroxton OX15 6PZ (☎ **01295/730777**).

GOLF   Courses near or along the itinerary include the following: In **Gloucestershire,** try the 18-hole **Broadway Golf Club,** Willersey Hill, Broadway (☎ **01386/853683**); the 18-hole **Cotswolds Hills Golf Club,** Ullenwood, Cheltenham (☎ **01242/522421**); the 18-hole **Tewkesbury Park Golf and Country Club,** Lincoln Green Lane, Tewkesbury, 12 miles north of Cheltenham (☎ **01684/295405**); or the 18-hole **Glouces- ter Golf and Country Club,** Matson Lane, Gloucester (☎ **01452/ 411331** or 01452/25653).

   In **Oxfordshire,** there's the 18-hole **Burford Golf Course,** Burford (☎ **01993/2149**), and the 18-hole **Chipping Norton Golf Course,** Southcombe, Chipping Norton (☎ **01608/642383**). On weekends the Chipping Norton course is reserved for members only.

   In **Bath,** try the 18-hole **Bath Golf Club,** Sham Castle (☎ **01225/ 463834**); the 18-hole **Lansdown Golf Club,** Lansdown (☎ **01225/ 422138**); or the 9-hole **Entry Hill Golf Course** (☎ **01225/834248**).

HORSEBACK RIDING   Beginners and experts can both saddle up for rides through the Cotswold countryside from the town of Stanton (see "Exploring," below). Riding centers in or near towns on the itinerary include the following: In **Gloucestershire,** try the **Talland School of Equitation,** Church Farm, Siddington, Cirencester (☎ **01285/652318**). In **Bath** call **01225/462831** for information. In **Hampshire,** try the **Arniss Riding Stables,** Godshill, Fordingbridge, 27.2 kilometers (17 miles) south of Salisbury (☎ **01425/654114**); closed Tuesday.

   You can also ride at **Harroway House Riding School,** Penton Mewsey, Andover SP11 ORA, west of Andover, 32 kilometers (20 miles) northeast of Salisbury (☎ **01264/772295**).

TENNIS   In **Bath,** try Royal Victoria Park, Sydney Gardens, and Alice Park (☎ **01225/425060**); Recreation Ground (grass courts) (☎ **01225/ 462563**).

WALKING   For free brochures describing paths and trails, contact the **Cotswold Wardens,** c/o County Planning Dept., Shire Hall, Gloucester (☎ **01452/425000,** ext. 7542). Also useful are the *Cotswold Way Handbook* from the **Rambler's Association,** c/o R. A. Long, 27 Lambert Ave.,

Shurdington, Cheltenham (☎ **01242/862594**); *The Cotswold Way, a Walk-er's Guide* by Mark Richards (Thornhill Press); and *A Guide to the Cotswold Way* by Richard Sale (Constable).

DINING

The myth of pale overboiled vegetables and tough overdone meats fades slowly. The emphasis today is on local produce prepared simply to enhance natural flavors. Traditional English fare is beginning to disap-pear, but you can still find game soups, roast beef with Yorkshire pudding, roast lamb with mint sauce, and shepherd's pie (so-called because the shepherds took something similar with them to the fields), usually filled with ground beef and a variety of vegetables and topped with mashed potatoes. Other traditional pies include veal and ham, steak and kidney, and beef and oyster. The most reasonably priced lunches are in pubs, which now serve both hot and cold food, including sausages ("bangers" to the British) with mashed potatoes and Cornish pasties (crescent-shape pies filled with meat, onions, and vegetables).

Even towns in the Cotswolds have reasonably priced Indian restau-rants. The curries are usually not very hot. Fish and chips are a staple for travelers on the run; an ordinance has forbidden the sale of fish and chips wrapped in newspapers, so you can no longer read about the IRA while eating.

Imported liquor is heavily taxed and therefore expensive. Drinks are cheaper in pubs than in restaurants. There's a great variety of Scotch whiskies to sample—light or heavy; made with malt, grain, or blended. Try sweet or dry cider, too—but remember that it's not as innocent as it tastes.

The most popular drink in pubs is beer. Bitter is the standard draft beer and is served at room temperature. Lager is akin to German beer and is nearly always served chilled; it's similar to many American beers. Other traditional beers include brown ale, light ale, mild (all of which may prove an acquired taste to Americans), and stout (equally inaccessible to first-timers and similar to Guinness).

Wine is also heavily taxed and can be very expensive; a decent vin-tage could double the cost of your meal. If you're on a tight budget, check prices before you buy.

Restaurants must by law add a 12½% service charge to the bill. Don't tip more unless the service is exceptional.

CATEGORY	COST
Very Expensive	Over £50
Expensive	£30–£50
Moderate	£20–£30
Inexpensive	Under £20

Per person, for a three-course meal, including tip but not wine.

THE ITINERARY

ORIENTATION

Nothing is far away in England, so your trip will never take you more than 2 hours from London. You'll head southwest to Salisbury and Stonehenge. After a night in a Tudor inn or a Georgian manor house, it's on to Wells and then Bath, where you can dine in the home of Beau Nash's mistress and end the day in a hotel where the elegance of 18th-century Bath hasn't been forgotten.

Next you can visit Lacock and then head north through the Cotswolds. Stow-on-the-Wold has some wonderful antiques shops and makes a great base from which to explore the region—by car, by horse, or on foot. Farther north is Stratford-upon-Avon, where the play's the thing. On your way back to London you can visit Blenheim Palace and wander through Oxford University.

THE MAIN ROUTE

3–5 DAYS

Day excursion to Salisbury and Stonehenge.

One Night: *Bath*.

One Night: *Lacock*.

Two Nights: *Cotswold, around Stow-on-the-Wold*.

ACCOMMODATIONS

If you haven't been to England for a while, you may be dismayed by the high price of a night's lodgings. You may be disappointed, too, by the standards of service. The sorry truth is that many English hotels, especially middle-ranking ones, are both expensive and badly run, especially in comparison with those elsewhere in Europe. Of course, there are exceptions.

You'll find that luxury hotels are in a class by themselves. Likewise, private homes offering bed-and-breakfast accommodations are usually spotless and offer you a great opportunity to make new friends. Large English breakfasts (though not private baths) are standard. (You can take your chance with B&B signs along the road or make reservations through regional tourist offices.) It may also be that for you staying in an old inn with creaky staircases and low-beamed ceilings is compensation for high rates, fading carpets, chipping paintwork, and uncertain plumbing.

5–7 DAYS

Day excursion to Winchester, Stonehenge, Salisbury.

One Night: *Lacock.*
Day in Bath, with side trip to Wells.

Two Nights: *Bath.*

Two Nights: *Cotswolds, around Stow-on-the-Wold.*

One Night: *In or near Stratford-upon-Avon.*

7–14 DAYS

Day excursion to Winchester, Stonehenge, Salisbury, Wilton, Longleat.

One Night: *Near Salisbury/Wilton.*

One Night: *Lacock.*
Day in Bath, with excursions to Wells and Glastonbury.

Two Nights: *Bath.*
Day excursion to Castle Combe, Cirencester, Fairford, Bibury, Burford, Northleach.

Three Nights: *Cotswolds, around Stow-on-the-Wold.*

One Night: *Near Stratford-upon-Avon.*
Excursions to Warwick Castle.

One Night: *Woodstock.*
Excursion to Blenheim Palace and Oxford.

Adding insult to injury, the dead hand of hotel chains, like Forte, is evident everywhere, especially in cities and larger towns.

The best answer is to mix and match. You could, for instance, stay in a Georgian town house in Bath, a 350-year-old country inn in Lacock (near Bath), and both a B&B and a great manor house in the Cotswolds. But steer clear of fading second-class hotels.

Bath scores strongly on hotels in all price ranges. Hotels in Winchester and Salisbury offer little more than convenience. The best reason to stay overnight in Salisbury is to see the floodlit cathedral. If you're following my itinerary, there's little reason to stay in Winchester. In Stratford there are several hotels perfectly adequate for a night or two—you'll need to stay over if you're going to the Royal Shakespeare Theatre—but none is legendary. The best hotels are a few miles out of town. Dotted around the Cotswolds are scores of hotels and ancient inns, among them some of the best in the country. But if you blanch at the prices, stay at B&Bs.

Breakfast is usually, but not always, included in room rates. Most hotels quote prices per room, not per person.

CATEGORY	COST
Very Expensive	Over £100
Expensive	£80–£100
Moderate	£60–£80
Inexpensive	Under £60

All prices are for a standard double room for two, including tax.

EXPLORING

WINCHESTER

Winchester is a cathedral town 104 kilometers (65 miles) from London by car on M3 and A33 or 63 minutes from London's Waterloo Station by rail.

The Anglo-Saxons—Germanic-speaking peoples who settled in England after the Romans left—made Winchester the capital of their kingdom of Wessex. Threats from the Danes forced rulers from all over England to unite under the Wessex king, Egbert (reigned 802–39), and Winchester became, in effect, the capital of all England. The town flourished under Alfred the Great (871–99) and was later the seat of Canute (1016–35) and Edward the Confessor (1042–66). When the Normans conquered England in 1066, William the Conqueror (1066–87) made Winchester his capital, too, and power didn't shift to London for another 100 years.

Winchester Cathedral (☎ **01962/853137**)—the largest church in Christendom when first built (1079–93)—is what draws most visitors to Winchester today. As you enter, you'll see long avenues of Norman columns encased in Gothic shells.

Walk down the left aisle. Set into the floor of the fourth bay is Jane Austen's gravestone. As the bronze plaque on the wall points out, it makes no mention of her talents as a writer because her fame followed her death. Farther down the aisle is a dark marble 12th-century **baptismal font,** where children were being baptized little more than 100 years after the Battle of Hastings.

Stand in the **north transept** (the transepts are the arms of a cross-shape church) and compare the sturdy grace of its rounded arches with the elegant pointed arches of the nave. These transepts are all that remain above ground of the original Norman church. To see more of the Norman building, go to the **crypt;** the entrance is in the north transept. It's the country's largest and oldest Norman crypt and gives a strong sense of the simple style of the first cathedral. Access is limited in winter.

Then climb the rough-hewn stone steps to the **choir**—or quire, as they call it here (English cathedrals guard their idiosyncrasies jealously)—one of the glories of Winchester. The choir stalls are among the oldest in England. Behind the quire is the **retrochoir** (*retro* means "behind"). Many of its battered red floor tiles date from around 1230.

Look along the north aisle for the tomb of Stephen Gardiner. When the Protestants under Cromwell ransacked the cathedral, they gave Gardiner's effigy the same rough treatment Gardiner gave the "heretics" during his lifetime. The Protestants were kinder to the blind and universally loved Bishop Richard Fox (1448–1528), whose effigy you'll find along the south aisle. Fox commissioned his own tortured effigy while he was still a young man—perhaps to remind himself that no one, not even a bishop, is free from corruption. How unlike the effigy of Cardinal Beaufort, all decked out in red, placidly awaiting his call to paradise.

As you walk through the chancel, look up at the painted **mortuary chests** that hold the bones of several Saxon kings: Egbert; Ethelwulf (839–58), who was the father of Alfred the Great; and Canute, among others. The bones were scattered during the Civil War against Cromwell, so Egbert's head may be spending eternity with Ethelwulf's arms and Canute's legs.

A door on the south side of the south transept leads to the **Cathedral Library** and the **Triforium Gallery.** The library contains a 10th-century copy of the Venerable Bede's *Ecclesiastical History* and a 12th-century painted Bible.

Free admission, but suggested donation of £2. Open daily 7am–6:30pm (restricted access during services). Crypt, admission 20p; open Easter–Oct, daily 7:30am–6:30pm (water level permitting); tours 10:30am and 2:30pm. Library and Triforium Gallery, admission 50p; open mid-May to mid-Sept, Tues–Sat 7:30am–6:30pm; Oct–Apr, Sat and Mon only (closed Jan). Treasury, admission 20p; open mid-May to Oct, daily 11am–5pm.

Make a sharp left as you leave the cathedral and another left along a path beneath the buttresses. Notice how these buttresses (a Gothic invention, though what you see are late 19th-century reconstructions of the Gothic originals) keep the walls from splaying out beneath the weight of the roof, and thus permit the building of churches with higher, thinner walls, using glass instead of solid masonry. Bear right. Ahead of you is a redbrick building; to your left, the flinty stone of the **Deanery,** the official residence of the Dean. Walk around it to the left, following a sign to the College/Water Meadows. Leave the cathedral close (where the clergy lived) and pass through the 14th-century town gate. To the right of the gate is the **Parish Church of St. Swithun upon Kingsgate,** founded in 1263. It seems odd that a tiny parish church would be built so close to a cathedral until you realize that cathedrals were used mainly by the clergy;

TAKE A BREAK

Ahead of you as you pass through the gate is **The Wykeham Arms,** *75 Kingsgate St. (☎ 01962/853834), dating from 1775. What was once one of the most run-down pubs in the city now houses an upscale restaurant (see "Dining," below). It's also a good spot for an inexpensive ploughman's lunch and a pint.*

that they had no seats or pulpits; that the naves were used primarily for processions; and that the laymen were encouraged by the clergy to build churches of their own.

Turn left on College Street. A plaque indicates the privately owned **house where Jane Austen died** from Addison's disease at age 42. She was born and spent most of her life elsewhere, but she was often in ill health and in 1817 put herself in the care of a Winchester doctor.

On the right side of College Street, at the end of a long, unbroken stone wall, is the arched entranceway to **Winchester College.** Founded in 1382, it's the oldest public school—an English public school is the equivalent of an American private school—in England. The college was established as a training ground for applicants to New College in Oxford. Continue down College Street. On your left is the **Bishop's Palace,** a handsome 17th-century building reputedly designed by Sir Christopher Wren. It's not open to the public, but you can admire its facade from the footpath. Just beyond are the ruins of the **Old Bishop's Palace,** College Street (☎ 01962/854766), destroyed by Cromwell's forces in 1646. Admission £1.50 adults, 80p children, £1.10 seniors. Open Easter–Oct, daily 10am–6pm.

Directly across from the palace is a sign to **St. Cross via Water Meadows.** If you have time, take this pleasant 1.6-kilometer (1-mile) walk through the meadows and school playing fields. At the lock, cross the road and continue along the river.

The Hospital of St. Cross, St. Cross Road (☎ 01962/851375), founded in 1133 by a grandson of William the Conqueror, may be the country's oldest functioning almshouse. The gatekeeper maintains an ancient tradition of doling out beer and bread to all visitors, but you have to ask—and get here early: He has only two pints and two loaves. The 25 brothers wear gowns (black gowns if they're members of the original foundation, red if members of the 15th-century order of the Brothers of Noble Poverty) and live in 15th-century quarters. You can tour a 15th-century kitchen and a 12th-century Norman chapel with a bell tower that you can get permission to climb. Admission £1.50 adults, £1 students and seniors, 50p children. Open Apr–Oct, Mon–Sat 9:30am–12:30pm and 2–5pm; Nov–Mar, Mon–Sat 10:30am–12:30pm and 2–3:30pm.

From the Hospital, take a mile walk or a bus ride back to town. St. Cross Road turns into Southgate Street. At High Street, turn left to the **Great Hall,** High Street (☎ 01962/841841), all that's left of a Norman castle. Hanging here is the legendary Round Table of King Arthur, now known to be from the 14th century and looking very much like a giant dart board. Was there really a King Arthur? Of course. When the Romans left Britain in 410, towns decayed and the country was plunged into a dark age of lawlessness and civil unrest. Into this vacuum swept a number of military leaders and kings. One of them was Arthur. In the mid-6th century, the invasion of German-speaking Anglo-Saxons began. Arthur defended the Romanized Britons against the advancing Saxons in southwest England. Fighting like Roman cavalrymen against the Saxon foot soldiers—wearing helmets and chain mail against Saxon infantrymen with nothing but swords and spears—Arthur was able to keep them at bay for 50 years. He was probably Christian. Later English kings played up the Arthur legend to unite the country. Stories of Arthur and his Round Table were creations of the Age of Chivalry and have no known basis in fact. Free admission (contributions welcome). Open Mar–Oct, daily 10am–5pm; Nov–Feb, Mon–Fri 10am–5pm, Sat–Sun 10am–4pm.

DINING

Brann's, 9 Great Minster St., The Square (☎ **01962/864004**). Brann's is about the best restaurant in Winchester and the most conveniently located—right across the close facing the main (west) facade of the cathedral. The food, like the mood, is busy modern/chic and accordingly popular with Winchester's conspicuous movers and shakers. You can eat in the wine bar or in the more formal restaurant on the second floor. Saddle of venison with braised cabbage and game sauce and monkfish with shellfish sauce number among the specialties. Critics proclaim the wine list to be "thoughtful." Reservations advised for dinner. Casual chic at lunch; jacket/tie required at dinner. AE, DC, MC, V. Closed Sun. Expensive.

Old Chesil Rectory, 1 Chesil St. (☎ **01962/851555**). The Old Chesil Rectory, with its gnarled black-and-white exterior, is the oldest house in Winchester (1450) and complete with the requisite low-beamed ceilings and creaky floors. Come for coffee in the morning, a snack or something more substantial at lunch, afternoon tea, or a full-blown Old English dinner, with roast beef, steak-and-kidney pie, sweetbreads, and boiled beef and carrots. Locals cite the food for its "gutsy, punchy flavours." Finish your meal with a prune-and-Armagnac parfait. The building is a 10- to 15-minute walk from the cathedral along Stockbridge Road. Reservations advised. Casual chic at lunch; jacket/tie required at dinner. AE, DC, MC, V. Moderate/Expensive.

The Wykeham Arms, 75 Kingsgate St. (☎ **01962/853834**). What was once a city-center dive is now an appealing pub/restaurant that combines sophisticated English food with the warm bustle of an old pub, just a step or two south of the cathedral close. The main dining room is at the rear of the building, divided from one of the two bars by an open fireplace. Have a drink first in the appealing cluttered main bar, then move into the candlelit dining room. Try the beef-and-venison casserole flavored with juniper or the duck breast marinated in plum sauce. The desserts often are inspired by recipes 200 years old, as exemplified by the carrot-and-ginger pudding. Reservations advised for dinner. Casual chic at lunch; jacket/tie required at dinner. No credit cards. Expensive.

ACCOMMODATIONS

Dellbrook, Hubert Rd., St. Cross, Winchester, Hants. S023 9RG (☎ 01962/865093). Set in an Edwardian house close to the town center, this friendly B&B features a terrace overlooking St. Cross Hospital. The guest rooms are large, bright, and simply furnished. 3 rms, 1 with bath. Facilities: dining room, terrace. No credit cards. Inexpensive.

Lainston House, Sparsholt, Hants. S021 2LT (☎ 01962/863588; fax 01962/776672). For luxury lodging, the best in the area is Lainston House, about 3.2 kilometers (2 miles) northwest of Winchester on A272 (well signposted). A driveway lined with lime trees winds through parkland to an ivy-covered 17th-century manor house built by staunch supporters of Cromwell. There's an ancient dovecote, the ruins of a 12th-century chapel, birdsongs, and peace. Inside are beautifully turned moldings, a mahogany staircase, and a wonderful cedar-paneled bar. The furnishings, while tasteful, fall short of the tone of a 17th-century manor house. The rooms are large and comfortable, if rather simply decorated; ask for one in the main building. The hotel caters principally to business types during the week and has an unmistakable expense-account atmosphere. 37 rms with bath. Facilities: restaurant, bar, tennis, clay-pigeon shooting, croquet, fishing, horseback riding, golf, helicopter landing pad, numerous business amenities. AE, DC, MC, V. Very Expensive.

The Royal Hotel, St. Peter St., Winchester, Hants. S023 CBS (☎ 800/ 528-1234 or 01962/840840; fax 01962/841582). While offering nothing special, this is a comfortable place to spend a night. The public areas are soothingly decorated in autumnal colors, and the guest rooms are standardized Motel Modern but adequate; those in the annex are definitely more functional. The restful glassed-in restaurant serves reasonable international food. Nonetheless, it's hard not to be reminded that this is now a Best Western. 75 rms with bath. Facilities: restaurant, bar, garden, conference room. AE, DC, MC, V. Expensive.

SALISBURY

From Winchester, drive 30 kilometers (18.6 miles) west on A272/A30; from London, bypassing Winchester, drive 149 kilometers (93 miles) on M3 and A30. By train from Winchester, backtrack to Basingstoke and catch another train to Salisbury; from London, it's a 90-minute ride from Waterloo Station.

Salisbury is the home of the most perfect English cathedral ever built. **Salisbury Cathedral** (☎ 01722/328726) owes its unity to the fact that it was constructed in 38 years, from 1220 to 1258—unheard of in those times—and therefore stands almost exactly as its designers conceived it more than 700 years ago. Winchester Cathedral is typical of most cathedrals, for it's an amalgam of styles, from Norman/Romanesque to

Perpendicular/Late Gothic. Salisbury, in contrast, is in a single style, Early English—the purest expression of Early English in Britain.

Take your time walking around the grounds and looking up at the cathedral from different angles, appreciating its confidence, restrained dignity, and strength. Walk around on summer nights, too, when the cathedral is floodlit. The masons had trouble securing the weighty spire, which was added a century later, and it still leans slightly, despite the use of heavy arches to support it. At 121.1 meters (404 ft.), it's the tallest medieval spire ever built in England.

It has been said that the outside is all decoration and the inside all lines. You may find the uncluttered interior disappointing in comparison: all ribs without flesh, appealing more to the mind than to the senses. This was the result of an 18th-century housecleaning by some ill-advised ecclesiastical rationalists.

Near the west end of the north aisle—the aisle on your left as you face the altar—is the **oldest clock mechanism** (1326) in England, perhaps in the world. As you walk down the aisles, you'll see the tombs of knights who went on the Crusades or who died at Agincourt, where Henry V routed the French in 1415. In Salisbury, as in other English cathedrals, you'll notice that the aisles are lined with small chapels enclosing an altar and an effigy. These are called **chantries.** Wealthy laymen endowed these chapels, paying priests to say daily masses for their souls and for the souls of their families, in perpetuity or for a fixed number of years.

In the **Trinity Chapel** is a sheet of blue stained glass: the *Prisoner of Conscience,* glazed in 1980. Turn and compare it to the medieval shields and figures in the west window.

Leave by the **cloisters,** the earliest and longest in any English cathedral, and visit the adjoining **chapter house** (the room in a cathedral where business was conducted). You'll find here one of four extant copies of the **Magna Carta,** the foundation of English, and American, liberty. The Barons prepared it and King John put his seal to it at Runnymede in 1215. In an effort to circumscribe the arbitrary powers of the king, Article 39 states that "no free man shall be seized or imprisoned, or stripped of his rights or possessions, or outlawed or exiled, or deprived of his standing in any other way, nor will we [the king] proceed with force against him, or send others to do so, except by the lawful judgment of his equals or by the law of the land." Cathedral, free admission but suggested donation of £2.50 adults, £1.50 seniors; open daily 8am–6:30pm (restricted access during services). Chapter House, admission 30p; open May–Aug, daily 8am–8pm; off-season, daily 8am–6:30pm (restricted access during services).

Salisbury has the best **cathedral close** in the country, with houses from the 13th to the 18th century. It was in these stone-and-brick buildings surrounding the cathedral that the clergy lived. The clergy of monastic cathedrals consisted of monks who lived around a cloister. The clergy of Salisbury Cathedral were secular canons—clergymen who went out into the community and weren't bound by monastic vows. These canons could live where they wanted, but usually chose to stay in houses near the cathedral, called a close. The secular cathedrals had cloisters, too, but they were often merely decorative.

Of particular note in the close are **King's House,** 65 The Close, home of the **Salisbury and South Wiltshire Museum** (☎ **01722/332151**), which has some models of Stonehenge that'll make your visit there more meaningful (admission £1.50 adults, 50p children; open Mon–Sat 10am–5pm; July–Aug, Sun 2–5pm); the **Museum of the Duke of Edinburgh's Royal Regiment,** The Wardrobe, 58 The Close (☎ **01722/ 414536**) (admission £1.80 adults, £1 children—free if accompanied by adult; open Apr–June and Sept–Oct, Sun–Fri 10am–4:30pm; July–Aug, daily 10am–4:30pm; Feb, Mar, and Nov, Mon–Fri 10am–4:30pm); and, above all, the beautifully furnished **Mompesson House** (1701), Choristers' Square, The Close (☎ **01722/335659**), with an exquisite Queen Anne interior (admission £3.20 adults, £1.60 children; open Apr–Nov, Sat–Wed noon–5pm).

Exit through the north door of the cathedral and cross the lawn to where North Walk intersects with High Street. If you have only a few minutes, follow High Street past Mompesson House and beneath North Gate. There's a **National Trust Gift Shop** here. Turn left on Crane Street. Just after the bridge cut left through the Queen Elizabeth Gardens to another bridge over the River Nadder. It was from here that John Constable painted his famous portrait of the cathedral. If time permits, follow a footpath from this bridge through open countryside and enjoy changing views of the cathedral.

TAKE A BREAK

*Any number of pubs offering reasonable food and atmosphere dot the city center. A good one to try is **The New Inn,** 41–43 New St. (☎ **01722/327679**), built in the 15th century and boasting an impressively warped timbered facade. The gnarled mood is continued inside. To reach it, take the first right after leaving North Gate (the close's main entrance). It's about 90 meters (100 yd.) down the street on your right.*

If you have an extra half an hour, *don't* go up High Street; instead, turn right on North Walk to **St. Ann's Gate.** Handel is said to have given his first public concert in the room above. Turn left on St. John Street, which turns into Catherine Street and then into Queen Street. On your left is **Market Square,** where outdoor markets (Tues and Sat) have been held since 1361. Cross through the market to **St. Thomas's Church,** founded about 1220 in honor of Thomas Becket. It was rebuilt in the 15th century in the Perpendicular style and has a notable fresco (1475) of the *Last Judgment* above the chancel arch (the arch separating the nave from the front of the church). From St. Thomas's, take High Street back toward the cathedral, turn right on Crane Street, and take the abbreviated walking tour described above.

WILTSHIRE, AVON & SOMERSET

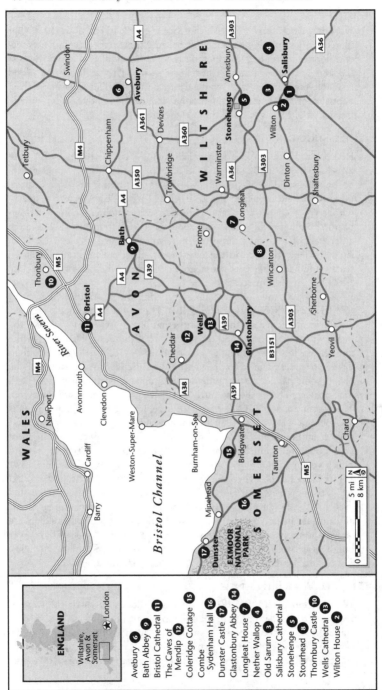

DINING

Harper's, 7 Ox Row, The Market Square (☎ 01722/333118). Other than the city's hotel restaurants, this friendly spot on the light and airy second floor of a building overlooking the Market Square is about the best Salisbury, not a town for gourmets, can muster. The English/French food is wholesome rather than sophisticated. Try the filet of salmon from Scotland or the beef bourguignonne. Reservations advised for dinner. Casual. DC, MC, V. Closed Sun. Moderate.

ACCOMMODATIONS

Red Lion Hotel, Milford St., Salisbury, Wilts. SP1 2AN (☎ 800/528-1234 or 01722/323334; fax 01722/325756). The Red Lion claims to be England's oldest purpose-built hotel, constructed in the 13th century (almost entirely rebuilt in the 17th). Now, it's a Best Western property with a Ye Olde atmosphere, complete with sagging floors and low-beamed ceilings. The best rooms, some with floral four-posters, are in the older part of the hotel; those in the newer wing are smaller. The hotel is conveniently located in the city center. 57 rms with bath. Facilities: restaurant, bar, conference room, golf, horseback riding, fishing, shooting. AE, DC, MC, V. Moderate.

Rose and Crown, Harnham Rd., Salisbury, Wilts. SP2 8JQ (☎ 01722/399955; fax 01722/339816). The two reasons for staying here are the location, just south of the cathedral but entirely removed from the bustle of the city center, and the splendid half-timbered black-and-white facade. Inside it's something of a disappointment, especially if you end up in the charmless annex (redeemed only by the views). But some of the older rooms have a certain time-honored appeal, particularly those with four-posters. There's also an attractive garden on the banks of the Avon. The restaurant serves Olde English Fayre, featuring deviled mushrooms and Butcher's Row pork filet; an outdoor riverside garden offers hot food daily from noon to 2:30pm. Although the food isn't special, it's the most scenic place for a lunch in Salisbury. 28 rms with bath. Facilities: restaurant, two bars, conference room, garden. AE, DC, MC, V. Expensive.

White Hart Hotel, 1 St. John St., Salisbury, Wilts. SP1 2SD (☎ 01722/327476; fax 01722/412761). A Georgian building not far from the cathedral, the White Hart is plushly comfortable, with spacious public rooms and tasteful guest rooms. The guest rooms in the original building are larger and more traditional than the faintly functional ones in the newer building at back. Some have four-posters. 68 rms with bath. Facilities: restaurant, bar, conference room. AE, DC, MC, V. Expensive.

ON TO WARMINSTER

Wilton House (☎ 01722/743115), 6.4 kilometers (4 miles) west of Salisbury on A30, is one of England's most opulent mansions, designed by Inigo Jones and his nephew by marriage, John Webb. The home of the earls of Pembroke for more than 400 years, it contains a world-famous collection of paintings, furniture, and sculpture; an exhibit of 7,000 model soldiers; a palace dollhouse; a working model railroad; even a lock of Elizabeth I's hair. Jones's state rooms are among the most palatial 17th-century rooms left in England.

In about 1530, a Welshman named William Herbert married the sister of Catherine Parr, who became Henry VIII's last wife. When Henry confiscated the church's lands, he abolished Wilton Abbey and gave the property to his brother-in-law. Herbert's eldest son later married Mary Sidney, sister of poet Philip Sidney, who wrote *Arcadia* while staying here. Scenes from this famous poem are painted on the walls of the Single Cube room. There's also a nude painting of the seventh earl's wife.

The famous Double Cube and Single Cube rooms, built to show the paintings of Van Dyke, follow the rules of proportion Jones learned from the Renaissance architect Palladio (1508–80): namely, that beauty consists of fixed, mathematical relationships between parts, none of which can be changed without destroying the harmony of the whole. The assumption is that God ordered the universe according to immutable mathematical laws and that beauty comes from creating a similar order on Earth. Admission £6.50 adults, £4 children 5–15 (under 4 free). Open Easter to mid-Oct, Mon–Sat and bank holidays 11am–6pm, Sun noon–6pm.

You can reach **Stonehenge** (☎ **01980/623108**) from Salisbury by taking A360 north 12.8 kilometers (8 miles) and turning right about 3.2 kilometers (2 miles) on A303. From Wilton House, take A36 north to Stapleford, take B3083 north, and turn right on A303. Buses leave from Salisbury Train Station frequently Monday to Saturday from mid-April to mid-December. There's more frequent service from Salisbury Bus Station near Market Place, a few blocks from the cathedral.

The best time to visit Stonehenge is early in the morning or just before closing, when the shadows are longer than the lines. A fence keeps you from wandering among the stones, so you may want to avoid the entrance fee and look from the road. Even if the site is officially closed, you can see it well from the embankment, another reason to visit at sunrise or sunset, when the dim light creates an even greater sense of mystery.

What was this circular group of standing stones? An astronomical observatory? A Druidic temple? A navigational aid for flying saucers? Evidence seems to point to its being an open-air temple dedicated to sky gods. It was built from about 2200 to 1550 B.C.—later than the Great Pyramid, contemporary with the Minoan civilization on Crete, and 1,000 years earlier than the Great Wall of China. The Druids, a Celtic priesthood, didn't get here until 250 B.C.

The stones were shaped with hammers and upended in holes dug with antler picks and spades made from the shoulder bones of cattle. The lintel stones (henges) were set in place with the help of log platforms. The bluestones, which weigh up to 4 tons each, were brought some 384 kilometers (240 miles) on logrollers and sledges or lashed to the sides of rafts. The other stones, which weigh up to 50 tons each, were brought mostly uphill from 32 kilometers (20 miles) away. At the time, only nomadic hunters lived on Salisbury Plain, so whoever built Stonehenge must've come from another, more sophisticated civilization.

The most important clues are the blue beads called *faience* that have been found in many parts of Britain and could only have come from workshops in Egypt and Mycenae. The Egyptians and Greeks made these beads for trade with Europe. If you look where they've been discovered, you'll find that they follow a trail along the southern coasts of France and Spain, up to Brittany, up to the Dorset coast of England, to the greatest concentration—around Stonehenge. It was here that these beads were traded for Irish gold; here that Mycenaean civilization, through the medium of these traders, was introduced in Britain; and here that one of the traders or his associates must've been commissioned to build Stonehenge. It may seem farfetched, but how else do you explain the Mycenaean-type dagger carved into one of the Stonehenge stones or the fact that the very same technique used to fasten the stone lintels to the uprights was used to construct the stone gateways at Mycenae?

Stonehenge—a temple dedicated to the sun—was needed by a people moving from a female-dominated society that worshiped earth goddesses to a male-dominated society that worshiped gods of the sky. The same transition went on in Greece, when the old Achaean earth gods were replaced by Zeus and his cronies on Olympus. The transition took place in Greece about 1600 B.C.—the very same time that the Beaker Folk were engineering the final remodeling of Stonehenge.

If you stand at the center on the summer solstice, you can see the sun rising over the Heel Stone. So sophisticated were the techniques of these early astronomers that posts were placed to indicate where the moon rises over the horizon, as it shifts every 2 weeks in 18.61-year cycles. Yet Stonehenge was probably not an early version of Palomar Observatory but a temple where planetary movement was observed for religious reasons. Admission £3.50 adults, £2.60 students, £1.80 children. Open Mar 16–May 31 and Sept 1–Oct 15, daily 9:30am–6pm; June–Aug, daily 9am–7pm; Oct 16–Mar 15, daily 9:30am–4pm.

Warminster

From Stonehenge, drive 28.8 kilometers (18 miles) west on A303 and A36 to Warminster, where there's an outstanding hotel.

ACCOMMODATIONS

Bishopstrow House, Bishopstrow, Warminster, Wilts. BA12 9HH (☎ **01985/212312;** fax 01985/216769). About 3.2 kilometers (2 miles) outside of Warminster on A36 is an elegant late-Georgian mansion that's certainly a contender for the best hotel between London and Bath, if not actually the best. There's no disputing the charm of the building, nor the substantial luxuries within. The formal lounge has Persian carpets, jade-green upholstery, antiques, and French windows overlooking the extensive grounds. The furnishings have a formal decorated look but are comfortable and in good taste. The small guest rooms aren't quite worth the price, but the suites are wonderfully luxurious, some with Jacuzzis made for two. The tiled indoor pool, surrounded by classical pillars, is as elegant as the pool at the Palace Hotel in St. Mortiz. The dining room offers sumptuous nouvelle-inspired dishes in a light, sophisticated atmosphere. 28 rms with bath. Facilities: restaurant, bar, indoor and outdoor tennis, indoor and outdoor pools, fishing, golf. AE, DC, MC, V. Very Expensive.

ON TOWARD WELLS

A trip to **Stourhead House and Gardens** (☎ 01747/840348) will add about 24 kilometers (15 miles) to your drive, but anyone who loves gardens will find the trip worthwhile. From Stonehenge, take A303 about 40 kilometers (25 miles), then turn north on B3092 for about 4.8 kilometers (3 miles). These are among the finest 18th-century gardens in England, laid out by the century's foremost landscape gardener, Lancelot "Capability" Brown. A river was dammed to create a three-part lake, whose shores are surrounded by various Italian temples and grottoes. You can also visit the handsome Palladian house, furnished by Thomas Chippendale. Admission £4.20 per person for house or gardens; joint ticket for £7.50 includes admission to both house and gardens.

From Stourhead House and Gardens, take B3092 north about 9.6 kilometers (6 miles) and follow the signs to **Longleat House** (☎ 019858/44400); from Stonehenge, drive 28.8 kilometers (18 miles) west on A303 and A36 to Warminster and follow the signs. What I remember most about Longleat is the guide shaking the change in his pocket so we wouldn't forget to tip him at the end of the tour. The house itself is an exercise in wowmanship, with busloads of tourists tramping through the gilded halls among the priceless antiques, some more tasteful than others. Longleat is the only surviving 16th-century example of a Renaissance-style house in England. It was redecorated in the Italian Renaissance style during the 19th century and stuffed with a dizzying collection of artifacts the fourth marquess gathered on a grand tour of Europe. Chinese vases, Venetian ceilings lifted from the Doge's palace, Sicilian clocks, 19th-century saltshakers—Longleat has them all. Highlighting the tour are the erotic murals—apples hanging from phallic trees and so on—painted in 1973 by the good Lord Weymouth, who is said to have had an unhappy childhood.

For children, the highlight of the trip to Longleat is a visit to the Dolls' Houses and a drive through Safari Park among the not-very-wild animals. There's also a maze, a 15-inch narrow-gauge railway, a 1:25 scale model of Longleat House, and safari-boat rides through a lake full of hippos and sea lions. This is a place that takes mass tourism seriously. Admission for all attractions, £11 adults, £9 children 4–14 and seniors; for house only, £4.50 adults, £2.50 children 4–14 and seniors; for gardens only, £2.50 adults, children 4–14 and seniors free; for Safari Park only, £5.50 adults, £4 children 4–14 and seniors; charges for other attractions vary from 50p to £1. House open Easter–Sept, daily 10am–6pm; Oct–Easter, daily 10am–4pm. Safari Park and Pets Corner open Mar–Oct, daily 10am–6pm (or dusk if earlier). Other attractions open Mar–Oct, daily 11am–6pm (dusk if earlier).

TAKE A BREAK

A good bet for lunch near Longleat is the **Bath Arms,** *Horningsham (☎ 01984/4308), en route to Frome. Lord Christopher from Longleat likes to come here for a pint with the locals. In Frome itself, 5.6 kilometers (3.5 miles) from Longleat on A362, try the* **Settle Inn,** *Cheap St. (☎ 01373/465975). The food and pastries are as memorable as the atmosphere. The lunch menu includes Somerset gammon (ham) with Damson sauce, pork in rough cider, and rabbit pie. The inn is open in the evenings and on Sunday for lunch.*

WELLS

From Frome take A361 east for 17.6 kilometers (11 miles), or from Bath take A39 south for 33.6 kilometers (21 miles) to Wells. The 33.6-kilometer/21-mile trip by bus from Bath takes 80 minutes. Buses leave hourly during the week, less frequently on Sunday, from the bus terminal one block from the train station.

If you're spending several days in Bath, it makes sense to settle in and make a side trip to Wells. If your time is limited, however, save time by visiting Wells en route to Bath.

Wells is England's smallest cathedral city, but its cathedral, built by secular canons, is the most graceful in the country. Because the complex of church buildings is so well preserved, it makes a great introduction to life in the Middle Ages. Try to visit on market days—Wednesday and Saturday.

The **Wells Cathedral** (☎ 01749/674483) took 3 centuries to plan and build (1175–1508) and therefore offers a lesson in the history of architectural styles. As you enter, look up at the famous west facade and try to imagine the statues colored and gilded, as they were in the 13th century. The Puritans destroyed some of the 400 statues, but 297 remain—the greatest and richest display of 13th-century sculpture in England.

Ahead of you is a pair of strangely inverted scissor arches added to support the new tower, which was so heavy it threatened to tumble into the nave. The arches look modern but were built 600 years ago. Some think them gross, others graceful, but all agree that they're unique and that they worked.

Follow the left (north) aisle to the transept and look up at the clock. Knights rush out every quarter hour and fight with lances. One has been knocked down each time—since 1390. On the hour Jack Blandiver kicks the bells with his heels and hammers one in front of him. No one knows how he got his name. Below the clock is a life-size 1955 carving of Christ rising from the tomb.

Continue toward the front (east) end of the church and look for the door to the **Chapter House**—the finest in the country. A flight of worn stone steps, themselves almost as memorable as anything else in the cathedral, leads up to it. In the octagonal room, 32 ribs fan out from the central pier like fronds on a giant palm tree.

Look at the capitals (the heads of columns) in the south transept—on your right as you face the altar—and find the heads and animal masks hidden among the leaves. One has a toothache and seems to be waiting for a dentist to pass by.

The cathedral has some wonderful **chantry chapels.** Look especially for Bishop Thomas Bekynton's. The two views of him, in this life and the next, say more about mortality than a hundred sermons. Look, too, for chantries of Nicholas Bubworth, Bishop of Bath, and John Drokensford, who is waiting for Judgment Day with his feet on a lion and his head on a pillow. Cathedral admission free, but suggested donation of £3 adults, £1.50 students and children. Open daily 7:30am–7pm (may sometimes close earlier in winter; restricted access during services).

From the cathedral walk through the 15th-century cloisters to the grounds of the **Bishop's Palace** (☎ 01749/678691), the only medieval bishop's palace still occupied. Because the bishop still lives here, the rooms we'd all like to see—bedrooms, baths, and so on—are closed to the public. The walls, 4.5 meters (15 ft.) thick, and moat were added in the 14th century to protect the bishop from town riots. Guidebooks tell you that swans in the moat ring a bell for dinner; but the swans find it easier to be fed by tourists and the bell hasn't tolled for years. Admission £2.50 adults, £2 students and seniors, under 16 free. Open Easter–Oct, Tues–Thurs 10am–6pm, Sun 2–6pm; Aug and bank holidays, daily 10am–6pm.

Wookey Hole (☎ 01749/672243) is a cave and paper mill 3.2 kilometers (2 miles) from Wells and very well signposted. If you dismiss it as a tourist trap run by Madame Tussaud's, you're making a mistake. It *is* commercial but great fun, too, and families in particular will want to see it. What makes a tour worthwhile is that prehistoric folk once lived here and you can imagine their lifestyle. Watercolorists can buy handmade paper here, and children of all ages can play prehistoric penny-arcade games and tour a room filled with Madame Tussaud's retired wax figures. Admission £6 adults, £3.50 children 16 and under; £7.50 family ticket. Open Apr–Oct, daily 9:30am–5:30pm; Nov–Mar, daily 10:30am–4:30pm.

BATH

From Wells, take A39 for 33.6 kilometers (21 miles) northeast; from Salisbury, take A36 for 64 kilometers (40 miles) northwest. **Bath** is England's most elegant city, famous for its history, architecture, and hot springs. It's also a clean, comfortable town with sophisticated restaurants and first-class hotels. The shopping, along traffic-free pedestrian malls, is in some ways the equal of London's. The major sights are the Roman Baths, the Abbey, and the Georgian buildings where British society stayed in the 18th century. None of this will mean much, however, unless you know something about Bath's history.

The Romans knew about the springs and their restorative powers when they began moving west in the 1st century A.D. to mine lead. They built the baths around them—nothing as grand or elegant as the baths in Rome, but luxurious for such a distant outpost. The baths are still well preserved and are today the best Roman ruins in Britain.

The fame of Bath disappeared with the Romans in the 5th century. Medieval chroniclers knew about the health-giving properties of the waters, but the spa was neglected until the 17th century. Diarist Samuel Pepys wrote in 1668, "Methinks it cannot be clean to go so many bodies together in the same water." Among those who disagreed was Charles II, who brought Queen Catherine here to make her fertile and give the crown a legitimate heir. It didn't work; but others followed, including Queen Anne, who, suffering from dropsy and gout, came in 1702 and 1703, bringing the rest of English society in her fashionable wake.

In 1704, a 31-year-old gambler, Richard "Beau" Nash, was chosen to oversee the spa's restoration. In the next 40 years this obscure Welshman virtually invented the resort business and became the Arbiter of Elegance. His famous Code of Behavior, posted in the Pump Room for all to see, included the following rules:

- That ladies coming to the ball appoint a time for their footmen coming to wait on them home, to prevent disturbance and inconvenience to themselves and others.

- That no gentleman give his ticket for the balls to any but gentlewomen.—NB: Unless he has none of his acquaintance.

- That the elder ladies and children be content with a second bench at the ball, as being past or not come to perfection.

On three points Nash was particularly insistent: that there should be no dueling and wearing of swords; that women should never appear at assemblies in white aprons; and that men should never appear at fashionable gatherings in riding boots. The fight against white aprons was particularly severe. The climax came when the duchess of Queensberry arrived at the Assembly Room in an apron that Beau ruthlessly stripped from her and threw among the ladies-in-waiting. The duchess took the insult in stride and meekly submitted to the uncrowned king of Bath.

Once Nash freed Bath from its rustic associations, the *beau monde* began to flock here, certain that dignity and decorum would prevail. By mid-century, Bath had become the center of Fashion and Polite Society during the long summer months. Richard Sheridan wrote *The Rivals* here in the 1770s while living on Terrace Walk. Jane Austen, who was often sick, came for the cures in the early 19th century. When you visit the

BATH

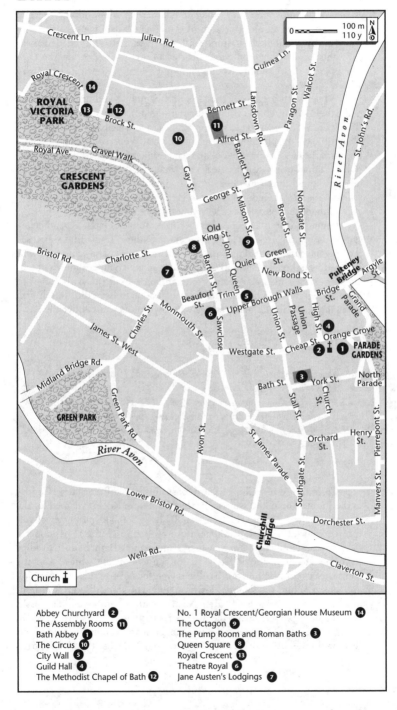

0 ——— 100 m
0 ——— 110 y

N

Crescent Ln.
Julian Rd.
Guinea Ln.
Walcot St.
Royal Crescent
Paragon St.
Lansdown Rd.
Royal Victoria Park
Bennett St.
Alfred St.
Brock St.
Bartlett St.
St. John's Rd.
River Avon
Royal Ave.
Gravel Walk
CRESCENT GARDENS
George St.
Gay St.
Milsom St.
Broad St.
Northgate St.
Old King St.
John St.
Quiet
Green St.
Bristol Rd.
Charlotte St.
Barton St.
Queen
New Bond St.
Beaufort St.
Trim
Upper Borough Walls
Pulteney Bridge
Bridge St.
Argyle St.
Grand Parade
Charles St.
Monmouth St.
Sawclose
Union Passage
Union St.
High St.
Orange Grove
James St. West
Westgate St.
Cheap St.
PARADE GARDENS
Midland Bridge Rd.
Bath St.
York St.
North Parade
Green Park Rd.
Stall St.
Church St.
GREEN PARK
Orchard St.
Henry St.
River Avon
Avon St.
St. James Parade
Southgate St.
Pierrepont St.
Manvers St.
Lower Bristol Rd.
Churchill Bridge
Dorchester St.
Wells Rd.
Claverton St.

Church †

Abbey Churchyard ②	No. 1 Royal Crescent/Georgian House Museum ⑭
The Assembly Rooms ⑪	The Octagon ⑨
Bath Abbey ①	The Pump Room and Roman Baths ③
The Circus ⑩	Queen Square ⑧
City Wall ⑤	Royal Crescent ⑬
Guild Hall ④	Theatre Royal ⑥
The Methodist Chapel of Bath ⑫	Jane Austen's Lodgings ⑦

Assembly Rooms you can imagine Catherine Morland, heroine of *Northanger Abbey,* and a projection of Jane herself as a young girl, being snubbed by fashionable visitors until she finds a suitable gentleman to show her around. A little later, Charles Dickens hung out in the card rooms (now the Assembly Rooms) and put the city in several chapters of *The Pickwick Papers.*

While Nash organized concerts and gambling and lit the streets to make them safe, architect John Wood (1700–54), with his son, also called John (1728–81), was busy transforming Bath into a city suitable for "people of quality." Inspired by Bath's Roman past, Wood conceived a scheme to return the city to what he took to be its former architectural glory. Little of his original plan was executed, but what was built serves to underline just how much more magnificent Bath might've become. Not only can you still see these buildings, you can stay in some of them, in hotels with appointments as splendid as the buildings themselves.

Begin your tour at the **Abbey,** a fine example of late Perpendicular-style—one of the last great achievements of Catholic England. Do you see the angels climbing ladders on the west facade? The sculpture was inspired by a dream of Bishop Oliver King, in which he saw angels climbing to heaven and heard voices commanding a king (his own name) to restore the church. The designers were anxious to have the church well lit, so they built the large clerestory windows in the walls above the nave.

TAKE A BREAK

*Combine your sightseeing with a bite to eat at **Sally Lunn's,** 4 N. Parade Passage (☎ 01225/461634), a Tudor building close to the Abbey that claims to be the city's oldest house. Downstairs is a small museum (☎ 01225/461634); closed Monday. For more substantial meals, try the **Pump Room** itself, Abbey Church Yard (☎ 01225/444477), where you can eat surrounded by 18th-century elegance.*

Cross the Abbey Church Yard, past the Tourist Information Centre, to the **Pump Room and Roman Baths.** The Pump Room—named for the reservoir below that provides 1,064,000 liters (280,000 gal) a day of sulfurous water at a constant temperature of 46.6°C (116°F)—is in fact a Georgian assembly hall. For a taste of 18th-century Bath, be sure to come from 9am to noon for coffee, a sip of the evil-tasting waters, and the sounds of violins. Be on your best behavior, for Nash—at least a painting and statue of him—is looking down on you. The Pump Room was actually built from 1789 to 1999, after Nash's death, when the middle classes had begun to gate-crash and the high-born and low-born were engaged in a frantic round of pleasure and diversion, both an easy prey to sharks and fortune hunters. Close your eyes and think of the Pump Room as described by novelist Tobias Smollett through the eyes of one of his heroines, Lydia Melford:

All is gaiety, good-humor, and diversion. The eye is continually enter-tained with the splendour of dress and equipage; and the ear with the sound of coaches, chaises, chairs, and other carriages. We have music in the Pump-room every morning, cotillions every forenoon in the rooms, balls twice a week, and concerts every night, besides private assemblies and parties without number. The Squares and the Circus put you in mind of the sumptuous palaces represented in prints and pictures. At eight in the morning we go déshabillé to the Pump-room, which is crowded like a Welsh fair; and there you see the highest qual-ity and the lowest tradesfolks, jostling each other, without ceremony. Hard by the Pump-room is a coffee-house for the ladies; but my aunt says young girls are not admitted, inasmuch as the conversation turns upon politics, scandal, philosophy, and other subjects about our capacity.

Descend to the **Roman Baths** (☎ 01225/477000). Most of the excavations were made in the late 19th century, long after Nash's reign. The **Great Bath**—in essence, a warm swimming pool—is still unroofed and has the original Roman lead plumbing; the columns and statues above are Victorian. There were no luxurious changing rooms in the 18th cen-tury; visitors arrived in carriages, wrapped in robes; after wallowing in the rather scuzzy waters, they wrapped themselves up, returned to their car-riages, and niddlenoddled home. After you've seen the Great Bath, you can walk through the extensive excavations of Roman remains discovered on the site. Admission £5.60 adults, £3.30 children 5–16; 4 and under free. Open Apr–Sept, daily 9am–6pm; Oct–Mar, Mon–Sat 9:30am–5pm, Sun 10:30am–5pm. Evenings in Aug, daily 8–10pm.

Leave the Baths and turn right on Stall Street. You'll find many fash-ionable shops on this pedestrian mall and along the side streets. Follow Stall Street as it becomes first Union Street, then Milsom Street. After about 450 meters (500 yd.), you come to the **Octagon,** Milsom Street (☎ 01225/462841), an 18th-century hall housing the National Centre for Photography, the world's oldest photographic society. It offers a var-ied program of quality exhibits and contains a small permanent collection. Admission £2.50; under 7 free. Open daily 9:30am–5:30pm.

Milsom Street runs into George Street. Turn right, then make the first left onto Bartlett Street, which has several **antiques shops,** and con-tinue to Alfred Street. Turn left. On your right are the famous **Assembly Rooms** (☎ 01225/477000), built by John Wood's son from 1769 to 1771 so that visitors didn't have to go all the way to the baths to socialize. The Assembly Rooms soon became the center of the town's social life, with balls, card playing, tea drinking, entertainments, and an endless stream of gossip and scandal. The Assembly Rooms, along with the famous

Museum of Costume beneath them, are open to visitors. Admission £3.20 adults, £2 children; £9 family ticket. Open Mon–Sat 10am–5pm, Sun 11am–5pm.

From the Assembly Rooms, turn left onto Bennett Street. This takes you to the **Circus,** a circle of identical Georgian houses that many consider John Wood's finest work. (A "circus" is a circle or ring.) Wood designed it, and it was completed by his son, who also designed the Royal Crescent (see below).

To appreciate the Georgian architecture of John Wood and his son, keep in mind that it was based largely on the concepts of the Italian Renaissance architect Palladio. If Wood's buildings seem cold to you, it's because they're meant not to overwhelm your senses, as, say, a Gothic or baroque building would, but to appeal to your mind—to your sense of order and harmony and proportion. Every part has a fixed size and shape in relation to every other and to the whole. This harmony, in the 18th century's rationally conceived universe, was thought to be an echo of the harmony of the universe—a universe that, like a clock, was set in motion by a rational God. As you walk around the Circus, try to appreciate these harmonic ratios and think fondly of an age when people could believe that Truth was known and that the world was ruled by reason.

Leave the Circus and walk down Brock Street, which was built by John Wood the Younger in 1767. The street was conceived as an avenue connecting the town's two architectural masterpieces, the Circus and the Royal Crescent. You won't know what's in store for you until the moment you turn into the Crescent—exactly as Wood planned it more than 200 years ago.

The **Royal Crescent** is the severest expression of the Palladian style in England. Built from 1767 to 1774, it consists of 30 houses with a continuous facade of 114 Ionic columns. Would you rather live here or in the Circus? I'd prefer the Circus; it seems more human. Yet Smollett seems unfair when he dismisses the Royal Crescent as "a pretty bauble, contrived for show, [that] looks like Vespasian's amphitheater [the Colosseum] turned inside out." Note that though the facade gives the buildings a uniform face, the interiors were designed differently, by various contractors, and that the back sides, which no one was supposed to see, are, in comparison, rather shabby. How 18th-century, this distinction between a person's private life and the face he presents to the world.

In the **Georgian House Museum,** 1 Royal Crescent (☎ 01225/428126), you can capture a sense of life in 18th-century Bath. Admission £3 adults, £2.50 children 5–18, students, and seniors; 4 and under free. Open Mar–Oct, Tues–Sun 10:30am–5pm; Nov to mid-Dec, Tues–Sun 10:30am–4pm.

In the center of this noble arc is the **Royal Crescent Hotel** (see "Accommodations," below). Note the fashionably understated hotel sign beside the door.

From the Royal Crescent, return to the Circus. Turn right (counterclockwise) in the Circus, past the hotel at no. 6, and make your first right down Gay Street, across Queen Square and then into Barton Street. On your right is the town's most popular restaurant, **Popjoy's** (see "Dining"), where Nash once lived with his mistress, Juliana Popjoy. Beside the restaurant is the beautifully restored **Theatre Royal,** Sawclose (☎ 01225/448844), where you should get seats for an upcoming performance.

Cross the open square and turn left on Westgate Street, which will take you back to Stall Street, the Baths, and the Abbey. Between the Abbey and the River Avon are the lovely **Parade Gardens,** where you can rest your feet. To the right of the gardens (facing the river) is a bridge. Cross over and turn immediately left on a path along the riverbank. There's a place here to catch a boat for a peaceful 60-minute cruise on the Avon: on the river's east bank, adjacent to the Pulteney Bridge, across the water from the Parade Gardens. (Walk down a slipway/boat ramp to reach the departure point.) Boat cruises lasting 50 minutes cost from £3 to £3.70 for adults and £1.50 to £2 for children. The big-windowed junket carries you about 3 miles upstream to Bathamp-

ton, then reverses and leisurely returns to Bath. River tours are offered from Easter to October on two boats maintained by **The Boating Station** (☎ 01225/466407) and its competitor, a one-ship outfit, the *Pulteney Princess* (☎ 01453/ 836639).

Continue along the river to the next bridge, Pulteney Bridge, which has shops on it, inspired by the ponte Vecchio in Florence. Cross the bridge, into Bridge Street. Turn left on High Street. On your left is the Guildhall, the banquet room of which is one of best interiors in Bath. Next door is the covered market. Continue down High Street and you'll be back at the Abbey.

DINING

Dower House Restaurant, 16 Royal Crescent (☎ 01225/319090). The restaurant of the Royal Crescent Hotel, the Dower House, is set in its own elegant building in a garden and is the town's most formal restaurant. If you're not staying at the Royal Crescent, this is a great opportunity for you to tour John Wood's masterpiece and learn what 18th-century elegance was all about. The imaginative menu includes lamb cutlets with tarragon mousse and pigeon with wood mushrooms and glazed turnips. Reservations required. Jacket/tie required. AE, DC, MC, V. Very Expensive.

Hole in the Wall, 16 George St. (☎ **01225/425242**). In the 1970s this was hailed as the West Country's finest restaurant. Chefs Christopher Chown and Adrian Walton have too much competition to maintain that title today, but their bistro cuisine is still among the finest in Bath. They operate in a cheerful atmosphere of polished copper pots, a large fireplace, whitewashed walls, and darkened ceiling beams. Traditional British cookery is combined with Mediterranean flair. The results are worth the trip across town—especially to taste the richly flavored lamb shank, daube of beef with mild horseradish dumplings, or braised pork tenderloin wrapped in bacon with brandy cider and applesauce. Reservations advised. Casual. AE, MC, V. Closed Sun. Moderate.

Popjoy's, Beau Nash's House, Sawclose (☎ **01225/460494**). This is the place to dine if you have only one evening in Bath. It's conveniently next door to the theater and comes closer than any restaurant in town to capturing the elegant atmosphere of 18th-century Bath. The menu features local fish and game, with such specialties as terrine of duck and chicken liver wrapped in bacon with tomato coulis; watercress-and-potato soup; sautéed lamb kidneys with crispy smoked bacon; braised lamb shoulder with sage-and-garlic dressing; and tagliatelle with leeks and cream sauce. Coffee is served upstairs. Nash lived here with his mistress; when he died she vowed never to sleep in a bed again and ended her life in a hollow tree in Wiltshire. Reservations required. Casual. AE, DC, MC, V. Closed Sun. Moderate.

Priory Hotel, Weston Rd. (☎ **01225/331922**). The Priory Hotel, a late-Georgian villa a mile or so west of the city center, is considered Bath's best restaurant by many locals. The cuisine leans toward traditional French with *moderne* flourishes. Roast beef remains a consistent favorite, as do the asparagus (in season) and braised quail with wild mushrooms. Some critics maintain that, though excellent, the wines are overpriced. Reservations required. Jacket/tie required. AE, DC, MC, V. Expensive.

ACCOMMODATIONS

Bailbrook Lodge, 35–37 London Rd. W., Bath, Avon BA1 7HZ (☎ **01225/859090**). One mile east of Bath along the A4, this John Everleigh–designed Georgian mansion from the 1780s will appeal if you wish to stay somewhere that's more like a private home than a hotel. The tastefully decorated suites, some with four-posters, others with brass bedsteads, survey the garden and Avon Valley. Downstairs is a sitting room with leather and velvet chairs and sofas, plus an inviting dining room. 12 rms with bath. Facilities: dining room, garden. AE, DC, MC, V. Inexpensive/Moderate.

The Priory Hotel, Weston Rd., Bath, Avon BA1 2XT (☎ **01225/ 331922;** fax 01225/448276). If the Royal Crescent has the atmosphere of a city hotel, the rambling Priory, though little more than 1.6 kilometers (1 mile) west of the city center, seems more like a country estate. The atmosphere is refined, but much more relaxed than at the Royal Crescent. There are rooms to curl up in—one would never curl up in the Royal Crescent, at least not in public. Pay extra for the deluxe doubles; they're worth it. The best standard rooms are in the older wing. The restaurant is justly famous. 19 rms with bath. Facilities: restaurant, croquet, heated outdoor pool. AE, DC, MC, V. Very Expensive.

Royal Crescent Hotel, 16 Royal Crescent, Bath, Avon BA1 2LS (☎ **01225/319090;** fax 01225/339401). The Royal Crescent was the best address in Bath 200 years ago—and still is. Staying in one of these lovingly restored town houses is as close as you'll come to recapturing the grandeur of Georgian Bath. The rooms in the renovated building behind the crescent are tastefully decorated in hushed pastels, but if you know the history of Bath, you may feel cheated unless you stay in the original building designed by John Wood. The atmosphere is formal and discreet, with most guests on the far side of 35. The larger rooms and suites are exquisite; the smaller, least expensive rooms are equally tasteful. The service is polished. 13 suites and 32 rms with bath. Facilities: restaurant, bar, heated pool. AE, DC, MC, V. Very Expensive.

Ston Easton Park, Ston Easton, Avon BA3 4DF (☎ **01761/241631;** fax 01761/241377). Located 19.2 kilometers (12 miles) from Bath on A37, the Ston Easton is one of England's most elegant country hotels, with period antiques, a grand salon with ornate plaster ceilings, and other Palladian-style details. Forests of flowers protrude from huge vases. Some rooms have four-posters, and all are sumptuously decorated. The staff is discreet, attentive, and welcoming. The hotel stands in 11.2 hectares (28 acres) of beautiful gardens landscaped in the 18th century by Sir Humphrey Repton, with panoramic views in every direction. 5 suites and 15 rms with bath. Facilities: two restaurants, private dining room, croquet, archery, horseback riding, fishing, ballooning, helicopter landing pad. AE, DC, MC, V. Very Expensive.

LACOCK

Take A4 about 19.2 kilometers (12 miles) east of Bath, then turn right (south) on A350 if you want to see **Lacock,** an 18th-century village that hasn't been prettified or overwhelmed with tourist shops. It can be mobbed on summer days by tourists stalking the *real* England, so stay overnight—before or after your trip to Bath—and explore the town when the day-trippers are gone. In the Middle Ages Lacock was a weaving community on an important Bath–London route. Prosperity continued through the 18th century, when—as with other towns you'll be visiting— the Industrial Revolution put the cottage weaving industry out of business. Unlike other towns, however, Lacock was owned largely by a single family, the Talbots, who preserved its heritage and in 1944 put it safely in the hands of the National Trust. Thanks to the preservationists, the newest houses are 18th century, and the village remains one of the most homogeneous in England.

The main street, leading to the abbey, is High Street, lined with moss-covered stone houses spanning at least 4 centuries. Church Street, paralleling High Street, leads to **St. Cyriac Church.** This is a Perpendicular-style wool church — so called because it was built by prosperous wool merchants from the 14th to the 17th century. Note the memorial brass in the south transept to Robert Raynard and his 18 children. Note, too, the weird faces in the arches of the Lady Chapel (on the left, facing the altar).

TAKE A BREAK

For better-than-average pub food and a satisfying old-world atmosphere (only partly spoiled by the piped music), try **The Carpenter's Arms** *(☎ 01249/ 730203). It can get crowded in summer, so it's best to arrive early. The newer Barn Restaurant in the back offers more substantial meals. The pub is located in the little square by the church.*

Lacock Abbey (☎ 01249/730227) was the last religious house in England to be suppressed at the Dissolution — when Henry VIII established the Church of England and appropriated church lands to fill his coffers. It's a good example of a medieval Augustinian priory that was converted into a private home, incorporating both the chapter house and the cloister. Admission £4.20 adults, £2.20 children (cloisters and grounds only, £3 adults, £1.50 children). House, cloisters, and grounds open Apr–Oct, Wed–Mon 11am–5pm (Tues, cloisters and grounds only open).

Outside the gates of the abbey is the **Fox Talbot Museum** (☎ 01249/730459), which contains photos by Fox Talbot, who made the first photographic prints in 1833. Admission £2.40. Open Mar–Oct, daily 11am–5pm.

DINING

At the Sign of the Angel, Church St. (☎ 01249/730230). You'll have to search long to find a more perfect example of Merrie England than this beautifully maintained inn. Roasts predominate, with roast beef and Yorkshire pudding an enduring favorite (it's almost always rare, so be sure to tell the waiter if you prefer it well done). Pan-fried lamb kidneys in Madeira sauce, salmon with lemon hollandaise, homemade pies, and treacle-and-walnut pudding are other long-standing offerings. Though a bit touristy for some tastes, the restaurant nevertheless is once again delivering sound English cookery following a bit of a slump. Reservations required. Casual. AE, MC, V. Closed Mon lunch, Christmas, and New Year's. Moderate/Expensive.

ACCOMMODATIONS

At the Sign of the Angel, Church St., Lacock, Wilts. SN15 2LA (☎ **01249/730230;** fax 01249/730527). If you're going to experience southwestern England, you should spend at least 1 night in a Georgian town house, another in a restored manor house, and a third in an old inn. The best of the inns, this 15th-century wool merchant's house has low oak-beamed ceilings, even in the bathrooms, and whitewashed stenciled room walls. What makes the inn unique is that it hasn't been mucked up with tasteless modern furnishings. A cottage annex has been added, but try to stay in the old part, where each room is different. No. 3 is more spacious than some; if noise bothers you, avoid no. 1. The breakfast omelets, with ham, mushrooms, and tomatoes, should see you through the day. 9 rms with bath. Facilities: restaurant, bar, garden. AE, V. Expensive.

Beechfield House, Beanacre, Melksham, Wilts. SN12 7PU (☎ **01225/703700;** fax 01225/790118). If you want to experience an old Tudor inn, you can't do better than Sign of the Angel (above), but if you prefer the more polished atmosphere of an English country house, drive 3.2 kilometers (2 miles) to Beechfield. It's south of Lacock on A350 and well signposted. The hotel is in a sturdy late-Victorian building and stands on 3.28 hectares (8 acres) of grounds. It lacks the finesse of some of the country's grander country hotels, but the rooms are comfortable and large, with most decorated in a variety of floral prints and wallpapers. 24 rms with bath. Facilities: restaurant, heated outdoor pool, conference rooms. AE, DC, MC, V. Expensive.

The Old Rectory, Lacock, Wilts. SN15 2JZ (☎ **01249/730335**). For a superior B&B, try this handsome Victorian house on the edge of town with 3 hectares (7 acres) of land. It's run by Margaret Addison, a friendly, intelligent woman who turns guests into friends. The spacious rooms feature pastel Laura Ashley fabrics, Moiret linings, and Designer Guild furnishings; two have four-posters. 3 rms with bath. Facilities: tennis, croquet. No credit cards. Inexpensive.

CASTLE COMBE

From Bath take A46 north for 9.6 kilometers (6 miles) to A420. Turn right (east) to Ford and follow the signs north to Castle Combe. From Lacock take A350 north to Chippenham, A420 west, and follow the signs on your right to Castle Combe.

The film *Dr. Doolittle* was a financial disaster, but it seems to have brought a lot of attention to **Castle Combe,** where it was filmed and which subsequently won a national poll as the prettiest town in England. The old wool weavers' village hasn't changed much in the past 250 years, except for the sea of tourists in which, each summer, it threatens to drown. The problem with Castle Combe is that it's a one-street town jammed with traffic; there are no side streets to get lost in, no alleyways to discover. If you're collecting lovely villages, try to include this one, but don't expect to be overwhelmed by local color.

ACCOMMODATIONS

Manor House Hotel, Castle Combe, Wilts. SN14 7HR (☎ 01249/ 782206; fax 01249/782159). The hordes of visitors that pour through Castle Combe during the day can make this seem more like a madhouse than a manor house. But if you spend your afternoons exploring, you'll return at night to one of the most romantically situated country house hotels in England. The building stands on 10.4 hectares (26 acres) with a trout-stocked lake, Italian gardens, and wooded trails. The public areas are filled with heirlooms and rich wood paneling. If there's anything wrong with the Manor House it's that it's so "discovered"—a place one does as part of the "olde Englande" experience. It's also expanding at an alarming rate. Be sure to get a room in the main house; the workmen's cottages look lovely from without but are in fact charmless, with worn carpets and small basic baths. Two rooms have four-posters. 41 rms with bath. Facilities: restaurant, bar, pool, tennis. AE, DC, MC, V. Expensive.

THE COTSWOLDS

The Cotswolds are England's "green and pleasant land"—a region of soft stone villages and rich, rolling pastureland, where nothing seems to change, or matter, but the seasons. Americans love these picturesque villages because they have everything America lacks: tradition, homogeneity, local color, and a sense of place. The towns seem to spring organically from the soil, and no one needs an advanced degree to appreciate their timelessness, their beauty, and their strength.

A "wold" is an upland common—a stretch of high land or plateau that's owned in common, usually as pastureland. The **Cotswold Hills** are about 160 kilometers (100 miles) long and 64 kilometers (40 miles) wide and rise to about 300 meters (1,000 ft.); the surrounding countryside, extending northeast roughly from north of the M4 expressway at Malmesbury to Stow-on-the-Wold, is often considered part of the Cotswolds, too.

From the 13th to the 15th century, the wool raised here was England's main export. The wool trade created great wealth and much of the money went into the construction of cottages, manor houses, and the so-called wool churches—buildings that give the Cotswold villages their unique architectural charm.

The cotton mills of Lancashire unraveled the wool trade. The commons were enclosed and turned into private farms by the Enclosure Acts (1795–1812). The drystone walls put an end to the small farmer and the great sheep runs; and when the bottom fell out of the wool trade in the 17th and 18th centuries, construction stopped and the towns remained suspended in time—until the tourists arrived and put the Cotswolds back on the map.

The challenge is to find some way to enter this world—not merely to pass through. It's not an easy task when you're one of hundreds of Americans sniffing around a tiny stone village, all searching for the "elusive past."

THE COTSWOLDS

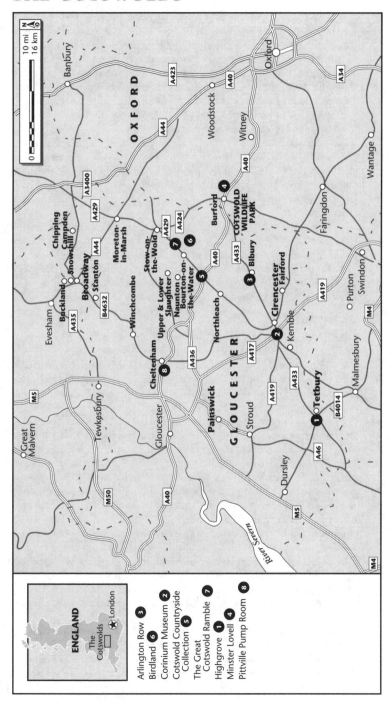

ENGLAND

The Cotswolds

★ London

Arlington Row 3
Birdland 6
Corinium Museum 2
Cotswold Countryside Collection 5
The Great Cotswold Ramble 7
Highgrove 1
Minster Lovell 4
Pittville Pump Room 8

Rule 1 is to avoid the main roads whenever possible. Get yourself a 1:50,000 map and drive down the backest of the back roads. Rule 2 is to pick your towns carefully. The itinerary below should give you some sense of which ones to visit or avoid. The area around Stow-on-the-Wold makes a great base, because it's centrally located; has restaurants, hotels, and shops for every taste and budget; and is large enough to absorb the crowds.

Rule 3 is to leave the pavement at least once and walk from one town to another, following a footpath through the meadows. One popular walk is from Stow-on-the-Wold to Lower Swell, Upper Slaughter, and Lower Slaughter; but wherever you are, ask a police officer or desk clerk to suggest a route or pick up one of the hiking guides sold throughout the region. Among the best are *Along the Cotswolds Ways* by G. R. Crosher (Pan) and *A Visitor's Guide to the Cotswolds* by Richard Sale (Moorland).

There are 2,560 kilometers (1,600 miles) of pathways in the Cotswolds—among country lanes, footpaths, and ancient sheep tracks as old as Stonehenge. Most are marked with signposts and indicated on 1:50,000 maps. Villages are so close together that you rarely need more than an hour or two to hike between them. If a circular route is unfeasible, walk from A to B and arrange for a taxi to take you back.

CIRENCESTER

From Castle Combe the fastest route is to Malmesbury and then north on A429 and A433. The more scenic route is via Tetbury.

Cirencester, known locally as Ciren, is a busy district center, with markets and shops. It was once the second-largest Roman town in Britain after London. During the Middle Ages it was the country's largest wool-market town.

The main reason to stop here, other than to admire the town's elegant and harmonious streets, is to visit **St. John the Baptist Church,** the finest of all the wool churches and one of the largest parish churches in England. Because of its unusual length, 54 meters (180 ft.), it looks more like a small cathedral. The aisles are wide to accommodate the faithful and give the church a sense of being of and for the people—an impression you don't always get in English cathedrals. The church was begun in the 12th century, but the **Tower,** the **Trinity Chapel,** and the **Lady Chapel** were built in the early 15th century. The Norman nave was raised 4.5 meters (15 ft.) a century later in the new Perpendicular style. The 15th-century wine-glass **pulpit** is one of a few left in the region from before the Reformation. To the right of the chancel arch is the **Boleyn Cup,** which Henry VIII gave to Anne 2 years before he ordered her beheaded. The Trinity Chapel has some great 15th-century brasses, which you can rub (contact Reverend Lewis at 01285/3142).

From the church turn right and go down Castle Street. Bear right on Silver Street, which turns into Park Street. On your right is the **Corinium Museum** (☎ 01285/655611), the finest museum of Roman remains in the country, with reconstructions of a Roman kitchen, dining room, and workshop. (Corinium was the Roman name for Cirencester.) It also houses well-preserved mosaic pavements in replicas of rooms where they once stood. Admission £1.50 adults, £1.25 students and seniors, 75p children. Open Apr–Oct, Mon–Sat 10am–5pm, Sun 2–5:30pm; Nov–Mar, Tues–Sat 10am–5pm, Sun 2–5pm.

Continue down Park Street. Bear right on Thomas Street and make your first right on Coxwell Street, which has many lovely old houses. At the end of Coxwell, turn right and return to the church.

A 5-minute walk from the church will take you to the **Cirencester Workshops,** Brewery Court (☎ **01285/657181**), where you can buy hand-printed textiles and other crafts. To get there from the church, turn right to the light; turn left on Cricklade, then make your first right. Free admission. Open Mon–Sat 10am–5pm.

Cirencester has the best of the **wool churches.** If you want to see some of the others, drive east on A417 to Fairford; north on A361 to Burford, and east on A40 to Northleach. From here take A429 north to Stow-on-the-Wold. If you've seen enough churches, take A429 directly from Cirencester to Stow-on-the-Wold.

FAIRFORD

From Cirencester drive east 14.4 kilometers (9 miles) on A417. The main attraction of **Fairford** is **St. Mary's Church,** and the main attraction of St. Mary's is the stained-glass windows. No other parish church in England has retained its complete set of medieval glass. The 28 windows serve as a picture book meant to teach the story of the Bible, beginning with Adam (the green glass you'll see when you stand with your back to the organ) and ending with the Last Judgment. The "Short Guide," sold at the entrance, gives a brief description of each panel. Except for the base of the tower, itself very curious—it's at the head of the nave, in the crossing—the wool church was completely rebuilt in the Perpendicular style by John Tame (1470–1534), a rich wool merchant, and his son Edmund. Below the carpet in the Lady Chapel are commemorative brasses to Edmund and his two wives. His second wife commissioned it.

For some examples of medieval humor, look for the misericords—the seat projections on the choir stalls. You'll see carvings of a woman giving grief to her husband, a couple draining a cider barrel, and so on.

As you leave, seek out the little statue that commemorates Tiddles, the church cat, gravely dated 1963–1980. It's opposite the main door.

Accommodations

Bull Hotel, Market Sq., Fairford, Glos. GL7 4AA (☎ **01285/712535;** fax 01285/713782). Standing in Fairford's attractive Market Square, the long, low, gray-stone exterior of the Bull promises rather more than the interior delivers. It's very much a traditional Cotswold inn, with old beams, uneven floors, and exposed stone woodwork. The owners have revamped the rooms along Victorian lines. One has a four-poster, another a sunken bath. 21 rms, 18 with bath. Facilities: restaurant, bar, conference room. AE, DC, MC, V. Moderate.

BIBURY

From Cirencester take A433 northeast for 11.2 kilometers (7 miles). From Fairford, follow the back-road signs.

Bibury is the town most often used on British Tourist Association posters—minus the crows. In season, you'll find yourself among a gaggle of tourists on what is essentially a tiny one-street village, much like Castle Combe. Yet Bibury is worth a stop because it's so pretty a town—William Morris thought it the most beautiful in England—and the Parish Church, Arlington Row, and Country Museum are all worth seeing. Here, as elsewhere in the Cotswolds, the ideal time to visit is in the early spring or fall.

About 90 meters (300 yd.) before the museum is a left turn leading to **St. Mary's Parish Church,** in an area of the town many visitors miss. At Bibury the wool merchants didn't completely rebuild the original Romanesque church, as they did at Cirencester, Fairford, and Northleach, so you'll be able to identify features going back to Saxon times, like a great Norman north door and Saxon capitals. The north aisle is the earlier of the two—you can tell by the massive columns. The large windows of the north aisle are 14th-century work in the Decorated style. You won't see this in many Cotswold churches, because by the time the wool merchants had money for restorations, the Perpendicular style was in. The wall-cupboards (ambries) indicate that the church must once have had a great collection of plates or relics.

Arlington Row is a group of old Cotswold cottages dating to the 14th century. Once the homes of shepherds, they were converted into houses in the 17th century to accommodate weavers from Arlington Mill. Don't peer into the windows; people are still living here. If you're ready for a walk, take the path uphill from Arlington Row to the gate and follow the sign.

The **Cotswold Country Museum** (☎ 01451/860715), in the former mill, has a fine collection of old carts and machines and rooms showing how people lived and worked. Admission £1.50 adults, £1.25 seniors, 75p children. Open mid-Mar to mid-Nov, Mon–Sat 10:30am–5pm, Sun 2–5pm (or dusk if earlier); mid-Nov to mid-Mar, Sat–Sun only 10:30am–dusk.

Visit the **Bibury Trout Farm** (☎ 01285/740212) next door to feed the fish (or to buy some—provided you have somewhere to cook them). It's a rather aggressively tourist-oriented place, with an Adventure Island, picnic areas, and the inevitable gift shop. But children appreciate it. Admission £1.90 adults, £1.50 seniors, 90p children. Open Mon–Sat 9am–6pm, Sun 10am–5pm.

Accommodations

Bibury Court Hotel, Bibury, Glos. GL7 5NT (☎ 01285/740337; fax 01285/740660). The stately stone Jacobean mansion that's Bibury Court, approached via a crunching gravel drive, stands on 2.4 hectares (6 acres) of land. Expansive lawns sweep away from the front of the building.

Dark wood paneling and antique furniture establish a convincingly old-fashioned mood inside. Nonetheless, and despite a scattering of four-posters, a number of the rooms exude a certain dowdiness. The management is actually proud of this maiden-aunt feel, and it seems to appeal to guests. The best is the Sackville Suite. The restaurant offers substantial, if unexceptional, English food. 19 rms, 16 with bath; 1 suite. Facilities: restaurant, fishing, gardens. AE, DC, MC, V. Moderate/Expensive.

Swan Hotel, Bibury, Glos. GL7 5NW (☎ **01285/740695;** fax 01285/740473). The Swan is another hotel that promises more than it delivers. The creeper-clad exterior, overlooking the River Coln, suggests something memorable inside, but, though the rooms are spacious, they remain faintly drab. The public rooms, too, bear witness to unsympathetic 1960s modernization. Probably the best reason to stay here is to wake up to the view of the village outside your window—before the tour buses arrive. 18 rms with bath; 1 suite. Facilities: restaurant, bar. MC, V. Moderate/Expensive.

BURFORD

From Bibury, take A433 northeast 14.4 kilometers (9 miles). **Burford** isn't directly on the route from Bibury to Stow-on-the-Wold; to get there you have to swing east. The extra miles are worthwhile, however, if you want to see one of the most beautiful wool churches and visit a half-dozen quality antiques shops strung along the main street of town.

The **Church of St. John the Baptist** is a late 12th-century Norman church that was transformed over the next 300 years into the Perpendicular building you see today. That's why the chapels and aisles are all at different levels.

TAKE A BREAK

*There's a lovely 4-kilometer (2¹/₂-mile) country walk east along the Windrush River to Asthall, where you can stop at the **Maytime Inn,** Asthall (☎ 01993/822068) for lunch. Ask locally for directions.*

NORTHLEACH

From Burford take A40 west for 14.4 kilometers (9 miles). From Bibury, follow the back-road signs from outside the Swan Hotel; it's a twisting 8.1 kilometers (5 miles) to Northleach.

Northleach was a medieval wool-trading center on high ground between the valleys of the Coln and the Windrush rivers. The wool church is one of the grandest—and a favorite among brass-rubbers.

The **Church of St. Peter and St. Paul** was built by God-fearing wool merchants and looks as if it were made to last forever. Like most other wool churches, it's a Norman building that was reconstructed in the

15th century in the Perpendicular style. There's lots to see here: a 15th-century pulpit, a 14th-century carved baptismal font, and wonderful brasses of wool staplers, their feet resting on wool packs or sheep. For permission to rub brasses, contact the post office or the Tudor house on the Green.

Dining

Old Woolhouse, The Square (☎ 01451/860366). Northleach is something of a gastronomic hot spot. The Old Woolhouse, an unpretentious building in the town square, is the kind of place where the French chef/owner's personality tends to dominate from the moment you step over the threshold. Your choices are limited: There are typically no more than two first courses and three main courses, followed by cheese and dessert. What's more, the cooking is idiosyncratically moderne: Most separate vegetable dishes, for example, are outlawed. Calf's sweetbreads and kidneys in cassis is a chef's specialty. Count on a surprise every night, depending on the day's shopping—perhaps turbot, mussels, and scallops cooked in a savory blend with a spicy sauce. The wines, though overpriced, are first class. Reservations (a week or two in advance) essential. Casual. No credit cards. Dinner only (lunch sometimes by arrangement); closed Sun and Mon. Expensive.

Wickens, Market Place (☎ 01451/860421). Come here for sturdy English cooking enlivened by sophisticated lighthearted touches. Cotswold cassoulet of local lamb, salmon fish cakes (more subtle than they sound), and braised pigeon in Yorkshire brown ale number among the specialties. The desserts often are from 19th-century English kitchens—try gooseberry jelly with elderflower syrup. The atmosphere is intimate; you dine in one of a series of small tastefully decorated rooms. Those who visit the Cotswolds seeking no more than pretty towns and pub grub will be pleasantly surprised. If you're feeling adventurous, order one of the English wines. Reservations required. Casual at lunch; jacket/tie required at dinner. MC, V. Dinner and light lunch; closed Sun and Mon. Expensive.

Accommodations

Cotteswold House, The Square, Northleach, Glos. GL54 3EG (☎ 01451/860493). On the corner of the main square, this B&B is set in a Georgian town house with zigzagging passages that lead to substantial rooms with firm beds, plain carpets, bare stone walls, and exposed oak beams. There are two shared baths. You breakfast in the paneled hall, which features a low carved oak chest. 3 rms without bath. No credit cards. Inexpensive.

STOW-ON-THE-WOLD

From Northleach take A429 14.4 kilometers (9 miles) north. **Stow-on-the-Wold** is an ancient hilltop market town. At over 700 feet, it's the highest town in the Cotswolds. It sits at the junction of seven important roads, but—and this is what makes Stow unique—none runs through the town itself. The 17th-century stone buildings are clustered around a market square as a defense against the wind; if you squint you can imagine yourself back in the Middle Ages, when the town was famous for its fairs. Stow makes a great base for exploring the Cotswolds because it's so centrally located and has all the facilities you'd want, including what looks like an antiques shop in every building (hotels and restaurants aside). In fact, Stow is now one of the most important centers of the antiques trade outside of London—and that includes Bath.

St. Edward's Church, in the town center, is Norman with many additions, including a Perpendicular tower dominating the square. The name has a notable 17th-century Belgian painting of the Crucifixion.

Dining

Mill House, Kingham (☎ **01608/658188**). Located 8.1 kilometers (5 miles) east of Stow on B4450 in the village of Kingham, the restaurant of the Mill House hotel is light, somewhat formal, and truly upscale. Surrounded by its pastel-colored walls, accented by voluminous curtains and soft lighting, you'll dine on ambitious British modern dishes such as breast of duck with mango-and-lime sauce, breast of chicken stuffed with spinach, hot prune-and-Armagnac soufflé with kirsch-based cream, and hazelnut mousse. Reservations essential. Jacket/tie required. AE, DC, MC, V. Expensive.

Prince of India, 5 Park St. (☎ **01451/831198**). For good-value Indian food, served swiftly and expertly, the centrally located Prince of India is hard to beat. The decor, with lurid tapestries of bullfighters and assorted Indian scenes, may not be to all tastes, but the sheer value for money may well outweigh aesthetic considerations. Casual. Reservations not required. AE, DC, MC, V. Inexpensive.

Wyck Hill House, Burford Rd. (☎ **01451/831936**). The formal surroundings of the Wyck Hill's restaurant (see "Accommodations," below) provide a satisfying setting for French food. If you're in the mood for a fancy night out you won't be disappointed. A favorite appetizer is charcoal-grilled tuna on a purée of roasted eggplant flavored with rosemary and garlic. Chef Ian Smith changes his menu daily, but typical main courses are red mullet charcoal-grilled and placed on fennel with a warm pesto dressing, grilled polenta with sautéed wood pigeon, and local oak-smoked salmon. Reservations required. Jacket/tie required. AE, DC, MC, V. Expensive.

Accommodations

Cross Keys Cottage, Park St., Stow-on-the-Wold, Glos. GL54 1AQ (☎ **01451/831128**). If you're in search of a good B&B, the best in the area is Cross Keys, a minute's drive east of the town's center. Margaret and Roger Welton are known for the care and attention they devote to guests, the warmth of their welcome, and the quality of their breakfasts (included in the rates). The site includes three interconnected stone cottages, the oldest of which dates from 1660. In the 17th century this place was a brewery. 3 rms, 1 with bath. No credit cards. Inexpensive.

Royalist Hotel, Digbeth St., Stow-on-the-Wold, Glos. GL54 1BN (☎ **01451/830670;** fax 01451/870048). The Royalist is the oldest inn in England, in business since 947 and with an entry in the *Guinness Book of Records* to prove it. In fact, most of today's building is a positive youngster, having been put up only in 1615 (and much altered since). Stone walls and ancient beams still show its antiquity; many rooms have four-posters and all are individually decorated. 12 rms with bath. Facilities: restaurant, bar, conference room. MC, V. Inexpensive/Moderate.

Unicorn, Sheep St., Stow-on-the-Wold, Glos. GL54 1HQ (☎ **800/ 225-5843** or 01451/830257; fax 01451/831090). The mellow 17th-century stone facade of the Unicorn encloses a slick interior, revamped by the Forte chain, which now owns it. Steep stairs lead to beamed rooms with bright furnishings. 20 rms with bath. Facilities: restaurant, bar, conference room. AE, DC, MC, V. Moderate.

Wyck Hill House, Burford Rd., Stow-on-the-Wold, Glos. GL54 1HY (☎ **01451/831936;** fax 01451/832243). Set in expensive grounds about 3.2 kilometers (2 miles) from town on A424, the Wyck Hill House is one of the most tastefully restored grand manor houses in the country. The cedar-paneled library, high French windows, Oriental lamps, plants, and thick carpets show a fine attention to detail, which is matched by the attentive service. The hilltop view of the Windrush Valley is glorious. 30 rms with bath. Facilities: restaurant, bar, conference room, tennis, horseback riding, golf. AE, DC, MC, V. Expensive/Very Expensive.

COTSWOLD DAY TRIPS

The following towns can all be reached on a 1-day excursion from Stow-on-the-Wold. They're listed in the order in which you would reach them on a circular tour.

BOURTON-ON-THE-WATER

Kids and grown-ups who want "Things to Do" will love Bourton-on-the-Water.

Birdland, Rissington Rd. (☎ **01451/820480**), is a world-famous 17th-century manor house with more than 600 species of birds from around the world, including, as it likes to boast, "the largest colony of penguins outside America." Admission £3.50 adults, £1.75 children, £2.50 seniors. Open Apr–Oct, daily 10am–6pm; Nov–Mar, daily 10:30am-4pm.

The enterprising owner of Birdland also runs the **Cotswold Motor Museum;** a **Village Life Exhibition;** and the **Oscar Collection of Street Jewellery,** which contains the world's largest collection of vintage advertising signs. These are all under one roof, in an 18th-century water mill (☎ **01451/821255**). Admission £1.40 adults, 70p children 4–14, 3 and under free; £3.95 family ticket. Open Feb–Nov, daily 10am–6pm.

On the opposite side of the High Street you'll find a **Model Railway** (☎ 01451/820686), housed in a superior toy shop. Admission £1.25 adults, £1 children 4–15 and seniors; 3 and under free. Open Apr–Sept and school holidays, daily 11am–5:30pm; Oct–Mar, Sat–Sun only 11am–5:30pm.

Finally, play Gulliver in Bourton's most famous attraction, the **Model Village,** High Street (☎ 01451/820467). It's an exact scale replica of the village, complete with miniature trees, made before World War II by the obsessive landlord of The Old New Inn, behind which the model is located. Admission £1.30 adults, £1.10 children. Open daily 9:30am–6pm (or dusk if earlier).

Dining

The Old New Inn, High St. (☎ 01451/820467). The home-style food here is the type of English fare that's been served for decades. In spite of the enormous appeal of this Cotswold village, Bourton-on-the-Water remains a gastronomic wasteland. Until someone opens a really top-notch restaurant, you can dine on standard set lunches and dinners here — English roast beef, shepherd's pie, and the like. You may want to spend an evening in the redecorated pub lounge playing darts or chatting with the villagers. Casual. MC, V. Inexpensive.

LOWER & UPPER SLAUGHTER

These are two delightful back-road villages — unspoiled except for the tourists searching for an unspoiled village. If you're here in summer, visit in the early morning or evening, when the day-trippers are gone. The short distance (.8km/half a mile) between the villages makes an ideal walk. Lower Slaughter is neater and prettier, with lovely stone bridges — which is why some people prefer Upper Slaughter.

Accommodations

Lords of the Manor Hotel, Upper Slaughter, Glos. GL54 2JD (☎ 01451/820243; fax 01451/820696). A mellow honey-colored 17th-century onetime rectory, the Lords of the Manor stands in 3 hectares (7 acres) of gardens. Ancient trees shield the house; lawns sweep down to the River Eye. The furnishings are old-fashioned in an understated way, with floral drapes and hushed pastels predominating. The stable block has been converted into more rooms; if you value space, character, and views, opt for the main house, where three rooms have four-posters. That this is a privately owned hotel is evident from the relaxed, friendly service. 27 rms with bath. Facilities: restaurant, bar, croquet, fishing. AE, DC, MC, V. Expensive.

Lower Slaughter Manor, Lower Slaughter, Glos. GL54 2HP (☎ 01451/820456; fax 01451/822150). An idyllic setting, a 17th-century manor house, and an expensive renovation have combined to create one of the most gracious of the Cotswolds' many luxury hotels. Open fires, enormous sofas, handwoven carpets, and fine draperies strike sophisticated notes in the handsome public rooms. The guest rooms, many with four-posters, are large and tasteful; the restaurant is imposingly formal. The bells from the village church next door add a touch of Olde Englande to the designer chintz. 14 rms with bath. Facilities: restaurant, bar, conference room, indoor pool, sauna, solarium, croquet, tennis, fishing. AE, DC, MC, V. Very Expensive.

NAUNTON

For being less picturesque than other Cotswold villages and for committing the unpardonable sin of permitting modern buildings, **Naunton** is blessed with an absence of tourists. The village won the 1981 Bledisloc Cup as Best Kept Village in England. "Most pleasant looking petrol station seen anywhere on the judge's rounds," says the award. "The telephone kiosk [behind the sign to the petrol station adjoining the bus shelter] cut into the face of the old building is ingenious."

COTSWOLD FARM PARK

Cotswold Farm Park (☎ 01451/850307) is 4.8 kilometers (3 miles) northeast of Guiting Power. Kids will love the rare breeds of farm animals, including the breed of sheep that brought prosperity to the region and some Iron Age pigs. You're 270 meters (900 ft.) up—a great setting for walks among the enclosed animals. Admission £3.50 adults, £2.50 seniors, £1.50 children. Open Apr–Sept only, daily 10:30am–5pm.

SUDELEY CASTLE

If your schedule is crowded, go directly from Naunton or the Cotswold Farm Park to Stanton (see below). But if time permits, take an hour out for **Winchcombe,** stopping at **Sudeley Castle** (☎ 01242/604357), 8 kilometers (half a mile) southeast of Winchcombe.

The fortified 14th-century manor house contains the tomb of Catherine Parr (1512–48), the sixth and last queen of Henry VIII. The king was Catherine's third husband—her second having died only months before the royal wedding. In the same year that Henry died, Catherine married a former lover, Thomas Seymour (brother of Jane Seymour, Henry's third wife), who owned Sudeley Castle—and a year later she died in childbirth. Catherine of Aragón stayed here; so did Anne Boleyn. Elizabeth I lived here as a child. The modern **Queen's Garden** is laid out in authentic Tudor-style. Inside you'll find a wonderful collection of toys and dolls; 18th-century Aubusson tapestries that belonged to Marie Antoinette; and paintings by Constable, Turner, Rubens, and Van Dyck. Admission £5.40 adults, £3 children 5–16 (4 and under free), £3.20 seniors. Open Easter–Oct, daily 11am–5pm.

WINCHCOMBE

St. Peter's, on Queen Square (☎ 01242/602368), is a fine Perpendicular-style church (1465), with a great gilded weathercock on top of the tower and some 40 grotesque gargoyle waterspouts around the façade. The bullet marks are from the English Civil War. The framed altar cloth behind blue curtains on the north wall is said to have been made by Catherine of Aragón. Look for the kneeling effigy of Thomas Williams of Corndean (d. 1636) in the chancel—he's staring at a space where his wife's image used to be: She remarried and is spending eternity with her second husband.

Opposite is the **Jacobean House** (1619), which is attributed to Inigo Jones and was restored in 1876. Exit the church, turn left, then turn right on Vineyard Street, which has some lovely old cottages running down to the river. It's also called Duck Street because of the "witches" who had their heads held under the water. If instead of turning right on Vineyard, you continue straight, you'll come to the Town Hall, where you can put your kids in the stocks. In the Town Hall is a tourist office, open May to October.

Kids will also enjoy the **Railway Museum,** 23 Gloucester St. (☎ **01242/620641;** admission £2.25 adults, 50p children; open daily 1–6pm or dusk if earlier). At **Toddington,** 6.4 kilometers (4 miles) away, you can tour the disused **train station** (admission 80p adults, 40p children). You can also ride on a steam train, a proud survivor from the once-mighty Great Western Railway, a precursor of the very much less-than-mighty British Rail (☎ **01242/69405;** trains operate Sun, Easter–Oct).

The Cotswold Way runs south from Winchcombe to Belas Knap and then circles back to Cleeve Hill on A46, 3.2 kilometers (2 miles) south of Winchcombe. You'll need an extra day for this, but if you like walking, this is one of the most memorable hikes you can make. After passing a Stone Age burial mound—the finest in the Cotswolds—you'll continue to **Cleeve Common,** the highest point in the Cotswolds, which has panoramic views. The bleak open wolds give you a wonderful sense of what the Cotswolds were like before the Enclosure Acts.

About 2 kilometers (1 mile) north of Winchcombe, on A46, turn left to **Greet** and greet the potters who sell their wares at Winchcombe Pottery.

STANTON

From Winchcombe, take A46 north about 8 kilometers (5 miles) and look for signs on the right to **Stanton** (north of Stanway, west of Snowshill).

With a terrain of steep pastures and much unclaimed marshland, there was nothing at Stanton to attract speculators and profiteers. Any move to commercialize the village was stopped in 1908, when Philip Sidney Stott, a builder of cotton mills, bought virtually the entire village. The restoration work that followed his arrival was tastefully done, and Stanton today seems unchanged from the 17th century. The result is a village that has kept its integrity and wins the Mike Spring award for the most perfect, unspoiled village in the Cotswolds. It's likely to stay that way, too.

TAKE A BREAK

Above the town is **Mount Inn** *(☎ 01386/584316), a newish stone building with not much atmosphere, but some outdoor tables with a splendid view. A good bet for drinks or lunch.*

Arrange with the owners of the **Vine** (see "Accommodations," below) to saddle up for a ride through the surrounding countryside.

The **Church of Saint Michael and All Angels'** is a 15th-century version of a Norman church, with a rare Decorated (1375) pulpit and a splendid font adorned with hares. The poppyheads on the medieval benches at the back of the nave are deeply ringed with marks of the chains of obedient sheepdogs, who sat through sermons with their masters.

Accommodations

The Vine, Stanton, near Broadway, Glos. WR12 7NE (☎ 01386/73250). There's only one place to stay in Stanton: It's a B&B housed in a substantial vine-covered house at the junction of the village's only two streets. The owners, the Gabbs, have horses and can take you on rides through the glorious countryside. 5 rms, 2 with bath. No credit cards. Inexpensive.

BUCKLAND

Just over 3 kilometers (2 miles) north of Stanton is **Buckland,** a small, quiet village. **St. Michael's Church** is Early English, with three panels of 15th-century glass releaded by William Morris and some humorous gargoyles. **Buckland Rectory,** still in use, is the oldest, best-preserved parsonage in England. The main reason to visit Buckland, however, is to dine or lodge at the Manor (see below).

Dining & Accommodations

Buckland Manor, Buckland, Glos. WR12 7LY (☎ 01386/852626; fax 01386/853557). Surely not *another* glorious Cotswold manor house hotel? Yes, indeed. And this one, as everyone seems to agree, is the best of all, an old honey-colored house sitting among 4 hectares (10 acres) of gardens and fields next to the village church. Inside, fine china, antiques, and crystal complement the exposed beams, dark paneling, and open fires to create a mood that's both formal and relaxed. The guest rooms are decorated with taste and great attention to detail. The restaurant offers sophisticated modern British food that makes good use of fresh local produce. 13 rms with bath. Facilities: restaurant (reservations required), bar, heated outdoor pool, tennis, croquet, horseback riding, putting. MC, V. Very Expensive.

BROADWAY

Just over 3 kilometers (2 miles) north of Buckland is the popular resort town of **Broadway,** so named for its single main street. Most houses were built in the 17th and 18th centuries when Broadway was an important staging post. The coming of the railway led to its decline. But it was redis-covered in the late 19th century by William Morris and restored under his influence. It became an artists' colony before it was discovered by people like you and me.

What you'll do in Broadway is walk down one side—at a faster pace, probably, than the traffic—and back up the other, browsing in antiques stores and gift shops and stopping for lunch or drinks in any of several restaurants and pubs. The quality of goods is geared more to the package-tour trade than it is, say, in Stow-on-the-Wold, but you'll find lots to choose from: Paddington dolls, lady mice, model Cotswold cottages, woolens, cashmeres.

If you've had enough sightseeing for a day, take A44 directly back to Stow-on-the-Wold. Just west of Broadway, A44 climbs to **Broadway Tower,** the second-highest point in the Cotswolds. There's a park here for lovely walks and a 12-county view.

Dining

Lygon Arms, Broadway (☎ **01386/852255**). If you want a serious lunch, stop in the hotel's Great Hall Restaurant and enjoy such dishes as smoked game consommé with herb dumplings and grilled halibut with baby leeks. You'll dine in a royal hunting lodge atmosphere, complete with rich wood paneling and red barrel-vault ceiling—a real conversation piece. Reservations required. Jacket/tie required. AE, DC, MC, V. Very Expensive.

The Tapestry Restaurant, in Dormy House, Willersey Hill (☎ **01386/852711**). Lying 2 miles from the center of Broadway on the road to Moreton-in-the-Marsh and Oxford, this restaurant surpasses even the food served at Lygon Arms (see above). A British/French cui-sine is innovatively created by master chefs Alan Cutler and Simon Boyle, who change their menu every 3 months to take advantage of the best sea-sonal products. In a converted 17th-century farmhouse, they serve rela-tively simple dishes, such as Lincolnshire sausage, or more elaborate fare, such as Barbary duckling with fig-and-ginger confit. They prepare the tastiest vegetarian dishes in the northern Cotswolds, as exemplified by a saffron-laced tagliatelle. Casual. AE, DC, MC, V. Expensive.

Accommodations

Broadway Hotel, The Green, Broadway, Hereford and Worc. WR12 7AA (☎ **01386/852401;** fax 01386/853879). This is a 150-year-old half-timbered stone house with cheerful modern furnishings and more charac-ter than a motel. Stick to rooms in the old inn. 18 rms with bath. Facilities: restaurant, bar, conference room. AE, DC, MC, V. Moderate.

Lygon Arms, Broadway, Hereford and Worc. WR12 7DU (☎ 01386/852255; fax 01386/858611). The Lygon Arms is a distinguished old hotel, as famous as the town. Both Charles I and Oliver Cromwell stayed here during the Civil War. Every year hundreds of groomed riders use the courtyard as the starting point for the North Cotswold Hunt. With so much expansion—there's a new wing and a newer wing—the Lygon Arms is less an inn than a luxury hotel with an inn theme. The rooms in the modern wing are tasteful but conventional, some with unattractive views. Ask for no. 17 or something similar. No. 8 is nice, as are the rooms with four-posters. Your best bets are the more expensive rooms in the old section; the smaller rooms are disappointing for the price. 58 rms with bath; 5 suites. Facilities: Goblet's wine bar, restaurant, tennis, snooker, conference room. AE, DC, MC, V. Very Expensive.

SNOWSHILL

The most scenic route back to Stow-on-the-Wold—indeed, one of the loveliest drives in the Cotswolds—is along a narrow country road from Broadway to **Snowshill** ("Snozzle" to locals), Taddington, and Ford, then east on B4077.

The main attraction of this secluded village is **Snowshill Manor** (☎ 01386/852410), a 16th- and 17th-century manor house. Charles Wade bought it in 1919 and filled it with everything from toys to musical instruments, old clocks, farm carts, dead beetles, and butterflies. He gave it to the National Trust, which left it just as they found it. Admission £5 adults, £2.50 children. Open May–Sept, Wed–Mon 1–6pm; Apr and Oct, Wed–Mon 1–5pm. Grounds open at noon. Closed Good Friday.

CHIPPING CAMPDEN

Chipping Campden isn't directly on our route, but it's too lovely to miss, should you have time to visit en route from Broadway or Stow-on-the-Wold to Stratford-upon-Avon.

Chipping means "market"—and by 1247, Chipping Campden had one every week. In the 14th century it was a major wool-market center, whose wealthy merchants built the Perpendicular church (**St. James**) and houses that make the town so special. The church has a handsome tower and some outstanding brasses.

High Street has several interesting craft and antiques shops, with a vitality that doesn't diminish at the end of the tourist season. Historian G. M. Trevelyan called it "the most beautiful village street in England."

If you care about gardens, stop at **Hidcote Manor Garden,** Midcote Batrim (☎ 01386/438333), a National Trust Property north of town en route to Stratford-upon-Avon. These world-famous gardens were some of the first to group plants in "rooms," using hedges as walls—each room devoted to a particular color, species, or combination of species. Admission £5 adults, £2.50 children. Open Apr–Oct, Mon, Wed–Thurs, and Sat–Sun 11am–7pm.

Accommodations

Noel Arms, High St., Chipping Campden, Glos. GL55 6AT (☎ 01386/840317; fax 01386/841136). This is the oldest inn in town, built in the 14th century. In 1650, after the Battle of Worcester, Charles II, it's said, stayed here, when he was Prince of Wales. The mood is suitably timeworn, the furnishings friendly and old-fashioned, particularly in the older wing. There are four-posters in some rooms. 26 rms with bath. Facilities: restaurant, bar. MC, V. Moderate.

STRATFORD-UPON-AVON

From Stow-on-the-Wold take A429 north for 20.8 kilometers (13 miles), then take A34 for 12.8 kilometers (8 miles) to **Stratford-upon-Avon,** the most popular destination in Britain after London. More than half a million tourists parade through its streets every year, visiting the Bard's birthplace and taking in a play at the Royal Shakespeare Theatre. Many Americans come prepared to sacrifice an evening in the name of Culture—as they would at home—and come away surprised at the wonderful fun a good Shakespeare production can be. It's only a half-hour drive from Stratford to Broadway or 40 minutes to Stow-on-the-Wold, so you don't have to spend the night in Bardland; but should you decide to stay, you have a whole folio of hotels from which to choose.

Mid–16th-century Stratford was a prosperous market town. People who wanted to rise in the world came here from the surrounding farms. One was John Shakespeare, who succeeded beyond his dreams, first as a maker of gloves, then as a justice of the peace and mayor. He had a son named William who did quite well for himself, too. John's wife, Mary, came from one of the region's oldest families, so the image of Will as an untutored country lad is just not true.

Begin your tour where Will began his life (1564), in a half-timbered house on partly pedestrianized Henley Street: **Shakespeare's Birthplace** (☎ 01789/204016). The houses on either side were destroyed to reduce the chances of fire. Admission £3.50 adults, £1.50 children. Open Mar 20–Oct 19, Mon–Sat 9am–5pm, Sun 9:30am–5pm; off-season, Mon–Sat 9:30am–4pm, Sun 10am–4pm. Closed Dec 23–26.

The house is owned by the Shakespeare Birthplace Trust, whose headquarters, the **Shakespeare Centre,** are next door. The Trust owns five of the most important Shakespearean buildings in and around Stratford: the Birthplace, New Place (Nash's House), Hall's Croft, Anne Hathaway's Cottage, and Mary Arden's House and the Shakespeare Countryside Museum. If you have any serious interest in the man, it's worth seeing them all. You can buy a joint ticket (£9 adults, £4 children) to all five at any of the properties. Otherwise, visit whichever interests you most, paying separately each time.

Turn left from the house and continue down Henley Street. The **Tourist Information Centre** is at the major crossing. Turn left on Bridge

THE ARTS IN STRATFORD & BATH

Stratford-upon-Avon

The **Royal Shakespeare Theatre** season runs from mid-April to December. Tickets are on sale from late March through **Keith Prowse & Co., Ltd.,** 234 W. 44th St., New York, NY 10036 (☎ 212/398-1430); and **Edwards and Edwards,** 1 Times Sq., New York, NY 10036 (☎ 800/223-6108 or 212/944-0290). For ticket information in Stratford, call 01789/269191; for reservations, call 01789/295623.

The Royal Shakespeare Company also performs at **The Other Place,** Southern Lane (☎ 0789/26919 for information; 01789/295623 for reservations). Plays include new musicals and dramas on their way to London's West End.

Bath

Nothing could be more pleasant than an opera or a play at the historic **Theatre Royal,** Sawclose (☎ 01225/465065). Try to get seats while you're in London or before you leave home. A good ticket agency is **Tickets,** Kingston House, Pierrepont St. (☎ 01225/466541).

The internationally famous **Bath Festival** runs from late May to early June and features everything from choral music to opera and jazz. Get tickets when you reserve your hotel room.

Street. You'll pass some lovely Shakespeare-period houses as you approach Clopton Bridge over the River Avon.

Turn right on Waterside (before the bridge). On your right is **Heritage Theatre,** the home of the **World of Shakespeare** (☎ 01789/ 269190), where you can submit to a continuous 30-minute multimedia introduction to Elizabethan England. Admission £4 adults, £3 children and seniors. Open year-round, daily 9:30am–5pm (to 9:30pm in summer).

Walk through the **Bancroft Gardens** (lit at night)—watched over by a statue of the Bard surrounded by Hamlet, Lady Macbeth, Falstaff, and Prince Hal— and over to the **Royal Shakespeare Theatre.** No, this wasn't the Globe—that was in London and burned down in 1613 (however, in the mid-1990s the new Globe Theatre was reopened as a replica of Shakespeare's original). The original Stratford theater was built in 1874, destroyed in a 1926 fire, and rebuilt in 1932. You should have reserved seats, but it's sometimes possible to get them on the day of a performance (see the box "The Arts in Stratford & Bath," above).

Take the river path to the **Brass Rubbing Centre,** Avon Bank Gardens (☎ 01789/ 297671), where you can make your own souvenirs. Free admission. Rubbing charges (includes materials and instruction) 95p–£20. Open Apr–Sept, daily 10am–6pm; Oct, daily 10am–4pm; closed winter.

Continue to **Holy Trinity Church** (☎ 01789/266316), where Shakespeare was baptized and buried. The 12 trees, as you approach from the north, are said to represent the 12 tribes of Israel; the 11 on the right, the 11 faithful apostles; and the one slightly back, Mathias, who took the place of Judas. The slab covering Shakespeare's grave was replaced a century ago, after the footsteps of tourists had almost

STRATFORD-UPON-AVON

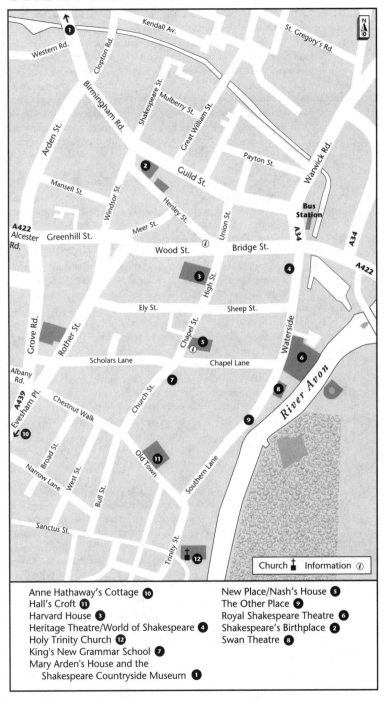

Anne Hathaway's Cottage ❿
Hall's Croft ⓫
Harvard House ❸
Heritage Theatre/World of Shakespeare ❹
Holy Trinity Church ⓬
King's New Grammar School ❼
Mary Arden's House and the
    Shakespeare Countryside Museum ❶

New Place/Nash's House ❺
The Other Place ❾
Royal Shakespeare Theatre ❻
Shakespeare's Birthplace ❷
Swan Theatre ❽

obliterated the words on it. Look for the bust of Shakespeare in a monument in the north chancel wall (on your left as you face the altar)—it's believed to be the Bard's most authentic known portrait. The charnel house—did it inspire the one in *Romeo and Juliet?*—is behind the north wall. Old bones were moved to make room for new ones—which is probably why Shakespeare wrote on his tomb, "And curst be he that moves my bones." Of course, he may also have wanted to prevent his wife, Anne—who lived 7 years after his death—from spending eternity beside him. Free admission to church; Shakespeare's tomb, donation 50p adults, 30p children. Open Mar–Oct, Mon–Sat 8:30am–6pm, Sun 2–5pm; Nov–Feb, Mon–Sat 8:30am–4pm, Sun 2–5pm.

Leave by the north door and bear left on Old Town Road to **Hall's Croft** (☎ 01789/292107), on the right. It's another Shakespeare Birthplace Trust building. It was here that Dr. John Hall lived with Shakespeare's daughter Susanna. He had no medical degree, but that wasn't expected then. The timber-framed late–16th-century house is carefully restored and gives a good sense of life in a middle-class Tudor home. The enclosed gardens are authentic, too, though replanted during restorations in 1950. Admission £2 adults, £1 children. Open Mar 20–Oct 19, Mon–Sat 9:30am–5pm, Sun 10am–5pm; off-season, Mon–Sat 10am–4pm, Sun 10:30am–4pm. Closed Dec 23–26.

Continue down Old Town Road and turn right on Church Street. On your right, behind a row of almshouses, is the **King's New Grammar School,** closed to the public, where Shakespeare learned "small Latin and less Greek." The sons of the most prominent men went to the same free grammar school as everyone else. The curriculum bore no relation to life after school, for it was meant to turn out clerks for church positions, and little was taught but Latin. Every weekday, summer and winter, Shakespeare went here from 7am (6am in summer) to 5pm, with a 2-hour midday break to go home for dinner.

Continue down Church Street. On your right, on the corner of Chapel Lane, is the 15th-century **Guild Chapel,** which has a famous fresco of the *Last Judgment* above the chancel arch.

Church Street turns into Chapel Street. On your right is **New Place** (☎ 01789/292325), also a Shakespeare Birthplace Trust property. In 1597, Shakespeare, now rich and famous, bought the house and realized his father's dream of becoming a gentleman. If your name is Gastrell, don't tell anyone: In 1759, a neighboring clergyman named Francis Gastrell was so furious at the tourists trooping through that he had New Place torn down. The town fathers were so angry, they ordered that no one with that name could ever live here again. Only the cellar steps remain. The foundations are planted with an Elizabethan-style garden containing all the plants and shrubs mentioned in Shakespeare's plays. Admission £2 adults, £1 children. Open Mar 20–Oct 19, Mon–Sat 9:30am–5pm, Sun 10am–5pm; off-season, Mon–Sat 10am–4pm, Sun 10:30am–4pm. Closed Dec 23–26.

TAKE A BREAK

*The bar of the **Falcon Hotel**, Chapel St. (☎ 01789/205777), opposite New Place, is a fine place for some sustaining pub food and a pint of whatever takes your fancy. With its heavily beamed rooms, it was founded as a tavern in 1640.*

Continue down Chapel Street, which turns into High Street. On the left is the **Harvard House** (☎ 01789/204507), built in 1576 by a butcher and alderman (local magistrate) named Thomas Rogers. His daughter Katherine was the mother of John Harvard, one of the founders of Harvard College. Admission £1.25 adults, 50p students and children. Open May 19–Sept 21 only, daily 10am–4pm.

You can drive to **Anne Hathaway's Cottage** (☎ 01789/292100) or take the lovely 1.6-kilometer (1-mile) walk the 18-year-old Shakespeare took to woo (or be wooed by) the 26-year-old Anne. From Harvard House, make a right on High Street and a quick right again on Ely Street. Where the street ends, turn left on Rother Street. Where Rother intersects with Grove Road, there's a marked path leading to the cottage. Anne lived in this thatched cottage until Will married her in 1582. She was pregnant at the time, and some iconoclasts, like Anthony Burgess, delight in the notion that Anne did hath-her-way and Shakespeare was forced to act against his Will. Controversy still rages over the meaning of the rushed marriage. It was customary for couples to proclaim banns on three Sundays so anyone who objected could be heard. The alternative was to get a special license and to post a bond to indemnify the court if objections were made later. Two farmer friends of Anne's father posted such a bond — were they also holding a shotgun to young Will? Anne may have been a Puritan who viewed actors not just with contempt but as threats to salvation. If that's the case, it's no wonder that Will skipped town and lived alone in London for 20 years in hired lodgings. Perhaps, though, he simply left because Stratford was too small for him, as the village of Shottery had been too small for his ambitious father. Admission £2.40 adults, £1.20 children. Open Mar 29–Oct 19, Mon–Sat 9:30am–5:30pm, Sun 10am–5:30pm; off-season, Mon–Sat 9:30am–4:30pm, Sun 10am–4pm.

STRATFORD SIDE TRIPS

Mary Arden's House, Wilmcote, north of Stratford off A34 (☎ 01789/293455), is where Shakespeare's mother lived before her marriage. It, too, belongs to the Shakespeare Birthplace Trust. It was still used as a farmhouse until the 1930s and has seen little modernization. Mary was the youngest of eight. Before marrying John she would have slept on the kitchen or living-room floor with the servants. Getting married meant, among other things, having a bed. Admission £3.30 adults, £1.50 children. Open Mar 20–Oct 19, Mon–Sat 9:30am–5pm, Sun 10am–5pm; off-season, Mon–Sat 10am–4pm, Sun 10:30am–4pm. Closed Dec 23–26.

Warwick Castle, 14.4 kilometers (9 miles) north on A46 (☎ **01926/ 40800**), is a great 14th-century castle, the most impressive in England after Windsor, with imposing towers and turrets on a steep rock over the Avon. You'll need 2 hours to tour some 30 state rooms (a number with tasteless waxworks, supposedly figures from an Edwardian country weekend), visit the grisly dungeons, and explore the gardens. Admission £8.75 adults, £5.25 children, £6.25 seniors; 3 and under free. Open daily 10am–5pm.

Charlecote Park, 6.4 kilometers (4 miles) east of Stratford off B4086 (☎ **01789/470277**), is an Elizabethan mansion in a 91.2-hectare (228-acre) park. It was here, it's said, that Shakespeare poached deer, for which he was fined by the owner and local magistrate, Sir Thomas Lucy. Shakespeare got even by turning Lucy into Justice Shallow in *Henry IV, Part II,* and *The Merry Wives of Windsor.* The main buildings were greatly altered in the mid-19th century. The gardens were laid out by Lancelot Brown, nicknamed "Capability," in 1760. Brown (1716–83) designed some Palladian country houses but won lasting fame as a landscape gardener who broke away from the geometric formality that had been imposed on gardens and created wide expanses of lawns, clumps of trees, and serpentine lakes. Kids will love the collection of carriages in the coach house. Admission £4.40 per person. Open Easter–Oct, Fri–Tues 11am–1pm and 2–6pm.

DINING

Billesley Manor, Billesley (☎ **01789/400888**). Shakspeare was a frequent visitor and may have written *As You Like It* on site. You're sure to like Mark Naylor's elegant country house–style cuisine, featuring such dishes as steamed chicken with a basil-flavored mousse and mushroom risotto or John Dory in puff pastry with a Chablis sauce. The prices can be high, especially for the wines, but the standards are reliable. The hotel is 6.4 kilometers (4 miles) west of Stratford on A422. Reservations required. Jacket/tie required. AE, DC, MC, V. Expensive.

Marlowe's Elizabethan Room, 18 High St. (☎ **01789/204999**). The oak-paneled walls of this second-floor restaurant in the town center establish a satisfactorily Tudorish atmosphere. Specialties are predominantly English. Try medaillon of beef or any of the duck and lamb dishes. It's a good place for pre- or posttheater dining. Reservations advised. Casual. AE, DC, MC, V. Moderate.

Shepherd's, 18 Sheep St. (☎ **01789/268233**). This is the restaurant of the Stratford House Hotel, in the town center. The decor is light and airy, with an almost Middle Eastern touch. The cuisine is a harmonious blend of English and French dishes, with such delights as grilled goat's cheese with marinated peppers or a velvety-smooth terrine of scallops and salmon. Chicken filets are likely to be flavored with fresh herbs and classic boeuf bourguignon is regularly featured, as are vegetarian main dishes. The fare is reliable and solid. Reservations required. Jacket/tie required. AE, DC, MC, V. Closed Sun dinner and Mon. Moderate/Expensive.

ACCOMMODATIONS

Billesley Manor, Billesley, Warwks. B49 6NF (☎ **01789/400888**). A peaceful 16th-century gabled manor house in splendid grounds, the Billesley, 6.4 kilometers (4 miles) west of Stratford on A422, offers your best chance of a memorable night in Shakespeare country. Ask for one of the large rooms in the main house, some with four-posters. 41 rms with bath. Facilities: restaurant, bar, indoor pool, tennis, pitch and putt, croquet. AE, DC, MC, V. Very Expensive.

Caterham House, 58–59 Rother St., Stratford-upon-Avon, Warwks. CV37 6LT (☎ **01789/267309;** fax 01789/414836). Set in a Georgian town house a 5-minute walk from the theater, this B&B is run by a friendly Frenchman and his English wife. The rooms are tastefully rustic with brass beds, cotton sheets, and pine furniture. The road is quite busy; ask for a room at the back. 12 rms, 10 with bath. MC, V. Inexpensive.

Shakespeare, Chapel St., Stratford-upon-Avon, Warwks. CV37 6ER (☎ **800/225-5843** or 01789/294771; fax 01789/415411). Of the hotels actually in Stratford, this Trusthouse Forte property is the best. The black-and-white exterior is newer than it looks, and a certain functional quality is evident inside, especially in some of the newer, smaller rooms. But for reliable standards and just a little authentic Stratford atmosphere, this isn't a bad bet. 62 rms with bath. Facilities: two restaurants, bar, conference room. AE, DC, MC, V. Expensive.

White Swan, Rother St., Stratford-upon-Avon, Warwks. CV37 6NH (☎ **01789/297022;** fax 01789/268773). If you're seeking atmosphere and want to avoid the sterile modern hotels, head here where the exterior of this old inn still appears as it did in Shakespeare's time. The interior has been modernized, though in a traditional style, with old beams and time-darkened timbers. Try for the two antique-furnished rooms in the original building, as those in the rear aren't as authentic or stylish; however, they're still quite comfortable, varying in size, shape, and age (the newest are 60 years old). 37 rms with bath. Facilities: limited on-site parking, restaurant, oak-beamed pub. AE, DC, MC, V. Moderate.

ON TO WOODSTOCK

This tour ends at Stratford-upon-Avon, a 2½-hour drive to London. If you want to extend your trip, drive south on A34 (follow the signs to Oxford) to the village of **Woodstock** to visit **Blenheim Palace,** one of England's greatest stately mansions, where American-born Jenny Jerome Churchill gave birth to Winston and where you can visit his modest grave. Two of England's most famous inns are here (both moderate): **The Bear,** Woodstock, Oxfordshire OX7 2SZ (☎ **01993/811511;** fax 01993/813380), and **Feathers,** Market St., Woodstock, Oxfordshire OX7 2SZ (☎ **01993/ 812291;** fax 01993/813158).

From Woodstock, it's only a short drive to **Oxford,** where you can tour the venerable colleges and chapels of one of the world's most famous universities. If time permits, stop at **Windsor Castle** en route back to London, and send my regards to the Queen.

GERMANY

Heidelberg, the Romantic Road, Munich & the Alps

Peopople who speak of romantic Germany usually think of the south, with the ancient university town of Heidelberg, the winding Neckar Valley, the Romantic Road, and the fortified medieval town of Rothenburg ob der Tauber, filled with gabled houses and narrow cobbled streets. But it also includes Munich, a cosmopolitan city with the feel of a small town; Garmisch-Partenkirchen, Germany's most complete four-season resort and the most convenient and comfortable base for excursions into the Bavarian Alps; and the fairyland castles of "mad" Ludwig II.

BEFORE YOU GO

GOVERNMENT TOURIST OFFICES

The major source of information is the **German National Tourist Board.**

In the U.S.: 122 E. 42nd St., 52nd Floor, New York, NY 10168-0072 (☎ **212/661-7200**); 11766 Wilshire Blvd., Suite 750, Los Angeles, CA 90025 (☎ **310/575-9799**).

In Canada: North Tower, Suite 604, 175 Bloor St. East, Toronto, Ontario M4 W3R8 (☎ **416/968-1570**).

In the U.K.: Nightingale House, 65 Curzon St., London W1Y 8NE (☎ **0171/495-0081**).

When to Go

The tourist season in Germany runs from May to late October, when the weather is at its best. This period boasts hundreds of folk festivals as well as many tourist events. The winter sports season in the Bavarian Alps runs from Christmas to mid-March. Prices everywhere are generally higher during summer, so you may find considerable advantages in visiting out of season. Most resorts offer out-of-season (Zwischensaison) and "edge-of-season" (Nebensaison) rates, and tourist offices can provide lists of hotels offering low-price inclusive weekly packages (Pauschalangebote). Similarly, many winter resorts offer lower rates for the periods immediately before and after the Christmas–New Year high season (Weisse Wochen, "white weeks").

The other advantage of out-of-season travel is that crowds are much less in evidence. The disadvantages of visiting out of season, especially in winter, are that the weather, which is generally good in summer, is often cold and gloomy and many tourist attractions, especially in rural areas, are closed.

HIGHLIGHTS ALONG THE WAY

- Heidelberg—the heart of German romanticism.

- The Romantic Road, with two of Europe's most perfect medieval towns—Rothenburg and Dinkelsbühl.

- Munich, the capital of Bavaria.

- The fantastic castles of King Ludwig II.

- The breathtaking scenery of the German Alps, including the country's highest peak, the Zugspitze.

Currency

The unit of German currency is the **Deutsche mark (DM),** which is subdivided into 100 **pfennig.** Bills are issued in denominations of 5, 10, 20, 50, 100, 200, 500, and 1,000 marks; coins come in 1, 2, 5, 10, and 50 pfennig. What the Deutsche mark is worth in terms of U.S. money is a tricky question, the answer to which you determine by consulting the market quotations from day to day. As of this writing, $1 U.S. = 1.42DM or 1DM = 70¢. In Britain, £1 sterling = 2.21DM or 1DM = about 45p. A Canadian dollar is worth about 1.05DM (1DM = about 95¢ in Canada).

Customs

The following items are permitted into Germany duty-free (imports from European Union countries in parentheses): 200 (300) cigarettes, 1 (1.5) liter(s) (.26/.40 gal.) of liquor above 44 proof, or 2 (3) liters (.53/.79 gal.) of liquor less than 44 proof, or 2 (4) liters of wine; 50 (75) grams (1.8/2.6 oz.) of perfume and 0.25 (0.375) liters (.53/.79 pt.) of eau de cologne; 500 (750) grams (18/26 oz.) of coffee; 100 (150) grams (3.5/5.3 oz.) of tea. All duty-free allowances are authorized only when the items are carried in the traveler's personal baggage.

GERMANY

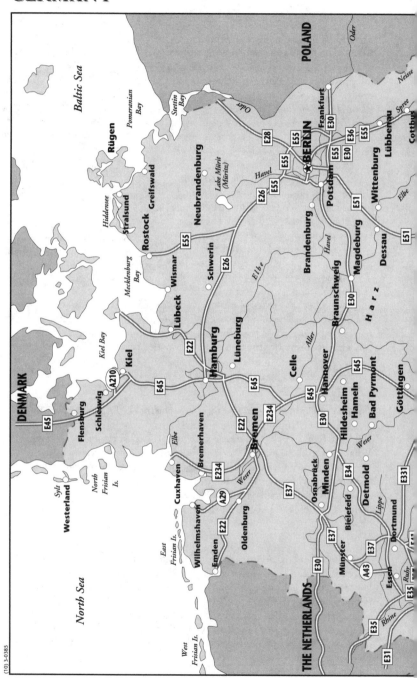

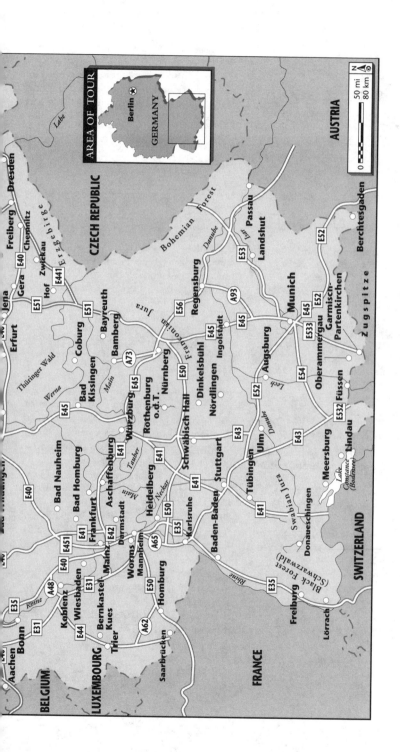

SPECIAL EVENTS & NATIONAL HOLIDAYS

Special Events

January: International ski-jumping competitions, Garmisch Partenkirchen. For more information contact the tourist bureau there on Dr.-Richard-Strauss-Platz (☎ 08821/1806).

March–April: International Fashion Fair, Munich.

May, July, and September: Augsburg Opera and Operetta Festival.

June: Munich Film Festival.

June–July: Der Meistertrunk Festival, Rothenburg.

July: Munich Opera Festival and Kinderzeche Festival, Dinkelsbühl.

August: Heidelberg Open-Air Theater in the castle grounds.

Late September–early October: Munich Oktoberfest—2 weeks of beer drinking, dancing, and entertainment.

National Holidays

January 1 (New Year's Day); January 6 (Epiphany); Easter Friday, Easter Monday; May 1; May 20 (Ascension); May 31 (Pentecost Monday); June 10 (Corpus Christi); October 3 (German Unity Day); November 1 (All Saints' Day); November 17 (Repentance Day); December 24–26 (Christmas Eve, Christmas Day, and Boxing Day; the holiday begins at noon on the 24th).

Tobacco and alcohol allowances are for visitors 17 and over. Other items intended for personal use may be imported and exported freely. There are no restrictions on the import and export of German currency.

LANGUAGE

The Germans are great linguists, and English is spoken in virtually all hotels, restaurants, airports and train stations, museums, and other places of interest. However, English isn't always widely spoken in rural areas.

If you speak a bit of German, you may find some regional dialects hard to follow, particularly in Bavaria. At the same time, however, all Germans can speak "high," or standard, German; even in the backwoods of Bavaria, the locals can alternate between dialect and standard German at will.

ARRIVING & DEPARTING

BY PLANE

Because the air routes between North America and Germany are heavily traveled, you have many airlines and fares from which to choose. But fares change with stunning rapidity, so consult your travel agent on what bargains are currently available.

The U.S. airlines serving Germany are **Northwest Airlines** (☎ 800/447-4747), **Delta** (☎ 800/241-4141), **TWA** (☎ 800/892-4141), **United** (☎ 800/538-2929), and **American Airlines** (☎ 800/433-7300). **Lufthansa** (☎ 800/645-3880) is the German national airline.

British Airways and **Lufthansa** are the main airlines flying from London to Germany. For reservations and information: **British Airways** (☎ 0181/745-7321), **Air U.K.** (☎ 01345/666777), and **Lufthansa** (☎ 0134/573-7747).

BY TRAIN

British Rail runs four trains a day to Germany from London. Of course, many travelers will want to take the Eurostar service running between London and Brussels direct via the Channel Tunnel. You can purchase tickets through British Rail travel centers in London (call **0171/834-2345** for a location near you). Four trains leave daily from Victoria Station in London, going by way of the Ramsgate-Ostend ferry or jetfoil. Two trains depart from Liverpool Street Station in London, via Harwich-Hook of Holland. If you go by jetfoil, Cologne is just 9½ hours away; it's 12½ hours with the Dover-Ostend ferry. Most trains change at Cologne for destinations elsewhere in Germany. Travel from London to Munich—depending on the connection—can mean a trip of 18 to 22 hours. Most visitors find it cheaper to fly from London to Munich than to take the train. You can reach Berlin in about 20 hours, with connections via Cologne.

By Bus

Bus travel to Germany's major cities is available from London, Paris, and many other cities in Europe. The continent's largest bus operator, **Eurolines,** operates out of Victoria Coach Station in central London and also within a 35-minute subway ride from central Paris, at 28 av. Général-de-Gaulle, 93541 Bagnolet (Métro: Gallieni). For information about Eurolines in Britain, call **01582/40-45-11** or 0171/730-8235, or contact any National Express bus lines or travel agent; for info about Eurolines in France, call **01-49-72-51-51.** Some buses cross the Channel on Sealink's Dover-Zeebrugge ferry service and then drive via the Netherlands and Belgium into Germany. The run to Munich, for example, takes 22¾ hours. Buses on long-haul journeys are equipped with toilets and partially reclining seats. Eurolines doesn't maintain a U.S.-based sales agent, though any European travel agent can arrange for a ticket on the bus lines that link Europe's major cities.

By Car

British motorists are advised to acquire a green card from their insurance companies. This gives comprehensive insurance coverage for driving in Germany. The most comprehensive breakdown insurance and vehicle and personal security coverage is sold by the **Automobile Association (AA)** in its Five Star scheme.

GETTING AROUND

By Car

Find a car-rental company that'll let you pick up a car at Frankfurt Airport and return it to Munich Airport with no additional drop-off charges. Munich's newest airport opened in 1992, 28 kilometers (18 miles) from the city; there are excellent connections via the A92 Autobahn or S8 train.

One-way rentals are offered by **Avis** (☎ 800/331-2112), **Hertz** (☎ 800/654-3001), **Budget** (☎ 800/527-0700), and **Eurodollar** (☎ 800/800-6000). There's no speed limit on most Autobahns—except in the eastern states of Saxony, Thuringia, Saxony-Anhalt, and Mecklenburg, where 100 kilometers per hour (62 m.p.h.) is the permitted maximum. The experience of cruising along at 112 kilometers per hour (70 m.p.h.) and having a car going twice as fast screech on its brakes only inches from your rear bumper is something you won't quickly forget. Always stay to the right (except when passing), keep your cool, and remind yourself that the Germans drive by different rules. (At home we call it madness.)

By Public Transportation

If you plan to travel through Europe, get a Eurailpass. Here's how it works: You can't purchase the **Eurailpass** in Europe—you must buy it before you go. The pass costs $522 for 15 days, $678 for 21 days, $838 for 1 month, $1,148 for 2 months, or $1,468 for 3 months.

If you're under 26, you can obtain unlimited second-class travel, wherever the Eurailpass is honored, on a **Eurail Youthpass,** which costs $598 for 1 month or $798 for 2 months. In addition, a Eurail Youth Flexipass is good for travelers under 26. Two passes are available: $438 for 10 days of travel within 2 months and $588 for 15 days of travel within 2 months.

Eurailpasses eliminate the hassles of buying tickets—just show your pass to the ticket collector. Note, however, that some trains require seat reservations and many have *couchettes* (sleeping cars) for which an additional fee is charged. Obviously, the 2- or 3-month traveler gets the greatest economic advantage; the Eurailpass is ideal for extensive trips. To obtain full advantage of the ticket in 15 days or a month, however, you'd have to spend a great deal of time on the train.

Travel agents or national rail offices of European countries can provide further details. General brochures are available by contacting **GermanRail,** 9501 W. Devon Ave., Rosemont, IL 60018-4832 (☎ **708/692-6300**).

Groups of two or more can purchase a Eurail Saverpass for 15 days of discounted travel in first class for $452. To be entitled to the discount, the members of the group must travel together. The Saverpass is valid all over Europe from September 30 to April 1, when the group must comprise at least two members. During the rest of the year (the warm-weather months) the group must comprise three persons or more to be valid.

The **Eurail Flexipass** allows you to visit Europe with more flexibility. It's valid in first class and offers the same privileges as the Eurailpass. However, it provides a number of individual travel days you can use over a much longer period of consecutive days. That makes it possible to stay in one city and yet not lose a single day of discounted travel. Two passes include $616 for 10 days of travel within 2 months and $812 for 15 days of travel within 2 months. Children 4 to 11 pay 50% of the adult fares.

These passes are available from travel agents in North America.

If your travel is limited to Germany, then a **GermanRail Pass** is the best deal. The German railroad offers discount fares to Americans and Canadians who buy tickets before leaving home, as well as lower round-trip fares for long-distance trips inside Germany if you buy tickets in advance. GermanRail Passes are available from travel agents and GermanRail offices in the United States.

Since the fall of the Berlin Wall, the opening of eastern Europe, and the completion of German unification, GermanRail has increased service and offers new rail passes, packages, and additional trains. Its **Flexipass** includes unlimited travel on the entire German rail system. Under the Flexipass, you get 5 days of travel in coach for $178 or $260 in first class, 10 days for $286 in coach and $410 in first class, and 15 days for $386 in coach and $530 in first class. Children 4 to 11 pay half fare; those 3 and under go free.

The Flexipass is good for unlimited rail travel for any 5, 10, or 15 consecutive days within 1 month. The pass entitles the bearer to the following exclusive bonuses: free travel on selected routes operated by Deutsche Touring/Europabus, such as the Romantic Road and the Castle Road; free travel on KD German Rhine Line day steamers on the Rhine, Main, and Mosel Rivers; and free admission to the Museum of Transportation in Nürnberg.

Other travel plans include "Rail and Drive" packages, programs for senior and junior citizens, city-to-city weekend tours, and district tickets.

German Federal Railroad (GermanRail/DB—Deutschebundes-bahn) offices or agents are at 747 Third Ave., New York, NY 10017 (☎ 212/308-3100), and 9575 W. Higgins Rd., Rosemont, IL 60018 (☎ 847/692-4209).

All major towns on the itinerary can be reached by public transport. Trains leave almost every hour from Frankfurt to Heidelberg and make the trip in about 60 minutes. A train goes from Heidelberg to Rothenburg (along the Romantic Road), but the Romantic Road Bus is more direct. By train, you need to change at Würzburg or Heilbronn and Steinach. The train trip takes about 3½ hours. The bus ride direct from Heidelberg to Rothenburg takes about an hour longer. Again, you could take the train or the Romantic Road Bus from Rothenburg to Munich, but the bus is preferable. Both train and bus take about 4½ hours. By train, however, you need to change at Ansbach. From Munich to Garmisch-Partenkirchen there's train service almost every hour, taking about 90 minutes. Tour buses leave daily in summer from Garmisch to the royal castles.

ESSENTIAL INFORMATION

IMPORTANT ADDRESSES & NUMBERS

VISITOR INFORMATION   The main regional office for this itinerary is the **Upper Bavarian Regional Tourist Office (Fremdenverkehrverband**

München-Oberbayern), Bodenseestrasse 113, D-81203, München (☎ 089/82-92-180), open Monday to Friday from 9am to noon and 1 to 5pm. The local tourist-information offices (Verkehrsverein) in the cities and towns on this itinerary are located as follows:

Dinkelsbühl:	On the main square, Marktplatz (☎ 09851/90-240); open Monday to Friday from 9am to 6pm and Saturday from 10am to 1pm.
Garmisch-Partenkirchen:	Verkehrsamt, on Richar-Strasse-Platz (☎ 08821/1806); open Monday to Saturday from 8am to 6pm and Sunday from 10am to noon.
Heidelberg:	Main office in the Pavillon am Hauptbahnhof (☎ 06221/14-22-11); open Monday to Saturday from 9am to 7pm.
Munich:	Main office, Fremdenverkehrsamt, at the Hauptbahnhof (☎ 089/233-302-56), found at the south exit opening onto Bayerstrasse; open Monday to Saturday from 9am to 9pm and Sunday from 11am to 7pm.
Nördlingen:	Verkehrsamt, Marktplatz 2 (☎ 09081/4380); open Monday to Thursday from 9am to 6pm and Friday from 9am to 4:30pm, Saturday and holidays from 9:30am to 12:30pm.
Rothenburg ob der Tauber:	Stadt Verkehrsamt, Rathaus (☎ 09861/4-04-92); open Monday to Friday from 9am to 12:30pm and 2 to 6pm and Saturday from 9am to noon.

EMERGENCIES   In **Heidelberg:** Police (☎ 06221/110); Ambulance (☎ 06221/13013). In **Munich:** Police (☎ 089/110); Urgent medical help (☎ 089/558661).

CONSULATES   **U.S. Consulate General,** Königinstrasse 5, D-80536, München (☎ 089/2888-0). **U.K. Consulate General,** Burkleinstrasse 10, D-80538, München (☎ 089/21-10-90). **Canadian Consulate,** Tal 29, D-80331 München (☎ 089/290-650).

OPENING & CLOSING TIMES

BANKS   Times vary from state to state and city to city, but banks are generally open Monday to Friday from 8:30 or 9am to 3 or 4pm (to 5 or 6pm Thursday). Some banks close from 12:30 to 1:30pm. Branches at airports and main train stations open as early as 6:30am and close as late as 10:30pm.

MUSEUMS Most museums are open Tuesday to Sunday 9am to 5pm. Some close from noon to 1pm. Most are closed Monday, but many stay open to 8 or 9pm Thursday.

SHOPS Most shops are open Monday to Friday from about 9am to 6:30pm. On Saturday they close at 1pm, except on the first Saturday of the month, when they remain open to either 4pm (summer) or 6pm (winter). Big stores also stay open to 8:30pm Thursday.

GUIDED TOURS

In **Heidelberg,** walking tours depart from the Universitätsplatz, at the base of the lion-shaped fountain (Löwenbrunnen). They're conducted in English from April to October, daily from 2 to 4pm; off-season, tours in German only depart on Saturday at 2pm. The cost is 10DM for adults and 7DM for children. Call **06221/142211** for more information. In **Munich,** blue buses, with sightseeing tours conducted in English, leave year-round from the square in front of the Hauptbahnhof, at Hertie's. Tickets are sold on the bus and no advance booking is necessary. A 1-hour tour, costing 15DM for adults and 8DM for children 6 to 12, departs daily at 10am, 11:30am, and 2:30pm. A 2½-hour tour, including the Olympic Tower, costs 27DM for adults and 14DM for children. Departures are daily at 10am and 2:30pm from May to October and daily at 10am and 2:30pm from November to April. For details about a wide range of other tour options, contact **Panorama Tours,** an affiliate of Gray Line at Arnulfstrasse 8 (☎ **089/59-15-04**).

Pedal pushers in Munich will want to try Mike Lasher's **Mike's Bike Tour,** St. Bonifatiusstrasse 2 (☎ **089/651-8275**). His bike-rental services for 25DM include maps and locks, child and infant seats, and helmets at no extra charge. English and bilingual tours of central Munich run from March to November at a cost of 28DM, leaving at 11:30am and 4pm daily (call to confirm).

In **Rothenburg,** walking tours of the city, organized by the tourist office at Marktplatz (☎ **09861/40492**), depart from a point in front of the Rathaus (Town Hall), near a sign that reads STADTSFÜHRUNG. The cost is 6DM per person, adult or child. Tours depart daily year-round at 2pm and 8pm, lasting 90 minutes. Horse-drawn carriage rides start at Marktplatz.

SHOPPING

VAT REFUNDS Germany imposes a tax on most goods and services known as a **value-added tax** (VAT, Mehrwertsteuer in German). Nearly everything is taxed at 15%. Note that the goods for sale, such as German cameras, have the 15% tax already factored into the price; whereas services, such as paying a garage mechanic to fix your car, will have the 15% added to the bill. Stores that display a "Tax Free" sticker work with the **Tax Free Shopping Service.** They'll issue you a Tax Free

Shopping Check at the time of purchase. When leaving the country before you check your baggage (customs will want to examine what you purchased), have your check stamped by the German Customs Service as your proof of legal export. You may then be able to obtain a cash refund at one of the Tax Free Shopping Service offices in the major airports and many train stations, even at some of the bigger ferry terminals. Otherwise, you must send the checks to Tax Free Shopping Service, Mengstrasse 19, D-23552 Lübeck, Germany. If you want the payment to be credited to your bank card or bank account, request it.

BEST BUYS Popular items include cameras, binoculars, and optical lenses; Rosenthal crystal, china, and cutlery; Nymphenburg porcelains (Munich); leather goods; gourmet delicacies; handcrafts; and antiques.

In **Heidelberg,** Hauptstrasse is a pedestrian mall with many gift shops. The region is noted for its glass and crystal. **Edmund von König,** 124 Hauptstrasse (☎ 06221/20929), has the most interesting collection, including Rosenthal, Meissen, and colored crystal from the Bavarian forest made by Nachtmann. Nearby, Sofienstrasse houses antiques, jewelry, and chic fashion shops. Try **B & B Antiques,** Sofienstrasse 27 (☎ 06621/23003), for old clocks and furniture; **Michael Kienscherff,** Hauptstrasse 177 (☎ 06221/24255), is the best place to shop for handcrafts—from western and eastern Germany; **Muchkels Maus,** Plöck 71 (☎ 06221/23886), has an intriguing collection of toys, including dolls and puppets.

In **Munich,** the most elegant shops are on Theatinerstrasse, Maximilianstrasse, and Residenzstrasse. The pedestrian shopping mall runs from Karlsplatz to Marienplatz. Many of the trendiest boutiques are in the suburb of Schwabing, a 10-minute subway journey from Marienplatz (subway routes U3/6).

For two floors of mugs, folk costumes, and antiques, try **Wallach,** Residenzstrasse 3 (☎ 089/22-08-71). **Loden-frey,** Maffeistrasse 7–9 (☎ 089/21-03-90), offers an exclusive and expensive range of traditional Bavarian clothes (Trachten), including dirndls. To see what contemporary artisans are up to, visit the **Galerie für Angewandte Künst München,** Pacellistrasse 8 (☎ 089/29-01-47-0), established in the 1840s by the Bavarian government as a showcase for local artists.

The famous porcelain factory **Nymphenburger Porzellanmanufaktur** (☎ 089/17-91-970; open Mon–Fri 8:30am–noon and 12:30–5pm) is on the grounds of the castle, 8 kilometers (5 miles) northwest of the city. There's also a factory shop in the city at Odeonsplatz 1 (☎ 089/28-2428). For gourmet food specialties, go to **Dallmayr,** Dienerstrasse 14–15 (☎ 089/21350). For clocks, seek out **Andreas Huber,** Weinstrasse 8 (☎ 089/29-82-95). For cameras and camera equipment, the biggest selections can be found in **Karstadt's** department store (ground floor), opposite Michaelskirche (☎ 089/290-230). For optical goods try **Sohnges,** at Kaufingerstrasse 34 (☎ 089/272-90-251).

For china, crystal, and cutlery, visit **Rosenthal,** Dienerstrasse 17 (☎ 089/22-26-17), or **Kunstring Meissen,** Briennerstrasse 4 (☎ 089/281-532). For suitcases and leather goods, **Rosy Maendler,** Maximiliansplatz 12 (☎ 089/291-3322), has a good selection.

There are numerous antiques and artwork shops in the university quarter along Türkenstrasse and Amalienstrasse, as well as in the streets around the Viktualienmarkt. Expensive but worth checking out is **Seidl Antiquitäten,** Siegelstrasse 21 (☎ 089/349-568). Ideal for browsers are the bits-and-pieces Auer Dult market weeks, held at the end of April, in July, and in October at Mariahilfplatz (check the tourist office for exact dates). To seek out the best purveyors of chocolate and marzipan, head for **Confiserie Reber,** Herzogspitalstrasse 9 (☎ 089/26-52-31). A rival, in business since 1861, is **Confiserie Kreutzkann,** Maffeistrasse 4 (☎ 089/29-32-77). If you can't make it to that little old wood-carver shop deep in the Bavarian forest, head for **Firma Kraus,** Rindermarkt 10 (☎ 089/260-4196), a cozy shop near Marienplatz that sells the city's worthiest assortment of carved wooden figures.

SPORTS

BICYCLING   In **Dinkelsbühl,** inquire at the tourist office. In **Heidelberg,** rentals are at the parcel counter in the main train station (Apr–Sept). In **Munich,** you can rent bikes at the English Gardens at the corner of Königinstrasse and Veterinärstrasse (☎ 089/282-500; May–Oct). You can also try **Lenbach + Pöge,** Hans Sachs Strasse 7, near Sendlinger Tor Platz (☎ 089/266-506).

BOATING   Part of the fun of a tour through the Rhineland involves taking to the mighty river whose current raised the level of art and culture to much-envied heights in medieval Europe. The concierge of whatever hotel you happen to be staying at can advise about outlets for boat tours and boat rentals, but one of the better companies, **Rhein-Neckar Fahrgastschiffart,** in the city's Kongresshaus (☎ 06621/20-181), operates 75-minute excursions on the rivers for 30DM per person. They also rent a collection of small boats to qualified persons, but because of busy barge traffic on the polluted waters, I don't recommend this.

HIKING   From Garmisch-Partenkirchen, serious hikers can take overnight trips, staying in mountain huts belonging to the German Alpine Association (Deutscher Alpenverein). Some huts are staffed and serve meals. At unsupervised huts, you'll need to get a key. For information, inquire at the local tourist office or write to the German Alpine Association (Deutscher Alpenverein), Am Perlacher Forst 186, D-80997, München (☎ 089/651-0720).

DINING

Bavarian food is solid and not for people concerned about their daily caloric intake. The emphasis is on pork of exceptional quality—from roast suckling pig to tender schnitzel. Traditional accompaniments include dumplings (knödel), made from either potato or bread and herbs, and salad with a variety of lettuces. Many menus are being internationalized, and beefsteak and the ubiquitous french fries are widely available. In the most expensive restaurants, modern French cuisine with Bavarian touches is often featured.

The main meal is at midday. The fixed-price menu (Tageskarte) is the best bargain and sometimes includes soup, a main dish, and usually a dessert. All restaurants display menus outside. Though prices include taxes and service, it's customary in lower-priced restaurants to round out the bill to the nearest mark and in expensive restaurants to add 5%. Coffee is widely available, from cake shops to beer restaurants.

Department stores (Kaufhäuser) are a good bet for inexpensive lunches. Butcher shops, such as the Vinzenz-Murr chain in Munich, often serve hot snacks, such as Warmer Leberkäs mit Kartoffelsalat (baked meat loaf with mustard and potato salad).

Germany has some 1,300 breweries, more than the rest of Europe combined. The average German consumes 144 liters (254 pt.) of beer annually—in Bavaria, he or she drinks 200 liters (352 pt.), the world's highest per capita consumption. Even the tiniest villages have breweries serving beer comparable to the best in the world but drunk only locally: Ask for the local brew as you're passing through. Lantern-hung Bavarian beer gardens are the center of life in summer, particularly in Munich.

The most widely available draft beer styles are Export (known in Bavaria as Helles, "pale") and the slightly stronger, more bitter, pilseners. The cloudy amber brew served in tall glasses shaped like flower vases is wheat beer (Weissbier), a slightly sour but very refreshing drink. Dark beer (dunkles) is usually available on request, but from the bottle.

Most German wines come from the midwest. The exceptions are around Lake Constance, along the Neckar River, and in Franconia in northern Bavaria. Ask for Lake Constance wines when you're touring the Garmisch area, and for Neckar (Württemberg) wines when you're in Heidelberg or driving through the Neckar Valley between Heidelberg and Rothenburg. If you're uncertain about which wine to order, remember that German wines are grouped in one of three categories: Tafelwein (table wines), Qualitätswein (quality wines), or Qualitätswein mit Prädikat (award-winning wines).

CATEGORY	COST
Very Expensive	Over 100DM
Expensive	65–100DM
Moderate	45–65DM
Inexpensive	30–45DM

Prices are per person for a three-course meal, excluding drinks.

ACCOMMODATIONS

If you're looking for Laura Ashley–land, you're in trouble. Even in many first-class hotels, the furnishings tend to be functional. On the positive side, the rooms tend to be cheerful (at least in an open-eyed, red-cheeked sort of way) and are always immaculate.

Taxes, service charges, and continental breakfast are usually, but not always, included in quoted rates. Ask before you sign.

You can't go terribly wrong staying in one of some 70 **Romantik Hotels,** many of them old postal inns along medieval trade routes. To belong to this association a hotel has to be privately owned and at least 100 years old, and more than 85% of the rooms must have private baths. Prices range from moderate to expensive. For a hotel's brochure and other information, contact **Euro-Connection,** 7500 212th St. SW, Suite 103, Edmonds, WA 98026 (☎ **800/645-3876**). A free list of Romantik Hotels is available both from the association and from the German National Tourist Office.

GermanRail sells a package that includes lodging in Romantik Hotels, unlimited rail travel, sightseeing trips, and bicycle rentals. **Castle Hotels** is an association of more than 100 privately owned historic castles in attractive locations. Prices run from moderate to very expensive. The German National Tourist Office has a free Castle Hotels brochure and information about Castle Hotels packages; you can also contact Euro-Connection directly (see above).

Lufthansa has several fly/drive packages, some including lodging in Romantik Hotels, Castle Hotels, and other properties.

CATEGORY	COST
Very Expensive	Over 300DM
Expensive	200–300DM
Moderate	150–200DM
Inexpensive	Under 150DM

Prices are for two people sharing a double room.

EXPLORING

FRANKFURT TO HEIDELBERG

Take the Autobahn (A5) south from Frankfurt to Darmstadt. From here you can continue south on A5 down the center of the Rhine Valley, through flat agricultural country; or you can turn off on the slower but more scenic Bergstrasse (Route 3). The drive along Bergstrasse, the old main road on the east side of the valley, is a pleasant rather than dramatic trip through wine-producing villages at the foot of gently sloping hills

THE ITINERARY

ORIENTATION

From Frankfurt, head south to Heidelberg. The drive through the Neckar Valley takes you to the Romantic Road and Rothenburg. Then you'll reach Munich, where you can explore the past in palaces and museums, shop along convenient pedestrian malls, and succumb to elegant restaurants, pastry shops, and beer halls. From Munich, it's only an hour's drive to Garmisch-Partenkirchen for skiing (Dec–May), mountain walks, dramatic cable-car rides, and visits to the Passion Play town of Oberammergau and the castles of Ludwig II. After Garmisch you can head home or continue south to Austria or Switzerland.

THE MAIN ROUTE
3–5 DAYS

One Night: *Heidelberg.*
 Excursion along the Romantic Road.

crowned with ruined medieval castles, some of them converted into restaurants and hotels.

About 19.2 kilometers (12 miles) south of Darmstadt, between the towns of Zwingenberg and Auerbach, look for signs to **Auerbach Schloss** (☎ **06251/72-923**). A 10-minute drive takes you through a wooded Natur-park, with lovely hillside trails, to the romantic ruins. Though the castle is losing its battle against nature, the ramparts are still intact, and children of all ages will love scurrying through its broken battlements. Free admission. Open May–Oct, daily 10am–11pm; Nov–Apr, daily 10am–6pm.

AUERBACH

If you're partial to apple strudel and lovely parks, turn left at the Hotel Krone in the center of **Auerbach** and drive to **Fürstenlager Park.** Leave your car at the Park Hotel Herrenhaus, spend an hour walking among the tropical trees and pavilions, and then reward yourself with some strudel and a glass of the hotel's own white Auerbach Fürstenlager wine.

Accommodations

Park Hotel Herrenhaus, 6140 Bensheim 3, D-64625 Auerbach (☎ **06251/72-274;** fax 06251/78-473). This is the former summer

One Night: *Munich.*

One Night: *Garmisch-Partenkirchen.*
Tour of the Alps and the royal castles.

5–7 DAYS

One Night: *Heidelberg.*
Excursion through the Neckar Valley and along the Romantic Road.

One Night: *Rothenburg.*

Two Nights: *Munich.*

Two Nights: *Garmisch-Partenkirchen.*
Tour of the Alps and the royal castles.

7–14 DAYS

Two Nights: *Heidelberg.*
Excursion through the Neckar Valley and along the Romantic Road.

One Night: *Rothenburg.*

Three Nights: *Munich.*

Four Nights: *Garmisch-Partenkirchen.*
Tour of the Alps and the royal castles.

residence of the grand dukes of Hesse-Darmstadt. The mansion, once a bit run-down, has been beautifully modernized. There are just nine guest rooms in the spacious interior. The owners are very friendly, and you couldn't ask for a more peaceful setting within a lovely 52-hectare (125-acre) park. 9 rms with bath. Facilities: restaurant (dinner for nonguests only by reservation), gardens. AE, MC, V. Moderate.

HEPPENHEIM

About 8 kilometers (5 miles) south of Auerbach, still on Route 3, is the town of **Heppenheim.** Stop at least long enough to appreciate the 16th-century town hall and pharmacy.

Park where you see on your left the brown marker with the words *Historischer Marktplatz* and spend a few minutes soaking up the atmosphere of the historic Marktplatz, surrounded by 16th-century buildings and a Gothic church, the so-called Bergstrasse Cathedral. Heppenheim offers only a taste of what you'll see in Rothenburg, but it's virtually tourist-free, with a sense of reality you won't find in the postcard towns along the Romantic Road.

HEIDELBERG

Heidelberg has the mellow flavor of old Germany. The country's oldest university town, it nestles along the banks of the fast-flowing Neckar River, beneath an imposing red sandstone castle. In the early evening the sun turns the red to gold; a deep radiance lies on the town and prints itself upon the inner eye.

The students transform what could be just another pretty tourist town into a place of youthful vitality. You'll mingle with them as you walk among the fashionable shops and cafes along the .8-kilometer (half a mile) pedestrian mall or wander down narrow alleyways in search of Heidelberg's past.

The city was the political center of a German state called the Rhineland Palatinate—the name deriving from the title palatines, which was given to the highest officers in the Holy Roman Empire. After the Thirty Years' War (1618–48) the Protestant Elector (hereditary ruler) Karl Ludwig married his daughter to the brother of Louis XIV in the hope of bringing peace to the Rhineland. But when the Elector's son died without an heir, Louis XIV used the marriage alliance as an excuse to claim Heidelberg, and in 1689 the town was sacked and laid waste. From the ashes of a devastating fire 4 years later arose what you see today: a baroque town built on Gothic foundations, with narrow twisting streets and alleys. The new Heidelberg is changing under the influence of U.S. Army barracks and industrial development stretching into the suburbs; but the old heart of the city remains unchanged and continues to exude the spirit of romantic Germany.

Longfellow wrote that "next to the Alhambra of Granada, the castle of Heidelberg is the most magnificent ruin of the Middle Ages." You should see **Heidelberg Castle** (☏ 06221/53-84-14) early in the morning because it's the town's leading attraction and you can spend 30 minutes in afternoon lines for the 60-minute guided tour. The imposing ruin is at its romantic best from a distance. You can drive up Neue Schlosstrasse, but parking can be a problem, so leave your car at your hotel and take the Königstuhl funicular (4.50DM adults, 2.90DM children).

The castle, dominating the town, should remind you of the time when Heidelberg was the capital of the Palatinate. There has been a fortress here since the 13th century, but it didn't become the principal residence for the electors for another 300 years. Construction began around 1300 and continued for the next 400 years; the courtyard through which you enter is like the public square of a medieval town, surrounded by buildings representing 4 centuries of changing architectural styles. The best wings were built during the Renaissance and show a fine balance of strength and refinement, of might and grace. The late-Renaissance **Heinrichs Wing,** on the right side of the courtyard as you face the river, was built by Elector Otto-Heinrich in the mid-16th century. It's pure Italian Renaissance, made of warm red sandstone from the Neckar Valley, and has a dignity and a simplicity that stand in marked contrast to the

HEIDELBERG

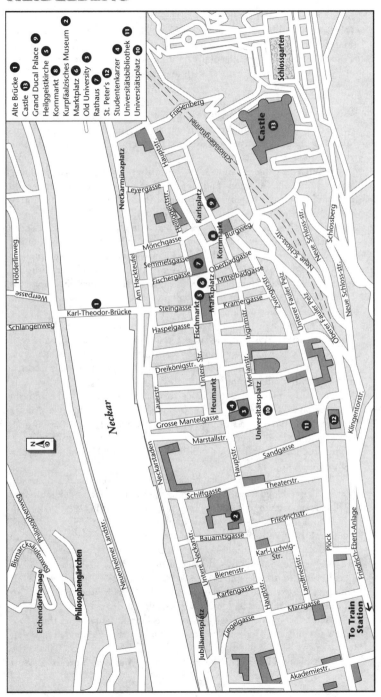

Alte Brücke ➊
Castle ⑬
Grand Ducal Palace ➒
Heiliggeistkirche ➎
Kornmarkt ➑
Kurpfälzisches Museum ➋
Marktplatz ➏
Old University ➌
Rathaus ➐
St. Peter's ⑫
Studentenkarzer ⑪
Universitätsbibliothek ⑩
Universitätsplatz ⑩

baroque ornamentation flourishing elsewhere. Otto's son Friedrich IV (1592–1610) added the **Friedrichs Wing,** also in late-Renaissance style. In 1693, less than 100 years later, the castle was badly damaged by the French and in 1764 was struck by lightning and left in ruins until the end of the 19th century, when the shell and interior of the Friedrichs Wing were restored.

Do you see, over the entrance, the relief of two angels holding a wreath of five roses enclosing a pair of compasses? The story goes that the twins of the master builder fell from the scaffolding and appeared as angels in the father's troubled dreams, holding the wreath of roses that covered their grace.

The castle's interiors are filled with a modest number of artifacts, arranged museum fashion, and don't breathe much living history; you may find the rooms much less impressive than the facades. What you're not supposed to miss is the mid–18th-century 186,200-liter (49,000-gal.) **Great Vat.** This isn't a joke. It was built at a time when the Elector's subjects paid him one-tenth of their wine in taxes. No one sent his best tenth, so it was customary to pour the whole amount into one cask and make a table wine for public celebrations or payments to officials. The vat is made from 130 oak trees. The guardian was the jester dwarf Perkeo, known for his capacity to drink from its contents. Local lore says he died when he drank his first glass of water.

The one sight you'll want to see inside the castle is the **Pharmaceutical Museum,** the largest in the world. In a setting worthy of *The Sorcerer's Apprentice,* you can view all the paraphernalia of medieval doctors. Kids in particular will love the dried beetles and toads and the mummy with a full head of hair.

If you haven't time or patience to wait in line, don't leave without standing on one of the balconies and enjoying the panoramic view of the town, with its spires and orange roof tiles spread along the river, and, stretching beyond them, the wooded mountains of the Palatinate. Admission, including the tour, 4.50DM adults, 2.90DM children. Open daily 8am–5pm.

Walk or take the funicular back into town. From the funicular station, walk one block toward the river to the **Kornmarkt,** which has a fine 1718 baroque statue of the Madonna. To your left is the oldest quarter of town, with narrow passageways leading to cozy wine taverns and pubs. You'll return here later. For now, make a short side trip to the right to **Karlsplatz.** On the far right corner of this square (as you face the river) are two historic student pubs, the **Seppl** and the **Roter Ochsen** (Red Ox).

Return to the Kornmarkt. On the riverside is the **Town Hall** (Rathaus). Next to it is another square, the **Marktplatz,** which has an outdoor flower market and good views of the castle.

Across from the Rathaus is the late Gothic **Church of the Holy Spirit** (Heiliggeistkirche). Note how the aisles, though divided into galleries, are as high as the main body (the nave) of the church. This is the hallmark of the Hall style. Slim pillars force your eyes upward toward

God. In 1705 a wall was raised between the choir and the nave so that rival Christian sects could enjoy separate places of worship. The Roman Catholics fell heir to the choir and the Protestants were awarded the nave. Climb the tower for a view.

Leave by the west end of the church. On your left is the **Ritter Hotel.** When the armies of Louis XIV destroyed the town and castle in 1693, the only Renaissance building to survive was the Ritter. Its carefully preserved Renaissance facade is the finest and most fantastic you'll see in Germany.

Continue down **Hauptstrasse,** a pedestrian street and the commercial center of town, which has many stores and restaurants. Here and on side streets you'll find some first-rate antiques shops.

Continue to a large open square, **Universitätsplatz.** This is the entrance to the **Old University,** founded in 1386 by Paris professors and students who were offered asylum when they refused to recognize the opposition Pope the French king had installed in Avignon. It was the first university in Germany and, after the Reformation had swept Europe, the chief Protestant center of learning in the country.

In the back of the Old University is the **Students' Jail** (Studentenkarzer) Augustinerstrasse 2 (☎ 06221/54-23-34). Ancient tradition dictated that students couldn't be thrown in the town clink, so from 1712 to the early 20th century the Studentenkarzer was filled with unruly undergraduates who spent their leisure time carving inscriptions commemorating their imprisonment—a distinction of which they were proud. Students could be confined for up to 14 days for such offenses as drunkenness, playing practical jokes, or disturbing the peace at night. After 3 days of bread and water they could accept food from outside, attend lectures, and receive visits from fellow prisoners. The walls are covered with cartoons, drawings, ribald verse—anyone who takes the time to examine the signatures can probably find names of many who have achieved distinction in the arts, business, and politics. Admission 1.50DM adults, 1DM children. Open Tues–Sat 10am–noon and 2–5pm.

Nearby is the **University Library** (Universitätsbibliothek), Plöck 107–109 (☎ 06221/542380), in which you'll find some illustrated (illuminated) medieval books on display. Free admission. Open year-round, Mon–Sat 10am–7pm; Easter to Nov 1, Sun 11am–4pm.

Return to Hauptstrasse, turn left, and continue to the **Electoral Palatinate Museum** (Kurpfälzisches Museum), Hauptstrasse 97 (☎ 06221/683402), and see the Altarpiece of the 12 Apostles (1509) by Tilman Riemenschneider. Riemenschneider was the greatest late-Gothic German wood-carver, and this is his finest work. Compare the spiritual faces of the Apostles closest to Christ to the more worldly, worn faces of those farther away. During the Peasants' War, Riemenschneider sneaked the peasants of Würzburg into town by a secret path, and the Bishop of Würzburg punished him by mutilating his hands. Admission 4DM adults; children free. Open Tues and Thurs–Sun 10am–5pm, Wed 10am–9pm.

WHAT TO SEE & DO WITH CHILDREN

In Heidelberg: Boat trips, bike rides, a visit to the castle.

In Rothenburg: The whole medieval town is a child's dream come true.

In Munich: The largest science-and-technology museum in the world; the famous Glockenspiel at the New Town Hall; bike riding, boating, and buggy rides in the English Gardens; ice-skating at the Olympia Tower; Hellabrunn Zoo, which has a children's section where animals can be hand-fed.

In Garmisch-Partenkirchen: Four seasons' worth of outdoor sports, including skiing (Dec–May) and hiking, cable-car and cog railway rides, and a stagecoach ride from Garmisch to Grainau. The former site of the Winter Olympics has seven indoor pools, including one with waves and artificially created surf; indoor tennis; three indoor skating rinks.

Now cross Hauptstrasse and head toward the river on Grosse Mantelgasse (Big Coat Lane). When you can't go any farther, turn right. From here to the **Old Bridge** (Alt Brücke) are several small side streets to explore. Cross the bridge and enjoy an unforgettable view of the town.

Go for a walk along the far side of the river, on Neuenheimer Landstrasse and Ziegelhäuser Landstrasse. You'll get your best views of the castle from here—preferably in the late afternoon, when the sun colors the town gold.

A more challenging and rewarding walk is along **Philosopher's Walk** (Philosophenweg), on the slopes above the riverside path. After you cross the Old Bridge, take Schlangenweg, the street that zigzags up the mountain.

DINING

Hirschgasse, Hirschgasse 3 (☎ 06221/45-40). The oldest inn in Heidelberg (built 20 years before Columbus discovered the West Indies) is across the river on the edge of town. Le Gourmet is the name of the unpretentious, small hotel restaurant serving both traditional and modern specialties. Casual. AE, DC, MC, V. Dinner only except for Sun lunch. Closed Sun night and Dec 23–Jan 7. Very Expensive.

Kurfürstenstube, in the Hotel Europa, Friedrich-Ebert-Anlage 1 (☎ 06221/5150). This is Heidelberg dining at its best—either in a wood-paneled tavern or on a terrace. It serves regional specialties with a delicate modern touch. Reservations required. Casual. AE, DC, MC, V. Expensive.

Kurpfälzisches Museum Restaurant, Hauptstr. 97 (☎ 06221/24-050). This garden restaurant is back from the main street—a peaceful oasis for a piña colada, a milkshake, or lunch. Reservations required. Casual. AE, DC, MC, V. Moderate.

Simplicissimus, Ingrimstr. 16 (☎ 06221/18-33-36). Heidelberg's best kitchen provides an elegant setting for dinner. Chef Johann Lummer envelops regional style in French taste. Try his rabbit filets in herbs or duck in a zesty sauce. Reservations required. Jacket/tie required. AE, DC, MC, V. Dinner only. Closed Tues, a week in Mar (dates vary), and first 3 weeks in Aug. Very Expensive.

Inexpensive student restaurants include **Zum Roten Ochsen,** Hauptstrasse 217 (☎ 06221/20-977); the 585-year-old **Schnookeloch,** Haspelgasse 8 (☎ 06221/22-733); and the more touristy **Zum Seppl,** Hauptstrasse 213 (☎ 06221/23-085).

ACCOMMODATIONS

Before you leave home, check with the German National Tourist Board for budget holiday packages that include 3 nights' accommodations, meals in student restaurants, entry fees, and guided tours.

Anlage, Friedrich-Ebert-Anlage 32, D-69117 Heidelberg (☎ 06221/2-64-25; fax 06221/164426). The small but comfortable Anlage nestles beneath the castle. Breakfast is the only meal served. 20 rms, most with bath. AE, DC, MC, V. Moderate.

Hirschgasse, Hirschgasse 3, D-69210 Heidelberg (☎ 06221/45-40; fax 06221/454-111). This hotel is across the river on the edge of town — a bit inconvenient if you want to go back and forth more than once a day. The original folksy look has been replaced by trendy Laura Ashley furnishings. A farmhouse was here when Columbus was crossing the Atlantic, and later it was a tavern and is referred to by Mark Twain in *A Tramp Abroad.* 20 suites. Facilities: restaurant. AE, DC, MC, V. Closed Dec 23–Jan 7. Very Expensive.

Hotel Europa, Friedrich-Ebert-Anlage 1, D-69115 Heidelberg (☎ 06221/5150; fax 06221/51-55-55). The Europa is a family-owned luxury hotel — the sort of place where an educated, well-heeled German would stay. The Red Baron would find himself outclassed in this hostelry, which has a marble entranceway flanked by carpeted lounges with wood newspaper racks, leather chairs, and crystal chandeliers. Celebrated guests have included Richard Strauss, the Duke and Duchess of Windsor, and Maria Callas. Muhammed Ali signed the guest book, "Love is the net where hearts are caught like fish. Peace." The rooms vary significantly in size and decor, and many are decorated with money rather than taste; if you're unhappy, ask to see more. 120 rms with bath; 15 suites. Facilities: restaurant, bar, summer patio. AE, DC, MC, V. Very Expensive.

Hotel Holländer, Neckarstaden 66, D-69117 Heidelberg (☎ 06221/12-091; fax 06221/22085). This renovated, centrally located 17th-century house boasts scenic river views. The rooms are clean but fitted with undistinguished Sears-like modern furnishings; the headboards are covered with velour in Halloween colors. Room 452 has a skylight. 39 rms with bath. Facilities: restaurant. AE, DC, MC, V. Expensive.

Perkeo, Hauptstr. 75, D-69117 Heidelberg (☎ 06221/1-41-30; fax 06221/141337). This hotel was recently renovated, so all the rooms have the same decor. The ambiance is a bit motelish, but with some old-fashioned touches you may find more agreeable than the deliberate Lederhosen look of other hostelries. It's on a busy pedestrian street, so ask for a quiet room. Try for no. 25; it's extra quiet and very cozy. 25 rms

with bath. Facilities: restaurant. MC. Closed Dec 23–Jan 6.
Moderate/Expensive.

Prinzhotel, Neuenheimer Landstr. 5, D-69120 Heidelberg
(☎ 06221/40-320; fax 06221/403-21-96). This well-known 80-year-old
luxury hotel is across the river from the old town. The atmosphere is
trendy European, with some smart un-Teutonic colors—pink and gray.
What the hotel lacks in warmth it makes up for in sophistication. Fight for
a room with a river view. 50 rms with bath. Facilities: California restaurant, piano bar (closed Tues), sauna, Jacuzzi. AE, DC, MC, V. Very
Expensive.

Romantik Hotel Zum Ritter St. Georg, Hauptstr. 178, D-69117
Heidelberg (☎ 06221/24-272; fax 06221/12683). This hotel occupies the
only surviving Renaissance house in town. The Red Baron would feel
right at home in the dining room, complete with suit of armor, rough plaster walls, arched doorways, and ceiling beams. The hotel was fully modernized in the late 1980s, and its rooms have been refurnished in a
mixture of "ancient and modern." Room 34 on the top floor is for romantics—it's under the roof and very cozy. 40 rms, most with bath; 1 suite.
Facilities: restaurant. AE, DC, MC, V. Expensive.

THE NECKAR VALLEY

Take Route 37 southwest through the **Neckar Valley** from Heidelberg
toward Bad Wimpfen. The road is busy, particularly in summer, so don't
expect to make rapid progress. Not that you'll be tempted to speed
through the gentle rural landscape of orchards and vineyards, where
wooded hills crowned with castles rise above the soft-flowing river. When
you reach Neckarelz, you have a choice of continuing to Bad Wimpfen or
turning left on Route 27 to Mosbach.

Route 27 is the most direct way to the Romantic Road. Turn left
on Route 27 through Mosbach and continue to Route 292. Turn right to
Bad Mergentheim. Drive east to Weikersheim and head south along the
Romantic Road.

If you have time, are enjoying the scenery, and are partial to castles
and medieval towns, continue south from Neckarelz to Bad Wimpfen.
This is the route I've described below.

NECKARGEMÜND

During the busy tourist season you may want to leave Heidelberg and
spend the night in the quiet surrounding of **Neckargemünd** (12.8km/
8 miles east of Heidelberg) to get an early start to the Romantic Road.

Accommodations

Hotel zum Ritter, Neckarstrasse 40, D-69151 Neckargemünd
(☎ 06223/92350; fax 06223/73339). This hotel began life as a castle in
1286. It has a good restaurant serving a multicourse Rittermahl (knight's
banquet)—if you order in advance. 38 rms with bath. Facilities: restaurant. AE, MC, V. Expensive.

THE NECKAR VALLEY

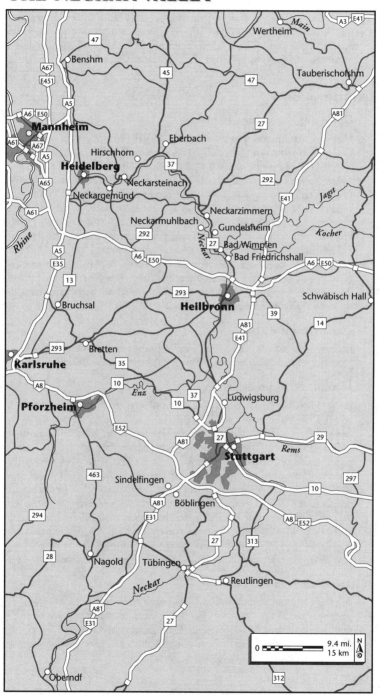

Hotel zum Rössl, Heidelberger Strasse 15, D-69151 Neckargemünd (☎ **06223/2665;** fax 06223/6859). This bed-and-breakfast–style hotel boasts a restaurant with a fine reputation. 12 rms, with bath. Facilities: restaurant (closed Mon–Tues). AE, MC, V. Closed 2 weeks in July. Inexpensive.

HIRSCHHORN

Dining & Accommodations

Hirschhorn Castle Hotel, Schloss Hotel, Auf Burg Hirschhorn, D-69434 Hirschhorn (☎ **06272/1373;** fax 06272/3267). About 12 kilometers (7.5 miles) east of Neckargemünd, the Hirschhorn isn't so much a castle hotel as a pleasant if undistinguished modern hotel inside an old castle. The hallways have that medieval rough-plaster look, lest you forget you're in a castle, and some rooms have double sinks, swagged velvet curtains, and canopied four-poster beds. The Grünes Zimmer and Hochzeitzimmer are the best rooms, but all have river views. The Student Prince furnishings tend at times to confuse ornateness with class. Your best bet may be to come for a meal (breakfast perhaps, after leav-ing Heidelberg) on a terrace overlooking the river. The view is splendid and the restaurant enjoys a good reputation for lunch or dinner. 25 rms with bath. Facilities: terrace/garden restaurant. AE, MC, V. Expensive.

NECKARZIMMERN

Follow the signs 1.6 kilometers (1 mile) to the left of **Neckarzimmern** to Hornberg Castle, part of which has been converted into a hotel.

Dining & Accommodations

Berg Hornberg, D-74865 Neckarzimmern (☎ **06261/4064;** fax 06261/18864). Your best bet here is lunch or dinner on the terrace overlooking the Neckar Valley. Specialties include fresh fish and venison at reasonable prices. The guest rooms are comfortable but haven't much panache for an 11th-century castle. Ask for one with a view and for no. 26. The castle was the home of the picaresque knight Götz von Berlichingen, who died here in 1562 and was immortalized in Goethe's drama of the same name. You can stroll around the rooms he once lived in, now a bit worse for wear and some of them roofless. His armor is on show in the castle museum. 24 rms with bath. Facilities: restaurant (with occasional medieval-style banquets arranged; wines from the hotel's own vineyards), miniature golf. V. Closed Dec 20–Feb. Expensive.

GUNDELSHEIM

A bridge beyond **Gundelsheim** takes you 3.2 kilometers (2 miles) out of your way to the romantic, fortified **Berg Guttenberg.** Sights worth stop-ping for include a library and an 18th-century herbarium, with plants grown in trick wood boxes. Return to the main road and drive about 6.5 kilometers (4 miles) south to Bad Wimpfen.

BAD WIMPFEN

The old fortified quarter of **Bad Wimpfen** was an imperial residence in the 13th century. The network of picturesque streets, such as Klostergasse, are lined with timber-framed houses, and are well worth an hour of your time. The 13th-century Gothic church, **St. Peter's** (Stiftskirche), has a lovely cloister. Other than that, the town's most famous monuments, each built during the 13th century, include a historic and cultural museum, the **Steinhaus** (Imperial Palace) (☎ 07063/8779). Within a few minutes' walk are the panoramic heights of the **Blue Tower** (Blauer Turm) (☎ 07063/8968), and the smaller and less impressive **Red Tower** (Roter Turm) (no phone). All three are open Tuesday to Sunday from 10am to noon and 2 to 4:30pm. Entrance to the Steinhaus and the Blue Tower is 2DM per person; the Red Tower is free. Wander down **Schwibbogengasse,** a street of broken cobbles, full of warmth and character. The four-story house beside the Hotel Sonne belongs in a fairy tale.

From Bad Wimpfen take country roads to Domeneck, Schöntal, and Krautheim, then turn north on Route 19 to Bad Mergentheim. The best restaurants in Bad Mergentheim are **Zirbelstube** in the Hotel Victoria (☎ 07931/5930) and the less expensive **Weinstube** in the same hotel. Drive to Weikersheim and head south along the Romantic Road.

THE ROMANTIC ROAD

The **Romantic Road** follows a medieval trade route through peaceful, rolling countryside, past vineyards and fields planted with sugar beets, potatoes, and wheat. This isn't ooh-and-ah country, but a rural daytime world of tractors and butterflies. The real romance is in the medieval towns along the route—the best preserved in Germany—particularly Rothenburg, Dinkelsbühl, and Nördlingen.

WEIKERSHEIM

The town of **Weikersheim** developed around a castle (1580–1680), **Schloss Weikersheim,** Marktplatz (☎ 07934/8364); it boasts a first-rate collection of 16th- to 18th-century furniture and a marvelous Great Hall (Rittersaal), which is part Renaissance, part baroque. Huntsmen track their prey on the ceiling, and carved deer and bear seem poised to spring from the walls. You pass beneath the unblinking gaze of local royalty, each in his own regal frame, each one uglier than the next. Admission 5DM adults, 2DM children. Open Apr–Oct, daily 9am–6pm; Nov–Mar, daily 9am–noon and 2–6pm.

Dining

Hotel Laurentius, Marktplatz 5 (☎ 07934/7007). This hotel is known for its fresh regional cuisine served at reasonable prices in two separate restaurants. It offers fixed-price low-cost lunches in its simple but appealing Filius restaurant, and somewhat more elaborate fixed-price lunches in its more formal dining room, Laurentius. Both restaurants closed Tues. Casual. AE, DC, MC, V. Reservations not necessary. Moderate/Inexpensive.

CREGLINGEN

A 1.6-kilometer (1-mile) side trip from **Creglingen** takes you to the **Chapel of Our Lord** (Herrgottskirche), which has a famous carved wood altarpiece (1505–10) of the Virgin by Riemenschneider. Open Apr–Oct, daily 8am–6pm; Nov–Mar, Tues–Sun 10am–noon and 1–4pm.

Dining & Accommodations

Gasthof Krone, Hauptstrasse 12, D-97993 Creglingen (☎ **07933/558;** fax 07933/1444). This place shares with the restaurant in Weikersheim a sound reputation for regional cuisine at reasonable prices. The Gasthof is also a comfortable hotel, run with a friendly touch by the Ebert family. 14 rms with bath. Facilities: restaurant (closed Mon). No credit cards. Closed Dec 10–Jan. Inexpensive.

ROTHENBURG OB DER TAUBER

In spite of its museumlike atmosphere and spate of tourists, **Rothenburg ob der Tauber** is one of Europe's most colorful medieval towns. Every street has its own arrangement of beautiful churches, gateways, fountains, and wrought-iron signs. No roof is like its neighbor. The gabled houses are half-timbered or plastered and dripping with flowers and vines. In America a street is an open road that could, it seems, go on forever; but in medieval Rothenburg the streets turn in on themselves and seem to shelter you from the world outside.

The town developed around two 12th-century castles that were destroyed in a mid–14th-century earthquake. From the ruins, the wealthy burghers built public monuments, such as **St. James's Church** (St. Jakobskirche), the **Town Hall,** and the **gabled houses** on Herrngasse. The town turned Protestant and never recovered from the depression caused by the Thirty Years' War (1618–48). It languished through the 17th and 18th centuries—a sleepy, forgotten regional market town, too poor to expand beyond its medieval walls. It was this neglect, ironically, that preserved the town, keeping it a perfect gem of a 16th-century village.

Begin at the **Marktplatz** (main square). Notice how all main streets converge here, in the geographic and spiritual heart of town—and that wherever you go within the medieval walls, you're always moving in relation to this central space. It must've been very satisfying, psychologically, always moving toward or away from a defined point; and it says something about our spiritual pilgrimage over the centuries that cities today no longer have this common center, these protective walls.

Look up at the **Rathaus** (Town Hall) off this square and see if you can distinguish between the 14th-century Gothic section, with a gable topped by a belfry, and the newer Renaissance section facing the Marktplatz, built after a fire in 1501. Standing in the Marktplatz, you can appreciate the contrast between the horizontal lines of Renaissance architecture and the soaring vertical lines of the earlier Gothic building. (The arcade in front was added in 1681.) Inside the town hall is a museum and a tower with striking views. Admission to tower 1DM adults,

THE ROMANTIC ROAD

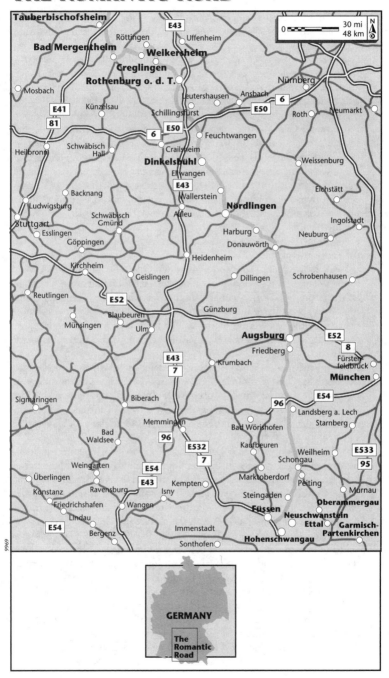

Tauberbischofsheim
Röttingen
E43
Uffenheim

Bad Mergentheim
Weikersheim
Creglingen
Rothenburg o. d. T.
Nürnberg

Mosbach
Leutershausen
Ansbach
6

E41
Künzelsau
Schillingsfürst
E50
Roth
Neumarkt

81
Schwäbisch Hall
6
E50
Feuchtwangen

Heilbronn
Crailsheim
Weissenburg

Dinkelsbühl
Ellwangen

Backnang
E43
Wallerstein
Eichstätt

Ludwigsburg
Schwäbisch Gmünd
Aalen
Nördlingen

Stuttgart
Esslingen
Harburg
Neuburg
Ingolstadt

Göppingen
Donauwörth

Kirchheim
Heidenheim

Reutlingen
Geislingen
Dillingen
Schrobenhausen

E52
Günzburg

Blaubeuren
Münsingen
Ulm
Augsburg
E52

Friedberg
8
Fürsten-feldbrück

E43
Krumbach
München

7
E54

Sigmaringen
Biberach
96
Landsberg a. Lech

Memmingen
Bad Wörishofen
Starnberg

Bad Waldsee
96
Kaufbeuren
Weilheim
E533

Weingarten
E532
Schongau
95

Überlingen
E54
7
Marktoberdorf
Peiting
Murnau

Konstanz
E43
Kempten
Steingaden
Oberammergau

Friedrichshafen
Ravensburg
Isny
Füssen
Neuschwanstein

Lindau
Wangen
Ettal
Garmisch-Partenkirchen

E54
Bergenz
Immenstadt
Hohenschwangau

Sonthofen

GERMANY

The Romantic Road

0 — 30 mi
0 — 48 km
N

50pf children. Rathaus open Mon–Fri 8am–6pm, Sat–Sun 7am–4pm. Tower open Apr–Oct, daily 9:30am–12:30pm and 1–5pm; Nov–Mar, Sat–Sun noon–3pm.

Also on the Marktplatz is the **City Councillors' Tavern** (Ratsherrn-trinkstube), which you can recognize by the three clocks on its baroque gable. If you're here at 11am, noon, or 1, 2, 3, 8, 9, or 10pm, you'll see the principal figures appear in what's called the "Drinking Feat of the Thirty Years' War." Rothenburg, a Protestant town, lay in the path of Catholic forces under Gen. Cserklas Tilly and was taken on October 30, 1631. The following day it was to be destroyed and its officers executed; but during the night the victorious general was offered a 3¼-liter (.8-gal.) tankard of wine, which, to his embarrassment, he was unable to empty in a single gulp. With his manhood at stake — so the story goes — he offered to pardon the town if one of its officials could down it in one go. A former mayor named Nusch succeeded in 10 minutes. It took him 3 days to recover, but the town was saved. The story is a bit hard to swallow, but who wants to question it? Skeptics can see the tankard in the museum and draw their own conclusions.

Cross the Marktplatz and walk down Obere Schmiedgasse (Upper Smith's Lane). The second house, the **Master Builder's House** — the one with the dragons on the gables — is the finest in town. The supporting figures at the upper windows represent alternately the seven vices and virtues; in the lower row Compassion, Gluttony, and Motherly Love stand side by side. The inner courtyard, unchanged for centuries, is today a cafe.

On the right, where Obere Schmiedgasse turns into Untere Schmiedgasse, is the Gothic **St. John's Church** (Johanniskirche). Adjoining it is the **Kriminal Museum** (☎ 09861/53-59), where kids can unlock their imaginations among the instruments of torture. Admission 5DM adults, 3.50DM children. Open Apr–Oct, daily 9:30am–6pm; Nov–Mar, daily 2–4pm.

Continue down Untere Schmiedgasse to Plönlein, a picturesque corner where two streets meet, both ending at gateways. If you have time, bear left and continue down Spitalgasse to the **Hospital** (Spital), a colorful group of 16th- and 17th-century buildings, including a notable Gothic **chapel** (Spitalkirche). Retrace your steps down Spitalgasse, back through the gate. Turn left and pass beneath the Koboldzell Gate.

If you skip the hospital, bear right to the Koboldzell Gate, make a sharp right turn, and follow the path along the outside of the wall, above the river. Pass through the arched entranceway into the **Burggarten.** Flowers bloom now where the two fortified castles used to be.

Follow the path through the public gardens. Pass through the fortified gateway (Burgtor), which was part of one of the castles, and head back toward the center of town. Bear right on Herrngasse, a commercial street lined with mansions of the medieval burghers, and peer into some of the courtyards. Soon you'll be back to the Marktplatz. Behind the well—which supplied the town's water needs 555 years ago—is a half-timbered house where artists display and sell their wares. To the left is the picturesque Hofbronnengasse (Court Well Lane), leading to the **Puppen und Spielzeugmuseum** (Doll and Toy Museum), Hofronnengasse 13 (☎ 09861/2339). Admission 5DM adults, 1.50DM children. Open Mar–Dec, daily 9:30am–6pm; Jan–Feb, daily 11am–5pm.

Turn left on Kirchgasse and right on Klostergasse to **St. James's Church** (St. Jakobskirche), Klostergasse 15 (☎ 09861/7000620). In the south aisle (on your right, facing front) is the famous 1504 Riemenschneider altarpiece, called the Holy Blood Altar because three drops of Christ's blood are said to be contained in a capsule of rock crystal in the gold-plated cross. Look closely at the facial expressions, particularly of Judas, in The Last Supper. Only John remains unperturbed. Admission 2.50DM adults, 1DM children. Open Mon–Sat 9am–5:30pm, Sun 10:30am–5:30pm.

Dining

Baumeisterhaus, Obere Schmiedgasse 3 (☎ 09861/94-700). This restaurant, in a 16th-century building, displays irresistible pastries. This is a good stop for a lunch of regional specialties, like dumplings in consommé, veal schnitzel, or sauerbraten. Reservations required for courtyard tables. Casual. AE, DC, MC, V. Moderate.

Eisenhut, Herrngasse 3–5 (☎ 09861/7050). The number-one hotel in town, the Eisenhut has an attractive terrace restaurant overlooking the Tauber River. Popular dishes include "Franconian wedding" soup, saddle of venison with fresh mushrooms, and walnut ice cream with blackberries. Try the wines made from the hotel's own grapes. Reservations required. Jacket/tie required. AE, DC, MC, V. Very Expensive.

Zum Greifen, Obere Schmiedgasse 5 (☎ 09861/2281). Another inn with a long and colorful past, Zum Griefen serves time-honored dishes. Reservations not necessary. Casual. AE, MC, V. Closed Sun and Mon lunch, Aug 22–Sept 2, Dec 19–25, and Jan. Inexpensive.

Accommodations

Burg Hotel, Klostergasse 1–3 (☎ 09861/5037; fax 09861/1487). This hotel is a bit flairless but clean and comfortable. Ask for a room overlooking the Tauber River. 14 rms with bath; 5 suites. AE, DC, MC, V. Expensive.

Eisenhut, Herrngasse 3–5, D-91541 Rothenburg (☎ 09861/7050; fax 09861/70545). This is the town's top choice, so be sure to reserve rooms well in advance at this centuries-old hotel that was stitched together from four patrician houses. The old Bavarian furnishings are colorful in a busy, undisciplined sort of way; state your preference for modern or traditional decor. Smaller rooms are in back, facing the garden. Some of the marbleized baths have twin sinks. Try for Room no. 102 or 108 or something comparable. The restaurant is excellent (see above). What a lovely way to start the day, eating breakfast in the courtyard. 80 rms with bath; 4 suites. Facilities: restaurant, garden terrace, piano bar. AE, DC, MC, V. Very Expensive.

Goldener Hirsch, Untere Schmiedgasse 16–25, D-91541 Rothenburg (☎ 09861/7080; fax 09861/708100). The better rooms here are comparable in price to those at the Eisenhut, but the standard rooms are considerably cheaper—and just as nice. The hotel has a delightful Louis XVI–style restaurant on a terrace overlooking the town. 72 rms with bath. Facilities: restaurant. AE, DC, MC, V. Closed Jan 8–30. Expensive.

Hotel Reichs-Küchenmeister, Kirchplatz 8, D-91541 Rothenburg (☎ 09861/9700; fax 09861/86-965). One of the city's oldest structures, this hotel was salvaged and restored after a firestorm in World War II and is running smoothly today. Set near St. Jakobskirche, it's built on different levels and contains more amenities than most hotels in town, including a solarium, Turkish bath, and Finnish sauna. Try for one of the beautifully furnished rooms in the main house and not one of the lackluster though comfortable accommodations in the annex across the street. The hotel also has one of the town's best restaurants. 50 rms with bath; 3 suites. AE, DC, MC, V. Moderate.

Landwehrbräu Hotel, Reichelshofen, D-91628 Steinsfeld (☎ 09865/98-90; fax 09865/989686). A short way north of town on Route 25, this traditional country hotel is also a brewery. The 18th-century half-timbered structure has a distinctive steeply arched roof. The cherry wood–paneled restaurant serves regional specialties like seasonal carp and local asparagus, plus four home-produced draft beers (try the rich dark Dunkel). The rustic guest rooms have pinewood furnishings. 30 rms with bath. Facilities: restaurant. DC, MC, V. Closed Jan. Moderate.

Romantik Hotel Markusturm, Rödergasse 1, D-91541 Rothenburg (☎ 09861/20-98; fax 09861/26-92). This family-type hotel just outside the walls is only a few minutes' walk from town center. Some rooms have canopied four-posters; most are small and unpretentious and not without a certain character. Room 17 is as nice as any. In summer, you'll hear the night watchman going his rounds below your window. 27 rms with bath; 2 suites. Facilities: restaurant serving local specialties. AE, DC, MC, V. Very Expensive.

DINKELSBÜHL

Dinkelsbühl offers a smaller, less perfect portrait of the Middle Ages than Rothenburg—but it's also less precious. Rothenburg exists to be looked at, Dinkelsbühl to be lived in. There are fewer tourists here and more people getting on with the business of life. If you have time for only one town along the Romantic Road, make it Rothenburg; but try to find time to see Dinkelsbühl, too. It's small enough that you can "do" it in less than an hour. On any street you can glance back through the centuries at 15th- and 16th-century houses—both gabled and frescoed—and at great half-timber structures up to six stories high. Look for the houses with rich

Renaissance decoration on Martin-Luther Strasse. Particularly notable is the 15th-century **Deutsches Haus,** which now has a small 17th-century Virgin over the entrance. Two other streets to explore are Segringer Strasse, its houses adorned with flowers and picturesque signs, and Nördlingen Strasse, where the houses are out of line.

St. George's is one of the finest Gothic churches of its type in southern Germany. The Romanesque tower rises nearly 200 feet and affords fine views. The interior is a Gothic hall with wonderful fan vaulting and a notable 15th-century Franciscan altar in the south aisle (on your right, facing the main altar).

Accommodations

Deutsches Haus, Weinmarkt 3, D-91550 Dinkelsbühl (☎ **09851/6058;** fax 09851/7911). This 550-year-old half-timbered beauty is the first choice of most visitors. The small privately owned hotel has recently modernized its rooms to a high standard of comfort. 6 rms with bath; 1 suite. Facilities: restaurant serving local specialties. AE, DC, MC, V. Expensive.

Gasthof Weisses Ross, Steingasde 12, D-91555 Dinkelsbühl (☎ **09851/ 2274;** fax 09851/6770). This inexpensive guest house has long been popular with artists, and the rooms have old-fashioned family furniture. The kitchen has a sound reputation for fresh local food: asparagus with spicy ham, trout or carp from local ponds with melted butter and potatoes. Accompany your meal with a glass of Frankenwein Bocksbeutel. 23 rms with bath. AE, DC, MC, V. Closed Jan 15–Feb 15. Moderate.

Goldene Rose, Marktplatz 4, D-91550 Dinkelsbühl (☎ **09851/5-77-50;** fax 09851/577575). The Goldene Rose is as venerable as the Deutsches Haus—Queen Victoria stayed here in 1891—but hasn't as much atmosphere. The restaurant, however, has a good reputation and is the scene of an annual "gourmet week." 33 rms with bath. Facilities: restaurant. AE, DC, MC, V. Moderate.

NÖRDLINGEN

Nördlingen is a less perfect medieval town than Rothenburg or Dinkelsbühl, and its buildings, made from a grayer stone, don't have the same ruddy glow. But the town does have some venerable buildings and you may enjoy walking along the crumbling 14th- and 15th-century ramparts, punctuated by five huge gate towers.

Like every self-respecting German town, Nördlingen has a mighty church near the center, thrusting its stately tower hundreds of feet into the sky. The late 15th-century **St. George's Church** is near Marktplatz. A late Gothic Hall-style building, it has attractive fan vaulting, a baroque organ gallery decorated with hanging keys, a late 15th-century pulpit, and a notable statue of Mary Magdalene that belonged to the original baroque altarpiece. Climb the church steeple for a grand view. Tower accessible Mon–Fri 9am–noon and 2–5pm and Sat–Sun 9am–5pm. Admission 2.50DM adults, 1.50DM children.

Dining

Meyer's Keller, Marienhöhe 8 (☎ 09081/4493). Overlooking the old town, this Bavarian rustic restaurant offers lunch specials ranging from bouillabaisse to venison. Casual. AE, MC, V. Closed Mon. Moderate.

MUNICH

If you arrive in **Munich** from Hamburg or Berlin, you'll realize how much more easygoing the Bavarians are than their neighbors to the north. There life is seen as serious business; here life is seen as short and so should be enjoyed.

Munich, the capital of Bavaria, is the center of rapidly expanding technology and computer industries, yet it retains the status of being the German cultural capital. As well as housing important art galleries and museums, it's home to the greater part of the country's film industry. Munich is also renowned for its beer, breweries, and BMWs. Its festive quality and proximity to the Alps make it the most popular city with Germans.

Why visit Munich? To shop and dine along its pedestrian malls, to wander among the dizzying smells and colors of the outdoor Viktualienmarkt food market, to clink mugs in a funky beer hall, to dine in an elegant three-star restaurant. You'll also want to ride bikes or row boats through the beautiful English Gardens; visit two of Europe's most important museums (one for art, the other for science); and go to the opera. Above all you'll want to soak up the atmosphere of a city impressed with the stamp of royalty—and an "old" city center that was 70% destroyed by bombs during World War II but has been lovingly rebuilt.

The monk on the Munich's coat of arms recalls the city's origin as a monastic settlement (*München* comes from *Mönch*, "monk") around 1100. Eighty years later Bavaria was given to Otto of Wittelsbach—an underling of Holy Roman Emperor Friedrich Barbarossa—and for the next 7 centuries, until 1918, the history of Bavaria and that of this family were intertwined. Munich became the ducal residence in 1255 and the capital of Bavaria in 1503.

People say that the medieval **Church of Our Lady** (Frauenkirche) captures the essence of Munich today, but the city is basically modern and owes its beauty to the taste of Ludwig I of Bavaria (1825–48). Soon after he was crowned, he proclaimed, "I shall make Munich such an honor to Germany that no one who has not seen it can pretend to know the country"; and he proceeded to lay out avenues and found galleries, libraries, and churches. Through his love of Italy and Greece, he attracted architects and artists who built the **Pinakotheken** (art museums), enlarged the **Residenz** (Palace), and constructed Ludwigstrasse.

Ludwig was forced to abdicate as the result of an 18-month affair, at the age of 60, with Irish-born Maria Gilbert, better known as the scandalous dancer Lola Montez. She had burst into his quarters one day to protest her being banned from the stage.

Following the rule of Ludwig's son, Maximilian II (1848–64), the so-called mad King Ludwig II assumed the throne (1864–86). Ludwig II built the castles you'll see during your stay in Garmisch-Partenkirchen. It says much about the people of Munich that they still love Ludwig and protect his memory as a person would protect his dreams.

When Ludwig II was declared insane and removed from the throne, his uncle, Prince Luitpold, son of Ludwig I, assumed the regency. It was he who laid out the great thoroughfare that bears his name, Prinz-regentenstrasse; built the **German Museum** (Deutsches Museum); and completed the **New City Hall** (Neues Rathaus) on Marienplatz.

Begin at **Karlstor,** one of the old city gates on **Karlsplatz,** popularly known as Stachus. Beneath the square is an underground shopping arcade. Pass through the Karlstor and enter the old part of the city, largely destroyed in the war, now the pedestrian street Neuhauserstrasse. On your left is **Bürgersaal Chapel,** which has a rococo interior with some notable frescoes. Still on your left is the single-columned **Richard Strauss fountain,** decorated with scenes from the Munich-born composer's opera *Salome.* Next to the fountain is the **Church of St. Michael** (Michaelskirche; 1583–97), the first large Renaissance church in south Germany and the inspiration for many others. Don't be surprised if you think you're in Rome, because this spacious white stucco building was modeled on the Gesù. It was built for the Jesuits and restored after the war. In the crypt is the tomb of Ludwig II of Bavaria (see "The Royal Castles," below, for notes on Ludwig).

Keep this church in mind as you visit the Church of Our Lady (Frauenkirche), the Church of the Theatines (Theatinerkirche), and the Church of the Asam Brothers (Asamkirche). In these churches you can trace the history of German architecture from Gothic to baroque: The Frauenkirche is Bavarian late Gothic, the Michaelskirche is Renaissance, the Theatinerkirche is late Renaissance but with the rich designs of the Italian baroque, and the Asamkirche shows the full riotous flowering of south German baroque.

Neuhauserstrasse turns into Kaufingerstrasse. On your left, a block past St. Michael's is a street leading to the **Church of Our Lady** (Frauenkirche; 1468–88), Munich's Gothic cathedral. The Frauenkirche has more character than originality, but its onion-shaped domes have been symbols of Munich since they were added in 1525. One of them, purists will be glad to note, is 3 feet higher than the other. Notice, too, the absence of buttresses and the walls running smoothly up to the roof. The redbrick exterior is strikingly plain but massive and has a strength and an integrity missing from many of the more ostentatious, imitative churches around town.

The purity of line is unbroken inside, too. The nave has 22 powerful pillars dividing it into three parts, with simple white walls framing the light from the stained-glass windows. The interior is memorable for its stark whiteness, its height, and the way in which the pillars seem to hide the aisles. The ancient art and furnishings—hidden during

MUNICH

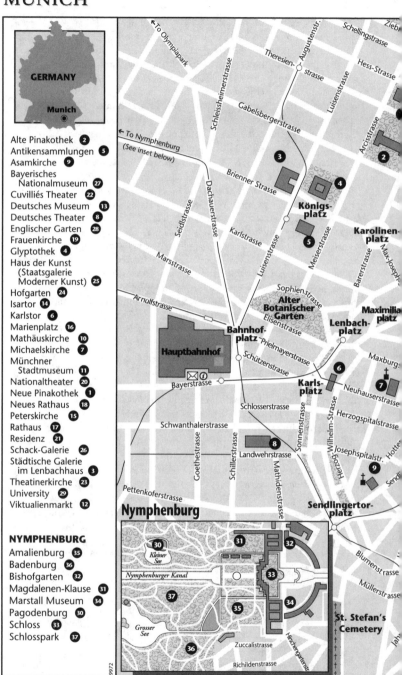

GERMANY

Munich

←To Olympiapark

←To Nymphenburg
(See inset below)

Schellingstrasse

Ziebl

Hess-Strasse

Theresien- strasse

Augustenstr.

Luisenstrasse

Arcisstrasse

Schleissheimerstrasse

Gabelsbergerstrasse

Brienner Strasse

Königs-
platz

Karolinen-
platz

Barerstrasse

Max-Joseph

Dachauerstrasse

Seidlstrasse

Karlstrasse

Luisenstrasse

Meiserstrasse

Marsstrasse

Arnulfstrasse

Sophien-
strasse

Alter
Botanischer
Garten

Elisenstrasse

Maximilia
platz

Lenbach-
platz

Bahnhof-
platz

Prielmayerstrasse

Maxburg

Hauptbahnhof

Schützenstrasse

Karls-
platz

Neuhauserstrasse

Bayerstrasse

Schlosserstrasse

Herzogspitalstrasse

Schwanthalerstrasse

Herzog- Wilhelm-Strasse

Josephspitalstr.

Hotte

Sonnenstrasse

Goethestrasse

Schillerstrasse

Landwehrstrasse

Mathildenstrasse

Sendi

Pettenkoferstrasse

Nymphenburg

Sendlingertor-
platz

Blumenst rasse

Kleiner
See

Nymphenburger Kanal

Bishofgarten

Müllerstrasse

St. Stefan's
Cemetery

Grosser
See

Höchergartenstr.

Zuccalistrasse

Richildenstrasse

Jah

9972

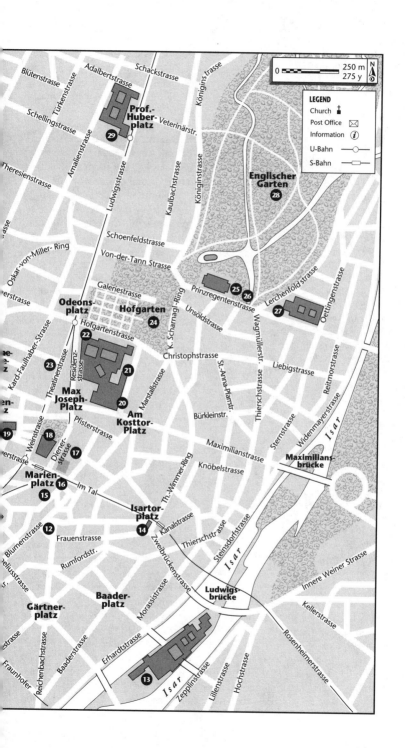

THE ARTS IN HEIDELBERG & MUNICH

In **Heidelberg** summer performances are given in the Castle (Schlosspiele), including *The Student Prince.* Check for organ recitals in the Church of the Holy Ghost (Heiliggeistkirche).

In **Munich,** the tourist office publishes a monthly events brochure, available in bookshops and newspaper kiosks. Munich has a fairy-tale Opera House (Bayerisches Nationaltheater) on Max-Joseph-Platz. The renowned company, which goes back 450 years, performed two premieres by Mozart and no fewer than five by Wagner. Richard Strauss conducted the opera orchestra for 7 years. Tickets are sold at agencies and at the Opera Ticket Office at Maximilianstrasse 11 (☎ 089/221-316; open Mon–Fri 10am–6pm, Sat 10am–1pm). Tickets are in great demand, so arrange to buy them when you make your hotel reservations.

If you want to attend any of Munich's musical, sporting, or theatrical events, you can visit the box office of whatever theater or stadium will host the event and see what tickets are available. A more convenient way, however, involves calling any of the city's three most reputable ticket agencies. They include **München Tickets** (☎ 089/54-81-81-81), specializing in everything from soccer matches, sporting events at the Olympic stadium, operas, and classical concerts; **Bauer & Hieber** (☎ 089/29-00-80), specialists in musical and theatrical events ranging from the intensely formal to the folkloric and Bavarian; and **Won** (☎ 089/260-9942), whose forte is pop and rock concerts.

the war—stand out dramatically against the modern decor. The cathedral houses the tombs of many Wittelsbachs—the royal dynasty that ruled Bavaria for 7 centuries—including that of Ludwig the Bavarian, a 14th-century Holy Roman Emperor. In 1994, celebrations marked the 500th anniversary of the cathedral's consecration.

Continue along Kaufingerstrasse to the square known as **Marienplatz**—the heart of the city, where you'll find luxury shops, cafes, and restaurants. Marienplatz was the central market until 1853 and is still a lively meeting place for people from all walks of life. During summer, street musicians, jugglers, and clowns perform. At Christmas there's a big outdoor market, the Christkindlmarkt, with rows of gaily colored stalls selling tree decorations, small gifts, or Gluhwein (a hot, punchlike alcoholic drink).

To the left of the square is the **New Town Hall** (Neues Rathaus; 1867–1908). One of Ludwig's more fanciful creations, it looks back on the golden age of the city during the Middle Ages, when the Wittelsbach realm included both North and South Germany and the Low Countries. Built in Flemish Gothic style, it was also meant to recall the rich autonomous towns of Flanders and thus the emancipation of Bavaria from the royal house. The Rathaus is nothing but a pastiche of styles, but it's fun and impressive nonetheless. On clear days the view from the **tower** extends as far south as the Alps (elevator operates Apr–Oct, Mon–Sat 10am–5pm; admission 2DM adults, 1DM children). If you're in the square at 11am (also 5pm in summer) or 9pm, you can watch the figures in the Glockenspiel (the town hall clock) spring to life. Two knights joust in honor of a celebrated 16th-century marriage, ending in victory for the Bavarian nobleman. The coopers (makers of wood casks) dance in gratitude for the town's escape from a 16th-century plague. If you arrive too early, find a window table in a third-floor cafe across the square.

South of Marienplatz is **St. Peter's** (Peterskirche), an old Gothic basilica in rococo dress. The archways seem to squeeze the walls together, forcing your eyes upward to God. At the same time, the 12 gilded apostles direct your gaze forward to the golden altar. The 90-meter (300-ft.) tower ("Old Peter") offers another view of the Alps.

From Marienplatz take a short trip down Sendllingerstrasse (a quality shopping street) to the **Church of the Asam Brothers** (Asamkirche; 1733–46) on the right. This jewel box, this spiritual ballroom, built by the brothers Asam, is the town's best example of late German baroque architecture. The brothers constructed it at their own expense in a narrow space between two buildings—which is why the usual east-west axis (the entrance to the west, the altar to the east) has been reversed. Making a virtue of necessity, the brothers installed windows above the door. The light filtering through them forces your eyes from the altar to the suspended figure of Christ and upward to the picture of the Ascension.

The Asams would've understood what Descartes, that master of reason, meant when he said, "The nature of men is such that they value only those things which arouse their admiration, and which they cannot entirely grasp." Note how the walls are molded, as if made of wax or clay. Form, the essence of Renaissance art, dissolves. Everything moves, undulates, flows. Nothing is; everything becomes.

You may not like the Asamkirche because it's the art of the facade. In friends as in furnishings, you don't like to be fooled by surface charm but want things to be what they seem. To the Asam brothers, however, as to all baroque artists, the essence was revealed through appearances. The facade wasn't an escape from or a distortion of reality, but proof of God's kingdom here on Earth.

From the Asamkirche, walk to the busy, colorful outdoor **Food Market** (Viktualienmarkt). A wide selection of wines, cheeses, fruits, vegetables, and flowers is displayed daily, together with game meat like deer and boar. You can also buy some of the best and most intricate dried-flower posies.

TAKE A BREAK

*There are numerous snack (imbiss) stalls here offering sausages and spicy meat-balls (Fleischpflanzerl). Try the **Schlemermeyer** kiosk, or the **Nordsee** buffet for delicious fish nibbles. There's also a beer garden in the square.*

Return to St. Peter's Church, near Marienplatz. On the northeast side is Burgstrasse. At no. 5 is the **Weinstadl** (1552), the oldest house in town. At no. 10, take the passage right to Lederstrasse and turn left on the pedestrian Orlandostrasse to Platzl. Here you'll find the **Hofbräuhaus,**

Am Platzl 9 (☎ 089/22-16-76), the most famous of Munich's beer halls. The atmosphere is as heady as the ale, which is drunk from large glass mugs. Take Pfisterstrasse to the **Old Castle** (Alter Hof) on your left and turn right on Hofgraben to Maximilianstrasse. Cross over to Max-Joseph-Platz. On your right is the **National Theater** (Nationaltheater), which houses the Bavarian State Opera.

Ahead of you, across the square, is the entrance to the **Residenz** (Palace), Max-Joseph-Platz 2 (☎ 089/29-06-71) — the home of the dukes of Wittelsbach for more than 650 years. Restored since the war, the Residenz contains a Treasury with beautiful crucifixes, diadems, and illuminated books; and a Palace Museum with both gilded State Rooms and Porcelain Rooms displaying masterpieces from Nymphenburg and Sèvres. Admission to both 5DM adults, 3DM students and seniors; under 15 free. Open Tues–Sun 10am–4:30pm.

The Residenz is bordered on the west by Residenzstrasse, which takes you to Odeonsplatz, overlooked by the lofty **Church of the Theatines** (Theatinerkirche; 1663–75). The elaborate stucco work in the chancel and dome are indicative of baroque at its best. From Theatinerkirche, head back down Residenzstrasse to Maximilianstrasse. Many of Munich's most expensive shops are along this street.

If you find the following places too far to reach by foot and you're taking public transportation, save money with multijourney blue Streifenkarten (strip tickets) or a Tageskarte, which allows unlimited travel for up to two adults and three children for a whole day. Both are valid for use on the city's network of buses, subways (U-Bahn), and trams.

Schwabing, a 10-minute subway ride from the city center, is a fashionable suburb bordering the English Gardens (Englischer Garten). A onetime Greenwich Village–style student quarter, Schwabing is now a place for the chic sidewalk cafe set by day and the dance club or jazz bar crowd by night. Schwabing's heart is Münchener Freiheit (take subway no. 3 or 6), home of the best ice-cream parlors. Try **Café Münchener Freiheit,** Münchener Freiheit (☎ 089/383-9080), and be sure to notice the wonderful marzipan figures in the shop window.

While visiting Schwabing, stroll through the lovely **Englischer Garten** — Munich's most famous park and Europe's largest city park. You can jog, ride rented bikes, row boats on a lake, or quench your thirst under the chestnut trees at the Chinese Tower beer garden, which actually has a Chinese pagoda where a Bavarian brass band entertains the crowd (weekends and Wednesdays). Here you can hire a horse-drawn carriage for a ride around the park (bus no. 54 stops at the beer garden).

Anyone with even a passing interest in art will want to visit the **Alte Pinakothek** (the old picture gallery), Barer Strasse 27 (☎ 089/238-05215), housing the painting collections of several centuries of Wittelsbachs, beginning in the early 16th century. Under Ludwig I, the Alte Pinakothek became one of the top art museums in Europe. The collection includes notable works by Dürer, Altdorfer, Raphael, Titian,

Leonardo, Van Dyck, Rubens, Rembrandt, and El Greco. Since the gallery was closed at press time, before heading here, call to see if it's open or check with the tourist office; reopening is scheduled for sometime in 1997.

Nearby is the **Neue Pinakothek,** Barer Strasse 29 (☎ 089/23-80-51-95), featuring works by the French impressionists (Monet, Degas, and others) and modern German painting, beginning with the wonderfully tasteless sentimental works of the German Romantics. Admission 6DM adults, 3.50DM students and seniors; 15 and under free. Open Tues and Thurs 10am–8pm, Wed and Fri–Sun 10am–5pm.

Straddling an island in the Isar River is the **Deutsches Museum** (German Museum), Museumsinsel 1 (☎ 089/2-17-91), one of the world's outstanding museums of science and technology. You can travel from prehistory to the space age in an hour, but the scale models and hands-on exhibits could keep you and your kids happy for days. Admission 9DM adults, 6DM seniors, 3DM students, 2.50DM children 6–12; 5 and under free. Open daily 9am–5pm (closed second Wed in Dec and major holidays).

Nymphenburg, Schloss Nymphenburg 1 (☎ 089/17-908-668; take tram no. 12 from Rotkreuzplatz or U-Bahn 1 from the Haupfbanhof), is the former summer palace of the Bavarian rulers. The oldest part dates from 1664, with buildings and arcades added during the next century. The rococo Hall of Mirrors is an exercise in wowmanship. In the Gallery of Beauty (Schönheitengalerie) Ludwig I collected portraits of beautiful women, both rich and poor, including his beloved Lola, for whom he forfeited his kingdom; see if you share his taste. It's not surprising that a back room upstairs was Ludwig II's favorite—it's so remote. In the peaceful park of woodland and lakes behind the palace you may spot wild deer. The park adjoins the colorful **Botanic Gardens,** which include tropical-plant greenhouses. The park also houses the **Amalienburg hunting lodge,** a rococo masterpiece, where no one seems to have hunted for anything but pleasure. Animals, birds, leaves—all join in a dance that captures the joy and movement of the chase.

Kids in particular will love the **Museum of Royal Carriages** (Marstallmuseum), where a mermaid holds the lamp on Ludwig II's carriage. Could anything be less appropriate? One floor above the Marstallmuseum is a Museum of Porcelain, containing the finest examples of Nymphenburg porcelain made between 1747 and the 1920s. Combined ticket to the palace, Marstallmuseum, Museum of Porcelain, and the pavilions of the park, 8DM adults, 5DM children 6–14; 5 and under free. For Nymphenburg palace, Amalienburg, Marstallmuseum, and Museum of Porcelain only, 6DM adults, 4DM children. Open Apr–Sept, Tues–Sun 9am–5pm; Oct–Mar, Tues–Sun 10am–4pm.

"Those who cannot remember the past are condemned to repeat it," says the brochure for the 4-hour morning tours to the Concentration Camp memorial at **Dachau.** In this ultimate symbol of Nazi atrocities, 20 kilometers (12 miles) northwest of Munich, more than 32,000 prisoners lost their lives. The camp, **KZ-Gedenkstätte Dachau,** lies at Alte-Roemar-Strasse 75 (☎ 08131/84566), reached by frequent S-Bahn trains (S-2) from Munich's Hauptbahnhof. Free admission. Open Tues–Sun 9am–5pm.

DINING

Müncheners, with their appetite for Bavarian specialties, keep scores of snack-bar stalls (schnell imbiss) busy all day long. Try Leberkäs, a beef-and-pork meat loaf served with sharp mustard; Fleischflanzerl, spicy meatballs; or Schweinswürstl, small grilled pork sausages often served with sauerkraut. The best stalls are in the **Viktualienmarkt.**

A favorite late breakfast (Brotzeit) dish is Weisswurst, the succulent white sausage made with veal and parsley. The best ones—made right on the premises—are served at **Franziskaner,** Perustrasse 5 (☎ 089/231-8120), to which locals flock in the early morning, downing almost as much beer as Weisswurst. The place is filled with long wooden tables and cavernous rooms off of which are several *intime* dining areas.

Beer-garden specialties include Steckelfisch, charcoal-grilled mackerel on a stick; Radi, a giant white radish sliced wafer thin; and Obatz'n, a spicy cocktail of Camembert cheese, butter, spring onions, paprika, and caraway seeds.

A. Boettner's, Theatinerstr. 8 (☎ 089/221-210). This is Munich's longest-running upscale culinary experience. In business since 1901, Boettner's has the decor to match its history—dark mahogany woodwork and attentive, stiffly collared waiters. Fresh seafood is the specialty, from oysters (flown in daily) to lobster, which sometimes appears in a soufflé or stew. Reservations required. Jacket/tie required. AE, DC, MC, V. Closed Sat evening, Sun, holidays. Very Expensive.

Alois Dallmayr's, Dienerstr. 14–15 (☎ 089/213-5100). This is Munich's answer to London's Fortnum & Mason: a black-tie gourmet food shop with a busy, sophisticated upstairs restaurant. It's an ideal trysting place for a hot lunch or salad or a gooey dessert you'll be talking about for years. Reservations required. Jacket/tie required. AE, DC, MC, V. Closed Sat evening, Sun, holidays. Expensive.

Augustiner Gastätte, Neuhauserstr. 27 on the pedestrian mall (☎ 089/551-99257). This restaurant serves a broad selection of good-quality Bavarian dishes at reasonable prices. Wash down your meal with the favorite beer of the locals in a bustling Central European atmosphere. Best bets: Schweinehaxen, crispy knuckle of pork, or spanferkel, tender grilled chops. Don't confuse this place with the much more famous Augustinerkeller. Reservations advised early evening. Casual. AE, DC, MC, V. Inexpensive.

Chesa Rüegg, Wurzerstr. 18 (☎ 089/297-114). Close to the Hotel Vier Jahreszeiten, this excellent Swiss restaurant features a yodelly Engadine look, with copper pans and beamed ceilings. Popular dishes are fresh lobster, Geschnetzeltes (shredded veal), and traditional Swiss fare like

Flädi-suppe (pancake soup) and Rösti (pan-fried potatoes). Reservations advised. Casual. AE, DC, MC, V. Closed weekends and holidays. Moderate.

Käferschänke, Schumannstr. 1 (☎ 089/416-82-47). This is another food delicacy stopover, offering fresh fish, Caspian caviar, and Hungarian goose liver. The seafood is imported daily from the south of France. The relaxed restaurant adjoining the store is a mixture of small wood-paneled rooms (Stuben) and elegant Victorian-style furnishings. A daily-changing menu concentrates on fish. Reservations required. Jacket/tie advised. AE, DC, MC. Closed Sun and holidays. Moderate.

Königshof, Karlsplatz 25 (☎ 089/551-360). This place serves the best hotel food in town. The belle epoque terrace restaurant has picture windows overlooking the busy Karlsplatz. The international cuisine is a mix of moderne and classical, with such favorites as lobster soufflé, loin of lamb with fines herbes, and sea bass suprême. Reservations advised. Jacket/tie advised. AE, DC, MC, V. Very Expensive.

Ratskeller München, Im Rathaus, Marienplatz 8 (☎ 089/22-03-13). Here's the best Town Hall dining hall in Bavaria, although a bit touristy because of its location at Marienplatz in the exact center of Munich. Nevertheless, you get the widest assortment of solid and robust Bavarian cookery in town, a virtual showcase of regional food. Many dishes are too heavy and "porky" for modern tastes, but a selection of lighter continental fare is available, including dishes prepared with the vegetarian in mind. Bavarian music adds to the gemütlich atmosphere. Reservations advised. Casual. AE, MC, V. Moderate.

Straubinger Hof, Blumenstr. 5 (☎ 089/260-8444). Near St. Peter's Church and the Outdoor Market (Viktualienmarkt), this is the place for hard-to-find Bavarian specialties, such as baked udder and pudding as well as pork with root vegetables. If you can pronounce it, try kälberne Briesmilzwurst in aufgeschmelzter Brotsuppe—a soup that'll keep you strong for the rest of the day. Other popular dishes are roast suckling pig with potato dumplings and Kaiserschmarren, a pancake with eggs and apples. One portion per family, please! Reservations required only for six or more. Casual. AE, MC, V. Closed Sun, holidays, and Sat evening. Inexpensive.

Tantris, Johann-Fichte-Strasse 7 (☎ 089/36-20-61). Munich's best restaurant is the domain of chef Hans Haas, voted Germany's top chef by the country's food critics in 1994—if anything, he's better than ever. Bavaria has no more innovative chef than this culinary wiz who likes to dazzle visiting celebrities and others with his moderne dishes. Try his terrine of smoked fish with a green cucumber sauce, roasted wood pigeon with scented rice, or classic roast duck with a mustard-seed sauce. The chef shops for only the finest and freshest of ingredients, which he cleverly transforms into dishes designed to enhance natural flavors. Reservations required. Jacket/tie required. AE, DC, MC, V. Closed lunch Sat–Mon and all day Sun. Very Expensive.

A visit to Munich would be incomplete without sampling the atmosphere of a **beer hall** or **beer garden** in summer. The city has six big breweries, plus a growing number of fashionable "house" breweries, where the beer is brewed in the pub and you can watch the process as you sit and sip. The most famous hall is the **Hofbräuhaus,** Am Platzl 9 (☎ 089/22-16-76), but it's now so overrun with tourists it's worth a miss. For local earthiness try the **Hirschgarten,** Hirschgartenstrasse 1 (☎ 089/17-25-91), in the Nymphenburg Park sector, west of the center. In a 500-acre park with hunting lodges and lakes, this is Munich's largest open-air restaurant, seating some 8,000 beer drinkers. The **Biergarten Chinesischer Turm,** Englischer Garten 3 (☎ 089/38-38-730), attracts those who flock to the English Garden, lying between the Isar River and Schwabing. The beer steins are enormous, and on weekends a brass band plays from inside the tower. The train deposits you virtually in the pub. The most central Biergarten is in the center of the Viktualienmarkt.

Munich is also famous for its **wine taverns,** where the emphasis is on drinking rather than eating. Try the **Pfälzer Weinprobierstube,** Residenzstrasse 1 (☎ 089/225-628), for a wide selection of wines served in stone arched rooms with a thigh-slapping atmosphere; or the **Weinstadl,** Burgstrasse 5 (☎ 089/290-40-44).

ACCOMMODATIONS

Reservations are advisable, but if you arrive without a booking, go to the city **tourist office** (☎ 089/233-302-56; open Mon–Sat 9am–9pm, Sun 11am–7pm) in the main train station (Hauptbahnhof) opposite Track 11. Bookings aren't accepted by phone. Munich's larger hotels are extremely expensive, with double rooms upward of 350DM, but most also offer significant weekend discounts.

An der Oper, Falkenturmstr. 11, D-80331 München (☎ 089/290-0270; fax 089/290-02-729). This small, cheerful, but fairly plain hotel in an ancient side street wedged between the Opera House and the Hofbräuhaus is popular with show-business people. 55 rms with bath. Facilities: restaurant, wine bar. AE, MC, V. Expensive.

Bayerischer Hof, Promenadeplatz 6, D-80333 München (☎ 089/21-200; fax 089/2120906). This is a very large, traditional hotel with a well-heeled clientele. The lobby has Italian marble floors, painted marble columns, and raw wood—an interesting blend of Caesar and Ludwig. The older rooms provide ornate comfort; the newer ones offer functionalism. State your preference. For a taste of something different in central Europe, try the Polynesian food in Trader Vic's restaurant in the basement. 440 rms with bath; 5 suites. Facilities: three restaurants, nightclub, rooftop pool, garage, sauna, masseur, hairdresser. AE, DC, MC, V. Very Expensive.

Domus, St. Annastr. 31, D-80538 München (☎ 089/221-704; fax 089/228-53-59). Close to the heart of the city but also handy for the Englischer Garten and Haus der Kunst, an art gallery, and one of the few surviving examples of Nazi-commissioned architecture, this isn't cheap for a small hotel but provides personal, friendly service. 45 rms with bath; 2 suites. Facilities: bar serving snacks. AE, DC, MC, V. Expensive.

Gästehaus Englischer Garten, Liebergesellstr. 8, D-80802 München-Schwabing (☎ **089/392-034;** fax 089/39-12-33). This converted ivy-covered 19th-century mill is only steps from Munich's largest and loveliest park. The rooms are plain, but the hotel is beautifully located and booking is necessary well in advance. Bed and breakfast only. 12 rms, 6 with bath. No credit cards. Moderate.

Hotel Pension Beck, Thierschstr. 36, D-80538 München (☎ **089/ 220-708;** fax 089/22-09-25). This is very much a functional pension, though clean and well run. It's convenient to the old center, museums, and the Englischer Garten. Tram no. 20 stops outside. 44 rms, 8 with bath. No credit cards. Inexpensive.

Hotel Splendid, Maximilianstr. 54, D-80538 München (☎ **089/ 296-606;** fax 089/29-131-76). The Splendid offers excellent homey service in cozy surroundings. In warm weather, breakfast is served in a pretty inner courtyard. 40 rms with bath, 1 suite. Facilities: bar serving light meals. AE, DC, MC, V. Expensive.

Königin Elizabeth's, Leonrodstr. 79, D-80636 München (☎ **089/ 126-860;** fax 089/126-86459). The restored neoclassical facade hides a modern but tasteful hotel, 15 minutes northwest of the center on a street-car route. If you like the color pink you'll feel extra cozy here. 79 rms with bath. Facilities: restaurant, bar, whirlpool, steam bath, sauna, fitness club, masseuse (by appointment). AE, DC, MC, V. Expensive.

Kriemhild, Guntherstr. 16, D-80396 München (☎ **089/178-09912;** fax 089/177-874). Here's an attractive place to stay if you're on a tight budget, have your family along, and don't mind being some distance from center city. It's very close to the Nymphenburg Palace, Botanic Gardens, and Munich's biggest and most famous beer garden, the Hirschgarten, and is reached by tram no. 17 from the main station. The family-run pension lays on the sort of breakfast that'll keep you going through the day. 18 rms, 12 with bath. Facilities: bar. AE, MC, V. Inexpensive.

Uhland Garni, Uhlandstr. 1, D-80336 München (☎ **089/54-33-50;** fax 089/54-33-5250). This small family-run hotel is in a pretty four-story Victorian house on a tree-lined street close to the site of the Oktoberfest. The rooms are bright and cheerful but not luxurious. A buffet breakfast is served. 27 rms with bath. DC, MC, V. Moderate.

Vier Jahreszeiten, Maximilianstr. 17, D-80539 München (☎ **089/ 221-50;** fax 089/212-52-000). The Four Seasons is on Munich's most exclusive shopping street and is one of the city's renowned hotels. It's part of a chain but still retains its old charm and continues to attract the famous. A quiet dignity pervades the public rooms, with their rich mahogany paneling. The rooms have a friendly, residential hotel feel—more Teutonic than Bavarian, with old-fashioned couches and framed botanicals. The less expensive rooms are smaller but thoughtfully furnished. 316 rms with bath; 48 suites. Facilities: restaurant, nightclub, pool, sauna, garage, car-rental service. AE, DC, MC, V. Very Expensive.

The Alps

The Autobahn (A95) whirls you through the **Alps** from Munich to Garmisch-Partenkirchen in only an hour. A slower, more scenic route is described below.

Andechs

Take A96 west of Munich and follow the exit signs to the Ammersee. If you're a beer drinker, you may want to take a roundabout route to Garmisch to taste what many Bavarians tell their overseas guests is one of the best beers in Germany—the dark, rich Andechser Bergbock—not a beer to be trifled with, especially if you're driving. It's made in a genuine monastery brewery (Klosterbrauerei), next door to the abbey in the village of **Andechs,** 6.4 kilometers (4 miles) south of Herrsching—a terminus town on the Munich S-Bahn rail system—and the 17.6-kilometer (11-mile) Ammersee (Ammer Lake). The Gothic **Abbey Church** (Klosterkirche), now in rococo dress, is in itself well worth a visit.

Murnau

The fast route is south from Munich on A95 for about 45 minutes to the **Murnau** exit. The more scenic route is via Andechs and Route 2.

Accommodations

Alpenhof Murnau, Ramsachstr. 8, D-82418 München (☎ **08841/1910;** fax 08841/5438). Here's a tasteful, comfortable modern hotel with traditional furnishings and the area's best dining. The hotel is in a peaceful rural setting with a distant view of the Alps: a sensible place to stay if you leave Munich in the afternoon and don't want to deal with Garmisch until the following day. 44 rms. Facilities: restaurant, outdoor heated pool, gardens. AE, MC, V. Expensive.

Garmisch-Partenkirchen

Garmisch-Partenkirchen is Germany's largest winter-sports complex, built almost entirely since World War I. The two towns—the hyphen is the stream that flows between them—sit in a valley ringed by the Bavarian Alps, including Germany's highest peak, the Zugspitze. Though originally a ski resort (the host for the 1936 winter Olympic Games), Garmisch-Partenkirchen has become a town for all seasons—the base for year-round sports and excursions into the countryside.

What Garmisch-Partenkirchen isn't is a quaint alpine village like Zermatt, huddled beneath towering peaks. It also lacks the panache of St. Moritz and seems to insinuate itself, rather than grow out of the alpine setting. On the positive side, it can give you all the pampering you want after a day in the great outdoors and has hotels and restaurants for all tastes and budgets. It makes an ideal base for hikes, scenic drives, cable-car rides, and visits both to the royal castles of Ludwig II and to the Passion Play village of Oberammergau. If that's not enough, the town has six Olympic-size pools and three indoor skating rinks that seat 12,000! Furthermore, despite its success, Garmisch-Partenkirchen has remained small in scale, with nothing higher than an alpine roof. Garmisch itself is the more fashionable and expensive part of town — more central to the cafes and nighttime activities; Partenkirchen is more low-key and family-oriented. But should both Garmisch and Partenkirchen be too commercial for your taste, you can stay in any of dozens of charming family-run chalets on the roads up to the mountains, and, like the American troops stationed nearby, come into town for R&R.

The ski slopes are open from December to May, but the cog railway and cable car to the highest peak, the **Zugspitze,** 2,966 meters (9,734 ft.), are open year-round, and a trip to the top is the area's number-one tourist attraction. The train trip from Garmisch station takes 75 minutes. Cable cars operate from Eibsee, about halfway up from Garmisch. You can buy a combination ticket (72DM adults round-trip; 42DM children under 16; under 4 free) for the train and cable car, which also includes a separate cable ride for the final 316 meters (1,037 ft.) from the Hotel Schneefernerhaus, just below the peak. More information is available from the **Bayerische Zugspitzbahn,** Olympiastrasse 27, Garmisch-Partenkirchen (☎ 08821/79-70). The train bores through a 4-kilometer (2½-mile) tunnel to the Hotel Schneefernerhaus. The hotel, despite panoramic views, is more for serious skiers than for lovers or tourists, since it has only single beds; and when the last train or cable car descends, there's nowhere to go. (The hotel does serve dinner, which is included in the rate.)

A popular cable-car ride if you have less time is a 20-minute trip direct from Partenkirchen to the 1,751.9-meter (5,840-ft.) summit of the **Wank.** The most dramatic high-altitude hike for the casual traveler in good condition is to take the cable car to the top of the Wank and walk along the ridge.

Another dramatic walk — one anyone can make if the route is not blocked by snow — is through **Partnachklamm Gorge,** following a trail gouged from a ledge of rock above the frothing or frozen water. Park near the Partenkirchen Sports Stadium and walk or take a horse-drawn carriage to the Graseck cable car (the road is closed to cars). Take the cable car to the lower station. There's a modern hotel here, the **Forsthaus Graseck Inn,** Am Graseck 4, D-82467 Garmisch-Partenkirchen (☎ 08821/54-006), where you can stop for lunch or drinks and take in the view on the sun terrace at 899.75 meters (2,950 ft.). If you like high-altitude living, you can stay in one of its 75 well-furnished rooms with bath. From the inn, a path leads up one slope of the valley. Don't take the first right, which descends into the valley; continue past the Wetterstein-Alm Inn (a friendly place for a snack but closed Saturday), and then turn right, to the bottom of the gorge, which you follow downstream. It's an easy walk, all downhill, back to your car.

You can test your luck at the town's casino, **Spielbank Garmisch-Partenkirchen,** Am Kurpark 74 (☎ 08821/53-099; open daily 3pm–2am). Admission is 5DM per person and presentation of a passport is required. Between 3 and 8pm, only roulette and the slot machines are available, and men must wear jackets. Beginning at 8pm, men must wear jackets and ties and noise of the roulette tables and slot machines are enhanced with blackjack tables. Baccarat, because of lack of interest, is no longer offered within the casino, but every Friday and Saturday, games of seven-card stud poker are arranged.

Dining

Gasthof Fraundorfer, Ludwigstr. 24 (☎ 08821/2176). This place offers a more down-to-earth evening. Try the schnitzel or the schweinebraten. Closed Tues and Nov 6–Dec 6. Casual. AE, MC, V. Inexpensive.

Reindl-Grill, in the Hotel Partenkirchner Hof, Bahnhofstr. 15 (☎ 08821/58-025). This place focuses more on food than on decor. It's not just a grill, it's an above-average restaurant serving the very freshest fish, veal, venison, and seasonal vegetables. Try the veal filets in Sauerrahmsosse (sour-cream sauce). For dessert, the homemade apple pie is justly popular. Casual. AE, DC, MC, V. Closed mid-Nov to mid-Dec. Moderate.

Restaurant Alpenhof im Casino, Bahnhofstr. 74 (☎ 08821/59-055). Here you'll find one adequate restaurant with local dishes at moderate prices, and a smaller Casino Stube for people who are willing to pay for a top French meal. Jacket advised. DC, MC, V. Moderate/Expensive.

Riessersee, Reiss 6 (☎ 08821/9-54-40). This restaurant lies on the shore of a small lake with emerald-green waters. Signposted from the center of town, it's reached after one of the loveliest 2-kilometer (1¼-mile) strolls in the area. Ideal for a leisurely lunch or afternoon tea, it offers solid Bavarian fare and homemade cakes along with luscious fruit-studded ice cream. Many stop over here after exploring the Zugspitze, soothing their nerves with the sound of zither music played on weekends. Some of the best veal dishes in the area are served here. Casual. No credit cards. Inexpensive.

Romantik Clausings Posthotel, Marienplatz 12 (☎ 08821/7090). This hotel offers two dining venues to suit different tastes: romantic candlelit gourmet dinners are served in the Klause restaurant, or you can eat Bavarian style in the noisier Post Hörndl tavern, with dancing and folk music. Tavern, casual; restaurant, jacket/tie required. AE, DC, MC, V. Expensive.

Tonihof, Walchenseestr. 42, Eschenlohe (☎ 08824/1021). About 14.4 kilometers (9 miles) from Garmisch is one of the best restaurants south of Munich. The moderne menu features fresh fish, poultry, vegetables, and fruit. Reservations advised. Jacket/tie required. No credit cards. Closed Wed. Expensive.

Garmisch has many pleasant outdoor cafes where you can people-watch under a crowd of stars. Try the moderately priced **Café-Konditorei Krönner,** Achenfelderstrasse 1 (☎ 08821/3007 or 08821/950713; closed Mon).

Many of the smaller restaurants and hotels in the town and surrounding countryside take a holiday break mid-November to mid-December before the hectic winter season.

Accommodations

Almost all the hotels here are low-roofed alpine chalets with carved wood balconies. Ask for a room with a view.

Dorint Sporthotel, Mittenwalderstr. 59, D-82467 Garmisch-Partenkirchen (☎ 08821/7060; fax 08821/706618). This hotel offers a wide range of facilities, particularly for the athletic, but you can also retire to your rustic-style apartment after an unenergetic evening at the in-house wine tavern. If your children are along, they can keep themselves busy in the playroom while you try your hand at tennis or bowling or take a skiing lesson in the hotel school. 152 apts. Facilities: two restaurants, two bars, gardens, indoor pool, solarium, sauna. AE, DC, MC, V. Very Expensive.

Garmischer Hof, Chamonix 10, D-82467 Garmisch-Partenkirchen (☎ 08821/51-091). Centrally located close to the train station, this hotel offers country Bavarian-style comfort, rooms with mountain views, and pleasant gardens. The room price includes a generous Bavarian buffet breakfast—just the thing to set you up for a day in the fresh mountain air. 49 rms with bath. Facilities: cafe, bar. AE, DC, MC, V. Moderate.

Gasthof Fraundorfer, Ludwigstr. 24, D-82467 Garmisch-Partenkirchen (☎ 08821/2176; fax 08821/71-073). You'll find this colorful family-run Bavarian inn in old Partenkirchen. Josef and Bärbel Fraundorfer provide traditional Bavarian hospitality—from the kitchen to the musical evenings featuring accordion music and folk dancing. 30 rms with bath. Closed Tues and Nov 6–Dec 6. AE, MC, V. Inexpensive.

Grand-Hotel Sonnenbichl, Burgstr. 97, D-82467 Garmisch-Partenkirchen (☎ 08821/7020; fax 08821/70-21-31). This old-world hotel, which welcomes you with an Italianate marble foyer, is fed by Arab money. The hotel's symbol is the peacock—could anything be more un-Bavarian? The only drawbacks are the hotel's lack of privacy (it's close to the road) and the necessity of looking out over the traffic to see the distant mountains. Be sure to get an upstairs room with a mountain view; at these prices, you don't want to stare out at the parking lot. 90 rms with bath; 3 suites. Facilities: restaurant Blauer Salon (moderne cuisine), Bavarian-style bar, sauna, solarium, heated pool, tennis, golf. AE, DC, MC, V. Very Expensive.

Haus Kornmüller, Höllentalstr. 36, D-82467 Garmisch-Partenkirchen (☎ 08821/3557; fax 08821/57426). This ornate wood-balconied guest house is set in gardens, a 2-minute walk from the center of town. Because of the presence of small kitchens in each unit and its low prices, it appeals to budget-conscious travelers. Although the main house no longer offers accommodations of any kind, an adjoining apartment building contains 8 units. 8 units with kitchen, 6 with bath. AE, MC, V. Inexpensive.

Hotel Roter Hahn, Bahnhofstr. 44, D-82467 Garmisch-Partenkirchen
(☎ 08821/54-065). This hotel is only 3 minutes from the station and the
Zugspitzbahn, the special railway to the mountain peak. It's a fairly functional place for people who aren't going to spend a lot of time at home;
surprisingly for a hotel of its class, it does boast an indoor pool. 32 rms
with bath. Facilities: pool. V. Moderate.
Obermühle, Mühlstr. 22, D-82467 Garmisch-Partenkirchen (☎ 800/
528-1234 or 08821/7040; fax 08821/70-41-12). An old waterwheel turns
outside to remind you of the hotel's antiquity—it dates from 1634, though
there's not much of the original left to see. It has all the modern facilities
of a Best Western, plus some Bavarian-style rustic decor. 87 rms with
bath; 4 suites. Facilities: restaurant, wine bar, indoor pool, sauna, solarium. AE, DC, MC, V. Expensive.
Posthotel Partenkirchen, Ludwigstr. 49, D-82464 Garmisch-
Partenkirchen (☎ 08821/51-067; fax 08821/78568). This, one of the
oldest buildings in the locality, dates from 1542 and claims to have enter-
tained Bavarian kings on their journeys through the district. It's a classic
of the "post house" style—that of the staging places where horse-drawn
coaches carrying travelers and mail stopped to rest. There's lovely paneling and stuccowork, and some colorful antiques, including old painted
chests and carved armoires. 56 rms with bath; 3 suites. Facilities: restaurant (a mix of French style and Bavarian cooking). AE, DC, MC, V.
Expensive.

ON TO ETTAL

Everybody's favorite trip from **Garmisch** is to the three royal castles iden-
tified with Ludwig II: Neuschwanstein, Hohenschwangau, and Linderhof. You have a choice of two routes: a northern route through
Oberammergau, and a southern route past Linderhof. The mountainous
southern route is more dramatic and has the added perk of a trip to
another country (Austria). Your best bet is to take one route going and the
other coming back. If you plan to visit Linderhof, begin with the southern
route so you reach the castle early in the day; otherwise, you won't get
here until after it's closed.

The following itinerary takes you to the castles by this southern route
and returns you by the northern route. It's going to be a long day, so leave
early and don't expect to return to Garmisch until dark.

ETTAL

Take Route 23 north from Garmisch-Partenkirchen to Oberau, and
continue about 4.8 kilometers (3 miles) to **Ettal.** The size of the abbey—
now a boarding school—is extraordinary. It was founded by Ludwig the
Bavarian in 1330 but wears 18th-century baroque dress.

The road splits past Ettal. The right fork (Route 23) continues north
to Oberammergau. Take the left fork to Linderhof.

Dining

Ludwig der Bayer, Kaiser Ludwig Platz 10, Ettal (☎ **08822/6601**). This hotel/restaurant is in the center of town, opposite the abbey. Stop for some yellow or green Kloster liqueur produced by the monks or for one of the five varieties of beer they brew. Reservations recommended. Casual. No credit cards. Moderate.

THE ROYAL CASTLES (KÖNIGSSCHLÖSSER)

Of the three castles, Neuschwanstein is the most impressive, Linderhof the least. But whether you have time to see one castle, two, or all three, it helps to know about the man whose life was intimately entwined with all of them—Ludwig II. It's important, too, to understand the symbolism of the swan, which you'll see so often as you tour the castles.

Ludwig II, the son of Maximilian II, was born in 1845 in Nymphenburg Castle (in Munich) but spent almost all his youth at his father's castle, Hohenschwangau, in the Bavarian Alps. This was a fairy fortress, capturing the spirit of the Middle Ages, where Maximilian could escape the pressures of Munich's official life. The walls of Hohenschwangau were covered with paintings of the swan knight Lohengrin, and the impressionable young Ludwig fell under their spell. Maximilian gave his son a spartan education, seldom allowing him to see the real world. The boy turned his back on his stern father and played not with soldiers but with puppets and dolls. His mother—one of the few women he ever saw—read him the Greek myths, including the story of how Zeus created swans from the waves.

When news came that his father was dying, Ludwig was absorbed in the text of Wagner's *Lohengrin,* based on a medieval German story of the knight Lohengrin, son of Parsifal, who sets off from the Castle of the Grail on the back of a swan to rescue the Princess Elsa. In the German legend, he saves her and is given her hand in marriage; but when she asks his name, in violation of a pledge, he must return to his castle and the swan turns into Elsa's brother.

In 1864, at the age of 18, Ludwig became the king of Bavaria. One of his first royal wishes was to meet with the German composer Richard Wagner, who was at the time living at the Bayerischer Hof in Munich, in flight from his creditors. Ludwig had seen *Lohengrin* 4 years earlier and lived for the moment when he could meet its creator and help produce his plays. The 51-year-old composer met the 19-year-old king at Hohenschwangau and thereafter became his soul mate, his confidant, his adviser.

Three years after assuming the throne, Ludwig became engaged to his cousin, Princess Sophie of Bavaria, a sister of the Austrian empress, Elizabeth. He is said never to have kissed her on the lips, only on the forehead, but he was wildly in love with her—why else would he have spent his days rowing with her in a swan-shaped boat? And why else would he have called her Elsa?

As the wedding day approached, Ludwig ordered his trousseau bro-caded with scenes from *Lohengrin.* But then at a ball for the royal couple, he rushed off to catch the last act of an opera without saying good-bye to anyone, including Sophie, and everyone knew the engagement was in trouble. Sophie, he had discovered, was only human. "When I marry, I want a Queen, a Mother for my country, not an imperious mistress," he explained later. But he never married. Instead, he flew back to Wagner. And on the ruins of an ancient castle near his father's, he decided to build an even grander castle of his own.

Neuschwanstein is a child's idea of a medieval knight's castle. It took 17 years to build but was never finished. As Ludwig became embroiled in hopeless wars, he withdrew more into himself and emptied his country's treasury to satisfy his fantasies. He began Linderhof, a rococo pleasure palace with an artificial Blue Grotto in imitation of the one at Capri. And he built Herrenchiemsee, modeled on Versailles, on an island in the Chiemsee, a large lake in southeast Bavaria.

In June 1886, Ludwig was declared insane by a state commission that visited Neuschwanstein and diagnosed him to be suffering from advanced paranoia. He was taken to Berg, overlooking Starnberg Lake, near Munich. On June 13—3 days after his uncle Luitpold had been named his successor as prince regent—both Ludwig and Dr. Bernhard von Gudden, the psychiatrist into whose care he'd been entrusted, were found dead in the lake. The official version of the deaths is that Ludwig committed suicide and von Gudden died trying to save him. But there has been considerable speculation over the years that Ludwig was mur-dered because he'd become an embarrassment to the authorities. In the stables of a nearby friend there were 10 horses instead of the usual 2— was he trying to escape? Most important of all, was he truly insane or merely the victim of a plot? After all, he was judged by physicians who never examined him. What was taken for madness may have been merely hypersensitivity. "If I were a poet I might be able to reap praise by putting my thoughts into verse," Ludwig once told an interviewer. "But the talent of expression was not given me, and so I must bear being laughed at, scorned at, and slandered. I am called a fool. Will God call me a fool when I am summoned before Him?"

The Bavarian people have always loved Ludwig, and if they could play God, even today, they would redeem him or at least forgive him. An affront to him is an affront to their fierce sense of regional pride. In a workaday world, here was a man who played. In a land of beer and sausages, here was a man who dreamed. The Bavarians know that the final laugh is on those who condemned Ludwig, for the castles that almost bankrupted the royal treasury now bring fortunes in tourist revenues; and the money taken from the public coffers to support Wagner gave the world some of its most treasured music.

LINDERHOF

The royal villa of **Linderhof** (1869–79) (☎ **08822/3512**) was once an annex of Ludwig's father's hunting lodge. It's said to have been inspired by the Petit Trianon at Versailles—though, as one critic has pointed out, it looks more like a small casino in southern France. Ludwig reportedly spent hours in the Moorish Pavilion—bought at the Paris Exhibition of 1867—playing the oriental potentate dressed in a bearskin. The grotto is a modern version of Aladdin's cave, where a rock moves back at the touch of a button. On an illuminated pond is a conch-shaped boat recalling the Venusberg episode in Wagner's *Tannhäuser*. More attractive than the house is the surrounding parkland—once the royal hunting grounds—with pools, Italian villa–style waterfalls, and formal gardens with pyramid-shaped hedges.

The influence of the Bourbons is seen in the royal sun—symbol of Louis XIV—on the ceiling. In the ornate Gobelin or Music Room, notice how the rococo wall paintings are meant to simulate tapestries. The Hall of Mirrors is a stage set for Ludwig's fantasies, in which nothing is what it seems. The bedchamber is a child's dream of luxury and opulence. Royal insignias, gilt-edged angels, and tapestries fill every inch of space, as if Ludwig were afraid of what lay beyond. Admission 7DM adults, 4DM students; under 15 free. Open Apr–Sept, daily 9am–5:30pm; Oct–Mar, daily 10am–4:30pm.

HOHENSCHWANGAU

From Linderhof drive 27.2 kilometers (17 miles) through Austria to Reutte and 12.8 kilometers (8 miles) north to Füssen. Follow the signs east 3.2 kilometers (2 miles) to the castle of **Hohenschwangau,** Alpseestrasse (☎ 08362/81-127).

Ludwig's father purchased the ruins of a 12th-century castle and restored it from 1832 to 1836. Ludwig spent most of his youth here; you can imagine him as a child, staring up at the murals depicting scenes from medieval legends. What he saw must have encouraged his own romantic inclinations without satisfying them, for the young visionary built an even more fanciful castle of his own. Maximilian's castle, unlike his son's, looks almost livable—which is why visitors prefer Neuschwanstein.

Today, 14 rooms are furnished for public view. The Authari Room is where Wagner stayed; he never set foot in Neuschwanstein. The Music Room or Room of the Hohenstauffen contains the square maple-wood piano on which Wagner played his works for Ludwig—who was an accomplished pianist himself. The bedchamber ceiling is painted to look like a night sky, with stars that could be made to light up. From a window the king could watch through a telescope the work progressing at Neuschwanstein. In the Hall of Heroes is a bust of Ludwig by an American sculptor; the king posed for it in 1869. Admission 10DM adults, 7DM children under 14 and seniors. Open Apr–Sept, daily 8:30am–5:30pm; Oct–Mar, daily 10am–4pm.

NEUSCHWANSTEIN

Bavarian kitsch—that's how you'd describe **Neuschwanstein,** Neuschwansteinstrasse 20 (☎ 08362/81-035). Yet in its own tacky, overstated way it has the purity of, say, Versailles, because it remains faithful to a single vision. As a 19th-century fortress, its bulwarks and its position on a mountain spur are wonderfully useless—which somehow makes Ludwig's vision even grander.

Maximilian II had thought of building a castle here, too, on the ruins of an ancient family fortress, so in a sense Ludwig was merely carrying out his father's designs. In 1869, influenced by Wagner's operas, Ludwig asked the court stage designer, Christian Jank, to draw up plans. Only later did he consult an architect. What he got, therefore, was a stage set where he could play the role of Lohengrin.

The castle tour takes you through an artificial stalactite cavern that recalls Wagner's *Tannhäuser*. The bedroom is decorated with a young boy's dreams—14 sculptors worked 4½ years to build it. The curtains and coverings are light Bavarian blue, Ludwig's favorite color. Throughout, the upper walls are covered with paintings from a world of fantasy—windows into a world of the mind. There's something sadly appropriate about the Oriental Throne Room without a throne. Ludwig lived in his castle only 102 days and died before the gold-and-ivory chair could be completed. Admission 10DM adults, 7DM students and seniors; under 15 free. Open Apr–Sept, daily 9am–5:30pm; Oct–Mar, daily 10am–4pm.

After the tour, take an hour's walk (round-trip) to the **Pöllat Gorge** and stand on the same bridge (Marienbrücke) across the ravine where Ludwig II came at night to look up at his empty castle.

WIES CHURCH

Returning to Garmisch-Partenkirchen by the northern route, drive north for 24 kilometers (15 miles) on Route 17, about 3.2 kilometers (2 miles) past Steingaden, and look for signs on the right to **Wies.** A 2.4-kilometer (1½-mile) side trip (one-way) takes you to this baroque masterpiece. The pilgrimage church (1746–52) is the work of the celebrated baroque architect Dominikus Zimmerman. The simple exterior is in marked contrast to the intensely rich interior. There's a similar contrast between the plain lower walls (symbolizing the Earth) and the rich stucco work of the "heavens." The pulpit and organ loft are high points of rococo art in southern Germany.

OBERAMMERGAU

Return to the T-junction and turn right for Route 23, where you cross the River Ammer and head south through Saulgrub to **Oberammergau** (17.6km/11 miles), a town famous for its Passion Play. When a devastating plague stopped short of the town in 1634, the villagers vowed to perform the play every 10 years. The first took place in that same year, and since 1680 it has been performed every decade, with an additional 350th-anniversary performance in 1984. When villagers aren't acting out the Passion of Christ they're turning out wood carvings in their colorfully painted homes. The **Heimat Museum,** Dorfstrasse 8 (☎ 08822/94136), has a large collection of handmade Christmas crèches (nativity scenes).

Admission 3DM adults, 1DM children. Open mid-Apr to mid-Oct, Tues–Sun 2–6pm; off-season, Sat only 2–6pm.

It's 19 kilometers (12 miles) on Route 23 by way of Ettal back to Garmisch-Partenkirchen—where your trip ends. From here, you can take one of four main routes:

- Return to Munich and fly back home.

- Drive to Salzburg, Austria, and follow the Austrian itinerary described in chapter 4. (The most scenic route is south from Garmisch-Partenkirchen through the lovely town of Mittenwald to Innsbruck.)

- Drive to Zurich for a tour of Switzerland. (If you're going to Switzerland, don't return to Garmisch-Partenkirchen but continue from the royal castles to Konstanz.)

- Return to Frankfurt through the Black Forest and fly home.

AUSTRIA 4

Salzburg to Vienna

The region between Salzburg, where Mozart was born, and Vienna, former capital of the Habsburg empire, is a trove of natural and cultural riches. The lakes and wooded hills of the Lake Country are a paradise for sailors and hikers, and the Wachau River Valley enchants with crumbling castles, terraced vineyards, and walled medieval towns. Throughout the year, outstanding music is performed not just in modern concert halls but also in baroque palaces under painted stucco skies filled with saints and angels. The history and art of 7 centuries of Habsburg rule are embodied in Vienna's churches and palaces.

BEFORE YOU GO

GOVERNMENT TOURIST OFFICES

The major source of information is the **Austrian National Tourist Office.**

In the U.S.: P.O. Box 1142, New York, NY 10108 (☎ 212/944-6880); 500 N. Michigan Ave., Suite 1950, Chicago, IL 60611 (☎ 312/644-8029); P.O. Box 491938, Los Angeles, CA 90049 (☎ 310/478-8376). Because of budget cutbacks, U.S. residents seeking information about Austria must now write instead of walk into various tourist offices. Write to the Austrian National Tourist Office, P.O. Box 1142, Times Square Station, New York, NY 10108-1142 (☎ 212/944-6880).

In Canada: 1010 Sherbrooke St. W., Suite 1410, Montréal, Québec H3A 2R7 (☎ 514/849-3709); 200 Granville St., Suite 1380, Granville Sq., Vancouver, British Columbia, V6C 1S4

(☎ 604/683-5808); 2 Bloor St. E., Suite 3330, Toronto, Ontario M4W 1A8 (☎ 416/967-3381).

In the U.K.: 30 St. George St., London W1R 0AL (☎ 0171/629-0461).

WHEN TO GO

Austria has two main tourist seasons. The summer season starts at Easter and runs to about mid-October. The most pleasant months are May, June, September, and October. June to August are the peak tourist months, and aside from a few overly humid days when you could wish for wider use of air-conditioning, even Vienna is pleasant; the city literally moves outdoors in summer. The winter cultural season starts in October and runs to June. Some events—the Salzburg Festival is a prime example—make a substantial difference in hotel and other costs. Nevertheless, bargains are available in the almost nonexistent off-season.

HIGHLIGHTS ALONG THE WAY

• The imperial city of Vienna, home of the Spanish Riding School, the world famous Boys' Choir, Schönbrunn Palace, and a baroque confection of music and art.

• The Wachau Valley, the most romantic stretch of the Danube, with magnificent abbeys and castles overlooking terraced vineyards and medieval towns.

• Salzburg, a city of historic beauty and natural charm—an ideal stage set for the world-famous music festival.

• The Lake Country, a natural setting of sparkling blue lakes and wooded hills.

CURRENCY

The unit of currency is the Austrian **schilling (AS),** divided into 100 **groschen.** There are AS 20, 50, 100, 500, 1,000, and 5,000 bills; AS 1, 5, 10, and 20 coins; and groschen 1, 2, 10, and 50 coins. The 1- and 2-groschen coins are scarce and the 20AS coins unpopular—though useful for some cigarette machines. The 500- and 100-schilling notes look perilously similar; confusing them can be an expensive mistake.

As of this writing, $1 U.S. = 10.5 schillings or 1 schilling = about $9^{1}/_{2}$¢ U.S. The British pound = about 16.8 schillings or 1 schilling = about 6p. The Canadian dollar is worth about 7.65 schillings or 1 schilling = about 13¢ Canadian.

CUSTOMS

Austria's duty-free allowances are as follows, divided into two categories: those for nonresidents arriving from European Union countries and those for nonresidents arriving from non–European Union countries (like the U.S. and Canada).

Visitors arriving from other European Union countries may import 800 cigarettes or 200 cigars or 1,000 grams (35 oz.) of tobacco, 20 liters (5.2 gal.) of liquor (up to 44 proof) or 10 liters (2.6 gal.) of distilled liquor (more than 44 proof).

AUSTRIA

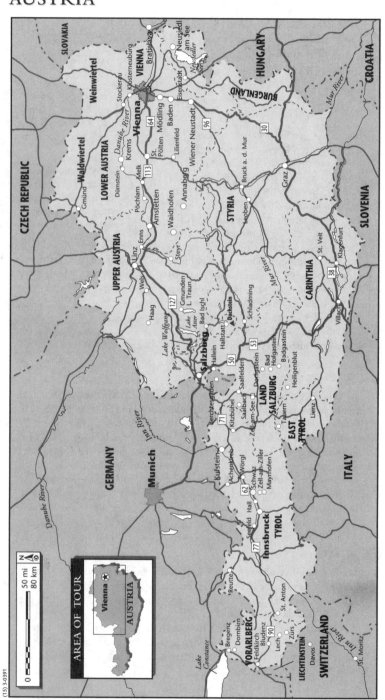

Visitors arriving from non–European Union countries may import 200 cigarettes or 50 cigars or 250 grams (8.70 oz.) of tobacco, 2 liters (.53 gal.) of wine or 1 liter of liquor (either distilled or nondistilled), .25 liter (.53 pt.) of eau de toilette or 50 grams (1.8 oz.) of perfume.

LANGUAGE

German is the official national language. In larger cities and most resort areas, you'll have no problem finding people who speak English; hotel and restaurant staffs, in particular, speak English reasonably well. Most younger Austrians speak at least passable English, even if fluency is relatively rare.

READING

Diane Buregwyn, *Salzburg: A Portrait* (sold in local gift shops).
Edward Crankshaw, *Vienna: The Image of a Culture in Decline* (Macmillan).
Henriette Mandl, *Vienna Downtown Walking Tours* (Ueberreuter).
Richard Rickett, *A Brief Survey of Austrian History* (Heinemann) and *Music and Musicians in Vienna* (Heinemann. Out of print; check your library).
Vienna from A to Z (Vienna Tourist Bureau).

SPECIAL EVENTS & NATIONAL HOLIDAYS

Special Events

Late July to late August: Salzburg Summer Festival, an international festival of concerts, opera, and ballet.
Early May to mid-June: Vienna Music Festival, with concerts in baroque palaces and gardens.

National Holidays

January 1 (New Year's Day); January 6 (Epiphany); Easter Monday, May 1; Ascension Day; Whitmonday; Corpus Christi Day; August 15; October 26 (Nationalfeiertag); November 1 and 26; December 25–26 (Christmas Day and Boxing Day).

ARRIVING & DEPARTING

BY PLANE

For the 3- to 5-day trip, fly to and from Vienna. **Austrian Airlines** (☎ 800/843-0002) flies nonstop to Vienna from New York, and **Lauda Air** (☎ 800/645-3880) offers direct service between Miami and Vienna three times a week. Lauda also operates flights into Vienna from Barcelona, Brussels, Manchester, Hamburg, Lisbon, Paris (Orly), Madrid, Düsseldorf, and London (Gatwick).

For stays of 5 to 7 or 7 to 14 days, fly to Munich and return home from Vienna. (If you need to arrive and depart from the same European airport, end your trip with a train ride from Vienna back to Munich.) Germany's reliable airline, **Lufthansa** (☎ 800/645-3880), flies nonstop from New York and Chicago to Munich. Lufthansa also flies to Munich via Frankfurt from San Francisco, Los Angeles, Dallas, Houston, Philadelphia, Boston, Miami, and Atlanta. TWA (☎ 800/221-2000) flies nonstop to Munich from New York. **Delta** (☎ 800/241-4141) flies direct to Munich from New York and also offers services from Atlanta with a change of equipment in Frankfurt.

BY TRAIN

Vienna has four principal rail stations, with frequent connections to all Austrian cities and towns and to all major European cities, such as Munich and Milan. You can get train information for all stations by calling **0222/17-17.**

The **Wien Westbahnhof,** Europaplatz, is for trains arriving from western Austria, western Europe, and many eastern European countries. It has frequent train connections to all major Austrian cities. Trains from Salzburg and Linz, for example, pull in at the rate of one per hour daily from 5:40am to 8:40pm. Trip time from Salzburg is $3^{1}/_{4}$ hours, and from Linz just under 2 hours.

The **Wien Südbahnhof,** Südtirolerplatz, has train service from southern Austria, including the new countries of Slovenia, Croatia (formerly part of Yugoslavia), and Italy. It also has links to Graz, the capital of Styria, and to Klagenfurt, capital of Carinthia. Seven daily trains arrive from Graz (trip time: $2^{1}/_{2}$ hours) and seven also arrive from Klagenfurt (trip time: $4^{1}/_{4}$ hours).

Other stations include **Franz-Josef Bahnhof,** Franz-Josef-Platz, used mainly by local trains, though connections are made here to Prague and Berlin. **Wien Mitte,** Landstrasser Hauptstrasse 1, is also a terminus of local trains, plus a depot for trains to the Czech Republic and to Schwechat Airport.

BY BUS

The **City Bus Terminal** is at the Wien Mitte rail station, Landstrasser Hauptstrasse 1. This is the arrival depot for Post and Bundesbuses from points all over the country and also the arrival point for private buses from various European cities. The terminal has lockers, currency-exchange kiosks, and a ticket counter open daily from 6:15am to 6pm. For bus information, call **0222/711-01** daily from 6am to 9pm.

BY CAR

Vienna can be reached from all directions via major highways (Autobahnen) or by secondary highways. The main artery from the west is Autobahn A-1, coming in from Munich (291 miles), Salzburg (209 miles), and Linz (116 miles). Autobahn A-2 arrives from the south, from Graz (124 miles) and Klagenfurt (192 miles). Autobahn A-4 comes in from the east, connecting with Route E-58, which runs to Bratislava and Prague. Autobahn A-22 takes traffic from the northwest and Route E-10 connects to the cities and towns of southeastern Austria and of Hungary.

Figure your driving time at 50 to 65 miles per hour, but this estimation varies depending on traffic, road conditions, and time of year.

GETTING AROUND

BY CAR

If you're taking the **3- to 5-day trip,** you'll be flying directly to Vienna. It makes no sense to rent a car at the airport. Parking in the city is difficult and public transportation is good. Rent a car only for the visit to Melk and the Wachau Valley—preferably at the end of the trip, when you can return the car to the airport.

If you're taking the **5- to 7- to 14-day trip,** fly directly to Munich and take the train to Salzburg, where your trip begins. The train from Munich to Salzburg takes 90 minutes. The drive takes under 2 hours, but a car in Salzburg is far more bother and cost than it's worth. The center of the city is a pedestrian zone and parking is limited in many other areas. After seeing Salzburg, drive to Vienna and return your car at the Vienna airport on your way home.

Is it better to rent your car in Munich or Salzburg? If money is no issue and you can pick up the car at the Munich airport and return it at the Vienna airport, do so. Otherwise, catch a train directly from Munich to Salzburg and pick up your car in Salzburg when you're ready to leave. The bus ride from Munich's airport to the city train station takes 30 to 45 minutes.

If you have to pick up and return your car from the same location, fly to Vienna, drive directly to Salzburg on A1 (a 3-hour trip), and then follow the itinerary below back to Vienna. You can also fly to Munich, follow the itinerary to Vienna, and then drive directly back to Munich.

BY PUBLIC TRANSPORTATION

You can follow essentially the same itinerary by car or by a combination of bus, train, and boat. What you'll miss traveling by public transportation are a few towns in the Lake District and the side trip to Mühlviertel.

Austrian Rail Passes, sold at train stations, are good for reduced rates on trains and Danube cruises. Several rail passes are available (check the **Rabbit** card, obtainable at rail stations in Austria, with unlimited travel on any 4 of 10 days), but if you're basically following the Salzburg-Vienna route with side trips, regular tickets will cost less and give more flexibility than special tickets.

If you're taking the **3- to 5-day trip,** which begins in Vienna, you have three ways to reach Melk and the Wachau Valley: (1) Join an escorted tour, which you can arrange through any hotel or travel agency in Vienna. Make sure the tour includes a boat ride between Melk and Dürnstein. (2) Take a Danube cruise from Vienna to Melk, tour the abbey, cross the river and take the train back to Dürnstein, spend the night in Dürnstein, and take a train or a boat back to Vienna. You can't take the steamship round-trip because it arrives in Melk at 4:10pm and doesn't return until 3:20 the next afternoon. Your nights away from Vienna should be spent not in Melk but in Dürnstein. (3) The third and best alternative is to take the train from Vienna to Melk, visit Melk Abbey, take the steamship back to Dürnstein, spend the night in Dürnstein, and take a train or a boat back to Vienna.

The evening sail from Dürnstein back to Vienna takes 4 hours. It's not nearly as scenic as the trip along the Wachau, so if you're pressed for time take the train instead.

Make sure you arrive in Melk in time to tour the abbey, which closes at 4 or 5pm, depending on the season. Melk has two docks, one for the local Wachau ferry and one for the ship to Vienna. If you want to sail directly back to Vienna, ask a taxi driver to take you to the Schiffahrt-Wien. Both ferries stop at Dürnstein, where you'll be spending the night.

The local ferries leave Melk in season at 9am and 12:30, 2:30, and 6pm. The trip from Melk to Dürnstein, along the most beautiful stretch of the Danube, takes less than 2 hours. (Check current schedules.)

You can purchase combination train/ship tickets through travel agencies or from the **First Danube Steamship Company** (DDSG Travel Dept., A-1021 Vienna, Handelskai 265 (☎ **0222/727-50-0**).

If you're taking the **5- to 7-day trip,** you'll be flying to Munich. Take the 30- to 45-minute bus ride from the airport to the train station. The ride to Salzburg takes 90 minutes. After touring Salzburg, take the 3-hour train ride to Melk. (One train leaves Salzburg at 10:05am; change at Amstetten to the 12:15pm local, which arrives in Melk at 12:50pm; there are no direct connections from Salzburg.) For the boat and train ride along the Danube, see the 3- to 5-day trip above.

If you're taking the **7- to 14-day trip,** you'll also be flying to Munich. It's a 30- to 45-minute bus ride from the airport to the train station, and a 90-minute train trip to Salzburg. After touring Salzburg, take a train or a bus to Hallstatt in the Lake Country. Both take about 90 minutes, plus connecting time. A boat meets the train at the opposite side of Hallstatt Lake (Hallstätter See) and brings you to the village of Hallstatt. If bus or train connections are poor, join an excursion bus directly from Salzburg to Hallstatt. You can purchase tickets through hotels and tourist offices in Salzburg. From Hallstatt, return by bus or train to Salzburg.

St. Florian is difficult to reach from Salzburg by train, so save the abbey for another trip and take the train directly from Salzburg to Melk. If you're determined to visit St. Florian, take the train from Salzburg to Linz, then change to a local train to Asten–St. Florian. After visiting St. Florian, return to Linz and continue by train to Melk. For the boat and train ride from Melk to Vienna, see the 3- to 5-day trip above.

ESSENTIAL INFORMATION

IMPORTANT ADDRESSES & NUMBERS

VISITOR INFORMATION For general information on travel in Austria, contact **Österreich Information,** Margaretenstrasse 1 (☎ **0222/588-660**).

Dürnstein: Parkplatz Ost (☎ **02711/360** or 02711/200); open May 1 to October 30, Thursday to Saturday from 3 to 6pm.

Krems: Undstrasse 6 (☎ **02732/82676**); open April to mid-November, Monday to Friday from 9am to 6pm, Saturday and Sunday from 10am to noon and 1 to 6pm (off-season, Mon–Fri 8am–5pm).

Melk: Babenbergerstrasse 1 (☎ **02752/230732** or 02752/230733); open July to August, daily from 9am to 7pm; September to October, Monday to Friday from 9am to noon and 2 to 6pm, Saturday from 10am to 2pm; April to June, Monday to Friday from 9am to noon and 3 to 6pm, Saturday from 10am to 2pm.

Salzburg: Platform 2A of the Hauptbahnhof, Südtirolerplatz (☎ **0662/873638**); open July to August, daily from 8am to 10pm; April to June and September to October, daily from 9am to 7pm; November to March, Monday to Saturday from 9am to 6pm. There's also an information center at Mozartplatz 5 (☎ 0662/84-75-68).

Vienna: City Tourist Office, Kärntnerstrasse 38, behind the Opera (☎ **0222/513-88-92**); open daily 9am to 7pm.

If you're driving from Salzburg or Dürnstein, there's an **Auto Information Center** off the Autobahn (A1) as you approach Vienna; call **0222/97-12-71.** You can make hotel reservations here. There's another information office at the airport; call **0222/711-10-2617.** For directions for any point in the city public transportation system, call **0222/587-31-86.** For airport information, call **0222/711-10-2233.**

EMERGENCIES In **Salzburg: Police** (☎ **0662/133**). In **Vienna: Police** (☎ **133**); **ambulance** (☎ **144**); **doctor,** for medical assistance, call Allgemeines Krankenhaus, Währinger Gürtel 18–20 (☎ **0222/404-00**).

CONSULATES & EMBASSIES In **Salzburg: U.S. Consulate,** Herbert-von-Karajan-Platz 19 (☎ **0662/848776**); open Monday, Wednesday, and Friday from 9am to noon.

In **Vienna: U.S. Embassy,** Boltzmanngasse 16, A-1090 Vienna (☎ **0222/31339**); open Monday to Friday from 8:30am to noon and 1 to 3:30pm. **Canadian Embassy,** Laurenzerberg 2, A-1090 Vienna (☎ **0222/531-38-30-00**); open Monday to Friday from 8:30am to 12:30pm and 1:30 to 3:30pm; **U.K. Embassy,** Jauresgasse 12, A-1090 Vienna (☎ **0222/713-1575**); open Monday to Friday from 9:15am to noon and 2 to 5pm.

OPENING & CLOSING TIMES

BANKS Doors open Monday to Friday from 8am to 12:30pm and 1:30 to 3pm, though afternoon hours vary from city to city. Principal offices in cities stay open during lunch.

MUSEUMS Opening days and times vary considerably from city to city and depend on the season, the size of the museum, budgetary constraints, and assorted other factors. Your hotel or the local tourist office will have current details.

PHARMACIES These are open Monday to Friday from 8am to noon and 2 to 6pm and Saturday from 8am to noon (at night and on Sunday you'll find the names of shops whose turn it is to be open at those times listed on a sign outside every shop).

SHOPS These are open Monday to Friday from 8 or 9am to 6pm, Saturday from 8 or 9am to noon or 1pm only, except the first Saturday of every month, when they stay open to 5pm. Many smaller shops close for 1 or 2 hours at midday.

GUIDED TOURS

Escorted walking tours leave from various points in Vienna and cover various subjects, such as Freud, *The Third Man,* and musicians. Ask at your hotel or at travel agencies for details.

Bus tours are convenient to the Belvedere, Schönbrunn Palace, and the Vienna Woods. Two companies offer escorted bus tours: **Elite Tours,** Operngasse 4 (☎ **0222/513-22-25**), and **Vienna Sightseeing Tours,** Stelzhamergasse 4–11 (☎ **0222/712-468-30**). Make reservations through hotels or travel agencies. Some leave from the Opera, others from in front of the Stadtpark subway station across from the Intercontinental Hotel. Most tours will pick you up at your hotel.

SHOPPING

VAT REFUNDS For purchases more than 1,000 schillings (about $95), ask for the special forms to be filled out at the shops where you've made your purchases and get a refund on the 20% or 34% **value-added tax (VAT)** when you leave the country.

BEST BUYS In **Salzburg,** the best buys are folk costumes (Lederhosen and dirndls), leather goods, sporting equipment, pottery, and candles.

In **Vienna,** you can shop for porcelain, crystal, petit point, leather goods, folk costumes, local handcrafts, and antiques. The **Dorotheum,** Dorotheergasse 17 (☎ **0222/515-600**), is the state-run auction house, which has sales almost every day. There's also a flea market on Saturday from 8am to 6pm at the end of the Naschmarkt, between districts V and VI. From May to September, an art-and-antiques market is held on Saturday from 2 to 7pm and Sunday from 10am to 7pm in District I alongside the Danube Canal below Schwedenplatz.

The shops listed below are along the streets and squares you'll be visiting in District I. Almost all are on three connecting streets, Kärntnerstrasse, Graben, and Kohlmarkt. Serious shoppers should begin at the Opera, stroll down Kärntnerstrasse to St. Stephen's, turn left on Graben, and turn left again on Kohlmarkt.

For porcelain and glass, try **J. & L. Lobmeyr,** Kärntnerstrasse 26 (☎ **0222/512-05-08**). For dirndls and Lederhosen, try **Lanz,** Kärntnerstrasse 10 (☎ **0222/512-24-56**); **Loden-Plankl,** Michaelerplatz 6 (☎ **0222/533-80-32**); ir **Niederösterreichisches Heimatwerk,** Herrengasse 6 (☎ **0222/533-34-95**). You can find local handcrafts at **Österreichische Werkstätten,** Kärntnerstrasse 6 (☎ **0222/512-24-18**). For leather, head to **Nigst,** Neuer Markt 4 (☎ **0222/512-4303**); for silverware try **Rozet & Fischmeister,** Kohlmeister 11 (☎ **0222/533-8061**); for music, stop by the **Arcadia Opera Shop,** Wiener Staatsoper, Kärntnerstrasse 40 (☎ **0222/513-95-68**); and for jewelry check out **A. E. Köchert,** Neuer Markt 15 (☎ **0222/512-58-28**).

DINING

Take your choice of sidewalk Wurstl (frankfurter) stands, quick-lunch stops (Imbisstube), cafes, Heuriger (wine restaurants), self-service restaurants, modest Gasthäuser neighborhood establishments with local specialties, and full-fledged restaurants in every price category. Most establishments post their meals outside. Many butcher shops (Fleischhauer) offer various cooked foods for on-premises or take-out consumption, a fine source of picnic fare. A number of Anker bakery shops also have coffee and delicious substantial snacks (Schmankerin). Shops selling coffee beans (such as Eduscho) also offer coffee by the cup at considerably lower prices than those in a cafe.

Austrians often eat up to five meals a day—a very early continental breakfast of rolls and coffee; a slightly more substantial breakfast (Gabelfrühstück) with eggs or cold meat, possibly even a small goulash, at midmorning (understood to be 9am sharp); a main meal at noon; afternoon coffee (Jause) with cake at teatime; and, unless dining out, a light supper to end the day. Cafes offer breakfast; most restaurants open somewhat later.

A jacket and tie are generally advised for restaurants in the top price categories. Otherwise, casual dress is acceptable, though in Vienna somewhat more formal dress (tie, jacket) is preferred in some moderate restaurants at dinner. When in doubt, it's best to dress up.

Prices include taxes and service (you may wish to leave small change, in addition). Currently, there are about 10.5 schillings (AS) to the U.S. dollar.

CATEGORY	MAJOR CITY	OTHER AREAS
Very Expensive	Over 800AS	Over 600AS
Expensive	500–800AS	400–600AS
Moderate	200–500AS	170–400AS
Inexpensive	Under 200AS	Under 170AS

Prices are per person and include soup and a main course, usually with salad, and a small beer or glass of wine. Meals in the top categories will include a dessert or cheese and coffee.

ACCOMMODATIONS

Austrian hotels and pensions are officially classified from one to five stars. These gradings broadly coincide with our own four-way rating system. No matter what the category, standards for service and cleanliness are high. All hotels in the upper three categories will have tub or shower in the room; even the most inexpensive accommodations will offer hot and cold water. Accommodations include castles and palaces, conventional hotels, country inns (Gasthof), motels (considerably less frequent), and the more modest pensions.

Though exact figures will vary, a single room will generally cost more than 50% of the price of a comparable double. Breakfast—which can be anything from a simple roll and coffee to a full and sumptuous buffet—is included in the room rate in all but the most expensive hotels. Currently, there are about 10.5 schillings to the U.S. dollar. At high season in Salzburg (July to mid-Oct) room prices may rise to 50% above normal.

CATEGORY	MAJOR CITY	OTHER AREAS
Very Expensive	Over 2,700AS	Over 2,000AS
Expensive	1,250–2,700AS	1,000–2,000AS
Moderate	950–1,250AS	700–1,000AS
Inexpensive	Under 950AS	Under 700AS

Prices are for two people in a double room.

AUSTRIAN BAROQUE ARCHITECTURE

In this region are the greatest examples of Austrian baroque: Salzburg Cathedral (very early baroque), the abbeys of St. Florian and Melk, and the Karlskirche in Vienna. The baroque style was imported from France and Italy, but for the Austrians it expressed architecturally the joy they felt after their triumph over the Turks in 1683. It was also the art of the Counter-Reformation—a form of visual propaganda to win Catholic

Austrians back to the Mother Church by a direct appeal to the senses. It's hard to believe today that a person could get very close to God in such a worldly setting, but each age approaches God in its own way.

In Austrian baroque churches, the original Gothic columns direct your eyes both upward to God and forward to the altar; but the flowing lines and ornate decorations force your eyes to stop along the way, almost as if you were being diverted by this world on your way to the next.

Renaissance architects worked on the Platonic assumption that there was an order in the universe that a building could capture by following certain rules—a certain ideal relationship, say, between the width of a column and its height. What the baroque artist tried to do was not to satisfy some ideal form of beauty, but to satisfy the direct emotional needs of the worshiper. Perhaps that's why Renaissance art has always belonged to the cultivated minority, whereas baroque belongs to the masses.

One might be tempted to dismiss these baroque churches as spiritual ballrooms—as ill suited for repentance as for salvation. But this would miss the essence of baroque, which is to bring heaven down to earth and to hold out an image of joy unsullied by guilt of sin. The baroque church was meant to be God's castle. Created in the spirit of the age, heaven became a dwelling place for God's appointed, the Habsburg kings and queens. Overwhelmed by such splendid surroundings, worshipers became royal, too.

The three great baroque architects whose major works you'll be seeing along the route are **Johann Bernhard Fischer von Erlach** (1656–1723), who designed Karlskirche (Vienna) and the University Church (Salzburg); **Johann Lukas von Hildebrandt** (1668–1745), who designed the Upper and Lower Belvedere (Vienna); and **Jakob Prandtauer** (1660–1726), who designed the abbeys of St. Florian and Melk.

EXPLORING

Salzburg

Vienna absorbs its tourists; Salzburg exists for them. Vienna spreads out; Salzburg nestles. Vienna merely acknowledges the seasons; Salzburg opens its arms to them. Vienna is ethnically diverse; Salzburg is so homogeneous that Hitler chose nearby Berchtesgaden as the headquarters for his dream of a Thousand-Year Reich.

Like Vienna, Salzburg was redone in baroque dress. Both cities are monumental, but Salzburg, with its clusters of ancient homes and narrow cobbled streets, has a much more intimate, medieval feel.

When visitors speak of Salzburg, they refer not to the modern town but to Old Salzburg, nestled on both sides of the Salzach River, below the cliffs of Mönchsberg and the Hohensalzburg fortress on one side and the Kapuzinerberg on the other. It's difficult not to love Old Salzburg—its setting is idyllic, its streets are safe and clean, its people are friendly and

THE ITINERARY

ORIENTATION

This itinerary takes you on a scenic and historic route eastward from Salzburg to Vienna, with stops in the Lake Country and along the most romantic stretch of the Danube. You'll begin in Salzburg and then relax in the Lake Country. After exploring the magnificent baroque abbeys of St. Florian and Melk, you'll wander through the gentle, rolling farmland of the Mühlviertel. From here you'll drive or sail through the romantic Wachau Valley. Rested by the slow, dreamy pace of the Danube, you'll be ready for Vienna.

polite. This is a show town, a pretty stage set with no apparent purpose but to entertain its paying guests. During the day everything is yours to peek into, buy, listen to, and explore—but by 11pm all shutters are closed and you can hear your footsteps echoing on the empty squares. There's something unreal about all this, but who needs reality on vacation?

You'll find yourself drawn down picturesque alleys, exploring monuments to this world and the next. Nearly everything is within walking distance: the baroque churches, the humble apartment where Mozart was born, the shopping streets with wrought-iron signs as intricate as lacework. Ideally, you should come during the summer music festival, but there are concerts all year long, performed in a baroque setting as sumptuous as any in the world.

The **cathedral** (Dom), on the south side of Residenzplatz (☎ 0662/84-11-62), is the physical and spiritual center of the town, so let's begin here. A Romanesque cathedral once stood on this spot; however, Archbishop Wolf Dietrich either set fire to it or did nothing to stop it from burning down. He wanted the cathedral to be another St. Peter's but died before its completion. Though its interior is influenced by St. Peter's, particularly in its geometric use of space, it's more closely modeled on Rome's Il Gesù.

The Main Route

3-5 Days

One Night: *Salzburg.*
Two Nights: *Vienna.*
One Night: *Dürnstein.*

5-7 Days

Two Nights: *Salzburg.*
Two Nights: *Dürnstein.*
Two Nights: *Vienna.*

7-14 Days

Two Nights: *Salzburg.*
Two Nights: *Lake Country.*
Two Nights: *Dürnstein.*
Four Nights: *Vienna.*

Wolf Dietrich was the most notorious of the prince-archbishops who ruled Salzburg and the surrounding territory for more than 1,000 years, controlling everything from breweries to the salvation of souls. When he became archbishop in 1587, he wasn't yet ordained. Educated in Rome, he shared with Alberti and Palladio the notion that a house of worship should stand isolated on a beautiful square; and so he tore down much of the medieval city and built Italian-style piazzas with lovely fountains, both around the cathedral and around the Residenz, where he planned to live.

Living with Wolf Dietrich, probably out of wedlock, was a Jewish woman named Salome Alt, who bore him 15 children. She tolerated his extravagances more than the townspeople, who rose up and imprisoned him in the Hohensalzburg—a fortress built, ironically, to protect archbishops from the people. When Wolf Dietrich died 5 years later, his only finished project was his mausoleum, which you can see in St. Sebastian's Cemetery, not far from the tombs of Mozart's wife and father.

After Wolf Dietrich came Archbishop Markus Sittikus, a man who apparently played as hard as he prayed, building a fun palace called Hellbrunn and renaming Salome's castle Mirabell after one of his own mistresses.

The last of the three great archbishops who gave Salzburg the face it wears today was Paris Lodron (1619–53), who completed the Residenz and a more modest version of the cathedral in Italian mannerist style. Though he was a more gentle, peace-loving fellow than his predecessors, he was accompanied wherever he went by 30 personal guards, 14 lords chamberlain carrying enormous gold keys, and a dozen children of the nobility dressed in red velvet.

It was Napoléon who put an end to the line of prince-archbishops; should we be grateful to him? The rulers of Salzburg were often selfish autocrats who led extravagant lives at the expense of their people, yet they loved art and created beauty, Can they be forgiven? (Salzburg still has an archbishop, but his domain is limited to matters of the spirit.)

The cathedral's **bronze doors** and **altar** are postwar. To the left of the entrance is the **baptismal font** in which Mozart was christened in 1756. In the **crypt** is the grave of an early Irish bishop named Virgil, who created waves 12 centuries ago by insisting that the world was round. In the treasury are baroque chalices, Romanesque miters, and a traveling flask belonging to the late 7th-century priest Rupert of Worms. Rupert founded St. Peter's Church, which you'll be visiting soon. Free admission to cathedral, excavations, 20AS adults, 15AS children 6–15, 5 and under free; museum, 40AS adults, 10AS children. Cathedral open daily 8am–8pm (to 6pm in winter); excavations open Easter to mid-Oct, daily 9am–5pm; museum open May 10–Oct 18, daily 10am–5pm.

Head south, away from the river, and cross Kapitelplatz. The square has an 18th-century drinking trough for horses in the shape of a monumental fountain—a reminder that some prince-archbishops may have treated their animals better than their subjects. Walk to the funicular that goes to the **Hohensalzburg,** Nönchsberg 34 (☎ **0662/842-430-11**). Buy a one-way ticket. This fortress—one of the best-preserved medieval structures in the world—gets top billing in Salzburg, so go in the morning to beat the lines. (Tours begin at 9am.) The Hohensalzburg was built to protect the prince-archbishops and was virtually impregnable. The fourth-floor apartments offer fine examples of late Gothic secular architecture, but there's little else that's memorable on the tour, so if the lines are long, pass it up and admire the panoramic view of Salzburg. Admission (excluding tour but including museum) 35AS adults, 20AS children 6–19; 5 and under free. Fortress and museums open Nov–Mar, daily 9am–5pm; Apr–June and Oct, daily 9am–6pm; July–Sept, daily 8am–7pm.

Near the fortress is **Nonnberg Convent,** with a late 14th-century church. It was while staying here that Maria heard the sound of music, or at least the voice of Baron George von Trapp. The real Maria, according to a delightful account in *Salzburg: A Portrait,* lost both parents at age 9 and was turned over to Salzburg and asked to be placed in the strictest convent. While at Nonnberg, she was sent to care for the baron's children, fell in love with him, and in 1938 escaped with him to the United States. After *The Sound of Music* was released, the von Trapps bought 600 acres in Vermont and turned a farmhouse into a Salzburg-type chalet with a Trapp family gift shop selling Trapp family postcards. The real von Trapps lived not in Leopoldskron Castle, as the film suggests, but in a Salzburg suburb. Maria was much sturdier than Julie Andrews and married George von Trapp not in the church in Mondsee but in the convent; and if they had followed the mountain route they took in the movie they would've ended up in Germany. The people of Salzburg don't appreciate songs like "Do Re Mi," which insult their religiously inspired folk melodies; but this doesn't stop them from cheerfully exploiting the film for every tourist dollar they can get—much as they exploit Mozart, who was born here but fled to Vienna.

TAKE A BREAK

*Stay on the ridge above the city and enjoy a delightful 30-minute walk through parklands to the **Winkler Café**, Am Mönchsberg 32 (☎ 0662/847-738). (If you make this walk in reverse, starting at the Winkler, you'll have a steep climb to the fortress.) The Winkler terrace is overrun with tourists but is still a scenic spot for coffee or lunch. Reservations advised. Casual, but no shorts. AE, DC, MC, V. Closed Mon, except during festival period. Expensive.*

A more peaceful and elegant alternative is the terrace at the **Hotel Schloss Mönchstein,** Mönchsberg Park 26 (☎ 0662/8485550), a 10-minute walk farther along the bluff. Reservations required. Elegant casual or jacket/tie. AE, DC, MC, V. Expensive.

From the Winkler, take the elevator back down to the town and wander along Getreidegasse, the main shopping street. Here and on Judengasse, the continuation of Getreidegasse, you can buy dirndls, needlework, leather goods, candles, and ski equipment.

At **Getreidegasse 9** (☎ 0662/84-43-13) is the humble apartment, now a museum, where Johannes Chrysostomus Wolfgangus Theophilus (Amadeus) Mozart was born in 1756. Mozart's clavichord is here; you can imagine his father, Leopold, standing over him while he played. When Mozart was 4, a court musician named Andreas Schatner came here with a friend to play trios with Leopold. Wolfgang begged to play the violin, but Leopold said no: The boy had never taken a lesson in his life. Schatner convinced Leopold to let Wolfgang try. The 4-year-old took up the same violin you see on display here and played the piece so perfectly that Schatner couldn't compete with him, and Leopold was reduced to tears.

At age 6, when most children were reading nursery rhymes, Wolfgang was brought to Vienna, where he performed for Empress Maria Theresa at Schönbrunn Palace. Six years later the Emperor commissioned him to write an opera. Mozart's problems with Salzburg began in 1771, when a new archbishop tried to limit what he called Mozart's "begging expeditions" across Europe. What the archbishop really wanted was a less brilliant, less ambitious court musician—someone content to fulfill his obligations at court. Mozart, in turn, felt unappreciated in provincial Salzburg, where "the audience is all tables and chairs." Eventually he left Salzburg for good. Admission 65AS adults, 47AS students, 17AS children. Open July–Aug, daily 9am–7pm; Sept–June, daily 9am–6pm.

In 1890, Mozart's fame was sweetened by the arrival of Mozartkugeln (Mozart balls) — pistachio-flavored marzipan rolled in nougat cream and dipped in dark chocolate; you can buy them anywhere along Getreidegasse. The factory at Mirabell turns out 150,000 of these tin-wrapped morsels every day; look for the word *echte*, which distinguishes them from the competition.

The next stop are the catacombs of **St. Peter's Church** (Stiftskirche St. Peter), St.-Peter-Bezirk (☎ 0662/844-578). If you want to trace Salzburg's history through its monuments, begin not at the cathedral or fortress, but here. A landslide in 1669 killed 200 people and revealed these crude stone chambers where the early Christians came to pray as far back as A.D. 200. On the 20-minute tour you can try to imagine the faith of these early believers, who prayed in secret and died for their beliefs. Some 2 centuries later a Christian church was built nearby. In the 7th century, Rupert of Worms poured the church's profits from salt mining into the monastery and church of St. Peter. Salzburg (which means "castle of salt") thus began life as a monastic settlement long before the era of the prince-archbishops. The secular town, where employees of the monastery lived, grew up along the river. You'll get a sense of these early days when you look at the massive Romanesque walls of the church and compare them to the 18th-century baroque interior. It was here in St. Peter's that Mozart first performed his C Minor Mass, with his wife, Constanza, singing solo soprano. Nearby is a peaceful 17th-century cemetery where anyone would be happy to spend eternity. The seven old iron crosses belonged to the family of a stonemason named Stumpfegger who died at 79 after burying six wives. Free admission. Open daily 9am–12:15pm and 2:30–6:30pm.

You can trace the history of Western architecture in the nearby **Church of the Franciscans** (Franziskanerkirche), Sigmund-Hoffner-Gasse (☎ 0662/841-327-72). Stand near the back and let the massive Romanesque columns pull your eyes forward to the baroque altar. The effect is that of standing in the 14th century and looking toward the 18th; of standing in a shaded forest and staring out at a distant sunlit clearing in the woods. The Gothic choir was begun by the Tyrolean wood sculptor Michael Pacher, whose work you'll see again in St. Wolfgang. He worked on the High Altar, too; but then Fischer von Erlach, the greatest of all Austrian baroque architects, was called in and put Pacher's gentle madonna in a baroque heaven. Free admission. Open daily 9am–6pm. Von Erlach's other masterpiece in Salzburg is the **University Church** (Kollegienkirche), Universitätplatz.

To understand the worldly power of the prince-archbishops, tour the 180-room Renaissance-style **Residenz,** Residenzplatz 1

SALZBURG

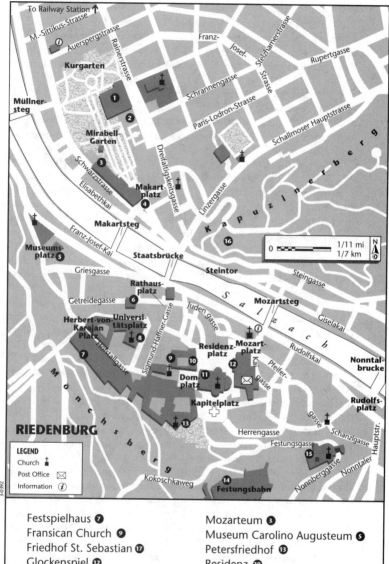

LEGEND
Church ✝
Post Office ✉
Information ⓘ

Festspielhaus ❼	Mozarteum ❸
Fransican Church ❾	Museum Carolino Augusteum ❺
Friedhof St. Sebastian ⓱	Petersfriedhof ⓭
Glockenspiel ⓬	Residenz ❿
Hohensalzburg Fortress ⓮	Salzburg Cathedral ⓫
Kapunzinerkloster ⓰	Salzburger Barockmuseum ❷
Kollegienkirche ❽	Schloss Mirabell ❶
Mozart Geburtshaus ❻	Stift Nonnberg ⓯
Mozart Wohnhaus ❹	Stiftskirche St. Peter ⓭

(☎ 0662/80-42-26-90). The staircase, commissioned by Wolf Dietrich, was built to be ascended on horseback. The cathedral, St. Peter's, and the Church of the Franciscans were all so close to the archbishop's home that he could commute from palace to pulpit without stepping outdoors. Admission to Residenz state rooms, 50AS adults, 40AS students 16 to 18 and seniors, 15AS children 6–15, free for children 5 and under. Combined ticket to state rooms and gallery, 80AS. Residenz Gallery, 50AS adults, 40AS students 16–18 and seniors, free for children under 16. Conducted tours of the Residenz state rooms, July–Aug, daily 10am–4:40pm; Sept–June, Mon–Fri 10am–3pm. Residenz Gallery, Mar 26–Sept 30, daily 10am–5pm; Oct–Jan, Thurs–Tues 10am–5pm (closed Feb 1–Mar 25). Across the Residenzplatz is the **New Building** (Neugebäude), Mozartplatz 1 (☎ 0662/80-42-27-84), which Wolf Dietrich began in 1590 for visiting royalty. Climb up at 10:45am or 5:45pm—weather permitting—to see the **Glockenspiel** (carillon) in action. It came broken from Antwerp in 1695 and is still slightly off-key. Admission 20AS adults, 10AS children 6–14; 5 and under free.

If you've had enough walking for a day, rent a Fiaker—a horse-drawn carriage—and clip-clop around town. In the early evening, cross over the Salzach River, turn left, and enjoy a delightful walk or bike ride along the water.

The same walk will take you at another time to the Mozarteum, Mirabell, and the Marionettentheater. The **Mozarteum,** Schwarzstrasse (☎ 0662/88-940), has two concert halls and a one-room summer house imported from Vienna where Mozart supposedly wrote *The Magic Flute.*

Mirabell, off Marktplatz (☎ 0662/8072-0), was the palace Wolf Dietrich built for Salome. Because of an early 19th-century fire, little remains of the baroque alterations except for the Marble Room upstairs and the playful white marble staircase, where stubby-legged cherubs ride the waves. The gardens, left as Dietrich designed them, are a delightful place to doze or sunbathe. Archbishop Franz Anton von Harrach was partial to dwarfs and commissioned the squat hunchbacked marble figures in the Dwarf Garden. Free admission. Open Mon–Fri 8am–6pm.

The elegant dining hall of the 90-year old former Hotel Mirabell is the home of the famous **Salzburger Marionettentheater,** Schwarzstrasse 24 (☎ 0662/87-24-06). Holography—the art of the laser—creates the illusion of 3-D sets for abbreviated, taped performances of *The Magic Flute, Die Fledermaus,* and other famous operas and operettas. *The Nutcracker* uses more than 100 lifelike puppets. Performances are in a sense more realistic than live opera, because there are no actors behind the masks, no real people standing between the characters and our vision of who they should be.

A few miles south of town is **Schloss Hellbrunn,** Fürstenweg 37 (☎ 0662/820-372), the pleasure palace of Archbishop Markus Sittikus. It was apparently built in 1612 for Madame de Mabon, the wife of the captain of the guard; look for her likeness in the Orpheus Grotto, wearing a portrait of Sittikus around her neck. The archbishop had a child's fascination with water and a child's sense of play. The stone dining table, for instance, has a trough down the center to cool wine and holes in the benches where jets of icy water drenched unsuspecting guests. The warbling in the Birdsong Grotto is created by water pressure. In the Neptune Grotto is a Groucho Marx–type figure who, when his mouth fills with water, sticks out his tongue and rolls his eyes. Admission 60AS adults, 30AS children. Open Apr and Oct, daily 9am–4:30pm; May, June, and Sept, daily 9am–5pm, July–Aug, daily 9am–10pm. Closed Nov–Mar.

DINING

Alt Salzburg, Bürgerspitalgasse 2 (☎ 0662/84-14-76). This restaurant has several small, relatively elegant dining rooms. After a lapse, it's on the way to recovering its former excellent reputation, particularly for its tafelspitz (boiled beef), filet of river char, and sautéed lamb chops, but the quality can be uneven. Reservations useful. Jacket/tie required. AE, DC, MC, V. Closed Sun except during Festival weeks and Feb 3–16. Expensive.

Mirabell, Auerspergstr. 4 (☎ 0662/88-99-90). Though it's housed in a chain hotel (the Sheraton), some will argue that the Mirabell is the city's top restaurant. The menu mixes international dishes with adventurous versions of local specialties, such as Wiener schnitzel and Wildschwein (wild boar). Reservations advised. Jacket/tie required. AE, DC, MC, V. Expensive.

Mundenhamer Bräu, Rainerstr. 2 (☎ 0662/87-56-93). Dark wood sets the mood in this popular restaurant serving Austrian and international fare. A welcome feature is the half-portions for after-theater dining as well as lighter items like steak sandwiches. Reservations advised. Casual but neat. AE, DC, MC, V. Closed Sun and holidays. Moderate.

Zum Eulenspiegel, Hagenauerplatz 2 (☎ 0662/84-31-80). The intimate rooms of an old city house contribute to the charm of this restaurant. Reservations advised. Jacket/tie required. AE, DC, MC, V. Closed Jan 5–Mar 20. Expensive.

Zum Mohren, Judengasse 9 (☎ 0662/84-23-87). Arched ceilings in the lower rooms of this historic house add atmosphere to the tasty local and international specialties, such as duck and venison. Reservations advised. Casual but neat, jacket/tie advised evenings. AE, MC, V. Closed Sun and June 10–July 12. Moderate.

Coffeehouses

For a morning or afternoon coffee break along one of the narrow winding streets near Getreidegasse, stop at a coffeehouse.

Café Tomaselli, Alter Markt 9 (☎ 0662/84-44-88). The coffee could be better, the cake fresher, and the waiters more polite, but you haven't been to Salzburg (some say) until you've been here. Reservations essential at festival time. Elegant casual. No credit cards. Moderate.

Konitorei Ratzka, Imbergstrasse 45 (☎ 0662/64-00-24). This place has the best pastries, including petit fours and fresh-fruit tarts. Reservations essential but often impossible to get. Elegant casual. No credit cards. Closed Sun–Mon. Moderate.

ÖH-Café, in the Hotel Österreichischer Hof, Schwarzstrasse 5–7 (☎ 0662/889-77). Here's a great place for afternoon coffee and pastries. Ask for a Sachertorte—the best this side of Vienna. Reservations useful. Elegant casual. AE, DC, MC, V. Expensive.

Schatz Konditorei, Passageway Getreidegasse 3 (☎ 0662/84-27-92). This is the oldest pastry shop in Salzburg, established in 1866. A delectable well worth a try are Mozartkugeln (cakes with candied fruit). You may take your coffee to go, or stay to enjoy the atmosphere in this dollhouse of a cafe. No reservations. Casual. No credit cards. Closed Sun. Moderate.

ACCOMMODATIONS

Goldener Hirsch, Getreidegasse 37, A-5020 Salzburg (☎ 0662/8084; fax 0662/8485-178-45). A 600-year-old house with rag rugs and old painted chests, this is a young American's idea of what a charming Austrian inn should be. It's on the main pedestrian street, which is a plus or minus, depending on how close to center city you want to be. 71 rms with bath; 3 suites. Facilities: restaurant, AE, DC, MC, V. Very Expensive.

Kaserer Bräu, Kaigasse 33, A-5020 Salzburg (☎ 0662/84-24-45; fax 0662/84-24-45-51). Keep your head up so you can ignore the carpets and appreciate the lovely old painted furniture and ornate armoires. Request a room with antiques. 37 rms with bath. Facilities: restaurant. AE, DC, MC, V. Expensive.

Österreichischer Hof, Schwarzstr. 5–7, A-5020 Salzburg (☎ 800/223-5652 or 0662/88-97-70; fax 0662/889-77-14). Salzburg's grande dame occupies a lovely riverside location, and some of the rooms give views of the fortress and the old city. All the restaurants are excellent so reservations are essential. 120 rms with bath; 17 suites. Facilities: four restaurants. AE, DC, MC, V. Very Expensive.

Schloss Mönchstein, Mönchsberg Park 26, A-5020 Salzburg (☎ 800/448-8355 or 0662/84-85-550; fax 0662/84-85-59). This castle in a peaceful garden overlooks the city. Filled with serious antiques and softened with dark wood paneling, it has more the atmosphere of a private residence than of a hotel. Some of the rooms are exquisite, others small and tasteless. Rooms 20 and 23 are good bets; avoid no. 34. 11 rms with bath; 6 suites. Facilities: restaurant, garage, tennis. AE, DC, MC, V. Very Expensive.

Other friendly hotels include **Weisse Taube,** Kaigasse 9, A-5020 Salzburg (☎ 0662/84-24-04; fax 0662/84-17-83; 33 rms with bath; nearby parking garage; AE, DC, MC, V; Moderate), and **Elefant,** Sigmund-Haffner-Gasse 4, A-5020 Salzburg (☎ 0662/84-33-97; fax 0662/84-01-09-28; 36 rms with bath; AE, DC, MC, V; Moderate).

THE LAKE COUNTRY

East of Salzburg is the **Salzkammergut,** a land of lakes and green mountains, where you can swim, boat, fish, or simply slow down to the pace of the season. This is a popular tourist area, but a short stroll or sail will take you away from the crowds and leave you in the company of birds and pines.

Salt (salz) was mined here for at least 1,500 years before the Romans came and was the principal source of wealth for the prince-archbishops of Salzburg. Because the managers permitted no visitors, it remained a sealed domain. The situation changed when Emperor Franz Josef (1867–1916) moved his summer court to Bad Ischl. Great families soon moved in and built their estates overlooking the lakes. Painters drew postcards of the Lake Country, and soon the region became one of the country's most popular resort areas.

LAKE FUSCHL (FUSCHLSEE)

From Salzburg, continue your tour on Route 158, traveling 24 kilometers (15 miles) to **Lake Fuschl.**

Dining & Accommodations

Hotel Schloss Fuschl, Hof bei Salzburg, am Fuschlsee, A-5322 Lake Fuschl (☎ 800/223-6800 or 06229/22530; fax 06229/2253-531). This elegant 16th-century hotel/castle overlooks the delightful lake. It's only 24 kilometers (15 miles) from Salzburg, so consider staying here while you tour the city or just stopping by for lunch. No lunch setting could be lovelier than the terrace above the lake. 62 rms with bath; 22 suites. Facilities: outstanding restaurant, swimming, sauna, tennis. AE, DC, MC, V. Very Expensive.

ST. GILGEN

Continue on Route 158 for 8 kilometers (5 miles) to **St. Gilgen,** where Mozart's mother was born.

Dining

Nannerl, Kirchenplatz 2 (☎ 06227/368). This is a good cafe and pâtisserie for snacks or lunch. No reservations. Casual. AE, DC, MC, V. Moderate.

ST. WOLFGANG

Continue south on Route 158 along the southern shore of **Lake Wolfgang** (Wolfgangsee). Either leave your car at Gschwandt, near the eastern end of the lake, and take the ferry; or drive to Strobl, turn left, and head back up the western side of the lake about 5.6 kilometers (3.5 miles). The boat trip is the best part of a visit to **St. Wolfgang,** so if time permits, take the ferry, checking the schedule the night before.

WHAT TO SEE & DO WITH CHILDREN

In Salzburg: The Glockenspiel (carillon); the catacombs at St. Peter's; the torture chamber in the fortress; the mummified Ice Age rhinoceros in the Natural History Museum; Schloss Hellbrunn, especially the mechanical theater; above all, the Marionettentheater.

In the Lake District: Windsurfing, swimming, fishing, and boating on all the lakes.

In the Abbey of St. Florian: The 6,000 skeletons in the crypt.

Along the Wachau: The ramparts of Aggstein Castle; bike riding along the less-traveled southern route (you can rent bikes at train stations in Melk and Krems and return them to these or other stations).

In Vienna: The children's armor collection in the Neue Burg; the Prater amusement park, particularly the Ferris wheel; the zoo; the royal coaches in the Wagenburg coach house outside Schönbrunn Palace; the walk to the top of St. Stephen's; a Sunday-morning concert by the Vienna Boys' Choir; a training session or performance of the Lipizzaner horses at the Spanish Riding School.

From the ferry landing at St. Wolfgang, walk to the **Parish Church,** wander down the narrow lanes, lunch on a terrace overlooking the lake, rent a rowboat, and then enjoy a peaceful boat ride back to your car. The drawing cards of St. Wolfgang are the lake view and Michael Pacher's altarpiece in the 16th-century Parish Church, one of the most famous Gothic wood carvings in the world. The work is done with such detail that you can see the stitches in the Virgin's robes. Perspective had just been mastered in 1481, and Pacher delights in it like a child who has just learned to walk. Give thanks to the artist who sculpted the baroque side altar; he was commissioned to update Pacher's work in baroque style and deliberately made it the wrong size so that the original wouldn't be replaced.

Dining & Accommodations

Lachsen, Reid 5, A-5360 St. Wolfgang (☎ 06138/2432). This is the best restaurant around, up the road in the smaller town of Ried. Reservations advised. Jacket/tie required. No credit cards. Closed Nov–Mar. Expensive.

White Horse Inn, in the Hotel Weisses Rossl, St. Wolfgang (☎ 06138/2306-0; fax 06138/2306-41). The pilgrims who visited St. Wolfgang 7 centuries ago have been replaced by busloads of tourists who saunter in and out of the famous hotel during the day. The rooms are clean and comfortable, but renovations have eclipsed much of the hotel's natural charm. Request a room with traditional furnishings and a balcony overlooking the lake. 72 rms with bath; 12 suites. Facilities: restaurant, lake swimming, indoor pool. AE, DC, MC, V. Closed Nov–Dec 22. Expensive.

BAD ISCHL

Continue east about 19.2 kilometers (12 miles) on Route 158 to **Bad Ischl.** From May to September, take the 60-minute tour of **Kaiservilla,** where Emperor Franz Josef held his summer court. His bedroom, with an iron bedstead, plain pine wardrobe, and uncomfortable armchair, is simplicity itself and reflects his austere tastes. The emperor was a great hunter who shot selectively, protecting the breeds of deer. His nephew, Archduke Franz Ferdinand—the one assassinated at Sarajevo with his wife, Sophie, precipitating World War I—wasn't permitted to hunt here because of his passion for indiscriminate slaughter. As you stand in the emperor's bedroom, think of him as a man so set in his Imperial ways that he refused to carry money or speak on the phone—a man who drove in a car only once, as a gesture to Edward VII of England, who came here to offer the emperor an alliance with Britain if Austria-Hungary would agree to break with Germany. If only Edward VII had been more persuasive or Franz Josef less obstinate—"You must not forget that I am a German prince," he said—World War I might've been averted.

Dining

Café Zauner, Pfarrgasse 7 (☎ 06132/23310). This cafe is world-renowned for its pastries. Reservations advised. Casual. AE, DC, MC, V. Closed Tues in winter. Expensive.

Weinhaus Attwenger, Lehárkai 12 (☎ 06132/23327). Try this place for a complete meal. Reservations advised. Jacket/tie required. AE, DC. Closed Sun eve, Mon, and 1 month beginning around Christmas. Expensive.

HALLSTATT

From Bad Ischl take Route 145 south about 16 kilometers (10 miles) and make a right turn on Route 166. **Hallstatt** is about 11.2 kilometers (7 miles) farther south along Lake Hallstatt.

The charming village of Hallstatt clings to the side of Dachstein Mountain above the deep-blue Hallstatt Lake. Consider spending the night; there are no first-class hotels, but when the day-trippers have left you'll enjoy one of the loveliest natural settings in the Lake Country. You can rent boats and use the town as a base for excursions. The **Parish Church** is reached by steps from the center of the village.

Hallstatt is the oldest known settlement in Austria, and many prehistoric graves have been discovered nearby. The cemetery is overcrowded, and skeletons have been periodically dug up and displayed in the **charnel house**—some inscribed with dates and causes of death. Kids will love it!

Dining & Accommodations

Gasthof Zauner, A-4830 Hallstatt (☎ 06134/8246; fax 06134/82468). At this simple but friendly guest house, ask for a room with antiques. 10 rms with bath. DC, MC, V. Closed Nov to late Dec. Moderate.

Seehotel Grüner Baum, Marktplatz 104, A-4830 Hallstatt (☎ 06134/8263; fax 06134/420). This terrace restaurant overlooks the lake. Reservations useful. Casual. AE, DC, MC, V. Closed Oct 15–Dec 15. Expensive.

SIDE TRIPS FROM HALLSTATT

LAKE OF GOSAU   From Hallstatt, turn left on Route 166 to Gosau, then turn left again to the Lake of Gosau. The surface of this small lake reflects the rock walls and majestic peaks of the nearby mountains. This is the most dramatic setting in the Lake Country, particularly if you arrive in the morning or evening, when the lake is still and the busloads of tourists are absent. The hour-long walk around the lake is a delightful experience.

SALT MINES   From Hallstatt, drive to Lahn, take the funicular to the restaurant, and then walk for 10 minutes to the salt mines. You can descend by a staircase or down the same smooth woodslide used by the miners. The trip ends with a mile-long underground train ride. Guided tours of the mines are conducted in May and from mid-September to mid-October, daily from 9am to 3pm; June to mid-September, daily from 9am to 4:30pm. Tours cost 135AS for adults and 65AS for children 4 to 14 (3 and under not admitted). Dress warmly and be sure to wear sturdy walking shoes for the 2¹/₂-hour hike.

THE ICE CAVES & MOUNT KRIPPENSTEIN   From Hallstatt, drive around the southern end of the lake. Just before Obertraun, turn right on the road to the Ice Caves (Dachsteineishöhle). Take the cable car to the station Schönbergalpe and follow signs to the Eishöhle. The ice cave is open May to mid-October, daily from 9am to 4pm; a guided tour costs 89AS for adults and 40AS for children. After the tour, continue up the cable car to Mount Krippenstein (2,075.6m/6,919 ft.) for lunch. The view is panoramic, particularly from Pioneer's Cross (Pionierkreuz), a short walk from the cable car.

ON TO LINZ

Return to Bad Ischl and take Route 145 about 17.6 kilometers (11 miles) north to **Ebensee.** If you're partial to panoramic views, take the cable car to the winter sports area of **Feuerkogel.**

From Ebensee, continue for about 4 kilometers (2¹/₂ miles) along the lovely west shore of the Traunsee to **Traunkirchen.** The Parish Church has ornate baroque furnishings and a famous Fisherman's Pulpit in the form of a boat, representing the Apostle's craft with dripping nets. Overhead is the scene of a lobster returning to St. Francis Xavier a crucifix he lost when shipwrecked near Japan.

Continue north about 8 kilometers (5 miles). **Gmunden** is famous for its ceramics. Stretch your legs on a 1.6-kilometer (1-mile) walk under chestnut trees along the shores of the Traunsee. **Ort Chateau** is on an island linked to the mainland. A nephew of the emperor acquired it in 1878. He gave up his title after the death of Franz Josef's son Rudolf (who committed suicide at Mayerling with his mistress, Baroness Maria Vetsera), and lived here under the assumed name of Johann Ort.

Linz

Take Route 144 north to A1 and drive east to **Linz.**

Dining

Traxlmayr, Promenade 16 (☎ **0732/77-33-53**). Here's a typical Austrian cafe where you can read the *International Herald Tribune* for the price of a cup of coffee at an 1890s-style round marble table. Reservations useful. Casual. No credit cards. Closed Sun. Inexpensive.

Ursulinenhof, Landestr. 31 (☎ **0732/774686**). This is the best and most expensive restaurant in the old town. It's housed in a former Ursaline convent, which contains two *Jugenstil* (art nouveau) dining rooms. The menu items are the most innovative in town, a modern update on classic Austrian cuisine but with a more lighthearted touch. Dishes change seasonally but include such treats as a terrine of sweetbreads with a kohlrabi sauce or braised breast of goose in Calvados butter. Reservations essential. Jacket/tie required. AE, DC, MC, V. Expensive.

THE MÜHLVIERTEL

If you're in a hurry, go directly to the Abbey of St. Florian. But if time permits and the weather cooperates, consider a loop north through the district of **Mühlviertel.** This will take you down back roads, through rolling farmland seldom seen by tourists. There's a Grandma Moses quality to this landscape, with stone barns, milk cans, laundry lines flapping their shadows on lengths of lawn, and everywhere the smells of the good earth.

It's about an 80-kilometer (50-mile) round-trip from Linz to Freistadt. Leave A1 and follow A7 north toward Linz. Continue past Linz, following the signs to Route 125 and Freistadt. About 11.2 kilometers (7 miles) before Freistadt, turn right on a small country road to **Kefermarkt.** In the chancel of the Gothic **Church of St. Wolfgang** is a great carved wood altarpiece about 11.9 meters (40 ft.) high. (If the church is locked, ask in the building behind, no. 2, for the key.) Continue north to **Freistadt.** The town has a lovely main square with a **Parish Church** and old arcaded houses.

DINING & ACCOMMODATIONS

Zum Goldenen Adler, Salzgasse 1, A-4240 Freistadt (☎ **07942/2112;** fax 07942/211244). This informal, reasonably priced hotel restaurant has been in the same family for 200 years. The regional dishes popular with tourists are roast pork with Speckkrautsalat (bacon-and-cabbage salad) and Zweibelrostbraten (roast beef) with Bratkartoffeln (roasted potatoes). Don't miss the Apfelstrudel (apple strudel), the best in town. 37 rms with bath. Facilities: restaurant, pub, pool, solarium, sauna, fitness room. MC. Moderate.

ON TO ST. FLORIAN

You can continue your back-road tour from Freistadt to **Bad Leonfelden** on Route 128, then south to **Glasau** on Route 126 and back to Linz. Part of this trip takes you through a forest and along a broodingly romantic gorge; but if you've had enough of back roads or need to reach St. Florian before the last tour (4pm), take Route 125 directly from Freistadt to Linz and continue to St. Florian.

ST. FLORIAN

The abbey at Melk, crowning a bluff above the Danube, is more imposing; but **St. Florian** has a greater variety of things to see, so it would be a mistake to pass it up for Melk. The **abbey** has been occupied for more than 900 years by the Canons of St. Augustine (canons, unlike monks, aren't confined to an abbey but do ministerial work in their district). It was entirely rebuilt under Carlo Antonio Carlone and Jacob Prandtauer (1686–1751) and is today one of the purest examples of baroque architecture in Europe.

St. Florian was a Roman administrator who was martyred in A.D. 304 and thrown into the nearby River Enns with a millstone around his neck; it was on the site of his grave that the monastery was built. The saint is traditionally invoked against fire with the prayer, "Good St. Florian, spare my house and rather burn my neighbor's." His figure can still be seen in many Austrian houses, dressed as a Roman legionary holding a pail of water to douse the flames.

A great stairway leads to the **Marble Hall,** which has a ceiling depicting Austrian victories over the Turks. Science and Virtue join hands with Religion in allegorical paintings on the **Library** ceiling—a reminder that the Augustines have always regarded the intellect as an ally in their search for spiritual truth.

There were no hotels fit for royalty in those days; hence, the **Imperial Apartments,** lavishly furnished as they were when Empress Maria Theresa and other members of the royal family stayed here. On display, too, is the bed of Anton Bruckner, who died here in 1896. Bruckner, the country's greatest 19th-century composer of organ music, was accepted into the abbey's choir school at 13, when his father died. Most of his symphonies and masses were composed here after 1845, when he was appointed church organist. He became famous when he went to Linz and Vienna as an organist/teacher, but his roots were here, and he was buried, as he requested, in the crypt beneath the church organ.

The exuberant baroque **Abbey Church,** Stiftskirche 1 (☎ 07724/89020), is the chief attraction. You'll wonder why the architect tried so hard to keep you in this world when you should be thinking of the next—until you realize that he has tried to bring God's kingdom down to you and overwhelm you with its glory. The organ's 7,343 pipes make music during summer concerts, daily at 4:30pm. In the crypt below lie Bruckner's coffin and the unbaroque bones of some 6,000 early Christians, dug up when the original Gothic church was built and arranged like so many oranges in a market.

The abbey's most valuable paintings, which you'll see on the tour, are 14 works by Albrecht Altdorfer (1480–1538), the master of the early

16th-century Danube school of painting. The works are noted for their warm, rich colors, their expressiveness, and their use of landscapes not just to provide background but to influence the total mood of the painting—a technique that foreshadowed the Romantics several centuries ahead of its time. You can enter the church free, but guided tours of the monastery cost 50AS for adults and 40AS for children. Tours are conducted from April to October, daily at 10 and 11am and at 2, 3, and 4pm. Otherwise, you must write to the abbey for permission to visit.

ON TO MELK

If you're anxious to reach Dürnstein or to make the last tour at Melk (summers at 5pm; off-season at 4pm), take A1 directly from Linz to Melk Abbey. The alternative is to follow A1 only as far as Enns, cross the Danube on Route 123, take Route 3 east along the Danube, and recross the river at Melk. This route takes you to **Mauthausen** (25.6km/16 miles from Linz), the granite quarry used as a concentration camp where nearly 200,000 prisoners were killed. A 90-minute tour takes you to the remaining huts where prisoners waited to be summoned to their deaths. Open Feb–Apr and Oct–Dec 15, daily 8am–3pm; May–Oct, daily 8am–5pm; closed Dec 16–Jan. For more information, call **07238/2269.** Admission 25AS for adults, 10AS for children.

MELK

There's nothing modest about **Melk;** straddling a rocky bluff 45 meters (150 ft.) above the Danube, it's the embodiment of the Church Militant and the Church Triumphant. The Babenbergs—the family that ruled Austria for 270 years, before the Habsburgs took over—established their rule here in the late 10th century. The second Babenberg, Heinrich I (994–1018), founded the monastery and turned it over to the Benedictines. The Turks gutted it in 1683, and 19 years later Jacob Prandtauer turned it into what many consider the greatest monument to the baroque imagination in Austria.

The high points of the tour are the **Library,** one of the richest in Europe, where the light of learning continued to burn during the Middle Ages; and the **Abbey Church,** Dietmayerstrasse 1 (☎ **02752/2312**). Leaving the church is like stepping from daylight into a shaded room. The abbey is open daily, with the first tour departing at 9am, the last at 5pm in summer or 4pm in winter. Adults pay 70AS for guided tours or 55AS for unguided tours; for children it's 45AS or 30AS, respectively.

THE WACHAU VALLEY

From Melk take Route 3 east along the north shore of the Danube to Krems.

The region along the Danube from Melk to Krems, scarcely 56 kilometers (35 miles) long, is known as the **Wachau Valley:** one of the dreamiest, most romantic river valleys in the world. Imposing castle ruins loom above as you drive along the wide, silent river past terraced orchards and vineyards. In spring, apple, plum, and apricot trees burst into bloom. Medieval vintners' towns with narrow cobbled streets and fortified churches spread along the banks. You're only 90 minutes from Vienna, yet there's little commercial development to mar the beauty of the landscape.

The economy rests on the vineyards, the source of Austria's finest white wines. In 1301 a man named Ritzling, whose vineyards lay along the brook that meets the Danube just west of Dürnstein, developed his own grapes, which were cultivated in Germany's Rhineland and then brought back to Austria under the name Riesling. Today more than 1,000 winegrowers belong to the Wachau cooperative, with headquarters in the 1719 castle outside Dürnstein. Wherever you stay, you'll be able to enjoy these local wines from family-owned vineyards. Route 3, the most popular, takes you through the most historic towns, including Dürnstein, where you should spend the night. Another town of interest is Weissenkirchen.

From Melk, cross the Danube and turn right on Route 3. About 5 kilometers (3 miles) along, on the opposite shore, you'll see an early 19th-century castle (closed to the public) called **Schönbühel.** The orchards begin after Grimsing. Looming up from the highest point across the river, past the village of Aggsbach Markt (11.2km/7 miles east of Melk), is **Aggstein Fortress.** You'll return here later.

SPITZ

After Aggsbach Markt comes **Spitz,** an ancient market town hidden behind apricot and pear trees. Schlossgasse is one of its most picturesque streets. The Gothic **Parish Church** has an elegant chancel that's out of line with the nave (the central aisle). If you need to stretch, hike through the vineyards to the **Red Door,** a wall built to keep out the Turks, and enjoy a sweeping view of the valley.

Dining

The Strand Restaurant, Donaulände 7 (☎ 02713/2320). At this delightful spot for lunch or dinner, overlooking the river at the far end of town, try the venison or some fresh Danube fish with a glass of homemade apricot brandy. Reservations useful. Casual. No credit cards. Closed Tues–Wed and Nov–Mar. Moderate.

Accommodations

Frühstückspensionen Hans Burkhardt, Kremstr. 19, A-3620 Spitz (☎ 02713/2356). You might enjoy this friendly guest house. 5 rms with bath. No credit cards. Closed Nov–Mar. Inexpensive.

Wachauer Hof, Hauptstr. 15, A-3620 Spitz (☎ 02713/2303-20; fax 02713/2403). This is the traditional choice for dining or lodging. Close to the vineyards, it's a mellow old place that has been run by the same family for generations. They pride themselves on their hospitality and gemütlich atmosphere. You can order the wines of the region in their shaded garden in summer or in their Gastube. The restaurant serves typically

Austrian fare, more hearty and filling than innovative. You can spend the night in one of the old-fashioned rooms with a rustic decor. 30 rms with bath. Facilities: restaurant. MC. Closed mid-Dec to mid-Feb. Moderate.

WEISSENKIRCHEN

Weissenkirchen is a charming medieval village dominated by a fortified Gothic church, 14.4 kilometers (9 miles) past Aggsbach. It's less perfect than Dürnstein but also less precious and less well known to tourists.

Dining

Florianihof, Weissenkirchen/Wösendorf 74 (☎ 02715/2212). This is one of the best restaurants along the Danube. The family Mandl takes credit for the friendly service and top cuisine. Popular dishes include fish from the Danube and Vanillerostbraten ("poor man's roast," flavored with garlic). For an aperitif, try a dry Dürnsteiner Auslese; and with your meal, a Riesling or Veltiner. Reservations advised. Jacket/tie required. No credit cards. Closed Wed and Thurs and mid-Jan to mid-Feb. Expensive.

Jamek, Joching 45 (☎ 02715/2235). Jamek is more expensive than Florianihof but enjoys a somewhat better reputation for its local wines and daily specials, particularly the cream soups, filet of beef, and pork cutlets with caraway. Reservations essential. Jacket/tie required. No credit cards. Closed Sun–Mon, mid-Dec to mid-Feb, and first week in July. Very Expensive.

Prandtauerhof, Joching 36 (☎ 02715/2310). This is a perfect choice for an outdoor lunch or dinner of lamb, venison, and excellent wines from the owner's own vineyards. Reservations useful. Casual. No credit cards. Closed Tues, Sun, and mid-Feb to mid-Mar. Expensive.

Accommodations

Raffelsbergerhof, Weissenkirchen, A-3610 Weissenkirchen(☎ 02715/2201; fax 02715/220127). At this former home of the controller of river traffic, not even the modern furnishings can destroy the charm of this 16th-century manor house. 13 rms with bath. MC. Closed Nov–Apr. Expensive.

DÜRNSTEIN

Dürnstein, 4 kilometers (2½ miles) past Weissenkirchen, is the most picturesque village along the Danube, sitting below terraced vineyards at the river's most dramatic turn. The main road passes through a tunnel beneath the town, so the modern world — except for the tourists — hardly intrudes. Richard the Lion-hearted would probably recognize Dürnstein, though he might wonder what has happened to the castle where he was imprisoned, as it lies today in ruins.

During the Third Crusade, Richard the Lion-hearted, king of England, offended Leopold V, duke of Austria, by removing his banner from a tower during the assault on Acre in Palestine. On his way home Richard was shipwrecked off the Yugoslavian coast and had to pass through his rival's lands dressed as a peasant. His royal ring gave him away near Vienna, however, and he was shuttled off to prison in Dürnstein. In the spring of 1193, so the story goes, Richard's faithful servant, Blondel, was wandering from town to town in search of his master, when Richard, standing in a fortress window, overheard Blondel singing his favorite song and finished the verse himself. The king was later set free, after paying a king's ransom.

It's only a 10-minute walk from one end of Dürnstein to the other. Wander along the main street (Hauptstrasse), lined with turreted 16th-century houses dripping with flowers. The 15th-century **Parish Church** was redone in baroque dress—compare the simple Gothic nave to the ornate 18th-century pulpit and high altar.

The best view of Dürnstein is possible from the ruins of the castle above the town. You should try to make the 20-minute walk in the early morning or at dusk. Two other hikes to enjoy are the mile-long walk along the riverfront promenade and the 4-kilometer (2½-mile) walk through the vineyards to Weissenkirchen. Time your trip so you can return by ferry.

If you're partial to boat rides on romantic rivers, take the local ferry round-trip from Dürnstein to Melk. You can get off the ferry at Melk if you missed seeing the abbey en route from Salzburg, then catch another ferry back to Dürnstein later in the day.

The road along the southern bank of the Danube is just as scenic as the one you took (Route 3) along the north shore. The southern route misses the major towns but lets you see them from a distance, framed by vineyards and orchards. To get to the southern route, drive east from Dürnstein toward Krems, cross the bridge at Mautern, and head west along the Danube, back to **Aggstein Fortress**—one of Austria's most romantic castle ruins. The present owner runs a modest restaurant in the old retainer's hall. From the ramparts, 288 meters (960 ft.) above the Danube, there's a panoramic view of the Wachau Valley. Standing at this dizzying height you can decide whether you'd rather jump or starve to death—a choice given to prisoners of Schreckenwald ("Terror of the Forest"), the robber baron who stretched a chain across the Danube here and imprisoned those who didn't pay a toll. (Justice was served when an escaped prisoner set the castle on fire and the Terror was reduced to a wandering beggar.)

You can rent bicycles at train stations in Krems and Melk and return them at other stations along the route. The ferries take bicycles (for a fee), so you can bike, say, from Dürnstein to Aggsbach, and then return by ferry. Most tourists take the north route, so the relatively flat south one is ideal for biking, though there are developed bicycle routes along both river shores. A ferry recrosses the Danube at Spitz.

Dining

Bacher, Südtirolerplatz 2, Mautern (☎ 02732/829370). Landhaus Bacher is one of Austria's best restaurants, elegant but entirely lacking in pretension. Dining in the garden in summer adds to the experience.

Reservations required. Jacket/tie advised. DC, V. Closed Mon–Tues. Very Expensive.

Sänger Blondel, Dürnstein (☎ 02711/253). At this family restaurant popular with tourists, the food inclines toward local and regional cuisine, including Danube fish. Try the clear soup with liver dumplings, the roasted pork or stuffed brisket of veal, and the house specialty, the Sänger-Blondel Torte. Reservations advisable. Jacket/tie required. No credit cards. Closed Dec–Feb and the first week in July. Moderate.

Zum Goldenen Strauss, Dürnstein (☎ 02711/267). In this attractive onetime post office, you'll find excellent local specialties such as roast pork and veal, along with good wines. No reservations. Casual but neat. No credit cards. Closed Tues and mid-Jan to Feb. Moderate.

Accommodations

Hotel Richard Lowenherz, A-3601 Dürnstein (☎ 02711/222; fax 02711/22218). This is more a hotel you check into than a castle where you become a privileged guest, and antiques are in the halls, not in the rooms; yet the hotel does have some character, and the rooms are less expensive than at the Schloss (see below). 40 rms with bath. Facilities: restaurant, terrace cafe, pool. AE, DC, MC, V. Expensive.

Pension Altes Rathaus, Beate Fürtler, A-3601 Dürnstein (☎ 02711/252). This private home provides budget lodging for travelers. 7 rms, 4 with bath. No credit cards. Closed Dec–Apr. Inexpensive.

Schloss Dürnstein, A-3601 Dürnstein (☎ 02711/212; fax 02711/351). This place spares no pains to capture the elegance of the original 17th-century castle, high on a cliff overlooking the Danube. There's a pool, a good restaurant, and a shaded terrace where you can sip local wines and watch the boats gliding along the river. The vaulted salons are decorated with antique furniture from the family of Count Starhemberg, who kept the Turks from Vienna in 1683. 37 rms with bath. Facilities: restaurant (reservations required), sauna, pool. AE, DC, MC, V. Closed Nov–Mar. Very Expensive.

Vienna

It's about 96 kilometers (60 miles) from Dürnstein to Vienna. As you head east from Dürnstein to Krems, the mountains recede and the scenery loses much of its drama. Cross the bridge at Krems and drive south past Herzogenburg to A1. There's a Tourist Information Office on A1 before you reach Vienna.

Vienna says Empire—that's why Americans love it so much. Only a people raised under Jefferson could embrace an imperial city so uncritically and with such longing. We may have left behind the Old World but not our need for splendor. And splendor, imaginary or not, is what Vienna has to offer.

The people, the palaces—everything about Vienna seems suspended in the 18th century, frozen in time. It's a city under glass. The people, born

VIENNA

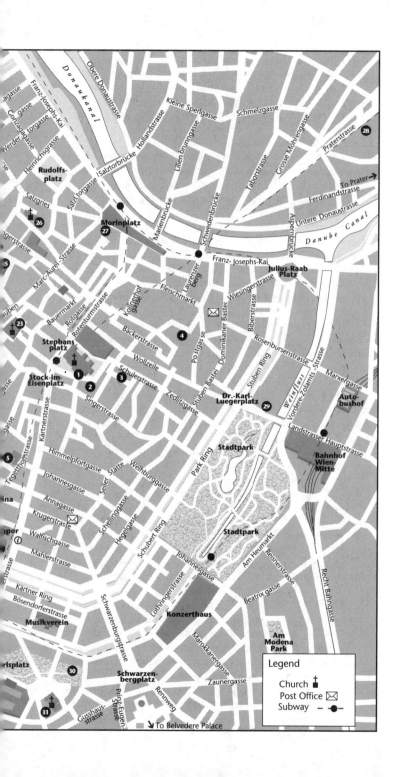

Legend

Church ✝

Post Office ⊠

Subway ─●─

to another age, still hold to courtly forms: addressing each other by titles long abolished, kissing hands, loving food and beauty, ignoring time. It is, literally, a city of dreams—dreams that become your own as you wander through palaces, sip champagne at the opera, or indulge yourself in pastry shops once frequented by Haydn and Mozart, Adler, and Freud.

There's a reverse side to this dream, of course. Strauss wrote "The Blue Danube" partly to make Austrians forget their humiliating defeat by Prussia, which reduced them to a second-rate power. Coffeehouses thrive in part because of a housing shortage and cramped living conditions. Few cities have been so unkind to their musicians—while they were alive. The Viennese loved Schubert's pretty songs, but the poignancy of his greatest works escaped them.

Between the Franco-Prussian War and World War I, Vienna changed from the center of an empire of 50 million to the capital of a small alpine nation. It remains today an imperial city without an empire. It's fitting that it is a baroque city, for baroque is the art of the facade, the perfect stage set for fantasy. To say that its splendor exists only in the mind's eye, however, makes it no less splendid. If Vienna is a dream, then I say let's dream on.

The oldest part of Vienna, bounded by the Ringstrasse and the Danube (Donau) Canal, is called District I. The major sights of District I are described below on the walking tour of "Old Vienna & the Ring." Other sights—Schönbrunn, the Belvedere, and the Prater—are then described under "Outside the Ring."

The Hofburg (the Habsburg Palace) is Vienna's number-one attraction, so visit in the morning, particularly because the Spanish Riding School and the National Library, both part of the Hofburg, are open only then. In the afternoon either visit museums near the Hofburg (the Fine Arts Museum for paintings; the Neue Burg for porcelain and silver, arms and armor) or wander the streets of Vienna, shopping and visiting churches and pastry shops. Save whichever you choose not to do for the following day and combine it with tours of Schönbrunn Palace, the Belvedere, and the Prater. If you have any time left, take a streetcar ride around the Ring. The "1" line does the full circuit clockwise, the "2" line counterclockwise. Plan to spend at least 1 evening dining in Old Vienna and going to a concert or an opera. Save another evening for a drive through the Vienna Woods and dinner at a Heuriger (new wine tavern) at Grinzing or Nussdorf.

OLD VIENNA & THE RING

Let's begin at the **Vienna Booking Service Tourist Office** in the subway station/shopping mall beneath Opera Square. Pick up maps, brochures, and listings of weekly events. Be sure to get the latest schedule of opening and closing times, which can vary from building to building; ignoring these times could ruin your trip. Buy a valuable city publication called *Vienna from A to Z*, which describes the major sights by numbers that match numbered plaques on the buildings. Also purchase a money-saving

Three-Day Transportation Ticket valid on all subways, streetcars, and buses.

From the Tourist Office, cross back inside the Ring and head down Kärntnerstrasse, past the **State Opera House** (Staatsoper), Opernring 2 (☎ 0222/51444-29-60). If you don't plan on going to the opera, take a tour (given almost daily year-round, depending on rehearsal schedules), costing 40AS per person. Tickets to performances cost 120 to 2,3000AS.

Continue down Kärntnerstrasse toward **St. Stephen's Cathedral** (see below). Just past the Opera House is Philharmonikerstrasse. Turn left. At no. 4 is one of Vienna's most illustrious hotels, the **Sacher,** where the nobility conducted its affairs, both political and social, during the days of the Empire. Franz Josef's guests used to come here after dining at the Imperial Palace (the Hofburg); etiquette demanded that no one eat after the Emperor finished a course, and Franz Josef, who had spartan tastes, was a light eater. If the hotel lobby is quiet, a porter may be willing to show you the paneled lounge, private dining rooms, and collection of autographed menus. The Sachertorte, a chocolate-frosted cake with a side of whipped cream, was first made here for one of Metternich's banquets.

It's said that here is where Franz Josef's son and heir, the Crown Prince Rudolf, began his affair with 17-year-old Baroness Maria Vetsera. Probably because Franz Josef refused to delegate authority to his son, the 31-year-old boy found his own way of growing up by drinking, partying, and associating with liberals and other freethinkers. In late 1888, Rudolf wrote a letter to the Pope. What he said nobody will ever know, but when his father got wind of it, he severely chastised the boy, and the next day Rudolf and Maria were found dead at his hunting lodge at **Mayerling,** about 32

MEMORIALS TO VIENNA'S GREAT COMPOSERS

Why did Vienna spawn so many musicians, but so few writers? Perhaps because ideas were censored under the Habsburgs and one can say most anything in music. Perhaps, too, music is the voice of nostalgia.

Musicians came here in the 18th and early 19th centuries because the aristocracy maintained small orchestras and groups of performers. A musician who joined a household was treated as a footman and lived and ate with the servants. The intimacy among the Viennese composers is legendary: Mozart and Haydn were friends; Beethoven took lessons from Haydn; Schubert was a pallbearer at Beethoven's funeral; Arnold Schönberg taught his 12-tone system here to Alban Berg and Anton von Webern.

The **Haydn Memorial House & Brahms Memorial Room,** Haydgasse 19, is where Haydn gave lessons to Beethoven and composed *The Creation.* When Franz Josef Haydn arrived in Vienna at 17 he was alone and friendless; at the time of his death, here at this house, he was the greatest composer in Europe. He came of peasant stock from a nearby village and was brought to sing in the choir of St. Stephen's. To make ends meet he sang at weddings and funerals. Eventually he was offered the position of Kapellmeister to a prince, at whose estate he composed most of his works. Admission 25AS adults, 10AS children. Open Tues–Sun 9am–12:15pm.

(continues)

For the **Mozart Memorial** (Figarohaus), see "Old Vienna & the Ring," above.

The **Pasqualati House,** Mölker Bastei 8 (☎ 0222/535-89-05), is where the Beethoven lived from 1805 to 1815. Ludwig van Beethoven came to Vienna from Bonn at 22 and stayed for life. He was a terrible neighbor, playing piano at odd hours, and was forced to move some 25 times. It was at this charming house that he composed *Fidelio* and the Fourth, Fifth, and Seventh symphonies. Here, too, he wrote the Moonlight Sonata, dedicated to an early love. It was a walk in the Vienna Woods that may have inspired the Pastoral Symphony. In his house in Heiligenstadt, which you can visit on a trip to Grinzing, Beethoven wrote his bitter Heiligenstadt Testament: "What humiliation when someone is standing near me and hears a far-off flute and I cannot hear it, or when someone hears the shepherd singing and I can hear nothing. Such experiences nearly drove me to despair, and it would have taken little to make me end my own life. One thing alone, the art of music, restrained me." When Beethoven conducted the Ninth Symphony in Vienna in 1824, the orchestra watched not him but the concert master. After the second movement there was thunderous applause, but Beethoven didn't hear it; the singer had to turn him around so he could see the clapping hands and acknowledge the ovation. Beethoven died in Vienna. According to one source, he died saying to his friend Hümmel: "I had a certain talent, hadn't I?" Admission 25AS adults, 10AS children. Open Tues–Sun 11am–12:15pm and 1–4:30pm.

The **Schubert Museum,** Nussdorferstrasse 54 (☎ 0222/317-36-01),

(continues)

kilometers (20 miles) southwest of Vienna. Maria had been shot first and covered with flowers. To cover up the scandal, she was spirited away in a rainstorm, sitting up fully dressed in a carriage between two uncles, and buried in a nearby monastery under police supervision. Rudolf left notes for his wife and mother, but not for his father. That the young couple had a suicide pact seems clear, but that the lovers took their lives because Franz Josef demanded they part seems doubtful. Rudolf was a man of many affairs—he had, in fact, spent the night before with an actress he'd been seeing for some time—so more than likely he was in trouble for his liberal views.

At the end of Philharmonikerstrasse is a large plaza, Albertina, now the site of a disputed war memorial.

Turn down the Tegetthoffstrasse to the **Capuchin's Crypt,** Neuer Markt (☎ 0222/512-68-53). Three centuries of Habsburgs are buried here—or at least their bodies: Their hearts are gathering dust in the crypt of the Augustinerkirche (see below) and their entrails are resting in the catacombs of St. Stephen's (see below). Empress Maria Theresa used to pay respect to her husband, Franz Stephan, here, and an elevator was installed when she got too stout for the trip. Stuck one day, she cried out, "Look, the dead don't want to let me go"; a week later she, too, was dead. Maria and Franz now stare into each other's eyes on the lid of their sarcophagus—an angel waits at their heads with a trumpet to awaken them on Judgment Day. The only non-Habsburg here is Caroline Fuchs, governess to Maria Theresa's 10 surviving children, including the ill-fated Marie Antoinette. History should note that it was Caroline Fuchs who made it possible for Maria Theresa to have both a family and a career. The most recent—and presumably last—burial in the crypt took place in 1989, when Zita, widow of Austria's last Kaiser, was interred with all state honors, those of Hungary included.

Backtrack, turning right on the Fürichgasse behind the disputed "Memorial to Oppression" and right again into Augustinerstrasse. On your left is the **Albertina Gallery,** Augustinerstrasse 1 (☎ 0222/53-483). Stop here now or return another day on your visit to the museums. The Albertina houses one of the largest and best collections of graphic art in the world, including many drawings by Albrecht Dürer. Unfortunately, many works are shown only in facsimile, except during special exhibits. Admission 45AS adults, 20AS students; under 11 free. Open Mon–Thurs 10am–4pm, Fri 10am–2pm, Sat–Sun 10am–1pm.

Continue down Augustinerstrasse to the 14th-century **Augustinerkirche,** Augustinerstrasse 3 (☎ 0222/533-70-99), entrance on Josefsplatz. Though remodeled, it gives off an aura of great age and captures the spirit of the early Habsburgs, who came here to pray. They all left their hearts here—buried in urns. Franz Josef gave *his* heart away here to 17-year-old Elisabeth. And it was here that Napoléon decided to marry his second wife, Marie-Louise (niece of Marie Antoinette), though he chose not to show up and sent someone to marry her by proxy. (He did eventually marry her in person, however, in Paris.) On your left on Josefsplatz is the **National Library.** The **Great Hall** is a masterpiece of baroque decoration.

is the birthplace of the only one of the major composers who was actually born in Vienna. Franz Peter Schubert was the son of a poor schoolmaster—a boy with glasses and an angelic voice. When his voice broke, he had to leave the Vienna Boys' Choir and find some other way to earn a living. He started teaching in his father's school but hated it and spent most of his time writing music instead. He was never able to afford his own room (except for a short time) or even his own piano. Many of his songs were written on the backs of menus in neighborhood cafes, where he went with devoted friends. At Beethoven's deathbed he toasted, "To the one of us who is next"; and 19 months later, at age 31, he himself was dead. Admission 25AS adults, 10AS students and children. Open Tues–Sun 9am–12:15pm and 1–4:30pm.

In the **Central Cemetery** (Zentralfriedhof) is Musician's Square, where you'll find the graves of Schubert, Hugo Wolf, Christoph Willibald Gluck, Johannes Brahms, Beethoven, and Johann Strauss (father and son).

You are now in the **Hofburg,** Michaelerplatz (☎ 0222/587-55-54), the winter residence of the Habsburgs and still the seat of Austrian government. The palace was begun in the 13th century and continued to grow and change for the next 700 years. Styles change from one building to the next—the public halls are usually lavish, the private rooms relatively plain and comfortable.

Your tour of the Hofburg is a voyage into Austria's past. In 976 the Holy Roman Emperor Otto I gave land to a German nobleman named Leopold of Babenberg for his help in crushing a Bavarian revolt. The Babenbergs ruled Austria for the next 270 years. And when the last

Babenberg died without an heir, Count Rudolf of Habsburg fought his way to power. From this family of minor Swiss nobility came the Habsburg dynasty, the strongest in European history, ruling continuously from 1278 to 1918. The emperors were brilliant and mad; they wrote music; they built palaces. Their goal wasn't to win slavish allegiance to Austria but to acquire wealth and land, and they accomplished this less by aggression than by diplomacy, marrying their daughters off to foreign kings. From the Hofburg they ruled most of Central Europe, as well as Spain and Spanish colonies in South America.

Vienna has always been a frontier town on the border between East and West. The Turks attacked in 1529 and were repelled. More than 150 years later, the Turks tried again. While the Emperor and his court fled the city, 24,000 men under Count Starhemberg held out for 2 months against a force of 200,000. With the aid of Polish King John Sobieski, the Turks were finally routed, ending forever the Ottoman threat to Europe. If Vienna had fallen, so might have Christendom. For decades the Viennese had faced outward, bracing themselves for the attack. Victory released a flood of pent-up energy, and with joy, pride, and relief the Viennese created the baroque city you see today.

Before Maria Theresa came the three so-called baroque emperors: Leopold I (1658–1705), Josef I (1705–11), and Karl VI (1711–40). Maria Theresa had much in common with Queen Victoria: a long reign (1740–80); a large family (16 children); an insistence on duty and morality; goodness and sincerity; and an enlightened despotism. With her death the age of monuments and, some would say, the glory of the Habsburgs came to an end.

Her son Josef II (1780–90) tried to continue his mother's reforms, but he pushed too hard and too fast. He reacted against excesses of luxury, but the people loved pomp and splendor. He tried to protect nightingales in the public gardens, but the people preferred keeping songbirds caged.

When Napoléon's empire fell apart, the crowned heads of Europe gathered in Vienna to pick up the pieces. Vienna was now the center of Europe. The main figure at the Congress of Vienna (Sept 1814–July 1815) was the Austrian statesman Prince von Metternich. For centuries, European powers had struggled to dominate by force; what Metternich sought was a balance of power, with Austria as the vital buffer between Russia and France. While Metternich schemed, the Congress danced and dined its way from one wild entertainment to the next. This was the laughing, licentious Vienna that lives on in our dreams: Czar Alexander of Russia dancing for 40 nights; the fat King of Würtemberg cutting a hole in the dinner table so he could reach his plate; Castlereagh's wife wearing a garter ribbon in her hair. *"Le Congrès danse, mais il ne marche pas"* is the quote to remember: "The Congress dances, but it gets nowhere."

The period from 1815 to 1848 is known as the Biedermeier Age, the age of the middle class. Tired of war, the country turned to Schubert songs, pastry, and new wine. Gone was the stately minuet—the dance of the aristocracy. In its place came the rhythms of a Jewish innkeeper's son named Johann Strauss. While twilight fell over Imperial Vienna, his son Johann Strauss the younger had some 230 musicians working for him in the resplendent ballrooms of Vienna. "Vienna, be gay!" they sang to the strains of "The Blue Danube." "Well, why court sorrow? / There's still tomorrow, / So laugh and be merry."

Metternich ruled under a weak emperor. Discontent grew as liberties were repressed, and Metternich was finally forced to flee to London in the Vienna uprising of 1848.

Franz Josef reigned for 68 years, from 1848 to 1916. When he was crowned, James Polk was in the White House; when he died, Woodrow Wilson had been elected to serve a second term.

Until the mid-19th century "Old Vienna" was encircled by the walls that kept the Turks from overrunning Europe. For the city to expand, Franz Josef had the walls torn down and replaced by the Ringstrasse—a ring of wide boulevards lined with the monumental late 19th-century public buildings you see today.

Tearing down the walls was one of Franz Josef's few gestures toward the future. He was a man of simple, austere tastes who hated reform. He was an anachronism—an 18th-century figure in a 19th-century world; a man who worked long hours, fumbling with documents while the world collapsed around him. His son Rudolf committed suicide at Mayerling; his wife, Elisabeth, was struck down by an assassin's dagger; his nephew Franz Ferdinand was assassinated at Sarajevo. It was perhaps a blessing that he died in 1916 and didn't live to see his successor, the Emperor Karl, renounce the throne in 1918, bringing to an end more than 6 centuries of Habsburg rule.

Across the Josefsplatz, on the far right, is the Stallburg, the stable for the **Spanish Riding School,** Michaelerplatz 1, Hofburg (☎ **0222/ 533-90-32**). A passage in front of the Stallburg leads to the Spanish Riding School itself.

The idea of noble purebred horses smacks of Empire, which helps explain the lasting appeal of the milk-white Lipizzaner stallions who perform to capacity crowds in the City of Dreams. Hitler, who, as the world knows, had a fondness for selective breeding, sent the horses to what was then Czechoslovakia to protect them during the war; General Patton, another horse lover, eventually brought them back.

It seems fitting that during the Congress of Vienna, kings and queens danced in the same sumptuous hall where the horses performed. As Edward Crankshaw wrote in 1938:

> *The cabrioling of the pure Lipizzaners is, by all our standards, the absolute of uselessness. The horses, fine, beautiful and strong, are utterly divorced from all natural movement, living their lives in an atmosphere of unreality with every step laid down for them and no chance whatsoever of a moment's deviation. And so it was with the 19th-century Habsburgs. The Court, intent on cabrioles and ballotades, was lost to all reality.*

True as this may be, what visitors seek and discover at performances today are qualities often missing from our modern world: grace, beauty, and dignity—all born of discipline and self-control. Regular performances are 240 to 800AS for seats and 190AS for standing room. Training performance with music are 240AS. Children under 3 aren't admitted, but children 3 to 6 attend free with adults. Training sessions are 100AS for adults and 20AS for children. Regular performances, Mar–June and Sept to mid-Dec, Sun at 10:45am, most Weds at 7pm. Training performances with music, May and Sept, Sat at 10am. Training sessions, mid-Feb to June and end of Aug to mid-Dec, Tues–Fri 10am–noon (except on public holidays).

Return to Josefsplatz. To your right, beside the National Library, is a passageway leading to the Swiss Court, named for the soldiers who once stood here on guard. On the right is the **Imperial Treasury,** Hofburg, Schweizerhof (☎ 0222/533-79-31), where you'll see the crown of the Holy Roman Emperor, Charlemagne's lance, and fabulous 15th-century embroidered vestments. Even when the imperial crown was padded it failed to fit most heads, and Maria Theresa had a good silent laugh when it slipped down over the ears of her husband at his coronation. Admission 60AS adults, 30AS children, seniors, and students.

From the Treasury, return to the Swiss Court. To your left are steps leading to the beautiful Gothic **Castle Chapel,** Hofburgkapelle (☎ 0222/533-99-27), where the Vienna Boys' Choir sings. The choir, founded in 1498 by Emperor Maximilian, is chosen from some 7,000 applicants every year (see the box "The Arts in Vienna" for ticket information).

Return to the Swiss Court, turn left, and pass into the central palace courtyard called In der Burg (Inside the Castle). Turn immediately right and pass beneath a rotunda directly inside the Michaelertor (Michael's Gate). On the left is the **Collection of Court Porcelain and Silver** (☎ 0222/533-7570). On the right are the Imperial Apartments. Admission 70AS.

The **Imperial Apartments** are impressed with the personalities of Franz Josef and Elisabeth. The emperor's iron bed is as austere as the one he slept in at Bad Ischl. Elisabeth had exercise equipment in the room next to her bedroom because she loved sports and was afraid of getting fat. In the Empire-style **Conference Room** is a portrait of Elisabeth with the face of both an empress and a playful little girl. What must it have been like for a 17-year-old to become an empress with 50 million subjects? According to British writer Rebecca West, it was Elisabeth who convinced her husband to create the Dual Monarchy with Hungary, which permitted the empire to survive into the 20th century. By 1860 Elisabeth had become a withdrawn, sensitive lady who hardly ever visited her husband and was seldom at Court. She may have gone a bit mad. If her tyrannical mother-in-law, Sophie, had let her raise her son Rudolf, who knows, the boy might have lived, and Elisabeth with him; and together they might have restrained Austria's imperialist ambitions and avoided World War I.

Without them, Franz Josef stood fast against reform. A conscientious but unimaginative man (though he liked people), he ruled a dying empire. Three years later Rudolf took his own life at Mayerling, and Franz Josef wrote to his wife, "I should like to put into words how very, very deeply I love you, though I am not very good at showing it and I would only bore you if I could." The most satisfying and disturbing room on your tour is the **Banquet Hall,** set for a royal feast to which the guests will never come.

Return to the rotunda and, leaving the Hofburg, turn right to **St. Michael's Church** (Michaelerkirche) on a square called Michaelerplatz. The high altar, with angels and saints in a golden heaven, is the essence of baroque.

At no. 3 Michaelerplatz is the 1910 **Loos House,** the first example of modern architecture. Adolf Loos was a New Functionalist who believed that style should be the servant of use. By eliminating meaningless detail and decoration—the essence of baroque—Loos paved the way for the familiar glass-and-concrete slabs that define our cities today. Now beautifully restored, the building houses bank offices instead of the tailors for which the lower floors were designed.

From St. Michael's, turn right along the pedestrian shopping street called Kohlmarkt. Turn right on another shopping street called Graben. If you want to see one of the most sumptuous baroque churches in Vienna, make your first left off Graben to **Peterskirche.**

Halfway up the Graben is the **Plague Monument,** designed by Fischer von Erlach to celebrate the end of a plague in 1679. Though it's not particularly satisfying—it looks like a mound of dirty whipped cream—it does capture the essence of baroque in the way that the artist completely transforms his material to satisfy his artistic needs.

The Graben ends at **St. Stephen's Cathedral** (Stephansdom), Stephansplatz 1 (☎ **0222/515-52**), the spiritual heart and soul of Vienna. This is one of the few Austrian churches whose Gothic austerity hasn't been retouched with the lightness and color of baroque. The slender south tower has been hit by lightning and artillery; search out the window where the watch keeper kept a lookout for Turks. The builder, Hans Puchsbaum, was told not to look down, but did anyway, and fell to his death. For a great view, climb 344 steps up the tower, past the bench where Count von Starhemberg watched the Turkish assault. An elevator takes you to the bell in the northern tower.

The Romanesque (13th-century) main doorway, decorated with stiff apostles, animals, and demons, is the oldest part of the church. In medieval times men and women sat on opposite sides, which is why there are only male saints over the southwest door, where the men entered; and only the Virgin and female saints over the northwest door used by women. Behind the cathedral is a suffering Christ called the "Toothache God."

Immediately on your left as you enter is the **Cross Chapel** (Kreuzkapelle), with the grave of military leader Prince Eugene (1663–1736). The iron grillwork on the doors is copied from the gates at Belvedere Palace. Look for reliefs depicting scenes from the Turkish wars.

Near the middle of the church, on the left, is the early 16th-century pulpit carved from solid blocks of stone. The artist peers through a window near the bottom, looking quite fatigued after so much work. The animals climbing up the railing represent sins.

More beautiful than the black marble main altar is the **Wiener Neustadt altarpiece** (1447) in the chapel to the left. This is one of the most richly carved altarpieces in the world. In the right chapel is the remarkable late 15th-century **tomb of Emperor Friedrich III,** made from red Salzburg marble. Evil animals try to disturb Friedrich's sleep, while good spirits, in the form of local personages, keep them away.

A 30-minute guided tour of the catacombs takes you past the entrails of the Habsburgs preserved in copper jars. Admission to Cathedral, free; tour of catacombs, 40AS adults, 15AS children under 14. Guided tour of cathedral, 40AS adults, 15AS children under 14. North Tower, 40AS adults, 15AS children under 15; South Tower, 25AS adults, 15AS students, 5AS children under 15. Evening tours, including tour of the roof, 130AS adults, 50AS children under 15. Cathedral open daily 6am–10pm (except times of service). Tour of catacombs, Mon–Sat at 10, 11, and 11:30am and 2, 2:30, 3:30, 4, and 4:30pm; Sun at 2, 2:30, 3:30, 4, and 4:30pm. North Tower, daily 9am–6pm; South Tower, daily 9am–5:30pm. Guided tour of cathedral, Mon–Sat at 10:30am and 3pm; Sun 3pm. Special evening tour Sat 7pm (May–Sept).

A block behind the cathedral is the **Mozart Memorial** (Figarohaus), Domgasse 5 (☎ 0222/513-62-94), where Wolfgang lived from 1784 to 1787 and wrote *The Marriage of Figaro.* Haydn came here as a guest and heard the first performance of Mozart's *Haydn Quartets.* Mozart died in 1791 about three blocks away in the Rauhensteingasse, in dire poverty. His body was taken to the cemetery on a cold, snowy day, and no one marked where it was placed. Freemasons at that time advocated extremely simple burials, without markers or tombstones. Admission 15AS adults, 5AS students and children. Open Tues–Sun 9am–12:15pm and 1–4:30pm.

The choice now is yours: to cross Stephansplatz and walk up the main shopping street, Kärntnerstrasse, back to the Opera; or to take a short side trip through the Old University district, the oldest part of the city. Let's begin with the Old University district; if your legs refuse to cooperate, skip down to the section below called Kärntnerstrasse and save the old town for another day.

THE OLD UNIVERSITY DISTRICT

As you exit through the main door of St. Stephen's, turn right and head down Rotenturmstrasse. Turn right at Lugeck and bear right on Bäckerstrasse. You're in the Old University district now (the university has since moved), with narrow lanes and beautiful courtyards. The courtyard at no. 7 has Renaissance arcades; the French writer Mme de Staël lived in no. 8 after Napoléon banished her from France. Continue to Old University Square, Dr.-Ignaz Seipel-Platz. To your left, at the far end of the square, is the dignified **Church of the Jesuits** (Jesuitenkirche). The domed ceiling isn't curved at all—a good example of baroque trompe l'oeil.

From the church entrance, walk straight on Sonnenfelsgasse (behind the Academy) and turn right on Schönlaterngasse, which is lined with houses that haven't changed much since the days of the Turkish siege. In a niche at no. 7 is an image of a beast, perhaps 750 years old. Legend has it that a dragon poisoned the water in the courtyard's well. A hero climbed down with a mirror. When the beast saw himself, he died of fright.

Just before the street turns right, you'll pass **Heiligenkreuzerhof,** with St. Bernard's Chapel and a peaceful courtyard where you can rest your feet. The monastery was the winter home of monks from the Vienna Woods.

Leave the courtyard by the far entrance, make your first right and then a left on Fleischmarkt (Meat Market). Turn left again on Rotenturmstrasse and right at Lugeck to the **Hoher Markt,** the old Roman forum, where Vienna began. In the Middle Ages the square was used as both a market and a pillory, where pickpockets and adultresses got their due. The great personages of Viennese history march from the **Anker Clock** as the hour strikes. Identify them from the plaque to the lower left of the clock archway; all march past at noon.

From the center of the square turn right up Judengasse to the Romanesque **Church of St. Rupert** (Ruprechtskirche), the town's oldest church. Though altered, its simplicity provides relief from the bright extravagances of the baroque and reminds you that the Viennese must have believed once in guilt and sin. Rupert was the patron saint of the Danube salt merchants, and you can see his salt bucket with his statue outside the church.

THE ARTS IN VIENNA

The **Vienna Festival** features 4 weeks of operas and concerts in late May and June. For details, contact any Austrian Tourist Office or contact the Wiener Festwochen, Bestellbüro, Lehargasse 11, A-1060 Vienna (☎ 0222/589-220).

The **Vienna Music Summer** (late June–Sept) is a summer-long festival of daily concerts. Complete programs are available at tourist offices or by mail from Laudongasse 29, A-1080 Vienna (☎ 0222/4000-8410; fax 0222/4000-7212).

The season at the **State Opera** (Staatsoper), Opernring 2, and the **Volksoper,** Währingerstrasse 78 (operettas, musicals), runs from September to June. Summer programs vary, but check for possible performances in the State Opera or Volksoper. It's worth a trip to the Staatsoper just to see the "show" at intermission when the Viennese, with their stiff collars and pearly bosoms, sip champagne and nibble on chocolate-dipped strawberries as they promenade up and down the hall. No monument gives you such a sense of living in a "city of dreams." Tickets are sold at box offices and travel agencies. From anywhere in the world you can make credit-card phone orders 6 days in advance of performance by calling 0222/ 51444-29-60.

The tourist office has monthly listings of concerts. The **Vienna Philharmonic** performs in the **Musikverein,** Dumbastrasse 3 (☎ 0222/505-8681-32). The

(continues)

Vienna Symphony and other groups perform in the **Wiener Konzerthaus**, Lothringerstrasse 20 (☎ 0222/712-12-11). Concerts are also held in the **Schubert Museum**, Nussdorferstrasse 54 (☎ 0222/ 317-36-01). Church music can be heard Sunday mornings at St. Stephen's, Karlskirche, and August-inerkirche. Special summer concerts are held in the Belvedere Garden and at Schönbrunn. Candlelit baroque concerts, with performers in 18th-century dress, are given in the Palais Pallavicini at Josefplatz. To see the **Vienna Boys' Choir** write at least 2 months in advance to Hofmusik-kapelle, Hofburg, A-1010 Vienna. You'll be sent a reservation card to present at the box office when you pick up your tickets. Additional tickets are sold at travel agencies and at the Burgkapelle (in the Hofburg) every Friday at 5pm. Line up by 4:30pm.

The two English-language theaters are the **English Theater**, Josefgasse 12 (☎ 0222/402-1260), and the **International Theatre**, Porzellan-gasse 8 (☎ 0222/319-6272).

Retrace your steps a short way down Judengasse and turn right on a narrow lane called Sterngasse. At the T-intersection, turn left, and then at the **Old Town** Hall (Altes Rathaus), next to St. Salvador Church, turn right down a narrow street to **Maria am Gestade.** Many consider this the loveliest church in Vienna. Before the Danube was diverted, an arm flowed by the church steps and fishers moored there to pray. The late 8th-century church was rebuilt in Gothic style in the early 15th-century and has been restored since World War II.

From Maria am Gestade, turn down the narrow Schwertgasse. The first wide street you come to is Wipplingerstrasse. Turn left and pass between the Altes Rathaus and the old **Chancellery of Bohemia,** with a baroque facade by Fischer von Erlach. Turn right around the chancellery, then right again, to a square called Judenplatz, the heart of the old ghetto. There was a synagogue here around 1200, but in the 15th century the Jews were burned or imprisoned and the synagogue razed. The Jews gradually returned but were again expelled during the Counter-Reformation.

Cross the square and turn left down another narrow street, Parisergasse, which empties into a small square. On your left are the **Municipal Clock Museum** (Uhren-museum der Stadt Wien), Schulhof 2 (☎ 0222/533-2265; admission 50AS adults, 20AS children; open Tues–Sun 9am–4:30pm), with a wonderful collection of timepieces, from medieval sundials to electronic clocks, which perform on the hour; and next door is the delightful **Doll and Toy Museum,** Schulhof 4 (☎ 0222/535-68-60; admission 60AS adults, 30AS children; open Tues–Sun 10am–6pm), whose collections of dolls and dollhouses is one of the most remarkable in the world, beginning in the 1740s. To your right, on the main square, Am Hof, is the **Church of the Nine Choirs of Angels** (Kirche am Hof), a 14th-century church with a simple early baroque facade. The church faces onto Am Hofsquare, surrounded by buildings with baroque facades. It was here that Franz II announced the end of the Holy Roman Empire in 1804. Turn left as you enter the square and at the corner turn left again on Borgnergasse or walk across into the Naglergasse, with its small shops and sidewalk restaurants. A quick right at the end of the street takes you back to Kohlmarkt. Turn left on Graben and return to St. Stephen's Cathedral.

In case you want to see the world.

At American Express, we're here to make your journey a smooth one. So we have over 1,700 travel service locations in over 120 countries ready to help. What else would you expect from the world's largest travel agency?

do more ®

Travel

In case you want to be welcomed there.

We're here to see that you're always welcomed at establishments everywhere. That's why millions of people carry the American Express® Card – for peace of mind, confidence, and security, around the world or just around the corner.

do more

Cards

In case you're running low.

We're here to help with more than 118,000 Express Cash

locations around the world. In order to enroll, just call

American Express before you start your vacation.

do more

Express Cash

And just in case.

We're here with American Express® Travelers Cheques and Cheques *for Two*.® They're the safest way to carry money on your vacation and the surest way to get a refund, practically anywhere, anytime.

Another way we help you...

do more

Travelers Cheques

From St. Stephen's walk along Kärntnerstrasse, the main shopping street, back to the Opera House (Staatsoper), where your walk began.

KÄRNTNERSTRASSE

If your feet are holding up, continue south along Kärntnerstrasse past the Ring to a large park. To your left, at the far end of the park, standing beneath a magnificent dome, is the **Karlskirche,** one of the most important baroque churches in Vienna. There's a story that Fischer von Erlach got the idea for it while standing on Pincio, Rome's famous hill, seeing Trajan's column and St. Peter's in a single vision in the setting sun. The Karlskirche is a fascinating synthesis of pagan Rome and Christianity, of East and West, of clerical and secular. There's no long nave (central aisle) leading to the altar, so you feel as though you're standing at the center of a cross, overwhelmed by color and light. It's not surprising that this was the first church built after the victory over the Turks.

Return to the Ring and turn left. The first park you come to on the right is the delightful **Burggarten.** There's a cafe on the back terrace. The park is bordered by the Neue Burg, which has museums of old musical instruments and of arms and armor.

Across the Ring is the **Museum of Fine Arts,** Schillerplatz 3 (☎ 0222/58-8160), which no one who cares about art will want to miss. Entire galleries are devoted to the paintings of Bruegel the Elder, Van Dyck, Rubens, and Dürer. The paintings come from the collection of the Habsburgs, who must have had a particular fondness for Venetian colors. Admission 30AS. Open Tues and Thurs–Fri 10am–1pm, Wed 10am–1pm and 3–6pm, Sat–Sun 9am–1pm.

If you're partial to wide, busy boulevards and monumental mid–19th-century public buildings, continue right around the Ring to the canal. The Ring that encircles the medieval city is a rather ponderous monument to a dying empire that barely survived its completion. The original ramparts, which stood along the Ring until Franz Josef tore them down, were so wide that carriages could ride on top, four horses abreast. Outside the walls was a moat, then a level area with no buildings, so that enemies could be spotted. The Ring today consists of eight interlocking boulevards, about 4 kilometers (2.5 miles) around and 18 meters (60 yd.) wide. Though its buildings aren't baroque, they are, in their monumental way, as much a part of Vienna as the baroque. A village lad, seeing them for the first time, wrote, "The entire Ringstrasse affected me like a fairy tale out of the Arabian Nights." The boy's name was Adolf Hitler.

OUTSIDE THE RING

The three most popular trips outside the Ring are to the Belvedere Palace, Schönbrunn Palace, and the Prater amusement park.

Belvedere Palace, Prinz-Eugen-Strasse 27 (☎ 0222/795-57), the summer residence of Prince Eugene of Savoy (1663–1736), is marked by lightness and grace. You may prefer visiting Schönbrunn because of its historic importance as summer residence of the Court, but you'd probably prefer living here. The Prince lived, between campaigns, in the Lower Belvedere; today it houses a museum of baroque and medieval art. Modern paintings are in the Upper Belvedere. Be sure to enjoy a peaceful stroll through the gardens. Admission 60AS adults, 30AS children. Open Tues–Sun 10am–5pm.

The grounds of **Schönbrunn Palace,** Schönnbrunner Schlossstrasse (☎ 0222/81-113), Austria's answer to Versailles, are rigidly formal. In the gardens of the Belvedere man has tried to cooperate with nature; here he has tried to conquer it. The Belvedere is a graceful tribute to the baroque in the years of peace following the Turkish defeat; Schönbrunn, in contrast, depends for effect on size and is decorated with all the frivolity of rococo. Aristocratic and voluptuous in a pale, fleshy sort of way; pleasant rather than strong or spiritual—these are the impressions associated with the rococo, the last flowering of the baroque. What's extraordinary is that this world of leaping tendrils and gilded peacocks, this riot of curved and twisted lines, was the choice of Maria Theresa—that model of sobriety, that pillar of church and state. Can you imagine Queen Victoria, whom Maria Theresa is often compared to, decorating Schönbrunn? Yet what a pleasant relief it must have been for the empress, with all her awesome responsibilities, to have this opportunity to set her imagination free. And what a pleasure it must have been to stay in Schönbrunn after a winter in the dark and gloomy Hofburg.

It was here in Schönbrunn that Marie Antoinette, ninth child of Maria Theresa, spent her youth, and here that the 6-year-old Mozart amazed Maria Theresa with his skill. (In the white-and-gold music room little Mozart slipped on the polished floor, and when Marie Antoinette, who was about the same age, helped him up, he vowed to marry her.) Here, too, Napoléon established his headquarters from 1805 to 1809; here Franz Josef was born and died; and here the empire came to an end, in 1918, when Franz Josef's successor, Karl I, signed the renunciation papers in the Chinese salon. After touring the apartments, stroll through the formal gardens. You can see the grand carriages in the old palace coach house (Wagenburg). Admission 95AS adults, 40AS children 6–15; under 6 free. Apartments open Apr–Oct, daily 8:30am–5pm; Nov–Mar, daily 9am–4:30pm.

The **Prater** was once the Court game preserve, but Maria Theresa's son Josef II turned it over to the people, and now it's a lovely public park with biking and jogging trails, lakes with rowboats to rent, a golf course, tennis courts, and an amusement park highlighted by a miniature railway (Liliputbahn) and a giant 19th-century Ferris wheel. You can rent bikes (Apr–Oct) from the **Radverleih Hochschaubahn,** 113 Prater (☎ 0222/729-5588), bear slightly right after you pass the big wheel, for 200AS per day.

THE VIENNA WOODS (WIENERWALD)

City planners could take a lesson from the Habsburgs, who—from a wish to protect their hunting grounds as much as a sense of civic duty—declared that the woods and mountains surrounding Vienna should forever remain inviolate, free from development. Hence the pastoral charm of the Vienna Woods, encircling the city. When people speak of the Vienna Woods they refer to one of two distinct areas—one to the southwest that includes Baden and Mayerling, where Rudolf and his mistress took their lives; and the other, the Kahlenberg Heights, to the west and northwest. If you must choose between the two, go to the Heights: They're closer and offer splendid views of Vienna. A scenic highway takes you from one vantage point to another. It makes sense to combine tours of Schönbrunn and the Heights and to stop on your way back to Vienna at a new wine tavern in Grinzing.

The best approach is from the south. Take the scenic mountain road called the Höhenstrasse for 8.8 kilometers (5½ miles), then drive another 24 kilometers (15 miles) to Klosterneuburg Abbey. There are scenic lookouts, restaurants, and hiking trails along the route. Turn right and follow a winding road to the summit of **Gallitzinberg**, where there's a restaurant. Walk to **Hermannskogel**, one of the less touristy areas.

Turn left on Sieveringerstrasse toward **Weidlingbach** and drive to the **Jägerwiese Restaurant**. Park and walk to the summit. (If you're using public transportation, take bus no. 39A to the end and follow Sieveringerstrasse.)

Continue to **Kahlenberg**. There's a church, hotel, and restaurant near the summit, and the view is impressive. By public transportation, take the streetcar to Grinzing and then a bus. It was on this summit that the Polish King John Sobieski gathered his forces for the attack that routed the Turks. Take a few minutes' drive or a 30-minute walk to **Leopoldsberg**, the mountain with the best view and the biggest crowds.

Continue north to **Klosterneuburg**, Stiftsplatz 1 (☎ **02243/411-212**). The 11th-century monastery wears baroque dress. The high point of the visit is the famous Verdun Altar, which has 51 enameled scenes by a late 12th-century goldsmith. The Museum of the Monastery can be visited May 1 to November 15 on Friday from 2 to 5pm and Saturday and Sunday from 10am to 5pm. Guided tours of the monastery are possible on Sunday and holidays throughout the year at 11am and on the half hour between 1:30 and 4:30pm. From April to October, tours are Monday to Saturday every hour from 9 to 11am and 1:30 to 4:30pm. From November to March, tours leave Monday to Saturday at 10 and 11am and then every hour from 1:30 to 4:30pm. For the tour and the museum, adults pay 50AS; students, children, and seniors 40AS.

From the monastery, either drive 11.2 kilometers (7 miles) east along the Danube back to Vienna or return south on the Höhenstrasse, past Leopoldsberg and Kahlenberg, and turn left on Cobenzlgasse to the wine town of Grinzing.

If you want to "do" Vienna, you need to visit a Heurigen tavern, many of them in the suburb of **Grinzing.** Streetcar no. 38 goes directly there. When the new wine is ready, vintners hang an evergreen branch over their doors. The wine tastes as innocent as soda water—until you stand up. When the weather cooperates, tables are set in outdoor gardens. The Viennese used to bring their own picnic dinners, but most Heurigen now serve meals. When you're not drinking, you can sing along with the musicians playing old Viennese folk songs on violins, accordions, and zithers. Among the best Heurigen are **Kirchenstöckl**, Himmelstrasse 4 (☎ 0222/32-66-62), and **Figlmüller**, Wollzelle 5 (☎ 0222/512-61-77). For additional names, pick up a booklet called *Heuriger in Wien* at any tourist information office.

DINING

Viennese food makes up in heartiness what it lacks in subtlety. A legacy of the Austro-Hungarian Empire is **Hungarian goulash** and **stuffed cabbage and peppers** (gefüllte Paprika and gefülltes Kraut). **Soup with dumplings** is another specialty, particularly Leberknödelsuppe (liver dumpling soup). **Veal** is featured on most menus, particularly Wiener schnitzel—veal dipped in egg batter and fried. Other specialties include Backhuhn (fried chicken), Rehfilet (venison), and gebackene Champignons (fried mushrooms). For dessert, try the small wild strawberries from the Vienna Woods, topped, of course, with fresh whipped cream.

Dö & Co, Akademiestr. 2 (☎ 0222/512-64-74). This is the most sophisticated deli in Vienna, next to the State Opera. The freshest produce in any season is flown in—perhaps asparagus from Argentina or shellfish from the Bosphorus. You can take your purchases away for a picnic or consume them at the tiny, cramped tables. The treats are legendary, from lobster Thermidor to salmon quiche. Sprawling rows of glass cases are laden with freshly made Viennese pastries. Reservations recommeded for a table. Casual. AE, DC, MC, V. Moderate.

Figlmüller, Wollzeile 5 (☎ 0222/512-61-77). This folksy restaurant is in a historic courtyard. Popular regional dishes include its own huge Figlmüller schnitzel (veal cutlet), Tafelspitz (boiled beef), Palatschinken (small crepes with jam), and excellent fruity wines. Reservations essential. Casual. No credit cards. Closed weekends. Moderate.

Ofenloch, Kurrentgasse 8 (☎ 0222/533-88-44). Ofenloch offers Viennese specialties like rump steak served by costumed waitresses in its collection of small rooms decorated with antique accessories. Reservations required. Jacket/tie advised. AE, DC, MC, V. Inexpensive.

Oswald & Kalb, Bäckerstr. 14 (☎ 0222/512-69-92). Near the cathedral, this is an old-world restaurant with a young crowd. Reservations essential. Elegant casual. No credit cards. Dinner only 6pm–midnight. Moderate.

Steirereck, Rasumovskygasse 2 (☎ 0222/713-31-68). Located near the Rotunden Bridge across the Danube Canal, this place is strong on elegant ambiance. The menu features fresh, lightly prepared international and regional dishes, including excellent cream soups, ravioli stuffed with Saibling (a freshwater fish), and wild duck in a juniper cream sauce. Reservations essential. Jacket/tie required. AE, V. Closed weekends. Very Expensive.

Zu Den 3 (Drei) Husaren (The Three Hussars), Weihburggasse 4 (☎ 0222/512-10-92). Just off Kärntnerstrasse, near St. Stephen's, is an elegant restaurant with an old-world atmosphere. Some 45 elegant but expensive hors d'oeuvres are wheeled around on four trolleys. The excellent French cuisine features goose-liver pâté, fresh lobster, and, best of all, a saddle of venison for two. Lunch prices are slightly lower than dinner. Reservations essential. Jacket/tie required. AE, DC, MC, V. Closed mid-July to mid-Aug. Very Expensive.

Zum Kuckuck, Himmelpfortgasse 15 (☎ 0222/512-84-70). On a side street between the Opera and the cathedral, this modern restaurant boasts a growing reputation for its creative Austrian cuisine. Reservations advised. Jacket/tie required. AE, DC, MC, V. Closed Sat lunch, Sun. Very Expensive.

Wine Cellars

Below the streets are a number of wine cellars with a cavernous, medieval feel to them that students and newcomers to Europe will love. Some serve modest meals. Among the best are **Melker Stiftskeller,** Schottengasse 3 (☎ 0222/533-55-30), and **Urbanikeller,** Am Hof 12 (☎ 0222/63-91-02).

Coffeehouses

Sitting at a cafe isn't a pastime but a way of life. Each Viennese has his or her own favorite, where he or she comes to talk, read, or dream. Here a patron becomes a person of leisure, a nobleperson from the Court. Once your order has been taken, feel free to stay all day; for a waiter to pressure you to move is un-Viennese. When the Turks fled in 1683, they left behind bags of a dark, bitter-tasting bean called coffee. The first coffee shop was opened by a Pole named George Kolschitsky, who was rewarded with some of these beans for having sneaked through Turkish lines with messages to relieving troops. The Kipfel (crescent-shape pastry) was conceived at the same time by a baker tasting victory over the Turks (whose symbol was a crescent). Among your choices: Einspänner (black coffee with whipped cream); Kapuziner (coffee with a little milk: brown in color like the habit of a Capuchin monk); Mit Schlag (with whipped cream and milk); Doppelschlag (with more whipped cream than coffee); Schale licht (with more milk than coffee).

Among the best are **Demel's,** Kohlmarkt 14 (☎ 0222/533-55-16), which also serves a fine lunch; **Café Dommayer,** Dommayergasse 1 (☎ 0222/877-54-65), where the Strausses (father and son) once played waltzes for members of Vienna's grande bourgeoisie; and **Café Landtmann,** Dr.-Karl-Lueger-Ring 4 (☎ 0222/532-06-21), one of the great cafes of the Ringstrasse, dating from the 1880s.

The historic **Café Central,** Herrengasse 14 (☎ 0222/533-37-63), is where Trotsky and Stalin used to play chess and where Trotsky still owes for an unpaid black coffee. At **Café Sacher,** Philharmonikerstrasse 4 (☎ 0222/514-56), you can decide whether the Sachertorte is worth its reputation. Eduard Sacher, the rebellious son of the owner of the Sacher Hotel, apparently slipped the recipe to the owner of **Demel's,** Kohlmarkt 14 (☎ 0222/533-55-16), and claimed that his recipe was the original.

After 10 years of litigation—only a city of dreams could have a 10-year court battle over pastries!—the judge decided that Sacher could claim the original and that Demel's should call its own Eduard Sacher Torte. Why not try both?

ACCOMMODATIONS

Ambassador, Kärntnerstr. 22, A-1010 Vienna (☎ **0222/51-4-66;** fax 0222/513-29-99). This hotel has rooms grouped around a central courtyard. The red plush draperies and upholstery are typically Viennese. If the top four hotels are booked or too expensive, stay here for comfort and old-world charm. 107 rms with bath. Facilities: restaurant, bar. AE, DC, MC, V. Expensive.

Astoria, Kärntnerstr. 32–34, A-1015 Vienna (☎ **0222/51-57-70;** fax 0222/515-77-82). Though the Astoria is one of Vienna's traditional old hotels, its rooms have been modernized. The paneled lobby, however, retains an unmistakable old-world patina. The location is central, but because of the street musicians and the late-night crowds in the pedestrian zone, rooms overlooking the Kärntnerstrasse tend to be noisy in summer. 108 rms with bath. Facilities: restaurant. AE, DC, MC, V. Expensive.

City, Bauernmarkt 10, A-1015 Vienna (☎ **0222/533-9521;** fax 0222/535-52-16). This is one of the most reasonable hotels in the center of the city, only steps from St. Stephen's. The rooms are modern and the baths attractive. 19 rms with bath. AE, DC, MC, V. Inexpensive.

Hotel Bristol, Kärntner Ring 1, A-1015 Vienna (☎ **0222/51-51-60;** fax 0222/515-16-550). The Bristol rivals the Sacher in prestige and tradition. Its location opposite the Opera House, at the head of the main shopping street, is equally convenient. The rooms are larger than those at the Sacher, and the black marble baths are more opulent. 137 rms with bath; 9 suites. Facilities: restaurants, bar. AE, DC, MC, V. Very Expensive.

Hotel Imperial, Kärntner Ring 16, A-1015 Vienna (☎ **800/325-3589** or 0222/50-11-00; fax 0222/501-10-440). The Imperial was completely restored after 10 years as the Russian headquarters during the Four Power occupation of Vienna (1945–55). Though it is a palatial indulgence (Wagner liked to stay here), it lacks the nostalgic feeling of the Sacher or Bristol. The service is faultless, however, and many consider the Imperial their favorite. 150 rms with bath. Facilities: beauty parlor, conference rooms. AE, DC, MC, V. Very Expensive.

Hotel im Palais Schwarzenberg, Schwarzenbergplatz 9, A-1030 Vienna (☎ **0222/798-45-15;** fax 0222/798-47-14). This hotel occupies part of a palace set within 7.6 hectares (19 acres) of gardens. The rooms are decorated with modern French elegance. If you want to be in walking distance of the shops and sights, stay at the Sacher or Bristol; if you want a quiet retreat and the sense of staying in a private palace, stay at the Schwarzenberg, a 10-minute cab ride to center city. 38 rms with bath. Facilities: restaurant, bar. AE, DC, MC, V. Very Expensive.

Hotel Kaiserin Elisabeth, Weihburggasse 3, A-1010 Vienna (☎ **0222/51-5-26;** fax 0222/515-267). This hotel is in a building dating back to the 14th century. Home to Wagner, Liszt, and Grieg, it offers all the creature comforts of the five-star hotels, without the trappings of luxury or the expense. 70 rms with bath. AE, DC, MC, V. Expensive.

Hotel Sacher, Philharmonikerstr. 4, A-1010 Vienna (☎ **0222/51-45-6;** fax 0222/51-45-78-10). Next to the Opera, the Sacher is still the place to stay for character and tradition. The baths can be small, but the hotel is truly 19th century, with hallowed, paneled lounges regal in crystal and Habsburg maroon. The Sacher attracts a crowd of intellectuals and artists, which makes its appeal perhaps a bit narrower and deeper than that of the equally opulent Bristol. 116 rms with bath. Facilities: restaurant, cafe. AE, DC, MC, V. Very Expensive.

König von Ungarn, Schulerstrasse 10, A-1010 Vienna (☎ **0222/ 51-58-40;** fax 0222/515-848). This utterly charming, centrally located hotel is tucked away in the shadow of the cathedral. The historic facade belies the modern efficiency of the interior, from the atrium lobby to the rooms themselves. The restaurant (just next door in a house that Mozart once lived in) is excellent, though not inexpensive, and is always packed at noon. 34 rms with bath. Facilities: restaurant, bar. AE, DC, MC, V. Expensive.

Pension Zipser, Lange Gasse 49, A-1080 Vienna (☎ **0222/404-54-0;** fax 0222/408-52-666-13). This has become a favorite with regular visitors to Vienna. It's slightly less central than some others on this list, but very comfortable. 47 rms with bath. Facilities: bar. AE, DC, MC, V. Moderate.

Wandl, Petersplatz 9, A-1010 Vienna (☎ **0222/53-45-50;** fax 0222/ 53-455-77). Wandl faces St. Peter's Church off Graben. The rooms are comfortable and reasonably priced. 134 rms with bath. No credit cards. Moderate.

I T A 5 L Y

Pompeii, Capri &
the Amalfi Coast

The region south and west of Naples offers you an extraordinary variety of landscapes and experiences. Volcanic ash and mud preserved the Roman towns of Pompeii and Herculaneum almost exactly as they were on the day Vesuvius erupted in A.D. 79. What you'll see are not just archeological ruins, but living testimony of daily life in the ancient world. You'll walk through the baths and brothels, the bars and bakeries, the sumptuous villas of wealthy patricians, and the cramped quarters of servants. You'll even see the food they ate, the wooden beds they slept in, and the graffiti they wrote on the walls. "Many a calamity has happened in the world," wrote Goethe, "but never one that has caused so much entertainment to posterity as this one."

When the ancients imagined the entrance to hell they had a specific place in mind—Lake Avernus—a silent, lonely spot in the Phlegrean Fields just west of Naples. Here also is the dark, vaulted chamber where the Cumaean Sibyl rendered her oracles. This was one of the most venerated sites in antiquity; English writer H. V. Morton called it the most romantic classical site in Italy today.

The magnificent Amalfi Drive snakes above deep gorges and fantastically shaped rocks. Sparkling white towns cling to the precipitous walls among lemon trees and vineyards. Here you can dine on fresh fish and sleep in rooms overlooking the sea.

Offshore are the islands of Ischia and Capri. The volcanic isle of Ischia offers mineral springs surrounded by tropical gardens and white wine-growing villages. The pleasure island of Capri is famed for its hotels and restaurants, its grottoes, its rich tropical vegetation, and its scenic walks. On the mainland, south along the coast, lies Paestum. Though unknown to many tourists, Paestum has three magnificent Greek temples—one of them as wonderful in its own way as the Parthenon in Athens.

BEFORE YOU GO

GOVERNMENT TOURIST OFFICES

The major source of information is the **Italian National Tourist Office.**

In the U.S.: 630 Fifth Ave., Suite 1565, New York, NY 10111 (☎ 212/245-4822); 401 N. Michigan Ave., Chicago, IL 60611 (☎ 312/644-0990); 12400 Wilshire Blvd., Suite 550, Los Angeles, CA 90025 (☎ 310/820-0098).

In Canada: 1 place Ville Marie, Suite 1914, Montréal, Québec H3B 2E3 (☎ 514/866-7667).

In the U.K.: 1 Princes St., London W1R 8AY England (☎ 0171/408-1254).

HIGHLIGHTS ALONG THE WAY

- The most spectacular drive in Italy, along the wild, romantic Amalfi Coast.

- Positano—the most scenic town on the Amalfi Drive.

- The excavated Roman town of Pompeii—brought back to life as it was almost 2,000 years ago.

- The magical island of Capri, with fairy-tale grottoes, comfortable hotels, dozens of first-class seafood restaurants, and dramatic walks high above the sea.

- Paestum—site of the Greek Temple of Neptune, a building as memorable as the Parthenon.

- The National Museum of Naples, housing the world's most important collection of classical art.

WHEN TO GO

The main tourist season runs from mid-April to the end of September. The best months for sightseeing are April, May, June, September, and October, when the weather is generally pleasant and not too hot. If you can avoid it, don't travel to Italy in August, when much of the population is on the move. The heat can be oppressive, and vacationing Italians cram the roads, trains, and planes.

CURRENCY

The unit of currency in Italy is the **lira (L).** There are bills of 100,000, 10,000, 5,000, 2,000, and 1,000 lire. Coins are 500, 100, and 50L. Currently, the exchange rate is about 1,565L = $1 U.S., 1,110L = $1 Canadian, and 2,380L = £1 sterling.

CUSTOMS

Non–European Union visitors can bring the following into Italy duty-free: 200 cigarettes or 100 cigarillos or 250 grams (17.5 oz.) of tobacco; 1 liter (1 qt.) of alcohol or 2 liters of wine; 50 milliliters (1.7 fl. oz.) of perfume; 250 milliliters (8.5 fl. oz.) of eau de toilette. European Unionvisitors can bring in the following duty-free: 800 cigarettes or 400 cigarillos or 400 cigars or 1 kilogram (2.2 lb.) of tobacco; 10 liters (2.6 gal.) of alcohol plus 60 liters (15.9 gal.) of sparkling wine and 90 liters (23.8

SPECIAL EVENTS & NATIONAL HOLIDAYS

Special Events

May (Saturday preceding the first Sunday) and September 19: Miracle of San Gennaro, Naples.
July 14–16: Feast of Santa Maria del Carmine, Naples.
Early September: Madonna di Piedigrotta, Naples.

National Holidays

January 1 (New Year's Day); January 6 (Epiphany); Easter Sunday and Monday; April 25 (Liberation Day); May 1 (Labor Day), August 15 (Assumption Day); November 1 (All Saints Day); December 8 (Immaculate Conception); December 25–26 (Christmas and Santo Stefano).

gal.) of table wine, and 75 milliliters (2.5 fl. oz.) of perfume and 375 milliliters (12.7 fl. oz.) of eau de toilette. Officially, 10 rolls of still camera film and 10 reels of video film may be brought in duty-free. Other items intended for personal use are generally admitted, as long as the quantities are reasonable.

LANGUAGE

In the main tourist cities, language is no problem. You can always find someone who speaks at least a little English, albeit with a heavy accent; remember that the Italian language is pronounced exactly as it's written (many Italians try to speak English as it's written, with disconcerting results). You may run into a language barrier in the countryside, but a phrase book and close attention to the Italians' astonishing use of pantomime and expressive gestures will go a long way.

Try to master a few phrases for daily use and familiarize yourself with the terms you'll need to decipher signs and museum labels. The exhortation *"Va via!"* (Go away!) is useful in warding off begging Gypsies and the advances of wolfish men.

READING

Edward Bulwer-Lytton. *The Last Days of Pompeii* (Buccaneer Books). The classic 1834 novel that brings Pompeii to life during its final days.
Michael Grant. *Cities of Vesuvius: Pompeii and Herculaneum* (Macmillan). The best unscholarly introduction to the two cities.
H. V. Morton. *A Traveller in Italy* (Dodd, Mead). Witty and intelligent.
Pompeii-Herculaneum: A Guide with Reconstructions. A guide to both sites with plastic overlays that let you see buildings as they are today and as they were before the eruption.
Virgil. *The Aeneid.* Book VI in particular is essential reading for a trip to the Sibyl's Cave and Lake Avernus in the Phlegrean Fields.

ARRIVING & DEPARTING

BY PLANE

There are no direct flights from the United States to Naples, where this trip begins. Your best bet is to fly to Rome, a 3-hour drive or a 2-hour train ride from Naples. Four airlines fly nonstop from the United States to

Rome: **TWA,** from New York and Los Angeles (☎ 800/221-2000); **Delta,** from New York (☎ 800/241-4141); **United,** from Washington, D.C. (☎ 800/241-6522); and **Alitalia,** from New York (☎ 800/223-5730).

Alitalia (☎ 0345/212121) and **British Airways** (☎ 0345/22211) operate direct flights from London (Heathrow) to Rome and Naples. Flying time is 2½ to 3 hours. There's also one direct flight a day from Manchester to Rome.

Capodichino Airport (☎ 081/7805763), 8 kilometers (5 miles) east of Naples, serves the Campania region. It handles domestic and international flights, including several flights daily between Naples and Rome (flight time: 45 min.).

BY TRAIN

If you're traveling by public transportation, take the modern express train from the airport to the Ostiense terminal (about 30 min.), then taxi or subway (Metropolitana) to the Termini train station. There are trains every hour between Rome and Naples. Intercity and Rapido trains make the trip in less than 2 hours. Trains take either the inland route (through Cassino) or go along the coast (via Formia). Express trains to Naples stop at **Stazione Centrale** (Central Station) on piazza Garibaldi (☎ 081/567111).

BY BUS

Eurojet (☎ 06/4744521), a Rome-based bus line, runs direct air-conditioned service from Rome to Campania, stopping at Pompeii and Sorrento year-round and Positano-Amalfi from June to mid-September only.

BY CAR

If you're renting a car, arrange to pick it up at the Rome airport. If you're driving from northern Europe and the distances seem too great, there's always the Motorail from the channel ports. However, no car/sleeper express runs beyond Milan. Italy's main north-south route, heading out of Rome (A2, also known as the Autostrada del Sole), connects the capital with Naples and Campania. In good traffic the ride takes less than 3 hours.

GETTING AROUND

BY CAR

To drive in Italy you need both a valid U.S. driver's license with Italian translation, available through your local AAA, and a Green Insurance Card. If you're driving your own car, get the Green Card from your insurance company. If you're renting a car in Europe, make sure the Green

ITALY

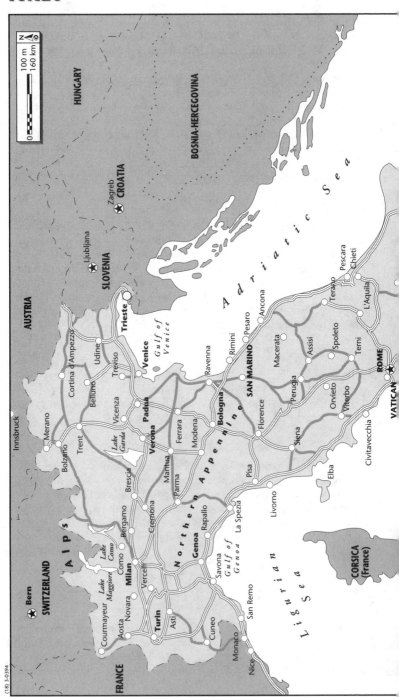

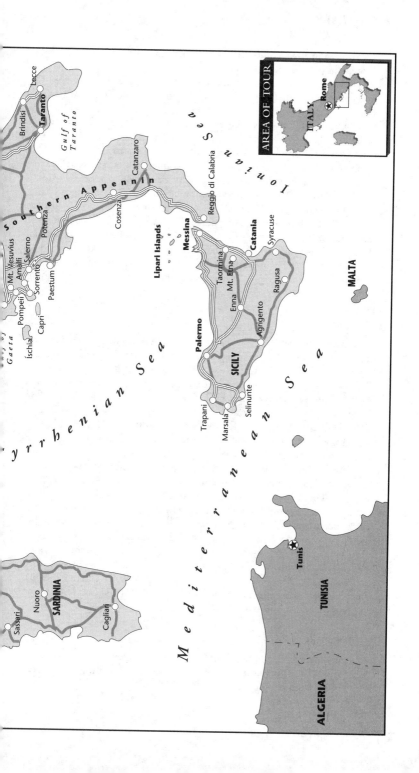

Card is in the glove compartment. You're required to have a red warning triangle in your car for use in emergencies.

Driving is on the right-hand side of the road. The speed limit is 130 kilometers per hour (81 m.p.h.) on the autostrada and 90 kilometers per hour (56 m.p.h.) on other roads. Other regulations are mainly as they are in the United States, except that police can levy on-the-spot fines—as high as $500.

Driving through Naples is a nightmare. Keep it to an absolute minimum and adopt tight security. Don't keep cameras or purses in sight, even when you're in the car, and never leave luggage, even in a locked trunk.

Autostrada A3, a southern continuation of A2 from Rome, runs through Campania and into Calabria, to the south. Take S18 south for Ercolano (Herculaneum), Pompeii, and the Sorrento peninsula; for the Sorrento peninsula and the Amalfi Coast, exit at Castellamare di Stabia. To get to Paestum, take A3 to the Battipaglia exit and take the road to Capaccio Scalo/Paestum. All roads on the Sorrento peninsula and the Amalfi Coast are narrow and tortuous, though they have outstanding views.

By Train

Save money on train tickets by purchasing an **Italian Railpass** before you leave home. Contact **CIT Tours,** the official representative of Italian State Railway, 342 Madison Ave., New York, NY 10173 (☎ **800/223-7987** or 212/697-2100), or a travel agent. If you phone CIT, be prepared to wait, as the phones are notoriously busy. Clients west of Colorado might fare better by calling the organization's Los Angeles office at **800/248-7245** or 310/338-8616. You can also fax the New York office at **212/697-1394,** or Los Angeles at **310/670-4269.** CIT also offers excellent rail tours, coach tours, hotel accommodations, spa bookings, and cruises.

Avoid lines at stations by buying tickets at authorized travel agencies. A network of suburban trains connects Naples with several points of interest. The **Circumflegrea** (☎ **081/5513328**) runs from the piazza Montesanto station in Naples to the archeological zone of Cumae, with three departures in the morning. Reached at the same number, the **Ferrovia Cumana** runs from the piazza Montesanto station to Pozzuoli and Baia. The line used most by visitors is the **Circumvesuviana** (☎ **081/7792444**), which runs from Corso Garibaldi station and stops at Stazione Centrale before continuing to Ercolano (Herculaneum), Pompeii, and Sorrento. Travel time between Naples and Sorrento on the express train is 45 minutes.

By Bus

There's an extensive network of local buses in Naples and throughout Campania. Buses connect Naples with Caserta in 1 hour, leaving every 20 minutes from piazza Garibaldi (☎ **081/7005091**).

SITA buses, departing from via Pisanelli 3 for Salerno, leave every 30 minutes on weekdays and every 2 hours on Saturday and Sunday from the SITA terminal, near piazza Municipio. SITA buses also serve the Amalfi Coast, connecting Sorrento with Salerno. For information and schedules in Amalfi, call **089/871009.**

BY BOAT

Hydrofoil and passenger- and car-ferries connect the islands of Capri and Ischia with Naples and Pozzuoli. Check ahead, as schedules and connections vary according to season. Boats and hydrofoils for these islands, and also for Sorrento, leave Naples from the **Molo Beverello,** piazza Municipio, near the Castle Nuovo. In Naples, call **081/70700** for schedules.

Caremar (☎ **081/991781**) has frequent passenger- and car-ferry services, as well as some hydrofoil services. **Lauro** (☎ **081/8377577**) and **SNAV** (☎ **081/7612348**) also provide hydrofoil services. In the summer, these lines have a "residents only" policy for cars.

ESSENTIAL INFORMATION

IMPORTANT ADDRESSES & NUMBERS

VISITOR INFORMATION The main **EPT (regional tourist board)** offices for Campania are in **Naples** at the following addresses: piazza del Gesù Nuovo 7 (☎ **081/5523328**); Stazione Centrale (☎ **081/5543188**); Stazione Mergellina (☎ **081/680635**); and Capodichino Airport (☎ **081/7092815**). These offices provide information on transportation, accommodations, and cultural events throughout the region. They're open Monday to Saturday from 9am to 2pm and 3 to 7pm and Sunday from 9am to 3pm.

Local tourist offices are useful for information on festivals, changing opening hours, and maps of towns and villages:

Amalfi:	corso del Repubbliche Marinare 19–21 (☎ **089/ 871107**).
Anacapri:	via G. Orlandi 19/A (☎ **081/8371524**).
Capri:	Marina Grande pier (☎ **081/8370634**), or piazza Umberto I no. 19 (☎ **081/8370686**).
Ischia Porto:	via Iasolino (☎ **081/991146**).
Naples:	piazza del Gesù (☎ **081/5523328**), or Hydrofoil pier at Mergellina (☎ **081/7614585**).
Paestum:	via Magna Gracia 151–156 (☎ **0828/811016**).
Pompeii:	via Sacra 1 (☎ **081/8507255**).
Positano:	via del Saracino 4 (☎ **089/875067**).

Ravello:	piazza del Duomo (☎ 089/857096).
Salerno:	piazza Ferrovia o Vittorio Veneto (☎ 089/231432).
Sorrento:	via de Maio 35 (☎ 081/8074033).

EMERGENCIES   **Police** (☎ 133). **Motoring** (☎ 116; Automobile Club of Italy). **Ambulance** (☎ 133). **Doctors/Dentists** (☎ 081/7513177 in Naples).

CONSULATES   **U.S. Consulate,** via Torrorio Veneto 121, Rome (☎ 06/46741); open Monday to Friday from 8:30am to noon and 2 to 4pm. **U.K. Consulate,** via Francesco Crispi 122, 80122 Naples (☎ 081/663511); open Monday to Friday from 9:15am to 1:30pm.

OPENING & CLOSING TIMES

BANKS   Banks are open Monday to Friday 8:30am to 1:30pm and 2 or 2:30 to 4 or 4:30pm.

CHURCHES   Churches are usually open from early morning to noon or 12:30pm, when they close for about 2 hours or more, opening again in the afternoon until about 7pm.

MUSEUMS   National museums are usually open to 2pm and closed on Monday, but there are many exceptions. Other museums have entirely different hours, which may vary according to season. Archeological sites are usually closed Monday. At all museums and sites, ticket offices close an hour or so before official closing time. Check with the local tourist office for current hours.

SHOPS   Shops are open, with individual variations, Monday to Saturday (but close a half day during the week) from 9am to 1pm and from 3:30 or 4pm to 7 or 7:30pm. For example in Rome most shops (except food shops) close Monday morning, or, in July and August, on Saturday afternoon.

SHOPPING

VAT REFUNDS   A **value-added tax** (called IVA) is imposed on all con-
sumer goods and services. The average tax is 19%, but it could be as high
as 35% on certain luxury items. If you spend more than 525,000L at any
one store, regardless of how many individual items are involved, you're
entitled to a refund. At the time of your purchase, collect a formal receipt
from the vendor. When you leave Italy, find an Italian Customs agent at
the airport (or at the point of your exit from the country if you're traveling by train, bus, or car). The agent will want to see the item you've

bought, confirm that it's physically leaving Italy, and stamp the vendor's receipt.

You should then mail the stamped receipt (keeping a photocopy) to the original vendor. The vendor will send you a refund of the tax you paid at the time of your original purchase. Reputable stores view this as a matter of ordinary paperwork and are very businesslike about it. Less honorable stores might lose your dossier. It pays to deal with established vendors on purchases of this size.

BEST BUYS Leather goods, coral, jewelry, and cameos are some of the best items to buy in Campania. In Naples, where many of the top leather and fashion houses have their factories, you'll find good buys in bags, shoes, and clothing, but it's often wise to make purchases in shops rather than from street vendors. The coast resorts have maintained some of their traditional crafts, though some shops try to pass off poor-quality machine-made goods as handmade items.

Capri: For trendsetting women's clothing that's well suited for the nonchalant permissiveness of Capri, head for **La Parisienne,** piazza Umberto I (☎ 081/8370283), and the much-respected **Ferragamo,** via Vittorio Emmanuele 21 (☎ 081/837-0499). Men appreciate the stylish inventories at **Grey Flannel,** via Camarelle 55 (☎ 081/8376805), and **Men,** via Camarelle 29 (☎ 081/8377012). Looking for a piece of sparkling jewelry to celebrate your romance with Capri? Check out the gems at **Angela Puttini,** via le Botteghe 12 (☎ 081/8378907). **Carthusia-Profumi di Capri,** via Camarelle 10 (☎ 081/8370368), specializes in island-made perfume, and has since 1947, attracting such notables over the years as Elizabeth Taylor before she started hawking her own scents.

Naples: The **Galleria** is a good introduction to shopping in Naples; a wide variety of retail outlets trade in the four glass-roofed arcades. Other areas and streets are more specialized: The area immediately around **piazza dei Martiri** is the heart of luxury shopping, with perfume shops, fashion outlets, and quality antiques. **Via Roma** and **via Chiaia** are better bets for bargains.

Positano: The picturesque streets of this coastal resort are lined with boutiques selling trendy casual fashions and beachwear in splashy colors and extravagant fabrics.

Sorrento: Sorrento has been famous for several centuries as a site where complicated marquetry work, intarsia, is crafted and showcased. Thin slices of wood from different species of trees are painstakingly inlaid into decorative patterns, using techniques that are transmitted through various generations of the same family. Within the central core of Sorrento, you'll find dozens of shops selling everything from jewelry boxes to trays, coffee tables, and religious plaques showing, for example, saints at prayer. One of the town's most interesting collections of intarsia, with a roster of objects more charming, eccentric, and idiosyncratic than

the usual, is **Intarsiatore Ferdinando Corcione,** via San Francesco 10–12
(☎ 081/878-2430).

SPORTS

Sun, sand, and sea combine in this region to offer you a number of sporting options, but be prepared to encounter pollution in some of the beaches nearest Naples. The top hotels often offer sports facilities such as
private beaches, pools, and tennis courts, and many will allow nonguests
to use these facilities. Contact the hotels themselves or the local tourist
office.

BEACHES The waters of the Bay of Naples are notoriously polluted.
Beaches tend to be pebbly and crowded. Capri and some, but not all, of
Ischia's beaches offer clean swimming. Pollution is intermittent along the
Amalfi Coast, where the deep waters are generally clean. It's best to avoid
the beaches in the Salerno area; the water is cleaner the farther south
you go.

FISHING For information on licenses and water quality, contact
Federazione Italians Pesca Sportiva, piazza Santa Maria degli Angeli,
Naples (☎ 081/7644921).

HORSEBACK RIDING For information on riding contact the **Centro
Ippico Agnano,** via Circumvallazione, Agnano, between Pozzuoli and
Naples (☎ 081/5702695).

SAILING Contact **Nantic Coop,** piazza Amedeo 15, Naples
(☎ 081/415371).

TENNIS Most top hotels have courts. Contact them or local tourist
boards about use of these courts. The following are public courts: In
Naples, via Giochi del Mediterraneo (☎ 081/5703910), and in **Porto
d'Ischia,** Lungomare Colombo (☎ 081/991013).

WATERSKIING Contact **Sci Nautico Partenopeo,** Lake Averno,
Pozzuoli (☎ 081/8662214).

DINING

The region is famous for its seafood, particularly shellfish soups and
grilled bass. Ask for the fresh fish of the day: triglie (red mullet), spigola
(sea bass), or tonno (tuna). Order vóngole (clam), cozze (mussel), or
other seafood sauces on pasta, the other specialty of the region. Pasta
comes in all shapes—not just spaghetti but also ziti, cannelloni, vermicel-
li, and so on. Most everything is served with local tomatoes; meat dishes

are often served alla pizzaiola (with tomato sauce and garlic). Naples is the birthplace of the pizza, so go ahead and try it. Neapolitan pizza tends to be served lukewarm, with a bit of runny tomato sauce floating on asea of oil; once I had to pour the oil into a cup and soak up the rest with a napkin.

This is mozzarella (buffalo cheese) country, which puts our own to shame. If it's made of cow's milk, it's called fior di latte. Other locally produced cheeses are scamorza and various types of smoked, fresh, or aged provolone.

For wines try Falerno, immortalized by Horace; the red and white Ischia and Capri wines; the wines from the volcanic slopes of Vesuvius — white Lacrima Christi (tears of Christ) with fish; red Gragnano with meat. Ravello (where you'll be staying) also has its own local wines.

For desserts try the famous sfogliatelle, a multilayered pastry filled with custard or ricotta. Happiness is a profiterole — a pastry puff filled with custard or whipped cream and topped with hot bittersweet chocolate sauce.

Prices are almost always listed in restaurant windows or just inside the door. Be prepared for a cover charge (pane e coperto) for the privilege of sitting down. The additional 15% service charge goes only partially to the waiter, so in finer restaurants be prepared to add another 5% to the tip.

CATEGORY	COST
Very Expensive	Over 90,000L
Expensive	65,000–90,000L
Moderate	30,000–65,000L
Inexpensive	Under 30,000L
Prices are per person, including house wine, service, and tax.	

ACCOMMODATIONS

The most attractive rooms overlook the water — some of them (usually upstairs) with full views, others (downstairs) with partial views. The better the view, as a rule, the higher the price. Ask for rates and then specify what you want.

The rooms even in better hotels tend to be decorated with a confusion of different brightly colored tiles — the more clashing the better. This busy Moorish-Italian look tends to compete with the naturally lush colors of the landscape.

Service charges and taxes are usually included in the rates, but it pays to ask in advance. It's a good idea, too, to check the quoted rates against those listed on the back of your hotel door.

THE ITINERARY

ORIENTATION

This Italian itinerary takes you through a wide range of countryside and atmospheres in a minimum amount of time. At no point are you more than 2 hours from Naples, yet you'll be exploring Pompeii and climbing to the heights of Vesuvius, dining on terraces above the spectacular Amalfi coast, and visiting fantastic grottoes on the magical isle of Capri.

THE MAIN ROUTE

3–5 DAYS

One to Two Nights: *Sorrento.*
Arrive Naples in morning, visit museum, then Pompeii or Herculaneum, and on to Sorrento; visit Vesuvius and Pompeii or Herculaneum.

One to Two Nights: *Capri or Positano.*
Boat to Capri for tour and overnight; or day tour, return boat to Sorrento or Positano (in summer).

One Night: *Positano or Ravello.*
Day trip along the Amalfi Drive; Salerno, Paestum.

Rooms with showers in the bath prevail. If you want a tub, specify when booking.

CATEGORY	COST
Very Expensive	Over 300,000L
Expensive	160,000–300,000L
Moderate	100,000–160,000L
Inexpensive	Under 100,000L

All prices are for a standard double room for two, including service and 9% VAT (19% for luxury establishments).

5–7 DAYS

One Night: *Naples.*
Arrive Naples in morning, visit museum, then Vesuvius and Pompeii or Herculaneum.

One Night: *Sorrento.*
Visit Pompeii or Herculaneum, then boat to Capri.

One to Two Nights: *Capri.*
Tour island, then return by boat to Sorrento, and on to Positano.

Two Nights: *Positano or Ravello.*
Trip along the Amalfi Drive; Salerno, Paestum.

7–14 DAYS

Two Nights: *Naples.*
Arrive Naples in morning, visit museum, then Vesuvius and Pompeii or Herculaneum; day trip to Phlegrean Fields and (in season) on to Pozzuoli for ferry to Ischia (off-season, ferry from Naples).

One to Two Nights: *Ischia.*
Explore, then (in season) boat to Capri (no tourists' cars allowed on Capri in season), or to Naples or Sorrento, then boat to Capri.

Three to Five Nights: *Capri.*
Explore, then boat to Sorrento.

Three to Four Nights: *Positano or Ravello.*
Amalfi Drive; Salerno, Paestum or . . .

Two to Three Nights: *Positano or Ravello.*

One Night: *Salerno or Paestum.*

EXPLORING

CASERTA

Visit Italy's answer to Versailles, **Caserta,** piazza Carlo III (☎ 0823/321400), only if you have a special interest in architecture and history or have time to spare. It's off Highway A2, 28.8 kilometers (18 miles) north of Naples, so you may want to stop here on the drive from Rome.

The baroque furnishings and decorations show you how Bourbon royalty lived in the mid-18th century. The Royal Palace was built by Charles III, the first Bourbon king of Naples, later to wear the crown of Spain. Charles was in his late thirties when he built this Hollywood-style extravaganza, this monument to megalomania. It was here, in what Eisenhower called "a castle near Naples," that the Allied High Command had its headquarters in World War II; and here that German forces in Italy surrendered in April 1945. Most enjoyable are the gardens and parks, particularly the Cascades, where a life-size Diana and her maidens stand waiting to be photographed. Admission to royal apartments 8,000L; to park 4,000L; to minibus 2,000L. Open Tues–Sun: royal apartments July–Oct, 9am–7pm, Sun 9am–2pm (closes 1:30pm off-season); park, 9am to 1 hr. before sunset; closed Mon and national holidays.

DINING

Antica Locanda Massa 1848, via Mazzini 55 (☎ 0823/321268). This large informal restaurant is decorated in brown and white in 19th-century rustic style. In fair weather you eat alfresco under an arbor. The specialties are linguine al cartoccio (pasta steamed with fresh tomato and shellfish) and gazzerielli alla borbone (gnocchi with cheese and truffle sauce). Reservations advised. Casual. AE, DC, MC, V. Closed Sun evening, Mon, and Aug 10–25. Moderate.

La Castellana, via Torre 4 (☎ 0823/371230). Located in Casertavec-chia, Caserta's medieval nucleus on the hillside overlooking the modern town, this tavern has atmosphere and hearty local specialties, such as stringozzi alla castellana (homemade pasta with piquant tomato sauce served in individual casseroles) and agnello allu Castellana (lamb sautéed in red wine). Reservations required Sat–Sun. Casual. AE, DC, MC, V. Closed Thurs (except July–Aug). Moderate.

NAPLES

Is it the sense of doom, living in the shadow of Vesuvius, that makes the people of **Naples** so volatile, so seemingly blind to everything but the pain and pleasure of the moment? Poverty and overcrowding are the more likely causes; but whatever the reason, Naples is a difficult place for the casual tourist to like. Security is a serious problem here—thieves commonly snatch purses or cameras from pedestrians or even out of cars stopped in traffic. The Committee of Ninety-nine (Napoli 99), formed to counter the city's negative image, has its work cut out. If you have the time and if you're willing to work at it, you'll come to love Naples as a mother loves her reprobate child; but if you're only passing through and hoping to enjoy a hassle-free vacation, spend as little time here as you can.

John Steinbeck must have had Naples in mind when he called Italian traffic "a deafening, screaming, milling, tire-screeching mess." I came to Naples determined to dismiss its noise, dirt, and confusion as so much local color; but after an hour, standing motionless in a traffic jam while a pride of police looked indifferently on, I was ready to search for color elsewhere.

Why visit Naples at all? First, Naples is the most sensible base—particularly if you're traveling by public transport—from which to explore Pompeii, Herculaneum, Vesuvius, and the Phlegrean Fields.

Second, it's home of the National Archeological Museum. The most important findings at Pompeii and Herculaneum are on display here—everything from sculpture to carbonized fruit—and seeing them will add to the pleasure of your trip to Pompeii and Herculaneum. The museum closes at 2pm (1pm Sun) except in summer, so spend the morning here and the afternoon visiting either the Phlegrean Fields or Herculaneum and Vesuvius (remembering that the last bus to the volcano is at 2pm). Spend the night back in Naples—perhaps at an opera or concert at the world-famous San Carlo Opera House—and the following morning set off on your tour of Pompeii.

The **National Archeological Museum,** piazza Museo (☎ 081/440166), was designed as a cavalry barracks in the 16th century. The ground floor is devoted to marble sculpture, notably the Farnese Hercules and Farnese Bull. On the mezzanine is a collection of ancient frescoes and mosaics, including *Alexander's Battle,* taken from the floor of the House of the Faun, which you'll see in Pompeii. On the first floor are works from Herculaneum. Don't miss the room with musical and surgical instruments. Admission 12,000L. Open June–Aug, Tues–Sat 9am–7pm, Sun 9am–1pm; Sept–May, Tues–Sat 9am–2pm, Sun 9am–1pm.

The **San Carlo Opera House,** via San Carlo (☎ 081/7972331), is famous for its near-perfect acoustics and sumptuous decoration. Box office open Dec–June, Tues–Sun 10am–1pm and 4:30–6:30pm.

DINING

Bergantino, via Milano 16 (☎ 081/5539787). This bustling trattoria, near the central station, is a favorite with businesspeople and is open for lunch only. Courteous and efficient waiters serve a variety of classic Neapolitan dishes, including hearty maccheroni con ragù (pasta with meat sauce) and sartù di riso (rice caserole with bits of meat and cheese). Anything made with mozzarella is sure to be good here, or order plain mozzarella—it's light and fresh. Reservations needed Sat–Sun. Casual. AE, DC, MC, V. Closed Sun and Aug 10–20. Moderate.

Bersagliera, borgo Marinaro 10 (☎ 081/7646016). Most first-time visitors to Naples want to dine once on the Santa Lucia waterfront in the shadow of the medieval Castel dell'Ovo, and this is one of the best places to do so. It's touristy but fun, with an irresistible combination of spaghetti and mandolins. The menu offers uncomplicated dishes like spaghetti alla pescatora (with seafood sauce) and melanzane alla parmigiana (eggplant with mozzarella and tomato sauce). Reservations advised. Casual. AE, DC, MC, V. Closed Tues. Moderate.

Casanova Grill, in the Hotel Excelsior, via Partenope 48 (☎ 081/7640111). Soft lights and a trendy art deco look set the tone in the Casanova. The seasonal specialties and antipasti arranged on the buffet will whet your appetite for such traditional Neapolitan dishes as the simple spaghetti al pomodoro (with fresh tomato sauce) and the classic carne alla pizzaiola (meat with tomato and oregano). Reservations advised. Jacket/tie advised at night. AE, DC, MC, V. Closed Mon. Expensive.

Ciro a Santa Brigida, via Santa Brigida 71 (☎ 081/5524072). Centrally located off via Toledo near the Castel Nuovo, Ciro is a straightfoward restaurant popular with business travelers, artists, and journalists who are more interested in food than frills. In dining rooms on two levels you can enjoy classic Neapolitan cuisine. Among the specialties: sarù di riso (rice casserole with meat and cheese) and scaloppe all Ciro (veal with prosciutto and mozzarella). There's pizza, too. Reservations advised. Casual. AE, DC, MC, V. Closed Sun and 2 weeks in Aug. Moderate.

Dante e Beatrice, piazza Dante 44–45 (☎ 081/5499438). A simple trattoria on central piazza Dante, this popular spot features typical Neapolitan dishes in an unassuming setting. The menu may offer pasta e fagioli (very thick bean soup with pasta) and maccheroni al ragù (pasta with meat sauce). Reservations advised in the evening. Casual. No credit cards. Closed Mon and Aug 15–30. Inexpensive.

Don Salvatore, strada Mergellina 4A (☎ 081/681817). Head just west to the little port of Mergellina to find an unpretentious-looking place known for good local dishes and seafood. Linguine cosa nostra (with shellfish) and other pastas with seafood sauces are specialties, and the fritto misto (mixed fried fish) is as light as a feather. Reservations advised. Casual. AE, DC, MC, V. Closed Wed. Moderate.

La Fazenda, via Marechiaro 58A (☎ 081/5757420). Overlooking the sea at Marechiaro, in one of the city's most picturesque spots, this is a favorite for leisurely dining and an invitingly informal atmosphere. The pastas, many with vegetable sauces, are particularly good. The specialty is seafood, but chicken and rabbit alla cacciatora (in a tangy sauce) also are good. The desserts are homemade. Note that you must take a taxi to get to La Fazenda. Reservations advised. Casual. AE, V. Closed Sun, Mon lunch, and Aug 12–18. Expensive.

La Sacrestia, via Orazio 116 (☎ 081/7611051). Popular with Neapolitans because of its location and the quality of its food, La Sacrestia is set on the slopes of the Posillipo hill, with marvelous views of the city and bay. The specialties range from appetizing antipasti to linguine con salsetta segieta (pasta with a sauce of minutely chopped garden vegetables). Seafood has a place of honor on the menu, and there are interesting meat dishes as well. If you swim clear of fish, the check can stay in the moderate category. Reservations required. Casual. AE, DC, MC, V. Closed Sun in July–Aug and 2 weeks in Aug (dates vary). Moderate.

ACCOMMODATIONS

Cavour, piazza Garibaldi 32, 80142 Napoli (☎ 081/283122; fax 081/287488). In the rundown Stazione Centrale area, on the square in front of the station and handy to all transportation, including the Circumvesuviana, the Cavour has been renovated and can now offer clean and comfortable rooms. It's especially convenient for those using Naples as a touring base. The hotel's contribution to urban renewal in the area is its elegant street-level restaurant and piano bar. 86 rms with bath. Facilities: restaurant, piano bar. AE, DC, MC, V. Moderate.

THE AMALFI COAST

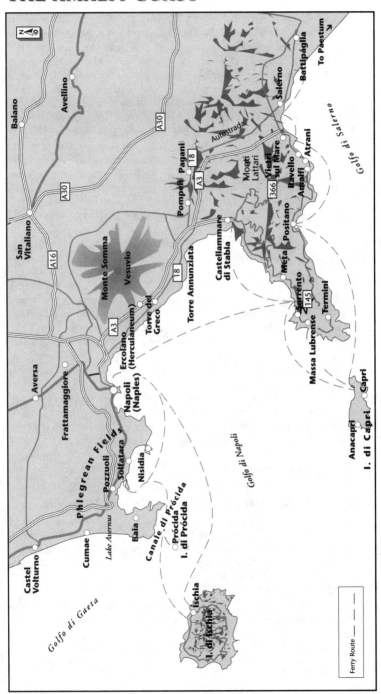

Excelsior, via Partenope 48, 80121 Napoli (☎ **800/325-3535** or 081/7640111; fax 081/7649743). This first-class hotel is on the shore dirve, with views of the bay from front rooms. The lobby and lounges are lavish, with Oriental carpets and gilt or glass chandeliers. Off the large semicircular lounge are a chic little bar and the Casanova restaurant. The rooms are decorated either in a standard Empire style (with ormolu trim and soft pastels) or in more typically Neapolitan floral prints. 124 rms with bath; 12 suites. Facilities: restaurant, bar. AE, DC, MC, V. Expensive.

Hotel Paradiso, via Catullo 11, 80122 Napoli (☎ **800/528-1234** or 081/7614161; fax 081/7613449). Stay here if you want something special a step or two off the beaten track. A modern air-conditioned building perched on the slopes of the hill above the port of Mergellina, the Paradise is just a few minutes by taxi or funicular from downtown and has fabulous views from huge window walls in the lobby and all the front rooms. The decor is restful and attractive. Be sure to ask for a room with a view; there's no extra charge. There are terraces for sitting, dining, and contemplating the entire bay as far as Vesuvius and beyond. 71 rms with bath; 2 suites. Facilities. restaurant, bar, garage. AE, DC, MC, V. Expensive.

Jolly Ambassador, via Medina 70, 80133 Napoli (☎ **081/416000;** fax 081/5518010). This hotel occupies the top 14 floors of the only skyscraper on the downtown skyline (if you don't count new business centers beyond the station), and the rooms and roof-garden restaurant command sweeping views of Naples and the bay. Decorated in the uninspired but functional style of the Jolly chain, with dark brown and white predominating, it promises comfort and efficiency in a city where these are scarce commodities. 251 rms with bath. Facilities: restaurant, bar, garage. AE, DC, MC V. Expensive.

Rex, via Palepoli 12, 80132 Napoli (☎ **081/7649389;** fax 081/7649227). At the lower end of this price range, the Rex has a fairly quiet location near the Santa Lucia waterfront. Situated on the first two floors of an art nouveau building, it has no elevator; the decor ranges from 1950s modern to fake period pieces and even some folk art, haphazardly combined. Though it has no restaurant, there are many in the vicinity. 40 rms with bath. AE, DC, V. Inexpensive.

On to Vesuvius, Herculaneum & Pompeii

If you're going directly from Naples to Ercolano (Herculaneum), take A3 to the Ercolano exit. The ruins of Herculaneum and Pompeii are here, as is the 12.8-kilometer (8-mile) road up the western face of **Vesuvius.** (There's another road from Pompeii up the south face of Vesuvius, but it's more difficult and requires more walking).

The road up Vesuvius splits twice. At the first split, a right turn takes you to the observatory. Stay left. At the second split, bear left to a parking area, where you set off on a 30-minute climb up a soft, slippery cinder track.

To drive directly from downtown Naples to Pompeii on A3 takes about an hour. To go by train, take the Circumvesuviana, which leaves from the Corso Garibaldi–Stazione Centrale stop. It's a 30-minute ride to the Pompeii–Villa dei Misteri Station. From here it's only a short walk to the Porta Marina (Sea Gate), the main entrance to Pompeii.

To drive to Pompeii from Herculaneum or Vesuvius, return to A3 and continue east about 11.2 kilometers (7 miles). To go by train, take the Circumvesuviana from the Ercolano Station to the Pompeii–Villa dei Misteri Station.

After touring Pompeii, you can get a train almost every 20 minutes to Sorrento, a 30-minute trip. If you're going to return to Pompeii, you can spend the night in Sorrento as an alternative to returning to Naples. From Sorrento, you can catch a boat to Capri or (in season) Ischia or begin your trip along the Amalfi Drive.

An Introduction to Vesuvius, Herculaneum & Pompeii

Lava is extremely fertile. In less than 20 years it sprouts greenery that in time becomes luxuriant vegetation. Memories of former eruptions are forgotten. The rich land attracts farmers, and villages are built. Two such towns, Herculaneum and Pompeii, grew up in the shadow of Vesuvius. On the slopes above the town, oaks and chestnuts grew; below were fig and lemon trees, chestnut forests, vineyards, and the yellow blossoms of mimosa.

In 80 B.C., Roman general Sulla turned Herculaneum and Pompeii into Roman colonies, where patricians came to escape the turmoil of city life and relax in the sun. The sea lapped against Herculaneum's walls then, and the citizens were mostly fishers. Pompeii was a thriving commercial center in a rich agricultural region. Herculaneum and Pompeii were ideal resort towns for overworked Romans seeking a delightful climate and a respite from Rome's frantic pace.

The towns were laid out on grid patterns, with two main intersecting streets. The wealthiest took a whole block for themselves; those less fortunate built a house and rented out the front rooms, facing the street, as shops. The facades of these houses were relatively plain and seldom hinted at the care and attention lavished on the private rooms within. When a visitor entered, he or she passed the shops and entered an open area (atrium). In the back was a receiving room. Behind was another open area, the peristyle, with rows of columns and perhaps a garden with a fountain. Only good friends ever saw this private part of the house, which was surrounded by the bedrooms and the dining area.

How different these homes are from houses today—and how much they say about changing attitudes toward family and society. Today we build homes that face the streets, that look out over the world; in Pompeii and Herculaneum, houses were designed around an inner garden so families could turn their backs on the world outside. Today we install picture windows that break down visual barriers between ourselves and our neighbors; the people in these Roman towns had few windows, preferring to get their light from the courtyard—the light within. How pleasant it must have been to come home from the forum or the baths to one's own secluded kingdom with no visual reminders of a life outside one's own.

Not that public life was so intolerable. Wine shops were on almost every corner and frequent shows were given at the amphitheater. The public fountains and toilets were fed by huge cisterns connected by lead pipes beneath the sidewalks. Because garbage and rainwater collected in the streets of Pompeii, the sidewalks were raised and huge stepping stones were placed at crossings so pedestrians could keep their feet dry. Herculaneum had better drainage, with an underground sewer that led to the sea.

The ratio of freemen to slaves was about three to two. A small, prosperous family had two or three slaves. As all manual labor was considered degrading, the slaves did housework and cooking, including the cutting of meat, which the family ate with spoons or with their fingers. Everyone loved grapes and figs. Venison, chicken, and pork were the main dishes. Oranges weren't known, but people used quinces (a good source of vitamin C) against scurvy. Bread was made from wheat and barley (rye and oats were unknown) and washed down with wine made from grapes from the slopes of Vesuvius.

The government was considered a democracy, but women, children, gladiators, and Jews couldn't vote. They did, however, express their opinions on election day, as you'll see in campaign graffiti left on public walls.

Some 15,000 graffiti were found in Pompeii and Herculaneum. Many were political announcements—one person recommending another for office and spelling out his qualifications. Some were bills announcing upcoming events—a play at the theater or a gladiator fight at the amphitheater. Others were public notices—that wine was on sale, that an apartment would be vacant on the Ides of March. A good many were personal and give a human dimension to the disaster that not even the sights can equal. Here are a few:

At the Baths: "What is the use of having a Venus if she's made of marble?"

At a hotel: "I've wet my bed. My sin I bare. But why? you ask. No pot was anywhere."

At the entrance to the front lavatory of a private house: "May I always and everywhere be as potent with women as I was here."

"Everyone writes on this wall but me."

"We are as full as wineskins."

"You sell us this watery liquid and drink pure wine yourself."

"Oh, I would rather die than be a god without you."

"Victoria, I greet you, and wherever you are, may your sneeze bring you good luck."

"Lucilla makes money from her lover."

"Virgula to her friend Tertius: Thou art too ugly!"

"Methea loves Chrestus with all her heart. May Venus favor them, and may they ever live in amity."

"Vivius Restitus slept here alone and thought with longing of his Urbana."

In the year A.D. 63 Vesuvius was considered an extinct volcano. The crater had become a dense forest filled with wild boars. Spartacus and his slaves had lived here during their rebellion against Rome.

An earthquake in that year caused so much destruction that the citizens of Pompeii and Herculaneum considered abandoning their towns and settling elsewhere. Nero was in the 10th year of his reign and the people had to turn to him for help. What was rebuilt was done in Roman style, splendid but not always in the best taste—a definite departure from the noble and simple lines of Greek art. Not that everyone minded or even noticed the difference. With so many wealthy visitors, it was only natural that the people in these provincial towns would imitate the manners of the Roman nobility and look to Rome for the latest styles. The Pompeiian artists mostly reproduced famous Greek paintings, not from inspiration but from memory. There were no allegories—just pleasant, agreeable images, mostly mythological love stories like Jupiter carrying off Europa, Apollo pursuing Daphne, and Venus in the arms of Mars. False pilasters were painted in fresco, imitating the example of the rich. Artists worked fast and art became an industry.

August 24, A.D. 79, was a hot summer day. On the previous day the annual Festival of Vulcan, the Roman fire god, had been celebrated. At both Herculaneum and Pompeii tremors had been felt for 4 days. Then came the explosion.

The younger Pliny, age 17, was at the house of his uncle, the elder Pliny, at Misenum (which you passed if you drove from Baia to Cumae), when the family's attention was drawn to a cloud of unusual size and appearance. As Pliny reported later in a famous letter to Tacitus (from *Letters,* VI, 20, 6, 8–9, 16; trans. B. Radice):

> *It was not clear at that distance from which mountain in the cloud was rising (it was afterwards known to be Vesuvius). Its general appearance can best be expressed as being like an umbrella pine, for it rose to a great height on a sort of trunk and then split off into branches . . . . In places it looked white, elsewhere blotched and dirty, according to the amount of soil and ashes carried with it. My uncle's scholarly acumen saw at once that it was important enough for a closer inspection, and he ordered a boat to be made ready, telling me I could come with him if I wished. I replied that I preferred to go on with my studies.*

Pliny the Elder, both a historian and a commander of the naval base at Misenum, was diverted by a note from the wife of a friend, begging him to rescue her husband, whose house was at the foot of Vesuvius. And so he ordered the warships launched with the intention of bringing help to those who were trapped. The letter continues:

He steered his course straight for the danger zone. He was entirely fearless. . . . Ashes were already falling, hotter and thicker as the ships drew near, followed by bits of pumice and blackened stones, charred and cracked by the flames: Then suddenly they were in shallow water, and the shore was blocked by the debris from the mountain. For a moment my uncle wondered whether to turn back, but when the helmsman advised this he refused, telling him that Fortune stood by the courageous. . . .

The wind was in my uncle's favor, and he was able to bring his ship in. He embraced his terrified friend, cheered and encouraged him . . . . Meanwhile, on Mount Vesuvius broad sheets of fire and leaping flames blazed at several points, their bright glare emphasized by the darkness of night. My uncle tried to allay the fears of his companions by repeatedly declaring that these were nothing but bonfires left by peasants in their terror, or else empty houses on fire in districts they had abandoned.

Then he went to rest. . . . By this time the courtyard giving access to his room was full of ashes mixed with pumice stones, so that its level had risen, and if he had stayed in the room any longer he would never have got out. He was awakened, came out and joined his friend Pomponianus and the rest of the household. They debated whether to stay indoors or take their chances in the open, for the buildings were now shaking with violent shocks, and seemed to be swaying to and fro as if they were torn from their foundations. Outside, on the other hand, there was the danger of falling pumice stones; however, after comparing the risks, they took the latter. As a protection against falling objects they put pillows on their heads tied down with cloths.

Elsewhere there was daylight by this time, but they were still in darkness, blacker and denser than any ordinary night, which they relieved by lighting torches and various kinds of lamps. My uncle decided to go down to the shore and investigate the possibility of escape by sea, but he found the waves still wild and dangerous. A sheet was spread on the ground for him to lie down on. . . . Then the flames and smell of sulphur which gave warning of the approaching fire drove the others to take flight and roused him to stand up. He stood leaning on two slaves and then suddenly collapsed, I imagine because the dense fumes choked his breathing by blocking his windpipe. . . .

When daylight returned on the sixteenth—two days after the last day he had been seen—his body was found intact and uninjured, still fully clothed and looking more like sleep than death.

This is the oldest-surviving realistic description of a major natural disaster.

The eruption actually began at 1pm, with flames and a cloud of ashes that whirled with the wind and covered the region in a shroud of darkness. Red-hot boulders were hurled thousands of feet into the air and rained down on the surrounding countryside. By the following day, Pompeii was covered to a depth of 3.7 meters (12 ft.) by a sudden fall of ashes, pumice, and stones. Later eruptions buried the town another 1.8 meters (6 ft.). When excavators uncovered the town, they found 600 bodies in the streets and the bodies of many others who had tried to flee. An estimated 2,000 people — one-tenth of the total population — had perished.

What covered Herculaneum was not pumice and ash, but mud. Vesuvius belched forth steam at 1,093°C (2,000°F), which mingled with seawater. Torrents of liquid mud swept down upon the city, leapt the walls, and penetrated into every crevice. Until a few years ago it was believed that most of the estimated 5,000 inhabitants had managed to escape by sea, as few skeletons were found in the city. Excavations at Porta Marina, the gate in the seawall leading to the beach, revealed instead that many perished there. As the mud solidified, it acted as a prop to buildings that otherwise would have collapsed. The pressure from this and subsequent eruptions converted the mud into a compact mass of rock (tufa) 18.3 to 30.5 meters (60 to 100 ft.) deep.

So effective was the covering that eggs and fish were found on a dining room table, and in a bakery 81 carbonized loaves were discovered in the half-opened oven. At Herculaneum, the mud scorched papyrus and cloth but didn't destroy them. Wood beds, stairs, cupboards — all were saved and are on view today. In one house excavators found the bread, salad, fruit, and cake that were being served for lunch when the catastrophe struck.

In 1864 Giuseppe Fiorelli, in charge of the excavations at Pompeii, had the idea of forcing liquid plaster into the lava molds that had solidified around the fallen bodies. The plaster forms (which you'll see) are so true to life that you can see the pubic hair shaved in semicircles to duplicate the look on certain statues as well as the tormented expressions on the faces.

The first deaths at Pompeii must have been caused by the huge stones falling from the sky. Some people hid in their homes; others fled. Many who stayed must have suffocated beneath the falling ash, or, like Pliny the Elder, been asphyxiated by fumes. Many who fled must have been struck down by falling pillars and masonry.

At the House of Meander at Pompeii the doorkeeper fled to his room with his little girl and covered their heads with pillows. That's how they were found 1,800 years later. In another house, a mother and daughter escaped through a skylight into a garden. That's where they were found. A woman and her three maids were found with the jewelry and the silver mirror they had squandered time gathering. A man with teeth marks in his flesh was found beside his dog. The Roman sentry at the gate at

Herculaneum was found trying to cover his dog with his cloak. Two glad-iators with manacled wrists were discovered in a prison cell. More than 60 gladiators were found dead in their barracks; with them was a richly dressed woman—no one will ever know why.

In 1748, when excavators turned over the ashes that for 1,700 years had covered Pompeii, they had one objective: to find masterpieces for the king's museums. Excavations were by chance; if nothing was found, the site was abandoned. Litter was thrown back; frescoes not worthy of the museum were left exposed to the influence of the sun and rain; walls cracked and fell. It was only in 1863 that the collection of artworks became secondary to the goal of restoring an ancient Roman city. That's why so much of the priceless art is found today in the National Museum in Naples and not where it belongs, in Pompeii. The situation in Herculaneum was somewhat different. Because the town was buried in solidified mud rather than ash, citizens couldn't return after the disaster, as many did in Pompeii, to recover possessions. Excavations began much later, so much of the art was left where it was found. Though Herculaneum had one-fourth the population of Pompeii and has been only partially excavated, the things that've been found here are generally better preserved than those discovered at Pompeii.

HERCULANEUM

The best guide is a small red book called *Pompeii-Herculaneum: A Guide with Reconstructions*. The photos are covered with plastic overlays, so you can see how various sites look today and looked 2,000 years ago.

If you want a personal guide, make sure he or she has certification papers (a booklet with a photo and a stamp). Agree beforehand on the length of the tour and the price. Write the figures down. Whether you're with a guide or not, be sure to have some 1,000L pieces handy to tip the guards who open the locked houses for you.

You could easily get lost in the streets of Pompeii, but not in **Herculaneum,** corso Resina (☎ **081/7390963**). You can see most impor-tant buildings in about 2 hours. If you feel closer to the past at Hercu-laneum than at Pompeii, it's in part because there are fewer hawkers here, and visitors tend to show a certain quiet respect for antiquity that's not always evident in such a famous spot as Pompeii. Though there's much less to see here, the houses are better preserved, with bright frescoes and mosaics. In some cases, you can even see the original wood beams, staircases, and furniture. Admission 12,000L; under 18 and over 60 free. Open daily 9am to 1 hr. before sunset; ticket office closes 2 hrs. before sunset.

The following route will help you locate the most important sights:

The sole entrance is at the east corner. You'll walk halfway around the perimeter of the site and enter on Cardo III. Only three main streets have been excavated: Cardo III, Cardo IV, and Cardo V. The two cross streets are Decumanus Inferior and Decumanus Maximus. As you walk around the excavated site, you can see how it was unearthed like hidden treasure from a pit below the surface of the existing town. Excavations are still going on; the best perhaps is yet to come.

On Cardo III, make the first right, in front of the badly damaged **Casa dell'Albergo,** and turn left on Cardo IV. The first building on the right is the **House of the Mosaic Atrium** (Casa dell'Atrio a Mosaico). The atrium (entranceway) is still paved with mosaics, but the floors rippled under the weight of the lava. You can still see the wood window frames in the courtyard (peristyle). Don't miss the bedrooms and the large dining room.

Continue up Cardo IV (to the right). On your left is the **Wooden Trellis House** (Casa a Graticcio). This is the only surviving example of the use of trellises to make walls—a money-saving technique used by the Romans for shops and secondary rooms. Next door is the **House of the Wooden Partition** (Casa del Tramezzo di legno), which has the charred remains of a bed and a well-preserved facade.

Cross Decumanus Inferior. The first house on the right is **Casa Sannitica,** which has a beautiful atrium surrounded by Ionic columns. The house retains the simple plan of the Samnites, the people who lived here before the Romans came.

A few steps farther along, across the street, is the entrance to the **Baths** (Terme), with separate rooms for men and women. The dressing room has cubicles for clothing. There's a series of chambers that grew progressively hotter, and a sweating room for people with bad livers. Hot air from furnaces circulated in cavities under the floor and through ducts in the walls and ceilings. Soap was reserved for medical treatment or hair dye, but bathers brought their own oils, scrapers, and towels. The baths usually opened at noon, when the furnaces were lit. Many bathers came to these early health and fitness clubs in the evening, after dinner. They sang, bathed, splashed, brawled, got massaged, drank wine, ate pastries and sausages, and sweated off the pressures of the day.

Continue (left) up Cardo IV. Across the street is the **House with Charred Furniture** (Casa del Mobilio Carbonizzato), an elegant small house with an attractive courtyard and the remains of furniture. Next to it is the **House with the Neptune and Amphitrite Mosaic** (Casa del Mosaico di Nettuno e Anfitrite). The annexed shop is the best-preserved example remaining of a Roman shop.

At the end of Cardo IV, turn right on Decumanus Maximus. The first entrance on the right is **Casa del Bicentenario,** so called because it was unearthed in 1938, 200 years after excavations began. The living room has a marble floor and frescoes. In a small upper room (many houses in Herculaneum had two floors) is a small cross in a panel above a wood altar—the oldest evidence of Christianity in the Roman Empire.

Make your first right down Cardo V. Halfway down the street, on the left, is the **Bakery** (Pistrinum), which has two original flour mills, an oven, and bread molds. Continue down Cardo V and turn left at the first cross street, Decumanus Inferior, for a look at the **Palestra,** the sports center, which has a pool in the shape of a cross.

Return to Cardo V and continue left. On your right is the **House of the Stags** or **Deer** (Casa dei Cervi), one of the most beautiful patrician houses, which has two marble statue groups of stags being assailed by dogs. At the end of Cardo V, outside Porta Marina, the **Suburban Baths** (Terme Suburbane) are elegantly decorated and illuminated by skylights. Now return to Cardo III and make your way back to the entrance.

VESUVIUS

You can visit **Vesuvius** either before or after Herculaneum. The mountain tends to be clearer in the afternoon, though then you must have your own car, as the last bus up the volcano is at 2pm. If possible, save the mountain until after you've toured the burned city and learned to appreciate the volcano's awesome power. The most important factor is whether the summit is lost in mist—when it is, you'll be lucky to see your hand in front of your face. The volcano is visible from Naples and everywhere else along the Bay of Naples; the best advice is, when you see the summit clearing, head for it. The view then is magnificent, with the curve of the coast and the tiny white houses among the orange and lemon blossoms.

If you decide to take the 30-minute walk, wear your hardiest shoes: It's a steep, relentless climb over pulverized ash and lapilli—definitely not for everyone. If the weather's bad and you've never seen a volcano, it's still worth driving to the parking area, past fields of black twisted lava from the 1944 eruption.

When you think of earlier generations being tougher than we are, imagine Goethe in 1787 making his way to the top hanging on to the belt of a guide.

To reach Vesuvius from Naples, you can take the Circumvesuviana Railway or (summer only) a motor-coach service from piazza Vittoria, which hooks up with bus connections at Pugliano. You get off the train at the Ercolano station, the 10th stop. SITA buses go from Herculaneum to the crater of Vesuvius at the rate of six per day, costing 4,000L round-trip. Once at the top you must be accompanied by a guide, costing another 5,000L.

POMPEII

If your time is limited and you have to choose between Herculaneum and Pompeii, choose **Pompeii:** The buildings aren't as well preserved as at Herculaneum, but the size of the town and the extent of the excavations are considerably more impressive. It would be a shame to miss either, however; and as the two towns are so close, there's no reason not to see both. This is one of the few times when it would be preferable to know two things superficially than to know one in somewhat greater depth.

If you want a personal guide, make sure he or she is registered and that the guide is standing inside the gate. Agree beforehand on the length of the tour and the price. Many houses will be locked. Ask one of the many guards to open them for you. Be persistent! And have some lire ready if persistence isn't enough.

For a self-guided tour, you'll need a map. Most, unfortunately, list only the major streets. The best comes with a useful English guide, *How to Visit Pompeii,* sold at the entrance. Also helpful, particularly for families with children, is the small red guide *Pompeii-Herculaneum: A Guide with Reconstructions,* which includes transparent overlays so you can see the various sites as they looked in A.D. 79.

You'll be spending many hours negotiating rough paving stones; be sure to wear your most comfortable walking shoes.

The following route will help you locate the most interesting sights:

Enter through **Porta Marina,** so called because it faces the sea. It's near the Pompeii–Villa dei Misteri Circumvesuviana Station. On your right is the **Antiquarium,** which contains a cast a dog caught in the agony of death.

Past the **Temple of Venus** is the **Basilica,** the law court and the city's economic center. These oblong buildings ending in a semicircular projection (apse) were the model for early Christian churches, which had a nave (central aisle) and two side aisles separated by rows of columns. Standing in the Basilica you can recognize the continuity between Roman and Christian architecture.

The Basilica opens onto the **Forum** (Foro), the public meeting place surrounded by temples and public buildings. It was here that elections were held and speeches and official announcements made. America's answer to the forum was the village green. The closest we come to it today is the mall.

Turn left. At the far (northern) end of the forum is the **Temple of Jupiter** (Tempio di Giove). Walk around the right side of the temple, cross the street, and continue north on via del Foro. On your left a low building houses a cafeteria, a coffee bar, a souvenir shop, and rest rooms. The next cross street becomes via della Fortuna to your right and via della Terme to your left. Turn right on via della Fortuna. On your left is **The House of the Faun** (Casa del Fauno), one of the most impressive examples of a luxurious private house, with wonderful mosaics (originals in the National Museum in Naples).

Retrace your steps along via della Fortuna to via del Foro. Cross the street. You're now on via della Terme. The first entrance on the right is the **House of the Tragic Poet** (Casa del Poeta Tragico). This is a typical

WHAT TO SEE & DO WITH CHILDREN

Capri: The Blue Grotto, the hotel pools, the walk to the Natural Arch, the cable car from Anacapri, the 960 steps from Anacapri back down to the harbor.

Pompeii: The casts of bodies and animals exhibited in the Antiquarium. (The more children read beforehand about Pompeii, the more interested they'll be.)

The Amalfi Drive: The Emerald Grotto, the hotel tennis courts and pools, the crowded pebbly beaches, the Italian ices and pizza.

middle-class house from the last days of Pompeii. Over the door is a mosaic of a chained dog and the inscription *Cave canem:* "Beware of the dog." Continue west on via della Terme to the end. Turn right and bear left along via Consolare. Pass through the beautiful **Porta Ercolano** (Gate of Herculaneum)—the main gate that led to Herculaneum and Naples.

Now outside of Pompeii, walk down **via dei Sepolcri,** lined with tombs and cypresses. The road makes a sharp left. At the four-way crossing, turn right to the **Villa of the Mysteries** (Villa dei Misteri). This patrician's villa contains what some consider the greatest surviving group of paintings from the ancient world, telling the story of a young bride (Ariadne) being initiated into the mysteries of the cult of Dionysus. Bacchus (Dionysus), the god of wine, was popular in a town so devoted to the pleasures of the flesh. But he also represented the triumph of the irrational—of all those mysterious chthonic forces that no official state religion could fully suppress. The cult of Dionysus, like the cult of the Cumaean Sibyl, gave people a sense of control over fate and, in its focus on the otherworld, helped pave the way for Christianity.

Return along via dei Sepolcri back into Pompeii. Retrace your steps down via Consolare, which joins with vicolo di Narciso. Make your first left on vicolo di Mercurio. Six blocks down is vicolo dei Vettii. Around the corner, to the left, is the **House of the Vettii** (Casa dei Vettii). This is the best example of a rich middle-class merchant's house, with beautifully frescoed walls and a garden.

Return back around the corner to vicolo di Mercurio. Turn left, the direction you took before you turned the corner to visit the House of the Vettii. Continue east one more block. You've now reached via Stabiana, one of the two major intersecting streets of the town. Around the corner to the left is **Casa degli Amorini Dorati** (House of the Gilded Cupids), a well-preserved elegant home with original marble decorations in the garden.

From the door of Casa degli Amorini Dorati, turn right down via Stabiana. Your third left should put you on via Augustali. Your first left will take you to the **Lupanare** (brothel) on vicolo del Lupanare. An uneaten plate of pasta and beans was found here. On the walls are scenes of erotic games that clients could request. The beds have shoe marks left by visitors.

Continue south on vicolo del Lupanare. Your first left will put you on via dell'Abbondanza, the other main street of the old town. The first door on your left is the **Stabian Baths.** It was here that people came in the evening to drown the day's burdens. The baths were heated by underground furnaces. The heat circulated among the stone pillars supporting the floor, rose through flues in the walls, and escaped through chimneys. Water temperature could be set for cold, lukewarm, and hot. Bathers took a lukewarm bath to prepare themselves for the hot room. A tepid bath came next, then a plunge into cold water to tone up the skin. A vigorous massage with oil was followed by rest, reading, horseplay, and conversation.

POMPEII

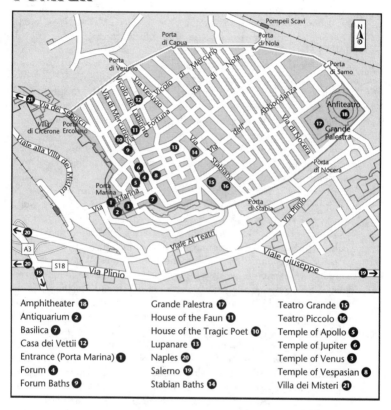

Amphitheater ⓲	Grande Palestra ⓱	Teatro Grande ⓯
Antiquarium ❷	House of the Faun ⓫	Teatro Piccolo ⓰
Basilica ❼	House of the Tragic Poet ⓾	Temple of Apollo ❺
Casa dei Vettii ⓬	Lupanare ⓭	Temple of Jupiter ❻
Entrance (Porta Marina) ❶	Naples ⓴	Temple of Venus ❸
Forum ❹	Salerno ⓳	Temple of Vespasian ❽
Forum Baths ❾	Stabian Baths ⓮	Villa dei Misteri ㉑

Continue in the same direction, east on via dell' Abbondaza (a left turn as you leave the baths). Two blocks down on your right is the **Fullonica Stephani,** a house converted into workshops for the cleaning of fabrics. All Roman citizens were required to wear togas in public, which weren't exactly easy to keep clean. It's not hard to imagine why there were more toga-cleaners (fullers) in Pompeii than anything else, except perhaps bakers. The cloth was dunked in a tub full of water and chalk and stamped on like grapes. Washed, the material was stretched across a wicker cage and exposed to sulfur fumes. The fuller carded it with a long brush, then placed it under a press. The harder the pressing, the whiter and brighter it became.

Go south, completely around the block. Behind the Fullonica Stephani is the entrance to the **Casa di Menandro,** a patrician's villa with many paintings and mosaics. Return to via dell'Abbontianza and turn right. If you've had enough walking, head back to Porta Marina, where your tour began, making a short detour to the left on via di Stabiana to the **Grand Theater** (Teatro Grande) and **Triangular Forum** (Foro Triangolare).

The recommended alternative is to continue east on via dell'Abbondanza seven blocks to the **Casa di Loreius Tiburtinus,** a richly decorated large patrician house. Two blocks farther is the **Villa di Giulia Felice** (House of Julia Felix), which has a large garden with a lovely portico. The wealthy lady living here ran a public bathhouse annex and rented out ground floor rooms as shops—no one knows why.

Turn right past the villa and continue to the **Amphitheater** (Anfiteatro). The games here were between animals, between gladiators, and between animals and gladiators. There were also Olympic Games and chariot races. The crowds rushed in when the gates opened—women and slaves to the bleachers. When the emperor or some other important person was in attendance, exotic animals—lions, tigers, panthers, elephants, and rhinos—were released. At "halftime," birds of prey were set against hares or dogs against porcupines—the animals tied to either end of a rope so neither could escape. Most gladiators were slaves or prisoners, but a few were Germans or Syrians who enjoyed fighting.

Teams of gladiators worked for impresarios, who hired them out to wealthy citizens, many of whom were running for office and hoping that some gory entertainment would buy them some votes. When a gladiator found himself at another's mercy, he extended a pleading hand to the president of the games. If the president turned his thumb up, the gladiator lived; if he turned his thumb down, the gladiator's throat was cut. The arena grew pretty bloody after a night's entertainment and was sprinkled with red powder to camouflage the carnage. The victorious gladiator received money or a ribbon exempting him from further fights. If he was a slave he was often set free. If the people of Pompeii had had trading cards, they would have collected portraits of gladiators; everyone had his or her favorite. Says one graffito: "Petronius Octavus fought 34 fights and then died, but Severus, a freedman, was victor in 55 fights and still lived; Nasica celebrates 60 victories." Pompeii had a gladiator school, the Caserma dei Gladiatori, which you can see behind the Grand Theater on your way back to Porta Marina. A main gate is at Porta Marina (☎ 081/8611051). Hours are daily from 9am to about 1 hour before sunset. Admission is 12,000L for adults; 17 and under and over 60 free.

Return to Porta Marina, where your walk began, or exit through the **Ingresso Anfiteatro** and find a cab for the 1.6-kilometer (1-mile) trip back to Porta Marina. You could, of course, begin your trip at Ingresso Anfiteatro and make the tour in the opposite direction.

From Pompeii return to Naples or head south through Castellammare di Stabia. Continue on Route S145 until it intersects with Route S163, then continue on to Sorrento on Route S145, unless you plan to skip it and go on to Capri from Positano.

THE PHLEGREAN FIELDS

The **Phlegrean Fields**—the "fields of fire"—was the name once given to the entire region west of Naples, including the island of Ischia. The whole area floats freely on a mass of molten lava very close to the surface. The fires are still smoldering. Greek and Roman notions of the underworld weren't the blind imaginings of a primitive people; they were the creations of poets and writers who stood on this very ground in the Phlegrean Fields and wrote down what they saw. The main sights today are the **Solfatara,** the sunken crater of a volcano, where you walk among the sulfurous steam jets and pools of bubbling mud; Italy's third-largest and best-preserved **Amphitheater at Pozzuoli; Lake Avernus,** which the ancients believed was the entrance to the underworld; **Baia,** the resort town of ancient Rome, where you can see the remains of a spa frequented by Pompey, Julius Caesar, Nero, and Cicero; and the **Cave of the Cumaean Sibyl,** described by Homer and Virgil.

Whether it's worth the half a day it takes to tour these sites really depends on your interests. If you've never seen volcanic activity, don't miss the Solfatara (it's quite safe, so long as you stick to the path). The Amphitheater at Pozzuoli is fascinating because of its well-preserved underground passages and chambers, which give you a good sense of how the wild animals were hoisted up into the arena. At Lake Avernus you'll be standing at the spot the ancients considered the entrance to Hades. The ruins at Baia won't mean too much unless you have more than a passing interest in antiquity. The Oracle at Cumae was as famous as the one at Delphi; if you've read *The Aeneid,* you'll want to enter the very cave described in Book VI, where Aeneas sought the Sibyl's aid for his journey to the underworld.

To reach the **Solfatara,** via Solfatara 161 (☎ 081/5267413), from Naples, take Route S7 Quater, "via Domiziana," 7.5 miles west toward Pozzuoli. About 2 kilometers (1.3 miles) before Pozzuoli you'll see a sign to the Solfatara on your right. The only eruption of this semiextinct volcano was in 1198. Admission 6,500L adults, 3,500L children. Open daily 8:30am to sunset.

Legends about this smoldering landscape are based on conflicts between the neolithic gods of the soil and the newer Olympian gods brought to Greece by the Achaeans around 1600. One legend tells of how Zeus hurled a 100-headed dragon named Typhon—the pre-Olympian god of volcanoes—down the crater of Epomeo on the island of Ischia; and of how every crater in the Phlegrean Fields is one of Typhon's mouths, flashing steam and fire. In a similar legend pitting old values against new, the sulfurous springs of the Solfatara are said to be the poisonous discharges from the wounds the Titans received in their war with Zeus before he hurled them down to hell. Both legends, of course, are efforts to dramatize man's struggle to overcome the mysterious and dangerous forces of nature.

The **Amphitheater** (Anfiteatro Flavio), via Nicola Terracciano (☎ 081/5266007), at **Pozzuoli** is about 2 kilometers (1.3 miles) farther west on S7. It's the third-largest arena in Italy, after the Colosseum and that of Santa Maria Capua Vetere, and could accommodate 40,000 spectators, who were sometimes treated to mock naval battles when the arena was filled with water. Admission 4,000L. Open daily 9am–1pm.

You may want to make a short side trip to Pozzuoli's harbor and imagine St. Paul landing here in A.D. 61 en route to Rome. His own ship had been wrecked off Malta, and he was brought here on the *Castor and Pollux*, a grain ship from Alexandria that was carrying corn from Egypt to Italy 18 years before the eruption at Vesuvius.

If your time is limited, visit Lake Avernus and Cumae (the Sibyl's Cave) and then return toward Naples on a highway called the Tangenziale. A longer route takes you on a 17.7-kilometer (11-mile) loop from Pozzuoli south to Baia, around Lake Miseno (a volcanic crater believed by the ancients to be the Styx, across which Charon ferried the souls of the dead), and around Lake Fusaro. This 30-minute side trip lets you see the baths at Baia and enjoy some fine views of Pozzuoli Bay and the Phlegrean Fields.

To reach **Lake Avernus** (Lago d'Averno) continue west on S7 toward Cumae and turn left (south) on the road to Baia. About 1.6 kilometers (1 mile) along this road, turn right and follow the signs to Lake Avernus. The best time to visit is at sunset or when the moon is rising. There's a restaurant on the west side, near the tunnel (closed to the public) to Cumae, where you can dine on the terrace. Forested hills rise on three sides; the menacing cone of Monte Nuovo rises on the fourth. The smell of sulfur hangs over this lonely landscape at the very gates of hell. No place evokes Homer, Virgil, and the cult of the otherworld better than this silent, mysterious setting.

The ancient city of **Baia** (5.7km/3.6 miles from Pozzuoli) is now largely under the sea, but it was once the Roman Empire's most opulent and fashionable resort area. Sulla, Pompey, Julius Caesar, Tiberius, Nero, Cicero—these are some of the men who built their holiday villas here. Petronius's *Satyricon* is a satire on the corruption and intrigue and the wonderful licentiousness of Roman life at Baia. (Petronius was hired to arrange parties and entertainments for Nero, so he was in a position to know.) It was here at Baia that Emperor Claudius built a great villa for his first wife, Messalina, who spent her nights indulging herself at public brothels and plotting to have her husband replaced by her lover (for which she was beheaded); here that Claudius was poisoned by his second wife, Agrippina, who was in turn murdered by her son, Nero; here that Cleopatra was staying when Julius Caesar was assassinated on the Ides of March. Admission 6,000L. Open 9am to 2 hrs. before sunset.

Cumae (19.25km/12 miles west of Naples) is perhaps the oldest Greek colony in Italy. In the 6th and 7th centuries it was the most important settlement in the Phlegrean Fields and in the entire Naples area.

The **Sibyl's Cave** (Antro della Sibilla) is here—one of the most venerated sites in antiquity. In the 5th or 6th century B.C., the Greeks hollowed the cave from the rock beneath the present ruins of Cumae's acropolis. You walk through a massive stone tunnel that opens into a vaulted chamber where the Sibyl rendered her oracles. Standing here, imagine yourself having an audience with her, her voice echoing off the dark, damp walls. The sense of mystery, of communication with the invisible, is overwhelming. "This is the most romantic classical site in Italy," wrote H. V. Morton. "I would rather come here than to Pompeii." Admission 4,000L. Open daily 9am to 2 hrs. before sunset.

Virgil wrote the epic *The Aeneid,* the story of the Trojan prince Aeneas's wanderings, partly to give Rome the historical legitimacy that Homer had given the Greeks. On his journey, Aeneas had to descend to the underworld to speak to his father, and to find his way in he needed the guidance of the Cumaean Sibyl. She told him about the Golden Bough, his ticket through the Stygian swamp to the underworld.

Virgil didn't dream up the Sibyl's cave or the entrance to Hades—he must have stood both in her chamber and along the rim of Lake Avernus—as you yourself will stand there. When he wrote, "The way to hell is easy"—*Facilis descensus Averni*—it was because he knew the way. In Book VI of *The Aeneid,* Virgil describes how Aeneas, arriving at Cumae, seeks Apollo's throne (remains of the Temple of Apollo can still be seen) and "the deep hidden abode of the dread Sibyl, / An enormous "cave."

The Sibyl wasn't necessarily a charlatan; she was a medium, a prophetess, a woman who the ancients believed could communicate with the otherworld. The three most famous Sibyls were at Erythrae, Delphi, and Cumae. Foreign governments consulted the Sibyls before mounting campaigns. Wealthy aristocrats came to consult with their dead relatives. Businessmen came to get their dreams interpreted or to seek favorable omens before entering into financial agreements or setting off on journeys. Farmers came to remove curses on their cows. Love potions were a profitable source of revenue; women from Baia lined up for potions to slip into the wine of handsome charioteers who drove up and down the street in their gold-plated four-horsepower chariots.

With the coming of the Olympian gods, the earlier gods of the soil were discredited or given new roles and names that reflected the change from a matrilineal to a patrilineal society. Ancient rites, such as those surrounding the Cumaean Sibyl, were carried out in secret and known as the Mysteries. The Romans tried in vain to replace these Mysteries by deifying the state in the person of its rulers. Yet even the Caesars appealed to forces of the otherworld. And until the 4th century A.D. the Sibyl was consulted by the Christian Bishop of Rome.

From the Phlegrean Fields, take S7 back from Cumae to Pozzuoli, where you can take the boat to Ischia or toward Naples. If you're going to Naples, less than 3.2 kilometers (2 miles) east of Cumae turn off on the Tangenziale, an expressway along the northern edge of Naples.

SORRENTO

Sorrento (27.2km/17 miles from Pompeii) is a large, attractive tourist town on the Gulf of Sorrento. You can stay here if you need an extra day to tour Pompeii. You may also need to stay here if you're headed for the island of Ischia or Capri and miss the ferry.

The most interesting historic site is the Gothic-cum-baroque **Church of St. Francis** (San Francesco di Paolo), with an attractive 13th-century cloister. The **Belvedere,** with orange and lemon trees and a terrace with a beautiful view, is behind the **Museo Correale di Terranova,** via Capasso 48 (☎ 081/8781846). The museum features a collection of decorative antiques. Admission 5,000L; gardens only, 2,000L. Open Apr–Sept, Mon and Wed–Sat 9am–12:30pm and 5–7pm, Sun 9am–12:30pm; Oct–Mar, Mon and Wed–Sat 9am–12:30pm and 3–5pm, Sun 9am–12:30pm.

DINING

La Favorita–O' Parrucchiano, Corso Italia 71 (☎ 081/8781321). Centrally located and popular, this is one of Sorrento's oldest and best restaurants. You walk up a few steps to glassed-in veranda dining rooms filled, like greenhouses, with vines and plants. The menu offers classic local specialties, among them panzerotti (pastry shells filled with tomato and mozzarella) and scaloppe alla sorrentina (veal with tomato and mozzarella). Reservations required. Casual. V. Closed Wed Oct 30–June 30. Inexpensive.

Russo-Zi'Ntonio, via De Maio 11 (☎ 081/8781623). The prices are reasonable at this bright, cheerful restaurant that has the look of a country inn. It's just off the main square, piazza Tasso. The specialties are classic spaghetti al pomodoro (with fresh tomato sauce and basil) and melanzane alla parmigiana (eggplant with mozzarella and tomato sauce). Reservations advised. Casual. AE, DC, MC, V. Closed Tues. Moderate.

ACCOMMODATIONS

Bellevue Syrene, piazza della Vittoria 5, 80067 Sorrento (☎ 081/8781024; fax 081/8783963). A palatial villa in a garden overlooking the sea, the Bellevue has solid old-fashioned comforts and plenty of charm, with Victorian nooks and alcoves, antique paintings, and worn Oriental rugs. The rooms are pleasant, with good views. 65 rms with bath. Facilities: restaurant, bar, garden, pool. AE, DC, MC, V. Expensive.

Cocumella, via Cocumella 7, 80065 Sant'Agnello (☎ 081/8782933; fax 081/8783712). This hotel surrounded by a clifftop garden is in a quiet residential area in the hamlet of Sant'Agnello, on the northern edge of Sorrento. Occupying a villa that was a monastery in the 17th century, it has been totally renovated and features a tasteful blend of antique and contemporary decor, with vaulted ceilings and archways, a dining veranda, and stunning tiled floors. It's exclusive and elegant without being stuffy. 60 rms with bath. Facilities: restaurant, bar, garden, pool, tennis court. AE, DC, MC, V. Very Expensive.

Eden, via Correale 25, 80067 Sorrento (☎ 081/8781909). In a quiet, central location, the Eden has a garden and bright but undistinguished rooms. The lounge and lobby have more character. Some smaller rooms are in the inexpensive category. 60 rms with bath. Facilities: restaurant, garden, pool. AE, V. Closed Nov–Feb. Moderate.

Grand Hotel Excelsior Vittoria, piazza Tasso 34, 80067 Sorrento (☎ **081/8071044;** fax 081/8771206). In the heart of Sorrento but removed from the bustle of the main square, this historic hotel perches on the cliff. It has art nouveau decor and some quite grand, though faded, furnishings. Tenor Enrico Caruso's room is preserved as a relic; guest rooms are slightly less elegant but spacious and comfortable. The views are panoramic. The winter prices are considerably lower than the high-season rates. 106 rms with bath; 12 suites. Facilities: restaurant, bar, pool, garden. AE, DC, MC, V. Expensive.

ISCHIA

Ischia takes time to cast its spell. Give Ischia a week and you'll probably grow attached to its special character, its hidden corners and familiar views. An overnight stay isn't long enough for the island to get into your blood. It does have its share of white, wine-growing villages beneath the lush volcanic slopes of Monte Epomeo; and it does enjoy a life of its own that survives when tourists head home. But there are few signs of antiquity; the architecture is unremarkable; the beaches are small and pebbly; and there's little shopping.

Ischia is volcanic in origin. From its hidden reservoir of seething molten matter come the thermal springs said to cure whatever ails you. As early as 1580 a doctor named Iosolini published a book about the mineral wells on Ischia. "If your eyebrows fall off," he wrote, "go and try the baths at Piaggia Romano. Are you unhappy about your complexion? You will find the cure in the waters of Santa Maria del Popolo. Are you deaf? Then go to Bagno d'Ulmitello. If you know anyone who is getting bald, anyone who suffers from elephantiasis, or another whose wife yearns for a child, take the three of them immediately to the Bagno di Vitara; they will bless you."

Today the island is covered with thermal baths surrounded by tropical gardens—if you've never been to one before, don't miss the opportunity. The most picturesque part of Ischia is the port (**Ischia Porto**), with small shops and charming seafront restaurants. If you're coming for the day, your best bet is to recapture your youth at one of the mineral baths, such as Poseidon Gardens, and then lose it at a harborfront restaurant in Forio or Ischia Porto.

Ischia also has some lovely hotel-resorts high in the hills, offering therapeutic programs and rooms with breathtaking views of the sea. If you want to plunk down in the sun for a few days and tune out the world, this is an ideal place to go—remembering that you're unlikely to find many Americans to talk with.

It's a 33.6-kilometer (21-mile), 2-hour drive around the island from Ischia Porto. Poseidon Gardens and the port of **Forio** are on the opposite side. Take the southern route and you'll come to **Fontana,** the start of an invigorating hour's climb to the top of **Mount Epomeo,** a huge volcano that last erupted in 1302.

Poseidon Gardens (south of Forio on the west coast) is a complex of thermal pools, waterfalls, limestone cliffs, and tropical vegetation. There's also a cafeteria and changing rooms. You can sit like a Roman senator on a stone chair recessed in the rock and let the hot water cascade over you. All very campy and fun. Baths, such as those on the north coast, at Lacco Ameno and Casamicciola, are more formal and reputed to be highly therapeutic.

Near the port is the Castello, which looks the way a fort is supposed to look. It was built by Alphonso V of Aragón in 1450. A sunset stroll in front of the castle, overlooking the Bay of Naples, is a treat.

DINING

La Bussola, via Marina 36, Forio (☎ 081/997645). On the harbor at Forio, La Bussola has a large rustic indoor dining room with a fireplace, as well as outdoor dining on a terrace. Its specialties include fettuccine alla bussola (with zucchini, prosciutto, onions, and cream), linguine alla aragosta (with lobster), and charcoal-grilled meat and fish. Reservations not necessary. AE, DC, MC, V. Closed mid-Nov to late Mar. Moderate.

Gennaro, via Porto 66 (☎ 081/992917). This small family restaurant on the seafront at the port where the boats from the mainland dock serves excellent fish. Reservations advised Sat–Sun and July–Aug. AE, DC, MC, V. Closed Nov to mid-Mar, Tues from mid-Mar to Apr, and Oct. Moderate.

Porticciullo, via Porto 42 (☎ 081/993222). This rustic restaurant, on the port at Ischia, is a friendly, well-managed place, specializing in shellfish. It's also the best place on the island for late-night dining, as service is until 2am. Reservations advised. AE, DC, MC, V. Closed Nov. Expensive.

Ristorante Damiano, via Nuova Circumvallazione (☎ 081/983032). This place offers a sunny terrace with a panoramic view over pine trees, guaranteed to put you in a relaxed mood for dining. As a true island restaurant, its specialty is fish. The meat dishes aren't as good, as the meat is shipped in frozen from the mainland. However, the chefs turn out a zesty Neapolitan seafood cuisine, including a sauté of clams and mussels and six seafood salads made with creatures ranging from shrimp to sea polyps. Reservations advised. No credit cards. Closed Oct–Mar and for lunch except on Sun. Moderate.

La Romantica, via Marina 46, Forio (☎ 081/997345). La Romantica has a terrace for outdoor dining. Seafood specialties include spaghetti con vongole (with clam sauce) and alla marinara (with seafood and tomato sauce). Reservations not necessary. AE, DC, MC, V. Closed Wed and Jan. Moderate.

San Montano Hotel, Lacco Ameno (☎ 081/994033). The terrace here is a peaceful setting for lunch. Reservations advised. AE, DC, MC, V. Closed Nov–Apr 26. Expensive.

ACCOMMODATIONS

Grand Hotel Punta Molino, Lungomare Colombo, 80077 Porto d'Ischia (☎ 081/991544; fax 081/991562). Right in the town of Ischia, but in a quiet zone near the sea and framed with pines and gardens, this is one of the island's best hotels. The decor is bright and contemporary, with some luxury touches, and many rooms have sea views. There's a heated pool on one of the terraces. Half-board is required. 82 rms with bath. Facilities: spa treatments, bar, restaurant, garden, outdoor pool, private beach, parking. AE, DC, MC, V. Closed Nov–Apr 24. Expensive.

Regina Palace, via Cortese 18, 80077 Porto d'Ischia (☎ **081/991344;** fax 081/983597). Near the beach of Ischia Porto is the Regina Palace. It has an elegant art deco look, with pink-toned wood the keynote. Almost all the rooms have terraces or balconies overlooking the grounds, on which there's a large pool. 63 rms with bath. Facilities: restaurant, garden, outdoor pool, tennis courts, spa treatments, parking. AE, DC, MC, V. Closed Jan–Feb. Expensive.

La Villarosa, via Giacinto Gigante 5, 80077 Porto d'Ischia (☎ **081/ 991316;** fax 081/992425). You'll find this welcoming hotel in the heart of Ischia Porto and only a short walk from the beach. It's a gracious family-run villa with bright and airy rooms. There's a heated pool in the villa garden. Half-board is required, and you must reserve well in advance. 37 rms with bath. Facilities: restaurant for guests only, garden, outdoor pool. AE, DC, MC, V. Closed Nov–Mar. Expensive.

CAPRI

The summer scene on **Capri** calls to mind the stampeding of bulls through the narrow street of Pamplona: If you can visit in spring or fall, do so. Yet even the crowds aren't enough to destroy Capri's very special charm. The town is a Moorish opera set of shiny white houses, tiny squares, and narrow medieval alleys hung with flowers. You can take a bus or the funicular to reach the town, which rests on top of rugged limestone cliffs, hundreds of feet above the sea.

The mood is modish but somehow unspoiled. The summer set is made up of smart, wealthy types and college kids. The upper crust bakes in the sun in private villas. The secret is for you, too, to disappear while the day-trippers take over—offering yourself to the sun at your hotel pool or exploring the hidden corners of the island. Even in the height of summer you can enjoy a degree of privacy on one of the many paved paths that wind around the island hundreds of feet above the sea—if you're willing to walk, you can be as alone here as you've ever wanted to be.

The **Blue Grotto** (Grotta Azzurra) is renowned, but there are lesser-known grottoes to explore at leisure on boat trips around the island. You can also make a day trip to the nearby island of Ischia. When you've seen enough and tanned enough, it's time to go shopping in some trendy boutiques or succumb to Capri's cafes, where you'll be watching everything but your waist. As for dinner—there are enough fine restaurants that you can try a different one each night.

In his book *Italian Holiday,* Ludwig Bemelmans offers an entertaining way to picture Capri. Turn a coffee cup upside down, he says, and next to it invert an oversize cup with a chipped lip. Put a matchbox between them and drape a green handkerchief on top. This is the island of Capri, about 6.4 kilometers (4 miles) by 3.2 kilometers (2 miles). The small cup is Mount Tiberio at 328.7 meters (1,096 ft.); the large cup, Mount Solaro at 576 meters (1,920 ft.). The matchbox is the saddle between them. On the saddle is the town of Capri. Lean a match against the matchbox and that's the funicular from the harbor (Marina Grande) to town. Put two pieces of limp spaghetti on the other side of the matchbox: These are the roads leading down to the smaller port and beach at Marina Piccola. A strand of spaghetti from the matchbox to the larger cup is the road to the town of Anacapri. Another strand from the matchbox to the top of the smaller cup is the path to Villa Jovis, where Emperor Tiberius spent his declining years. The chip in the cup is, of course, the Blue Grotto.

TAKE A BREAK

Just down via Roma from the piazzetta is **Verginiello** (☎ *081/8370944*), *one of the island's best-value restaurants for lunch. Try the calamari (squid).*

The boat will disgorge you in a north coast settlement called **Marina Grande.** Here you'll find a few medium-price restaurants, the tourist information office, boats to the Blue Grotto, and the funicular to the town of Capri. If you're staying at one of the larger hotels, a representative will be at the harbor to take your bags. To reach the upper town, take the funicular, a minibus, or a cab (expensive). The funicular lines can be long; if you're coming for the day, it helps to be the first off the boat.

The funicular lets you off at the piazzetta (piazza Umberto I), which was probably here when Emperor Tiberius was living on the island in the first century. This open-air drawing room is surrounded by the medieval quarter of the town.

There are three spectacular walks.

From the main square of Capri, follow either via Longano or via Le Botteghe to the crossroads. Take via Matermania to the **Natural Arch,** a remarkable phenomenon of geological erosion. Then descend the nearby steps to the **Grotto of Matermania,** a natural cave that was transformed by the ancient Romans into a nymphaeum (a shrine and resting place adorned with a fountain, plants, and statues). Then continue down the steps leading to the **Terrace of Tragara.** Here you'll enjoy views of the famous Faraglioni, rocky islets carved into fantastic shapes by the sea. (The best time to see the Faraglioni is in the early-evening light.) Follow the picturesque via Tragara amidst sumptuous villas and flowering gardens back to the town center. The walk takes about 90 minutes round-trip.

From Capri's central plaza, follow either via Longano or via Le Botteghe until you reach a crossroad. Take the road to the left that passes by the little **Church of San Michele.** In 45 minutes you'll reach the

CAPRI

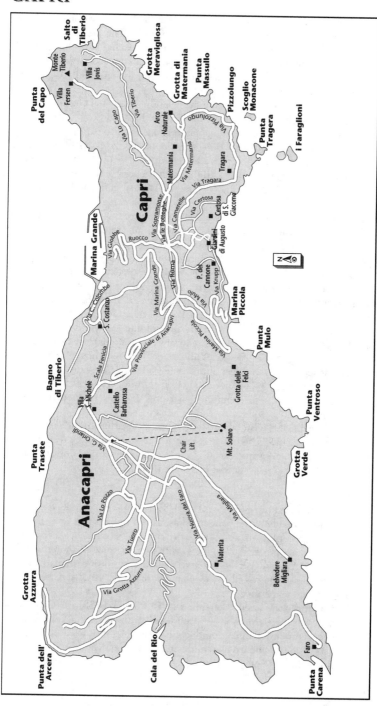

summit of **Mount Tiberio** and the ruins of the **Villa Jovis** on via Tiberio. This was the largest and most sumptuous of Tiberius's many villas on Capri. You can imagine him sitting here with Caligula on his 92-meter (300-ft.) front porch, planning an orgy in one of the grottoes or watching for imaginary enemies approaching by sea. Admission 4,000L. Open daily 9am to 1 hr. before sunset.

Via Krupp takes you below the beautiful **Augustus Gardens** (Parco Augusto) to the port and beach of **Marina Piccola.** Stop for a drink or pastry here, then take the 10-minute bus ride back to Capri.

An excursion to the **Blue Grotto** (a 45-min. trip from Marina Grande) is something you have to submit to, if only to have an opinion about one of the most celebrated tourist attractions in the world. The boat ride can be rough; if you have a weak stomach, sit in the back looking forward, rather than on one of the side seats. You can also reach the grotto by cab from Anacapri, but it would be a shame to miss the 10-minute boat ride beneath the towering cliffs. At the entrance to the grotto you'll step from your 14-passenger motorboat (expect to get a bit wet) into a tiny rowboat and duck low as you pass through the narrow entrance of the cave on a surge of the sea. The cliff wall doesn't extend to the bottom of the sea, so the sun's rays are refracted about a yard below the surface and indirectly illuminate the cavern from underneath. It's difficult to feel much wonder when it's paid for with a ticket and called for on demand—when in under 3 minutes you're spewed back out into the world again, among the fleets of boats bobbing at the entrance, waiting for their turn—but it's worth seeing what all the fuss is about and imagining how wonderful the experience might have been if only you had had this beauty to yourself. Cost, including 8,000-lire admission to the grotto, is 22,000L. Open daily 9:30am to 1 hr. before sunset; departures are less frequent in winter months.

To make this wish (almost) come true, at Marina Grande rent a boat that follows your schedule and visit the less frequented green, yellow, pink, and white grottoes around the island. The trip around the island takes 1½ hours by motorboat and costs 18,000L.

DINING

Al Grottino, via Longano 27 (☎ 081/8370584). This friendly family-run restaurant, handy to the piazzetta, has arched ceilings and lots of atmosphere; autographed photos of celebrity customers cover the walls. House specialties are gnocchi (dumplings) with tomato sauce and mozzarella as well as linguine al gamberetti (pasta with shrimp and tomato sauce). Reservations required in the evening. Casual. AE, MC, V. Closed Nov 3–Mar 30. Inexpensive.

La Capannina, via delle Botteghe 14 (☎ 081/8370732). La Capannina is only a few steps from the busy social hub of the piazzetta. It has a vine-draped veranda for dining outdoors by candlelight in a garden setting. The specialties, aside from an authentic Capri wine with the house label, are homemade ravioli alla caprese (with a cheese filling, tomato sauce, and

basil) and regional dishes. Reservations required in the evening. Casual.
AE, DC, MC, V. Closed Nov–Feb. Moderate/Expensive.

La Pigna, via Roma 30 (☎ **081/8370280**). Ensconced in a glassed-in
veranda and offering outdoor dining in a garden shaded by lemon trees,
the Pigna is among Capri's favorite restaurants. The specialties are a
house-produced wine, linguine alla Mediterranea (pasta with herbs), and
aragosta alla luna caprese (lobster). The waiters are courteous and efficient, and the atmosphere is nostalgic, as guitarists stroll by singing sentimental Neapolitan ballads. Reservations recommended. Casual. AE, DC,
MC, V. Closed Tues. Moderate.

ACCOMMODATIONS

Florida, via Fuorlovado 34, 80073 Capri (☎ **081/8370710;** fax
081/8370042). In the heart of downtown Capri off via Fuorlovado, this
modern building overlooks its own small garden and those of nearby
hotels. The rooms are cheery and functional; those on upper floors have
views and many have balconies. There's some degree of charm but few
frills. It's booked way ahead by regulars in season, so reservations are
essential. 19 rms with bath. AE, DC, MC, V. Closed Nov–Mar. Moderate.

Quisisana, via Camerelle 2, 80073 Capri (☎ **081/8370788;** fax
081/8376080). Catering largely to Americans, this is the most luxurious
and traditional hotel in the center of town. The spacious rooms are done
in traditional or contemporary decor with some antique accents; many
have arcaded balconies with views of the sea or the charming enclosed
garden, in which there's a pool. The bar and restaurant are casually elegant. 150 rms with bath; 15 suites. Facilities: restaurant, bar, garden, pool.
AE, DC, MC, V. Closed Nov 15 to mid-Mar. Very Expensive.

Scalinatella, via Tragara 8, 80073 Capri (☎ **081/8370633;** fax
081/8378291). The name means "little steps" and that's how this charming
but modern small hotel is built, on terraces following the slope of the
hill, overlooking the gardens, pool, and sea. The rooms are intimate,
with alcoves and fresh, bright colors. The hotel has a small bar, but no
restaurant. Ask for a room high up. 28 rms with bath; 8 suites. Facilities:
pool, air-conditioning. AE, MC, V. Closed Nov 15–Mar 15. Very
Expensive.

Villa Brunella, via Tragara 24, 80073 Capri (☎ **081/8370122;** fax
081/8370279). This quiet family-run gem nestles in a garden just below
the lane leading to the Faraglioni. Comfortable and tastefully furnished,
the hotel has spectacular views and a terrace restaurant known for good
food. 19 rms with bath. Facilities: restaurant (☎ **081/8370122;** reservations required for nonguests; moderate), pool. AE, DC, MC, V. Closed
Nov 6–Mar 20. Moderate.

Villa Krupp, via Matteotti 12, 80073 Capri (☎ **081/8370362l;** fax
081/8376489). Among the hotels open year-round, this historic hostelry is
a good choice. In a quiet location above the Gardens of Augustus, it has
marvelous views. The rooms are ample; some have balconies. 15 rms with
bath. Facilities: garden. MC, V. Inexpensive.

Villa Sarah, via Tiberio 3/a, 80073 Capri (☎ 081/8377817; fax 081/8377215). This quiet family-run hotel, about 10 minutes from the center of town, is on the path leading to Tiberius's Villa Jovis. The facility is a Capri-style villa with a pretty garden and nice views. The rooms are bright though simply furnished. 20 rms with bath. AE, MC, V. Closed late Oct–Mar 19. Inexpensive.

ANACAPRI

Anacapri (about 4km/2½ miles from Capri) has little to offer the casual visitor, so it's difficult to understand why one would choose to stay there; but the ride along the corniche road, gouged from the edge of the cliff, is spectacular. No cars are allowed in Anacapri from April to October. From Anacapri, take the chairlift to the top of **Mount Solaro** for panoramic views. Small buses run on schedule from Capri to Anacapri. If you have to catch an afternoon boat back to the mainland, leave plenty of time; lines both in Anacapri for the bus back to Capri and in Capri for the funicular back down to the harbor can be a good 30 minutes long in season. Most people wait for the return bus at the main square in Anacapri; to make sure you get on the bus, walk away from the square to an earlier stop. From the bus terminal in Anacapri follow via San Michele to the **Villa San Michele,** viale Axel Munthe, built for a Swedish doctor who lived here until 1910. Admission 6,000L adults; 10 and under free. Open daily: May–Sept 9am–6pm; Apr and Oct 9:30am–5pm; Mar 9:30am–4:30pm; off-season 10:30am–3:30pm.

ACCOMMODATIONS

Europa Palace Hotel, via Capodimonte 2/b, 80071 Anacapri (☎ 081/8373800; fax 081/8373191). A modern resort atmosphere prevails at this large Mediterranean-style hotel set in lovely gardens. Each of the three major suites has a private pool and terrace. The rooms are tastefully decorated in contemporary style, with white predominating; marble is featured in the baths, and many rooms have balconies. 92 rms with bath; 3 suites, 20 junior suites. Facilities: pool, garden, restaurant (moderate), AE, DC, MC, V. Closed Oct 31–Easter. Expensive.

Hotel San Michele di Anacapri, via G. Orlandi 1-3, 80071 Anacapri (☎ 081/8371427; fax 081/8371420). Surrounded by luxuriant gardens, this hotel offers solid comfort and good value along with spectacular views. The decor is contemporary, with some Neapolitan period pieces adding atmosphere. Most rooms have terraces or balconies overlooking the sea or island landscapes. 56 rms with bath. Facilities: two restaurants, garden, tennis courts, outdoor pool. AE, DC, MC, V. Closed Nov 5–Mar 27. Expensive.

THE AMALFI DRIVE

The **Amalfi Drive** is the most romantic drive in Italy, the road gouged from the side of rocky cliffs plunging down into the sea. Small boats lie in quiet coves like so many brightly colored fish. Erosion has contorted the rocks into mythological shapes and hollowed out fairy grottoes where the air is turquoise and the water an icy blue. White villages, dripping with flowers, nestle in coves or climb like vines up the steep terraced hills. The road must have 1,000 turns, each with a different view, on its dizzying 69-kilometer (43-mile) journey from Sorrento to Salerno.

POSITANO

The most popular town along the drive, particularly among Americans, is **Positano** (27.2km/17 miles from Sorrento), a village of white Moorish-type houses clinging dramatically to slopes around a small sheltered bay. When John Steinbeck lived here in 1953, he wrote that it was difficult to consider tourism an industry because "there are not enough tourists." Alas, Positano has since been discovered. The artists came first; and as happens wherever artists go, the wealthy followed and the artists fled. What Steinbeck wrote, however, still applies:

> *Positano bites deep. It is a dream place that isn't quite real when you are there and becomes beckoningly real after you have gone. Its houses climb a hill so steep it would be a cliff except that stairs are cut in it. I believe that whereas most house foundations are vertical, in Positano they are horizontal. The small curving bay of unbelievably blue and green water laps gently on a beach of small pebbles. There is only one narrow street and it does not come down to the water. Everything else is stairs, some of them as steep as ladders. You do not walk to visit a friend, you either climb or slide.*

In the 10th century Positano was part of the Amalfi maritime republic, which rivaled Venice as an important mercantile power. Another heyday was in the 16th and 17th centuries, when its ships traded in the Near and Middle East, carrying spices, silks, and precious woods. The coming of the steamship in the mid-19th century led to the town's decline, and some three-fourths of the town's 8,000 citizens emigrated to America, mostly to New York City. One major job of Positano's mayor has been to find space in the overcrowded cemetery for New York Positanesi who want to spend eternity here.

What had been reduced to a forgotten fishing village is now the number-one attraction on the coast, with hotels for every budget, charming restaurants, and dozens of boutiques. From here you can take hydrofoils to Capri in season, escorted bus rides to Ravello, and tours of the Emerald Grotto near the town of Amalfi.

If you're staying in Positano, your hotel may have a parking area; if not, you'll have to pay for space in an open-air garage. If you're here only for the day, a parking place in summer is almost impossible to find. If you're day-tripping, get to Positano early enough to find space in a garage. No matter how much time you spend in Positano, make sure you have some comfortable walking shoes—no heels, please!—and be aware that you'll have to negotiate steps.

Do you see the three islands offshore? They're called **Li Galli** (The Cocks). The local king wanted a castle quickly, legend says, and a sorcerer agreed to build one in 3 days if the king would give him all the roosters in Positano. (The sorcerer had a passion for fowl.) The king ordered them all slaughtered and sent to the sorcerer, but the young daughter of a fisherman hid her rooster under her bed. At dawn the rooster did what a rooster does. The workmen, flying by with rocks for the castle, realized that the king had broken his contract and dropped their loads into the sea.

Positano may not have a castle, but it does have another attraction that brings the town considerable wealth: extravagantly styled summer clothes. From January to March buyers from all over the world come to Positano to buy the trendy resort clothes that are sold in more than 50 boutiques. One-size loose-fitting cotton dresses; full skirts, plain or covered with lace—some in light pastel colors with handprinted designs, others in bold block colors: bright oranges, pinks, and yellows—the choice is endless, and the prices—well, you're on vacation, and the same dresses would cost twice as much in New York or Rome.

Because the streets are narrow and winding and many hotels are accessible only on foot, make sure you get explicit directions on how to reach your hotel. The tourist office is little help because it's down near the beach and inaccessible by car.

The town rises up on either side of a cove. Most shops and restaurants are near the beach on the east side (the side away from Sorrento), where you'll find both the domed Parish Church and Le Sirenuse Hotel. Le Sirenuse is in an ideal location: high enough for breezes and dramatic views, yet close enough to restaurants and shops. There are other, less expensive hotels in the same vicinity.

Dining

Buca di Bacco, via Rampa Teglia 8 (☎ **089/875699**). After an aperitif at the town's most famous and fashionable cafe downstairs, you dine on a veranda overlooking the beach. The specialties include spaghetti alle vongole (with clam sauce) and grigliata mista (mixed grilled seafood). Reservations required. Casual. AE, DC, MC, V. Closed Oct 31–Mar. Inexpensive.

Capurale, via Regina Giovanna 12 (☎ **089/875374**). Among the popular restaurants on the beach promenade, this one has the best food and lowest prices. Tables are set under vines on a breezy sidewalk in summer, upstairs and indoors in winter. Spaghetti con melanzane (with eggplant) and crêpes al formaggio (cheese-filled crepes) are among the specialties. Reservations advised for outdoor tables and Sat–Sun off-season. Casual. AE, DC, MC, V. Closed Tues and Nov 4–Mar. Moderate.

Accommodations

Casa Albertina, via Tavolozza 4, 84017 Positano (☎ **089/875143**; fax 089/811540). One of the few hotels here that's open year-round, Casa

Albertina is a pleasant place with a friendly owner/manager. The rooms are bright with color (some have views), and you can enjoy the panorama from the terrace, where you can have breakfast or drinks in fair weather. It's a few steps up from one of the town's social hubs, the Bar De Martino. There's a restaurant and roof garden. 20 rms with bath. Facilities: restaurant, bar, parking. AE, DC, MC, V. Inexpensive.

Palazzo Murat, via dei Mulini 23, 84017 Positano (☎ **089/875177;** fax 089/811419). The location is perfect—in the heart of town, near the beachside promenade, but set in a quiet walled garden. The old wing is a historic palazzo with tall windows and wrought-iron balconies; the newer wing is a whitewashed Mediterranean building with arches and terraces. You can relax in antique-accented lounges or in the charming vine-draped patio, and because there's no restaurant you'll avoid the half-board requirement applied in most hotels here in high season. 28 rms with bath. Facilities: bar, garden. AE, DC, MC, V. Closed Nov–Easter. Inexpensive.

San Pietro, via Laurito 2, 84017 Positano (☎ **089/875455;** fax 089/811449). Spreading across a rocky ledge outside of town, the spacious San Pietro is an elevator ride down from the road (there's a shuttle service to town and back). The decor is tasteful, with fabrics that complement, rather than fight against, the bright colors of the landscape. Nature intrudes everywhere: in the pitchers of wild purple orchids; in the bougainvillea spilling over the terraces and balconies; in the roses and hibiscus growing through the windows and spreading over the lounge and dining-room ceilings. 52 rms with bath; 5 suites. Facilities: restaurant, two bars, pool, private beach and dock, hotel boat, tennis court, garden, parking. AE, DC, MC, V. Closed Nov–Mar. Very Expensive.

Le Sireneuse, via Cristoforo Colombo 30, 84017 Positano (☎ **089/875066;** fax 089/811798). Older and somewhat smaller than the San Pietro, Le Sireneuse is a converted 18th-century villa with seven floors both above and below the road. Located in town, it appeals to a younger, snappier clientele. The rooms have panoramic views from balconies and terraces, and the top-floor suites have Jacuzzis. 58 rms with bath; 2 suites. Facilities, restaurant, bar, heated pool, parking. AE, DC, MC, V. Very Expensive.

ON TO AMALFI

Because you're heading directly east from Positano to Amalfi it's best to drive in the afternoon, with the sun behind you. Drive past the towns of Véttica Maggiore and Praiano. The 4.8-kilometer (3-mile) stretch of the Amalfi Drive between Praiano and the Emerald Grotto is the most dramatic. The road passes the gorge of Furore, where abandoned fishers' houses cling to the cliff above a tiny beach. Wild vegetation sprouts in the crevices and clambers up the sides. A path goes up one side of the gorge, which you'll see after you pass through two tunnels after Praiano. (Trails along the Amalfi Drive are indicated on a tourist map—carta turística—called Penisola Sorrentina, Costiera Amalfitana, which is sold in tourist shops in Positano and Amalfi.)

THE EMERALD GROTTO

About 4.8 kilometers (3 miles) farther along is the **Emerald Grotto** (Grotta Smeralda). An elevator takes you down to a rocky terrace (cost: 5,000L). A small rowboat then transports you around a cave with stalactites and an underwater Nativity scene. With tourists lined up to "do" the Grotto, it's not easy to experience the awe the first visitors must have felt; but the luminescent emerald-colored water is still magical, and a trip is worthwhile just to be able to enter into the argument over whether the Emerald Grotto is more beautiful than the Blue Grotto on Capri. You can also reach the Emerald Grotto by boat from Amalfi or Positano in season. Open daily: Mar–Apr 9am–5pm; May–Sept 8:30am–6pm; Oct–Feb 10am–4pm.

AMALFI

Amalfi (12.8km/8 miles from Positano) is your third choice after Positano and Ravello as a town to stay in along the drive. It would have to be a distant third, however, because of the congestion caused by tour buses that make Amalfi the main stop on their excursions. The town is romantically situated at the mouth of a deep gorge and has some quality hotels and restaurants. It's also a convenient base for excursions to the Emerald Grotto and to Ravello.

During the Middle Ages Amalfi was an independent maritime state—a little Republic of Venice—with a population of 50,000. The ship compass—trivia fans will be pleased to know—was invented here in 1302.

The main historic attraction is the **Duomo** (Cathedral of St. Andrew), piazza del Duomo (☎ **089/871485**), which shows an interesting mix of Moorish and early Gothic influences. The interior is a 10th-century Romanesque skeleton in an 18th-century baroque dress. The transept (the transverse arms) and the choir are 13th century. The handsome 12th-century campanile (bell tower) has identical Gothic cupolas (domes) at each corner. Don't miss the beautiful late 13th-century Moorish cloister, with its slender double columns. At least one critic has called the cathedral's facade the ugliest piece of serious architecture in Italy—decide for yourself. The same critic has snickered at the tourists who fail to note the cathedral's greatest treasure, the 11th-century bronze doors from Constantinople. Admission to cloister 3,000L. Open daily 8am–1pm and 3:30–7pm.

The parking problem here is almost as bad as in Positano. The small lot on the waterfront fills quickly.

If the sea is calm, you can take a boat back along the coast to the Emerald Grotto.

The main street leads back through town from the cathedral to the mountains and passes a ceramic workshop and some water-driven paper mills where handcrafted paper is made and sold.

TAKE A BREAK

*On the main piazza, facing the fountain, **Pansa** is Amalfi's best bakery, offering pastries, candies, and jumbo sfogliatelle (cream- or preserves-filled pastry dusted with confectioners' sugar) fresh from the oven.*

Dining

La Caravella, via M. Camera 12 (☎ 089/871029). You'll find this welcoming establishment tucked away under some arches lining the coast road, next to the medieval Arsenal, where Amalfi's mighty fleet once was provisioned. La Caravella has a nondescript entrance but pleasant interior decorated in a medley of colors and paintings of Old Amalfi. It's small and intimate; specialties include scialatelli (homemade pasta with shellfish sauce) and pesce al limone (fresh fish with lemon sauce). Reservations required. Casual. AE, V. Closed Tues, Sept 15–June 15, and Nov. Inexpensive.

Accommodations

Hotel dei Cavalieri, via M. Comite 32, 84011 Amalfi (☎ 089/831333; fax 089/831354). This terraced white Mediterranean-style hotel is on the main road outside Amalfi; it has three villa annexes in grounds just across the road that extend all the way to a beach below. The rooms are air-conditioned and functionally furnished, with splashy majolica tile floors contributing a bright note throughout. An ample buffet breakfast is served, and, though half-board is mandatory in high season, you can dine at the hotel or at several restaurants in Amalfi by special arrangement. 60 rms with bath. Facilities: restaurant, bar, beach (via stairs), parking, garage, minibus sevice into town. AE, DC, MC, V. Moderate.

Santa Caterina, Strada Amalfitana 9, 84011 Amalfi (☎ 089/871012; fax 089/871351). A large mansion perched above terraced and flowered hillsides on the coast road just outside Amalfi, the Santa Caterina is one of the best hotels on the entire coast, offering gracious living in a wonderfully scenic setting. The rooms are tastefully decorated; most have small terraces or balconies with great views. There are lovely lounges and terraces for relaxing, and an elevator whisks you to the seaside saltwater pool, bar, and swimming area. On grounds lush with lemon and orange groves are two romantic villa annexes. 70 rms with bath; 11 suites. Facilities: restaurant, bar, pool, swimming area, beach bar, parking. AE, DC, MC, V. Expensive.

Miramalfi, via Quasimodo 3, 84011 Amalfi (☎ 089/871588; fax 089/871588). A modern building perched above the sea, the Miramalfi has wonderful views, simple but attractive decor, terraces, a pool, and a sunning/swimming area on the sea. It boasts a quiet location just below the coast road, only a half mile from the center of town. Many rooms have balconies with sea views. 43 rms with bath; 3 suites. Facilities: restaurant, garden, swimming, parking. AE, DC, MC, V. Moderate.

ATRANI

A few minutes past Amalfi is the less-known but impressively situated town of **Atrani,** just waiting to be discovered. The valley here is narrower than at Amalfi and its flanks are steeper. Atrani's **parish church** is worth a visit.

Porcelain and ceramics are sold in Atrani and in nearby towns along the Amalfi Drive. Among the mass-produced turnpike ware are some lovely, simple, hand-painted plates, vases, pillboxes, and the like.

Just past Atrani is the road winding up the mountain to Ravello. The road heads east, paralleling the coast, then switches back. As it turns again and climbs up the valley, there's a turnoff that ends in a trail climbing 305 meters (1,000 ft.) up to Ravello. It's a walk you might want to make going down. Both the walk and the drive take you up the spectacular Dragon Valley (Valle del Dragone), which is planted with vines, fruit trees, and olives and offers a breathtaking view of Atrani and the Amalfi Coast.

RAVELLO

Envy Gore Vidal for living in what André Gide calls "a town closer to the sky than to the shore." Because **Ravello** (6.5km/4 miles from Amalfi) is a long, steep drive above the sea, tour buses are discouraged and crowds are less overwhelming than at Positano and Amalfi. By early afternoon the day-trippers have departed and Ravello becomes one of the most reposeful settings in the world.

Not that Ravello is everyone's glass of chianti: There's little to do here except walk through peaceful gardens, admire the view, and exist. Those who need a more active life, with shops and restaurants, should avoid the rarefied air and stick to Positano. But after so much traveling, you may welcome this excuse to come to a complete stop.

There are two estates to visit, Villa Cimbrone and Villa Rufolo. Don't miss either, but particularly don't miss Villa Cimbrone.

Villa Cimbrone, via Santa Chiara 26 (☎ 089/857459), is a scenic 15-minute walk from the main square. The cloister to the left of the entrance looks medieval but was built in 1917. The unusual crypt was finished in 1913. What makes the villa so memorable are its peaceful gardens, with small secluded grottoes and temples hundreds of feet above the sea. The Viale dell'Immensita, a long, straight avenue flanked by oleanders, leads to a belvedere with an unforgettable view of the coast. Few places lend themselves so thoroughly to contemplation. Most construction was carried out in the early 20th century by the former valet of a British lord. Was the mood of melancholy merely a pose that suited a classical garden? In the Belvedere of Mercury, the god faces away from the view as though tired of running; and on the bench is a quote from D. H. Lawrence:

Lost to a world in which I crave no part,
I sit alone and commune with my heart,
Pleased with my little corner of the earth,
Glad that I came, not sorry to depart.

Under the cupola of the little temple of Bacchus are verses by Catullus, which say, in translation, "What is sweeter than to return home free of care, and, tired of toiling for others, to repose in one's own bed?" Admission 5,000L adults; 3,000L children. Open daily 9am to 1 hr. before sunset.

Villa Rufolo, piazza Vescovado (☎ 089/857866), is a crumbling 11th-century palace that has a famous Moorish cloister, ancient trees, and a belvedere with a fantastic view. In 1880, while working on *Parsifal,* Richard Wagner stayed at the Villa Palumbo in Ravello and on a morning walk visited Villa Rufolo. In the hotel register he wrote, "The magic garden of Klingsor has been found: May 26, 1880." It's fitting that this beautiful garden-terrace has become the site of summer concerts dedicated to Wagner. Admission 4,000L adults; 2,000L children. Open daily: Nov–Mar 9am–1pm and 2–5pm; Apr–Oct 9am–1pm and 2:30–6:30pm.

The 13th-century **cathedral** (Duomo di San Pantaleone) was redone 5 centuries later in baroque dress and has a notable late 13th-century Byzantine pulpit decorated with fantastic beasts and resting on a pride of marble lions.

Dining

Cumpa'Cosimo, via Roma 44 (☎ 089/857156). This family-run restaurant a few steps from the cathedral square offers a cordial welcome in three simple but attractive dining rooms. There's no view, but the food is excellent. Among the specialties are cheese crepes and roast lamb or kid. Reservations recommended. Casual. AE, DC, V. Closed Mon Nov–Mar. Inexpensive.

Accommodations

Hotel Caruso Belvedere, via San Giovanni del Toro 52, 84010 Ravello (☎ 089/857111; fax 089/857372). Charmingly old-fashioned, spacious, and comfortable, this rambling villa hotel has plenty of character and a full share of Ravello's spectacular views from its terraces and balconied rooms. The restaurant is known for fine food and locally produced house wine. 24 rms with bath. Facilities: restaurant, garden. AE, DC, MC, V. Expensive.

Hotel Giordano e Villa Maria, via Santa Chiara 2, 84010 Ravello (☎ 089/857255; fax 089/857071). This family-run pension is set in a pretty garden where you can enjoy a drink or dine under the trees. The rooms are simple but homey, and the atmosphere is restful. 51 rms with bath; 2 suites. Facilities: restaurant, bar, garden. AE, DC, MC, V. Moderate.

Hotel Palumbo, via San Giovanni del Torro 28, 84010 Ravello
(☎ **089/857244;** fax 089/858133). Occupying a 12th-century patrician
palace furnished with antiques and endowed with modern comforts, this
hotel has a warm atmosphere that gives you the feeling of being a guest in
a private home, under the care of Swiss host Signore Vuilleumier. The
rooms are conversation pieces—a bit cramped for the price but marked
by character and good taste. 27 rms with bath; 3 suites. Facilities: restaurant, bar, garden. AE, DC, MC, V. Very Expensive.

SALERNO

The Amalfi Drive ends at **Salerno** (32km/20 miles from Ravello). There's
no overwhelming reason to stay here except to get an early start to
Paestum the next day or catch a morning train back to Naples. Worth
seeing before you leave are the **cathedral** and **via dei Mercanti,** a picturesque old street with shops selling jewelry and other gift items at less-
than-tourist-area prices. Drive along the harborfront, past the port. When
you see a wide, grassy seafront promenade on your right, park. Via dei
Mercanti is a few blocks in from the promenade, depending on where you
park. The cathedral won't be more than 15 minutes away. Built in 1085
and remodeled in the 18th century, it has an unusual Moorish atrium,
beautiful Byzantine doors (1099) from Constantinople, outstanding 12th-
and 13th-century pulpits, and a crypt bright with multicolored marble
inlays and frescoes.

Accommodations

Plaza, piazza Ferrovia, 84100 Salerno (☎ **089/244477;** fax 089/237311).
A dignified old building conveniently located opposite the train station,
the Plaza has been entirely renovated for comfort and efficiency without
losing its character. The rooms are quiet, with functional modular
furnishings and bright white-tiled baths; everything is well maintained,
with a fresh clean look. The management is friendly and helpful. 42 rms
with bath. Facilities: bar, air-conditioning on request. AE, DC, MC, V.
Moderate.

ON TO PAESTUM

Trains run several times daily from Salerno to Paestum. Buses leave about
every hour. To drive, take the road along the Salerno harbor and continue south to Paestum.

PAESTUM

For most visitors, a trip to **Paestum** (40km/25 miles from Salerno) is jus-
tified by three classical temples: the Basilica, the Temple of Ceres (Tempio
di Cerere) and, above all, the Temple of Neptune (Tempio di Netuno). If
a building like the Parthenon does nothing for you, don't waste your time
here. But if you can be moved by the harmony and proportion of Greek
architecture, Paestum may be the highlight of your trip.

You won't need more than an hour or two. On one side of the main street are the souvenir shops and a museum. On the other are three of the largest and best-preserved Greek temples in the world—surely the greatest Greek buildings in Italy—two of them older than the Parthenon.

The temples were originally part of a sacred area within a Greek colony founded about 600 B.C. by the people of Sybaris, located on the opposite (eastern) coast of Italy. The Sybarites didn't like the loss of revenues from ships sailing from Greece and Asia Minor through the Straits of Messina (between Sicily and the toe of Italy), so they convinced merchants to unload goods at Sybaris and send them overland to the new town of Paestum, rather than make the dangerous trip through the straits. Eventually Sybaris was razed in a war among competing political parties. Paestum became a Roman colony in 273 B.C. The opening of the via Appia from Rome to Brindisi in about 22 B.C. spelled the end of Paestum as an important port. Its harbor gradually silted up and the inhabitants succumbed to malaria from the marshes. An 11th-century visitor found the town deserted. Malarial marshes and thick forests hid the temples until road builders came on them in the 18th century. In the 19th century, only a few foreigners bothered traveling south of Pompeii; one of them was the poet Shelley. When a train station was built, the stationmaster was given gloves and veils against the mosquitoes (no problem today).

English writer H. V. Morton has pointed out that the **Temple of Neptune** has "a primitive grandeur that recalls the Great Hall of Karnak rather than the lighter constructions of classical Greece." It may be ruder, less perfect than the Parthenon, but it has a raw, almost animal power that the Parthenon lacks. What makes this temple so extraordinary is its blend of brutal strength and constraint; of defiance and grace. And there it sits, this 2,400-year-old temple, among the grasses in a forgotten field. It was called the Temple of Neptune (the Roman name for Poseidon) by some 17th-century visitors because the town was named Poseidonia before it became a Roman colony; but the temple was, in fact, dedicated to Hera (Juno).

The **Temple of Ceres,** originally dedicated to Athena (Minerva), dates from the end of the 6th century B.C. The **Basilica** (so called by some 18th-century archeologists who thought it was a secular building) is the oldest of the three temples, dating back to the mid-6th century B.C. This temple was also dedicated to Hera. Like all Greek temples, it faces east because it's from the east that the sun (the first god of all ancient peoples) rises daily. The **museum** (museo) contains bronze vases, unique 5th-century B.C. paintings, and decorated stone slabs from a nearby cemetery depicting details of daily life in the 4th century B.C. Admission 8,000L (ticket also valid for museum). Open daily 9am–sunset.

DINING & ACCOMMODATIONS

Martini, Zona Archeologica (☎ **081/811451;** fax 081/811600). Directly across the road from the Porta della Giustizia and only a few steps from the temples, the Martini has 13 cottage-type rooms, each with minibar, in a garden setting and a pleasant restaurant serving local specialties and seafood. 29 rms with bath. Facilities: restaurant (reservations advised; casual), beach 1 kilometer (half a mile) away. AE, DC, MC, V. Inexpensive.

ON TO NAPLES

If you're driving from Paestum to Naples, take Route SS18 north to Battipaglia and pick up Highway A3 toward Naples. Turn off on Highway A2 back to Rome. If you're taking the train, there's daily service from Paestum to Naples, with a change in Salerno.

F R A6N C E

The Riviera

I n the popular imagination, the Riviera is a golden stretch of beach along the southern coast of France. Life here is a dialogue of sun and flesh, where nothing is meant to be built, just to be burned up. That's one Riviera—but there's another, a few miles inland, where fortified medieval towns are perched on mountaintops, high above the sea.

It's impossible to be bored along the Côte d'Azur (Azure Coast). You can try a different beach or restaurant every day. When you've had enough sun, you can visit pottery towns like Vallauris, where Picasso worked; or perfumeries at Grasse, where three-quarters of the world's essences are produced. You can drive along dizzying gorges, one almost as deep as the Grand Canyon in the United States. You can dance or gamble the night away in Monte Carlo and shop for the best Paris has to offer, right in Cannes or Nice. Only minutes from the beaches are some of the world's most famous museums of modern art, featuring the work of Léger, Matisse, Picasso, Renoir, Chagall—artists who were captivated by the light and color of the Riviera.

The myths have changed, but not the beauty or the sybaritic pleasures. You can go in search of them or stand still and let them find you. The Riviera will always know where you are.

BEFORE YOU GO

GOVERNMENT TOURIST OFFICES

Contact the **French Government Tourist Office** for information on all aspects of travel to and in France.

In the U.S.:   444 Madison Ave., 16th floor, New York, NY 10022; 676 N. Michigan Ave., Suite 3360, Chicago, IL 60611; 9454 Wilshire Blvd., Beverly Hills, CA 90212. To request information at any of these offices, call the France on Call hot line at 900/990-0040; each call costs 95¢ per

HIGHLIGHTS ALONG THE WAY

- The fabulous casino at Monte Carlo. The colorful old town of Nice. Lavish festivals at Cannes. The beach scene at St-Tropez. And every-where, the luminescent light and brilliant sunshine of the Côte d'Azur.

- Historic churches and castles, modern-art museums, fortified medieval hill towns where dedicated artists work and sell their wares.

- A bouillabaisse of first-class restaurants, offering the best in classic, moderne, and Provençal cuisine.

- Hotels for every taste and budget—from friendly family-run pensions to some of the most palatial resorts in the world.

minute. Contact the Monaco Tourist and Convention Bureau, 845 Third Ave., New York, NY 10022 (☎ 800/753-9696 or 212/759-5227), for information on Monte Carlo.

In Canada: 1981 McGill College, Suite 490, Montréal, Québec H3A 2W9 (☎ 514/288-4264); 30 St. Patrick St., Suite 700, Toronto, ON M5T 3A3 (☎ 416/593-4723).

In the U.K.: 178 Piccadilly, London, W1V 0AL England (☎ 0171/629-9376).

WHEN TO GO

On the whole, June and September are the best months to be in France, because both are free of midsummer crowds. June offers the advantage of long daylight hours, whereas slightly cheaper prices and frequent extended summers (often lasting well into October) make September attractive. Anytime between March and November will offer you a good chance to soak up the sun on the Riviera, though, of course, you'll tan quicker between June and September.

CURRENCY

The units of currency in France are the **franc (F)** and the **centime.** The bills are 500, 200, 100, 50, and 20 francs. Coins are 10, 5, 2, and 1 francs, and 50, 20, 10, and 5 centimes. At press time, the exchange rate is about 5F = $1 U.S., 3.65F = $1 Canadian, and 7.70F = £ sterling.

CUSTOMS

For goods obtained in another European Union country, such as Great Britain, you may import duty-free 300 cigarettes or 150 cigarellos, or 75 cigars or 400 grams (14 oz.) of tobacco. You're also allowed 5 liters (1.3 gal.) of table wine and 1½ liters (.4 gal.) of alcohol over 22% volume; 3 liters (.8 gal.) of alcohol under 22% volume (fortified or sparkling wines), or 3 more liters of table wine; plus 90 milliliters (3 fl. oz.) of perfume, 375 milliliters (12.7 fl. oz.) of eau de toilette, and other goods to the value of 2,400F (620F for those under 15).

From such non–European Union countries as the United States and Canada, you may bring in duty-free 200 cigarettes or 100 cigarillos, or 50 cigars or 250 grams (8.8 oz.) of tobacco (these allowances are double if

FRANCE

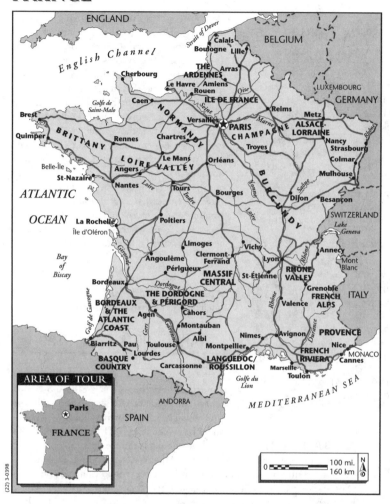

you live outside Europe), plus 2 liters (.53 gal.) of wine and 1 liter of alcohol over 22% volume; 2 liters of alcohol under 22% volume (fortified or sparkling wines), or 2 more liters of table wine; plus 60 milliliters (2 fl. oz.) of perfume, 250 milliliters (8.5 fl. oz.) of eau de toilette, and other goods to the value of 300F (150F for those under 15).

LANGUAGE

The French study English for a minimum of 4 years at school (often longer) but to little general effect. English is widely understood in major tourist areas, however, and, no matter what the area, there should be at least one person in most hotels who can explain things to you, if necessary.

SPECIAL EVENTS & NATIONAL HOLIDAYS

Special Events

January: Monte Carlo Auto Rally.
February: Nice Carnival, for 2 weeks before Shrove Tuesday.
May: Cannes Film Festival; Monaco Grand Prix motor race.
June: Nice Festival of Sacred Music.
July: Classical concerts in the palace courtyard in Monaco.
August: Menton Music Festival.

National Holidays

January 1 (New Year's Day); Easter Sunday and Monday; May 1 (Labor Day); Ascension Thursday (40 days after Easter); May 8 (V-E Day in Europe); May 19 (Whit Monday); July 14 (Bastille Day); August 15 (Assumption of the Blessed Virgin); November 1 (All Saints' Day); November 11 (Armistice Day); and December 25 (Christmas).

Be courteous and patient and speak slowly. The French, after all, have plenty of other tourists and aren't dependent for income on English-speakers. And while it may sound cynical, remember that the French respond quicker to charm than to anything else.

Even if your own French is terrible, try to master a few words: The French are more cooperative when they think you're at least making an effort. Basic vocabulary: *s'il vous plaît* (please), *merci* (thanks), *bonjour* (hello—until 6pm), *bonsoir* (good evening—after 6pm), *au revoir* (goodbye), *comment ça va?* (how do you do), *oui* (yes), *non* (no), *peut-être* (maybe), *les toilettes* (toilets), *l'addition* (bill/check), *où* (where), *anglais* (English), *je ne comprends pas* (I don't understand).

READING

What's Hot, What's Not: French Riviera Guide (available in shops along the coast).

ARRIVING & DEPARTING

BY PLANE

American Airlines (☎ 800/433-7300) offers daily flights to Paris's Orly Airport from Dallas/Fort Worth, Chicago, Miami, and New York City's JFK. **Delta Airlines** (☎ 800/241-4141) is one of the best choices for those flying to Paris from both the southeastern United States and the Midwest. In fact, Delta offers the greatest number of flights to Paris from the United States. From such cities as New Orleans, Phoenix, Columbia (S.C.), and Nashville, Delta flies to Atlanta, connecting every evening with a nonstop flight to Orly. Delta also operates daily nonstop flights to Orly from both Cincinnati and New York City's JFK. All these flights depart late enough in the day to permit transfers from much of Delta's vast North American network.

Continental Airlines (☎ 800/231-0856) provides nonstop flights to Orly from Newark and Houston. Flights from Newark depart daily, while flights from Houston depart four to seven times a week, depending on the season.

TWA (☎ 800/892-4141) operates daily nonstop service to Charles de Gaulle from Boston, New York City's JFK, and (in summer) several nonstop flights a week from Washington, D.C.'s Dulles Airport. In summer, TWA also flies to Paris from St. Louis several times a week nonstop and to Paris from Los Angeles three times a week nonstop. In winter,

love 0-800-99-0011

n the springtime.

All you need for the fastest, clearest connections home.

Every country has its own AT&T Access Number which makes calling from France and other countries really easy. Just dial the AT&T Access Number for the country you're calling from and we'll take it from there. And be sure to charge your calls on your AT&T Calling Card. It'll help you avoid outrageous phone charges on your hotel bill and save you up to 60%.* 0-800-99-0011 is a great place to visit any time of year, especially if you've got these two cards. So please take the attached wallet card of worldwide AT&T Access Numbers.

flights from Los Angeles and Washington, D.C., are suspended and flights from St. Louis are direct, with brief touchdowns in New York or Boston en route to Paris.

USAir (☎ **800/428-4322**) offers daily nonstop service from Philadelphia International Airport to Paris's Charles de Gaulle Airport.

Aircraft belonging to **Air France** (☎ **800/237-2747**) fly frequently across the Atlantic. Formed from a merger combining three of France's largest (and completely nationalized) airlines, the conglomerate offers routes that, until the merger, were maintained separately by Air France, UTA (Union des Transports Aériens), and France's internal domestic airline, Air Inter (now Air Inter Europe). In the process, many transatlantic routes that previously flew nonstop into France's provincial capitals were abandoned.

The airline offers daily or several-times-a-week flights between Paris's Charles de Gaulle Airport and such North American cities as Newark, N.J.; New York's JFK; Washington, D.C.'s Dulles; Miami; Chicago; Houston; San Francisco; Los Angeles; Montréal; Toronto; and Mexico City.

From London, **Air France** (☎ **0181/742-6600**) and **British Airways** (☎ **0181/897-4000**) fly regularly and frequently to Paris (trip time is 1 hr.). Air France and British Airways alone operate up to 17 flights daily from Heathrow, one of the busiest air routes in Europe. Many commercial travelers also use regular flights from the London City Airport in the Docklands.

BY TRAIN

Paris is one of Europe's busiest railway junctions, with trains arriving at and departing from its many stations every few minutes. If you're already in Europe, you may want to go to Paris by train, particularly if you have a Eurailpass. Even if you don't, the cost is relatively low—especially in comparison to renting a car. The one-way fare from London to Paris by train (including the Channel crossing) is $117 to $172 in first class and $68 to $121 in second class. Incidentally, you don't have to go to Paris from London. For example, there are direct trains from London to such places as the Côte d'Azur (French Riviera), the Alps, Strasbourg (capital of Alsace), Lyon (in Burgundy), and the Pyrénées.

If you're arriving in Paris and traveling by train, go by cab or by bus and subway from **Charles de Gaulle (Roissy) Airport** to the **Gare de Lyon** train station. The airport bus goes to the RER, a rural extension of the Paris Métro. Change at Châtelet–Les-Halles for the Gare de Lyon. There are about six trains daily from the Gare de Lyon to the Riviera. The trip takes slightly under 5 hours to Marseille (via Lyon), another 2 hours to Cannes, and an additional half an hour to Nice. The Paris–Lyon train is one of the fastest in the world—up to 272 kilometers per hour (170 m.p.h.). You can also take an overnight sleeper from Paris to Nice (about 12 hours) and save the cost of a hotel. One train, for instance, leaves Paris at 8:30pm and arrives at Nice at 8:20 the next morning.

The **French Railpass** provides unlimited rail transportation throughout France for 3 days, to be used within 1 month, and the **France Fly, Rail, 'n' Drive Pass** is an arrangement whereby air, rail, and car transportation in France are combined into one all-encompassing discounted purchase.

BY BUS

Bus travel to Paris is available from London. The arrival and departure point for Europe's largest bus operators, **Eurolines France,** is a 35-minute Métro ride from central Paris, at the terminus of Métro line 3 (Métro: Gallieni), in the suburb of Bagnolet. Despite this inconvenience, many people prefer bus travel. Eurolines France is at 28 av. du Général-de-Gaulle, 93541 Bagnolet (☎ 01-49-72-51-51). Because Eurolines doesn't have a U.S.-based sales agent, most people wait until they reach Europe to buy their tickets. Any European travel agent can arrange for these purchases. If you're traveling to Paris from London, you can contact **Eurolines U.K.,** Victoria Coach Station (the continental check-in desk) or call 01582/40-45-11 for information (0171/73-03-499 for credit-card sales).

BY FERRY

About a dozen companies run hydrofoils, ferries, and hovercraft across *La Manche* ("the sleeve," as the French call the Channel). Services operate day and night. Most ferries carry cars, but some hydrofoils carry passengers only. Hovercraft and hydrofoils make the trip in just 40 minutes, whereas slower moving ferries might take hours, depending on conditions. The major routes are between Dover or Folkestone and Calais or Boulogne (about 12 trips a day). It's important to make reservations, as vessels are always crowded. Prices and timetables can vary depending on weather conditions.

The most frequently used carriers are **SuperFerry** (conventional ferryboat service), **Hoverspeed catamarans** (travel on motorized catamarans), and **Sealynx,** which skim along a few inches above the surface of the water. Despite the differences in speed, transportation with a car aboard either mode of transport costs the same.

The shortest and busiest route between London and Paris is the one from Dover to Calais. By ferryboat, the trip takes about 90 minutes, although a Sealynx can make the run in about 45 minutes. The Sealynx also crosses from Folkstone to Boulogne in about 60 minutes but is designed only for foot passengers, not for cars.

Each crossing is carefully timed to coincide with the arrival and departure of trains from London and Paris, which disgorge passengers and their luggage a short walk from the piers. The U.S. sales agent for the above-mentioned lines is **Britrail** (☎ 800/677-8585 or 212/575-2667).

If you plan to take a rented car across the Channel, check carefully with the rental company about license and insurance requirements before you leave.

BY THE CHANNEL TUNNEL

In 1994, the *Eurostar Express* began twice-daily passenger service between London and both Paris and Brussels under the English Channel. The $15-billion tunnel provides a 31-mile journey between Great Britain and France taking 35 minutes, though the actual time spent in the Chunnel is only 19 minutes. **Rail Europe (☎ 800/94-CHUNNEL** for information) sells tickets for the *Eurostar* direct train service between London and Paris or Brussels. A round-trip fare between London and Paris, for example, is $312 in first class and $258 in second. But you can cut costs to $140 with a second-class, 15-day advance-purchase (nonrefundable) round-trip ticket. In London, make reservations for *Eurostar* at 01719/286-000; in Paris at 01-49-95-58-03; and in the United States at 800/387-6782.

BY CAR

If you're driving from Paris, it's 880 kilometers (550 miles) to Cannes and 912 kilometers (570 miles) to Nice. The Autoroute goes from Paris to Lyon and swings north of Marseille to Cannes and Nice. You can arrange to have your car transported on the train, but you must make the arrangements in France.

GETTING AROUND

BY CAR

You may use your own driver's license in France but must be able to prove you have third-party insurance. Drive on the right-hand side of the road. Be aware of the French tradition of yielding to drivers coming from the right. Seat belts are obligatory, and children under 12 may not travel in the front seat. Speed limits are 130 kilometers per hour (80 m.p.h.) on expressways, 110 kilometers per hour (70 m.p.h.) on divided highways, 90 kilometers per hour (55 m.p.h.) on other roads, 50 kilometers per hour (30 m.p.h.) in towns. French drivers break these limits and police dish out hefty on-the-spot fines with equal abandon.

The best regional maps are published by Michelin. If they're unavailable in local bookstores, order them directly from Michelin's North American depot: **Michelin Travel Publications,** P.O. Box 19008, Greenville, SC 29602-9008 (☎ **800/423-0485** or 800/223-0987). A road map that contains the entire mainland of France isn't detailed enough to help you negotiate the back roads of Provence. More appropriate is yellow regional map no. 245, Provence/Côte d'Azur.

If you're planning to rent a car in France for between 17 days and a year, look into the option of leasing a car directly from **Renault Inc.,** 650 First Ave., New York, NY 10016-3214 (☎ **800/221-1052** or 212/532-1221).

BY TRAIN

The **Metrazur** is the local train linking all major towns on the Riviera from Monte Carlo to St-Raphaël and Marseille. The ride from Nice to Monte Carlo takes 22 minutes; from Nice to Cannes, 40 minutes; from Nice to St-Raphaël, 60 minutes; from Nice to Antibes, 26 minutes. For information and reservations, contact **Gare SNCF**, av. Thiers, Nice (☎ 04-36-35-35-35).

If you want to reach St-Tropez by public transportation, take the train to St-Raphaël and then the bus or (preferably) the hydrofoil to St-Tropez. There's also helicopter service by **Heli Air Monaco** at Nice Airport (☎ 04-94-97-15-12).

BY BUS

Reacting to the flood of visitors pouring onto the Riviera, motor coaches run between the Nice Airport and most major towns in the region. For access from the airport into Nice, catch any of the yellow-sided buses maintained by the **Société, A.N.T.** (☎ 04-93-56-35-40). Beginning at 6:05am and running to 11:30pm (to 11pm Sunday), they depart from the Nice Airport at 20-minute intervals, depositing passengers anywhere along the town's seafront and in the old city for a fee of 21F each way. Alternatively, you can take municipal bus no. 23, which runs about once an hour from the airport to the railway station of Nice for a fee of 8F each way.

If you're traveling by public transportation, the perched towns of Eze and St-Paul-de-Vence are the most accessible by bus from Nice. To visit other medieval towns in season, sign up for bus excursions at any hotel or travel agency in Cannes or Nice.

BY HYDROFOIL

There's daily hydrofoil service in season along the coast. It's slower than the train, but can be faster than driving in high season. Check with hotels and travel agencies.

BY MOTORBIKE OR BICYCLE

Mopeds and motorbikes are ideal for negotiating traffic on crowded beachfront roads, particularly for short distances, such as from Cannes to Cap d'Antibes or from Nice to Cap Ferrat. Contact the following: **Nice,** Nicea Rent, Gare SNCF, 9 av. Thiers (☎ 04-93-82-42-71); **Cannes,** Mistral Location, 14 rue Georges-Clemenceau (☎ 04-93-39-33-60), and Cycles Daniel, 2 rue du Port Romain (☎ 04-93-99-90-30); **Antibes,** French Riviera Location, 43 bd. Wilson (☎ 04-93-67-65-67).

Bikes, mopeds, or motorbikes are particularly useful in **St-Tropez,** because the main beaches are several miles from town. Try Azur Motor Sport, 10 rue Joseph-Quaranta (☎ 04-94-97-77-20).

ESSENTIAL INFORMATION

IMPORTANT ADDRESSES & NUMBERS

VISITOR INFORMATION   Contact the following Offices de Tourisme:

Beaulieu: place Georges-Clemenceau (☎ 04-93-01-02-21); open Monday to Saturday from 9am to noon and 3 to 7pm, Sunday from 9am to noon.

Cannes: esplanade du Président-Georges-Pompidou (☎ 04-93-39-24-53); open July to August, daily from 9am to 8pm; September to June, Monday to Saturday from 9am to 6:30pm.

Cap Ferrat: 59 av. Denis-Semeria (☎ 04-93-76-08-90); open July to August, Monday to Saturday from 9am to 7pm, Sunday from 10am to 5pm; September to June, Monday to Saturday from 9am to noon and 2 to 6pm.

Monaco: 2a bd. des Moulins (☎ 337-92-16-61-16); open Monday to Saturday from 9am to 7pm, Sunday from 10am to noon.

Nice: avenue Thiers (☎ 04-93-87-07-07); open July to September 15, daily from 8am to 8pm; other months, Monday to Saturday from 8am to 7pm and Sunday from 8am to noon and 2 to 6pm.

St-Tropez: quai Jean-Jaurès (☎ 04-94-97-45-21); open August, daily from 8:30am to 2pm and 4:30 to 8pm; June to July, daily from 7:30am to 1pm and 2 to 7pm; September to May, daily from 10am to noon and 2 to 7pm.

St-Paul-de-Vence: rue Grande (☎ 04-93-32-86-95); open June to August, daily from 10am to 7pm; September to May, daily from 10am to noon and 2 to 6pm.

EMERGENCIES   For **Police:** Dial 17 anywhere in France.

CONSULATES   **U.S. Consulate,** 2 rue St-Florentin, 75008 Paris (☎ 01-42-96-12-02, ext. 2531); **U.K. Consulate,** 35 rue du Faubourg St-Honoré, 75383 Paris (☎ 01-44-51-31-00).

OPENING & CLOSING TIMES

BANKS   In general, banks are open Monday to Friday from 9:30am to 4:30pm, but times vary. Most close for an hour to an hour and a half for lunch.

Museums   Most museums are closed 1 day a week (usually Tuesday) and on national holidays. Usual times are from 9:30am to 5 or 6pm. Many museums close for lunch from noon to 2pm; many are open afternoons only on Sunday.

Shops   Large shops in big towns are open from 9 or 9:30am to 6 or 7pm without a lunch break. Smaller shops often open earlier (8am) and close later (8pm), but take a lengthy lunch break from 1 to 4pm. Corner grocery stores, often run by immigrants, frequently stay open to around 10pm.

SHOPPING

VAT Refunds   For refunds of up to 20% on purchases exceeding 2,000F, fill out a **value-added tax (VAT)** form in larger stores and give a copy to customs when leaving the country. A refund will be sent to you. Shops with duty-free signs in windows give this discount on the spot.

Best Buys   Jewelry, designer clothing, perfume—whatever you would buy in Paris is sold along the Riviera, particularly in Cannes, Monte Carlo, and Nice. The price and quality are about the same, too. Look for good buys in silk scarves, perfumes, scented soaps, sportswear, and swimsuits (particularly bikinis).

Handmade pottery is sold in Vallauris, some based on original Picasso designs, and in Moustiers-Ste-Marie (near the Grand Canyon of the Verdon). The town of Biot specializes in handblown glass. Paintings and local crafts—pewter, batik, jewelry, olive-wood carvings, handprinted cotton shoulder bags—are made and sold in the hilltop villages, particularly St-Paul-de-Vence and Tourrette-sur-Loup. The more commercial villages, such as Eze and Gourdon, also sell scented soaps, candles, herbs, and essences. The town of Grasse is famous for its (not particularly subtle) perfumes. Poivre d'âne is a wild savory found only in this region. There are some first-rate antiques shops in Nice and Antibes, and along the road from Cagnes-sur-Mer to Vence. Monaco is the place for stamps.

Cannes: La Croisette and rue d'Antibes, a few blocks behind La Croisette, are two of the Azure Coast's most glamorous shopping streets. Among the most appealing of the resort's emporiums is **Saint Laurent Rive Gauche,** 44 La Croisette (☎ 04-93-39-23-35), where women's clothing, from sportswear to evening gowns, is showcased. The prices of individual garments can easily surpass $1,200, so ask specifically for Saint Laurent Variations, a line of less-expensive sportswear that might fall more gracefully into your budget. (Regrettably, Saint Laurent menswear is no longer available in Cannes.)

Looking for something succulent to spoil your figure? **Chocolats Maiffret,** 31 rue d'Antibes (☎ 04-93-39-08-29), sells chocolates and candied everything, presented in elegant boxes suitable as gifts, unless you opt to consume the treats yourself. Other shopworthy boutiques lie on nearby streets, such as rue des Serbes and rue des Etas-Unis. Many, like **Cerruti** (☎ 04-93-38-25-20) and **Chevignon** (☎ 04-92-98-06-45), which share premises at 15 rue des Serbes, specialize in fashionable clothing for men. A worthy competitor in menswear is **Trabaud,** 48 rue d'Antibes (☎ 04-92-98-30-92).

Don't overlook the grand hotels, such as the Martinez, the Carlton, and the Gray d'Albion, as a setting for upscale and often imaginative boutiques. Looking for gemstones to set the Film Festival on fire? **Cartier** (☎ 04-93-99-58-73) and **Van Cleef & Arpels** (☎ 04-93-94-15-08) are both on La Croisette, at nos. 57 and 61, respectively.

Monte Carlo: The shop windows in Monte Carlo are for many visitors as interesting as the historic sites. Certainly, some of the couture clothing is as dazzling and, for many, as inaccessible as the furnishings in the prince's palace.

Most of the boutiques—Cartier, Dior, Yves Saint Laurent, and the like—are on streets surrounding the casino: place du Casino, avenue des Beaux-Arts, boulevard des Moulins, and avenue Princesse-Grace. The somewhat younger, trendier boutiques are in the Park Palace complex (Les Allées Lumières) at the head of the casino gardens.

To help support local artisans, the late Princess Grace set up two shops called **Boutique du Rocher,** selling handcrafts and goods made from Provençal fabrics. One is at 1 av. de Madone (☎ 93-30-91-17), the other at 11 rue Emile-de-Loth (☎ 93-30-33-99).

Nice: If you happen to be strolling along boulevard des Anglais, don't overlook the grand hotels lining its landward edge as venues for upscale, designer-conscious shopping. Both the **Hôtel Méridien,** 1 promenade des Anglais (☎ 04-93-82-25-25), and the **Hôtel Négresco,** 37 promenade des Anglais (☎ 04-93-16-64-00), contain several pricey, relentlessly chic boutiques for that spontaneous fling with conspicuous consumerism. More appealing, however, is a bout of wandering through the well-accessorized streets and alleys of Nice's historic core, where dozens of shops lure newcomers with finery.

The densest concentrations of shops lie along rue Masséna, place Magenta, and rue Paradis, as well as on streets funneling into and around them. Examples are **Façonnable,** 7 rue Paradis (☎ 04-93-87-88-80); **Gigi,** 7 rue de la Liberté (☎ 04-93-87-81-78); **Carroll,** 9 rue de la Liberté (☎ 04-93-16-15-25); and **Trabaud,** 10 rue de la Liberté (☎ 04-93-87-53-96). Timeless and endlessly alluring, despite the passage of time, are the products of **Yves Saint Laurent,** 4 av. de Suède (☎ 04-93-87-70-79).

St-Tropez: St-Tropez has many boutiques at the port, in the old town around the Hôtel-de-Ville, and along the narrow streets between quai Suffren and place des Lices. Place des Lices has a market for clothing and antiques on Tuesday and Saturday morning. The best place for unusual gift items is **Galeries Tropéziennes,** 56 rue Gambetta (☎ 04-94-97-02-21), near place des Lices. The inspiration is Mediterranean, breezy, and sophisticated. One of the best emporiums for women's fashions is **Choses,** quai Jean-Jaurès (☎ 04-94-97-03-44). Its specialty is clingy and often provocative T-shirt dresses that are snapped up by scores of Bardot wanna-bes. **Jacqueline Thienot,** 12 rue Georges-Clemenceau (☎ 04-94-97-05-70), is one of the best outlets on the Riviera for authentic Provençal antiques. Most of the furniture is crafted from walnut.

SPORTS

BEACHES   The beaches between Monte Carlo and Cannes are mostly small and pebbly. Cannes has a sandy beach (with imported sand). The best beach is at St-Tropez. Most resorts tend to have a single stretch of sand divided into a public area and a series of private beaches, each with its own distinctive character and clientele. The private beaches charge admission that includes use of a changing room and rental of a sun umbrella and mattress. They also usually serve light lunches. You're free to wander, so find a beach that suits your taste and budget and then go exploring.

Cannes: Of the public beaches, **Plage du Midi,** to the west of the old harbor, is best in the afternoon; **Plage Gazagnaire,** to the east of the new port, is best in the morning. Between the two are private beaches where anyone can swim for around 140F—a fee that includes a mattress, a sun umbrella, and waiters who'll take your orders for lunch. As elsewhere on the Riviera, each section of the beach has its own character. An older Middle Eastern crowd, for instance, gathers at the **Plage Gray d'Albion.**

Monte Carlo: The **Plage du Larvotto** is a man-made public beach squeezed between two pieces of man-made land. Next door is the private Monte Carlo Sea Club, which has a heated seawater pool free to guests at the Beach Plaza Hotel. If you want to come close to experiencing some of the dazzle Monte Carlo once knew, the only place to swim is at the exclusive **Monte Carlo Beach** (☎ 93-28-66-66). A fee of around 140F will admit you to a heated Olympic-size saltwater pool, restaurants, a pebbly beach with cabanas, and a bevy of pretty boys and aspiring Bardots.

St-Tropez: The beaches close to town—**Plage des Greniers** and the **Bouillabaisse**—are great for families; but holiday people snub them, preferring a 10-kilometer (6-mile) sandy crescent at **Les Salins** and **Pampellone.** These beaches are about 3 kilometers (2 miles) from town, so it helps to have a car, motorbike, or bicycle (see "By Motorbike or Bicycle," earlier in this chapter, for rentals).

The most magnificent stretch of beach is divided into a number of private beaches, each with its own atmosphere and clientele. **Tahiti,** for instance, tends to get a 30- to 35-year-old singles crowd. For around 140F you'll get a mattress and sun umbrella—then you're free to wander up and down the beach at will. Each beach has its own lunch area open to the public. The one at **Club 55** began as the canteen for the film crew of Bardot's *And God Created Woman.*

BICYCLING   In high season bicycles can be faster than cars. Two lovely trips on fairly level terrain are around Cap d'Antibes from Nice and around Cap Ferrat from Cannes. Bikes are ideal at St-Tropez, since the beach is a few miles from town. Bicycles can be rented at train stations in Antibes, Cannes, Juan les Pins, and Nice. They can be taken with you on trains.

In **St-Tropez,** to prepare yourself for Muscle Beach and to perhaps save some money on car rentals and taxis, rent a bike at **Chez Mas,** 5 rue Joseph-Quaranta (☎ 04-94-97-00-60), and bike to the beach every day.

BOATING   Windsurfers and sailboats are for rent at all major resorts. Waterskiing is also available.

Cannes: Sailboats and motorboats, and, in some cases, some rather impressive yachts, can be rented in Cannes at **Folie-Too,** Vieux Port de Cannes (☎ 04-93-43-17-03), or **Station Voile,** Porte de Moure Rouge (☎ 04-92-18-88-88). If you're looking for a larger, more prestigious vessel for rent by the day, week, or month, consider the services of **M.S. Yacht,** 57 La Croissette (☎ 04-93-99-03-51). For deep-sea fishing in the waters off Cannes, contact the region's most visible outfitter, **Club de Pêche Sportive,** Vieux Port de Cannes (☎ 04-93-63-78-30).

St-Tropez: Rentals for windsurfing at Tahiti and Pampelonne beaches are available from the region's biggest water-sports outfitter, **Club Watersport,** route de l'Epi (☎ 04-94-79-82-41).

GOLF   In **Cannes,** two of the most worthwhile and challenging golf courses include **Golf Club de Mandelieu** (sometimes referred to as Golf Club de Cannes La Napoule), Face Mer, La Napoule (☎ 04-93-49-55-39); and the **Country Club de Cannes Mougins,** 175 av. du Golf (☎ 04-93-75-79-13). Less convenient is the **Golf Bastide du Roy** (☎ 04-93-65-08-48), in the resort of Biot, about a 40-minute drive from Cannes.

In **Monte Carlo,** try the **Monte Carlo Golf Club,** Mont Agel (☎ 93-41-09-11), across the border in La Turbie, France.

TENNIS   Resorts that offer tennis (white outfits only, please!) include the following: **Antibes:** Hôtel du Cap and Résidence du Cap (☎ 04-93-61-39-01); **Cannes:** Complexe Sportif Montfleury, boulevard Montfleury (☎ 04-93-38-75-78), or Gallia Tennis Club, 30 bd. Montfleury (☎ 04-93-99-23-20). **Cap Ferrat:** Grand Hôtel du Cap (☎ 04-93-76-50-50); **St-Paul-de-Vence:** Mas d'Artigny (☎ 04-93-32-84-54); **Vence:** Château St-Martin (☎ 04-93-58-02-02); **St-Tropez:** Tennis de St-Tropez (☎ 04-94-97-80-76), Hôtel dei Marres (☎ 04-94-97-26-68), and Tennis de la Vernatelle (☎ 04-94-56-15-32).

DINING

A set or fixed-price menu is usually cheaper than ordering à la carte. The cuisine takes its inspiration from Paris, Provence, and Italy. The closer to the Italian border you are—from Nice eastward—the more pronounced the Italian influence will be. You'll find essentially three types of meals: classic French, cuisine moderne, and regional or Provençale. Classic and cuisine moderne are served in the more formal restaurants; regional cuisine in the small family-run establishments. The telltale sign of a classic meal is the use of rich, heavy sauces. Cuisine moderne emphasizes small portions of fresh local produce, cooked simply to enhance natural flavors and attractively arranged. Many meals, of course, are a blend of classic and moderne. A dinner served à la Provençale is usually cooked with garlic, tomatoes, and fresh herbs, particularly rosemary or thyme. The emphasis is on simple, robust flavors. A popular local taste is *aïoli:* mayonnaise with garlic, olive oil, and saffron. The most popular dish is fish—broiled, grilled, or cooked in a stew or in a sauce with pasta.

Bouillabaisse is a fish stew with eel, shrimp, crabs, and other fish and shellfish, cooked with olive oil, tomatoes, garlic, saffron, fennel, and a touch of anise liqueur—all served with garlic toast and a garlic-and-pepper mayonnaise. *Pistou* is a thick vegetable soup with beans, onions or leeks, fresh herbs (especially basil), garlic, and grated cheese. *Soupe de poisson* is fish soup made with tomatoes, saffron, garlic, and onions.

Salade Niçoise begins with tomatoes, anchovies, radishes, green peppers, olives, and a vinaigrette dressing. Added to these basics are green beans, tuna, and/or hard-boiled eggs. *Loup de mer* (sea bass) is a specialty of the Riviera, particularly flambéed with fennel. Less expensive is *daurade* (sea bream), often grilled or baked with onions, tomatoes, and lemon juice. *Rouget* is red mullet grilled or baked in foil with lemon. Grilled scampi is often imported, frozen. *Moules* (mussels) are served in white wine à la marinière or in soup.

Leg of lamb (*gigot d'agneau*) or brochettes of skewered lamb are best in the spring. *Daube de boeuf* is a beef stew with a wine-flavored mushroom sauce, popular in Nice. Chicken is served roasted with herbs (*poulet rôti*) or with white wine, herbs, tomatoes, and black olives (*Niçoise*). Also popular is *lapin* (rabbit) in a mustard sauce.

As you head east toward Italy, try various kinds of pasta, particularly with fresh fish sauce.

Of the various fresh vegetable dishes, the best is ratatouille—a vegetable stew with tomatoes, onions, eggplant, zucchini, and green peppers. Other local favorites are asparagus and artichokes with herb stuffing. You can try a different cheese every night for a year without having the same one twice. Be sure to try local goat and sheep cheeses.

For dessert, you can't go wrong with fresh local fruits: particularly melons and strawberries dipped in crème fraîche. Fruit sorbets are special, too.

For quick snacks on the beach, try a simple ham-and-cheese sandwich on a long thin loaf of French bread or *pain bagnat* (a sandwich with tomatoes, hard-boiled eggs, olives, anchovies, onions, olive oil, and sometimes tuna).

Anise-flavored pastis is the number-one drink.

CATEGORY	COST
Very Expensive	Over 500F
Expensive	300–500F
Moderate	150–300F
Inexpensive	Under 150F

Prices are per person for a three-course meal, including tax and service but not wine.

ACCOMMODATIONS

Most but not all hotels include a continental breakfast (coffee and crois-sant) in the price.

A salle de bain is a bathroom that may have a shower or a tub (baig-noire). Specify which you want. A tub is more expensive. In less expen-sive hotels with shared baths, you may have to pay extra each time you take a bath or shower.

Many of the most splendid properties—most of them castles and other historic buildings that have been converted into hotels—belong to an organization called Relais & Châteaux. For reservations or an illus-trated catalog, send $10 to **Relais & Châteaux,** 11 E. 44th St., Suite 704, New York, NY 10017 (for information and reservations of individual Relais & Châteaux, call **212/856-0115** or fax 800/860-4930). Their Web site address is http://www.integra.fr/relaischateaux.

The best of the simpler and less expensive hotels are grouped toge-ther in an organization called the **Féderation Nationale des Logis de France,** 83 av. d'Italie, 75013 Paris (☎ **01-45-84-70-00**). These clean and inexpensive family hotels are located in quiet neighborhoods or on back roads. (It helps to have a car to reach them.) About 30% of the rooms in the inexpensive hotels have private baths, and most have restau-rants that serve well-prepared family meals. You can recognize these hotels by the distinctive yellow-and-green signs in front. The association publishes an annual directory, priced at 95F. Copies are available from the **French Government Tourist Office,** Maison de la France, 444 Madison Ave., 16th floor, New York, NY 10020-2452 (☎ 212/838-7800), and also from stores specializing in travel publications, including the **Traveller's Bookstore,** 22 W. 52nd St., New York, NY 10019 (☎ **800/755-8728** or 212/664-0995).

A traditional itinerary—moving from place to place—makes no sense on the Riviera. What you should be doing is learning how to relax, not how to pack and unpack every day. Your best bet, therefore, is choos-ing a limited number of hotels and using them as bases from which to make daily excursions both inland and along the coast.

Begin by answering two important questions: Do you want to spend all your time in one or more seaside resorts or split your time between these resorts and one of the walled medieval towns in the interior? And of the time you spend on the coast, do you want to stay in towns where there's lots of activity, in relatively isolated resorts, or in a combination of the two?

If you want to spend all your time in seaside resorts: Stay in or around Cannes and/or in or around Nice. You can also stay in St-Tropez and/or Monte Carlo, but Cannes and Nice are more centrally located for excursions. (Picture the Riviera as a straight line along the southern coast of France. St-Tropez is at the southwest end and Monte Carlo at the northeast end. Cannes is in the middle. Nice is midway between Cannes and Monte Carlo.)

If you want to split your time between seaside resorts and perched villages: Stay in one or more of the seaside resorts described above and also in one of the hill towns, St-Paul-de-Vence or Peillon.

If you want to stay along the coast, but only in towns with lots of activity: Stay in the city of Nice, the city of Cannes, the village of St-Tropez, and/or Monte Carlo.

If you want to stay on the coast, but only in quiet, isolated resorts: Stay on Cap d'Antibes near Cannes and/or in Beaulieu or Cap Ferrat, near Nice. The two capes, though different in character, are off the main coastal road and more tranquil. Village and beach life in St-Tropez are pretty frenetic but there are some peaceful resorts (see "The Itinerary") outside of town.

If you want to stay on the coast and experience both quiet resorts and active towns: For a quiet resort, stay in either Beaulieu or Cap Ferrat or Cap d'Antibes. For city life, stay in Cannes, Nice, the village of St-Tropez, or Monte Carlo.

Return to these questions after you've read "The Itinerary."

CATEGORY	COST
Very Expensive	Over 1,000F
Expensive	600–1,000F
Moderate	300–600F
Inexpensive	Under 300F

All prices are for a standard double room for two, including tax (18.6%) and service charge.

EXPLORING

The first step is to find a place to stay. I begin with the most popular areas along the coast — Monte Carlo; the Nice area, including Beaulieu and Cap Ferrat; the Cannes area, including Cap d'Antibes; and St-Tropez. Then I discuss the various excursions, including visits to St-Paul-de-Vence and Peillon — two medieval hill towns where you might want to stay, too.

MONTE CARLO

Trains run directly from both Cannes and Nice to **Monte Carlo.** If you're driving, there are three scenic roads at varying heights above the coast between Nice and Monte Carlo, a distance of about 20 kilometers (12 miles). All are called corniches—literally, a projecting molding along the top of a building or wall. The Lower Corniche (Corniche Inférieure) is the busiest and slowest route because it passes through all the coastal towns. The Middle Corniche (Moyenne Corniche) is high enough for views and close enough for details; it passes the perched village of Eze. The Upper Corniche (Grande Corniche) winds some 390 to 480 meters (1,300 to 1,600 ft.) above the sea, offering sweeping coastal views. The Upper Corniche follows the via Aurelia, the great Roman military road that brought legions from Italy to Gaul (France). In 1806, Napoléon rebuilt the road and sent Gallic troops into Italy. The best route is to take the Middle Corniche one way and the Upper Corniche the other. The view from the upper route is best in the early morning or evening.

The Principality of Monaco is 190 hectares (473 acres) small and would fit comfortably inside New York's Central Park or a family farm in Iowa. Its 5,000 citizens—the Monégasques—would take up only a small percentage of seats in the Astrodome. The country is so tiny that residents have to go to another country to play golf.

The present ruler, Prince Rainier III, traces his ancestry back to Otto Canella, who was born in 1070. The Grimaldi dynasty began with Otto's great-great-great-grandson, Francesco Grimaldi, also known as Frank the Rogue. Expelled from Genoa, Frank and his cronies disguised themselves as monks and seized the fortified medieval town known today as the Rock. That was in 1297, almost 700 years ago. Except for a short break under Napoléon, the Grimaldis have been here ever since, which makes them the oldest reigning family in Europe. On the Grimaldi coat-of-arms are two monks holding swords: Look up and you'll see them above the main door as you enter the palace.

Back in the 1850s, a Grimaldi named Charles III made a decision that turned the Rock into a giant blue chip. Needing revenues but not wanting to impose additional taxes on his subjects, he contracted with a company to open a gambling facility. The first spin of the roulette wheel was on December 14, 1856. There was no easy way to reach Monaco then—no carriage roads or railroads—so no one came. Between March 15 and March 20, 1857, one person entered the casino—and won two francs. In 1868, however, the railroad reached Monaco, filled with wheezing Englishmen who came to escape the London fog. The effects were immediate. Profits were so great that Charles eventually abolished all direct taxes.

Almost overnight a threadbare principality became an elegant watering hole for European society. Dukes and their mistresses and duchesses and their gigolos danced and dined their way through a world of spinning roulette wheels and bubbling champagne—preening themselves for

THE ITINERARY

ORIENTATION

On your trip you'll be traveling both along the coast, from Monte Carlo to St-Tropez, and to the so-called perched villages. This makes sense, because until recently the beaches were nothing but extensions of the hill towns.

The Riviera trip, unlike others in this book, won't be taking you from Point A to Point B, checking off important sights along the way. Happiness, as all travelers know, is staying put whenever possible. Even if you're in southern France for several weeks, there's no need to stay in more than two hotels—three at most. From any of these bases you can make daily excursions to all the places recommended below, then come back to the same familiar room.

This itinerary, then, is divided into two main parts: The first is a description of the areas where most visitors prefer to stay: Monte Carlo; the Nice area, including Beaulieu and Cap Ferrat; the Cannes area, including Cap d'Antibes; and St-Tropez. Then follows a description of the various excursions you can take from any of these areas. Two of the excursions are to the perched villages of St-Paul-de-Vence and Peillon, where you may want to stay, too.

It's important to begin with a realistic sense of Riviera life so you won't spend your holiday nursing wounded expectations. The Riviera conjures up images of fabulous yachts and villas, movie stars and palaces, and budding Bardots sunning themselves on ribbons of golden sand. The truth is that most beaches, at least east of Cannes, are small and pebbly. In summer, hordes of visitors are stuffed into concrete high-rises or roadside campsites—on weekends it can take 2 hours to drive the last 10 kilometers (6 miles) into St-Tropez. Yes, the film stars are here—but in their private villas. When the merely wealthy come, they come off-season, in spring and fall—the best time for you to visit, too.

That said, I can still recommend the Riviera, even in summer, so long as you're selective about the places you choose to visit. Back from the

nights at the opera, where artists such as Vaslav Nijinsky, Sarah Bernhardt, and Enrico Caruso came to perform.

Monte Carlo—the modern gambling town with elegant shops, man-made beaches, high-rise hotels, and a few belle-époque hotels—is actually only one of four parts of Monaco. The second is the medieval town on **the Rock (Monaco-Ville),** 60 meters (200 ft.) above the sea. It's coast, the light that Renoir and Matisse came to capture is as magical as ever. Fields of roses and lavender still send their heady perfume up to the fortified towns, where craftspeople make and sell their wares, as their predecessors did in the Middle Ages. Some resorts are as exclusive as ever, and no one will dare argue that French chefs have lost their touch.

THE MAIN ROUTE

3–5 DAYS

Two Nights: *Nice, Beaulieu, or Cap Ferrat.*
Visits to Nice, Monte Carlo, St-Paul-de-Vence, Tourrette-sur-Loup.

Two Nights: *Cannes or Cap d'Antibes.*
Visits to Cannes, Antibes, L'Estérel, Vallauris, Cagnes.

5–7 DAYS

Two or Three Nights: *Nice, Beaulieu, or Cap Ferrat.*
Visits to Nice, Monte Carlo, Peillon, St-Paul-de-Vence, Tourrette-sur-Loup, Villefranche.

Two or Three Nights: *Cannes or Cap d'Antibes.*
Visits to Cannes, Vallauris, Antibes, Biot (Léger Museum), Cagnes, L'Estérel, St-Tropez.

One Night: *St-Paul-de-Vence or Peillon.*

7–14 DAYS

Three Nights: *Nice, Beaulieu, or Cap Ferrat.*
Visits to Nice, Cap Ferrat, Monte Carlo, Eze, Peillon, St-Paul-de-Vence, Vence, Tourrette-sur-Loup, Gorges du Loup, Grasse.

Three Nights: *Cannes or Cap d'Antibes.*
Visits to Cannes, Vallauris, Antibes, Biot, L'Estérel, St-Tropez, Cagnes, Grand Canyon of the Verdon, Moustiers-Ste-Marie.

One Night: *Peillon.* **Or two nights:** *St-Paul-de-Vence.*

Two Nights: *St-Tropez.*
Trips to Ramatuelle, Gassin.

here that Prince Rainier lives. From July to September the prince goes a-traveling and the palace is open to the public.

The third area is **La Condamine,** the commercial harbor area, with apartments and businesses. The fourth is **Fontvieille,** the industrial district on 8 hectares (20 acres) of reclaimed land.

Today only about 3% of the country's revenues come from gambling; other chips are invested in chemicals, glass, ceramics, plastics, food products, and beer. Monaco may be a handkerchief-size state, a golden ghetto, but it's also a serious country with some 95 consulates around the world. Rainier has been adept financially and his citizens still don't have to pay taxes. (If you're thinking of becoming a citizen, there are long residency requirements before you can even apply and even then it isn't easy: There are no huddled masses here.) Of some 33,000 residents, only about 5,000 are Monégasques, who aren't allowed to gamble.

The principality has the lowest crime rate in Europe, perhaps because it has one security officer for every 122 residents. The navy, such as it is, has the fastest boat on the coast—so don't think of robbing the casino and escaping by sea.

When the Monégasques want to expand, they build upward or reclaim land from the sea. The result is a clean, sparkling concrete jewel set in a ring of mountains at the edge of the sea. The climate is the next best after Southern California's. Unlike other towns along the coast, Monaco has a highly defined history and tradition. It's also a town dedicated to conspicuous consumption. The borders with France are open; one moment you're driving through France, the next, through Monaco. The spoken language is French. French money is freely circulated, though there are Monégasque coins stamped with the image of Rainier III.

The casino is worth a visit, even if you don't bet a centime. You might find it fun to count the Jaguars and Rolls-Royces parked outside and breathe on the windows of shops selling Saint Laurent dresses and fabulous jewels. The Oceanographic Museum under Jacques Cousteau is a treat, and so is the Exotic Garden. Should you decide to stay, there's one hotel straight out of the 19th century and a comfortable beach hotel where expensive people offer their oiled bodies to the sun.

Most of the very wealthy stay in their private villas, of course, barricaded behind a wall of old money, and the people you will meet are people like yourself—holidaymakers, sunseekers, coming to Monte Carlo to cloak themselves in the opulence of a world that no longer exists. But no matter. The contrast between yesterday and today is sad and wonderful, funny and obscene—but it's still worth seeing. And while you're mourning what has been lost, a bit of the old glamor, miraculously, will rub off, too.

As you approach Monte Carlo from Nice, you'll see signs on the right to the **Jardin Exotique** (Tropical Gardens), the **Musée d'Anthropologie Préhistorique** (Museum of Prehistoric Anthropology), and the **Observatory Caves** on boulevard du Jardin Exotique (☎ **93-30-33-65**). All three are worth a visit. The garden has some 9,000 species of cacti and succulents clinging to a rocky cliff 92 meters (300 ft.) above the sea. The view of the palace and the coast is spectacular. Steps take you down to the museum (which has a great collection of skeletons and stone-age tools of interest to the nonspecialist) and to the caves. The caves aren't enormous; but you'll still enjoy wandering through an Arthur Rackhamish world of

THE FRENCH RIVIERA

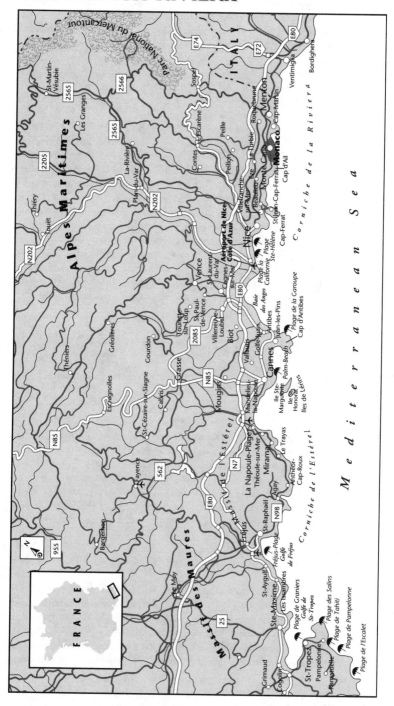

fantastic shapes and shadows. Keep in mind that it's a long, steep walk down to the caves and back again. Admission 36F adults, 18F children 6–18; 5 and under free. Open daily: June–Sept 9am–7pm, Oct–May 9am–6pm.

The next stop is Old Monaco—the Rock—to tour the palace. Leave your car in the Fontvieille Car Park on your way into town. From Easter to the end of October there's bus service between the car park and the Rock. The walk takes about 30 minutes.

There's little room on the Rock for anything but official buildings, tourist shops, and restaurants. The marble staircase in the **Palais Princier,** place du Palais (☎ 93-25-18-31), was inspired by the staircase at Fontainebleau. The tour takes you through ornate state rooms filled with priceless antiques and paintings, where Princess Grace once greeted visiting royalty. Families with kids should come early to see the Changing of the Guards in front of the palace, daily at 11:55am. Admission 30F adults, 15F children. Open daily: June–Sept 9:30am–6:30pm; Oct 10am–5pm.

One wing of the palace, open throughout the year, is taken up by a **museum** full of Napoleonic souvenirs and documents related to Monaco's history. Admission 18F adults, 9F children. Joint ticket with palace apartments, 20F adults, 10F children. Open Dec 17–May 31, Tues–Sun 10:30am–12:30pm and 2–5pm; June–Sept, daily 9:30am–6:30pm; Oct 1–Nov 11, daily 10am–5pm.

TAKE A BREAK

Take the museum's elevator to the roof terrace for a fine view and a restorative drink.

The **Oceanographic Museum,** avenue St-Martin (☎ 93-15-36-00), has an aquarium asplash with playful sea lions and turtles. Admission 60F adults, 30F children. Open daily: July 1–Aug 9am–8pm; Apr–May and Sept 9am–7pm; Mar and Oct 9:30am–7pm; Nov–Feb 10am–6pm.

Also on the Rock is the **cathedral,** a neo-Romanesque (1875–84) monstrosity with several important early paintings of the Nice School. This school, led by Louis Bréa—you'll see his work in churches along the coast—flourished from the mid-15th to the mid-16th century under strong Gothic and Italian Renaissance influence. The simplicity and humanity of Bréa's work have led some critics to call him a Provençal Fra Angelico.

The **casino,** place du Casino (☎ 92-16-21-21), is a must. Nowhere in the world will you see a more striking contrast between yesterday and today. Wandering through a world of gold-leaf splendor are gamblers looking as though they had just stumbled off the bus to Reno or Atlantic City. The main gambling hall, once called the European Room, has been renamed the American Room and fitted with 150 one-armed bandits from

MONACO

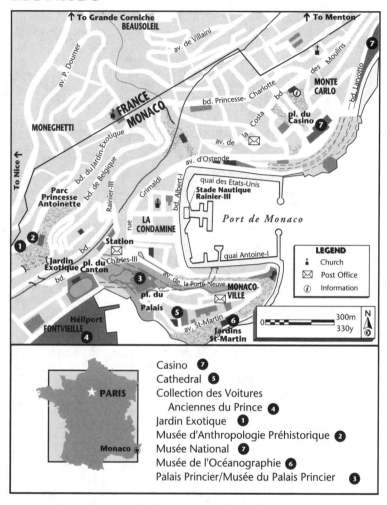

Chicago. Adjoining it is the Pink Salon, now a bar where unclad nymphs float about on the ceiling smoking cigarillos. The private rooms (Salles Privées) are for high rollers. Even if you don't bet, it's worth the price just to see them. The stakes are higher here, so the mood is more sober, and well-wishers are herded farther back from the tables. On July 17, 1924, black came up 17 times in a row on Table 5. This was the longest run ever. A dollar left on black would have grown to $131,072. On August 7, 1913, the number 36 came up three times in a row. In those days, if a gambler went broke the casino bought him a ticket home. Open 10am until the last die is thrown. The back rooms open at 4pm; jackets and ties are required. Bring your passport.

It seems in the true spirit of Monte Carlo that the **Opera House,** with its 18-ton gilt bronze chandelier, is part of the casino complex. The designer, Charles Garnier, also built the Opéra Garnier in Paris.

The serious gamblers, some say, play nearby at **Loews Casino,** 12 av. des Spélugues (☎ 93-50-65-00). You may want to try parking here, because parking near the old casino is next to impossible in season. Open Mon–Fri 4pm, Sat–Sun 1pm.

TAKE A BREAK

Head for **place d'Armes** *in the port below the Rock and munch on hot socca (a thick pancake made with chickpea flour) or a slice of pissaladière (thick pizza with onions) in the open-air market.*

The **Museum of Dolls,** 17 av. Princesse-Grace (☎ 93-30-91-26), is in the **National Museum,** a short walk to the left as you exit the casino. Your children will thank you for taking them. Admission 26F adults, 16F children. Open daily: Easter–Sept 10am–6:30pm; Oct–Easter 10am–12:15pm and 2:30–6:30pm.

DINING

Café de Paris, place du Casino (☎ 92-16-20-20). Here's a brasserie-type lunch spot for jet-setters who want to see and be seen and for ladies with poodles and heavy Arpels bracelets. Reservations advised. Elegantly casual. AE, DC, MC, V. Expensive.

Le Grill de l'Hôtel de Paris, place du Casino (☎ 92-16-29-66). Le Grill has the best classic French cuisine in town. There's no swankier place on the Riviera than the rooftop of this fabled hotel of the super wealthy and celebrities. The ceiling opens in summer to reveal a starry sky. Select one of some 20,000 bottles of wine and feast on such delectable fare as grilled sea bass or tender lamb from the Alps, the latter cooked with fresh aromatic herbs. The Charolais cut of beef is the tenderest you're likely ever to be served. You can also dine at the equally touted Le Louis XV at the same hotel. Reservations essential. Jacket/tie required. AE, DC, MC, V. Closed Jan 6–31. Very Expensive.

Pinocchio, 30 rue Comte Félix-Gastaldi (☎ 93-30-96-20). Featuring French-Italian specialties, this is the most popular eatery on the Rock. Bronzed women and men fighting their age relax in a cozy atmosphere beneath a vaulted ceiling. Reservations essential. Elegantly casual. MC, V. Closed Dec 10–Jan 23 and Wed out of season. Moderate.

Pizzeria Monégasque, 4 rue Terrazzani (☎ 93-30-16-38). This is a chic pizza house. Yes, there is such a thing. Reservations advised. Elegantly casual. AE, MC, V. Closed Dec 25–Jan 1. Inexpensive.

Rampoldi, 3 av. des Spélugues (☎ 93-30-70-65). Rampoldi draws a fashionable and exuberant yachting crowd with its Italian food in a

1930s-ish setting. Try the risotto primavera or grilled lamb. They also serve excellent pastas, the best of which is tortellini with a truffled cream sauce. The lobster ravioli is excellent. Reservations essential. Elegantly casual. AE, DC, MC, V. Expensive.

Restaurant du Port, quai Albert-Ier (☎ 93-50-77-21). This popular Italian restaurant has outside tables and efficient service. The varied large menu includes prawns, pastas, lasagna, fettuccine, fish risotto, and veal with ham and cheese. Reservations advised. Elegantly casual. AE, DC, MC, V. Closed Mon and Nov to early Dec. Expensive.

ACCOMMODATIONS

Monte Carlo is only half an hour's drive from Nice, so there's no need to stay here unless you're an inveterate gambler or like the idea of waking up in the land once frequented by Princess Grace. If you're looking for a luxurious hotel, the Négresco in Nice is as luxurious as the Hôtel de Paris in Monte Carlo, and the food is better; if you need a moderately priced or inexpensive hotel, you'll have a better choice in Nice. Don't come to Monte Carlo in season without a reservation.

The Balmoral, 12 av. Costa, 98000 Monte-Carlo (☎ 93-50-62-37; fax 93-15-08-69). Though some rooms have recently been renovated, the Balmoral remains a sad reminder of a lost age. The nicest thing a travel writer can say about it is that it's an old-fashioned family hotel. 80 rooms with bath. Facilities: snack bar/restaurant. AE, DC, MC, V. Closed Nov. Expensive.

Beach Plaza, 22 av. Princesse-Grace, 98000 Monte-Carlo (☎ 800/ 225-5843 or 93-30-98-80; fax 93-50-23-14). This large modern hotel is part of the respected Trusthouse Forte chain. 304 rms with bath; 9 suites. Facilities: restaurant, three pools, private beach. AE, DC, MC, V. Very Expensive.

The Hermitage, square Beaumarchais, 98005 Monaco (☎ 92-16-40-00; fax 92-16-38-52). The Hermitage is a grand belle-époque palace. The dining room is a tribute to a bygone age, with pink marble columns holding up a gilded frescoed ceiling. The recently reappointed rooms are comfortable but disappointing after you've seen the lavish public areas. 231 rms with bath; 16 suites. Facilities: restaurant, pool. AE, DC, MC, V. Very Expensive.

Hôtel de Paris, place du Casino, 98000 Monaco (☎ 92-16-30-00; fax 93-16-38-50). Located right near the casino, this is one of the most famous hotels in Europe. Just as the newer Loews Hotel is the offspring of the modern travel world of conventions and gambling junkets, so the ornate Hôtel de Paris is the child of a vanishing age of privilege and luxury. It was here in this Second Empire splendor that Escoffier worked his magic for empresses, dowagers, and queens. 206 rms with bath; 41 suites. Facilities: restaurant (closed Tues, Wed [except dinner July–Aug], Nov–Dec, and second half Feb). AE, DC, MC, V. Very Expensive.

Monte Carlo Beach Hotel, Monte Carlo Beach, 06190 Roquebrune (☎ 93-28-66-66; fax 93-78-14-18). This hotel has small, modern, elegant rooms with balconies overlooking the sea. It also has the best hotel food in town. It's exactly what its name says—a beach hotel, where you're given privileges at the exclusive Monte Carlo Beach Club, which occupies the same site. A minibus takes you to the casino and shops, which are too far to reach by foot. 41 rms with bath. Facilities: restaurant, pool, private beach. AE, DC, MC, V. Closed Oct 8–Apr 4. Very Expensive.

The Terminus, 9 av. Prince-Pierre, 98000 Monaco (☎ **92-05-63-00;** fax 92-05-20-10). Near the train station, this is the closest thing in Monte Carlo to a budget hotel. 54 rms, some with bath. DC, MC, V. Moderate.

A SIDE TRIP TO EZE

Almost every tour to Monte Carlo includes a visit to the medieval hill town of **Eze,** perched on a rocky spur near the Middle Corniche, some 390 meters (1,300 ft.) above the sea. (Don't confuse Eze with the beach town of Eze-sur-Mer, which is down by the water.)

Eze is one of several beautifully preserved medieval towns on mountaintops behind the coast. It would be a shame to tour the Riviera without seeing at least one of these towns, and Eze, on the road between Nice and Monte Carlo, is the most accessible. But because of this it's also the most crowded and commercial. Eze has its share of serious craftspeople, but most of its vendors make their living selling perfumed soaps and postcards to the package-tour trade.

If Eze is your first perched village, you'll be delighted with it, but if you've been to St-Paul-de-Vence (also commercial but visually more beautiful), Tourrette-sur-Loup, Peillon, or others, you may be disappointed with Eze. If your time is limited, certainly, visit Eze, particularly in the evening when the buses have returned to Nice.

You enter through a fortified 14th-century gate and walk down narrow cobbled streets with vaulted passages and stairs. The church is 18th century, but the small **Chapel of the White Penitents** dates to 1306 and contains a 13th-century gilded wood Spanish Christ and some notable 16th-century paintings. Tourist and craft shops line the streets leading to the ruins of a **castle** that has a scenic belvedere. Some of the most tasteful craft shops are in the hotel/restaurant **Chèvre d'Or,** rue Barri (☎ **04-92-10-66-66**).

Near the top of the village is the **Jardin Exotique,** boulevard du Jardin Exotique (☎ **04-93-41-10-30**), a garden with exotic flowers and cacti. Entrance is 12F, and it's open daily March to October from 9am to 7pm and November to February from 9am to noon and 2 to 8pm. It's worth the admission price, but if you've time for only one exotic garden, visit the one in Monte Carlo.

Dining & Accommodations

Château d'Eze, rue Pise, 06360 Eze (☎ **04-93-41-12-24;** fax 04-93-41-16-64). This hotel is trying hard to match the well-established Chèvre d'Or in comfort and class. The rooms here are more spacious, though the atmosphere is a bit "ye olde." The hotel occupies the former home of the King of Sweden. The view from the terrace is, as they say, breathtaking. 6 rms with bath; 4 suites. AE, DC, MC, V. Very Expensive.

Chèvre d'Or, rue Barri, 06360 Eze (☎ **04-92-10-66-66;** fax 04-93-41-06-72). This restored medieval manor house has well-appointed but smallish rooms and some apartments (no. 9 is a good bet). The small pool is surrounded by a terrace: a lovely, peaceful place to take the sun or end the day. The hotel belongs to the prestigious Relais & Châteaux group. Classic French cuisine is served in the restaurant, where specialties include filet de loup (local bass) and pigeon with fresh truffle pâté. The dining area is formal, without much warmth; the terrace may be more appealing if you're here only for the day. 23 rms with bath. Facilities: restaurant, cafe, bar, terrace, pool. AE, DC, MC, V. Closed Dec–Feb. Very Expensive.

NICE

Near the busy city of **Nice** is a cape called Cap Ferrat, jutting out into the sea. On the far side of the cape is the coastal village of Beaulieu. A village, a cape, a city—which of these three is right for you? Let's look at the alternatives.

Nice is less glamorous, less sophisticated, and less expensive than Cannes. It's also older—weathered and faded, like a wealthy dowager who has seen better days but still maintains a demeanor of dignity. Nice is a big, sprawling city of 350,000—five times as many people as in Cannes—and has a life and vitality that survive when tourists pack their bags and go home. Cannes, on the contrary, exists for its visitors; it was dreamed up by them and blinked into existence almost overnight.

The glitter has moved to Cannes, but Nice has kept some of the local Marseille flavor that Marseille has lost and Cannes never had. Cannes is smart, stylish, and international, like cuisine moderne; Nice has the simple robust flavor of a meal cooked à la Provençale, with lots of garlic, tomatoes, and herbs.

It's easy to picture Nice, stretching behind the beautiful blue Baie des Anges. Along a narrow strip of pebbly beach is the **promenade des Anglais,** lined with hotels and cafes. If you follow the promenade to the west, you'll come to the fabulous Hôtel Négresco. If you follow the promenade to the east, you'll reach a hill called the **Château,** crowned with the ruins of an old fortress. Below the fortress are both the old town—**Vieille Ville**—and the harbor. That's it, essentially, as far as visitors are concerned. After the promenade, the old town, and the museums and ruins in an area called **Cimiez,** you're left with a busy modern city where nothing goes on but life.

The old town of Nice is one of the delights of the Riviera. Cars are forbidden on streets narrow enough for their buildings to crowd out the sky. The winding alleys are lined with faded 17th- and 18th-century buildings where families sell their wares. Flowers cascade from window boxes

WHAT TO SEE & DO WITH CHILDREN

The Riviera is an ideal vacation spot for children. Every coastal resort has swimming, water sports, and bike rentals. For teenagers, there's a vigorous nightlife, particularly in Juan-les-Pins, St-Tropez, Cannes, and Nice.

Visit the walled medieval towns—the next best thing to sand castles, particularly Peillon. Hike through the Gorge of the Verdon, France's answer to the Grand Canyon. In Monte Carlo, don't miss the Aquarium on the Rock (under the supervision of Jacques Cousteau), the Doll Museum, and the Anthropological Museum. Cap Ferrat has a zoo with a trained-monkey show. There's a Marineland at the turnoff to Biot on the coastal road between Nice and Cannes.

on pastel-colored walls. You wander down cobbled streets, proceeding with the logic of dreams, or sit in an outdoor cafe on a Venetian-like square bathed in a pool of the purest, most transparent light. At the edge of the old town is the **flower market,** a swirl of colors and smells as intoxicating as wine.

Nice is certainly worth a visit, but should you stay here? On the negative side, its beaches are cramped and pebbly. Except for the luxurious Négresco, most of its hotels are either rundown or being refurbished for the convention crowd. On the positive side, Nice is likely to have hotel space when all other towns are full, and at prices you can afford. It's also a convenient base from which to explore Monte Carlo and the interior's medieval towns. It does have its share of first-class restaurants and boutiques, and an evening stroll through the old town or along the promenade des Anglais won't be easily forgotten.

Nice was "colonized" in the mid-18th century by Englishpeople fleeing the harshness of northern winters. The promenade des Anglais got its name because, in the 1820s, the Rev. Lewis Way got the English colony to pay for widening a 4-kilometer (2.5-mile) footpath along the Baie des Anges, thus creating jobs for fruit pickers thrown out of work by a terrible frost. The eastern end of the boulevard, bordering the old town, is now called the quai des Etats-Unis in deference to changing commercial realities. You can lunch in your swimsuit at any of the private beaches along the promenade.

A few blocks inland, to the west of the Hôtel Négresco, is a first-rate fine-arts museum, the **Musée des Beaux-Arts Jules Chéret,** 33 av. des Baumettes (☎ **04-93-44-50-72**). It contains paintings by masters of the belle époque and Picasso ceramics created in the pottery village of Vallauris in the 1950s. Admission 25F adults, 15F children. Open Tues–Sun: May–Sept 10am–noon and 3–6pm; Oct–Apr 10am–noon and 2–5pm.

The **Musée Masséna,** 65 rue de France (☎ **04-93-88-11-34**), a few blocks west of the Négresco, has a fine collection of Provençal ceramics and paintings by the early Nice School, including works by Bréa. Admission 25F adults, 15F children (free one Sun per month). Open Tues–Sun: May–Sept 10am–noon and 3–6pm; Oct–Apr 10am–noon and 2–5pm; closed holidays.

At the end of the quai des Etats-Unis are steps and an elevator leading to a viewing platform at the top of the **Château.** From here, continue

NICE

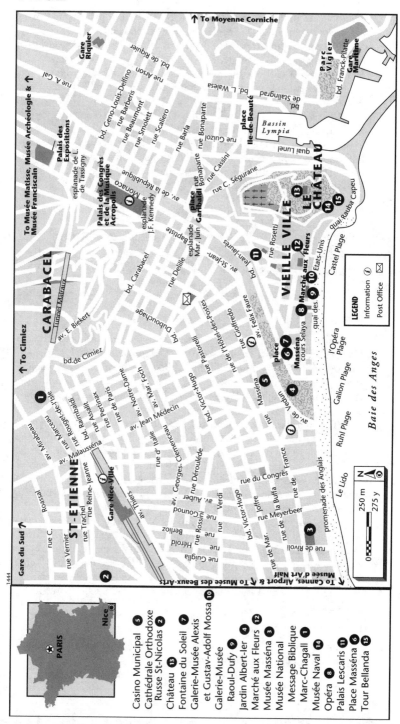

LEGEND

Information ⓘ

Post Office ⊠

Casino Municipal ⑤
Cathédrale Orthodoxe
Russe St-Nicolas ②
Château ⑬
Fontaine du Soleil ⑦
Galerie-Musée Alexis
et Gustav-Adolf Mossa ⑩
Galerie-Musée
Raoul-Dufy ⑨
Jardin Albert-Ier ④
Marché aux Fleurs ⑫
Musée Masséna ③
Musée National
Message Biblique
Marc-Chagall ①
Musée Naval ⑭
Opéra ⑧
Palais Lescaris ⑪
Place Masséna ⑥
Tour Bellanda ⑮

inland, down to the old town. At **place Garibaldi** is a morning fish market. Walk down **rue St-François** and bear left on **rue Droite.**

On your right is the **Palais Lescaris,** 15 rue Droite (☎ **04-93-62-05-54**). This mid–17th-century palace has an 18th-century pharmacy and a rococo interior with a grandiose staircase and an interesting trompe l'oeil ceiling. Admission free. Open Tues–Sun 10am–noon and 2–6pm; closed Nov.

Continue down **rue Droite.** On your left is the 17th-century **Eglise St-Jacques,** known as the Gesù, because it was modeled on that church in Rome. Three short blocks in from the bay, and paralleling it, is the tastefully restored **cours Saleya,** once the elegant promenade of Old Nice, now a street lined with shops and restaurants and home to a daily flower market.

TAKE A BREAK

*Shop for the best crystallized fruits in Nice at **Henry Auer,** 7 rue St-François-de-Paul (☎ **04-93-85-77-98**), and have an ice cream and pastry in his cozy tea room.*

Cimiez, site of ancient Nice, is now a residential neighborhood on a hill back from the bay. The **Musée Marc Chagall,** avenue du Dr.-Ménard (☎ **04-93-81-75-75**), houses the most important permanent collection of the painter's work, including the 17 canvases of the *Biblical Message.* Admission 28F adults, 18F ages 18–24; 17 and under free. Open Wed–Mon: July–Sept 10am–6pm; Oct–July 10am–5pm.

The ruins of a Roman bath and amphitheater won't be high on your list of musts unless you have a special interest in antiquity. Nearby is the 17th-century Villa des Arènes, which houses the **Musée Matisse,** 164 av. des Arènes-de-Cimiez (☎ **04-93-81-08-08**), with some 30 examples of the painter's work, drawn from different stages of his life. The museum was extensively renovated in 1992. Admission 25F adults, 15F children. Open Wed–Mon: Apr–Sept 11am–7pm; Oct–Mar 10am–5pm.

Also near the ruins is a **Franciscan Monastery** with several masterpieces of the Nice School, including a 1475 *Pietà* by Louis Bréa. Admission free. Open Mon–Fri 10am–noon and 3–6pm.

Nice is a good base for half-day or full-day excursions to Monte Carlo and Eze; to the perched villages of Peillon and St-Paul-de-Vence; to the Léger Museum at Biot; and to Cap Ferrat, Villefranche, Antibes, and Cannes.

DINING

Dining in Nice is a mixture of Italian, Provençal, and Parisian. Lunch specialties include pissaladière (pizza with black olives, onions, and anchovies) and pan bagnat (French bread soaked in olive oil and filled with tomatoes, radishes, hard-boiled eggs, black olives, and parsley).

Most tourists are directed to restaurants on the eastern side of the harbor, where glass-enclosed terraces muffle the sound of traffic. None has a very strong reputation among locals, except Le Taj (see below).

L'Ane Rouge, 7 quai des Deux-Emmanuel (☎ 04-93-89-49-63). This is the best of the many harborfront restaurants. Its specialties include bourride (a fish stew), lobster, sweetbreads, and chocolate cake. Reservations advised. Elegant casual. AE, DC, MC, V. Closed Wed. Very Expensive.

Le Chantecler, 37 promenade des Anglais (☎ 04-93-16-64-00). Le Chantecler is the top restaurant for cuisine moderne. The menu dégustation includes tiny, elegant portions of a dozen dishes. Other specialties include Charlotte de St-Pierre (a fish dish made with John Dory), lobster salad with asparagus tips, melon-and-grapefruit soup with Sauterne wine, and lobster ravioli in a shellfish bouillon. Chef Dominique le Stanc forged a name for himself in Monte Carlo. Jacket/tie required. AE, DC, MC, V. Very Expensive.

Chez Don Camillo, 5 rue Ponchettes (☎ 04-93-85-67-95). Tiny, quiet, and comfortable, this restaurant with attentive service and a good but limited menu serves Italian specialties. Try the fettuccine or filet of sole. Reservations essential. Elegant. AE, V. Closed Sun and Mon (lunch) and Dec 1–15. Expensive.

La Mérenda, 4 rue de la Terrasse (no phone). Here's a popular old town bistro near the flower market. Specialties cooked to order include tripes Niçoises, pâté au pistou (pasta with garlic-and-basil sauce), pizza, and stew Provençale. This is your best bet for a first-rate meal at a low price. Reservations not accepted. Casual. No credit cards. Closed Aug, Feb, and Sat–Mon. Moderate.

Le Florian, 22 rue Alphonse-Karr (☎ 04-93-88-86-60). This restaurant isn't quite as good as Le Chantecler. But on the many occasions when it's impossible to get a table at Chantecler, you'll do well to eat in these art deco dining rooms on the ground floor of a turn-of-the-century apartment building. Chef Claude Gillon is at least "second best" in Nice, turning out such dishes as shellfish-stuffed ravioli or oxtail with foie-gras sauce. His stuffed pig's feet is the best in Nice. Reservations required. Jacket/tie required. MC, V. Closed July–Aug. Expensive.

Le Taj, 87 quai des Etats-Unis (☎ 04-93-80-03-51). This restaurant serves Indian food in suitably Oriental surroundings. Reservations advised. Casual. AE, MC, V. Moderate.

ACCOMMODATIONS

Except for the Négresco, which has succeeded in maintaining the elegant standards of a bygone age, Nice's major hotels are either fading or undergoing restoration to satisfy the demands of the package-tour trade. The older hotels in all categories have beautifully ornate facades. Dining rooms, hallways, and stairways also have a certain fading charm. But the rooms are almost always a disappointment. It's not that they're uncomfortable or unclean, but that they lack character and fail to live up to the promise of the public areas.

Elysée Palace, 59 promenade des Anglais, 06000 Nice (☎ 04-93-86-06-06; fax 04-93-44-50-40). This glass-fronted addition to the Nice hotel scene lies close to the sea; all rooms feature views of the Mediterranean. The interior is spacious and ultramodern, with plenty of marble. The large restaurant is a sound bet for cuisine moderne, served amid contemporary works of art. 143 rms with bath. Facilities: restaurant, bar, pool, sauna, health club. AE, DC, MC, V. Very Expensive.

Grand Hôtel Aston, 12 av. Félix-Faure, 06000 Nice (☎ 04-93-80-62-52; fax 04-93-80-00-34). This hotel has a lovely roof garden overlooking the old city. 156 rms with bath. Facilities: restaurant. AE, DC, MC, V. Moderate.

Hôtel Busby, 38 rue du Mal-Joffre, 06000 Nice (☎ 04-93-88-19-41; fax 04-93-87-73-53). The Busby is one of a group of hotels back from the bay that cater heavily to the package-tour trade. If you're stuck for a room, they're likely to come up with something. 80 rms with bath. Facilities: restaurant. AE, DC, MC, V. Closed Nov 15–Dec 20. Moderate.

Hôtel Harvey, 18 av. de Suède, 06000 Nice (☎ 04-93-88-73-73; fax 04-93-82-53-55). The Harvey is just off the ocean behind the Méridien. Recent renovations have brought improvements to this hotel, but it remains a simple "two-star" selection and very provincial—cheap and cheerful. The location is great, though. 62 rms with bath. DC, MC, V. Closed late Oct to mid-Feb. Moderate.

Hôtel Négresco, 37 promenade des Anglais, 06000 Nice (☎ 04-93-88-39-51; fax 04-93-88-35-68). A turn-of-the-century turreted white castle, the Négresco is the only hotel in France that the government has declared a national monument. Doormen greet you in red-lined capes, knee-high boots, and blue hats with cockades. The massive suites are designed around different periods of French history—Romantic, Louis XIV, Empire, and others. The marble baths are big enough to throw parties in. The lobby is a huge rotunda encircled with columns reaching up to a stained-glass dome. Hanging above its center is a gigantic Baccarat crystal chandelier. The hallway carpet, when woven, represented one-tenth of the cost of the hotel. 132 rms with bath, 18 suites. Facilities: two restaurants, bar, private beach. AE, DC, MC, V. Very Expensive.

La Pérouse, 11 quai Rauba-Capéu, 06300 Nice (☎ 04-93-62-34-63; fax 04-93-62-34-63). This is at the eastern end of the Baie des Anges, near the Château. The reception area is tacky, but the rooms are clean and the rooftop pool is a quiet oasis with a spectacular view. 63 rms with bath. Facilities: restaurant, pool. AE, DC, MC, V. Very Expensive.

Méridien, 1 promenade des Anglais, 06000 Nice (☎ 04-93-82-25-25; fax 04-93-16-08-90). This is an impersonal modern hotel with a rooftop pool. 306 rms with bath; 8 suites. Facilities: restaurant, pool. AE, DC, MC, V. Very Expensive.

Splendid, 50 bd. Victor-Hugo, 06000 Nice (☎ **04-93-16-41-00;** fax 04-93-87-02-46). The Splendid is a family-run in-town hotel with a rooftop pool and sun terrace. 113 rms with bath. Facilities: restaurant, pool. AE, DC, MC, V. Expensive.

Beaulieu & Cap Ferrat

The **Beaulieu–Cap Ferrat** area, just east of Nice, is the quietest, most understated, most refined area along the Riviera. People come here not to see and be seen but to be left alone. Because of the limited nightlife, the absence of sandy beaches, and the distance from Cannes, guests tend to be families or couples on the far side of 30—particularly off-season. If a hotel is nothing more to you than a place to put your head after a full day of sightseeing, stay in Nice; but if you want to escape the frenetic pace of Riviera summer life and merely exist in the sun for a few days, stay in Beaulieu or on Cap Ferrat. You'll want to have a car and perhaps a rented bike for rides around the cape.

BEAULIEU

The one must-do in **Beaulieu** is visiting the **Villa Kérylos,** rue Gustave-Eiffel (☎ **04-93-01-01-44**). In the early part of the century a rich amateur archaeologist named Theodore Reinach asked an Italian architect to build him an authentic Greek house. The villa, now open to the public, is a faithful reproduction made from cool Carrara marble, alabaster, and rare fruitwoods. The furniture, made of wood inlaid with ivory, bronze, and leather, is copied from drawings of Greek interiors found on ancient vases and mosaics. Admission 35F adults, 15F children and seniors. Open daily: July–Aug 10am–7pm; Sept 10am–6pm; Dec 1–Mar 14 2–5:30pm; Oct and Mar 15–June 30 10:30am–12:30pm and 2–6pm.

Dining

Le Maxilien, 43 bd. Marinoni (☎ **04-93-01-47-48**). This is the best choice for dining outside the grand palaces. Try for a table on the shaded terrace of this old-fashioned place where the chef is known for his delectable cuisine and market-fresh produce. The dull international fare served at many establishments in Beaulieu has no place in this chef's creative repertoire. Some of the dishes may be for French-born-and-bred tastes, including calf's head salpicon. But don't judge a dish until you taste it. The fondant of eggplant studded with red peppers and served with a tangy tomato coulis is reason enough to visit. Even the bread is homemade. The welcome is professional, even friendly. Reservations essential. Jacket required. AE, DC, V. Closed Feb and Tues. Expensive.

La Pignatelle, 10 rue Quincenet (☎ **04-93-01-03-37**). This restaurant offers regional food in a home-style atmosphere. Reservations advised. Casual. MC, V. Closed mid-Oct to mid-Nov. Inexpensive.

Accommodations

La Réserve, 5 bd. Général-Leclerc, 06310 Beaulieu (☎ **04-93-01-00-01;** fax 04-93-01-28-99). A bit more reserved, in an elegant sort of way, La Réserve boasts a lounge resembling the reception room in Rome's Farnese Palace. 40 rms with bath; 3 suites. Facilities: restaurant, pool. AE, DC, MC, V. Closed Nov–Mar. Very Expensive.

Métropole, 15 bd. Général-Leclerc, 06310 Beaulieu (☎ **04-93-01-00-08;** fax 04-93-01-18-51). At the edge of the sea, the Métropole is visually relaxed, with comfortable couches in the public areas and 1 hectare (2.5 acres) of gardens leading past rocky ledges to the sea. 50 rms with bath. Facilities: restaurant, pool, private beach. AE, MC, V. Closed Oct 20–Dec 20. Very Expensive.

CAP FERRAT

Cap Ferrat (St-Jean-Cap-Ferrat), originally the southern tip of the cape, now gives its name to the entire peninsula. It resembles Cap d'Antibes, near Nice, in that it's a rocky finger extending into the sea, covered with sumptuous mansions hidden behind walls of lush vegetation. Because of its proximity to Cannes, Cap d'Antibes tends to attract a noisier, more aggressively star-studded clientele; guests on the more inaccessible Cap Ferrat want nothing but privacy, understated elegance, and seclusion. Land values on Cap Ferrat are second only to those in Monaco.

The cape is a fine, peaceful place to visit, even if you're not staying here. There's a lovely 1-hour **walk** along the coast from Paloma Beach around Pointe St-Hospice—ask for directions to the Tourist Path (Sentier Touristique). There's also the **Zoo de St-Jean-Cap-Ferrat,** chemin du Rox (☎ **04-93-76-04-98**), with a tropical garden and some 350 species of animals and exotic birds, including a condor and a school of chimps who put on a daily show. Admission 50F adults, 40F children 3–10 (2 and under free). Open daily: June–Sept 9:30am–7pm; off-season, 2:30–5:30pm.

Best of all is the **Ephrussi de Rothschild Foundation** (☎ **04-93-01-33-09**), a 7-hectare (17-acre) estate with magnificent gardens and a villa-museum called the Musée Ile-de-France. The museum reflects the sensibilities of its former owner, Mme Ephrussi de Rothschild, sister of Baron Edouard de Rothschild. An insatiable collector, she lived surrounded by an eclectic but tasteful collection of impressionist paintings, Louis-XIII furniture, rare Sèvres porcelain, and objets d'art from the Far East. Admission 45F adults, 30F children. Open daily: July–Aug 10am–7pm; Feb 15–June 30 and Sept–Oct 10am–6pm; Nov 1–Feb 14 2–6pm. Guided tours only.

Dining

Le Sloop, Nouveau Port (☎ **04-93-01-48-63**). Le Sloop serves meals on a terrace by the harbor. Reservations advised. Casual. AE, DC, MC, V. Closed Nov 15–Dec 15. Expensive.

Provençal, 2 av. Denis-Séméria (☎ 04-93-76-03-97). Overlooking the harbor of St-Paul-du-Cap, this is a first-class choice on the cape. Reservations essential. Elegantly casual. MC, V. Closed Nov–Mar. Moderate.

Voile d'Or, 31 av. Jean-Mermoz (☎ 04-93-01-13-13). Sited at this deluxe hotel, this restaurant serves classic cookery that hasn't changed much since the days of the moguls who flocked to Cap Ferrat after the war. The cuisine was good back then, and it's good today, though evocative of another time. Lunch is best on the canopied terrace, whereas chicly dressed evening diners head for the more formal restaurant. Provençal specialties share billing with international specialties. Sea bass appeared recently with two kinds of caviar and the saddle of Provençal lamb is delicately perfumed with herbs from the Alps. Reservations essential. Jacket/tie required. No credit cards. Closed Nov to mid-Mar. Expensive.

Accommodations

Brise Marine, 5 av. Jean-Mermoz, 06230 St-Jean-Cap-Ferrat (☎ 04-93-76-04-36; fax 04-93-76-11-49). This is a clean, friendly, unpretentious villa with lovely views (try room 3) and reasonable prices—reasonable, that is, for Cap Ferrat. 16 rms with bath. Facilities: restaurant. MC, V. Closed Nov–Jan. Moderate.

Grand Hôtel du Cap Ferrat, 71 bd. Général-de-Gaulle, 06290 St-Jean-Cap-Ferrat (☎ 04-93-76-50-50; fax 04-93-76-04-52). This is a grand but modernized resort standing back from the cliffs in isolated splendor at the southern tip of the cape. A walk across sweeping lawns takes you to the funicular, which leads down to the seaside pool. Anyone can use the pool for a fee (a plus for day visitors, a minus for guests), so if you're only passing through, bring your swimsuit and stay for lunch. The restaurant serves good classical French cuisine. 59 rms with bath; 11 suites. Facilities: restaurant, pool, private beach, tennis. AE, DC, MC, V. Very Expensive.

Voile d'Or, av. Jean-Mermoz, 06230 St-Jean-Cap-Farrat (☎ 04-93-01-13-13; fax 04-93-76-11-17). "The Golden Sail" is a smaller, smarter, younger hotel overlooking the pleasure boats in the colorful harbor of St-Jean-du-Cap. It has a private pool and is near the boutiques, restaurants, and antiques shops of an active but generally unspoiled seaside village. The sophistication of the clientele is reflected in the tasteful furnishings: white marble floors, chenille spreads, pastel-colored walls covered with hand-loomed tapestries. 50 rms with bath; 5 suites. Facilities: restaurant, pool. No credit cards. Closed Nov to mid-Mar. Very Expensive.

CANNES

Cosmopolitan, sophisticated, smart—these are words that describe the liveliest and most flourishing city on the Riviera: **Cannes.** It's a resort town (unlike Nice, which is a city) that exists only for the pleasure of its guests. It's a tasteful and expensive breeding ground for yuppies, a

AFTER DARK ALONG THE RIVIERA

Cannes

If you want to find out what Cannes is all about, splurge with a drink at the **Hôtel Carlton Bar,** 58 La Croisette (☎ 04-93-06-40-06) after 9pm. From 11pm nightly to dawn, you can dance at **Jane's,** in the Gray d'Albion hotel, 38 rue des Serbes (☎ 04-92-99-79-79). A rival club, **Le Blitz,** 22 rue Jean-Macé (☎ 04-93-39-31-31), offers a band downstairs, with funk music upstairs. Le Blitz is open nightly until dawn. If you're gay, head for **Disco 7,** 7 rue Rouguière (☎ 04-93-39-1036), which presents a sexy spectacle nightly at 11pm.

There's gambling at **Le Casino du Carlton,** La Croisette (☎ 04-93-38-12-11), which also contains the best nightclub in Cannes, **Le Jimmy's** (☎ 04-93-68-00-07), decorated in shades of red.

Nice

The hot spot is aptly named **Disco Inferno,** 10 Cité du Parc (☎ 04-93-80-49-84), a nightclub that's a continuous party until dawn (go after 9pm). The most active dance club in the center of town is **L'Ambassade,** 18 rue de Congrès (☎ 04-93-88-88-87). The hottest gay club is **Le Blue Boy,** 29 rue Alphonse-Karr (☎ 04-93-44-68-24).

St-Tropez

Les Caves du Roy, in the Hôtel Byblos, avenue Signac (☎ 04-94-56-68-00), is the resort's leading

(continues)

sybaritic haven for those who believe that life is short and that sin has something to do with the absence of a tan.

Whatever you'd want to buy in Paris you can find in Cannes, and at about the same price. There are hair-raising salons where trendies get their cuts and boutiques for the model man and woman. There are frozen kiwi parlors and late-night clubs for Arab princes, playgirls, and pretty boys. Everywhere—along the coast, high up in the hills—are restaurants where chefs make an art of arranging asparagus and peas. The day's catch is swaddled in ice outside bistros where film stars sit at tables covered with red-checkered cloths, trying not to get oyster juice on their black ties or down their cleavage. Couples sip wine at open-air cafes behind the beach. There are few historic monuments, but people come here for the present, not the past.

Picture a long, narrow beach. Stretching along it is a broad elegant promenade called **La Croisette** bordered by palm trees and flowers. At one end of the promenade is the modern Festival Hall, a summer casino, and an old harbor where pleasure boats are moored. At the other is a winter casino and a modern harbor for some of the most luxurious yachts in the world. All along the promenade are cafes, boutiques, and luxury hotels like the Carlton and the Majestic. Speedboats and water-skiers glide by; little waves lick the beach, lined with bronzed bodies. Behind the promenade lies the town, filled with shops, restaurants, and hotels; and behind the town are the hills with the villas of the very rich.

The first thing to do is stroll along La Croisette, stopping at cafes and boutiques along the way. Near the eastern end (turning left as you face the water), before you reach the new port, is the **Parc de la Roserie,** where some 14,000 roses nod their heads. Walking west takes you past the **Palais des Festivals** (Festival Hall), where the famous film festival is held each May. Just past the hall is a square called Place du Général-de-Gaulle. On your left is the old port, where boats leave for the Iles de Lérins. If you continue straight beyond the port on allés de la Liberté, you'll reach a tree-shaded area where flowers are sold in the morning, boules is played in the afternoon, and a flea market is held on Saturday. If instead of continuing straight from the square you turn inland, you'll quickly come to rue Meynadier. Turn left. This is the old main street, which has many 18th-century houses—now boutiques and specialty food shops, where you can buy exotic foods and ship them home.

traditional nightclub. Both gays and straights dance the night away at **Le Pigeonnier,** 13 rue de la Ponche (☎ **04-94-97-36-85**). **Chez Maggi,** 7 rue Sybille (☎ **04-94-97-16-12**), has the best draft beer in town and often live music. One of the largest nightclubs is **Le Papagayo,** in the Résidence du Nouveau Port, rue Gambetta (☎ **04-94-97-07-56**), filled nightly with some of the most attractive men and women in the Mediterranean.

TAKE A BREAK

Be sure to stop at no. 53 for ice cream; your best bet is La Marmite du Diable — a "devil's dish" laced with cocoa and nougat.

Rue Meynadier leads to a covered market, **Marché Forville.** Ahead of you is **Le Suquet,** the fortress in the center of medieval Cannes, and narrow, steep streets leading to a tower with a lovely view.

You, like St-Honorat almost 1,500 years ago, may want to visit the peaceful **Iles de Lérins** (Lerins Islands) to escape the crowds. The ferry takes 15 minutes to Ste-Marguerite, 30 minutes to St-Honorat (call **04-93-39-11-82** for information).

Ste-Marguerite, the larger of the two, is an island of wooded hills, with a tiny main street lined with fishers' houses. You can enjoy peaceful walks through a forest of enormous eucalyptus trees and parasol pines. Paths wind through a dense undergrowth of tree heathers, rosemary, and thyme. The main attraction is the dank cell in **Fort Royal** where the "Man in the Iron Mask" was imprisoned (1687–98) before going to the Bastille, where he died in 1703. The mask that he always wore was in fact made of velvet. Was he the illegitimate brother of Louis XIV or Louis XIII's son-in-law? No one knows.

St-Honorat is wilder but more tranquil. It was named for a hermit who came to escape his followers; but when he founded a monastery here in 410, his disciples followed and the monastery became one of the most powerful in all Christendom. A pope was among the pilgrims who came to walk barefoot around the island. It's still worth taking this 2-hour walk to the old fortified monastery, **Monastère de Lérins** (☎ 04-93-48-68-68), where noble Gothic arcades are arranged around a central courtyard. Next door to the "new" 19th-century monastery (open on request) is a shop where the monks sell handcrafts, lavender scent, and a home-brewed liqueur called Lerina. Admission 10F. Open daily 9am–noon and 2–4:45pm. High Mass at the abbey Sun 9:45am.

DINING

You may have great success with a classical or moderne meal, but your best bet is to stick with simply prepared seafood.

Au Bec Fin, 12 rue du 24-Août (☎ 04-93-38-35-86). Here the owner and his son turn out simple, homemade dishes—thick steaks, grilled fish with fennel, salad Niçoise, homemade tarts—in a cheerful crowded restaurant near the train station. Reservations advised. Casual. AE, DC, MC, V. Closed Sat dinner, Sun, and Dec 20–Jan 20. Inexpensive.

Félix, 63 La Croisette (☎ 04-93-94-00-61). This place is popular with film folk and with those who don't mind paying for the ambiance of La Croisette. Reservations advised. Elegantly casual. AE, MC, V. Closed 1 week in Mar. Expensive.

La Mirabelle, 24 rue St-Antoine (☎ 04-93-38-72-75). This is a popular bistro in the old quarter. The limited menu includes pastas with John Dory, salad with foie gras and honey, and homemade sorbets. Reservations advised. Jacket/tie required. MC, V. Closed Dec 1–20, Feb 1–15, and Tues. Expensive.

La Poêle d'Or, 23 rue des Etats-Unis (☎ 04-93-39-77-65). This is very plain, perhaps a bit somber, but it has a solid reputation for dishes like mousseline of trout and chicken in morel-cream sauce. Reservations essential. Elegant. AE, DC, MC, V. Closed July 1–7, Feb, Sun night, Mon, and Tues lunch. Expensive.

Le Festival, 52 La Croisette (☎ 04-93-38-04-81). Le Festival is busy and lively—exactly what you'd expect from a restaurant across from the Palais des Festivals. Lunchtime is best. Specialties include salmon à la menthe and pastries. Reservations essential. Elegant. AE, DC, MC, V. Closed mid-Nov to Dec 23. Moderate.

Mère Besson, 13 rue des Frères-Pradignac (☎ 04-93-39-59-24). This crowded, fashionable Provençal restaurant serves regional specialties. Reservations required. Casual. AE, DC, MC, V. Closed Sun except July–Aug. Moderate.

Part of the "Cannes experience" is to drive out of town for dinner, to the hills or to other resorts along the coast. Here are some possibilities.

In **Golfe-Juan** (about 15 minutes east of Cannes on the coastal road to Antibes):

Chez Tétou, avenue des Frères-Roustan (☎ 04-93-63-71-16). This friendly, informal restaurant has wood tables on a lovely terrace. The sole meunière and bouillabaisse are outstanding. Reservations advised. Elegant. AE, DC, MC, V. Closed Oct 30–Dec 20 and Mar. Very Expensive.

In **Mougins** (a hill town about 15 minutes north of Cannes on the road to Grasse):

Bistro de Mougins, place du Commandant-Lamy (☎ 04-93-75-78-34). This bistro features such regional dishes as beet pie, sardines with mint, stuffed rabbit, guinea hen with cabbage, and a good selection of local cheeses. The low prices keep the restaurant crowded. Reservations advised in midsummer. Casual. MC, V. Closed mid-Nov to mid-Dec and lunch July–Aug. Moderate.

L'Amandier, place du Commandant-Lamy (☎ 04-93-90-00-91). The chef and the old-olive-mill ambiance are the same as at Le Moulin de Mougins, but the prices are lower. The modern menu includes a creamy mussel-and-oyster soup with saffron, crayfish bisque, sea bass, rabbit pâté, farm cheeses, and homemade tarts. Reservations advised. Jacket/tie required. AE, DC, MC, V. Expensive.

Le Moulin de Mougins, Notre-Dame-de-Vie (☎ 04-93-75-78-24). This is one of the best-known restaurants in the country, where you can expect patrician treatment—and prices. An inventive cuisine moderne is served in a converted olive mill, with such specialties as lobster fricassée, escalope of fresh salmon, and cold wild-strawberry soufflé. Reservations required. Jacket/tie required. AE, DC, MC, V. Closed Jan 8–18, Feb 12–Mar 14, and Mon except from July 15–Aug 31. Very Expensive.

Le Relais à Mougins, 32 place du Commandant-Lamy (☎ 04-93-90-03-47). This is another favorite (though some say it rests too heavily on its reputation). Mougins is a lovely old town; consider coming here for lunch and try the good-value set menu. Reservations essential. Elegant. MC, V. Closed Sun night, Mon except in July and Aug. Expensive.

ACCOMMODATIONS

Because Cannes exists for its tourists, its hotels in season aren't cheap; expect to pay 800F to 1,600F or a lot more a night for a room for two on or near La Croisette. If you're on a budget, the best bets are the smaller hotels closer to the train station.

Beau Séjour, 5 rue Fauvettes, 06400 Cannes (☎ 04-93-39-63-00; fax 04-92-98-64-66). This hotel has its own pool and garden not far from the beach. 45 rms with bath. Facilities: restaurant, pool. AE, DC, MC, V. Closed Nov to mid-Dec. Expensive.

Beverly, 14 rue Hoche, 06400 Cannes (☎ 04-93-39-10-66; fax 04-92-98-65-63). Between La Croisette and the train station, the Beverly is a good value. 18 rms with bath. AE, MC, V. Closed Dec to mid-Jan. Moderate.

Cheval Blanc, 3 rue Guy-de-Maupassant, 06400 Cannes (☎ 04-93-39-88-60; fax 04-93-38-01-50). The Cheval Blanc is back from the beach but relatively low-priced. 16 rms with bath. MC, V. Moderate.

Gray d'Albion, 38 rue des Serbes, 06400 Cannes (☎ 04-92-99-79-79; fax 04-93-99-26-10). The Gray d'Albion provides free videos, bathroom phones, and other state-of-the-art amenities. The restaurant, **Le Royal Gray,** is one of the best in town, with an imaginative modern menu that includes rack of lamb with fresh herbs, salmon salad marinated in ginger on a bed of vegetables, prawn salad with orange dressing, and duck aiguillette with apple sauce. For dessert, succumb to the hot walnut cake. 172 rms with bath; 14 suites. Facilities: three restaurants, dance club, private beach. AE, DC, MC, V. Very Expensive.

Hôtel Carlton International, 58 La Croisette, 06400 Cannes (☎ 800/327-0200 or 04-93-06-40-06; fax 04-93-06-40-25). The Carlton has been modernized but still retains the feeling of a luxurious belle-epoque hotel. The west wing is quieter, with the best views. 326 rms with bath; 28 suites. Facilities: restaurants, bar, terrace, private beach. AE, DC, MC, V. Main restaurant closed Tues, Wed, and Nov–Christmas. Very Expensive.

Hôtel le Fouquet, 2 rond-point Duboys-d'Angers, 06400 Cannes (☎ 04-93-38-75-81; fax 04-92-98-03-39). This is a small boutique hotel that Parisians view as a secret address in Cannes. Though its boudoir decor and dainty design may be too "precious" for more masculine tastes, it has a devoted following. Set several blocks from the beach, it offers rooms that are airy—decorated in bold colors with a loggia. There's no restaurant. 10 rms with bath. AE, DC, MC, V. Closed Oct 30–Mar 20. Moderate.

Majestic, 14 La Croisette, 06400 Cannes (☎ 04-92-98-77-00; fax 04-93-38-97-90). The Majestic is another of the grand old hotels, perhaps just a notch below the Carlton. There's a great heated seawater pool in a palm grove. Ask for one of the renovated rooms. 263 rms with bath; 24 suites. Facilities: restaurant, pool, private beach. AE, DC, MC, V. Closed Nov 25–Dec 20. Very Expensive.

Novotel-Montfleury, 25 av. Beauséjour, 06400 Cannes (☎ 04-93-68-91-50; fax 04-93-38-37-08). The Novotel has 10 tennis courts, two heated pools, and two restaurants on a 9-acre hillside estate with great views. Its remoteness will be a plus or a minus, depending on your priorities. This is one of the most upscale of all Novotels in the chain, geared more for holidaymakers than business travelers. 181 rms with bath; 1 suite. Facilities: restaurants, two pools, tennis, ice-skating. AE, DC, MC, V. Expensive.

Victoria, 122 rue d'Antibes, 06400 Cannes (☎ 04-93-99-36-36; fax 04-93-38-03-91). The Victoria nestles among the fancy boutiques on the main shopping street. There's a garden with a small pool and stylish rooms with electrically controlled shutters and other amenities. 25 rms with bath. Facilities: pool. AE, DC, MC, V. Closed Nov–Dec. Expensive.

ON TO CAP D'ANTIBES

Strictly speaking, Cap d'Antibes refers to the southern tip of the cape, but it has come to mean the entire peninsula, including even the resort towns of Antibes and Juan-les-Pins. Though the three will be discussed together here, be sure to distinguish among them, for each has its own character and clientele. On the eastern side of the cape is the village of Antibes, which boasts a Picasso Museum and, like Nice, a charming old section with restaurants, antiques shops, and boutiques. You'll want to visit Antibes but probably not stay, for it has no memorable hotels. On the western side of the cape, closer to Cannes, is the village of Juan-les-Pins, which has a shoreline backed by ferroconcrete high-rises where French families spend their 2-week vacations.

Visitors under 30 will enjoy the crowded public beaches and the neon nightlife, but others may have less reason to linger. The place to stay is on the cape itself—a lush and peaceful garden with sumptuous villas, guest houses, and hotels. Cannes is perhaps 20 minutes away, so you can take advantage of everything the city has to offer and then return here at night. If you're single or into crowds, stay in Cannes. But if you want to be alone with yourself or with someone you want to be alone with, look no farther than Cap d'Antibes.

CAP D'ANTIBES, ANTIBES & JUAN-LES-PINS
CAP D'ANTIBES

The main reason to visit **Cap d'Antibes,** even if you're not staying here, is to enjoy the view at Pointe Bacon; to walk through the Jardin Thuret; to have lunch or a swim at the exclusive Hôtel du Cap; and to imagine yourself living in the palatial estates discreetly hidden behind hedges and trees.

Follow D2559 along the eastern shore to **Pointe Bacon,** where you should be able to see as far east as Nice and Cap Ferrat. Continue south along the eastern shore of the cape on boulevard de Bacon, which merges with boulevard de la Garoupe. At the end of the boulevard, turn left to visit the Hôtel du Cap d'Antibes (see "Accommodations") or turn right on boulevard F.-Meilland and right again on chemin des Nielles to the top of the hill, where the road ends. There's a great view here, plus a church, La Garoupe, which has two aisles, each built at a different time and dedicated to a different saint.

Return down chemin des Nielles and make the first right on boulevard du Cap to the **Jardin Thuret.** Created by a botanist in 1856, the garden contains exotic cacti, palms, mimosas, and some 141 species of eucalyptus. Free admission. Open Mon–Fri 8am–12:30pm and 2–5:30pm.

Continue straight on boulevard du Cap and make a left on chemin des Sables. Bear right and return to Cannes, about 11 kilometers (7 miles) west on N7.

Dining

Many day-trippers have their limousines take them to lunch at the **Eden Roc,** the restaurant of the exclusive Hôtel du Cap (see below). The menu is moderne.

Bacon, bd. de Bacon (☎ 04-93-61-50-02). This restaurant is near Pointe Bacon, which you'll pass as you drive down the east shore of the cape. The bouillabaisse is, some say, the best on the coast. Seafood dishes are served on a terrace with a lovely view. Specialties include steamed bass, prawn salad, and grilled mullet. Reservations essential. Jacket/tie required. AE, DC, MC, V. Closed Mon lunch (except July–Aug) and Nov–Feb 14. Very Expensive.

Accommodations

Hôtel du Cap d'Antibes, bd. Kennedy, 06601 Antibes (☎ 04-93-61-39-01; fax 04-93-67-76-04). This is the Riviera's best known and most expensive resort. The world's elite stay in this Second Empire–style resort, which is said to have a staff-to-guest ratio of one-to-one. The celebrity guest list is legendary, though often reading like "Who Was Who." Charles Graves tells in his book *The Azure Coast* how George Raft walked down from the hotel to the pool with Norma Shearer, passing hairy-legged Charles Boyer. While Marlene Dietrich was checking out, Edward G. Robinson and Erich Maria Remarque were sitting at the bar— Robinson looking at himself, Remarque just looking glum. F. Scott Fitzgerald stayed here with Zelda and is said to have used the hotel as his model in *Tender Is the Night.* That said, it should be added that the atmosphere today is a shade self-conscious. Day-trippers can pay to use the pool—great for them but not for guests. A child would be an anomaly here—unless he were dressed in white, with knee-high socks. There's no library, no sequestered bar, no place to relax except at the pool and in the privacy of your room. 130 rms with bath; 10 suites. Facilities: restaurant, tennis, pool. No credit cards. Closed mid-Oct to mid-Apr. Very Expensive.

Hôtel Levant, bd. de la Garoupe, 06160 Cap d'Antibes (☎ 04-92-93-72-99; fax 04-92-93-72-60). This rectangular motel-like building sits by the sea. It has no special charm but is clean and new and very friendly. 27 rms with bath. Facilities: private beach. V. Closed Oct–Easter. Expensive.

La Gardiole, chemin de la Garoupe, 06600 Cap d'Antibes (☎ 04-93-61-35-03; fax 04-93-67-61-87). This hotel has simple, quiet rooms among the pines, away from the sea. 21 rms with bath. Facilities: restaurant. AE, DC, MC, V. Closed Nov–Feb. Moderate.

ANTIBES

What makes a visit to **Antibes** worthwhile are the picturesque old streets, lined with shops and cafes, and the Picasso Museum.

The **Musée Picasso,** place du Château (☎ 04-92-90-54-20), is housed in a Grimaldi castle overlooking the sea. Picasso had part of the castle at his disposal when he arrived on the Riviera in 1946. His output was extraordinary—some 145 works in 6 months; and most of what you'll see was produced during his first season here. Particularly noteworthy are his ceramics from Vallauris and his joyful Antibes paintings, inspired by the Mediterranean's marine and mythological life. Admission 20F adults, 10F children and seniors. Open Tues–Sun: July–Sept 10am–noon and 2–6pm; Oct–June 10am–noon and 2–5pm.

Just north of the museum is the **Church of the Immaculate Conception,** which has a wood crucifix from 1447 in the choir and an early 16th-century altarpiece by Louis Bréa in the south transept.

From either the church or the museum walk inland one block and turn left to the colorful marketplace at **cours Masséna.** Ahead is rue de la Touraque. Spend an hour in this area, strolling through the streets of the old town, among the antiques and pastry shops.

Antibes is the rose capital of Europe. Some 250 hectares (625 acres) of carnations, tulips, and gladioli grow here, too. Anyone who loves color will want to visit the **flower market** near pont Vauban (Vauban Bridge).

Dining

Auberge Provençale, 61 place Nationale (☎ **04-93-34-13-24**). This restaurant is on a lovely old square behind the Picasso Museum. Specialties include smoked trout, seafood, and beef filet. Reservations advised. Elegant. AE, DC, MC, V. Closed Jan, Mon, and Tues lunch. Moderate.

La Bonne Auberge, Quartier de la Brague (☎ **04-93-33-36-65**). North of Antibes on N7, near La Brague, this place is expensive but is one of the most famous restaurants on the coast, though no longer enjoying the stellar reputation it once did. Dinner, a blend of classic and moderne, is served either in a Provençal dining room or on a flowery terrace. Specialties include lobster soup, artichoke salad with lobster, and grilled bass (loup). Reservations required. Jacket/tie required. MC, V. Closed end of Oct to Dec 5 and Mon in winter. Expensive.

Le Romantic, 5 rue Rostan (☎ **04-93-34-59-39**). Le Romantic lives up to its name in its regional setting of time-worn beams and hewn stone walls. The prices are reasonable, particularly for the fixed-price menu. Try the pork medallions with cranberries, fresh catch of the day (often red mullet), or regional cheeses. The wine list is limited but select. Reservations advised. Casual. AE, DC, MC, V. Closed Nov 25–Dec 9 and lunch June 15–Sept 5. Moderate.

Les Vieux Murs, 130 promenade Amiral-de-Grasse (☎ **04-93-34-06-73**). This restaurant sits on the ramparts close to the sea. The decor — stucco walls, arched ceilings — is regional. The classical menu includes fish soup and lobster Thermidor. Reservations advised. Elegant. AE, MC, V. Moderate.

L'Oursin, 16 rue de la République (☎ **04-93-34-13-46**). On the edge of the old town, L'Oursin is a crowded family restaurant with little atmosphere, but it has a solid reputation for fresh seafood and reasonable prices. Reservations advised. Casual. MC, V. Closed Aug, Sun eve, and Mon. Moderate.

JUAN-LES-PINS

Juan-les-Pins splashed into life in the 1920s, thanks to its mile-long beach (an improvement on the man-made beach at Cannes) and amenities. The ambiance is (with two notable exceptions) strictly fast food. If you're alone and don't want to be, hang out on the beach and wait for night, when the bar and disco lights outshine the stars.

Dining & Accommodations

The two luxury-class hotels in Juan-les-Pins have no trouble filling their rooms in-season, but it's not easy to understand why. What use is elegance in clubland?

Belles Rives, 33 bd. Edouard-Baudoin, 06160 Juan-les-Pins (☎ 04-93-61-02-79; fax 04-93-67-43-51). Here the rooms are rather small and basic, but the location is lovely, with a stone terrace overlooking the harbor. 41 rms with bath; 4 suites. Facilities: restaurant, private beach. AE, MC, V. Closed Oct 8–Mar 31. Very Expensive.

Eden, 16 av. Louis-Gallet, 06160 Juan-les-Pins (☎ 04-93-61-05-20; fax 04-92-93-05-31). Eden is located between the train station and the beach and is priced lower. 17 rms, some with bath. No credit cards. Closed Nov 6–Dec 26. Moderate.

Juana, av. Gallice, 06160 Juan-les-Pins (☎ 04-93-61-08-70; fax 04-93-61-76-60). Juana is more tasteful than Belles Rives. Though hidden behind hedges, the pool sits at the edge of a busy road near the center of town. Juan-les-Pins is only 10 minutes from Cannes by train (20 by car), so you may want to come for dinner at the **Terrasse Restaurant,** which enjoys a first-class reputation. 45 rms with bath; 5 suites. Facilities: restaurant, bar, pool. MC, V. Closed Nov–Mar. Very Expensive.

ST-TROPEZ

There's only one main road from Ste-Maxime to **St-Tropez,** and in season the 14-kilometer (8.5-mile) trip can take 2 hours. If you're planning to drive down from Cannes for the day, be sure to leave in the early morning and return in the early afternoon or late at night. Stick to A8 and avoid the coast as long as possible. The worst time to come is on summer weekends, when you're competing with the rest of France. Your best bet is to take a hydrofoil from Cannes or St-Raphaël and avoid the road altogether. If you want to combine trips to the Estérel and St-Tropez, drive southwest along the coast from Cannes to St-Raphaël and take the hydrofoil from there. Make arrangements through any travel agency or hotel. Cabs in St-Tropez are available by calling 04-94-97-05-27. For bus information, call 04-94-97-88-51.

Old money never came to St-Tropez, but Brigitte Bardot did. She came with director Roger Vadim in 1956 to film *And God Created Woman,* and the resort has never been the same. Actually, the village was "discovered" by writer Guy de Maupassant and painter Paul Signac, who came in 1892 and brought his friends—Matisse, Bonnard, and others. What attracted them was the pure, radiant light and the serenity and colors of the landscape. Colette moved into a village here between the wars and contributed to its notoriety. When the cinema people staked their claim in the 1950s, St-Tropez became known as St-Trop (*trop* in French means "too much").

Anything associated with the past seems either detestable or absurd in St-Tropez, so you may not want to hear the story of how it got its name. In A.D. 68, a Roman soldier named Torpes from Pisa was beheaded for professing his Christian faith in the presence of Nero. The headless body was put in a boat between a dog and a cock and drifted out to sea. The body eventually floated ashore, perfectly preserved, still watched over by the animals. The buried remains became a place of pilgrimage, which by the 4th century was called St-Tropez. In the late 15th century, under the Genovese, it became a small independent republic.

Nowadays, the beaches are filled with every imaginable type of human animal: aggressively cheerful volleyball players searching for one-night relationships, supergirls with Cartier bracelets, golden boys with big dogs, aspiring Bardots, college girls with organic faces, middle-aged men with mirrored shades, bare-breasted mothers with children and dogs. The atmosphere is part Benetton, part Tarzan-and-Jane. In summer the population swells from 7,000 to 65,000.

Off-season is the time to come, but even in summer you can find reasons to stay. The soft sandy beaches are the best on the coast. Take an early-morning stroll along the harbor or down the narrow medieval streets—the rest of the world will still be comatose from the night before—and you'll see just how pretty St-Tropez is, with its tiny squares and its pastel-colored houses bathed in light. There's a weekend's worth of trendy boutiques to explore (to be delighted by or shocked at) and many cute cafes where you can sit under colored awnings sipping wine and feeling very French. The restored harborfront has a reputable art museum. Travel 5 minutes from town and you'll be in a green world of vineyards and fields, where you'll see nothing more lascivious than a butterfly fluttering around some chestnut leaves or a grapevine clinging to a farmhouse. Above the fertile fields are mountains crowned with medieval villages, where you can come at dusk for wild strawberry tarts and fabulous views. Perhaps it's the soft light, perhaps it's the rich fields and faded pastels, but nowhere else along the coast will you experience so completely the magic of Provence.

TAKE A BREAK

*The food at the **Café des Arts**, place Carnot (☎ **04-94-97-02-25**), may be ordinary, but the cafe is a popular place to sit and feel part of the in-crowd. Closed Oct–Mar.*

Near the waterfront is the **Musée de l'Annonciade,** place Georges-Grammont (☎ 04-94-97-04-01), a collection of works by impressionists and postimpressionists who loved St-Tropez: Maurice de Vlaminck, Braque, Seurat, Bonnard, Dufy, Rouault, and others. Admission 30F adults, 15F children. Open Wed–Mon: June–Sept 10am–noon and 3–7pm; Oct and Dec–May 10am–noon and 2–6pm.

You may enjoy a trip through **Port-Grimaud,** a modern architect's idea of a Provençal fishing village cum Venice, built out into the gulf for the yachting crowd—each house with its own mooring. Particularly appealing are the harmonious pastel colors, which have weathered nicely, and the graceful bridges over the canals.

From St-Tropez take D93 south about 11 kilometers (7 miles) to the market town of **Ramatuelle.** The ancient houses are huddled together on the slope of a rocky spur 130 meters (440 ft.) above the sea. The central square has a 17th-century church and a huge 300-year-old elm. Surrounding the square are narrow twisting streets with medieval archways and vaulted passages.

From Ramatuelle, follow the signs to the village of **Gassin,** about 3 kilometers (2 miles) away. The ride is lovely, through vineyards and woods, and takes you over the highest point of the peninsula (320m/1,070 ft.), where you can stop and enjoy a splendid view. The perched village of Gassin, with its venerable houses and 12th-century Romanesque church, has somehow managed to maintain its medieval appearance. The best time to visit is in late afternoon, when the shadows deepen and the tourists have gone home. Find yourself a table at an outdoor cafe, order a fruit tart, and watch the sunlight turn the fields to gold. From Gassin, return to St-Tropez or continue back along the coast to Ste-Maxime and Cannes.

DINING

St-Tropez has many charming restaurants but no great ones. If celebrities like Catherine Deneuve leave the privacy of their villas, it's to dine in Le Mas de Chastelas or Le Byblos (see "Accommodations"). Your best bets are the restaurants big on atmosphere that specialize in fresh fish. The busy waterfront is lined with small restaurants where you can sit in tiny back rooms or people-watch in front, beneath colorful awnings.

Le Café des Arts, place Carnot 1 (☎ 04-94-97-02-25). In the quieter old part of town is where you can join the locals. The fixed-price menu here includes zucchini, stuffed eggplant, veal in wine sauce, grilled fish, and bouillabaisse. Reservations advised. Casually elegant. V. Closed early Oct to late Mar. Moderate.

L'Escale, 9 quai Jean-Jaurès (☎ 04-94-97-00-63). This is the best and busiest of the waterfront restaurants—try the bouillabaisse. Families come at 8pm, singles at 10pm. Reservations advised. Casual. AE, MC, V. Moderate.

Les Mouscardins, 16 rue Portalet (☎ 04-94-97-01-53). This is a busy Provençal-type restaurant in the old city, serving such local favorites as bouillabaisse and grilled sea bass. Reservations essential. Casually elegant. AE, MC, V. Closed Nov 1–Mar 15. Expensive.

Le Girelier, quai Jean-Jaurès (☎ 04-94-97-03-87). Near the port, Le Girelier offers fish at reasonable prices. Reservations not required. Casual. AE, DC, MC, V. Closed mid-Jan to early Mar. Moderate.

Pizzeria La Romana, chemin des Conquêtes (☎ 04-94-97-13-16). This popular eatery has a more ambitious menu and higher prices than its name implies. The fresh pasta is tops. Reservations advised in midsummer. Casual. MC, V. Expensive.

ACCOMMODATIONS

Byblos, av. Paul-Signac, 83990 St-Tropez (☎ 04-94-56-68-00; fax 04-94-56-68-01). The Byblos is a smart, flashy hotel-village where the gold-chain set should feel right at home. The look is New York Casbah, with Persian carpets on the dining-room ceiling, a genuine leopard-skin bar, raw stone and brick walls, and lots of heavy damask and hammered brass. It's a real conversation piece, with an imaginative use of space. 47 rms with bath; 55 suites. Facilities: restaurant, pool, sauna, exercise room, dance club, nightclub. AE, DC, MC, V. Closed Oct 15–Easter. Very Expensive.

Hôtel Ermitage, av. Paul-Signac, 83990 St-Tropez (☎ 04-94-97-52-33; fax 04-94-97-10-43). This hotel is next door to the Byblos, but the ambiance is more subdued. It's one of the few hotels with a view of the town. 26 rms with bath. AE, DC. Moderate.

Hôtel Le Levant, routes des Salins, 83990 St-Tropez (☎ 04-94-97-33-33; fax 04-94-97-76-13). Just out of town, the Levant has well-appointed modern rooms, a heated pool, and a beautiful garden. The hotel lies near the extreme tip of the peninsula of St-Tropez, near Brigitte Bardot's house. To get here requires navigating through the center of the resort's traffic and congestion. Once you're here, it's very appealing, though it no longer maintains a restaurant (snack lunches are served beside the pool). 28 rms with bath. Facilities: pool. AE, DC, MC, V. Closed mid-Oct to Easter. Expensive.

Le Mas de Chastelas, rte. de Gassin, Quartier Bertaud, 83580 St-Tropez (☎ 04-94-56-71-71; fax 04-94-56-71-56). You'll find this renovated 17th-century manor house in a rural setting just outside of town; it boasts heated pools, tennis courts, and sophisticated dining. The year-round hotel contains 12 rooms in the original manor house, plus 33 modern duplex units in the surrounding park. 45 rms with bath. Facilities: restaurant, two pools. AE, DC, MC, V. Very Expensive.

Lou Troupelen, chemin des Vendanges, 83990 St-Tropez (☎ 04-94-97-44-88; fax 04-94-97-41-76). This is a modernized farmhouse with gardens, not far from the beach or town. 45 rms with bath. AE, DC, MC, V. Closed Nov 4–Mar 28. Moderate.

Ponche, 3 rue des Remparts, 83990 St-Tropez (☎ 04-94-97-02-53; fax 04-94-97-02-53). This old but thoroughly renovated inn has a chic but peaceful terrace restaurant serving such specialties as saffron mussel soup, giant shrimp in tarragon sauce, lamb stew, and homemade lemon pie. 18 rms with bath. Facilities: restaurant. AE, MC, V. Closed Nov–Mar 15. Moderate.

There are several small, family-run hotels among the farms and vineyards along the road to Tahiti Beach—one of the most tranquil settings on the Riviera:

La Figuière, rte. de Tahiti, 83350 Ramatuelle (☎ **04-94-97-18-21;** fax 04-94-97-68-48). This hotel is the only one with dining facilities. 42 rms with bath. Facilities: restaurant, pool, tennis. MC, V. Closed Oct 8–Apr 3. Expensive.

St-Vincent, rte. de Tahiti, 83350 Ramatuelle (☎ **04-94-97-36-90;** fax 04-94-54-80-37). St-Vincent is pleasant and friendly, with vineyards outside the door. 16 rms with bath. Facilities: pool. MC, V. Closed Oct 16–Mar 22. Very Expensive.

EXCURSIONS FROM NICE & CANNES

Here are some of the most worthwhile excursions from the Nice area (including Beaulieu and Cap Ferrat) and the Cannes area (including Cap d'Antibes).

PEILLON

Peillon and Monte Carlo are both about 20 kilometers (12 miles) east of Nice and can be combined in a single excursion from Cannes or Nice. Monte Carlo is along the coast; Peillon is about 10 kilometers (6 miles) inland. From Nice take D2204 and turn right on D21; turn right again, up the mountain to Peillon. If you're returning to Nice, retrace your path. If you're continuing to Monte Carlo, return to D21. Turn right, then turn right again on D53 to the medieval town of Peille. Continue south on D53 to Monaco.

TAKE A BREAK

*Stop for lunch or dinner at the charming **Auberge de la Madone,** Peillon 06440, L'Escarène (☎ **04-93-79-91-17;** fax 04-93-79-99-36). The ideal arrangement is to arrive in the late afternoon and spend the night at this lovely family-run auberge (inn), far away from the traffic and heat along the coast.*

To picture Peillon, close your eyes and imagine a fortified medieval town perched on a craggy mountaintop more than 300 meters (1,000 ft.) above the sea. Of all the perched villages along the Riviera, Peillon is the most spectacular and the least spoiled. Unchanged since the Middle Ages, the village has only a few narrow streets and many steps and covered alleys. There's really nothing to do here but look—which is why the tour buses stay away. Some 50 families live in Peillon (including professionals from Paris who think it's chic summering in a genuine medieval village and artists who sincerely want to escape the craziness of the world below). Call at the studio of a very talented French sculptor, visit the **White Penitents' Chapel** (key available at the Auberge), spend half an hour exploring the ancient streets, and then be on your way.

ROQUEBRUNE

If you haven't seen enough medieval towns, continue south on D53 (en route from Peillon to Monte Carlo) and take the Upper Corniche road to **Roquebrune.** From here, head south to Monaco.

The ancient town of Roquebrune is spread out along the slopes. Its shops are filled with the wares of painters and artisans. The **Carolingian castle** was restored in the early 16th century by the Grimaldis. The keep is the oldest in Provence, with walls from 1.8 to 3.8 meters (6 to 13 ft.) thick.

Dining

Le Vistaero, in the Vista Palace, Grande Corniche (☎ **04-92-10-40-00**). Le Vistaero is about 3 kilometers (2 miles) from Roquebrune. A good deal of what you pay for is the fabulous view. Reservations essential. Elegant. AE, DC, MC, V. Closed Jan 4–Mar 14 and Nov 16–Dec 19. Expensive.

VILLEFRANCHE

Villefranche is on the coastal road (N98, the Lower Corniche), only 4 kilometers (2.5 miles) east of Nice on the way to Cap Ferrat and Beaulieu.

The harbor town of Villefranche, about 10 minutes from Nice or Cap Ferrat, is a miniature version of old Marseille, with steep narrow streets — one, rue Obscure, is an actual tunnel — winding down to the sea. The town is a stage set of brightly colored houses (orange with lime-green shutters, yellow with ice-blue shutters), the sort of place where *Fanny* could have been filmed. If you're staying in Nice, include Villefranche on a tour of Cap Ferrat.

If you arrive in late afternoon or early evening, you can see the Cocteau Chapel (see below), watch the sun set over the harbor as you take a walk around it (the sun turns the soft pastels to gold), and perhaps stay for dinner.

The 17th-century **St. Michael's Church** has a strikingly realistic Christ, carved of boxwood by an unknown convict. The **Chapel of St-Pierre-des-Pêcheurs,** known as the **Cocteau Chapel,** is a small Romanesque chapel once used for storing fishing nets, which the French writer/painter Jean Cocteau decorated in 1957. You walk through the flames of the Apocalypse (represented by staring eyes on either side of the door) and enter a room filled with frescoes of St. Peter, Gypsies, and the women of Villefranche. Open daily: July–Sept 10am–noon and 4–8:30pm; Oct–Mar 9:30am–noon; Apr–June 9:30am–noon and 3–7pm. Closed mid-Nov to mid-Dec.

Dining

La Campanette, 2 rue du Baron-de-Brès (☎ 04-93-01-79-98). Near St. Michael's Church, this inexpensive bistro boasts a turn-of-the-century decor, serving meals like fish ravioli in shellfish sauce, mussels in pastry with chicory, and chicken with clementines. Reservations unnecessary. Casual. AE, MC, V. Closed Sun late Sept to Easter and lunch. Moderate.

Mère Germaine, 7 quai Amiral-Courbet (☎ 04-93-01-71-39). This is the finest of a string of restaurants along the port, where you can dine on the best bouillabaisse in town while watching fishers repair their nets. It specializes in the freshest of seafood—none better than the grilled sea bass with fennel. Reservations advised. Casual. AE, MC, V. Closed Nov 18–Dec 19. Moderate.

CAGNES

From either Cannes or Nice take A8 to the Cagnes exit. There are actually three "Cagnes"—**Gros-de-Cagnes,** the seaside resort on the coast; **Cagnes Ville,** the modern commercial section; and **Haut-de-Cagnes,** the old town leading up to the castle. From Cagnes Ville follow the signs to the Renoir Museum.

The **Musée Renoir,** 19 chemin des Collettes (☎ 04-93-20-61-07), is at Les Collettes, the house Pierre-Auguste Renoir built for himself in 1908 and where he spent the last 12 years of his life. One of his well-known canvases, *Les Collettes Landscape,* is on view on the ground floor, and his bronze statue of *Venus* stands in the garden surrounded by fruit trees. But what you'll remember most are Renoir's studios, preserved just as he left them, and the gardens where he walked and painted. The sense of his presence is overwhelming as you stroll among the olive trees, gazing out across the fields through the most magical, luminescent light at the ancient town of Cagnes, rising in the distance like a fortress in a dream. Admission 20F adults, 10F children. Open May 1–Oct 14, daily 10am–noon and 2–5pm; Oct 15–29 and Dec–Apr, Wed–Mon 10am–noon and 2–5pm. Closed Oct 30–Nov 30.

If time is limited and you're planning to visit St-Paul-de-Vence and Tourrette-sur-Loup, consider seeing Haut-de-Cagnes only for Renoir's house and continuing to the Escoffier Museum in Villeneuve-Loubet (see below). Haut-de-Cagnes is a lovely old medieval village, but it doesn't have the craft shops you'll see in the other villages; and the streets are very steep and look down on a modern town. If you do decide to visit Haut-de-Cagnes (it's only a few minutes' drive from Renoir's house), park near the top of the town, at the Castle Museum.

The **Castle Museum,** 7 place Grimaldi (☎ 04-93-20-85-57), is a feudal castle restored by the Grimaldis when they lived here from the 14th century to the French Revolution, at which time it was looted and sold. The marble stairway, inspired by the one at Fontainebleau, leads to state rooms with ornately painted ceilings and notable collections of objets d'art and paintings. The throne room is most sumptuous. In the cellar the olive gets its due in the **Museum of the Olive Tree.** On the second floor is a **Museum of Modern Mediterranean Art.** Admission 20F adults, 10F students. Open Wed–Mon: June 15–Sept 30 10am–noon and 2–6pm; Oct 1–14 and Nov 16–June 14 10am–noon and 2–5pm. Closed Oct 15–Nov 15.

Dining

Josy-Jo, 8 place du Planastel, Haut-de-Cagnes (☎ **04-93-20-68-76**). Josy-Jo is well known for its regional cuisine, including duck pâté, calf's liver, mutton, and a dessert of lemon mousse. Reservations essential. Casually elegant. MC, V. Closed Apr 1–15 and Aug 1–17. Expensive.

Le Cagnard, rue du Pontis-Long, Haut-de-Cagnes (☎ **04-93-20-73-22**). This restaurant offers a cuisine moderne menu that includes duck liver pâté, crayfish in Sauterne au gratin, and veal with mushrooms. The 14th-century setting offsets the steep prices. Reservations essential. Elegant. AE, DC, MC, V. Closed Nov 1–Dec 18 and Thurs lunch. Very Expensive.

Peintres, 71 montée Bourgade, Haut-de-Cagnes (☎ **04-93-20-83-08**). Peintres has lovely views and reasonable prices. Reservations essential. Casual. AE, DC, V. Closed Dec 1–20. Moderate.

VILLENEUVE-LOUBET

From Cagnes Ville (the modern city below the old town) take avenue de la Gate and D2085 (avenue de Grasse) some 3 kilometers (2 miles) to the Escoffier Museum in **Villeneuve.** If this doesn't interest you, go directly from Cagnes to St-Paul-de-Vence.

The **Musée Escoffier,** 3 rue Escoffier (☎ **04-93-20-80-51**), is the birthplace of the king of chefs, Auguste Escoffier (1846–1935). It includes a Provençal kitchen with every sort of cooking utensil imaginable; mementos of his career as head chef of the Savoy in London, where he created peach Melba, and of his career at the Ritz in Paris; and his collection of some 15,000 menus dating back to 1820. Admission 10F adults, 7F students. Open Dec–Oct, Tues–Sun 2–6pm (to 7pm June–Aug).

ST-PAUL-DE-VENCE

Take D2 north about 11 kilometers (7 miles) to **St-Paul-de-Vence.** The atmosphere in this perfect gem of a town is Medieval Chic, for none of the hill towns is better preserved. Not even the hordes of tourists (for which the village now exists) can destroy its charm. You can walk the narrow cobbled streets in perhaps 15 minutes, but you'll need another hour to explore the shops—mostly galleries selling second-rate landscape paintings, but also a few serious studios and gift shops hawking everything from candles to dolls, dresses, and hand-dipped chocolate strawberries. Visit in the late afternoon, when the tour buses are gone, and enjoy a drink among the Klees and Picassos in the Colombe d'Or (see "Dining & Accommodations"). You'll want to light a candle in the 12th-century **Gothic church** to relieve its wonderful gloom. The treasury is rich in

12th- to 15th-century pieces, including processional crosses, reliquaries, and an enamel Virgin and Child.

The **Maeght Foundation** (☎ 04-93-32-81-63) is one of the world's most famous small museums of modern art. Founded in 1964 by Aimé Maeght, a Paris art dealer, and his wife, Marguerite, it sits on a grassy hill a 10-minute walk above St-Paul-de-Vence. In addition to regular exhibits, the museum has a permanent collection of ceramics by Miró, mobiles by Calder, bronze figures by Giacometti, and stained-glass windows by Braque. The building containing the museum is a masterpiece itself: Its white concrete arcs give the impression of a giant pagoda. Architect Luís Sert designed the building on several levels, its glass walls providing an indoor-outdoor vista at every turn. The setting is a perfect showcase for both nature and the artistic creations of men and women. Check for concerts in summer. Admission 40F adults, 30F children. Open daily: July–Sept 10am–7pm; Oct–June 10am–12:30pm and 2:30–6pm.

Dining & Accommodations

Château St-Martin, rte. de Coursegoules, 06140 Vence (☎ 04-93-58-02-02; fax 04-93-24-08-91). The castle sits on a 14-hectare (35-acre) property overlooking Vence, and its rooms are exquisitely decorated with antiques, needlepoint, and brocade. You're thought of not as credit-card numbers but as guests in a private castle. The rooms in the tower are smaller and less expensive but decorated with the same loving attention to detail. The formal dining room is one of the best along the coast. 14 rms with bath. Facilities: restaurant, garden, pool, tennis, helicopter landing pad. AE, DC, MC, V. Closed mid-Oct to mid-Apr. Very Expensive.

Colombe d'Or, place Général-de-Gaulle, 06570 St-Paul-de-Vence (☎ 04-93-32-80-02). Here Picasso, Klee, Dufy, Utrillo, and others—all friends of the former owner—paid with paintings, which hang today on the walls above the tables. What a vast difference there is between seeing a Calder in a museum and lunching on a terrace with a Calder mobile swaying among the lemon trees. So this is what it means to live with art! Unless you like being an Ugly American, don't visit without having a drink or stopping for lunch or dinner. The restaurant has a reputation for simple, adequate meals in an unforgettable setting. The building has great warmth and character, though it was constructed only after World War II. The rooms are booked far in advance. Staying here, you can explore St-Paul-de-Vence in the early morning, or under a full moon, when the only footfalls are your own. 15 rms with bath. Facilities: restaurant, pool. AE, DC, MC, V. Closed Nov to late Dec, part of Jan. Expensive.

Hôtel Marc-Hély, 535 rte. de Cagnes, 06480 La Colle sur Loup (☎ 04-93-22-64-10; fax 04-93-22-93-84). This cozy and unpretentious family home, built in the 1970s, is set amid a large garden with a pool, set back from the road that runs between the Mediterranean coast and the historic core of St-Paul-de-Vence. (It's 3 miles south of that famous town and offers a view of its skyline from the hillside on which the hotel sits.) 15 rms with bath. AE, DC, MC, V. Moderate.

Le Hameau, 528 rte. de La Colle, 06570 St-Paul-de-Vence (☎ **04-93-32-80-24;** fax 04-93-32-55-75). This hotel consists of four buildings on the grounds of an old farm set among fruit trees. Try room 11. 14 rms with bath. AE, MC, V. Closed Nov 15–Dec 22 and Jan 6–Feb 15. Moderate.
Mas d'Artigny, rte. de la Collet des Hauts de St-Paul, 06570 Vence (☎ **04-93-32-84-54;** fax 04-93-32-95-36). There's tranquillity and peaceful wooded trails; but unfortunately the public areas, though lavish, are more suited for a convention of professionals than for young lovers. It's not that anything is in bad taste but that the ambiance is chain-hotelish. The main reasons to stay are the private pools—one per suite—and the bathtubs for two. 53 rms with bath; 29 suites. Facilities: restaurant, private pools, tennis. MC, V. Very Expensive.

VENCE

From St-Paul-de-Vence continue north on D2, which runs directly into the old section (Vieille Ville) of **Vence** at avenue M.-Maurel. If you haven't seen enough medieval towns, park and walk around. In the center is the **Romanesque cathedral,** which has a nave (central corridor), four aisles, and no transepts (projecting arms). Of special note is a mosaic by Marc Chagall of Moses in the bulrushes and the ornate 15th-century carved wood choir stalls.

From D2, turn left on avenue M.-Maurel. Cross avenue Foch and turn right on avenue Henri-Matisse to the main attraction of Vence, the **Rosaire (Matisse) Chapel,** avenue Henri-Matisse (☎ **04-93-58-03-26**). "Despite its imperfections I think it is my masterpiece . . . the result of a lifetime devoted to the search for truth," wrote Matisse, who designed and dedicated the chapel in the late 1940s, when he was in his eighties and nearly blind. Admission 5F. Open Dec 13–Oct 31, Tues and Thurs 10–11:30am and 2:30–5:30pm.

TOURRETTE-SUR-LOUP

From Vence, drive west about 5 kilometers (3 miles) on D2210. There's a limit to how many medieval hill towns you'll want to see. The three I'd recommend are Peillon, because it's the most uncommercial and the most dramatically situated; St-Paul-de-Vence, because it's easy to reach, is surrounded by first-class hotels and restaurants, and is visually a gem; and **Tourrette-sur-Loup,** because it's less commercial and its shops are filled not with postcards and scented soaps but with the work of dedicated artisans. I also recommend the village of Moustiers-Ste-Marie, should you make the full-day trip to the Grand Canyon of the Verdon (see below).

The outer houses of Tourrette-sur-Loup form a rampart on a rocky plateau, 390 meters (1,300 ft.) above a valley full of violets. A rough stone path takes you on a circular route around the rim of the town, past the shops of engravers, weavers, potters, and painters. Ask any artisan for a map of the town that locates each of the shops. Also worth visiting is a single-nave 14th-century church, which has a notable wood altarpiece.

TAKE A BREAK

*If you have a sweet tooth, stop in Pont-du-Loup at **La Confiserie des Gorges du Loup**, rue Principale (☎ 04-93-59-32-91) and watch the good people making sugared tangerines, chocolate-covered orange peel, and rose-petal jam. Pretty unsubtle stuff from the land of the tarte aux pommes, but good to munch on as you drive around the gorge.*

Dining

Le Petit Manoir, 21 Grande-Rue (☎ 04-93-24-19-19). It'd be difficult to find a sweeter, friendlier place to eat than this tiny restaurant. Reservations advised. Casually elegant. MC, V. Closed Wed, Sun evening, Nov 15–Dec 10, and Feb. Moderate/Expensive.

GORGES DU LOUP

From Tourrette-sur-Loup, continue west about 8 kilometers (5 miles) on D2210 to Pont-du-Loup. Take D6 north for 6 kilometers (4 miles) along the east side of the **Gorges du Loup,** then head south on D3, past Gourdon, to D2085, the main road between Grasse and Cagnes.

This is a very scenic drive up one side of a dramatic gorge and down the other. It's less impressive than the Grand Canyon of the Verdon but a great deal closer to the coast.

As you head north on D6, park after the third tunnel and walk back for spectacular views into the depths of the gorge.

The road (D3) that takes you south along the western edge of the gorge reaches dizzying heights. Gourdon is touted as one of the "must" stops on the tourist route, which should be enough to dissuade you from stopping here unless you're desperate for scented soaps or lavender eau de toilette.

GRASSE

From Gourdon, continue south on D3 to D2085. From here, turn left (east), back to Cagnes and Nice; or turn right and make a short detour to **Grasse.** If you're headed back to Cannes, you have to pass through Grasse en route to N85.

Grasse is bottled and sold on every escorted tour along the coast. The reasons are its accessibility from both Cannes and Nice and its perfumeries, where tourists spend money. The town is also famous for its preserves and its crystallized fruits and flowers.

If touring a perfume factory in an attractive modern town is your idea of pleasure, visit Grasse. If you'd visited 4 centuries ago, when the town specialized in leather work, you would've come for gloves. In the 16th century, when scented gloves became the rage, the town began cultivating flowers and distilling essences. That was the beginning of the perfume industry. Today some three-fourths of the world's essences are made here from wild lavender, jasmine, violets, daffodils, and other sweet-smelling flowers. Five thousand producers supply some 20 factories and six cooperatives. If you've ever wondered why perfume is so expensive, consider that it takes 10,000 flowers to produce 1 kilogram (2.2 lb.) of jasmine petals, and that nearly 1 ton of jasmine is needed—nearly seven million flowers—to distill 1½ quarts of essence. Sophisticated Paris perfumers mix Grasse essences into their own secret formulas; perfumes made and sold in Grasse are considerably less subtle. You can, of course, buy Parisian perfumes in Grasse—at Parisian prices.

You can buy local perfumes and get some sense of how they're made at three perfumeries: **Fragonard,** 20 bd. Fragonard (☎ 04-93-36-44-65); **Galimard,** 73 rte. de Cannes (☎ 04-93-09-20-00); and **Molinard,** 60 bd. Victor-Hugo (☎ 04-93-36-01-62). All three are open weekdays during business hours.

A perfume museum, the **Musée International de la Parfumerie,** 8 place du Cours (☎ 04-93-36-80-20), explains the history and manufacturing process of perfume. You can admire old machinery, pots, and flasks; toiletry, cosmetics, and makeup accessories are displayed; and a section is devoted to perfume's sophisticated marketing aids, with examples of packaging and advertising posters. Admission 14F adults, 7F seniors; under 14 free. Open daily 9am–6pm.

From Grasse return to Cannes on N85, or to Nice on N85, D35, and A8.

Biot and Vallauris are just a mile or two inland from the coastal road between Cannes and Nice. If you're staying in the Nice area, visit these two towns as you head south along the coast to Cannes. If you're staying in the Cannes area, visit them as you drive north along the coast to Nice.

BIOT

On the road to Biot is the **Musée National Fernand Léger,** chemin du Val-de-Pome (☎ 04-92-91-50-30). Donated to France by Léger's widow, Nadia, in 1959, it offers a good opportunity to trace the artist's development from 1904 until his death in 1955. On its outside wall the building has a 1,200-square-meter (4,000-sq.-ft.) mosaic that's strikingly out of keeping with the surroundings. Admission 28F adults, 16F ages 18–24 and seniors; under 17 free. Open Wed–Mon 10am–12:30pm and 2–6pm (to 5:30pm in winter).

The houses of **Biot** cling to a hillside above the Braque Valley. The town is a handcraft center, specializing in gold and silver jewelry decorated with precious and semiprecious stones as well as glassblowing. Suspended in the heavy tinted glass are tiny bubbles that sparkle in the sun. You can buy the glass or simply watch the ancient process by which it's blown.

When you return to the coastal road (Rte. 7), you'll pass a replica of the kind of marine park made famous in such places as Florida and California, **Marineland,** rue Mozart, off RN7, direction Antibes (☎ 04-93-33-49-49), with some of the most appealing trained dolphin and seal shows in France. Admission 106F adults, 70F children 3–12; 2 and under free. Open Sept–June, daily 10am to between 6 and 9pm, with four trained seal or dolphin shows throughout the day and evening.

VALLAURIS

In **Vallauris,** the wares of more than 100 local potters overflow avenue Georges-Clemenceau and the neighboring streets, such as rue Sicard and rue du Plan—some of it high quality, most of it turned out for the high-volume tourist trade. With luck you'll find some tasteful cups and plates. Also for sale are handmade marionettes and olive-wood sculpture.

Since the time of Tiberius, bricks and pottery have been made here from a local seam of clay. Picasso revived the declining industry when he lived here from 1952 to 1959; his ceramics are on display in the 16th-century **Renaissance castle,** place de la Libération (☎ **04-93-64-16-05**); reproductions are for sale in the Madoura studio. Also in the castle is an enormous allegorical fresco by Picasso called *War and Peace.* Admission 13F. Open Wed–Mon 10am–noon and 2–6pm.

THE GRAND CANYON OF THE VERDON

Drive from the Nice area or the Cannes area to Grasse. Take N85 northwest toward Castellane and pass Seranon on your right. Just beyond the small village of Villaute, turn left on D21 to Comps-sur-Artuby and then turn right on D71. As you approach the gorge, you'll see the hill town of Trigance on your right.

This excursion will take the better part of a day—a full day or overnight if you plan to walk through the canyon. It's an unforgettable trip—the most spectacular you could make on a 1-day side trip from the coast. If you like wild gorges and dizzying heights, the **Grand Canyon of the Verdon** will be an outstanding experience. For thousands of years the Verdon River has dug a rift in the earth, making a winding corridor up to 690 meters (2,300 ft.) deep and in places only 7.5 meters (25 ft.) wide!

The route follows the southern rim of this 21-kilometer (13-mile) gorge to Moustiers-Ste-Marie, one of the loveliest and most unspoiled of the medieval hill towns, where you can buy pottery and dine in a charming country restaurant. Then it returns along the northern rim, with frequent vantage points where you can leave your car and peer down into the swirling depths. Highly recommended are two dramatic walks, neither particularly demanding: one a 2-hour trip down into the gorge and back; the other a 6- to 8-hour trek along the bottom. Should you decide to spend the night, a romantic castle-hotel overlooks the gorge at **Trigance.**

The route around the southern rim is the most dramatic. As you approach the gorge, you'll see the medieval town of Trigance crowning a hill on your right.

The views along the gorge are awesome, from a height that'll make you feel as though you're piloting a plane. Stop when the spirit moves you and don't leave your camera in the car. As you leave the gorge behind, the road turns into D19. At the town of **Aiguines,** which has a noble 17th-century château, you can buy a descriptive guide to the gorge that indicates the trails. At the lake (Lac de Ste-Croix), turn right on D957. In about 7 kilometers (4.5 miles), D957 intersects D952. You can turn right and head back along the northern rim of the canyon, but it's worth a 2.4-kilometer (1.5-mile) detour (a left turn on D957) to visit the unspoiled medieval village of **Moustiers-Ste-Marie,** where serious craftspeople work and sell their waves. There's an attractive **Romanesque church** with a three-tier bell tower, and a **Pottery Museum** (open summers, Wed–Mon 9am–noon and 2–7pm; earlier closings off-season) displaying the clear blue-glazed pottery that made the town famous in the 17th and 18th centuries, when there were 12 active potteries here. For good photographs, take the path that winds up above the village to the **Notre-Dame-de-Beauvoir Chapel.**

TAKE A BREAK

*The terrace of **Les Santons**, place de l'Eglise (☎ **04-92-74-66-48**), a delightful Provençal restaurant, overlooks a mountain torrent flowing through the town. It's a tiny family-run restaurant, so make reservations. Closed Tues.*

After resting up in Moustiers-Ste-Marie, return east on D952, along the northern rim of the gorge. Unless you're in a rush to get back, leave D952 at La Palud-sur-Verdon and take the circular Crest Road (D23) that hugs the edge of the canyon. The Crest Road will return you to D952 near where you left it. Turn right on D952 to Point Sublime and continue east to Castellane. From here, take N85 back to Grasse.

Two Spectacular Walks

The shorter 2-hour walk (round-trip) begins at the parking lot at **Samson Corridor.** Follow the marked route to the right just beyond the first tunnel (Tusset Tunnel) after **Point Sublime.** Walk down to the footbridge over the Baou, cross over, and continue through two tunnels to a promontory with a view of the Trescaïre Chaos. Bring a flashlight.

The 6- to 8-hour walk begins at the **Chalet de la Maline** (on the Crest Road) and continues for 14.7 kilometers (9.15 miles) to Point Sublime. Follow the red and white arrows along the footpath. Wear sturdy shoes and carry a flashlight, water, and food. Before setting off, phone 04-92-83-65-38 or 04-92-83-68-06 to make sure that a taxi is available; then call again when you reach Point Sublime and arrange to be picked up. (There may not be a phone at the Chalet de la Maline, which is why it's important to end your hike at the phone booth at Point Sublime.)

Dining & Accommodations

Château de Trigance, 83840 Trigance (☎ 04-94-76-91-18; fax 04-94-85-68-99). This château commands a splendid view of the valley and the surrounding mountains. There are a few small rooms with a medieval feeling to them—an ideal place to spend the night should you spend a full day at the gorge and not want to drive back after dark. 10 rms with bath. Facilities: restaurant. AE, DC, MC, V. Closed Nov 12–Mar 22. Expensive.

THE ESTÉREL

From Nice, take A8 south past Cannes to the La Napoule (N98) exit. Continue south along the coast to St-Raphaël.

This is a half-day trip from Cannes that takes you away from the crowds, into a silent world of tortured rust-colored rocks thrusting their jagged claws into the sea. The contrast between the fiery red rocks, the deep green pines, and the blue sea inspired Belgian writer Maurice Maeterlinck to call this region "closer to fairyland than any place on earth."

The **Estérel** is made up of volcanic rocks (porphyry) carved by the sea into dreamlike shapes. The harshness of the landscape is softened by patches of lavender, cane apple, and gorse. The deep gorges with sculpted parasol pines could've inspired Tang and Sung Dynasty landscape painters. The drive south from La Napoule to St-Raphaël takes you along the coast, past tiny rust-colored beaches and sheer rock faces plunging into the sea. The route back to Cannes takes you through the mountains of the Estérel, which have many trails and dramatic views.

You may want to stop in **La Napoule** at the **Château de la Napoule Art Foundation,** boulevard Henry-Clews (☎ 04-93-49-95-05), to see the eccentric and eclectic work of American sculptor Henry Clews. Clews, who saw himself as Don Quixote and his wife as the Virgin of La Mancha, came from a New York banking family. A cynic and sadist, he had, as one critic remarked, a knowledge of anatomy worthy of Michelangelo and the bizarre imagination of Edgar Allan Poe. His work—as tortured as the rocks of the Estérel—shows an infatuation with big bellies and distorted bodies; his nude of a man with a skull between his thighs is not easily forgotten. Admission 25F adults, 20F children. Guided visits Mar–Oct, Wed–Mon at 3 and 4pm.

From **Le Trayas** to **Anthéor** is the most scenic part of the drive, beneath the tormented mountains, with deep ravines and razorsharp ridges. **Agay** has the best protected anchorage along the coast. It was here that Antoine de Saint-Exupéry was shot down in July 1944. He had just flown over his family castle on his last mission.

St-Raphaël is a family resort with holiday camps, best known to tourists as the railway stop for St-Tropez. It was here the Allied forces landed in their offensive against the Germans in August 1944. Before returning through the Estérel, you can make a short side trip from St-Raphaël to **Fréjus** (the two towns border each other), but I don't

TAKE A BREAK

A good possibility for lunch is **La Calanque,** *boulevard Henry-Clews (☎ 04-93-49-95-11). This old inn was built on a foundation dating from the Roman Empire. Once it was a private villa, but it's been turned into a 17-room inn offering good food. Try for a table on the outdoor terrace. La Calanque offers the cheapest fixed-price menu in La Napoule, and nonguests are welcome. The food, though simple Provençal fare, is hearty and filling. Reservations not needed. Casual. MC, V. Closed Nov–Mar. Inexpensive.*

recommend it unless you have a special interest in antiquity. It was at Fréjus that Napoléon landed in 1799 on his way back from Egypt, and it was from here that he embarked for Elba.

Caesar made Fréjus a way station on the road between Italy and Gaul. When Emperor Augustus took over, he wanted a powerful fleet and turned the town into a huge naval base—the second largest in the Empire, where galleys were built and men trained for the victory over Mark Antony at Actium. Today there's little sense of the town's former glory. Remains of the 48-kilometer (30-mile) aqueduct can best be seen at the east end of the town. The forum is gone and the Temple of Jupiter is a hospital. The amphitheater (arena), where bullfights are sometimes held, is the most imposing site still to be seen. The **Episcopal Town,** built in the late 10th century, which includes a cathedral, baptistery, cloister, and bishop's palace may be of greater interest. The austere 4th-century baptistery, built with black granite columns from the Roman forum, is one of the oldest in France. The present cathedral dates back to the 10th century, with 12th-century vaulting and handsome 15th-century carved wood choir stalls. Ring the bell on the iron gate to see the graceful cloister and the amusing 14th-century carvings of creatures from the Apocalypse on the ceiling of the upper arcade.

From St-Raphaël return to Cannes on N7—the mountain route through the Estérel. There's a fine desolation here, with different views around every curve. At the sign FORÊT DOMANIALE DE L'ESTÉREL, turn right and drive to the top of **Mount Vinaigre** (609m/2,030 ft.). It's all of 30 meters (100 ft.) from the parking lot to the summit. Try to come in the late afternoon when the coastal views are most striking.

Return to N7 and continue east to Cannes.

S P A I N

Seville, Córdoba, Granada & the Costa del Sol

The mosque of Córdoba, the Alcázar of Seville, and the Alhambra of Granada—these are the three great monuments of Islamic Spain that you'll visit on your trip through Andalusia. Here's a brief look at the history behind them.

When the Visigoths gained control over Spain in the 5th century, they persecuted the Jews and overtaxed everyone else. When the Muslims took over in 711, they were greeted as liberators and they remained there until 1492.

These Muslims are often called Moors, but there really is no such person: The Spaniards used the term merely to designate those people (Arabs, Syrians, Egyptians, Berbers, and others) who settled in their country. To call them Arabs is equally misleading. The first wave of settlers were Berbers—there wasn't an Arab among them. The Arabs eventually rose to power in Spain, but they were never more than a small minority of the Muslim population, and their power and influence always exceeded their numbers. As it was the Muslim religion that united these settlers, let's refer to them collectively as Muslims and speak of their kingdom as Islamic Spain.

The three great centers of Muslim culture were Córdoba (756–1010), Seville (1010–1248), and Granada (1248–1492). Each rose to power, enjoyed a period of glory, and then faded.

The greatest flowering of Moorish culture was during the first 250 years under the Córdoba caliphate. (A caliph is a successor of Mohammed who enjoys both spiritual and temporal power; a caliphate is his office or kingdom.) Undermined by incompetent rulers, the caliphate disintegrated and Islamic Spain broke into 23 separate kingdoms (taifas), of which Seville became the most important.

In the meantime, the Christians, weakened by squabbles of their own—there was no unified Spain then, only a number of warring kingdoms—banded together in the north, where the Muslims had less control, and began what is called the Reconquest. This struggle to restore Christianity continued for more than 400 years.

The first major Christian victory was in Toledo in 1085. When Seville fell in 1248, Muslim culture moved to Granada, where it survived precariously for 244 years. The marriage of Isabella of Castile to Ferdinand of Aragón brought the two strongest Spanish kingdoms together and unified Catholic Spain against the Muslims. Granada finally fell in 1492, about 10 months before Columbus sailed for the New World.

Ferdinand and Isabella persecuted the Jews and Moors and hounded them out of Spain. The Spanish Inquisition, which lasted until 1834, was an effort to reestablish a Spanish identity after more than 700 years of Muslim rule. Its first victims weren't Jews but pure-blood Spaniards who had converted to Islam. By eliminating the Muslims and the Jews, the Inquisition virtually eliminated the Spanish middle class and plunged the country into a decline from which it has only recently recovered.

It's fashionable but unfair to build up Islamic Spain at the expense of the Catholics—to say that whatever is beautiful is the inheritance of Muslim culture. Only after many years on Spanish soil did Islamic culture flourish. On the other hand, it's fair to agree with Federico García Lorca that "an admirable civilization, a poetry, an architecture, and a delicacy unique in the world—all were lost."

HIGHLIGHTS ALONG THE WAY

- The palace and gardens of Granada's Alhambra—the greatest monument of Islamic Spain.

- The fabulous mosque of Córdoba, with a full-size cathedral inside.

- Tennis, golf, and sun along the fashionable Costa del Sol.

- A back-road adventure to the perched white villages of Andalusia.

- Accommodations in palaces and abbeys converted into first-class hotels.

BEFORE YOU GO

GOVERNMENT TOURIST OFFICES

The major source of information is the **National Tourist Office of Spain.**

In the U.S.: 666 Fifth Ave., 5th floor, New York, NY 10103 (☎ 212/265-8822); 845 N. Michigan Ave., Chicago, IL 60611 (☎ 312/642-1992); San Vicente Plaza Bldg., 8383 Wilshire Blvd., Suite 960, Beverly Hills, CA 90211 (☎ 213/658-7188); 1221 Brickell Ave., Suite 1850, Miami, FL 33131 (☎ 305/358-1992).

SPAIN

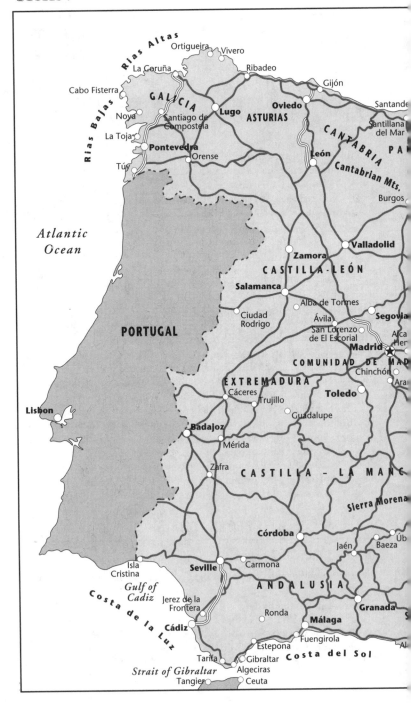

SPECIAL EVENTS & NATIONAL HOLIDAYS

Special Events

Palm Sunday–Good Friday: Holy Week festivities in Seville.
Late April: The Seville Fair, with dancing, processions, and bullfights.
May 1–12: Córdoba festival of decorated patios.
Late June: Seville folk-dance competitions.
Late June–early July: Granada Festival of Music and Dance, with concerts and ballet in the gardens of the Alhambra.

National Holidays

January 1 (New Year's Day); January 6 (Epiphany); March 19 (San José); Maundy Thursday, Good Friday, Easter Sunday; May 1 (Labor Day); Corpus Christi (May or June); July 25 (Santiago Apóstel); August 15 (Feast of the Assumption); October 21 (Fiesta Hispanidad); November 1 (All Saints' Day); November 9 (Our Lady of Almudena); December 6 (Spanish Constitution Day); December 8 (Immaculate Conception); December 25 (Christmas Day).

In Canada: 102 Bloor St. W., 14th floor, Toronto, Ontario M5S 1M9 (☎ 416/961-3131).

In the U.K.: 57–58 St. James's St., London SW1 1LD (☎ 0171/499-0901).

WHEN TO GO

The tourist season runs from Easter to mid-October. The best months for sightseeing are May, June, September, and early October, when the weather is usually pleasant and sunny without being unbearably hot. During July and August try to avoid the inland cities of Andalusia, where the heat can be stifling and many places close at 1pm.

As for crowds, Easter is always a busy time, especially in the main Andalusian cities of Seville, Córdoba, Granada, and Málaga as well as the Costa del Sol resorts. July and August, when most Spaniards and other Europeans take their annual vacation, see the heaviest crowds, particularly in the coastal resorts. Holiday weekends are naturally busy, and major fiestas, such as Seville's April Fair, make advance booking essential and cause prices to soar. Off-season travel offers fewer crowds and lower rates in many hotels.

CURRENCY

The unit of currency in Spain is the **peseta (PTA).** There are bills of 500, 1,000, 2,000, 5,000, and 10,000PTA. Coins are 1PTA and 5, 25, 50, 100, 200, and 500PTA. The 2PTA and 10PTA coins and the old 100PTA bills are rare but still legal tender. The exchange rate is about 125PTA = $1 U.S., 92PTA = $1 Canadian, and 188PTA = £1 sterling.

CUSTOMS

European Union citizens who travel only within the European Union (say, from England to Spain or France to Spain) are permitted to bypass most general customs procedures. Those traveling from non–European Union countries, such as Canada or the United States, or European

Union citizens coming directly from non–European Union countries, must follow guidelines. Those travelers in this category can take into Spain most personal effects and the following items duty-free: two still cameras and 10 rolls of film per camera; one video camera; tobacco for personal use; 1 liter each of liquor and wine; a portable radio; a tape recorder; a typewriter; a bicycle; and sports equipment and fishing gear that's intended for personal use.

LANGUAGE

In major cities and coastal resorts you should have no trouble finding people who speak English. In such places, the reception staff in hotels of three stars and up are required to speak English. Don't expect the person in the street or the bus driver to speak English, though you may be pleasantly surprised.

READING

Arturo Barea, *The Forging of a Rebel*, perhaps the finest account of the 1936–39 Spanish Civil War, told by a leading Republican official and literary personality.

Gerald Brenan, *The Spanish Labyrinth*, a serious-minded look at the roots of modern-day Spain.

John A. Crow, *Spain: The Root and the Flower*, the most readable introduction to Moorish Spain.

Ernest Hemingway, *Death in the Afternoon*, the best book ever written about the techniques of bullfighting; *The Sun Also Rises*, about Spain between the wars; and *For Whom the Bell Tolls*, about the Spanish Civil War.

Vicente Blasco Ibañez, *Blood and Sand*, a beautiful and tragic novel of bullfighting written from the point of view of an opponent.

Jan Morris, *Spain*, a classic, impressionistic guide.

H. V. Morton, *A Stranger in Spain*, a mid–20th-century English traveler's literate, absorbing reflections on visiting Spain.

George Orwell, *Homage to Catalonia*, in which the author of *Nineteen Eighty-Four* describes his frontline experience fighting with an anarchist unit during the Civil War.

V. S. Pritchett, *The Spanish Temper*, a perceptive, if at times dated, portrait of the Spanish people, with insights into the art of bullfighting.

Richard Wright, *Pagan Spain*, an irreverent and perceptive travelogue written during the Franco years.

ARRIVING & DEPARTING

BY CAR

Driving is on the right-hand side of the road, and horns and high-beam headlights theoretically may not be used in cities. The wearing of seat belts is compulsory on the highway but not in cities (except the M30 Madrid ring road). Children may not ride in front seats. At traffic circles give way to traffic coming from the right unless your road has priority. Your home driver's license is essential and must be carried with you at all times, along with your car insurance and vehicle registration document. You'll also need an International Driving License and a Green Card if you're bringing your own car into Spain. Speed limits are 120 kilometers per hour (75 m.p.h.) on autopistas, 100 kilometers per hour (62 m.p.h.) on N roads, 90 kilometers per hour (56 m.p.h.) on C roads, and 60 kilometers per hour (37 m.p.h.) in cities unless otherwise signposted.

If your trip begins in Madrid and you're traveling by car, stop in Toledo on your way south, taking Routes N401 and then N400 to NIV. It's a 5-hour drive from Madrid to Bailén, then another 1½ hours to Córdoba.

By Plane

If you don't plan to visit Madrid, either fly directly to and from Málaga, on the Costa del Sol, only 49.91 kilometers (31 miles) east of Marbella, or fly to Seville, changing planes in Madrid. **Iberia** (☎ 800/772-4642) is the only airline with direct flights between Málaga and the United States (from New York, Chicago, and Los Angeles).

If you do plan to visit Madrid, fly directly to Madrid and return from Málaga or Seville; or, conversely, fly directly to Málaga or Seville and return from Madrid.

Iberia also has direct flights between Madrid and New York, Miami, and Los Angeles. **American** (☎ 800/433-7300) offers direct service from Dallas to Madrid; **TWA** (☎ 800/221-2000) has direct flights between Madrid and New York; **United** (☎ 800/241-6522) has direct service between Washington, D.C. and Madrid. In Seville, Iberia Airlines is at the San Pablo Airport, Almirante Lobo 3 (☎ 95/451-53-20).

British Airways (☎ 0171/897-4000 in London) and **Iberia** (☎ 0171/437-5622 in London) are the two major carriers flying between England and Spain. More than a dozen daily flights, on BA or Iberia, depart from London's Heathrow and Gatwick. The Midlands is served by flights from Manchester and Birmingham, two major airports that can also be used by Scottish travelers flying to Spain. There are about seven flights a day from London to Madrid and back, and at least six to Barcelona (trip time: 2–2½ hours). From either the Madrid airport or the Barcelona airport, you can tap into Iberia's domestic network—flying, for example, to Seville or the Costa del Sol (centered at the Málaga airport). The best air deals on scheduled flights from England are those requiring a Saturday-night stopover.

Charter flights also leave from most British regional airports with a destination in mind (for example, Málaga), bypassing the congestion at the Barcelona and Madrid airports. Figure on saving approximately 10% to 15% on regularly scheduled flight tickets. But check carefully. British

Sunday papers are full of charter deals, and a travel agent can always advise what the best values are at the time of your intended departure.

By Train

If your trip begins in Madrid and you're using public transport, take the Madrid airport bus downtown to the airport bus terminal at Plaza Colón (30 min.) and a cab (20 min.) to the South Station (Atocha). Express trains take about 2 hours to Córdoba, 6 to 8 hours to Granada, about 2½ hours to Seville, and about 4 hours to Málaga.

GETTING AROUND

By Car

If you're driving, you need a Green Insurance Card. A rented car should have one in the glove compartment. If you're bringing your own car, get the Green Card from your insurance company before you leave home.

Roads marked A are turnpikes (autopista). N is for national roads, C for country roads. You'll frequently be driving on single-lane roads, so expect delays, though major highway improvements undertaken in connection with Expo '92 vastly improved a number of highways in southern Spain.

Almost all monuments and buildings close from 1:30 to 3 or 4pm and remain open to 7 or 8pm. Many close on Monday. Plan your itinerary accordingly. If you begin and end your trip in Madrid, take NIV from Madrid to Bailén (about 6 hr.). If you arrive in Madrid after an all-night flight, you may want to stop in Bailén before heading to Córdoba, which is another 105.6 kilometers (66 miles) west on NIV. Bailén has a good hotel, the Zodíaco, Carretera NIV, 23710 Bailén (☎ **953/67-10-62;** fax 953/67-19-06).

From Córdoba you have a choice of two roads to Seville. The faster is 142.4 kilometers (89 miles) on NIV, one of the roads dramatically upgraded in 1992. The slower but more scenic route is on C431 for 78.89 kilometers (49 miles) along the Guadalquivir River; south on C432 for 27 kilometers (17 miles) to Carmona (there's another parador hotel here); and then west for 38.4 kilometers (24 miles) on NIV to Seville.

From Seville, you have a choice of routes to Ronda and Marbella (described in the itinerary). Major improvements were made on both in 1992, making the drive not only beautiful but relatively easy. When you're ready to leave Marbella, take the coastal road N323 east to Málaga (54.4km/34 miles) and Motril (another 67.2km/57 miles); then take N323 north to Granada (67.2km/42 miles). The fastest route from Granada back to Madrid is on N323 through Jaén and Bailén. The more interesting route is Baeza and Úbeda.

If you plan to begin your trip in Madrid and end it in Málaga, follow the same route as above, except from Granada return to Málaga by the inland route—west on N342 and south on N321 (78 miles). Should you choose to drive between Granada and Seville, note that improvements on those highways have cut traveling time to just over 2 hours.

If you begin and end your trip in Málaga, what you have to decide is whether to do your sightseeing and then reward yourself with a few final days of indolence on the Costa del Sol; recover from your overnight flight to Spain on the Costa del Sol and then begin your sightseeing; or begin and end on the Costa del Sol. The following route lets you do all three. It's essentially the same route described above, but in reverse.

Head west along the coast from Málaga to Marbella. The drive takes less than an hour. You can either save Marbella for the end of your trip or stop here now. From Marbella, continue west on N340 to San Pedro de Alcántara and turn north on C339 to Ronda. There are two routes from Ronda to Seville, both discussed in the itinerary below. From Seville, there are two roads to Córdoba. The faster is 142.4 kilometers (89 miles) on NIV. The slower but more scenic route is east for 38.4 kilometers (24 miles) on NIV to Carmona; north on C432 for 27.2 kilometers (17 miles); and east on C431 for 78.4 kilometers (49 miles) along the Guadalquivir River to Córdoba. From Córdoba, the shortest route to Granada is on N432. The more interesting route is on NIV to Bailén; N22 to Úbeda; N321 to Baeza and Jaén; and N323 to Granada. From Granada, take N323 south to Motril, then head west along the coast back to Málaga. You can either fly directly home or spend more time in Marbella.

By Train or Bus

If you're taking public transportation, get a **Tarjeta Turística,** allowing 3, 5, or 10 days of unrestricted rail travel over a month, or ask about a **Family Pass,** granting 20% to 50% discounts to families (three or more relatives). The latter isn't valid on holidays or *some* Friday and Saturday afternoons. They're sold at main stations. When you're buying the actual tickets, get them from travel agents displaying blue-and-yellow RENFE signs, and avoid ticket lines at stations.

If you begin and end your trip in Madrid, there's good, fast train service among Madrid, Córdoba, and Seville; between Seville and Málaga; and between Granada and Madrid. The express from Madrid to Córdoba takes 2 hours and from Córdoba to Seville 1 hour. From Seville to Marbella, it's a 3½-hour train ride to Málaga and a 1-hour bus ride from Málaga to Marbella. The train takes 2 hours from Málaga to Granada and about 6 hours from Granada back to Madrid.

If you begin your trip in Madrid and end it in Málaga, follow the same route as above, but instead of taking the train from Granada to Madrid, take the train from Granada back to Málaga.

In Córdoba, contact **RENFE,** the national train company, for train information (in Spanish only, ☎ 957/49-02-02); or visit the RENFE office at Zaragoza 29 (☎ 95/454-0202). Trains to Seville and Granada leave from the station at Avenida de América (☎ 957/49-02).

In Marbella, bus information is at Av. Ricardo Soriano 21 (☎ 95/277-21-92).

For bus information in Seville, call 95/441-7111.

If you begin and end your trip in Málaga, buses leave almost every half an hour from Málaga to Marbella. The express trip takes about 1 hour. From Málaga take the train to Seville (3½ hours). From Seville take the train to Córdoba (1 hour). The bus trip from Córdoba to Granada takes 3 hours. The train from Granada back to Málaga takes about 2 hours.

ESSENTIAL INFORMATION

IMPORTANT ADDRESSES & NUMBERS

VISITOR INFORMATION   The major regional tourist offices of Moorish Spain are in the following cities:

Córdoba: Calle Torrijos 10 (☎ 957/47-12-35); open Monday to Saturday from 9:30am to 7pm and Sunday from 10am to 2pm.

Granada: Plaza de Mariana Pineda 10, about six blocks east of the cathedral (☎ 958/22-66-88); open Monday to Saturday from 9:30am to 2pm and 5 to 7:30pm.

Marbella: Glorieta de la Fontianilla s/n (☎ 95/277-14-42); open Monday to Friday from 9:30am to 9pm and Saturday from 10am to 2pm.

Seville: Av. de la Constitucíon 21, a short walk from the cathedral (☎ 95/422-14-04); open Monday to Saturday from 9am to 7pm and Sunday and holidays from 10am to 2pm.

Smaller, significantly less useful municipal offices are in **Córdoba** at the Palacio de Congresos y Exposiciones, Torrijos 10 (☎ 957/47-12-35), and **Seville** at Paseo de Las Delicias 9 (☎ 95/423-44-65).

EMERGENCIES   The national emergency number is **006** throughout Spain. For medical emergencies, contact: in **Marbella,** Hospital Comarcal, CN340, km 187 (☎ 95/286-27-48); **Seville,** Hospital Universitario Virgen Macareno, Avenida Dr. Fedriani (☎ 95/437-84-00).

CONSULATES   The **Canadian Consulate:** Av. Constitución 30, Seville (☎ 95/422-9413); Plaza de la Malagueta 3, Málaga (☎ 95/222-3346). The **U.S. Consulate:** Centro Comercial Las Rampas, Fuengirola (☎ 95/247-9891); Paseo de las Delicias 7, Seville (☎ 95/423-1833/84-85). The **U.K. Consulate:** Duquesa de Parcent 8, Málaga (☎ 95/221-75-71); Plaza Nueva 8, Seville (☎ 95/422-8875).

Opening & Closing Times

BANKS Banks are generally open Monday to Friday from 9:30am to 2pm and Saturday from 9:30am to 1pm. Money exchanges at airports and train stations stay open later.

MUSEUMS Most museums are open from 10am to 2pm and from 4pm to 6pm and are closed 1 day a week, usually Monday. Opening hours vary widely, so make sure to check before you set off.

SHOPS One of the most inconvenient things about Spain is that almost all shops close at midday for at least 3 hours. An important exception are the two major department store chains, Corte Inglés and Galerias Preciados, which stay open through the siesta hour. Generally store hours are Monday to Saturday from 9:30am to 8pm. Shops are closed all day Sunday.

Shopping

VAT REFUNDS If you're a non–European Union resident and make purchases in Spain worth more than 86,520PTA, you can get a tax refund. The internal **value-added tax,** known as VAT in most of Europe, is called IVA in Spain. Depending on the goods, the rate usually ranges from 7% to 13% of the total worth of your merchandise. Luxury items are taxed at 33%. To get this refund, you must complete three copies of a form that the store will give you, detailing the nature of your purchase and its value. Citizens of non–European Union countries show the purchase and the form to the Spanish Customs Office. The shop is supposed to refund the amount due you. Inquire at the time of purchase how they'll do so and discuss in what currency you wish your refund to arrive.

BEST BUYS In **Córdoba,** look for filigree silver and embossed leather in the shops of the old Jewish quarter, a short walk from the mosque. In the narrow streets of **Granada,** such as Zacatín and Angel Ganivet, between the cathedral and Reyes Católicos, is the old Moorish silk market (the **Alcaicería**), which has been turned into a tourist district with some interesting pottery and craft shops. Look for marquetry (inlaid wood chess sets, boxes, music boxes), ceramics, shoulder bags, rugs, and wall hangings. Reyes Católicos is the main shopping street leading toward the Alhambra. Other shops are on Cuesta de Gomérez, which goes from Reyes Católicos up to the Alhambra. Pottery is sold on Routes N323 and N342, north and east of town.

In **Marbella** you can find designer clothes (particularly beachwear) in the old Moorish quarter and in the boutiques of individual hotels.

Seville's main pedestrian shopping street, Calle de las Sierpes, will be a disappointment unless you're into Korean castanets, wood bulls stuck with swords, and imitation Moorish tiles. A few shops sell quality jewelry, pottery, and fans, however, so take a look. You may also find folk costumes and flamenco dresses.

At Plaza del Duque 10 is a department store, **Corte Inglés** (☎ 95/422-4931), and a daily craft and jewelry market. Your best bet for antiques and ceramics are the stores in the Barrio Santa Cruz. For ceramics in particular, try **Martian Ceramics,** Sierpes (☎ 95/421-3413). Note how the pottery is more intricate and sophisticated—less rustic and spontaneous—than the pottery made in Granada.

For embroidered tablecloths and handwoven blankets, try **Artesanía Textil,** Sierpes 70 (☎ 95/456-2840). For folk costumes, head to **Dardales,** Cuna 23 (☎ 95/421-3709).

SPORTS

FISHING Dozens of fishing boats are docked at Puerto Banús, 8 kilometers (5 miles) east of Marbella (toward Cádiz), waiting to take you angling for shark.

GOLF The Costa del Sol has several championship golf courses, many near Estepona (27.2km/17 miles west of Marbella) and San Pedro de Alcántara (11.2km/7 miles west of Marbella): These include **Atalaya Park** (☎ 95/288-48-01); **Las Brisas** (☎ 95/281-52-06); **Guadalmina** (☎ 95/288-22-11); and **Nueva Andalucía** (☎ 95/281-08-75). All these courses are in the western Costa del Sol. The best courses in the east are **Club de Campo de Golf de Málaga** (☎ 95/237-6677), just 10 kilometers (6 miles) from Málaga and 6 kilometers (4 miles) from Torremolinos, and **Golf Torrequebrada** at Costa Benalmádena (☎ 95/561-102), directly west of Torremolinos.

TENNIS Most hotels have their own courts. The best independent tennis club is **Club de Sportivo,** Carretera de Mijas, km 6.5 in Fuengirola (☎ 95/246-16-48), 25.6 kilometers (16 miles) east of Marbella.

DINING

There's a value-added tax (called IVA in Spain) of 7% or 13% on all meals, depending on the category of the restaurant. At the less expensive cafes and restaurants, this tax will be included in the cost of the dishes. At the more expensive establishments, it's added to the bill. Restaurants don't add a service charge. Ten percent of the total before tax is standard. At bars and cafes, it's customary to leave a tip when the waiter brings your change on a saucer (tip tray).

Ask for water and you'll get bottled mineral water, either sin gas (without bubbles) or con gas (with). For tap water, which is safe, ask for agua natural.

The main meal is lunch, which usually doesn't begin until 1pm. Dinner often starts at 9pm, sometimes as late as 11:30pm or midnight. Restaurants open at 1pm, so go early if you want quick service for lunch. For dinner, restaurants open around 9pm and dining rooms in paradors open at about 8:30pm.

The three-course menú del día (menu of the day) is the best bargain, though rarely the best meal. Restaurants are required to have a "menu of the day," but you may have to ask for it. The menu is typically offered at lunch; at dinner, if there's any left, it'll simply be lunch warmed over.

Spanish food is, as a rule, a food of the people; don't expect gourmet cuisine (with the notable exception of fine Basque cookery). The Spaniards usually don't serve their meals steaming hot (extreme heat, they argue, hides the taste), so if you like hot food ask to have it served *muy caliente*. Contrary to what many people think, the Spanish don't like their food highly seasoned; chili is almost never used and pepper is seldom on the table. Nearly everything is cooked with olive oil, which isn't necessarily heavy, and *al ajillo* (with lots of garlic). Desserts are usually a letdown; fresh fruit is usually the best choice.

The national dish is paella, a base of saffron-flavored rice with anything from mussels to chicken, pimientos, peas, and lobster. If it's properly prepared, you'll taste the separate flavor of each ingredient. It's heavy and takes some 20 minutes to prepare, so it's usually served at lunch. Your best bet near the coast is paella with fresh seafood.

Another universal dish is gazpacho, a cold blend of puréed tomatoes, cucumbers, green peppers, garlic, oil, salt, pepper, onions, and a touch of vinegar. Taste differs according to the region, but often garlic will be dominant. Try "white gazpacho" with ground almonds and grapes.

On the Costa del Sol, and to a lesser degree in Seville and Granada, you're usually better off with fish than with meat. Specialties include *lubina al sal* (sea bass baked in a shell of salt) and *fritura mista* (a delicate mix of lightly fried fish).

Don't leave Spain without trying some tapas. These tasty tidbits—potatoes, marinated beef, squid, ham, clams, mussels, fish roe, and so on—are served on the counters of bars and cafes and also as appetizers or main dishes in the paradors (government-run hotels). Like the Spaniards, you can go from bar to bar sharing tapas—a happy alternative to a formal dinner. *Raciónes* are larger portions.

Tortilla sacromonte, a potato omelet with diced ham and mixed vegetables, is popular in Granada. (Tortillas in Spain are omelets.) For dessert or for afternoon snacks, try *almendra* (almond-flavored ice cream) or rum raisin (Málaga-style) ice cream. *Granizado de café* is iced coffee.

Southern Spain produces sweet aperitif and dessert wines, not table wines. Sherry, produced near Jerez de la Frontera (which is not included on the itinerary described below, but is only an hour out of your way), is the most famous Spanish wine. There are three basic types: the light, dry aperitifs (*fino*), such as Tío Pepe and La Ina, that should be drunk as fresh as possible (don't get the last glass in an open bottle); the fuller-bodied, nutty-tasting *amontillados*—the cheap ones made from blended wines, the better ones from finos that've been left to mature; and the darker, fuller-bodied *olorosos*, with a higher alcohol content. Sherry has a slightly higher alcohol content than other wines because brandy is added while it's being made. You'll find a lower alcohol content in Spanish sherries than in those you drink at home because extra brandy is added in exported sherries to protect them in transit. There's no such thing as a vintage sherry.

Most restaurants have a cheap, adequate house wine. *Sangría* (a fruit punch with wine, fruit juice, soda, brandy, and slices of oranges and lemons) originated in southern Spain. *Sol y sombra* (brandy and anis) is another popular drink. *Sorbeta de limón* (champagne and sorbet) is a great antidote for hot weather.

CATEGORY	COST
Very Expensive	Over 8,000PTA
Expensive	6,000–8,000PTA
Moderate	3,000–6,000PTA
Inexpensive	Under 3,000PTA

Prices are per person, excluding drinks, service, and IVA.

ACCOMMODATIONS

You'll see three signs on Spanish hotels. H means "hotel." HR is a "residential hotel" with no formal restaurant but often a Spanish-style cafeteria. HA designates an "apartment hotel," often with cooking facilities.

Breakfast may or may not be included in the price; ask in advance. Rooms with bathtubs usually cost more than rooms with showers. On the Costa del Sol, rooms with sea views often cost more; specify what you want. Many hotels are undergoing restoration, so specify whether you want a newer or an older room. When possible, ask to see your room before checking in.

The five main hotel chains are Hotasa (look for the symbol of two animal heads), Husa, Meliá, Sol, and Entursa. All tend to be clean and comfortable, but only the Entursa hotels have any special character.

You'd think that government-run hotels would be institutionally bland, but the paradors—some 80 of them—are, as a rule, Spain's most tasteful and interesting hostelries. Many are restored castles, convents, palaces, and royal hunting lodges that've been modernized but allowed to keep their old-world charm. Most are spacious, with large baths, and decorated with antiques, armor, tapestries, and ceramic tiles. Many are also on high ground with magnificent views or in the historic sections of ancient cities. Dining rooms serve regional meals and local wines. The only minus—a plus for some—is the absence of after-dark entertainment and recreation, and a certain lack of warmth in the newer ones. Paradors generally have only a few rooms, so make reservations in advance. The National Tourist Office of Spain has a brochure that describes "parador vacations," which let you stay in one parador or in a different one every night as you travel. Following the itinerary below, you can stay in paradors in Bailén (on the road from Madrid to Córdoba), Córdoba (outside the city), Carmona (outside of Seville), Granada (here you'll need to reserve at least 3–4 months in advance), Pico de Veleta (outside of Granada), Málaga, and Úbeda.

CATEGORY	COST
Very Expensive	Over 24,000PTA
Expensive	12,000–24,000PTA
Moderate	8,000–12,000PTA
Inexpensive	Under 8,000PTA

Prices based on a standard double room, excluding IVA and service.

BULLFIGHTING

The bullfighting season runs from late March to mid-October. If you don't know anything about it, you're likely to be confused, repelled, or bored.

It's usual to divide the bullfight into a prelude and three acts:

The Prelude: There's a roar of applause as the president enters. He signals and the gates swing open. In come the participants, even the man who'll drag the dead bulls offstage. The first to enter are the matadors. Each has his own swagger. They're supposed to look grave and unconcerned. The main actor, on the right, will fight the first and fourth bulls. The youngest, in the center, gets to kill the third and sixth. Everyone now leaves the ring. The president signals again.

Act One, Scene One: Enter the bull. No one knows how he'll perform. Only the young heifers at the bull ranches are tested; if they charge bravely, they're bred; if not, they become meat. The bulls are never tested because they'd remember. It's assumed that they'll inherit bravery from their mothers.

If the bull comes out charging, he's a single-minded bull who is easy to handle. This one stops. He thought he was being set free to join the herd, but something is wrong. He sniffs. He has seen the flick of a cape. He has never seen one before; his owners have made sure of that. He charges. Of the three *peones* (assistants) now in the ring, he chooses one victim, who scurries over the stockade. The matador watches. He isn't a coward: He wants to see how the bull responds—if his vision is good, if he pulls to the left or to the right.

The matador approaches with his cape, red on one side, yellow on the other. The color really doesn't matter, for the bull is color-blind. The bull charges and the matador shows off his skill. The first pass of the cape, the verónica, is the most basic, deriving from the way in which St. Verónica is said to have held the cloth she used to wipe Christ's face. With each pass the matador gets closer to the bull, as he learns what he can and cannot

ANDALUSIA

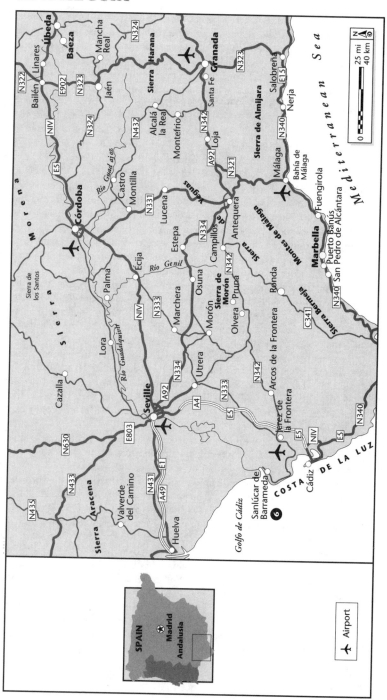

do. If the bull stakes a territory, it's more dangerous to fight him there, protecting his ground, than when he's headed for it and has nothing on his mind but getting back. *Olé!* shout the crowds—a word some say comes from the Moorish cry to Allah.

Act One, Scene Two: Enter the men on horseback, the picadores, holdovers from the days when matadors were royal sportsmen who fought bulls from horses. The horses are terrified, but you can't hear them complain because their vocal cords are cut. Their right eyes are bandaged so they won't see the bulls coming to rip them apart. The bull is goaded to attack the right side of the heavily padded horses while the picadores, in turn, thrust their 6-foot lances into his shoulders. The idea is to weaken the neck muscles so that the head drops and the matador can slay the bull with a sword. The motive isn't sadistic; if the picadores pump their pikes or take too long, the audience boos. The bull is encouraged to toss the horses so that he'll tire out. Much worse than the sight of a dying bull is the sight of a gored horse, writhing in pain, its insides spilling into the ring; pray you don't see this extremely rare event. What does happen occasionally is that the horse, when tossed, goes down, and with him, the picador, who scurries away while the matadors divert the bull.

Act Two: Enter the banderilleros, on foot, who dance away from the bull as he charges, thrusting three pairs of 45.7-centimeter (18-in.) darts, barbed like fishhooks, into the beast's shoulders. This is the least dangerous part of the show, done not to cause pain but to lower the bull's head further so the matador can slay him. The bull stands in pain, trying to lick the pools of blood pouring like paint down his back. "As the wounded bull stands there waiting for the kill," wrote English traveler H. V. Morton, "I am reminded of all the tortured Christs in Spain. They wear the same air of spent and hopeless exhaustion. The blood streaks their bodies in the same way." Morton added: "No one brought up on Beatrix Potter can understand this."

Act Three, Scene One: The matador sometimes dedicates the bull to one person; but if he takes off his hat and salutes the whole audience it means he's dedicating the bull to everyone, and we can expect a great performance. With the muleta, a small red cape that hides a sword, he now performs his most dangerous and exciting moves. The matador is judged by his artistry and by his willingness to put himself in danger. He shouldn't move his feet as the bull passes. The bull should avoid him, not he the bull. Arching his body shows less skill than standing straight. Kneeling is dangerous; so is passing the cape over his head (losing sight of the bull) and holding the cape behind his body. What he must do is destroy the bull's will—making the bull do what he wants, rendering him harmless. Getting the bull to perform in slow motion increases the danger.

Act Three, Scene Two: This is called the "Moment of Truth." The matador returns to the stockade for his killing sword and then advances toward the bull. He looks along the edge of his blade to the narrow space between the bull's shoulders that leads straight to his heart. This is the most dangerous moment.

The matador sweeps the cape in front of the bull to draw his head down; if the head doesn't drop, the horns will rip into the matador. The matador lunges forward. Rarely does he strike true. He thrusts again. The bull totters and begins to cough up blood. If the matador can't make a clean kill, the audience boos loudly to disassociate itself from the butchery. Once the bull is down, he's killed with a final thrust to sever his spinal cord.

EXPLORING

CÓRDOBA

Except for its great mosque and ancient Jewish Quarter, the modern city of **Córdoba** gives little evidence of its former glory. The two sights are a must on any tour of southern Spain, but once you've seen them, you'll probably be content to move on. During the time the mosque is closed in the off-season (1:30–3:30pm), tour the former Jewish Quarter and stop for lunch. At least two good restaurants are nearby.

As you wander through the mosque and the old Jewish quarter, imagine yourself back in the 8th century, when Córdoba was the first and greatest capital of Islamic Spain.

Your ruler is one-eyed Abd-er-Rahman I. His family belonged to a long line of Umayyads, who were slaughtered by another branch of Mohammed's family, the Abbassides. Abd-er-Rahman fled to Spain, where he began a dynasty that ruled for 300 years. It was in 785, under his rule, that the mosque was begun. In 929, his descendant Abd-er-Rahman III unmasked the fiction that the Arab world was united and declared himself Caliph. The Arab world was now formally split in two— as the Roman world was split between East and West—one capital in Baghdad, the other in Córdoba.

Americans tend to label Muslims as intolerant, but under the Córdoba caliphate nothing could have been more untrue. For almost 50 years the Muslims shared the Visigoth church with the Christians and made no effort to interfere with their services. When the Muslims decided to build a mosque, they gave the Christians money to construct themselves another cathedral. How unlike the intolerance the Christians showed the Muslims after the Reconquest!

For 300 years the caliphs of Córdoba ruled the most advanced state in Europe. Arabic, the official tongue, was spoken by both Jew and Christian. Córdoba was said to have had a population of 500,000—almost twice what it has today. While the rest of Europe was groping through the Dark Ages, Córdoba had illuminated streets. While education in Northern Europe was limited to a few monastic centers, nearly everyone in Córdoba could read and write. Universities flourished. The Renaissance began here with translations of classical learning.

The Spanish Muslims introduced Europe to waterwheel irrigation, peach trees, and dates. They introduced paper and glass, jasmine, and the

THE ITINERARY

ORIENTATION

Your trip takes you through Andalusia, on a voyage through almost 800 years of Islamic Spain. It also includes a few happy days of self-indulgence on the beaches of the Costa del Sol.

In Córdoba you'll visit an 8th-century mosque that's so vast it contains a 16th-century baroque cathedral within its walls. Nearby are the ancient white streets of the Jewish quarter, unchanged from a time when Jews and Arabs lived together in peace.

When people think of romantic Spain—of Carmens and Don Juans—they think of Seville. Here you can discover for yourself whether bullfighting is butchery or art. After visiting the Alcázar—a Moorish palace of gleaming tiles and arabesques—you'll dine in an old Andalusian house and watch flamenco in the Barrio Santa Cruz, a maze of white-washed streets overflowing with flowers.

Back roads take you south from Seville to the shining white villages of Andalusia, rising like castles above the fields of wheat and corn. From the past you move into the present in Marbella, the most tasteful and sophisticated resort along the Costa del Sol. You can lead an active life playing golf and tennis and enjoying a different restaurant every night— or spend your days lounging at your hotel pool at the edge of the sea.

The trip ends in Granada, where you'll check into a palace hotel and explore the Alhambra—a fabled palace worthy of the Arabian Nights.

lute. The world's most accomplished mathematicians, they showed the West how to use Arabic numerals. Without them we'd still be trying to multiply CCXII by MCLXI.

The caliphate eventually crumbled because of incompetent rulers and Islamic Spain split into warring states (taifas), the most powerful of which was Seville. In 1236, Córdoba fell to the Christians. About 100,000 Muslims fled to Granada, where they remained until the last caliph was ousted from power in 1492.

The first place to visit in Córdoba is the **mosque** (Mezquita) near the Guadalquivir River (☎ 957/47-05-12); the entrance is on Cardenal Herrero. Your initial feeling may well be of disorientation—of losing your way in a mysterious forest. Try to remember that in a mosque all paths are supposed to be good, because God is everywhere; that in God's house one can no longer lose the way. How different the feeling from that of a Christian church, where columns propel the worshiper's gaze forward to the altar and upward to God.

THE MAIN ROUTE

3–5 DAYS

Day excursion to Córdoba.

Two Nights: *Seville.*

One Night: *Marbella.*

One Night: *Granada.*

5–7 DAYS

Day excursion to Córdoba.

Two Nights: *Seville.*

Two Nights: *Marbella.*

Two Nights: *Granada.*

7–14 DAYS

Day excursion to Córdoba.

Three Nights: *Seville.*

One Night: *Parador of Carmona.*

Four Nights: *Marbella.*

Day excursions to Ronda and the perched white villages of Andalusia.

Three Nights: *Granada.*

Day excursion to Úbeda and Baeza.

It's important to realize also that the mosque doesn't serve the same function as a church. The side facing Mecca has a sanctuary indicating the direction worshipers should face while praying, but the rest of the mosque is a community gathering place—a huge rectangular desert tent where people come to stroll or study. In Islamic times, officials read proclamations here, scholars debated, and students attended classes.

The original mosque wasn't a place of self-abnegation where a worshiper escaped this life in order to find the next: It was a cool oasis (the columns are often compared to palm trees) where people could escape the heat of the sun. Arcaded porticos kept the mosque open to the outside world. The lines of columns were continued outside in the rows of orange trees in the perfumed courtyard, as if people and nature were working together in the service of God. When the Christians took power, they filled in the arcades to build shrines against the outer walls. The natural world was locked out and a living mosque became spiritually dead.

CORDOBA

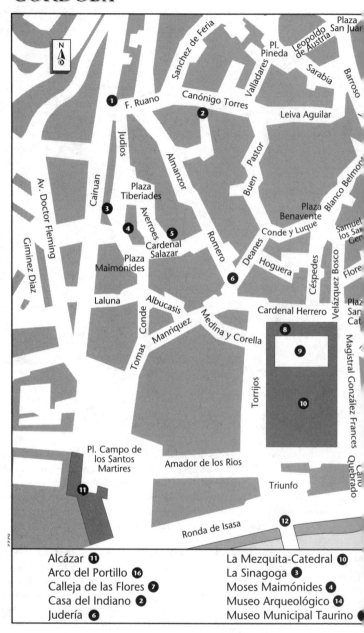

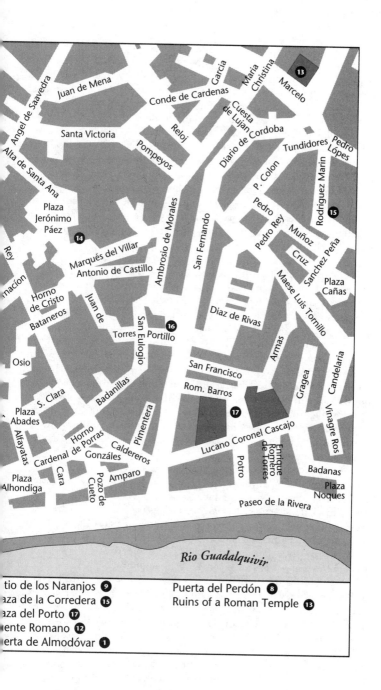

Notice how the columns are of different shapes and made from different materials: granite, marble, jasper, and other stones. These pillars were taken by the Muslims from various places they conquered. There are Roman pillars from Gaul, Visigoth pillars with fleur-de-lis designs, Byzantine pillars from Constantinople. The shorter ones are raised on bases; the longer ones are buried beneath the floor.

As the Muslim population increased, the mosque was enlarged three times. Completed, it measured 176.9 meters (590 ft.) by 127.4 meters (425 ft.), one-third of which was the open courtyard.

The horseshoe-shape arches, a trademark of early Moorish architecture, were used in the original Visigoth church that the mosque replaced. The double arches—one on top of the other—were added to raise the ceiling and create a sense of airiness; the idea may have come from the Roman aqueduct at Segovia. Many of the bronze and copper lamps were made from church bells.

It's mind-boggling that you can wander through this forest of pillars for perhaps 30 minutes without even knowing that within its midst is a full-size cathedral! At first, the Christians merely ripped out some of the pillars to create a space that resembled the nave (central aisle) of a church. This satisfied them for nearly 300 years, from 1236 to 1520. The local clergy then petitioned Charles V to build a transept, cover it, and close it in from the rest of the mosque. Charles, unaware of the desecration that was to be performed, gave his consent. When, 6 years later, he saw the results, he exclaimed, "If I had known what you were to do, you would not have done it. For what you have made here may be found in many other places, but what you have destroyed is to be found nowhere else in the world."

Enter through the **Patio de los Naranjos** (Courtyard of the Oranges). Try to imagine what it was like before it was walled in, when the ornamental fountains were used for ablutions by the faithful as they entered the mosque.

You'll enter into the oldest part of the mosque. Head to the right wall, turn left, and walk until you come to a break in the columns. This is where the original cathedral was. Continue to the far wall, turn left, and walk to the **Mihrab,** the sanctuary facing Mecca. This was the holiest part of the mosque. The gold dome is a synthesis of Byzantine and Islamic art—a reminder that the mosque was built by Christian workers lent by the Christian emperor in Constantinople. Note the paving stones worn smooth by centuries of worshipers kneeling in prayer.

Suddenly, in the midst of this forest, you step into a gilded baroque cathedral. What, you wonder, is it doing here? From a world of shadows you've stepped suddenly into a radiant clearing. James Michener called it a monument of "colossal ugliness." Others have called it a worm in a bright red apple and a Jonah in the whale. Still others are content to find it emblematic of southern Spain: the ruins of a Roman basilica incorporated into a Visigoth church, turned into a Muslim mosque with a Christian cathedral inside. Whatever you think of the cathedral, be grateful it was built, for without it the mosque would surely have been torn down. Admission 750PTA adults, 375PTA children. Open daily: Apr–Sept 10am–7pm; Oct–Mar 10am–1:30pm and 3:30–5:30pm.

Exit through the Courtyard of the Oranges and turn right to the famous Street of the Flowers (Calleja de las Flores). You can't miss it because it's filled with tourists. On this and adjoining streets are numerous shops selling leather goods, filigree jewelry, marquetry, fans, and pins. Other, less famous streets are just as beautiful, so walk around.

Directly behind the mosque is the **Jewish Quarter** (Judería). Like Seville's barrio, it's an ancient world of narrow twisted streets, cool courtyards, beautifully wrought window grilles, and whitewashed walls covered with flowers. The 14th-century **synagogue** (La Sinagoga; ☎ 957/20-29-28) is no more than a plain small room with some Mudéjar stucco on the upper walls, but it has rich historic associations and is one of three synagogues left in Spain. Admission 75PTA. Open Tues–Sat 10am–2pm and 3:30–5:30pm, Sun 10am–1:30pm.

For 3 centuries, under Muslim tolerance, the Jews of Córdoba enjoyed a golden age. They were doctors, philosophers, diplomats, and even generals. In the Judería is a statue of Moses Maimónides (1135–1204), a Jewish physician and one of the most brilliant men that Spain has ever produced.

Walk from the synagogue to the **Zoco,** Calle de los Júdio, s/n (☎ 957/296-262), a large courtyard where craftspeople work around a patio and where you can stop for a light lunch. Open Mon–Fri 9:30am–8pm and Sat–Sun 9:30am–2pm.

DINING

Ciro's, Paseo de la Victoria 19 (☎ 957/29-04-64). Ciro's has grown from a simple cafeteria into one of Córdoba's top three restaurants. It's tucked away in an air-conditioned enclave directly south of the rail station, about a quarter of a mile northwest of the Mezquita. The inventive chef tempts with his specialties, which include a savory pudding made with salmon and anchovies, followed by stuffed sweet peppers and hake in shrimp sauce. Reservations advised. Jacket recommended. AE, DC, MC, V. Closed Sun in summer. Moderate.

El Caballo Rojo, Cardenal Herrero 28 (☎ 957/47-53-75). This old converted mansion, near the mosque, has a terrace and dining rooms on three levels. The decor is regional. National specialties include cordero a la miel (lamb with honey). Reservations unnecessary. Jacket recommended. AE, DC, MC, V. Expensive.

La Almudaina, Plaza de los Santos Mártires (☎ 957/47-43-42). This top restaurant is located in an old converted school at the entrance to the Judería. Fish is a specialty, but the menu varies with the seasonal produce. Reservations essential. Casual. AE, DC, MC, V. Closed Sun July–Aug. Moderate.

ACCOMMODATIONS

Adarve, Magistral Gónzalez, Francés 15, 14003 Córdoba (☎ 957/48-11-02; fax 957/47-46-77). The Adarve was built in 1986 to face the

Mezquita on the side opposite its sibling hotel, the Maimónides. Constructed as part of an old house, it's furnished in smartly contemporary style, though the rooms are relatively small. 101 rms with bath. Facilities: garage. DC, MC, V. Very Expensive/Expensive.

Maimónides, Torrijos 4, 14003 Córdoba (☎ 957/47-15-00; fax 957/48-38-03). The Maimónides is small, friendly, and relatively reasonable. Its rooms are a bit worn but clean. The location, in the heart of the historic area next to the mosque, is ideal. The hotel doesn't have its own restaurant, but next door is the Bandolero with indoor and outdoor dining. 83 rms with bath. AE, DC, MC, V. Moderate.

Parador Nacional de la Arruzafa, Av. de la Arruzafa 33, 14012 Córdoba (☎ 957/27-59-00; fax 957/28-04-90). This modern parador, 4 kilometers (2½ miles) north of Córdoba, boasts lovely gardens, a restaurant serving Andalusian specialties, a children's dining area, and private terraces overlooking the city. 90 rms with bath; 6 suites. Facilities: restaurant, outdoor pool. AE, DC, MC, V. Expensive.

SEVILLE

When foreigners imagine romantic Spain, they think of **Seville,** Andalusia's largest city. It was here that Velázquez and Murillo were born; here that Don Juan, the model for *Don Giovanni,* lived; here that Don José first met Carmen. It was Seville that inspired *The Marriage of Figaro* and *The Barber of Seville.* Here Cervantes was imprisoned and Don Quixote was born.

The important sights—the cathedral, the Giralda, the Alcázar, and the Barrio Santa Cruz—are all within walking distance of one another. Not far away are the bullring and the María Luisa Gardens—among the loveliest in Spain.

When the Christians overran Córdoba, they decided to build their cathedral inside the mosque; in Seville they demolished the mosque and built **Seville Cathedral,** Plaza del Triunfo, Avenida de la Constitución (☎ 95/421-4971). The Christians were overwhelmed by the beauty of Seville and must have felt a need to prove that Christianity could do as well. The cathedral's size will overwhelm you; walking beneath those massive pillars—the vaults rising 55 meters (184 ft.) above the transept crossing—is like strolling through a forest of giant sequoias. The gloom is immense, too, the pillars disappearing upward into darkness. How unlike the Alhambra, where life is seen as something to enjoy, not escape.

To the left of the modern doors is the **Royal Chapel** (Capilla Real), a Renaissance building with an ornamented dome. The sanctuary contains some 15th- and 16th-century choir stalls, as rich as the Spanish imagination, and the tomb of Christopher Columbus. There's a school of thought that says Columbus's remains are still in Santo Domingo, but we're in Seville now, so let's assume he's here.

The **library** behind the cathedral contains 10 books owned by Columbus, including *Marco Polo,* Plutarch's *Lives,* Seneca's *Tragedies,* and Pliny's *History.* Can you imagine Columbus reading Seneca? His marginal

SEVILLE

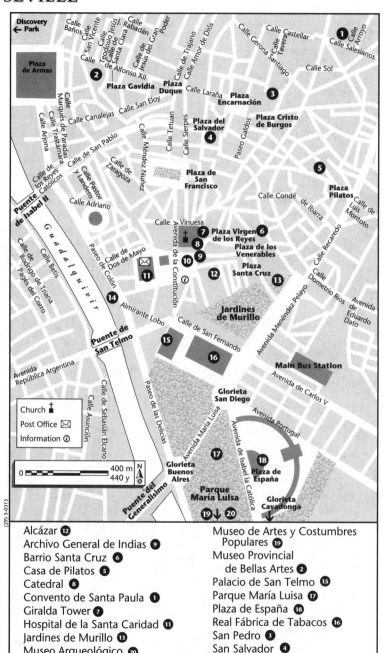

WHAT TO SEE & DO WITH CHILDREN

Córdoba: The mosque, which looks like a forest of zebras.
Costa del Sol: The pools, beaches, and tennis courts; the Nerja caves; the dance clubs at Puerto Banús.
Granada: The Gypsy caves on Sacromonte; a hike from Pico de Veleta.
Seville: A walk through the Old Quarter to a flamenco show at Plaza de Santa Cruz; a climb to the top of the Giralda; a horse-drawn carriage ride from the cathedral; a bullfight; a performance at the new opera house.

notes all have to do with gold, pearls, ivory, and pepper—in other words, making money.

The 96.5-meter (322-ft.) **Giralda** (minaret) was the only part of the original mosque (other than the Orange Tree Court) that the Christians didn't destroy. A 16th-century Renaissance belfry has been added to the original 12th-century structure: How typically Andalusian to have a church bell rung from the top of a Muslim minaret!

You'll notice that the Giralda has a solidity and a monumentality not usually associated with Muslim architecture. This is because it was built by the Almohades, a fundamentalist dynasty that eschewed all ostentation in an effort to restore the strict religious beliefs and simple lifestyle of the Prophet. Gone are the horseshoe-shape arches (inspired by the Visigoths) used in the Córdoba mosque; the arches here are more pointed, in the spirit of the Middle East.

Giraldas were built for the muezzin to call the faithful to service. In small mosques he stood at the door; in large ones he climbed the minaret, faced Mecca, put his forefingers in his ears, and cried, "God is most great" (four times) and "Come to salvation" (twice). In the morning he added, "Prayer is better than sleep." The muezzin couldn't be drunk, insane, or a woman. Climb the gentle ramp—two horses wide—to a platform at 68.9 meters (230 ft.) for a breathtaking view of Seville. Admission 500PTA, which includes entrance to the Giralda. Open daily 11am–5pm.

Outside the cathedral are horse-drawn carriages (coche caballos) waiting to take you for a ride. Be sure to bargain and to agree on a price beforehand. One lovely trip is through María Luisa Park.

On your way from the cathedral and the Alcázar consider a visit to the **Archives of the Indies** (Archivo General de Indias; ☎ 95/421-1234). Among the documents are signatures of Columbus and Magellan and a letter Cervantes wrote in 1590, at the age of 43, asking for a job in the New World. If accepted, Cervantes would probably have lived out his life as a public accountant and never written *Don Quixote;* but scrawled across his application are the words, "Let him look for something closer to home." Open for guided tours Mon–Fri 10am–1pm.

The **Alcázar** (☎ 95/422-7163) is an intricate maze of gleaming tiles, arabesques, carved wood ceilings, and lacelike stucco—a perfect setting, it would seem, for the Arabian Nights. Its stunning profusion of shapes and forms—H.V. Morton called it "the multiplication table set to music"—will enchant you. Equally fascinating is the fact that this Moorish palace was built for Catholic king Pedro the Cruel (1333–69).

When Pedro came to power in 1350, more than 70 years had passed since the Moors had relinquished power and the palace that the Almohades had built was nearly in ruins. A man as sensuous as he was cruel, Pedro loved the idea of living with his harem in an exotic Moorish palace, so he hired the finest Muslim craftsmen to emulate the Alhambra in Granada. These craftsmen were called Mudéjars, and their art was executed according to Muslim designs and techniques, but under a Christian yoke. Pedro's palace was a hybrid structure, half Visigoth, half Moorish; but the fact that it was built at all shows how completely Arabic ideas had infiltrated Spanish thought.

Restorations went on through the 19th century, destroying much of the palace's integrity; nonetheless, it remains one of the greatest and purest examples of Mudéjar architecture in the world. As you tour the rooms, have fun trying to distinguish Christian from Muslim elements and comparing the sometimes glaring harshness of the new tiles to the soft, subtle lyricism of the originals.

If you don't see any paintings, it's because the early Muslims, like the Jews, saw the use of idols as a threat to their concept of the One God, and therefore frowned on representational art. Their need for artistic self-expression found its outlet in geometric forms and calligraphy. The greatest mathematicians of the ancient world, they loved logical, coherent lines. Of all the arts, they respected calligraphy the most. In the West we think of the written word as nothing but an abstract symbol; but to the Arabs, language has a visual dimension as well. Words, to them, not only celebrate beauty, they *are* beauty.

A grand 16th-century staircase takes you to the **Royal Apartments** — the most touched-up part of the palace, some rooms altered as late as the 19th century. The lacelike delicacy of some of the work is Isabeline — a style named for Isabella, Ferdinand's wife, after they had ousted the Moors from Granada. The need to cover every inch of space with fine designs, as a woman's veil does, was inspired by the Moorish love for detail; yet note how the Spanish work is voluptuous for its own sake, whereas the Moorish work is only the outward expression of a mathematical love of form.

The Moorish **Court of the Maidens** (Patio de las Doncellas) was, sadly, given an upper story in the 16th century. Surrounding the court are rooms of finely carved stucco and glazed tiles. The room of Emperor Charles V — he was the one who allowed a Renaissance palace to be in the Alhambra — has a notable collection of tapestries. Also worth seeing is the domed ceiling (cupola) of the **Hall of the Ambassadors** (Salón de Embajadores). Did Pedro know that the verses on the wall were in praise of Allah?

Also off the Court of the Maidens are the **apartments of María de Padilla,** Pedro's mistress. Simple, pious, and beautiful, she alone gave beauty to Pedro's life. At the advice of the court, he married a French princess, Blanche of Bourbon, but after 3 days he imprisoned her and fled back to María. He married again, but after 1 day he was back in María's arms.

Don't miss the **terraced gardens** of the Alcázar, filled with exotic trees, shrubs, and ornamental fountains. You can sit here beneath the magnolia trees and imagine yourself back in the court of Pedro the Cruel. Admission 700PTA. Open Tues–Sat 10:30am–5pm, Sun 10am–1pm.

From the gardens, walk to the Flag Court (Patio de las Banderas) and follow a covered passage to the Barrio Santa Cruz, the former Jewish Quarter, where the Spanish nobility lived in the 17th century. The **Barrio Santa Cruz** is one of Spain's most picturesque sights. Narrow white streets open out into tiny squares that could be in North Africa. The sun-bleached walls give no indication of what's within; be sure to peer through the beautiful wrought-iron doors at the tiled courtyards with their gurgling fountains and orange trees. What a contrast between the simplicity of these homes and the rococo indulgences of the cathedral.

Among the houses are curiosity shops that sell everything from old jewelry to mirrors, antique ceramics, and daggers.

TAKE A BREAK

*On several squares are restaurants where you can pause for drinks or lunch. Be sure to return at night when the cafes blast their lights and music into the dark streets. At Plaza de los Venerables is **Casa Román** (☎ 95/421-6408), an atmospheric bar with hams hanging from the ceiling. At Plaza de Santa Cruz 11 is **Los Gallos** (☎ 95/421-6981), where you can watch flamenco. Plaza de Doña Elvira has a fountain, and benches for guitarists.*

North of the barrio is **Pilate's House** (Casa de Pilatos), Plaza Pilatos (☎ 95/422-5055). This is a smaller, less crowded version of the Alcázar, with carved wood doors from Lebanon, beautiful old tiles, and a fountain in a central courtyard. A 16th-century ancestor of the present owner returned from the Holy Land and built his palace in what he thought was the style of Pontius Pilate's home, yet it's much more Mudéjar than Roman. Upstairs are some lesser-known paintings by Goya, Murillo, and Velázquez. Admission to museum 1,000PTA; patio and gardens 500PTA. Museum open daily 10am–2pm and 4–6pm; patio and gardens open daily 9am–7pm.

The **Charity Hospital** (Hospital de la Santa Caridad), Calle Temprado 3 (☎ 95/422-32-22), is a baroque alms house with a single-nave church containing paintings by Murillo and Valdés Leal. The best-known work is Leal's morbid *Finis gloriae mundi*, in which a bishop in his coffin is being devoured by cockroaches or worms. Murillo said the painting made him want to hold his nose.

In the crypt below the altar lie the remains of Miguel de Mañara. Inscribed on his tomb are the words, "Here lie the ashes of the worst man the world has ever known." Mañara, who commissioned Leal's paintings, is often mistaken for the original Don Juan. Actually, he saw a play about Don Juan and was inspired to follow in his footsteps. One story tells of how, after a drunken orgy, he saw a funeral procession with a partially decomposed corpse that was himself. According to another legend he made advances to a beautiful nun, but when she turned her head aside he saw that her face was eaten away by a foul disease more horrible than death. Whatever happened, he was so overwhelmed by a sense of his own mortality that he gave away all his possessions, joined the brotherhood, and spent the rest of his life burying the bodies of executed prisoners. Somerset Maugham described the chapel he built as "a bed-chamber transformed into a chapel for the administration of the last sacrament." Admission 300PTA. Open Mon–Sat 10am–1pm and 3:30–6pm, Sun 10:30am–12:30pm.

After a day of sightseeing, nothing could be lovelier than an early-evening stroll along the Guadalquivir River between the **San Telmo** and **Isabel II bridges.** The walk takes you past the early 13th-century **Golden Tower** (Torre del Oro), Paseo de Cristóbal Colón (☎ **95/422-24-19;** admission 100PTA; open Tues–Fri 10am–2pm, Sat–Sun 10am–1pm), one of the few remaining monuments of Almohade Spain. Sixty-minute **river cruises** depart from near the tower, usually at 5:45pm. Contact **Cruceros Turísticos Torre del Oro,** Paseo Marqués de Contadero (☎ **95/412-13-96).**

To escape the summer heat, stroll through the peaceful **Parque María Luisa,** one of the prettiest in Spain, with pools and fountains and quiet, shaded nooks beneath towering beech trees. On one side of the entrance is the **Tobacco Factory** (Real Fábrica de Tabacos), where some 10,000 women and girls worked in the 19th century, including the fiery Carmen. The building is now part of the University of Seville.

DINING

Dinner usually doesn't begin until 9 or 10pm, so consider a drink first at the elegant Alfonso XIII (see "Accommodations," below) on San Fernando, close to the Alcázar.

El Burladero, Canalejas 1 (☎ **95/422-29-00).** With its bullfighting motif, this place near the bullring seems to have been gored by success. It's still popular, though, particularly among el toro fans. Try the clams in a sauce of onions, tomatoes, and white wine. Reservations suggested. Casual. AE, DC, MC, V. Closed Aug. Expensive.

El Rincón de Curro, Virgen de Luján 45 (☎ **95/445-02-38).** A 5-minute walk from the Alfonso XIII, regional specialties are formally and graciously presented in what some consider the best restaurant in the city. Reservations suggested. Jacket required. AE, DC, V. Closed Aug and Sun. Expensive.

Enrique Becerra, Gamazo 2 (☎ **95/421-30-49).** Off Plaza Nueva near the cathedral, this is an outpost of fine Andalusian cookery, using market-fresh ingredients deftly handled by a well-trained kitchen staff. In this friendly oasis, sample such fresh fish as hake and sea bream. The gazpacho is the city's best, and the sangría served icy cold mitigates the impact of the heat wave outside in summer. Reservations suggested. Casual. AE, DC, MC, V. Closed Sun. Moderate.

Hostería del Laurel, Plaza de los Venerables 5 (☎ 95/422-02-95). This restaurant is in the barrio, with hanging hams, herbs, and a good reputation for fresh fish dishes, such as fritura mixta. Reservations suggested. Casual. AE, DC, MC, V. Inexpensive.

La Albahaca, Plaza Santa Cruz 12 (☎ 95/422-07-14). Le Albahaca is a small restaurant in an old patrician house in the heart of the barrio. There's a limited menu but lots of atmosphere. Reservations suggested. Jacket suggested. AE, DC, MC, V. Closed Sun. Moderate.

La Dorada, Av. Ramón y Cajal (☎ 95/492-10-66). La Dorada specializes in fresh seafood, such as dorada (tuna) and lubina (flatfish), baked in a shell of salt. Reservations suggested. Jacket suggested. AE, DC, MC. V. Closed Sun dinner (Sept–June) and Aug. Expensive.

Los Alcázares, Miguel de Mañara 10 (☎ 951/421-31-03). This place looks a bit too much like something off a travel poster, but it offers good value. It's also conveniently near the cathedral. The meals are served in a quaint white-plaster building faced with tiles. Reservations unnecessary. Casual. Closed Sun. MC, V. Moderate.

Méson Don Raimundo, Argote de Molina 26 (☎ 95/421-29-25). This is a converted 1600s convent at the end of a flower-lined alley in the center of the Barrio de Santa Cruz. Its interior decor of brick and terra-cotta is Andalusian cliché, but the regional food is worth the trek. Soups are big in the chef's repertoire, including a smooth one made with clams and pine nuts. Try the casserole of partridge in sherry sauce or the wild rabbit. Some recipes are adapted from old Arab-Hispanic cookbooks. Reservations suggested. Casual. AE, DC, MC, V. Inexpensive.

Rio Grande, Calle Betis 70 (☎ 95/427-39-56). Rio Grande is another top restaurant, serving summer meals alfresco on a scenic terrace above the Guadalquivir River near the west end of San Telmo Bridge. The elegant (as opposed to regional) dining room has globe lamps, oil portraits, and potted plants. If you have only 1 night in Seville, you may prefer a place with more of a barrio atmosphere. Reservations essential. Jacket suggested. AE, DC, MC, V. Expensive.

ACCOMMODATIONS

Alfonso XIII, San Fernando 2, 41004 Seville (☎ 800/221-2340 or 95/422-28-50; fax 95/421-60-33). The Alfonso is in a class by itself. It was built to house wealthy guests for an Exhibition in 1929 and has retained the elegance of a stately palace. Despite some exterior and interior renovations completed in 1992, the rooms aren't as grand as you might expect from the price (the Alfonso is Spain's third or fourth most expensive hotel), and some of the furnishings are worn. However, the courtyard atrium is a museum of Spanish and Moorish tapestries and art. Come here for predinner cocktails even if you don't book a room. 130 rms with bath; 18 suites. Facilities: formal dining room, outdoor pool, shops, hairdresser, parking. AE, DC, MC, V. Very Expensive.

Doña María, Don Remondo 19, 41004 Seville (☎ **95/422-49-90;** fax 95/421-95-46). This hotel is tucked into a side street minutes from the barrio and the cathedral. No two rooms are alike—some charming with canopied brass beds, others cramped and plain. There's a top-floor pool and a comfortable Moorish-style lounge with antiques and couches for you to curl up in. The price is right, too; about half of what the Alfonso XIII charges. 60 rms with bath. Facilities: restaurant serving breakfast only, rooftop pool, bar. AE, DC, MC, V. Moderate.

Girarda, Justin de Neve 8, 41004 Seville (☎ **95/421-51-13**). One of several basic family-run hotels in the barrio, it's in a wonderful old Moorish-style building with a colorful enclosed patio that also serves as a basic restaurant, open daily for lunch and dinner. 4 rms without bath. AE, MC, V. Inexpensive.

Grand Hotel Lar, Plaza de Carmen Benitez 3, 41003 Seville (☎ **95/ 441-03-61;** fax 95/441-04-52). This slick modern hotel is a short walk from the barrio. 129 rms with bath. Facilities: gym, sauna, fax service. AE, DC, V. Very Expensive/Expensive.

Hotel Tryp Colón, Canalejas 1, 41001 Seville (☎ **800/387-8842** or 95/422-29-00; fax 95/422-09-38). This gets an olé! as one of the better large modern hotels, popular with bullfight aficionados. Seventh-floor rooms have private balconies. 204 rms with bath; 14 suites. Facilities: formal restaurant, 24-hour room service, gym, fax service. AE, DC, MC, V. Expensive.

La Rábida, Castelar 24, 41001 Seville (☎ **95/422-09-60;** fax 95/422-43-75). Here's a real find for the budget-minded: an old-fashioned hotel on a quietish street near the town center. Marble halls lead to basic rooms surrounding an open courtyard. The rooms are unmemorable but clean, with high ceilings. Breakfast is included in the rates. 100 rms with bath. No credit cards. Moderate.

Parador de Carmona, 41410 Carmona (☎ **95/414-10-10;** fax 95/ 414-17-12). This parador is in Carmona, west of Seville. It's a 40-minute drive, but how often do you get to sleep in the ruins of a Moorish fort? You won't want to commute more than once, so stay either the night before you arrive in Seville or the night you leave. 63 rms with bath. Facilities: outdoor pool. AE, DC, MC, V. Expensive.

Pasarela, Av. de la Borbolla 11, 41004 Seville (☎ **95/441-55-11;** fax 95/442-07-27). Pasarela is inviting and well run with modern facilities. 77 rms with bath. Facilities: restaurant serving breakfast only, gym, sauna, parking. AE, DC, V. Very Expensive/Expensive.

Residencia Murillo, Lope de Rueda 7–9, 41004 Seville (☎ **95/421-60-95;** fax 95/421-96-16). The Murillo is a picturesque hotel on a pedestrian-only street. The front rooms have balconies, and the hotel has many long-term tenants, even though it has no restaurant. 57 rms with bath. Facilities: bar. AE, DC, MC, V. Inexpensive.

Reyes Católicos, Gravina 57, 41001 Seville (☎ 95/421-12-00; fax 95/421-63-12). This is a small modern annex to the nearby Montecarlo Hotel. 26 rms with bath. AE, DC, V. Moderate.

ON TO MARBELLA

You have a choice of driving directly from Seville to Marbella or following back roads through the **perched white villages of Andalusia.**

If you're anxious to see these villages but have limited time, drive through them en route to Marbella. You'll see only a few of them—but some are better than none. Here's the route to follow: From Seville, take N334 to Morón. Continue south to Pruna and Olvera; then go 3.2 kilometers (2 miles) west on N342 and south to Setenil, Arriate, and Ronda. From Ronda, drive south on N339 to San Pedro de Alcantara and east on N340 to Marbella. Pick up a large-scale Costa del Sol map at tourist shops in Seville.

A better idea, if time permits, is to drive directly from Seville to Marbella, settle into your hotel, and then break the routine one day with a side trip through Ronda and the other perched villages.

MARBELLA

Marbella is the most fashionable and sedate resort area along the coast. There's a town with both a charming old Moorish quarter and a modern T-shirt–and–fudge section along the main drag; but when people speak of Marbella they refer both to the town and to the resorts—some more exclusive than others—stretching 16 kilometers (10 miles) or so on either side of town, between the highway and the beach. If you're vacationing in southern Spain, this is the place to stay. You'll find championship golf and tennis, fashionable waterfront cafes, and trendy boutiques in the charming medieval quarter of town.

The Golden Bachelor—like Prince Charming, the richest catch in Spain—hangs out at the Marbella Club. Petrodollars fill the Arab banks along N340. The Arabs, of course, stick to their own *wadi* (domain); what you'll see are people like yourself, shopping in Marbella and relaxing in one of the resorts surrounded by subtropical foliage at the edge of the sea. Marbella does have a certain Florida-land-boom feel to it, but development has been controlled, and Marbella, let's hope, will never turn into another tacky Torremolinos.

Most of your time should be devoted to indolence—swimming in the ocean, sunbathing on sandy beaches or by the hotel pool. When you need something to do, visit the old Moorish section and wander along the narrow whitewashed lanes radiating from **Plaza de los Naranjos.** Among the trashy souvenir emporia you'll find some tasteful crafts shops like **Pretty Table,** Ctra. de Cádiz, km 179 (☎ 95/282-5693), offering a wide range of crystal gifts and silver-plated items at affordable prices, plus an array of other merchandise. Most boutiques specialize in beachwear; there's a choice of charming cafes for lunch or drinks.

Another trip you won't want to miss is to **Puerto Banús,** 8 kilometers (5 miles) west of Marbella. Less than 25 years ago Puerto Banús was a quiet port with a few bars. Today it has more than 125 restaurants and shops. Blinked into existence by a group of developers with a sense of style and taste, Puerto Banús is an adult fantasyland, a Yuppieland of Benettons and Picasso Pizzerias, quality restaurants and designer boutiques—all stretching along two streets behind the harbor, with a small sandy beach at one end. Everything is fun and for sale—just as it is in the restored harborfronts of Boston, Newport, and New York. The uniformly whitewashed buildings lend a semblance of order and peacefulness to the profusion of shops—and create an atmosphere more Spanish than Spain. Many shops are open to 2am. The young take over the piano bars and dance clubs from around 11pm and straggle home at dawn.

DINING

Cipriano, Muelle de Levante, Puerto Banús (☎ 95/281-10-77). The Cipriano enjoys a good reputation for fresh fish. The prices are slightly lower than at Gran Marisquería Santiago, and the atmosphere is more casual. Reservations advised. Casually elegant. AE, MC, DC, V. Closed Feb. Moderate.

Don Leone, Muelle Ribera 45, Puerto Banús (☎ 95/281-17-16). Don Leone is a local favorite, with such specialties as artichoke soup, fresh homemade pastas, and fritta mista del pescados (a mixed fish fry). Reservations advised. Casually elegant. AE, MC, V. Closed Nov 21– Dec 21 and lunch from late June to mid-Sept. Expensive.

El Balcón de la Vírgen, Remedios 2 (☎ 95/277-60-92). Here's a friendly low-priced restaurant in a 16th-century building in Marbella's Old Quarter. Reservations advised. Casual. AE, MC, V. Closed Tues Nov–May. Moderate.

El Portalon, Carretera de Cádiz, km 178 (☎ 95/282-7880). El Portalon is a citadel of chic, a sophisticated rendezvous lying a mile west of the center on the road leading to Puerto Banús. Most of its patrons are guests at the ultra-expensive Marbella Club, adjacent to the restaurant. Time-honored dishes of Spain like suckling pig and lamb are the chef's specialties—emerging from an old-fashioned wood-burning oven. Impeccably fresh fish is imported daily, and it's often grilled—none better than the sea bass. Reservations suggested. Casually elegant. AE, DC, MC, V. Expensive.

Gran Marisquería Santiago, Av. Duque de Ahumada 5 (☎ 95/277-43-39). This restaurant is well known for its fresh seafood: sole meunière, halibut with mushroom sauce, fresh salmon with herbs, lobster from the tank. The atmosphere is informal—the restaurant is on the busy waterfront, in back of the main town beach. Reservations unnecessary. Casual. AE, DC, V. Closed Nov. Moderate.

La Hacienda, Ctra. Cadiz, km 193 (☎ 95/283-12-67). About 12.8 kilometers (8 miles) east of town, toward Málaga, is this white adobe building with rustic decorations (beamed ceilings, fireplace, tiled floor, wood tables). Specialties include veal cooked in foil, roast partridge in vine leaves, quail flambé, guinea hen, and maize pancakes. Reservations advised. Jacket required. AE, DC, MC, V. Closed Nov 15–Dec 15. Expensive.

La Meridiana, Camino de la Cruz, Las Lomas (☎ 95/277-61-90). This restaurant 4.8 kilometers (3 miles) west of town, toward Cádiz, serves meals on the garden terrace of a Bauhaus-type building. Reservations advised. Jacket suggested. AE, DC, V. Closed Mon, Tues lunch, and Jan 9–Feb 28. Expensive.

Marbella Club, Bulevar Principe Alfonso von Hohenlohe s/n (☎ 95/282-22-11). On N340, 3.2 kilometers (2 miles) west of town, toward Cádiz, this is where the private villa owners come to socialize, creating an intimate, community feeling you won't experience in other Marbella resorts. Reservations advised. Jacket required. AE, DC, MC, V. Expensive.

Mesón del Museo, Plaza de Los Naranjos 11 (☎ 95/282-5623). This place is set on Marbella's most famous and colorful old square, occupying the upper floor of an 18th-century structure housing one of the oldest art and antique galleries in Marbella. A Swedish/Chilean husband and wife team up to offer both Swedish and international dishes prepared with fresh ingredients. The cross-cultural menu ranges from Swedish meatballs to filet of beef stuffed with truffles or foie gras. Reservations suggested. Casual. AE, DC, MC, V. Closed Sun Dec 23–May 1 and Sun July–Aug. Moderate.

Taberna del Alabardero, Muelle Benabola, Puerto Banús (☎ 95/281-27-94). This restaurant serves seafood specialties in a setting overlooking the harbor. Reservations advised. Casually elegant. AE, DC, MC, V. Closed Jan–Feb. Expensive.

ACCOMMODATIONS

The only reason to stay in town is if you're on a tight budget and have no car. Students can stay in small family-run hotels in the Old Quarter. There are a few reasonably priced package tour–type high-rise hotels only a block from the busy town beach. For most visitors, air-conditioning in summer is a must. The ocean is uninviting at times, thanks to improper pollution controls, so a hotel pool is a plus.

You may prefer to stay at one of the sparkling white resorts strung along the beach on either side of town. Finding the right one is critical.

Andalucía Plaza, Urbanizacíon Neuva Andalucía, 29660 Apartado 21 Nueva Andalucía (☎ 95/281-20-00; fax 95/281-47-92). Stay here only if you like being surrounded by Americans or don't mind 600 conventioneers at dinner. 308 rms with bath; 67 suites. Facilities: restaurants, bars, subtropical gardens, indoor and outdoor pools, boutiques, tennis. AE, DC, MC, V. Expensive.

Don Carlos, Ctra. N340, km 192, 29600 Marbella (☎ 800/223-5652 or 95/283-11-40; fax 95/283-34-29). About 12.8 kilometers (8 miles) east of Marbella, on the road toward Málaga, is a 17-story white concrete slab at the edge of the sea. This former Hilton attracts an American crowd. Ask for an upper room facing the ocean. The isolated 5.2-hectare (13-acre) estate has lovely gardens, and you can walk along a natural beach away from the commercial areas. Otherwise, you need a car. 223 rms with bath; 15 suites. Facilities: restaurants, bars, large gardens, heated outdoor pool, boutiques, tennis. AE, DC, MC, V. Very Expensive.

El Fuerte, Fuerte s/n, 29600 Marbella (☎ 95/282-15-00; fax 95/282-44-11). This hotel offers simple, adequate rooms in town. There's a garden with palm trees and a certain faded elegance in the public areas. 261 rms with bath; 2 suites. Facilities: restaurants, bars, outdoor pool, tennis courts. AE, DC, MC, V. Moderate.

Hotel Baveria, Camino del Calvario 4, 29600 Marbella (☎ 95/277-29-50; fax 95/277-29-58). The Baveria is an eight-story two-star hotel built in the late 1960s; it's set on the main street of town, opposite the bus station. 41 rms with bath. MC, V. Inexpensive.

Los Monteros, Crta. N340, km 187, 29600 Marbella (☎ 95/277-17-00; fax 95/282-58-46). About 6.4 kilometers (4 miles) east of Marbella, on the road to Malága, Los Monteros prides itself on being one of Spain's most expensive hotels. It's minutes from the famous Rio Real golf course (free bus service to the greens). A large pool and lovely lawns separate a modern two-story section from a more old-fashioned seven-story building. The rooms and views vary; specify what you want. Eighty percent of the guests are English, which may explain the somewhat starched formality of many rooms, and the beach chairs perfectly aligned on manicured lawns, like so many pieces of sculpture. 160 rms with bath; 10 suites. Facilities: restaurants, bars, subtropical gardens, outdoor pools, private beach, horseback riding, boutiques, seven tennis courts. AE, DC, MC, V. Expensive.

Marbella Club, Bulevar Principe Alfonso von Hohenlohe s/n, 29600 Marbella (☎ 800/448-8355 or 95/282-22-11; fax 95/282-98-84). The Marbella Club is 3.2 kilometers (2 miles) west of town on the road to Cádiz. The grande dame of Marbella, it's old and aristocratic and tends to attract an older, established clientele, who request the same room year after year. The fact that the local patricians all belong to the club and come down from their villas for drinks and dinner gives it a certain color and class. The bungalow-style rooms range from cramped to spacious, and the decor varies from Beach Modern to regional; specify what you want, but ask for a room that's been recently renovated. The grounds are exquisite. Breakfast is served on a patio where songbirds flit through the lush subtropical vegetation. 85 rms with bath; 34 suites; 10 bungalows. Facilities: restaurant, piano bar, outdoor heated pool, private beach, boutiques, tennis. AE, DC, MC, V. Very Expensive.

Puente Romano, Ctra. N340, km 176, 29600 Marbella (☎ 95/277-01-00; fax 95/277-57-66). About 3.2 kilometers (2 miles) west of town on the road to Cádiz, this hotel is just past the Marbella Club. Though under the same management, it has a different atmosphere. More international, Puente Romano offers greater anonymity and hosts a greater number of

American guests. It's a modern hotel/apartment complex of low white stucco buildings on beautifully manicured grounds. The rooms here are more luxurious than at the Marbella Club—and more predictable. 217 rms with bath. Facilities: restaurant, piano bar, nightclub, two outdoor pools, private beach, boutiques, tennis. AE, DC, MC, V. Very Expensive.

Backpackers and students on a budget can stay in small family-run hotels in the Old Quarter of Marbella and pay between $24 and $40 for a double room, without breakfast. In rooms of this caliber, air-conditioning won't exist and the setting is likely to be well-used, a bit battered, and perhaps in need of a renovation, but the rooms will usually be clean and in some cases have private baths. Two worthy choices are the **Hostal del Pilar,** Mesoncillo 4, 29600 Marbella (☎ **95/282-99-36**), a raffish place run by a pair of expatriate Scots who maintain a bar with a pool table on the street level for a clientele of backpackers from around Europe. None of the 22 rooms has a bath; accommodations are in a second story added in the 1970s to a street-level architectural core that's at least a century old. Slightly more expensive is the more restrained **Enriqueta,** Calle Los Caballeros 18, 29600 Marbella (☎ **95/277-00-58**), whose 16 rooms have baths and access to a communal TV room.

ON TO RONDA

Perhaps it was the light after a late-afternoon storm, but the drive through the **perched white villages of Andalusia** was the highlight of my last trip to Spain. There are many such villages, blazing white, clutching the rocky mountainsides above the fields of sunflowers and wheat, grape, and maize.

The houses are painted white to ward off the summer heat. Up close, you see that the streets are dusty and the walls crumbling. But from a distance, the towns seem to rise from the plains like medieval castles. The uniform whiteness gives them an architectural integrity as soothing to the heart as to the eye: Here at last is a world where, visually at least, the individual is subsumed; where everything says "us," not "I." What you'll see is the seasonless monochromatic world; the family is still the wellspring of life in these Moorish towns, and the true colors come from the perfumed courtyards within.

You owe it to yourself at least once to leave the main highways and wander along the back roads, through fields and pasture land, beneath the perched white villages. The roads are as safe as any in Spain and marked well enough that with a detailed map you won't get lost—at least not for long. Drive west on N340 to San Pedro de Alcántara (10.7km/6.7 miles) and head north on C339 to Ronda (43.2km/27 miles).

RONDA

Both the modern district and the old Moorish quarter of **Ronda** are split in two by a great gorge. The bridge across it, which has a restaurant in the former prison cell above its central arch, is one of Spain's most spectacular sights. The only problem with Ronda is its popularity; you have no sense of discovery here as you do in the white villages. The old town lies behind walls built during the Moorish occupation, which lasted until 1485. Because of the high elevation, the houses are low and small, with steep roofs, as they are in the colder regions of the north. Park at the **Collegiate Church** (Colegiata de Santa María la Mayor), Plaza de la Ciudad, on your left as you drive through the old town. Of particular note in this former mosque are the Renaissance chancel (where the altar is) and the ornate choir stalls, as well as the minaret bell tower. Walk behind the church (the side away from the road) and turn right to the **Mondragón Palace,** El Campillo (☎ 95/287-08-18), with its twin towers. The terrace overlooks the gorge and the plains below. Admission 200PTA adults; under 14 free. Open Mon–Fri 10am–7pm and Sat–Sun 10am–3pm.

The view from the **bridge,** looking down 110 meters (360 ft.), is spectacular. Cross the bridge and enter the new town. On your left is the **bullring.** Built in 1785, it's one of the oldest in Spain. Francisco Romero, the father of modern bullfighting—he introduced the cape, the muleta, and most of the rituals—was born in Ronda in 1698. His son Juan Romero introduced the "supporting team," and his grandson Pedro Romero (1754–1839) became one of Spain's greatest bullfighters.

Also on your left, beyond the bullring, are the **Paseo de la Merced Gardens** (Alameda del Tajo). Stroll through the gardens and enjoy a dramatic walk along the cliffs.

For a short excursion from Ronda you should consider a visit to **Cueva de la Pileta** (Pileta Cave), just outside Benaoján (☎ 95/16-72-02). Not only are the caves fascinating for their multiple caverns filled with stalactites and stalagmites, but they contain black-and-red drawings predating those at Altimira and indicating that the caves were inhabited more than 25,000 years ago. Tours daily 10am–1pm and 4–6pm. Admission (including the 1-hour tour) 600PTA adults, 400PTA children.

Continue north through the modern section of Ronda on C339 to Puerto de Montejaque (16km/10 miles). Turn left on C344 to **Grazalema** (12.9km/8 miles), 814.7 meters (2,716 ft.) up, where you can visit the Church of the Encarnación and wander through the white streets, beneath balconies and patios bursting with flowers.

Now you have a decision to make. To reach **Zahara,** one of the most beautiful of the white villages, the most direct route, over a rough mountain road, is to take C344 another mile west and then to turn north (right) on Route 521 (12.8km/8 miles), past Puerto de las Palas. The longer, less dramatic route is to drive northeast 9.6 kilometers (6 miles) from Grazalema to Puerto de Asperilla on C339; then, at the T-intersection, turn left (north), go about 11.2 kilometers (7 miles), and turn left again on Route 521 to Zahara.

If you're addicted to back roads, follow the signs from Zahara to the pretty town of **El Gastor** and then head north to the major road, N342.

AFTER DARK IN ANDALUSIA

Granada

In Granada nightlife centers on the Gypsy caves on Sacromonte, the hillside opposite the Generalife. Tourists submit to and sometimes participate in 30-minute flamenco shows, which have been described as "a cosmic low in tourist-racketeering." Although very touristy, some of the most professional shows are presented at the **Jardines Neptuno,** Calle Neptuno (☎ 958/52-25-33), which often features regional music and ballet as well. The shows at **Reina Mora,** Mirador de San Cristobal (☎ 958/27-22-28), are more intimate and less touristy. If you absolutely insist on going to the Sacromonte caves, then the best shows are at **Zambra Maria la Canastera** (☎ 958/12-11-83), but always call before going here.

The origin of the Gypsies isn't known, but it's generally believed that they came from northern India and migrated to Persia around A.D. 1000. From there they split into two branches—one heading southwest to Egypt and North Africa, the other moving northwest to Europe and the Balkans. *Gypsy* means "Egyptian." Gypsies from Egypt migrated to Spain in the mid-15th century. They preserved the songs and dances of old Andalusia, but didn't create them—being better imitators than creators.

In Granada the Gypsies perform in caves carved from the hillsides. It's not as primitive as it sounds, for their whitewashed rooms are lit with electricity and

(continues)

If you've seen enough, skip El Gastor and from Zahara continue north on Route 521, then turn left (north) on C339, going 6.4 kilometers (4 miles) to **Algodonales.** This town seems even whiter than the other white towns, perhaps because of the striking contrast with the silvery-green olive groves that surround it.

Whether you go to Algodonales or El Gastor, you'll end up on N342. Turn right (east) to **Olvera** (20.8km/13 miles from Algodonales). The beauty of this village is compromised only by the presence of the main road. From Olvera, you can make a side trip northeast to **Pruna** (14.4km/9 miles round-trip).

Drive 3.2 kilometers (2 miles) east on N342, and head south 11.2 kilometers (7 miles) to the perched village of **Setenil,** where the rock forms a natural roof over the streets. This is the most dramatic part of the drive and should be made in the late afternoon, when the sun is less harsh. From Setenil continue south to **Arriate** and Ronda, and then take C339 back south to the coast. The trip will take the better part of a day.

If this tour hasn't satisfied your wanderlust, try the following itinerary to other white villages and a dramatic mountain peak. Drive east along the coast on Route N340 from Marbella to **Fuengirola** (27.2km/17 miles). Take the beautiful drive north to touristy **Mijas** (8km/5 miles). Continue north, past **Alhaurín** to the white village of **Cartama** (19.2km/12 miles). Cross the Guadalhorca River (3.2km/2 miles) and turn left (north) on C337 to the white village of **Alora** (20.8km/13 miles). Continue north on another beautiful road to the **Ruinas de Bobastro** (17.6km/11 miles). Drive to **Las Atalayas,** turn left at the edge of the lake to **Ardales** (6.4km/4 miles), return to Alora via **Carratraca** (22.4km/14 miles), and retrace your way back to Cartama (24km/15 miles). Take C337 to **Coin**

(12.8km/8 miles), **Monda,** and **Marbella** (12.8km/17 miles).

ON TO GRANADA

As you approach overdeveloped **Torremolinos,** the traffic increases and so do the real estate and video club signs. What Torremolinos has to offer are high-rise hotels with pools and shops along a highway, and a strip of beach. Life here is geared for the package-tour trade.

Accommodations

Málaga isn't a destination but a point of transit. The only place I'd recommend staying here is the 38-room **Parador de Gibralfaro,** Málaga 29016 (☎ **95/222-19-02;** fax 95/222-19-04), which sits on a mountaintop with breathtaking views, about 3.2 kilometers (2 miles) from the center of town. The rustic rooms are reasonably priced, and there's a pleasant dining room with the option of eating on a terrace that offers a spectacular view over Málaga's harbor. Facilities: restaurant, parking. AE DC, MC, V. Expensive.

Between Málaga and Salobreña is the **Nerja Cave** (Cueva de Nerja), Carretera de Maro s/n (☎ **95/252-95-20**). If you're partial to caves or are traveling with children, the Nerja Cave is worth an hour of your time. It's not the usual long, dark passageway, but a huge network of limestone caverns with lots of corners to explore. There's classical music, and, best of all, no guide comparing stalactites to Joe DiMaggio's bat or George Washington's nose. Most thrilling are the Cascade Chamber, which hosts an annual festival of music and dance, and a cathedral-like room with a pillar 59.9 meters (200 ft.) long—the longest known stalactite in the world.

heated with tiled stoves. The caves themselves are naturally warm in winter and dry and cool in summer. You may find a passionate or talented dancer here, but most just walk through the steps, clicking their imported castanets, squeezing the myth of Gypsy Spain for every tourist dollar they can get. Go for the experience, expect to be taken, and insist on having a good time.

Marbella

Marbella has two casinos, **Casino Nueva Andalucia,** Puerto Banús (☎ **95/281-40-00**), and **Casino de Juego de Torrequebrada,** km 226 on N340 Benalmádena (☎ **95/244-25-45**). The latter also has a nightclub.

Other bright spots in the town of Marbella include **Willy Salsa,** km 186 on N340 (☎ **95/277-0279**), and **Olivia Valere,** km 184 on N340 in Puerto Banús (☎ **95/277-0100**).

Seville

People who know flamenco are less than enthusiastic about the tourist shows in Seville—but they're the best you're going to find in southern Spain. For around $25 you get a seat at a table for a 60-minute performance and a drink. Shows begin at 9:30pm and 11:30pm. The most authentic is at **El Arenal,** Rodo 7 (☎ **95/421-64-92**).

Consider eating dinner in the barrio and then taking in the flamenco show at **Los Gallos,** Plaza de Santa Cruz 11 (☎ **95/421-69-81**). Shows are at 9 and 11pm. After the show, you can visit some of the quarter's colorful bars, such as **Casa Román,** Plaza de los Venerables (☎ **95/421-6408**).

Although the subject of many operas, Seville didn't get its own

(continues)

opera house until the 1990s. The **Teatro de la Maestranza,** Núñez del Balboa (☎ 95/422-6573), often presents operas with Seville as a setting, including Mozart's *Marriage of Figaro.* The most special bar in Seville is **Abades,** Abades 1 (☎ 95/455-15-69), a converted mansion in the Barrio de Santa Cruz that's been called "a living room in a luxurious movie set." The Spanish press hails it as "wonderfully decadent."

Admission 500PTA adults, 300PTA children 6–12; 5 and under free. Open daily 10:30am–2pm and 3:30–6pm

At **Almuñecar,** turn north on N323 for 65.6 kilometers (41 miles) to Granada. This is a beautiful trip along the western rim of the Sierra Nevadas—a world of wild red rock, orange and lemon groves, and silver olive trees.

GRANADA

The main attraction of **Granada**—perhaps of all Spain—is a Moorish fort and palace known as the Alhambra. You'll want to spend at least half a day here and at the palatial villa called the Generalife. The other musts are the cathedral and the adjoining Royal Chapel (Capilla Real), where Ferdinand and Isabella are buried. You'll also want to wander through the old Moorish quarter to see the Alhambra at dusk and journey 46.4 kilometers (29 miles) to Pico de Veleta to enjoy the wild mountain views of the Sierra Nevadas.

When Córdoba was at the height of its power, Granada was a mere provincial capital. It was then, in the 9th century, that construction of the Alhambra began—not the palace, but the original fortress that occupies part of the present site.

Granada came to its full glory under the Nasrid dynasty (1232–1492), when the rest of Spain had fallen to the Catholics. As many as 100,000 Muslim refugees fled here before the advancing Christian armies. The city was under constant siege, and its existence depended on the payment of tributes, skillful diplomacy, and the whims of the enemy. The situation was worse than precarious; it was just a matter of time before Granada fell into Christian hands.

When Mohammed V began the Alhambra Palace in 1377, he must have known that he was building the last and perhaps most splendid monument of 700 years of Moorish culture in Spain. It was the work of an old, dying civilization, the product of a reduced and threatened state. As you tour the palace, try to see it as an oasis of peace and beauty where Mohammed V and other sultans sought to escape impending doom— each room an Arabian tale told to stave off death.

Modern Granada is a busy, sprawling town, visually unmemorable. As you climb Alhambra hill, you leave the noise and confusion of modern life behind and enter a green world, where the air is clear and cool.

The **Alhambra** isn't one but a series of buildings on a 14-hectare (35-acre) plateau, a natural acropolis looming over the modern town of Granada. Think of it as a fortified medieval city with five sections: the **Alcazaba,** the oldest part of the Alhambra (and also the most touched up), dating back to the days when it served as a military fortress; the 14th-century **Alhambra Palace,** or **Alcázar,** where the sultan lived with his harem and entertained important guests; the **Royal City,** which included a college, houses, workshops, and a great mosque—virtually none of which remains; a **Christian palace** built after the Reconquest by Charles V (grandson of Ferdinand and Isabella); and the **Generalife** (technically outside the walls of the Alhambra), the summer villa of the sultan and his family.

Ask yourself as you walk around: Is the Alhambra the high point of Muslim architecture in Spain, or is it the dying gasp of a decadent culture? One critic has called it "foppish." Another has said it looks more like a boudoir than a king's palace. Still another has equated the Córdoba mosque with the robustness of early Christian architecture and the Alhambra to the flaccid self-indulgence of rococo. "No medieval Christian king lived in such feminine exotic surroundings," wrote H. V. Morton in *A Stranger in Spain.* "These pretty vistas, fountains, and arcades, designed it seems for eating of rose-petal jam, for tears, for sighs, provoke the thought that the Alhambra is not unlike a woman who has no other quality than beauty."

You'll probably be surprised by the smallness of the rooms. No effort has been made to overwhelm you, as at, say, Versailles. Even the Court of Lions is built on an intimate human scale. The sultans seemed to be seeking an inner peace, not a way of proving their worth in the eyes of the world.

The material of which the Alhambra is made is wonderfully flimsy. Beneath the ornate stuccowork is nothing but bricks, plaster, and rubble. The wood frame is crudely constructed. The ceilings are nothing but carved plaster, which you could break with a hand. The caliphs built schools and mosques to last, but not palaces, which were merely the headquarters of one man who would someday be replaced. That the decorations have survived 500 years is a miracle.

What you see is not the creation of one man but an accretion of styles over many generations. This explains the seemingly haphazard arrangement of some buildings and the absence of a defined axis. Notice how the builders concealed all solid functional components—walls, arches, ceilings—behind a decorative web of plaster and tile. Lightness was the aim of Moorish architecture as massiveness was for the Egyptians. The goal was worthy of a genie: Not only to fill space with beauty, but to make the walls disappear, to free them of weight—in short, to transcend matter.

As you walk through the Alhambra, try to think of it as a Moorish heaven: an oasis in a dry desert, with fountains, greenery, and shelter from the sun. Picture the slender columns as tent poles or date palms; the flowery capitals (the heads of columns) as vegetation; the designs on the walls as Oriental carpets in a nomad's tent. The desert is empty as a whitewashed wall: Is it any wonder that the Moors would want to fill it with color and life?

GRANADA

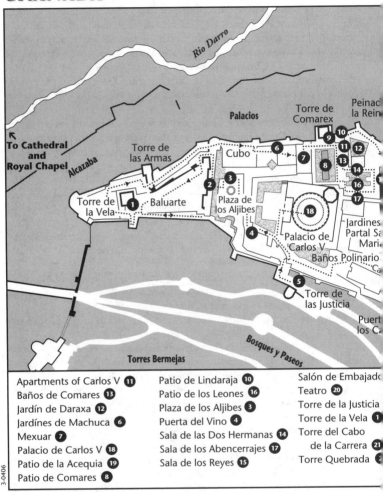

3-0406

Our own houses shelter us from nature; in the Alhambra, nature i⚬
integrated in the design. We admit sunshine from without; the Alhambr⚬
admits it from courtyards within. It's only in recent times that Wester⚬
architects have begun to catch up with the Arabs—using skylights an⚬
atriums, and, following the lead of Frank Lloyd Wright, integrating archi⚬
tecture with the natural environment. For this to happen we had to lear⚬
what the Moors apparently knew: that people and nature are one and tha⚬
happiness comes from experiencing this oneness.

The road to the entrance is lined, inappropriately, with elms: Th⚬
Spanish king gave Wellington an estate in return for his struggle agains⚬

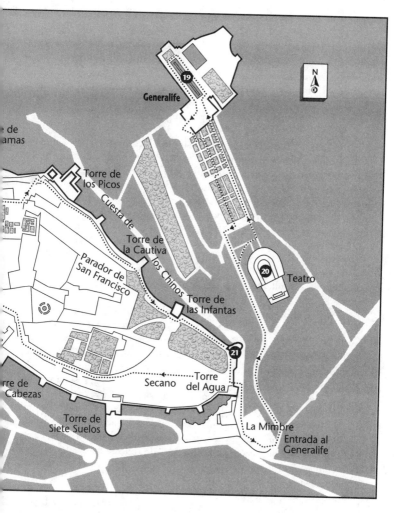

Napoléon, and Wellington returned the favor with a decidedly un-Moorish gift of elms.

Enter through the **Gate of Justice** (Puerta de la Justicial), so called because it was here that the sultans held court. In the keystone of the horseshoe-shape entry arch is a large open hand of Fátima, daughter of Muhammad by his first wife, each finger symbolizing one of the five re-quirements of the Islamic faith: belief in the oneness of God, prayer, fasting in the month of Ramadan, pilgrimage to Mecca, and the giving of alms.

Turn into the **Place of the Cisterns** (Plaza de los Aljibes), an open area where water was stored in case enemies destroyed the aqueduct. On your right is the 14th-century **sultan's palace** (Alcázar), where you'll want to spend most of your time. On your left, behind a wall, is the oldest part of the Alhambra, which contained military headquarters, government offices, a mint, guards' barracks, and apartments for members of court and official guests.

Turn left into the **Alcazaba** and climb the watchtower (Torre de la Vela) for a great view of Granada. It was on this terrace that the Catholics placed their first cross in 1492, proclaiming the end of 700 years of Muslim rule.

Return to the Place of the Cisterns. Ahead of you is **Emperor Charles V's Palace.** It's fashionable to denigrate this Renaissance structure, to dismiss it as a visual obscenity; but not all critics agree. The important thing is to make up your own mind and see what your verdict says about your own sensibilities. Charles V, the grandson of Ferdinand and Isabella, tore down many Moorish buildings to construct this palace, which was never completed. It's a perfect square with a circular inner court where bullfights were once held. Michener called its facade "grotesquely ugly, as if someone had set out to burlesque the worst taste of the time." Washington Irving dismissed it as an "arrogant intruder." Whatever its architectural virtues, Charles's palace is as inappropriately situated as the cathedral in the Córdoba mosque.

From Charles V's palace, turn into the **Court of the Myrtle Trees** (Patio de Comares), which has a long pool down the center, bordered by myrtles. This was the reception area for visitors to the Hall of the Ambassadors (Salón de Embajadores), so try to imagine yourself waiting here for a meeting with the sultan. Notice how nature is included in this Moorish version of paradise: in the dark green hedges standing out against the gleaming white marble; in the sky sailing across the water. Notice, too, how everything converges on the center: a very Eastern notion, where one looks inward (as opposed to outward, toward the world) to find peace, and where beauty is enclosed within walls as the spirit or the soul is encased in the body. The reflections create a playful ambiguity about the nature of reality (which is real, which reflection?). There's a sense of unreality as well in the narrow columns, which seem too slight to support anything.

At the north end of this court is the **Hall of the Blessing** (Sala de la Barca), which leads into the **Hall of the Ambassdors.** The sultan met official visitors and held state receptions here. The lavish decoration—the most splendid in the Alhambra—reflects the importance of this hall in a kingdom that depended on diplomacy, not warfare, for its survival.

Turn right down a gallery to the **Queen's Dressing Room** (Tocador de la Reina), located at the top of a small tower (Abul Hachach's Tower). The room has been modernized and painted with arabesques. Washington Irving lived here while writing *Tales of the Alhambra*.

Return to the Court of the Myrtle Trees and turn left into the famous **Court of Lions** (Patio de los Leones). This 14th-century court was the drawing room of the harem, at the heart of the palace. The lions offering their rumps to the fountain are probably Phoenician. The fountain was originally a sundial—at each hour water flowed from the mouth of a different lion.

To your right, off the Court of Lions, is the **Hall of the Abencerrajes** (Sala de los Abencerrajes). The honeycomb dome is carved from simple plaster: as one critic wrote, "a beehive whose honey is light." The hall is named after the noble family whose male members were lured here and executed by the last sultan of Granada; guides will insist you can still see their blood.

From the Hall of the Abencerrajes return to the Court of Lions. Turn right. At the end of the hall is the **Hall of the Kings** (Sala de los Reyes), which houses the portraits of the first 10 Nasrid rulers.

Return to the Court of Lions and take the passageway to the right. This leads into the **Hall of the Two Sisters** (Sala de las Dos Hermanas), which many consider the palace's loveliest room. It would be fun to dream up an Arabian tale about the sisters, but they're in fact nothing more than the two slabs of flawless white marble. The honeycomb ceiling seems the work of bees. Many compare it to stalactites or icicles—an appropriate sort of wish fulfillment for a people of the desert.

Exit through the Gate of Justice and walk left around the walls to the **Generalife** (☎ 958/22-75-27), the summer villa of the sultans. All here is cool and restful, sensual and intimate. The two lines of water jets make visual poetry and remind us again that the Arab heaven is a cool place with water. Admission 675PTA, which includes the Alhambra and the Generalife (free after 3pm Sun). Open Nov–Feb, daily 9am–6pm; Mar–Oct, daily 9am–7:45pm; floodlit visits Nov–Feb 9am–6pm, Mar–Oct 10pm–midnight.

The **Royal Chapel** (Capilla Real), Plaza de la Lonja (☎ 958/22-29-59), is the tomb of the Catholic Monarchs (Los Reyes Católicos), Ferdinand and Isabella. Built in the Isabeline style—a Catholic response to the Moorish love of decoration, but with none of the restraint—it's one of the world's most lavish sepulchres. Isabella's art collection of great Flemish, Spanish, and Italian paintings is in the sacristy. Admission 200PTA. Open daily 10:30am–1:30pm and 4–7pm (to 6pm in winter).

The Catholic Monarchs wanted to be buried in the city where they won their final victory over the Moors in 1492. Isabella was a year older than Ferdinand. She was a beautiful child who was pursued at age 14 by Edward IV of England; had she accepted his advances, she might've become Queen of England. Her modesty went to such extremes that when she was dying, she refused to show her bare foot for extreme unction, and her silk stocking was anointed instead. She was devoted to Christ's kingdom and thought God approved of the Inquisition and the expulsion of the Jews. It was she, not her husband, who believed in Columbus.

Isabella is looking away from her husband, just as, on another sepulchre, her daughter Juana is looking away from her husband, Philip the Handsome.

At age 17 Juana set sail for Flanders to marry 18-year-old Philip of Burgundy. She was insanely jealous of him and responded to his infidelities with hunger strikes and tantrums. The couple returned to Spain, but Philip hated the stuffiness of the court and fled, leaving Juana alone with her depressions. She tried to flee to him one cold November night, dressed in nothing but her nightgown; from that time she was known as Juana la Loca—Joan the Mad or Crazy Jane. When she was permitted to return to Flanders in 1504, she embarrassed the Spanish court by attacking Philip's lover and cutting off her rival's long hair in public.

When Isabella died, Juana returned to Spain with Philip to claim her inheritance as heir to Castile. Ferdinand acted as her regent, because she was considered unfit to rule. Within a year Philip died. Inconsolable, Juana refused to have him buried and set his corpse on a throne dressed in furs. After the body was embalmed, she never left the coffin and had it opened every night so she could kiss the dead man's face. For several years she wandered about the country, traveling by night with a hearse that carried her husband's body. Her father, Ferdinand, who outlived Isabella by a dozen years, finally convinced Juana to settle in a mansion, still accompanied by Philip's corpse; and there they remained for 47 years, until her death at 76. It was the child of Juana and Philip, Charles V, who built his palace in the Alhambra and who approved the construction of the cathedral in the Córdoba mosque.

A short flight of steps leads down to a vault where the simple coffins of Ferdinand, Isabella, Juana, and Philip lie on a stone slab. On the wall is a crucifix. The reality of death is poignantly brought home in the contrast between the splendid tomb and these four lead boxes.

Next to the Royal Chapel is the **cathedral,** built in the 16th and 17th centuries. Sit in its dim interior, preferably during one of the daily organ concerts, and contemplate the different values that went into the creation of this church and the Alhambra. What is unusual is the way in which you're made to enter through a rotunda rather than through a nave (the long central aisle). Admission 200PTA. Same schedule as Royal Chapel.

One of the highlights of your stay in Granada is the sweeping view of the Alhambra from the terrace of **St. Nicholas Church** (San Nicolás) in the **Albaicín,** the old Moorish quarter. Visit at sunset for a sight you won't forget.

If you're interested in architecture, visit the **Carthusian Monastery** (Monasterio de la Cartuja), east of the university on Calle Real de Cartuja, which has a lavishly decorated baroque church, a magnificent late-baroque sacristy, and a splendid view. Admission 350PTA. Same schedule as Royal Chapel.

To escape the heat and enjoy some spectacular mountain scenery, either on foot or from your car, drive 46.4 kilometers (29 miles) to **Pico de Veleta**—more than 3,000 meters (10,000 ft.) up in the Sierra Nevadas. You can ski here from mid-December to early May; one of the lifts is open in summer. The road to the top is passable only from July to October, but you don't have to reach the summit to appreciate the view.

DINING

There are several good to excellent restaurants in Granada, but none that is consistently first-rate. Several have a great deal of warmth and character.

Columbia, Antequereula Baja 1 (☎ **958/22-74-33**). Columbia presents live guitar music on a terrace overlooking the city. Reservations advised Fri–Sat. Casually elegant. AE, DC, MC, V. Closed Sun. Moderate.

Cunini, Pescaderia 14 (☎ **958/25-07-77**). Behind the flower market near the cathedral, Cunini takes top billing. Downstairs is a tapas bar; the upstairs restaurant is best known for its Basque-style soup-stews and fresh fish. Reservations advised. Casually elegant. AE, DC, MC, V. Closed Mon eve. Expensive.

Los Manueles, Zaragoza 2 (☎ **958/22-34-13**). This place is basic, busy, and friendly, with ceramic tiles, and smoked hams hanging from the ceiling. No reservations. Casual. AE, DC, MC, V. Inexpensive.

Mesón Antonion, Ecce Homo 6 (☎ **958/22-95-99**). Antonion is a simple, friendly place, offering good value, even though the food is unremarkable. It's quite decent, however, and based on fresh ingredients—try the roast lamb with aromatic herbs or a savory seafood zarzuela (mixed stew). Reservations not necessary. Casual. AE, MC, V. Closed Sun eve and Mon. Inexpensive.

Parador Nacional San Francisco, Recinto de la Alhambra (☎ **958/ 22-14-40**). On Alhambra hill, this parador has a restaurant worth visiting—perhaps more for its atmosphere than for its cuisine—if you're staying in the neighborhood. Reservations required. Casually elegant. AE, DC, MC, V. Expensive.

Polinaro, Real de la Alhambra 3 (☎ **958/22-29-91**). Polinaro is a good bet if you're visiting the Alhambra. Here you can forget about the long lines of Alhambra tourists and savor a typically Andalusian cuisine in one of the three restaurants within the walled confines of the Alhambra. Across from the Palace of Carlos V, it's best visited at lunch, when you can partake of a wide buffet (fixed price) with a vast array of dishes. Reservations not necessary. Casual. No credit cards. Inexpensive.

Ruta del Veleta, 44 Cenes de la Vega (☎ **958/48-61-34**). This restaurant is 4.8 kilometers (3 miles) from Granada on the road to the mountains, so you may want to stop there for lunch or dinner en route to the Pico de Veleta. Casual. Reservations advised. AE, DC, MC, V. Closed Sun eve. Expensive.

Sevilla, Oficios 12 (☎ **958/22-12-23**). A well-established restaurant near the cathedral, Sevilla serves traditional Andalusian cuisine, including a local fish soup recipe. The tapas bar is especially good. Reservations advised. Casual. AE, DC, MC, V. Closed Sun eve. Moderate.

ACCOMMODATIONS

Hotels that claim to be in the Alhambra aren't in fact within the walls but only on Alhambra hill, within walking distance from the palace. Try to stay here: It's quiet and cool and away from the congestion of the town below. Stay in town only if you need a budget hotel or want to be within walking distance of the nightspots.

América, Real de la Alhambra, Granada 18009 (☎ **958/22-74-71;** fax 958/22-74-70). An alternative hotel much in demand, América is closer to the Alhambra than the government parador. Its popularity stems from the warm hospitality expressed by its owners, who have filled the public rooms with an assortment of antiques. The guest rooms are on the small side, but they're comfortable and well maintained. 14 rms with bath. Facilities: restaurant. Closed Nov–Feb. AE, DC, MC, V. Moderate/ Inexpensive.

Brasilia, Rocogidas 7, Granada 18005 (☎ **958/25-84-50**). This hotel is aging but fine if you just need a place to put your head. Ask for one of the seventh-floor rooms with balconies. 68 rms with bath. Breakfast is the only meal served. AE, DC, V. Moderate/Expensive.

Britz, Plaza Nueva y Gomerez 1, 18009 Granada (☎ **958/22-36-52**). Britz is a clean, pleasant, small hotel conveniently located at the base of the Alhambra hill and close to downtown attractions—a good, cheap bet all around. English is spoken by the helpful staff, and the atmosphere is family oriented. 22 rms with bath. MC, V. Inexpensive.

Carlos V, Plaza de los Campos 4, Granada 18009 (☎ **958/22-15-87**). This is a quiet English-style hotel on the fourth floor of a government building in a residential area. The rooms are furnished with twin beds only. Breakfast is the only meal served. 28 rms with bath. No credit cards. Inexpensive.

Hotel Alhambra Palace, Peña Partida 2, Granada 18009 (☎ **958/28-14-68;** fax 958/22-64-04). This is a lavish Moorish-style modern palace halfway up the hill to the Alhambra. Its location on the main road, with cars and buses constantly pulling into and out of insufficient parking spaces, gives it a more harried mood than that of the more isolated parador. Despite its busyness, however, the Palace is still a conversation piece, with rich carpets, tapestries, and colorful Moorish tiles. The rear rooms, which look out over the city, are preferable. 132 rms with bath. Facilities: restaurant, lounge for afternoon tea and cocktails, limited parking. AE, DC, MC, V. Expensive.

Hotel Carmén, Acera del Darro 62, Granada 18009 (☎ **800/387-8842** or 958/25-83-00; fax 958/25-64-62). The Carmén is essentially a high-rise on a busy street not far from the cathedral. Its rooms are clean but somewhat basic. The inside ones are quieter—the higher up the better. 272 rms with bath; 11 suites. Facilities: restaurant. AE, DC, MC, V. Expensive.

Hotel Granada Center, Av. Fuentenueva s/n, 18002 Granada (☎ **800/387-8842** or 958/20-50-00; fax 958/28-96-96). Here's one of the best of the modern hotels in town, having opened in 1992 adjacent to the university. Rising seven stories, with a glass-covered atrium at its center, it has an impersonal group-tour ambiance. But the rooms are comfortable, monochromatically decorated in neutral earth tones, with modern but standardized furniture. 165 rms with bath; 7 suites. Facilities: restaurant, parking, shops. AE, DC, MC, V. Expensive.

Hotel Saray, Tierno Galbán s/n, 18006 Granada (☎ **800/387-8842** or 958/13-00-09; fax 958/12-91-61). The Saray, a 10-minute walk south of the historic core, rises nine salmon-colored floors. Its upper-floor rooms open onto the best hotel room views of the Sierra Nevadas. Since 1991, this has lured discriminating guests to its precincts. The lobby-level restaurant is only standard, but the outdoor pool is a welcome respite from the heat. 195 rms with bath; 8 suites. Facilities: pool, restaurant, shops, parking. AE, DC, MC, V. Moderate/Expensive.

Los Angeles, Cuesta Escoriaza 17, Granada 18008 (☎ **958/22-14-24;** fax 958/22-21-25). The Los Angeles caters to tour groups and is away from the center of town. But the surroundings are pleasant and peaceful, the staff is friendly, the price is right, and the hotel is one of the very few with a pool. Ask for one of the larger rooms added since 1983. 100 rms with bath. Facilities: restaurant, outdoor pool, parking. AE, MC, V. Moderate/Expensive.

Parador Nacional San Francisco, Recinto de la Alhambra, Granada 18009 (☎ **800/343-0020** or 958/22-14-40; fax 958/22-22-64). This is one of two hotels that are actually on the grounds of the Alhambra (though not within the walls). The former Arab palace was transformed into a Franciscan convent when Granada was reconquered in 1492. The rooms are simple and restrained; the public areas are full of rare icons, rugs, mosaics, and embroideries. The only noise is from the fountains in the gardens, beneath the vine-covered walls. If you want a tastefully subdued environment where you can experience the tranquillity of the Alhambra itself, this is the place to stay. (If you can't get a room in the Parador—and you'll need to reserve at least 3 to 4 months in advance—make reservations for lunch.) 36 rms with bath. Facilities: restaurant, terrace for afternoon tea and cocktails, garage. AE, DC, MC, V. Very Expensive.

Washington Irving, Paseo del Generalife 2, Granada 18009 (☎ **958/22-75-50;** fax 958/22-88-40). This is where the author of *The Alhambra* once stayed. The hotel is one of a kind, but many rooms are very small and plain. If you stay, ask for a large one. 60 rms with bath. Facilities: restaurant, banquet room, shops. AE, MC, V. Moderate.

SIDE TRIPS TO BAEZA & ÚBEDA
BAEZA

If you're driving from Granada back to Madrid (or from Granada to Córdoba), consider a short side trip to Baeza and Úbeda. Take N323 north to Jaén, then turn right on N321 for 46.4 kilometers (29 miles) to Baeza and another 9.6 kilometers (6 miles) to Úbeda.

Baeza was a former taifa capital—one of the feudal kingdoms that developed in Moorish Spain when the Córdoba caliphate collapsed. The Albaicín, the old Moorish quarter of Granada, is named for the Baezan Moors who fled to Granada when the Christians reconquered the town in 1227. This was the first reconquered town in Andalusia; the first mass of the Reconquest was held here on a balcony overlooking the Plaza of the

Lions. What you'll see in Baeza are some fine examples of early Spanish Renaissance architecture. The casual visitor can expect to spend less than an hour exploring the important sights, all within a few minutes' walk of each other.

Park at the lovely **Plaza of the Lions** (Plaza de los Leones), the square on your right as you drive through town on N321. Above the lions is a draped figure said to be Hannibal's wife. The head is new; the old one was removed during the Spanish Civil War by anticlerical Republicans who mistook her for the Virgin.

To the right of the square is the **tourist office,** Plaza del Pópulo (☎ **953/74-04-44;** open Mon–Fri 9am–2:30pm), where you can pick up a walking guide. To the left is the most elegant 16th-century slaughterhouse (*abatoir*) you'll ever see. Stairs lined with 16th-century Renaissance-Plateresque buildings lead from the square to the cathedral. The Plateresque style combines Gothic, Renaissance, and Arabic elements. Plateresque comes from *platero*, meaning "silversmith"; the design is so fine that it seems more the work of a silversmith than of a mason. Though this delicate ornamentation is Arab-inspired, the decorative themes and the symmetry and balance of the buildings themselves are inspired by the Italian Renaissance.

Follow the steps to the Plaza Santa María. Turn right to reach the **cathedral,** Plaza de la Fuente de Santa María (no phone), which was remodeled in the late 16th century and has some outstanding chapels. Free admission. Open daily 10am–1pm and 4–7pm.

Instead of returning to the lions, cross Plaza Santa María and follow a narrow street to the Romanesque church of **Santa Cruz.** Next door is the 16th-century university, which had a prison for unruly students. Across from the university is the **Jabalquinto Palace** (Palacio de Jabalquinto). The free-flowing lacelike facade is a great example of the Moorish-inspired Isabeline style, in which every inch of space is covered with intricate designs.

ÚBEDA

After the Christians took over in 1234, **Úbeda** became a stronghold for knights, who continued the fight against the Moors—and among themselves.

The focus of your trip has been Moorish Spain; an hour in Úbeda will introduce you to the art and architecture of Catholic Spain during the Renaissance. If you have more than a passing interest in the arts, you'll find many notable Renaissance palaces to explore; or you may be content visiting the buildings on Plaza Vázquez de Molina and the streets and pottery shops in the Gypsy quarter.

Stop at the **tourist office,** Plaza de los Caídos 2 (☎ **953/75-08-97;** open Mon–Fri 9am–2:30pm, Sat 11am–2pm), for a map and descriptive booklet. Leave your car here and walk to Plaza Vázquez de Molina. Around the corner from the tourist office, on your way to the square, is a crafts shop selling the green glazed pottery for which the town is known. You'll also pass some unique shops selling old ceramics.

Plaza Vázquez de Molina, the aristocratic center of the old town, is bordered by several historic buildings. **El Salvador Church** (Iglesia el Salvador) was designed in 1630 and has an ornamented sacristy of breathtaking exuberance. The Virgin averts her eyes from the pair of top-less Italian Renaissance caryatids guarding the door. For the key to the church, walk around the left side—to your left as you're facing the entrance—and down a street of whitewashed buildings. Ring the bell on the first door on the right. Free admission. Open daily 9am–1pm and 5–7pm.

Across the street from the church is a 16th-century palace that has been converted into the 31-room **Parador de Úbeda,** Plaza Vázquez de Molina 1, 23400 Úbeda (☎ **953/75-03-45;** fax 965/75-12-59).

Another church worth visiting is the Gothic **St. Paul's** (San Pablo)— particularly for its chapels.

If you liked the pottery near the tourist office, visit the studios where it's made, along Calle Valencia in the **Gypsy quarter,** a 10-minute walk from St. Paul's. You step through a Moorish stone archway and enter a world of immaculate white walls and angular shadows where time seems to have stopped. Men crouch in doorways as if waiting for time to begin, and old women huddle in doorways like petals of a black flower. The area is quite safe and, unlike the ancient quarters of Seville and Córdoba, completely unspoiled by the tourist trade.

From Úbeda, take N322 west for 40 kilometers (86 miles) to Bailén and then take N IV north (about 6 hr.) to Madrid.

APPENDIX: MENU TERMS

FRENCH

BASICS

beurre	butter
citron	lemon
déjeuner	lunch
dîner	dinner
fromage	cheese
moutarde	mustard
pain	bread
petit déjeuner	breakfast
poivre	pepper
sel	salt
sucre	sugar
vinaigre	vinegar

SOUP (POTAGE)

bouillabaisse	fish soup
consommé	clear broth
potage à la reine	cream of chicken soup
potage de volaille	chicken soup
potage aux lentilles	lentil soup
potage portugais	tomato soup
potage St-Germain	pea soup
soupe à l'oignon	onion soup

FISH (POISSON)

anguille	eel
brochet	pike
crevette	shrimp
escargots	snails
hareng	herring
homard	lobster
huîtres	oysters
maquereau	mackerel
moules	mussels
saumon fumé	smoked salmon
thon	tuna
truite	trout

MEAT (VIANDE)

agneau	lamb
ailes	chicken wings
aloyau	sirloin
bifteck	steak
boeuf	beef
canard	duck
caneton	duckling
cervelles	brains
charcuterie	cold cuts
chauteaubriand	filet steak
chevreuil	venison
côtelette d'agneau	lamb chop
dinde	turkey
foie	liver
foie gras	goose liver
grenouille	frog
jambon	ham
lapin	rabbit
mouton	mutton
oie	goose
pot au feu	beef stew
poulet	chicken
poussin	squab
ris de veau	sweetbreads
rognons	kidneys
saucisse grillée	fried sausage

tournedos	small filet steaks
veau	veal
viande en ragoût	meat stew
volaille	poultry

VEGETABLES/SALADS (LEGUMES/SALADE)

asperge	asparagus
aubergine	eggplant
choucroute	sauerkraut
choux	cabbage
cornichon	pickle
crudités	vegetable salad
épinards	spinach
haricots verts	green beans
navets	turnips
petits pois	green peas
pommes de terres	potatoes
pommes frites	french-fried potatoes
purée de pommes	mashed potatoes
radis	radish
riz	rice
salade de concombres	cucumber salad
salade de laitue	lettuce salad
salade niçoise	salad with tuna, olives, and capers

FRUIT (FRUIT)

ananas	pineapple
fraises	straw-berries
framboises	raspberries
oranges	oranges
pamplemousse	grapefruit
raisins	grapes

DESSERT (DESSERT)

compôte de fruits	stewed fruit
crème à la vanille	vanilla custard
fromage à la crème	cream cheese
fruits frais	fresh fruit
gâteau	cake
glace à la vanille	vanilla ice cream
macedoine de fruits	fruit salad
tartes	pastries

BEVERAGES (BOISSON)

bière	beer
café	coffee
cognac	brandy
crème	cream
eau	water
jus d'orange	orange juice
lait	milk
thé	tea
vin blanc	white wine
vin rouge	red wine

COOKING TERMS

à point	medium
bien cuit	well done
farci	stuffed
frit	fried
meunière, au beurre	buttered
rôti	roast
saignant	rare

GERMAN

BASICS

Abendessen	dinner
Brot	bread
Butter	butter
Eis	ice
Essig	vinegar
Frühstück	breakfast
Käse	cheese
Mittagessen	lunch
Salz	salt
Senf	mustard
Zitrone	lemon
Zucker	sugar

SOUP (SUPPEN)

Erbsensuppe	pea soup
Gemüsesuppe	vegetable soup
Hühnerbrühe	chicken soup
Kartoffelsuppe	potato soup
Linsensuppe	lentil soup
Nudelsuppe	noodle soup
Ochsenschwanzsuppe	oxtail soup
Schildkrötensuppe	turtle soup
Eier	eggs
Eier in Schale	boiled eggs
Rühreier	scrambled eggs
Spiegeleier	fried eggs
Verlorene Eier	poached eggs

FISH (FISCH)

Aal	eel
Forelle	trout
Hecht	pike
Karpfen	carp
Krebs	crayfish
Lachs	salmon
Makrele	mackerel
Schellfisch	haddock
Seezunge	sole

MEAT (FLEISCH)

Aufschnitt	cold cuts
Brathuhn	roast chicken
Bratwurst	grilled sausage
Deutsches Beefsteak	hamburger steak
Eisbein	pigs' knuckles
Ente	duck
Gans	goose
Geflügel	chicken
Hammel	mutton
Hirn	brains
Kalb	veal
Kaltes Geflügel	cold poultry
Kassler Rippchen	pork chops
Lamm	lamb
Leber	liver
Nieren	kidneys
Ragout	stew
Rinderbraten	roast beef
Rindfleisch	beef
Schinken	ham
Schweinebraten	roast pork
Speck	bacon
Taube	pigeon
Truthahn	turkey
Wiener schnitzel	veal cutlet
Wurst	sausage

VEGETABLES/SALADS (GEMÜSE/SALAT)

Artischocken	artichokes
Blumenkohl	cauliflower
Bohnen	beans
Bratkartoffeln	fried potatoes
Erbsen	peas
Gemischter salat	mixed salad
Grüne Bohnen	string beans
Gurken	cucumbers
Karotten	carrots
Kartoffelbrei	mashed potatoes
Kartoffelsalat	potato salad
Knödel	dumplings
Kohl	cabbage
Kopfsalat	lettuce salad
Reis	rice
Rohkostplatte	vegetable salad
Rote Rüben	beets
Rotkraut	red cabbage
Salat	lettuce
Salzkartoffeln	boiled potatoes
Sauerkraut	sauerkraut
Spargel	asparagus

Spinat	spinach
Steinpilze boletus	mushrooms
Tomaten	tomatoes
Weisse Rüben	turnips

FRUIT (OBST)

Ananas	pineapples
Äpfel	apples
Apfelsinen	oranges
Bananen	bananas
Birnen	pears
Kirschen	cherries
Pfirsiche	peaches
Weintrauben	grapes
Zitronen	lemons

DESSERT (NACHTISCH)

Bratapfel	baked apple
Kloss	dumpling
Kompott	stewed fruit
Obstkuchen	fruit tart
Obstsalat	fruit salad
Pfannkuchen	sugared pancakes
Pflaumenkompott	stewed plums
Torten	pastries

BEVERAGES (GETRÄNKE)

Bier	beer
Ein Dunkles	dark beer
Ein Helles	light beer
Eine Tasse Kaffee	cup of coffee
Eine Tasse Tee	cup of tea
Milch	milk
Rotwein	red wine
Sahne	cream
Schokolade	chocolate
Tomatensaft	tomato juice
Wasser	water
Weinbrand	brandy

COOKING TERMS

Gebacken	baked
Gebraten	fried
Gefüllt	stuffed
Gekocht	boiled
Geröstet	broiled
Gut durchgebraten	well done
Nicht durchgebraten	rare
Paniert	breaded

ITALIAN

BASICS

aceto	vinegar
biscotti	crackers
burro	butter
cena	dinner
colazione	breakfast
formaggio	cheese
ghiaccio	ice
marmellata	jam
mostarda	mustard
olio	oil
pane	bread
pepe	pepper
pranzo	lunch
sale	salt
sott'aceti	pickles
zucchero	sugar

SOUP (ZUPPA)

brodo	consommé
minestra	soup
minestrone	vegetable soup
pastina in brodo	noodle soup
riso in brodo	rice soup
zuppa alla pavese	egg soup
zuppa di fagioli	bean soup
zuppa di pesce	fish soup

EGGS (UOVA)

omelette, frittata	omelet
pan dorato	french-fried toast

uova a la coque	boiled eggs
uova affogate	poached eggs
uova fritte	fried eggs
uova strapazzate	scrambled eggs

FISH (PESCE)

acciughe	anchovies
aragosta	lobster
aringhe	herring
filetto di sogliola	filet of sole
frutta di mare	assorted sea food
gamberi	shrimp
merluzzo	cold
ostriche	oysters
sardine	sardine
scampi fritti	fried shrimp
sgombro	mackerel
sogliola	sole
tonno	tuna fish
trota	trout

MEAT (CARNE)

abbacchio	baby lamb
agnello	lamb
anitra	duck
bistecca	steak
carne fredda assortita	cold cuts
cervello	brains
cotoletta alla milanese	breaded veal cutlet
fagiano	pheasant
fegatini	chicken livers
fegato	liver
lepre	rabbit
lingua	tongue
maiale	pork
manzo lesso	boiled beef
pancetta	bacon
pollo	chicken
prosciutto	ham
reni	kidney
rosbif	roast beef

VEGETABLES/SALADS (VEGETALE/INSALATA)

antipasto	hors d'oeuvres
asparagi	asparagus
carciofi	artichokes
carote	carrots
cavolfiore	cauliflower
cavolo	cabbage
cetrioli	cucumbers
cipolle	onions
fagiolini	string beans
fettuccine	noodles
funghi	mushrooms
insalata mista	mixed salad
insalata verde	lettuce salad
lattuga	lettuce
melanzana	eggplant
olive	olives
patate	potatoes
peperoni	green, red, or yellow peppers
piselli	peas
pomodori	tomatoes
ravioli alla fiorentina	cheese ravioli
ravioli alla vegetariana	ravioli with tomato sauce
riso	rice
risotto	rice dish
sedano	celery
spinaci	spinach
zucchini	squash
verdura	vegetables

FRUIT (FRUTTA)

ananasso	pineapple
aranci	oranges
banane	bananas
ciliegie	cherries
frutta	fruit
frutta cotta	stewed fruit
limoni	lemons

mele	apples
pere	pears
uva	grape

DESSERT (DOLCI)

budino	pudding
cassata	ice cream with fruit
gelato	ice cream
macedonia di frutta	fruit salad
pasticceria	pastry
pesca alla Melba	peach Melba
torta	cake

BEVERAGES (BIBITE)

acqua	water
acqua minerale	mineral water
aranciata	orangeade
birra	beer
caffè	coffee
latte	milk
limonata	lemonade
tè	tea
vino	wine

COOKING TERMS

al sangue	rare
arrosto	roast
ben cotto	well done
fritto	fried
lesso, bollito	boiled

SPANISH

BASICS

aceite	oil
ajo	garlic
azucar	sugar
cena	dinner
comida	lunch
desayuno	breakfast
mantequilla	butter
miel	honey
mostaza	mustard

pan	bread
pimienta	pepper
queso	cheese
sal	salt
vinagre	vinegar

SOUP (SOPA)

caldo gallego	Galician broth
caldo de gallina	chicken soup
sopa de ajo	garlic soup
sopa de cebolla	onion soup
sopa clara	consommé
sopa espesa	thick soup
sopa de fideos	noodle soup
sopa de guisantes	pea soup
sopa de lentejas	lentil soup
sopa de pescado	fish soup
sopa de tomate	tomato soup
sopa de verduras	vegetable soup

EGGS (HUEVOS)

huevos escaltados	poached eggs
huevos fritos	fried eggs
huevos duros	hard-boiled eggs
huevos revueltos	scrambled eggs
huevos por agua	soft-boiled eggs
tortilla	omelet

FISH (PESCADO)

almejas	clams
anchoas	anchovies
anguilas	eels
arenque	herring
atún	tuna
bacalao	cod
calamares	squid
cangrejo	crab
caracoles	snails
centollo	sea urchin

chocos	large squid
cigalas	small lobsters
gambas	shrimp
langosta	lobster
langostinos	prawns
lenguado	sole
mejillones	mussels
merluza	hake
necoras	spider crabs
ostras	oysters
pescadilla	whiting
pijotas	small whiting
pulpo	octopus
rodaballo	turbot
salmonete	mullet
sardinas	sardines
trucha	trout
vieiras	scallops

MEAT (CARNE)

albondigas	meatballs
bistec	beefsteak
callos	tripe
cerdo	pork
chuleta	cutlet
cocido	stew
conejo	rabbit
cordero	lamb
costillas	chops
gallina	fowl
ganso	goose
higado	liver
jamón	ham
lengua	tongue
paloma	pigeon
pato	duck
pavo	turkey
perdiz	partridge
pollo	chicken
riñón	kidney
rosbif	roast beef
solomillo	loin
ternera	veal
tocino	bacon
vaca	beef

VEGETABLES/SALADS (LEGUMBRES/ENSALADA)

aceitunas	olives
alcachofa	artichoke
arroz	rice
berenjena	eggplant
cebolla	onion
col	cabbage
coliflora	cauliflower
ensalada mixta	mixed salad
ensalada de pepinos	cucumber salad
ensalada verde	green salad
esparragos	asparagus
espinacas	spinach
guisantes	peas
judías verdes	string beans
lechuga	lettuce
nabo	turnip
patata	potato
remolachas	beets
setas	mushrooms
tomate	tomato
zanahorias	carrots

FRUIT (FRUTA)

albaricoque	apricot
aquacate	avocado
cerezas	cherries
ciruela	plum
datil	date
frambuesa	raspberry
fresa	strawberry
granada	pomegranate
higo	fig
limón	lemon
manzana	apple
melocotón	peach
naranja	orange
pera	pear
piña	pineapple
plátano	banana
toronja	grapefruit
uvas	grapes

Dessert (Postre)

buñuelos	fritters
compota	stewed fruit
flan	caramel custard
fruta	fruit
galletas	tea cakes
helado	ice cream
pasteles	pastries
torta	cake

Beverages

agua	water
agua mineral	mineral water
café	coffee
cerveza	beer
ginebra	gin
jerez	sherry

leche	milk
naranja zumo	orange juice
sangría	red wine, fruit juice, and soda
sidra	cider
sifon	soda
té	tea
vino blanco	white wine
vino tinto	red wine

Cooking Terms

asado	roast
cocido	broiled
empanado	breaded
frito	fried
muy hecho	well done
poco hecho	rare
tostado	toasted

INDEX

FROMMER'S COMPLETE TRAVEL GUIDES

(Comprehensive guides to destinations around the world, with selections in all price ranges—from deluxe to budget)

Acapulco/Ixtapa/Taxco
Alaska
Amsterdam
Arizona
Atlanta
Australia
Austria
Bahamas
Bangkok
Barcelona, Madrid & Seville
Belgium, Holland & Luxembourg
Berlin
Bermuda
Boston
Budapest & the Best of Hungary
California
Canada
Cancún, Cozumel & the Yucatán
Caribbean
Caribbean Cruises & Ports of Call
Caribbean Ports of Call
Carolinas & Georgia
Chicago
Colorado
Costa Rica
Denver, Boulder & Colorado Springs
Dublin
England
Florida
France
Germany
Greece
Hawaii
Hong Kong
Honolulu/Waikiki/Oahu
Ireland
Italy
Jamaica/Barbados
Japan
Las Vegas
London
Los Angeles
Maryland & Delaware
Maui

Mexico
Mexico City
Miami & the Keys
Montana & Wyoming
Montréal & Québec City
Munich & the Bavarian Alps
Nashville & Memphis
Nepal
New England
New Mexico
New Orleans
New York City
Northern New England
Nova Scotia, New Brunswick & Prince
 Edward Island
Paris
Philadelphia & the Amish Country
Portugal
Prague & the Best of the Czech Republic
Puerto Rico
Puerto Vallarta, Manzanillo & Guadalajara
Rome
San Antonio & Austin
San Diego
San Francisco
Santa Fe, Taos & Albuquerque
Scandinavia
Scotland
Seattle & Portland
South Pacific
Spain
Switzerland
Thailand
Tokyo
Toronto
U.S.A.
Utah
Vancouver & Victoria
Vienna
Virgin Islands
Virginia
Walt Disney World & Orlando
Washington, D.C.
Washington & Oregon

FROMMER'S FRUGAL TRAVELER'S GUIDES

(The grown-up guides to budget travel, offering dream vacations at down-to-earth prices)

Australia from $45 a Day
Berlin from $50 a Day
California from $60 a Day
Caribbean from $60 a Day
Costa Rica & Belize from $35 a Day
Eastern Europe from $30 a Day
England from $50 a Day
Europe from $50 a Day
Florida from $50 a Day
Greece from $45 a Day
Hawaii from $60 a Day

India from $40 a Day
Ireland from $45 a Day
Italy from $50 a Day
Israel from $45 a Day
London from $60 a Day
Mexico from $35 a Day
New York from $70 a Day
New Zealand from $45 a Day
Paris from $65 a Day
Washington, D.C. from $50 a Day

FROMMER'S PORTABLE GUIDES

(Pocket-size guides for travelers who want everything in a nutshell)

Charleston & Savannah
Las Vegas

New Orleans
San Francisco

FROMMER'S IRREVERENT GUIDES

(Wickedly honest guides for sophisticated travelers)

Amsterdam
Chicago
London
Manhattan

Miami
New Orleans
Paris
San Francisco

Santa Fe
U.S. Virgin Islands
Walt Disney World
Washington, D.C.

FROMMER'S AMERICA ON WHEELS

(Everything you need for a successful road trip, including full-color road maps and ratings for every hotel)

California & Nevada
Florida
Mid-Atlantic
Midwest & the Great Lakes
New England & New York

Northwest & Great Plains
South Central &Texas
Southeast
Southwest

FROMMER'S BY NIGHT GUIDES

(The series for those who know that life begins after dark)

Amsterdam
Chicago
Las Vegas
London

Los Angeles
Miami
New Orleans

New York
Paris
San Francisco

WHEREVER YOU TRAVEL, *H*ELP IS NEVER FAR AWAY.

From planning your trip to

providing travel assistance along

the way, American Express®

Travel Service Offices are

always there to help.

American Express Travel Service Offices are found in central locations throughout Europe.

Travel

http://www.americanexpress.com/travel